D0374959

THE INVENTION OF NEWS

The
INVENTION
of NEWS

HOW THE WORLD CAME TO
KNOW ABOUT ITSELF

ANDREW PETTEGREE

YALE UNIVERSITY PRESS
NEW HAVEN AND LONDON

For information about this and other Yale University Press publications, please contact:

U.S. Office; sales.press@yale.edu   www.yalebooks.com
Europe Office: sales@yaleup.co.uk   www.yalebooks.co.uk

Set in Minion Pro by IDSUK (DataConnection) Ltd
Printed in Great Britain by TJ International Ltd, Padstow, Cornwall

Library of Congress Cataloging-in-Publication Data

Pettegree, Andrew.
  The invention of news: how the world came to know about itself/Andrew Pettegree.
    pages cm
  ISBN 978-0-300-17908-8 (hardback)
1. Journalism—Europe—History.   I. Title.
  PN5110.P48 2014
  070.09—dc23

                                                                            2013041978

A catalogue record for this book is available from the British Library.

10 9 8 7 6 5 4 3 2 1

Contents

Maps

Introduction

All the News that's Fit to Tell

IN 1704 the English writer Daniel Defoe embarked on the publication of a political journal: the *Weekly Review of the Affairs of France*.[1] This was not yet the Defoe made famous by his great novel *Robinson Crusoe*; he would discover his vocation as a novelist only late in life. Up to this point Defoe had tried his hand at many things, and often failed. The *Review* (as it soon became) was the latest of many attempts to find a way to make money. This time it worked. Within a few months Defoe's publication had found its new form, as a serial issued two or three times a week, consisting largely of a single essay on an item of topical interest.

Defoe was lucky. He had launched the *Review* at a time when the reading public was expanding rapidly, along with a market for current affairs. Naturally Defoe made the most of it. When, in an essay in 1712, he turned his mind to this buoyant market for news publishing, he did not hold back. The present times, wrote Defoe, had seen a media explosion. He recalled a time, even in his own lifetime, when there had been no such torrent of newspapers, state papers and political writing. The rage for news was transforming society, and Defoe was happy to be in the thick of it.[2]

Defoe was not the only one to remark the current passion for news, and the rancorous tone of political debate that seemed to come with it. But if he truly thought this was new he was very much mistaken. The conflicts of the English Civil War over sixty years previously had stimulated a torrent of pamphlets, news reports and abusive political treatises. The first continental newspapers were established forty years before that. Long before Defoe, and even before the creation of the newspapers, the appetite for news was proverbial. 'How now, what news?' was a common English greeting, frequently evoked on the London stage.[3] Travellers could buy phrase books that offered the necessary vocabulary, so they too could join the conversation: 'What news have you? How goeth all in this city? What news have they in Spain?'[4]

If there was a time when news first became a commercial commodity, it occurred not in Defoe's London, or even with the invention of the newspaper, but much earlier: in the eighty years between 1450 and 1530 following the invention of printing. During this period of technological innovation, publishers began to experiment with new types of books, far shorter and cheaper than the theological and scholarly texts that had dominated the market in manuscripts. These pamphlets and broadsheets created the opportunity to turn the existing appetite for news into a mass market. News could become, for the first time, a part of popular culture.

This book, which traces the development of the European news market in the four centuries between about 1400 and 1800, is the story of that transformation. It follows the development of a commercial news market from the medieval period – when news was the prerogative of political elites – to a point four hundred years later when news was beginning to play a decisive role in popular politics. By the time of the French and American revolutions at the end of the eighteenth century, news publications were not only providing a day by day account of unfolding events, they could be seen to play an influential role in shaping them. The age of a mass media lay at hand.

Trusting the Messenger

Of course the desire to be informed, to be in the know, is in one respect as old as human society itself. People would go to some lengths to find out the news. In the eleventh century two monasteries in rural Wales, one hundred miles apart across rugged terrain, would every third year exchange messengers who would live in the other house for a week, to share the news.[5]

This tale, related in a Tudor chronicle, points up one other important aspect of the information culture of that earlier period. Our medieval ancestors had a profound suspicion of information that came to them in written form. They were by no means certain that something written was more trustworthy than the spoken word. Rather the contrary: a news report gained credibility from the reputation of the person who delivered it. So a news report delivered verbally by a trusted friend or messenger was far more likely to be believed than an anonymous written report. This old tradition, where the trust given to a report depended on the credit of the teller, had an enduring influence over attitudes to news reporting. But this early news world is not easy to reconstruct. Verbal reports in the nature of things leave little trace for the historian: studying the early history of news is a matter of combing through scraps and fragments.

Bernard of Clairvaux, architect of the Cistercian order, sat at the centre of one of medieval Europe's greatest news networks. Those who visited Clairvaux in eastern France would bring him news of their travels; sometimes they would carry his letters away with them when they departed. We are unusually well informed about Bernard's news network, because over five hundred of his letters survive.[6] But in some respects Bernard is utterly characteristic of the news world of the medieval period. At this time regular access to news was the prerogative of those in circles of power. Only they could afford it; only they had the means to gather it. But even for these privileged individuals at the apex of society, news gathering was not unproblematic. They were fully aware that those who brought them news were likely to be interested parties. The travelling cleric who brought Bernard news of a distant episcopal election might be supporting one candidate; the ambassador writing home from abroad might be seeking to influence policy; merchants hoped to gain from a fluctuating market. Merchants, in particular, had a keen awareness of the value of information, and the dangers of acting on a false rumour. For the first two centuries of the period covered by this book merchants were both the principal consumers of news and its most reliable suppliers.[7]

Even as news became more plentiful in the sixteenth and seventeenth centuries, the problem of establishing the veracity of news reports remained acute. The news market – and by the sixteenth century it was a real market – was humming with conflicting reports, some incredible, some all too plausible: lives, fortunes, even the fate of kingdoms could depend on acting on the right information. The great events of history that pepper these pages were often initially mis-reported. In 1588 it was originally thought throughout much of continental Europe that the Spanish Armada had inflicted a crushing defeat on the English fleet; as in this case, the first definitive news was frequently outrun by rumour or wishful thinking, spreading panic or misjudged celebration. It was important to be first with the news, but only if it was true.

This troubling paradox initiated a second phase in the history of news analysis: the search for corroboration. As we will see, by the sixteenth century professional news men had become quite sophisticated in their handling of sensitive information. The first intimation of tumultuous events was reported, but with the cautious reflection 'this report is not yet confirmed'.[8] Europe's rulers would pay richly for the earliest report of a crucial event, but they often waited for the second or third report before acting upon it. But this was not a luxury all could afford: for the French Protestants hearing news of the St Bartholomew's Day Massacre in August 1572, only immediate action might save them from becoming one of the next victims. In these troubled times news could be a matter of life and death.

News, Rumour and Gossip

Not all news concerned events of such momentous or immediate relevance. Even before the publication of the first weekly newspapers in the seventeenth century, enormous quantities of news were available for those prepared to pay for it, or even just to follow the talk in the market square. To Defoe this abundance was a great miracle of modern society. To others it was deeply troubling. From this great mass of swirling information how could one extract what was truly significant? How could one tell the signal from the noise?[9]

Those who followed the news had to devise their own methods of making their way through the mass of rumour, exaggeration and breathlessly shared confidences to construct a reasonable version of the truth. First they tended to exclude the purely personal and parochial. Our ancestors certainly delighted in the tales of the ambitions, schemes and misfortunes of their families, neighbours and friends: who was to marry whom, which merchants and tradesmen faced ruin, whose reputation had been compromised by a liaison with a servant or apprentice. When in 1561 a citizen of Memmlingen in southern Germany rather unwisely decided to get to the bottom of who had spread a rumour that his daughter had fled town to conceal an unwanted pregnancy, fifty citizens could offer precise recollections of how they first heard this delicious gossip.[10] But however eagerly consumed and passed on, this sort of scuttlebutt was not generally what people thought of as news. When men and women asked friends, business partners or neighbours, 'What news?', they meant news of great events: of developments at court, wars, battles, pestilence or the fall of the great. This was the news that they shared in correspondence and conversation, and this was the news that fuelled the first commercial market in current affairs.

Very occasionally, through a diary or family chronicle, we have a window into the process by which early news readers weighed and evaluated these news reports. One such was Herman Weinsberg, who lived in the great German city of Cologne in the later sixteenth century. Weinsberg, it must be said, was a very odd man. It was only after his death that his appalled family discovered that he had memorialised all their doings in an expansive chronicle of their lives and times.[11] Weinsberg, who lived a comfortable existence on the rents from inherited property, took a close interest in contemporary events. Living outside the circles of the city elite, he was forced to rely on what he picked up from friends, or read in purchased pamphlets. Happily a news hub like Cologne was drenched in information, but not all sources could be relied upon. Weinsberg's technique was to weigh conflicting reports to discern the 'general opinion' or consensus. In this he unconsciously imitated precisely the process followed by the city's magistrates, or at Europe's princely courts. But sometimes it was simply impossible to discern the true state of affairs. When in 1585 the nearby town of Neuss was surprisingly captured by forces of the Protestant Archbishop Gerhard von Truchsess, Weinsberg heard no fewer than twelve different accounts of how the archbishop's soldiers had slipped into the town undetected. He interviewed eyewitnesses who told their own story. The city council sent messenger after messenger to find out what had happened, but they were prevented from entering the town. Weinsberg had eventually to conclude that the true facts might never be known: 'Each person cannot truly say and know more than what he had seen and heard at the place where he was at that hour. But if he heard about it from others, the story may be faulty; he cannot truly know it.'[12]

The exponential growth of news reporting did not necessarily make things easier; many believed it made things worse. In fact, for those traditionally in the know, the industrialisation of news, the creation of a news industry where news was traded for profit, threatened to undermine the whole process by which news had traditionally been verified – where the credit of the report was closely linked to the reputation of the teller. In the burgeoning mass market this vital link – the personal integrity of those who passed on the news – was broken.

The Commercialisation of News

In the first stages of our narrative almost no one made money from supplying news. On the contrary, the provision of news was so expensive that only the elites of medieval Europe could afford it. You either had to pay large sums to build up a network of messengers – a fixed cost that proved beyond the means even of some of Europe's wealthiest rulers – or rely on those under a social obligation to provide news for free: feudal dependants, aspirants for favour, or, in the case of the Church, fellow clerics. Even Europe's most mighty princes frequently cut costs by handing their despatches to friendly merchants, who would carry them for free.

It is only in the sixteenth century that we will encounter the systematic commercialisation of these services. The first to make money from selling news were a group of discreet and worldly men who plied their trade in the cities of Italy. Here in Europe's most sophisticated news market they offered their clients, themselves powerful men, a weekly handwritten briefing. The most successful ran a shop full of scribes turning out several dozen copies a week. These *avvisi* were succinct, wide ranging and remarkably well informed. They are one of the great untold stories of the early news market.[13]

This was an expensive service, yet such was the thirst for information that many of Europe's rulers and their advisers subscribed to several of them. But

such facilities only met the needs of those for whom access to the best sources
of information was a political necessity. The vast majority of the population
made do with what news they could come by for free: in the tavern or marketplace, in official announcements proclaimed on the town hall steps. These too
played an important role in shaping the climate of opinion, and would remain
an essential part of the news market throughout the period covered in this
book. Europe's more humble residents sought out news where they could find
it: in conversation, correspondence, from travellers and friends.

The real transformation of the news market would come from the development of a news market in print. This would occur only haltingly after the first
invention of printing in the mid-fifteenth century. For half a century or more
thereafter printers would follow a very conservative strategy, concentrating on
publishing editions of the books most familiar from the medieval manuscript
tradition.[14] But in the sixteenth century they would also begin to open up new
markets – and one of these was a market for news. News fitted ideally into
the expanding market for cheap print, and it swiftly became an important
commodity. This burgeoning wave of news reporting was of an entirely
different order. It took its tone from the new genre of pamphlets that had
preceded it: the passionate advocacy that had accompanied the Reformation.
So this sort of news reporting was very different from the discreet, dispassionate
services of the manuscript news men. News pamphlets were often committed
and engaged, intended to persuade as well as inform. News also became,
for the first time, part of the entertainment industry. What could be more
entertaining than the tale of some catastrophe in a far-off place, or a grisly
murder?

This was not unproblematic, particularly for the traditional leaders of society
who were used to news being part of a confidential service, provided by trusted
agents. Naturally the elites sought to control this new commercial market,
to ensure that the messages delivered by these news books would show them
in a good light. Printers who wanted their shops to remain open were careful
to report only the local prince's victories and triumphs, not the battlefield
reverses that undermined his reputation and authority. Those printers who
co-operated willingly could rely on help in securing access to the right
texts. Court poets and writers, often quite distinguished literary figures, found
that they were obliged to undertake new and unfamiliar tasks, penning texts
lauding their prince's military prowess and excoriating his enemies.[15] Many of
these writings made their way into print. For all that this period is often
presented as one of autocratic and unrepresentative government, we will
discover that from remarkably early in the age of the first printed books
Europe's rulers invested considerable effort in putting their point of view, and

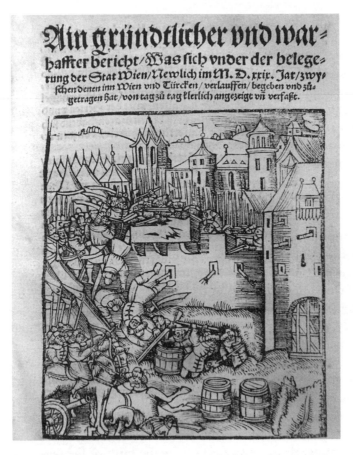

0.1 Good news from the front. The inspiring tale of the defeat of the Turkish attack on Vienna in a contemporary news pamphlet.

explaining their policies, to their citizens. This too is an important part of the story of news.

The patriotic optimism of the news pamphlets served Europe's rulers well in their first precocious efforts at the management of public opinion. But it posed difficulties for those whose decisions relied on an accurate flow of information. Merchants ready to consign their goods to the road had to have a more measured view of what they would find – news pamphlets that obscured the true state of affairs were no good to them if what was important was that their cargoes should safely reach their destination. The divisions within Europe brought about by the Reformation were a further complicating factor: the news vendors of Protestant and Catholic nations would increasingly reproduce only news that came from their side of the confessional divide. News therefore took on an increasingly sectarian character. All this led to distortions tending to obscure the true course of events. This might be good for morale, but for those in positions of influence who needed to have access to more dispassionate reporting the growth of this mass market in news print was largely a distraction. For this reason the rash of news pamphlets that flooded the market in the sixteenth century did not drive out the more exclusive manuscript services. The *avvisi* continued to find a market among those with the money to pay; in many parts of Europe confidential manuscript news services continued to prosper well into the second half of the eighteenth century.

The Birth of the Newspaper

The printed news pamphlets of the sixteenth century were a milestone in the development of the news market, but they further complicated issues of truth and veracity. Competing for limited disposable cash among a less wealthy class of reader, the purveyors of the news pamphlets had a clear incentive to make these accounts as lively as possible. This raised real questions as to their reliability. How could a news report possibly be trusted if the author exaggerated to increase its commercial appeal?

The emergence of the newspaper in the early seventeenth century represents an attempt to square this circle. As the apparatus of government grew in Europe's new nation states, the number of those who needed to keep abreast of the news also increased exponentially. In 1605 one enterprising German stationer thought he could meet this demand by mechanising his existing manuscript newsletter service. This was the birth of the newspaper: but its style – the sober, detached recitation of news reports inherited from the manuscript newsletter – had little in common with that of the more engaged and discursive news pamphlets.

The newspaper, as it turned out, would have a difficult birth. Although it spread quickly, with newspapers founded in over twenty German towns in the next thirty years, other parts of Europe proved more resistant – Italy for instance was late to adopt this form of news publication. Many of the first newspapers struggled to make money, and swiftly closed.

The trouble with the newspapers was that they were not very enjoyable. Although it might be important to be seen to be a subscriber, and thus to have the social kudos of one who followed the world's affairs, the early newspapers were not much fun to read. The desiccated sequence of bare, undecorated facts made them difficult to follow – sometimes, plainly baffling. What did it mean to be told that the Duke of Sessa had arrived in Florence, without knowing who he was or why he was there? Was this a good thing or a bad thing? For inexperienced news readers this was tough going. People who were used to the familiar ordered narrative of a news pamphlet found the style alienating.

News pamphlets offered a very different presentation of news, and one far better adapted to contemporary narrative conventions. Pamphlets concentrated on the most exciting events, battles, crimes and sensations; and they were generally published at the close of the events they described. They had a beginning, a middle and an end. Most of all, news pamphlets attempted an explanation of causes and consequences. By and large, this being a religious age, news pamphlets of this sort also drew a moral: that the king was mighty; that malefactors got their just deserts; that the unfortunate victims of natural catastrophe were being punished for their sins.

The news reporting of the newspapers was very different, and utterly unfamiliar to those who had not previously been subscribers to the manuscript service. Each report was no more than a couple of sentences long. It offered no explanation, comment or commentary. Unlike a news pamphlet the reader did not know where this fitted in the narrative – or even whether what was reported would turn out to be important. This made for a very particular and quite demanding sort of news. The format offered inexperienced readers very little help. The most important story was seldom placed first; there were no headlines, and no illustrations. And because newspapers were offered on a subscription basis, readers were expected to follow events from issue to issue; this was time-consuming, expensive and rather wearing.

This was not at all how most citizens of European society in these years experienced news. For them, great events might only be of interest when they impacted their lives directly. Even for the more curious, it was easy to dip in and out, to buy a pamphlet when it interested them, and, when not, to save the money for some other pursuit. This made far more sense in terms of the way events unfolded – sometimes momentous, sometimes frankly rather humdrum. The news pamphlets reflected this reality: that sometimes news was important, and provoked a flurry of activity on the presses, and sometimes it was not.

So it was by no means easy to persuade the inhabitants of seventeenth-century Europe that the purchase of news publications should be a regular commitment. It is not difficult to see why newspapers were so slow to catch on. Consumers had to be taught to want a regular fix of news, and they had to acquire the tools to understand it. This took time; the circle of those with an understanding of the world outside their own town or village expanded only slowly. For all of these reasons it would be well over a hundred years from the foundation of the first newspaper before it became an everyday part of life – and only at the end of the eighteenth century would the newspaper become a major agent of opinion-forming.

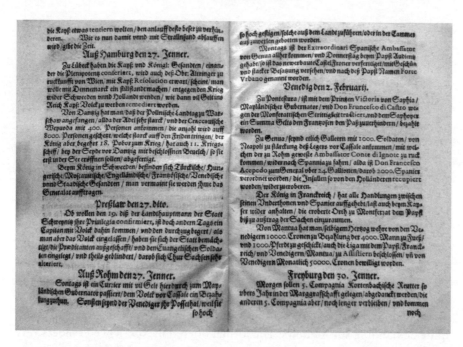

0.2 *Wochentliche Ordinari Zeitung*, Anno 1629. An early issue of a German newspaper. Crammed with information, but hard-going for the uninitiated.

The birth of the newspaper did not immediately transform the news market. Indeed, for at least a hundred years newspapers struggled to find a place in what remained a multi-media business. The dawn of print did not suppress earlier forms of news transmission. Most people continued to receive much of their news by word of mouth. The transmission of news offered a profound demonstration of the vitality of these raucous, intimate, neighbourly societies. News was passed from person to person in the market square, in and outside church, in family groups. Enterprising citizens celebrated exciting occurrences in song: this too became a major conduit of news, and one quite lucrative to travelling singers who otherwise would have struggled to make a living.[16] Singing was also potentially very subversive – magistrates found it much more difficult to identify the composer of a seditious song than to close a print-shop.[17] The more sophisticated and knowing could enjoy contemporary references at the theatre. Playgoing, with its repertoire of in-jokes and topical references, was an important arena of news in the larger cities.[18] All these different locations played their part in a multi-media news world that coexisted with the new world of print.

These long-established habits of information exchange set a demanding standard for the new print media. We need to keep constantly in mind that in these centuries the communication of public business took place almost exclusively in communal settings. Citizens gathered to witness civic events, such as the arrival of notable visitors or the execution of notorious criminals. They heard official orders proclaimed by municipal or royal officials; they gathered around the church door to read ordinances or libels; they swopped rumours and sung topical songs. It is significant that in this age to 'publish' meant to voice abroad, verbally: books were merely 'printed'.[19] Printed news had both to encourage new habits of consumption – the private reading that had previously been an elite preserve – and to adopt the cadences and stylistic forms of these older oral traditions. Reading early news pamphlets, we can often hear the music of the streets, with all their hubbub and exuberant variety. Readers of early newspapers, in contrast, were offered the cloistered hush of the chancery. They were not to everybody's taste.

News Men

The complexities of this trade called for agility on the part of those who hoped to make money from news. Many who tried were disappointed. Pamphlet publishing was highly competitive, and only those whose connections gave them access to reliable sources of information could expect to flourish. Many of the first newspapers were remarkably short-lived. Those that survived often did so with a discrete subsidy from the local prince – hardly a guarantee of editorial independence. For much of Defoe's time writing the *Review* he was paid a secret retainer by one or other of England's leading politicians to promote their policies.[20] Sir Robert Walpole coped with a critical press by buying the newspapers and making them his mouthpiece. He went on to become England's longest-serving eighteenth-century prime minister.

For most of this period there was not much money to be made from publishing news, and most of it went to those at the top of the trade. If some did grow rich, they were the proprietors: in the sixteenth century the publishers of the bespoke manuscript services, later the publishers of newspapers. A manuscript news-service was by and large the business of a single well-informed individual. As his reputation grew he might have found it necessary to employ an increasing number of scribes to make up the hand-written copies; but his was the sole editorial voice.

The first newspapers were put together in much the same way. The publisher was exclusively responsible for their content. His task was essentially editorial: gathering reports; bundling them up; passing them on. In many cases the publisher was the only person professionally involved in this stage of the production process. He employed no staff and no journalists in the modern sense. Much of the information that made up the copy of the first newspapers was provided free: information passing through the rapidly expanding European postal service or sent by correspondence. Some of the newspapers were quasi-official publications with close connections to local court officials, who provided access to reliable information from state papers. Publishers found other ways to augment the meagre pickings from cover-price sales and subscriptions. For many, advertising became the mainstay of the business model; for others, obliging politicians with their gifts, pensions or promises of office paved the way to a better life.

The nature of the newspapers and the means of their compilation left little scope for what we might regard as journalism. The reports were not long enough to leave room for much in the way of comment or commentary. As the newspapers became more established in the eighteenth century some publishers employed a few stringers, men who would hang around the law courts or stock exchange hoping to pick up snippets of publishable material.[21] But such men seldom leave much of a mark in the records. Although we will meet some colourful characters in these pages, this was not yet the age of the professional journalist. The information they provided was hardly ever valuable enough to command the exclusive service of one particular paper. Most sold their stories to whomever would have them. It is only with the great events at the end of the eighteenth century – the struggle for press freedom in England and the French and American revolutions – that newspapers found a strong editorial voice, and at that point a career in journalism became a real possibility. But it was always hazardous. As many of the celebrity politician writers of the French Revolution found, a career could be cut short (quite literally) by a turn in political fortunes. At least these men lived and died in a blaze of publicity. For others, the drones of the trade, snuffling up rumour for scraps, penury was a more mundane danger.

The Sinews of Power

The more sophisticated news market that emerged during this period depended on the construction of a network of communications. Between the fourteenth and eighteenth centuries this too was steadily improved. The European postal networks became more intricate and more reliable. News reports became more frequent. It became easier to verify what one had heard from a second or third independent source. That this was possible was largely the result of the creation of far more efficient means of exchanging written communication over long distances. At the beginning of the fourteenth century only the rich and powerful could afford the cost of maintaining a network of couriers; as a result, those in positions of power largely determined what information should be shared with other citizens. By the eighteenth century relatively ordinary citizens could travel, send and receive mail, or purchase news reports. The process of information exchange had been put on a rational commercial basis. Millions of communications now flowed along the arterial routes of European trade every year. News was abundant: now everyone could have an opinion, and many chose to express it.

In many respects the four prime considerations that governed the business of news – its speed, reliability, the control of content and entertainment value – were remarkably unchanging in these centuries. At different times one or other of these priorities would matter more to consumers of news than others; sometimes they would be in direct conflict. The truth was seldom as entertaining as tall stories; news men were often tempted to pass off the one as the other. But whatever the place and whatever the news medium, these four principles, speed, reliability, control and entertainment, express fairly succinctly the main concerns of those who gathered, sold and consumed the news.

The centuries with which this book is concerned witnessed a vast widening of horizons for Europe's citizens. The discovery of the Americas and the creation of new trade routes to Asia brought a fresh relationship with distant continents. But while these new discoveries have done much to shape our perceptions of those periods, just as important at the time was the quiet incremental revolution that brought citizens in touch with the neighbouring city, the capital and other countries in Europe. Sitting down to their weekly digest of news in any of a dozen European countries in 1750, men and women could experience the fascination of faraway events. They could obtain, through regular perusal, a sense of the leading personalities of European society, and the disposition of its powers. Four centuries previously such knowledge would have been far less widely shared. In this earlier period for the vast majority of citizens news of life outside the village, or the city walls, depended on chance encounters with strangers. Many such citizens would have little knowledge of the world beyond, unless directly affected by the local consequences of high politics or warfare. This was a very different time for news. What we do detect, however, even at this earlier date, is a hunger for information, even if it could only be satisfied for those in the highest reaches of politics and commerce. This was the same hunger that in the centuries that followed would set European society on the road towards a modern culture of communication.

PART ONE

THE BEGINNINGS OF NEWS PUBLICATION

CHAPTER 1

Power and Imagination

Maximilian I, Holy Roman Emperor between 1493 and 1519, was not the most astute of rulers. Despite a whirlwind of travel, diplomacy and optimistic dynastic alliances, he never succeeded in asserting control over his large and dispersed dominions. Even before his election as emperor, he had so inflamed opinion in the Low Countries that in 1488 the people of Bruges held him hostage for seven months until he capitulated to their demands. Always chronically in debt, on one other occasion he was forced to flee his German creditors by slipping out of Augsburg under cover of darkness. This was neither very dignified nor very imperial.

Yet Maximilian usually seemed to triumph over adversity. A combination of extraordinary resilience and restless scheming ensured that his grandson, Charles V, would inherit from Maximilian an even more formidable collection of territories, encompassing a large part of the European land mass. Maximilian also had imagination. He harnessed the power of the innovation of printing more effectively than any contemporary ruler.[1] And in 1490 he embarked on a project that would have enormous resonance for the history of communication: he determined to create an imperial postal service.

At this time Maximilian ruled over an unusual combination of territories. As co-administrator with his father, Emperor Frederick III, he ruled the Habsburg lands in Austria and south Germany; through his first wife, Mary of Burgundy, he was also effective ruler of the Netherlands as regent for his young son Philip. A later marriage, to the daughter of the Duke of Milan, opened the prospect of further dynastic aggrandisement but also brought him into persistent conflict with the kings of France, inevitable rivals for supremacy in Italy. Juggling these complex possessions and constantly on the move, Maximilian needed to have the most up-to-date political intelligence. It was with this in mind that in 1490 he summoned to Innsbruck two members of an

Italian family of communications specialists, Francesco and Janetto de Tassis.[2] The two men were the sons of Alessandro Tassis, who had built his reputation by organising the papal courier service, the *Maestri dei Corrieri*. Francesco had subsequently gained experience with similar projects in Milan and Venice. Now Maximilian engaged the two sons to establish a regular postal service that would cross Europe: from Innsbruck in Austria to his Netherlandish capital at Brussels. The agreement made provision for the establishment of regularly spaced and permanently manned stages: the couriers were to ride at an average speed of 7.5 kilometres per hour, covering up to 180 kilometres per day. In 1505 a new contract extended the range of this network to embrace stations in Spain, at Granada and Toledo, where Maximilian's son Philip now resided as co-ruler.

Like so many of Maximilian's grand schemes, this was only partly successful. It would take another hundred years before the imperial postal network was fully functioning. But from these beginnings would eventually emerge a communications network that underpins much of what we will encounter in this book: the beginnings of a commercial market for news, and the first regular serial news publications.

It is hard to know what inspired Maximilian to take this momentous step, but in creating such an ambitious scheme he, like so many of his Renaissance

1.1 Two portraits of the Emperor Maximilian. The Habsburgs were not a handsome family, though the artistry of Albrecht Dürer could at least invest Maximilian with a certain majesty.

contemporaries, sought inspiration from the ancients. With the help of Francesco de Tassis, Maximilian had the chance to recreate a plausible imitation of the postal network of the old Roman Empire – until this point the most spectacularly successful communications system known to civilisation.

The passage of time had done much to obliterate the physical remains, if not the memory, of the Roman Empire; but the imprint of the Roman communications system had proved remarkably enduring. It would be the ghostly presence hovering in the background as medieval Europe gradually began to construct its own system of news and communication.

The Ghosts of Vindolanda

Like so much of what had been created during the Roman Empire, the Roman postal service was an achievement of breathtaking imagination and administrative ambition. The Roman road network had been designed to move large bodies of troops around a militarised domain that stretched from Spain to Germany and from Britain to Asia Minor. A high-speed courier service was an essential part of the information and administrative infrastructure that underpinned this system. Although much of the engineering work was in place under the Republic, the postal service itself only became fully established during the reign of Emperor Augustus.[3] Couriers travelled by horse or by carriage. The main stage posts were established eight miles apart, with night quarters at every third stage. This suggests that a courier would normally progress at the rate of about 25 miles a day. Fifty miles would be possible if the news was especially urgent, but the journey would take a terrible toll on the messenger if the distance to be travelled was very large.

Normally a single courier would carry the message the entire length of the journey. In principle a relay of messengers could travel in greater comfort, but many messages were so confidential that they could only be entrusted to a particular individual. Very often the written message was little more than an introduction, confirming the credentials of the bearer; the substance would then be delivered verbally. The same messenger could then take back a reply. According to Suetonius, Augustus, who took a personal interest in the establishment of the post, also regularised the practice of dating letters, even to the exact hour, to document when they had been despatched.

The imperial postal service was created explicitly to serve the purposes of the vast Roman administrative machine. The upkeep of the service was extremely expensive, particularly after the development of more elaborate rest stations (*mansiones*), where travellers could find accommodation, stabling and a change of horses. The system was not generally open to the public. Yet the management of the Empire demanded the transport of a large quantity of military freight along the roads, alongside the express courier service, and it seems that this more mundane traffic provided plentiful opportunities for the citizens of the Empire, dispersed around the distant outposts, to maintain a surprising level of written communication.

The full extent of this can only be guessed at: most of the evidence has long since disappeared. But a glimpse into this lost world opened up quite recently, thanks to a remarkable find at Hadrian's Wall, near the northern British frontier of the Roman Empire. In 1973 a team of archaeologists was continuing routine excavations at Vindolanda, one of the military camp settlements adjacent to the wall. Excavating a trench they came across a mass of leather, textiles and straw, mixed with bracken and wood. Some of the wood was in small, thin fragments. When they inspected these slivers, it became apparent that these were covered in writing. What had been discovered were the first of nearly two thousand writing tablets, all written in ink on a wooden veneer – somehow miraculously preserved in the anaerobic soil of Northumberland.[4]

The wooden tablets found in this excavation have transformed what is known of the writing culture of the northern Empire. Britain was as far away as it was possible to be from the production centres of papyrus, the versatile

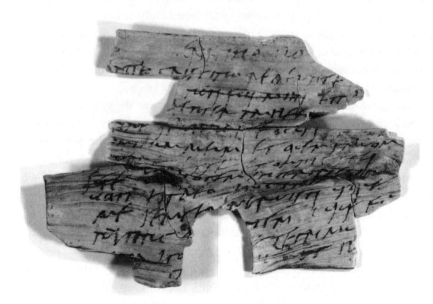

1.2 Fragments of a wooden writing tablet from Vindolanda. This contains the draft of a letter from a prefect of Vindolanda to a certain Crispinus.

reed that provided the cheapest and most abundant writing material in Roman times. Where papyrus was not available, officials used waxed wooden tablets, where notes could be inscribed in the wax. A large number of these were also found in the Vindolanda excavation, though with little or nothing still legible once the wax had disappeared. The slivers of wood discovered at Vindolanda, subsequently confirmed by other finds, reveal a whole new writing medium, and one open to a wide cross section of the general public. The tablets, now in the British Museum, preserve communications from over one hundred writers, from the local governor and his wife to relatively humble members of the garrison community.

The ghosts of Vindolanda are often no more than tiny and incomplete fragments of enigmatic and cryptic messages. Yet they reveal a writing community of depth and breadth even in a frontier outpost at the very edge of the Empire, manned, it should be remembered, not by Roman legionaries but by auxiliaries raised from other subject peoples. We do not know how widespread were the skills of reading and writing in the Roman Empire.[5] But what can be inferred from the Vindolanda tablets is that even when societies were not highly literate, systems of government and administration could be built around the assumption that written communication was a normative means of conveying news.

The Romans were of course masters in the exercise of power. The creation of the imperial postal service reflected a recognition that the control of information, and the swift passage of vital news, was essential to the government of widely dispersed and thinly garrisoned possessions. Roman Britain was an archetype of the large province managed by an astonishingly small occupying force. It was only possible because the control of communications meant that a larger, irresistible force could swiftly be marshalled.

The Roman postal service died with the Empire, to be resurrected only by the equally ambitious German emperors at the turn of the sixteenth century. But the main lesson of the Roman communications network, that control of news was an essential attribute of power, was fully grasped in medieval Europe. We will see it reflected in the conduct of all three of the major power brokers in the medieval world: the Church, the State and the merchant class. All three would develop a vivid culture of news.

From the Cloister

The Church was one of the great estates of medieval Europe. Its institutions had played a crucial role in the preservation of learning after the collapse of the Roman Empire. Since membership of the clerical estate was essentially defined by literacy, it was inevitable that the clergy would be the designated record-keepers of early medieval society. As the Church consolidated its reach across the whole of western Europe, it would also be in the forefront in the transition from a culture where inherited wisdom was preserved by memory to one of written record.[6] Not that the assumed superiority of writing would go entirely uncontested. In the various confrontations between secular and ecclesiastical power that erupted in the eleventh and twelfth centuries, lay folk were not always prepared to concede that verbal reports were any less authoritative than, as they put it, 'words written on animal skins'.[7] This well-turned insult drew attention to the rather unromantic origins of parchment, which was at this point the only abundantly available writing material. Parchment, made of the dried hide of sheep or calves, was a good, reliable and durable writing surface, but complex and expensive to prepare. The writing surface had to follow the irregular dimensions of the original hide, so notes were often written on thin slips cut from the edges. So for all but the most ceremonial purposes, such as a charter or treaty, there was a strong incentive to keep messages short. Often, as in Roman times, written communications would simply attest to the trustworthiness of the messenger, who could deliver the substance of the message verbally. Parchment could also be reused, but then important documentary information is often lost because a text has been scraped off and overwritten. This means that the information culture of the early medieval period often has to be reconstructed from very fragmentary remains.

Problems of this nature apply even to those at the very apex of medieval Europe's emerging news networks. The Cistercian monk Bernard of Clairvaux, for example, was one of the most distinguished voices of medieval Christianity. He was deeply involved in the major political and theological controversies of his day. He spoke out against the Cathars and the theologian Peter Abelard; he intervened freely in disputes over the election of bishops, and offered his counsels to the French king, Louis VI. Between 1146 and 1147 he preached passionately in favour of the Second Crusade. All of this required close attention to the maintenance of an active network of information, messengers and correspondence.

In the conditions of twelfth-century Europe this was by no means easy, but Bernard possessed one priceless advantage. As Abbot of Clairvaux, the mother house of an extensive network of monasteries, Bernard could call upon the assistance of a willing band of peripatetic and literate churchmen. A remarkable number of Bernard's letters survive – around five hundred – far more than for his contemporary (and rival) Peter the Venerable, Abbot of Cluny.[8] These were just the visible remains of an information network that extended far beyond regular communications with Rome, even as far as Constantinople

and Jerusalem. The maintenance of such a network was not without its chal-
lenges. As was the case with Roman couriers, the written communication was
often little more than a letter of introduction, with the substance of the
message intended to be conveyed verbally. Bernard would sometimes have to
wait patiently for a suitable envoy who could be trusted to deliver a sensitive
communication accurately. He was lucky that Clairvaux was a regular stopping place for numerous pilgrims and clerics on official business, situated as
it was in prosperous Champagne, between Paris, Dijon and the Alpine passes.

Bernard was, by the standards of the time, exceptionally well informed. But
there was still a large element of chance in the individuals who passed by and
the news they brought. It was seldom possible to corroborate a report brought
by a visitor – Bernard would have to make his own estimate of the reliability
of the source. Many of those who brought news – of a disputed episcopal election, for instance – had their own axes to grind. If the news was important
enough for Bernard to send his own messenger, it might be many months
before he received a reply. Even a journey back and forth to Rome, the hub of
Europe's most intensive traffic in information, might take up to four months,
as the messenger inevitably had his own business to conduct, and might not
be planning a return trip to Clairvaux. Contact with more occasional correspondents was even more sporadic. A complex negotiation, which required
the passage back and forth of several despatches, was hard to envisage.

Chronicles

Bernard of Clairvaux was an exceptional figure: a true prince of the Church.
But the wish to stay abreast of events, and an awareness of the significance of
life outside the cloister, was shared by many of his fellow clerics. Medieval
monasteries served an important function as custodians of the collective social
memory: monks were the first historians of western Christendom. To perform
this function required that they make assiduous efforts to gather information
on the world's follies and travails; in the words of the chronicler Gervais of
Canterbury, 'such deeds of kings and princes as occurred at those times, along
with other events, portents and miracles'.[9]

Some of these events had a decidedly contemporary character, and this
trend becomes far more pronounced in the chronicle-writing of the fourteenth and fifteenth centuries. This development was partly the consequence
of the increasing predominance of chroniclers who were secular priests and
even laymen, many with close access to the centres of power in the royal
courts. The monastic chroniclers in contrast had, by nature of their vocation,
been largely confined to their own houses. These new chroniclers could get

out and about: they frequently wrote from their own experience, or recorded having personally spoken to eyewitnesses or participants.

These medieval chroniclers offer a precocious and unexpected sense of developing news values. Naturally they write from a religious perspective: events reflect the unfolding of God's purpose and must be interpreted within the context of divine revelation. But the chroniclers also reveal a profound concern that the events they record should be credible and recognised as such. They offer repeated testimonials to the quality of their sources, the social status or number of the witnesses, and whether the writers were personally present. Even the recording of distant events reflects a clear concern to report only what was credible. Thus the chronicler of St Paul's Cathedral in London recorded, of an exceptionally severe frost in Avignon in 1325 in which many froze to death, that 'according to the testimony of those who were there and who saw it, for one day and night the ice covering the Rhône, which is an extremely fast-flowing river, was more than eight feet thick'.[10] Note how the addition of a seemingly precise but unverifiable detail, the thickness of the ice, adds greatly to the credibility of the account.

Many medieval chroniclers were partisan – fierce critics or passionate supporters of the kings whose deeds they record. But they also exhibit a precocious instinct for the ethics of news reporting. If they rely on second- or third-hand accounts, these are identified as such: 'so it is said', 'so people said' (*ut fertur; ut dicebantur*). When they know of conflicting accounts they are often scrupulous in reporting this fact. Of course chronicles are written with the benefit of hindsight, when events have been resolved; this was reporting without any of the hazards of contemporaneity. The chroniclers were able to look back and draw the appropriate morals: that a comet had portended great evil, that a king had been rewarded for his virtue or laid low by his vices. News was never fleeting or ephemeral, but always imbued with purpose. This form of moralising was equally characteristic of much of the news reporting of the following centuries, as we shall see. In this and so many other respects the medieval chroniclers' views of contemporary history would prove profoundly influential in the development of a commercial news market. They reflected a shared vision of the continuum of history, linking past, present and future events in one organic whole.

The Pilgrim Way

Medieval travel was never undertaken without purpose. The hardships and dangers of the road were well known, and there were few with the resources or leisure to undertake journeys not directly connected to their occupational needs. A traveller passing through a town or village on the road, if he was not one of the traders who plied that route, was likely to be either a pilgrim or a fighting man. Pilgrims often traded conversation for charity. Sometimes they could be persuaded to carry letters or messages to an intermediate destination. Few would have approached a band of armed soldiers for a similar favour.

For large parts of the high Middle Ages the eyes of both groups were turned towards Palestine. The mustering of crusader armies were major public events from the eleventh to thirteen centuries. Calls to arms and for pious donations to underwrite the costs of the Crusades reverberated around Europe. Many of Europe's citizens would have known someone who had joined the holy hosts, and returning knights and camp-followers brought their own accounts of these strange and unforgiving lands. Jerusalem was the ultimate test of pilgrim devotion, the more so because after the fall of Acre in 1291 the holy sites were never again in Christian hands.

Those setting off on these arduous journeys could, in the centuries that followed, avail themselves of a quite considerable body of travel literature offering routes and a tour of the sacred places. By the fourteenth century such travelogues offered a wealth of observation on local customs and exotic beasts (travellers were particularly amazed by the giraffe).[11] The time such written guides took to filter through to a wider public undermines their claims to be news publications – this was a time, remember, when each book had to be laboriously copied by hand. But they do mark the first stage of a certain broadening of horizons, and an expansion of the geographical frame of reference, which will be one of the key aspects of news culture in the centuries that follow.

The Crusades must certainly have impacted on most communities in the western countries where the crusader armies were recruited. In a society where speech was still the main means of delivering facts, people were eager to hear tales of faraway places. In the eleventh century, it has been said, an ordinary Christian would likely have been more familiar with the existence of Jerusalem than the name of their nearest big city.[12] But this came at a price. By inflaming Christian opinion against Islam, the seemingly endless Crusades canonised a series of lurid stereotypes that proved remarkably enduring. Even the most anthropological pilgrim narratives of the fourteenth and fifteenth centuries seem to have had little impact in challenging the exotic fantasies of Islamic society that resonated through the literature of the period. If Christian society knew anything of the Saracens, it would have been from the popular epic poems of the *Chansons de geste*, rather than eyewitness accounts.

This created a challenging environment for the reception of news. Throughout the medieval period and into the sixteenth century, news, especially news of faraway events, had to compete with marvels, horrors and deeds of valour related in the travelogues and romantic epics.[13] The truth was often more prosaic, and therefore vastly less entertaining. Telling truth from fiction was never easy. Even if we confine ourselves to literature that purported to be factual, none of the pilgrim writings enjoyed a shadow of the success of Marco Polo's accounts of more distant lands, or the even more spurious *Travels* of John de Mandeville. These two works survive from the medieval period in more than five hundred manuscripts.[14] Both lived on to populate the imagination of Renaissance travellers including, most influentially, Christopher Columbus.

Faith and Commerce

Not all pilgrimages were as arduous as a trip to the Holy Land. The majority of those undertaken, particularly by laypeople, were to local destinations. Geoffrey Chaucer's pilgrims, we may remember, made the relatively simple trip from Southwark to Canterbury, a journey of about 60 miles. Since this was along one of England's best established and well-maintained roads, one wonders how they had time for more than two or three stories. Of course the leisured circumstances of Chaucer's pilgrims and the undemanding nature of their journey are part of the joke.

By this point the rage for pilgrimage was already attracting a degree of criticism from more austere religious, who feared pilgrims like these might act as a distraction for the more pious and aesthetic. The distinguished theologian Jacques de Vitry was one who had scathing things to say about 'light-minded and inquisitive persons going on pilgrimages not out of devotion, but out of mere curiosity and a love of novelty'.[15] Nevertheless Chaucer does encapsulate very effectively the opportunities that pilgrimage provided for conviviality, gossip and the exchange of news.

In the later Middle Ages pilgrimage was part of the intricate fabric of church life. Canterbury was one of a number of locations that attracted both English worshippers and pilgrims from farther afield. France had a proliferation of medieval pilgrimage sites including Limoges, Poitiers and Bourges.[16] The more austere locations included St Andrews in Scotland and Santiago de Compostela in northern Spain, though many pilgrims to Santiago went by boat, rather than enduring the long trek overland. Competition between pilgrimage sites was intense, not least because local rulers were very aware of the monetary benefit of receiving pilgrims and the attendant sales of trinkets and souvenirs. The extent of this commerce, and by implication the number of pilgrims criss-crossing Europe's roads, can be judged by the fact that an enterprising German entrepreneur entered into a contract to provide 32,000

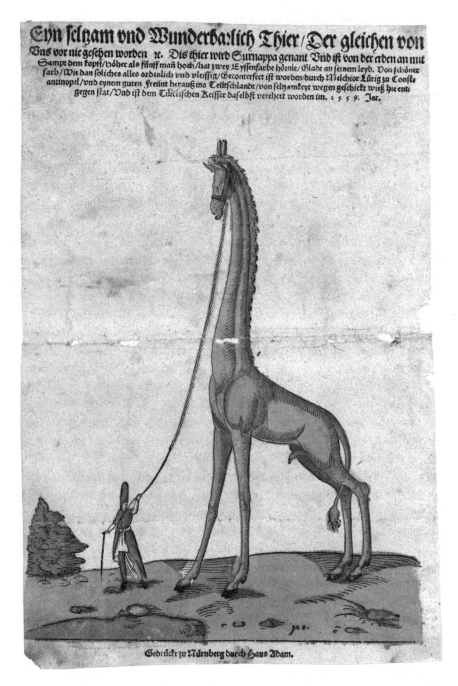

1.3 *A rare and unusual animal*: the giraffe. It is easy to see why so many, to us impossible, travellers' tales were believed, when something as implausible as the giraffe turned out to be true.

pilgrims' mirrors for the septennial display of holy relics in Aachen in 1440.[17] It was only the failure of this enterprise (the partners had mistaken the year, and could not repay their loans in the stipulated term) that caused the projector, one Johannes Gutenberg, to redirect his energies towards a different experimental commercial technology: the printing press.

The most famous of all pilgrimage sites, and one of the most popular, was the fountainhead of the Western Church, Rome.[18] A remarkable number of pilgrims made what was truly a demanding journey, involving as it did, for non-Italians, either a perilous sea journey or a trek across the Alpine passes. When Pope Boniface VIII declared a plenary indulgence for pilgrims who visited the Holy Basilica in 1300, about two hundred thousand pilgrims made the trip. The Jubilee was repeated in 1350 and at intervals thereafter. As pilgrims converged on the Italian Peninsula, finding the right road would have been made easier by having to hand one of a number of route maps prepared for their benefit. These route finders were convenient handwritten rolls, listing the staging points on the route, often with the distances between them. One such route map, the itinerary of Bruges, carries the traveller from the heart of Flanders and down the Rhine.[19] It sketched out what would become, in later centuries, Europe's first great information super-highway.

The pre-eminence of Rome as a pilgrimage site had been greatly enhanced by the role of successive popes in leading calls for the recovery of the Holy Land during the three centuries of the Crusades. In the later Middle Ages the city was a natural centre of news and international politics. Its right to claim financial support from all provinces of the Western Church led to large transfers of money, for which purpose the Church made extensive use of the emerging network of international finance. The need to seek papal approval for appointments, dispensations and annulments required a constant flow of letters and petitioners. The medieval papacy's active intervention in European power politics also attracted attention, from fellow Italians in particular but potentially also from other states. Rome was therefore the first place where many states established their own representatives. The birth of diplomacy, a natural generator of news, gossip and intrigue, was in many respects partly accidental. The journey to Rome was long and papal business slow. While travellers recuperated and waited patiently to conduct business, they would see the sights and often write home. They became, more by chance than intention, the first ambassadors.[20]

For much of this period the authority and even the location of papal power were fiercely contested. Between 1309 and 1376 seven successive popes resided in the papal enclave of Avignon in southern France, after the newly elected Clement V declined to move to Rome. For these seventy years, before the Great Schism led to the establishment of competing centres of authority in Avignon and Rome, Avignon became the centre of Church business, drawing to it much of the bureaucratic apparatus previously established at Rome. This included a very considerable information network. Fourteenth-century paper registers include at least six thousand pieces of correspondence: twenty letters a day left the secretariat for some place in Europe, and this required the elaboration of a considerable infrastructure.[21]

Only a tiny proportion of this correspondence was carried by the Pope's own messengers. The papal couriers were persons of dignity and privileged members of his household. During the fourteenth century there were generally about forty. But they could not all be on the road. Carrying despatches was only one of their responsibilities; they also played a considerable role in provisioning the papal household, negotiating in the markets roundabout. In any case to send all correspondence by courier would have been enormously expensive. The papal secretariat made every effort to minimise expense, sending letters with returning emissaries or other travellers leaving Avignon in the right direction. As in Rome, emissaries from other church or lay potentates could be kept waiting many months for a despatch, and then leave with a considerable bundle of letters to be sent on to other recipients. Letters could also be sent out with papal agents departing to collect revenues, or with bishops and abbots visiting their charges. These, though, were opportunities that would arise only exceptionally. For the largest volume of routine correspondence the popes availed themselves of merchant couriers passing back and forth between Avignon, their Italian headquarters, and other branch offices dispersed around Europe. In the first half of the fourteenth century all the major Italian companies established permanent residencies in Avignon. The Bardi, Peruzzi and Acciaiuoli were the Pope's principal bankers, and much of the correspondence concerned the raising of funds and servicing of debt. After the mid-century crisis of the Florentine financiers the papacy was forced to rely on firms who did not necessarily run their own couriers, or, indeed, on private professional services set up specifically to accommodate the needs of papal correspondence. Some of these freelance operators, like Piero di Gieri, ran a business of considerable size, in his case combining his activities as a hotelier in Avignon with an on-demand courier service. This gave Piero wide-ranging influence; as a sort of unofficial postmaster from 1355 he accumulated both wealth and benefices.[22]

In the variety of mechanisms it could call upon to receive and despatch the news the papacy was not unlike a royal court, though with the added facility of a large infrastructure of volunteer informants and messengers spread throughout the Western Church. Even so, the maintenance of such a sophisticated information network, particularly in such troubled times for the Church, put a considerable strain on its finances. The need to save money often led to delays; routine correspondence for a destination such as Rome or Venice would be accumulated until enough letters were ready to fill the messenger's bag, and this might take several weeks.[23] Economy and efficiency were in constant tension in the medieval news networks.

Beloved Parents

Another group who established their own postal service were a less distinguished part of Europe's clerical class: university students. Universities were church communities of a very particular type. They were dedicated, as were monasteries, to training young men for the service of God. But theirs was a far more transient population. They brought together groups of young men who stayed for a relatively short time. Although life in the medieval university was very austere, students were not subject to the strict discipline of monastic life.

The largest universities drew their students from all over Europe. These young men, far from home, were often homesick, and the universities developed a sophisticated letter service to allow them to keep in touch with their families. The first documented case of a university postal service is that of Bologna, established by 1158; such a service was a common feature of almost all universities by the fifteenth century. The university of Salamanca in Spain employed fifteen muleteers for its messengers; Bourges, in France, had six couriers from the date of its foundation. The best documented example is that of the university of Paris.[24] Founded in around 1300, its messengers were appointed by the different student 'nations' to serve their locality.[25] The longer journeys were made once or twice a year, shorter routes were covered more frequently. The university messengers were privileged individuals, exempted from a variety of taxes and duties. The positions were very much sought after, and became more lucrative when, from the fourteenth century onwards, the couriers began to carry letters also for other customers. This private postal service was remarkably enduring. Jean de Ravillac, the man who in 1610 would murder King Henry IV of France, was one of the *petits messagiers* of the university: he made his living carrying letters for a consortium of eighty students.

The examples that survive of student correspondence are undoubtedly only a tiny proportion of the anxious communications that shuttled back and forth between the universities and home. But the letters are sufficiently numerous for us to hope to discover in them some informed commentary on current affairs. Universities were placed in some of Europe's most vibrant cities, close to the ebb and flow of political life. Yet for all this the harvest of insights and comment on the great events of the day is decidedly meagre. Students writing home had two things uppermost in mind: to impress their parents with their progress in the art of letter writing, and to ask for cash.[26] The medieval epistolary style was formal and highly structured, and students, often destined for a career as an official or a clerk, were keen to demonstrate their progress in mastering this art. If they happened to be less diligent in attending the classes of masters who taught these skills, there were copy-books and manuals with model letters to draw on as shortcuts.[27] The formal salutations over, the writer cut to the chase: money had run out; it was hard for family back home to realise how expensive a university could be; send more. This letter from Oxford University written around 1220 could stand for thousands in a similar vein:

> This is to inform you that I am studying at Oxford with the greatest dili-
> gence, but the matter of money stands greatly in the way of my promotion,
> as it is now two months since I spent the last of what you sent me. The city
> is expensive and makes many demands: I have to rent lodgings, buy neces-
> saries, and provide for many other things which I cannot now specify.
> Wherefore I respectfully beg your paternity that by the promptings of divine
> pity you may assist me, so that I may be able to complete what I have well
> begun.[28]

Few parents found it easy to resist the pleas of a starving child even if the protestations of ceaseless industry were treated with healthy scepticism. 'I have recently discovered,' wrote one exasperated parent from Besançon to his son at Orléans,

> that you live dissolutely and slothfully, preferring license to restraint and
> play to work, and strumming a guitar while the others are at their studies,
> whence it happens that you have read but one volume of law while your
> more industrious companions have read several. Wherefore I have decided
> to exhort you herewith to repent utterly of your dissolute and careless ways,
> that you may no longer be called a waster, and that your shame may be called
> to good repute.[29]

This letter is interesting because it indicates parents were not solely dependent on their own children for knowledge of what was going on: other locals travel-ling back and forth would bring news. Students would describe their living quarters, their (reassuringly respectable) housemates, and the hazards of travel to their place of study. But they seem not much interested in the great events swirling around them. Private correspondence, as we will see, is frequently disappointing in this respect.[30] What these letters do offer is access to a remarkable network of communications radiating out from many of Europe's largest urban centres, a network licensed, and to some extent regulated, but operating independent of the apparatus of state.

The King's Command

The Church could rely on willing and trustworthy messengers travelling between communities or on pilgrimage. The universities identified sufficient demand to establish a regular paid messenger service. But only Europe's rulers could dispose of the resources, and authority, to establish something approaching the Roman system of relay couriers. Even so this became possible only towards the very end of the Middle Ages. Until then, a formal system of news-gathering proved beyond the capacity of most medieval states. For the most part princes concentrated on establishing the mechanisms to convey their wishes to their own subjects. Keeping abreast of events abroad relied on more ad hoc arrangements.

The volume of business generated by state administration in the medieval period is extremely impressive. The Exchequer or financial administration of King Henry I of England logged over four thousand despatches during his lengthy reign from 1100 to 1135.[31] The deposited record could have been even more impressive had not the English Exchequer made use of wooden tally sticks to record tax receipts. Unlike the strips from Vindolanda, these were all consumed by fire in the nineteenth century. The Italian city states, which were among the first to adopt paper for their bookkeeping, chose what proved to be the more durable medium. For their part the English kings devoted particular attention to making their wishes known in the different parts of the kingdom. Messages, writs, summonses and notification of new laws were disseminated by mounted messengers. Each was responsible for four counties. By the fourteenth century the county sheriff could expect to receive several thousand writs a year.[32] Every writ required action to be taken, as the king's will was thereby advertised. Collectively they made a material contribution to building a sense of a national, as well as a local, community.

At this point the nation states of western Europe were devoting far greater resources to enforcing authority within their own domains than to news gathering. This was an understandable priority, given that establishing authority over a dispersed land mass created its own logistical challenge. In southern Europe the situation was rather different. In Italy highly competitive, rich but volatile city states lived cheek by jowl. In these compact and well-organised communities it was far easier to communicate with the citizenry; but potentially hostile neighbours were also close at hand. Having accurate information about the intentions and manoeuvres of rival states was absolutely critical to survival. In the Mediterranean region as a whole, vulnerability to the consequences of political events in the Levant and Middle East, as well as competition for territory, made the need for reliable intelligence a high priority. We know from the letter-books of King Jayme II of Aragon (1291–1327) that he cultivated an extensive network of informers in Italy and elsewhere. His surviving letter-books record an impressive fifteen thousand items of incoming intelligence.[33] The king received information from a wide variety of correspondents, including Cristiano Spinola, a merchant who had inherited a connection with the Crown of Aragon from his father. Between 1300 and his death in 1326, Cristiano wrote King Jayme almost thirty letters from his native Genoa, and, while on his travels, from Avignon and elsewhere. The king rewarded him with trade concessions and royal protection. The Spinola company factors in Sicily were another reliable source. Cristiano relayed information largely without comment; he offered the king no advice on what action should be taken.

Jayme's intelligence gathering was highly reliant on merchant contacts, both for information and for ensuring that the letters reached him. The interlocking of these two networks is encapsulated in the rather charming cypher designed by one of Jayme's correspondents: 'Where I make mention of florins, galleys of Genoa are to be understood, and when I make mention of doubloons, galleys of Savona.'[34] The rather different news priorities of the Mediterranean states can also be discerned in the precocious development in Italy of diplomacy, with its formal system of resident emissaries. News gathering was quickly identified as a primary responsibility of those sent to represent their country abroad.[35]

In northern Europe the landscape gradually shifted, as the monarchical states began to see the need for more systematic systems of news gathering. Not coincidentally this occurred during a period of intense dynastic competition and fluid alliance politics connected to the contests between England, France and Burgundy in the Hundred Years War. Relying on the despatch of envoys to pursue particular tasks was exceptionally expensive. The head of a mission to Aquitaine in 1327 charged £19 for the twenty-one messengers despatched back to England to inform the king of his progress. A special envoy to the Papal Court in Avignon in 1343 charged £13 for a single journey. The English Crown believed much could be achieved by correspondence. Edward, Prince of Wales, the future Edward II, despatched around eight hundred letters in a single year (1305–6). His wife Isabella employed two mounted and eleven unmounted messengers, mostly to keep in touch with her family abroad.[36]

As these examples show, diplomatic correspondence was a major drain on resources. It was important, therefore, that much of the news received by Europe's rulers should not have to be paid for. Courts were great news hubs in their own right. Those drawn to the court included regional magnates with their own networks of communications, and there was constant movement of arrivals and departures of those with favours to ask, or rewards to claim. All courts by the fourteenth century would have their resident poets and chroniclers. Here the victorious knights would repair to ensure that their deeds of renown were known and recorded. When Jean Froissart, the quintessential chronicler of chivalry, set about collecting the information for the third volume of his *Chronicles*, he travelled to the court of Gaston, Count of Foix, at Orthez in southern France. Here he found gathered men eager to provide him with copy:

> In the hall, in the chamber and in the courtyard, worthy knights and esquires came and went, and one heard them talking of arms and adventures. Every subject of honour was discussed there. News from every country and kingdom was to be heard there, for, because of the reputation of the master of the house, they were brought there from every country. There I was informed of most of the feats of arms which had taken place in Spain, Portugal, Aragon, Navarre, England, Scotland and within the frontiers and borders of Languedoc, for while I was staying there knights and esquires from all those nations came to visit the count. And so I gathered information either from them or from the count himself, who was always willing to talk to me.[37]

Europe's rulers were in a unique position to command service and appropriate the necessary resources for news gathering. But as this example shows, many great nobles also established what was in effect a royal court in miniature, sending out messengers to enforce authority in their lands, and exchanging letters with allies or far-flung relatives. By the fourteenth century many city governments also felt the need to maintain their own couriers. In London the volume of letter-writing demanded by civic authorities, guilds and private individuals led to the incorporation of a formal craft, the Scriveners' Company.[38]

News Management

These embryonic systems suffered considerable disruption in the century after 1350. First the Black Death, then prolonged periods of warfare, put strains on both royal finances and royal authority. It became less easy to enforce the duty to provide horses and hospitality for royal messengers. Roads were less safe and appear to have deteriorated in quality. In France this was a period first of near disintegration, then gradual reconstruction after the Hundred Years War. Such events made the need for reliable information all the more urgent, even while its provision became more hazardous.[39] In England the turmoil of the Wars of the Roses, when the Crown changed hands repeatedly and most of the leading protagonists died a violent death, made it exceptionally difficult to stay abreast of events. On hearing an apparently authentic report of the death of King Edward IV on 6 April 1483, the mayor of York ordered a requiem Mass to be said the following day. In fact, the king was still alive until 9 April.[40]

With so much false information swirling around, it was sometimes necessary to take extraordinary steps to ensure that true reports were given credence. Since the battle of Barnet (1471) took place very close to London, wild rumours circulated in the city, and the first reports of the Yorkist victory were not believed. It was only when a mounted rider rode through Westminster carrying the king's gauntlet, his token to the queen of his success, that Londoners knew the outcome. King Edward's decision to exhibit the corpse of the defeated Earl of Warwick in St Paul's Cathedral was also shrewd. When reports began to circulate that Warwick had survived, too many people were able to give this the lie.

In these febrile times, both contending parties gave more attention to news management. After the battle of St Albans in 1455 and again after Towton (1461) and Tewkesbury (1471), the victorious party circulated written reports detailing events. These are sometimes referred to as newsletters, though there is no evidence of systematic mass production. The surviving copies are manuscripts circulated to influential figures in local society keen to align themselves to the change in events.[41] The most significant events were made known to the citizens of London and other towns in proclamations which would be publicly read in the churches or marketplace. This form of law-making and news management was an enduring feature of government in many parts of Europe until at least the seventeenth century.[42]

The French Crown too gave attention to the manipulation of opinion. An early and precocious example was the flurry of writings that followed the assassination of John, Duke of Burgundy, in 1419. These were intended to win over those wavering in their loyalty to the dauphin Charles, the leader of French resistance to the Anglo-Burgundian alliance who had certainly been involved in the duke's murder.[43] Although such manuscripts undoubtedly circulated at this point in rather restricted circles, they prepared the way for a more intensive propaganda in defence of French rights, which at some point engaged most of France's greatest medieval writers.[44]

Despite the considerable progress made in the development of information networks, credible information could still arrive in curiously haphazard ways. A Norfolk man learned the outcome of the battle of Barnet when he saw the dead body of the Earl of Warwick exhibited at St Pauls. Wanting to be first to carry the news home, he left London by boat the same day, but was waylaid at sea and landed by his captors on the coast of Holland. His story was quickly relayed to Margaret, Duchess of Burgundy, at Ghent, who immediately passed this vital intelligence to her husband Charles, at Corbie near Amiens.[45] Thus Edward IV's influential ally had news of his success within four days, but only by happenstance.

In all these circumstances it is no surprise that Europe's rulers began to pay increasing attention to the establishment of a regular, reliable postal service that would give them privileged and rapid access to vital political information. This was the motivation behind the creation in the fifteenth century of a series of royal postal relays. The first successful experiment of this sort was the achievement of the aforementioned Frederick III, then King of the Romans, who in 1443 established a relay between Feldkirch and Vienna in his Austrian dominions. More ambitious by far was the national network of postal couriers established by King Louis XI of France (r. 1461–83). As a child Louis had experienced at first hand the humiliating weakness of the French Crown before the expulsion of the English. Even after the recovery of Paris and northern France, his reign was plagued by internecine feuding in the royal family and with the great nobility. So his creation of a communications network under royal control was both a potent symbol of restored Crown authority and an important tool in the endless struggle to keep one step ahead of restless subjects. Louis's scheme called for the establishment of relay stations on all of the main routes leading through and out of the kingdom.[46] Salaried postmasters were appointed to man each station; their duties required them to maintain horses for the royal couriers speeding through. Following the practice established in the Roman Empire, and continued by the Tassis for the imperial post, the postmaster was to note on the docket the time of arrival and departure of each courier. The system, in principle at least, was closely regulated, and exclusively for royal service. Sentence of death was prescribed for postmasters who allowed their horses to be used by other customers. The couriers carried detailed passports specifying their destination, and they were not permitted to deviate from the route. Foreign couriers were also obliged to keep to the postal routes, or they would be stripped of their safe conducts.

The French experiment inspired Edward IV of England to devise a similar system for the kingdom's most critical news artery: the road to Scotland. The short route between London and the Channel ports was already covered by a system of posts, which obliged the towns along the way to bear most of the cost of speeding royal messengers to the coast. The longer distance to the northern border was more challenging. In 1482 King Edward devised a scheme whereby a mounted messenger was posted at 20-mile intervals. When an important message was to be transported, each messenger would ride to the next sector, before returning to their post.[47] This was ruinously expensive and hardly likely to be maintained outside the present emergency.

The French system, too, proved over-ambitious, and far too expensive to be maintained for any length of time. After the death of Louis XI it was scaled back and fell into disuse. Both Edward and Louis had faced two apparently intractable problems: they could only command the necessary resources for this system to function within their own dominions, which was very limiting from the point of view of international news gathering; and the postal routes could not be made financially self-supporting. These travails, which continued for much of the sixteenth century, point up the particular brilliance of the Habsburg imperial post. By employing a family of private contractors, Emperor Maximilian had passed the problem of making the system work to a group of

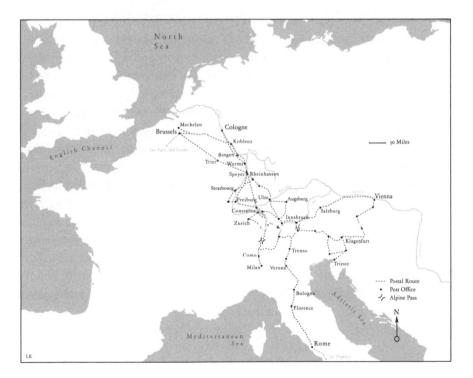

Map 1 The imperial postal system in the sixteenth century.

specialists who were working for profit. The contract of 1505 specified a fixed yearly payment of 12,000 livres. In return the Tassis agreed guaranteed times of delivery between the major postal destinations. Significantly, these included Paris: being private contractors, rather than a royal service, they could operate to some extent outside the Habsburgs' own domains.

The accession of Charles V and his succession as Holy Roman Emperor in 1519 allowed the imperial postal service to extend its range still further. A new contract with Charles in 1516 did one other remarkable thing: it allowed the Tassis to open their postal service to private customers. As a consequence the imperial postal service vastly increased the volume of business, which meant most of those involved could hope to share in the profits. This was a major contrast with the English and French systems, which remained closed royal networks into the seventeenth century. With these restrictions English post-masters were grudgingly aware that their meagre fees would hardly ever cover their expenses. The imperial post was in a highly advantageous situation, since Habsburg domains sat astride many of Europe's major trade routes. But it was also an acknowledgement that to be effective a European communications system had also to serve the needs of Europe's merchant traders.

The centuries before the inauguration of the Habsburg postal system had seen enormous strides in the development of a concept of news. The practical diffi-culties in creating such an infrastructure were very significant, but the notion of news also required a considerable intellectual reorientation, which was far from complete by the end of this period. The increase in written communica-tion and the accumulation of documentation since the twelfth century did not immediately challenge the perceived superiority of the spoken word.[48] Medieval society was built around the transmission of information in face-to-face meet-ings. The main modes of communication were all oral: preaching, lectures in the universities, the proclamation of new laws, tales of wandering minstrels, and this included the sharing of news. 'My cosyn John Loveday can tell you, for he hath walked in London and so do not I,' wrote John Paston in 1471 in response to a request for news, and he reflected a common contemporary perception of the superiority of eyewitness reports transmitted verbally.[49] The trust and reliability of a news report were closely attached to the credit of the bearer: this could hardly be judged in the case of an anonymous writing. Even with the vast increase of written documentation, many of these letters were, as we have seen, highly stylised and uninformative. They were intended to demonstrate the learning of the writer or attest to the credit of the bearer: the critical information was still delivered by word of mouth.

Much of the news communicated in medieval society was still a matter of the spoken word, and thus frustratingly often lost. We have to delve into other sources, such as chronicles, to attest the lively interest in receiving and sharing news. The one main exception, which has been left to its own chapter, is the correspondence generated by the growing international network of trade. Long-distance commerce of necessity separated merchants from their partners and agents. They had, therefore, to develop systems of sharing news, in an atmosphere of trust, and with a reasonable expectation that their correspondents would act on the information. It was a critical development in the history of news gathering.

CHAPTER 2

The Wheels of Commerce

W HEN one considers the problems and expense that Europe's crowned
heads experienced in keeping abreast of events – and how often they
failed to do so – the smooth, efficient progress of merchant correspondence
provides a vivid contrast. Between 1200 and 1500 the economy of Europe was
transformed by the rise of the great merchant companies, trading between Italy
and northern Europe, Germany, the Mediterranean and the Levant. The appetite for eastern luxuries, spices and costly fabrics, exchanged for northern wool
and cloth, created a large and expansive marketplace, full of opportunity for the
bold and ingenious trader. The hazards were also obvious. A ship could be lost
at sea, consignments of goods waylaid on Europe's perilous roads. The intrica-
cies of the money markets created new complexities for those who failed to
master the ever-changing exchange rates. And politics – war, dynastic conflicts
or civil disorder – could derail even the most carefully managed enterprise.

To succeed in this labyrinthine and unpredictable world, merchants had to
remain informed. In the thirteenth century a certain class of merchant ceased
to travel with their goods and instead attempted to manage their business
through brokers and agents. At that stage the growth of a network of merchant
correspondence became inevitable. The essential building blocks were already
in place. Unlike the princes, who had to create such a network from scratch,
merchants had ships, and a far-flung network of agents and warehouses. Carts,
couriers and pack animals passed back and forth every day between Europe's
major trading towns. They carried with them news and, increasingly, written
correspondence.

Even so, the volume of this correspondence is breathtaking. We get a flavour
of its magnitude by examining the well-documented example of Francesco
Datini, a merchant of Prato in Tuscany. Datini was never a member of one of
the great merchant families. A self-made man, he had amassed his fortune

trading in armaments in Avignon before returning to his home town in middle age. Operating through a series of ad hoc partnerships, he consolidated his wealth by shrewd diversification into banking and general trade. Between 1383 and 1394 he established branch offices at Pisa, Genoa, in Spain and Majorca.[1] For all this Datini remained a man of the second rank: his fortune, when he died in 1410, was a respectable 15,000 florins. Yet he also left behind five hundred account books and ledgers, several thousand insurance policies, bills of exchange and deeds, and a staggering 126,000 items of business correspondence.[2] Thanks to this survival (the childless Datini left all his property to the local poor) they comprise one of the greatest archives for understanding the international medieval economy.

That a middle-ranking merchant could accumulate such an extraordinary documentary archive seems highly exceptional, but in its day it was probably routine: the Datini archive was unusual only in its survival. It was contingent, however, on one further technological revolution, as significant in its way as any other of the medieval period: the introduction of paper. Parchment (often known as vellum), made from scraped animal skins, had served the medieval world well. It was hardy, took ink smoothly and evenly, and was very durable, as witnessed by the quantities of parchment documents that survive today. Parchment was also, to an extent, reusable. But it was brittle, and could not easily be folded. It had to be cut from the shape of the skin, with considerable waste from trimming. It was also expensive. The raw material was finite, and took a long time to prepare. The volume of documentation generated by commerce and the expanding state bureaucracies demanded a more flexible and cost-effective writing medium.

Paper entered Europe via Moorish Spain in the twelfth century. Within a hundred years paper mills had been established in Italy, France and Germany. The technology, though capital intensive, was relatively simple. Paper-making demanded an abundance of linen rags and swift running water to power the mills that pounded the rags into mulch. Paper mills were usually constructed in hilly regions close to major centres of population. By the thirteenth century they were turning out a sophisticated range of paper products in carefully graded weights and sizes. Parchment continued to be preferred for precious documents intended to be preserved: charters, deeds and manuscript books. Paper also took longer to enter general use in northern Europe, where the raw materials were harder to come by, because in the colder weather people wore clothes made of wool rather than linen. In England there was no domestic paper manufacture until the eighteenth century, so all paper had to be imported. But despite this, by the fourteenth century paper was the preferred medium for all mundane purposes of record-keeping and correspondence throughout Europe. This humble artefact had established the dominant role in information culture that it retained into the last decades of the twentieth century.

In Bruges

The northern axis of the great network of European trade was Bruges, the vibrant Flemish city that still retains much of its medieval charm. Bruges was the hub of the trade in wool and cloth. To this city came the finest English wool, from whence it was either shipped south or manufactured into the high-quality dyed Flemish cloths which commanded a high price in Italy, France and Germany. All the major Italian trading families of Genoa, Venice and Florence maintained offices in Bruges. Its great square provided space for the exchange of goods from all over Europe.

The fortunes of Bruges were assured with the arrival in 1277 of the first Genoese seaborne fleet.[3] The groups of foreign traders who settled in the city were organised into separate nations, each with their own residential head-quarters and charter of privileges. The Italians were particularly numerous. At a time when Italian overseas trade was dominated by the so-called super-companies, each was heavily represented in Bruges.[4] Technically nothing could be sold in Bruges except through a licensed native broker. Although this stipulation was frequently evaded, brokerage fees yielded large gains for local men. Managing the enormous demand for monetary instruments was also lucrative. By the fourteenth century Bruges had become, in effect, a highly sophisticated service economy. It was also the largest money market in northern Europe.[5]

Communications played an essential role in oiling the wheels of trade. Though many of the bulk goods from southern Europe continued to be trans-ported by sea, letters were sent overland. They travelled along the settled routes familiar to pilgrims and the first generation of international traders in the twelfth century. The roads from Bruges to Italy were recorded in hand-written itineraries which guided the traveller in carefully delineated stages between the largest towns. From Flanders the road went either east to Cologne and down the Rhine, or south to Paris, and thence, via the plains of Champagne, to the Alpine passes.[6]

The merchants and travellers who met on these routes would inevitably exchange news. Pilgrims could also sometimes be persuaded to carry letters with them on their way home. But the sheer volume of documentary traffic demanded something more settled and permanent. In 1260 the Italian merchants set up a formal courier service between Tuscany and Champagne, home at this time to the most important of the great medieval trade fairs. The rhythms and itineraries of trade were built around these fairs. Merchants were enticed to do business by the promise of a large international gathering. Cities competed for the valuable business by offering exemptions from customary dues and tolls in transit. The fairs of Champagne offered a fixed sequence of markets that lasted through most of the year from spring to autumn.[7] They were the centre of a European network that spread out through the fourteenth and fifteenth centuries to embrace Geneva and Lyon to the south, St Denis north of Paris, and Frankfurt in Germany. Further afield lay Leipzig, Medina del Campo in Spain and Antwerp, the rising rival to Bruges in the Netherlands. Fairs provided the opportunity for face-to-face bargaining and the exchange of information. Much of this commercial and political news was never committed to paper. Merchants had to have a highly developed capacity to retain information on commodity prices, exchange rates, distances and commercial rivals. A good memory was a precious financial gift and one that was consciously trained and nurtured. The account book of Andrea Barbarigo of Venice records in 1431 a cash payment of 13 ducats to 'Maistro Piero dela Memoria for teaching me memory'.[8]

In the fourteenth century the wealthier merchants travelled less. Although the fairs still attracted merchandise, much bulk commerce was now shipped by sea. This only increased the need for reliable intelligence. In 1357 seventeen Florentine companies banded together to create a shared courier service. The most important routes ran from Florence to Barcelona, and from Florence to Bruges. The Bruges service ran along two routes: one via Milan and then up the Rhine to Cologne; the other diverted from Milan via Paris. The rival *scarzelle Genovesi* ran services from Genoa to Bruges and from Genoa to Barcelona.[9] In addition to the trans-continental routes, the Italian merchant communities established numerous shorter-distance services within the Italian Peninsula. A twice-weekly service ran between Venice and Lucca. The weekly post between Florence and Rome arrived in Rome on a Friday and set off back on Sunday. It was now only a short step to the establishment of commercial courier services, run on behalf of the merchant companies by independent entrepreneurs. The firm headed by Antonio di Bartolomeo del Vantaggio in the fifteenth century operated a whole network of routes, including a weekly service between Florence and Venice.

Couriers were expected to keep to strict timetables. In the 1420s couriers from Florence were expected to reach Rome in five or six days, Paris in twenty to twenty-two, Bruges in twenty-five and Seville, a journey of two thousand kilometres, in thirty-two days. The annotations on the letters exchanged between Andrea Barbarigo in Venice and correspondents in Bruges, London

2.1 The birth of a paper culture. Merchants and other writing professionals were forced to develop systems for filing incoming documents and correspondence.

and Valencia suggest this timetable could generally be adhered to: only the Seville itinerary seems unfairly demanding.[10] The most sustained evidence for the efficiency of the courier service around the year 1400 comes from the Datini archive. An examination of his correspondence, together with notes of arrival and despatch of letters in the account books, produces evidence of around 320,000 dated epistolary transactions. The seventeen thousand letters between Florence and Genoa and the seven thousand letters between Florence and Venice took between five and seven days to arrive. Delivery times to London were more variable, depending as they did on the vagaries of the Channel crossing. On the other hand the post between Venice and Constantinople was remarkably reliable: letters would arrive between thirty-four and forty-six days of despatch.[11]

Merchants were not the only users of these courier services. Notwithstanding the resources they poured into building their own postal networks, Europe's rulers were perfectly aware that the earliest and most reliable news often came through the merchant communities. With a fair wind news could travel remarkably quickly. The murder of Charles the Good in Bruges on 2 March 1127 was known in London two days later, thanks to the good offices of the Flemish merchants. When in 1316 a papal emissary arrived in England with news of the election of the new Pope, John XXII, he was graciously received and richly rewarded. But the king, Edward II, had in fact already heard this news, a month earlier, from Lawrence of Hibernia, the messenger of the Bardi of Florence.[12] As late as 1497 the Milanese ambassador in London was recommending use of the courier service of the Florentine or Genoese merchants when speed was of the essence. Their confidentiality could also be relied upon.[13]

The merchants were often remarkably well informed. A long report compiled by the manager of the Medici office in Bruges in 1464 offered a detailed commentary on recent political events in both England and the Low Countries.[14] A decade earlier he had correctly predicted that the loss of Rouen would spell the end for the English in Normandy. If one leaves aside the detail of business information (for the political manoeuvres obviously had implications for various ongoing transactions), then these letters have almost the character of diplomatic despatches. Certainly the long-established branch managers were seasoned observers of the local political scene, and often had better local connections than the foreign ambassadors who established residence in the sixteenth century. Diplomats, particularly if they arrived as representatives of a hostile power, struggled to establish relationships of trust.[15] So they frequently turned for information, as did their hosts, to the ostensibly neutral foreign (usually Italian) merchants. This neutrality could become strained if the relationship between the merchants and the host power became too close. At one point the Medici manager in Bruges became personally involved in the secret negotiations surrounding a proposed continental marriage for Edward IV. During the Hundred Years War the Bardi and Peruzzi companies both received substantial payments from the English Crown for spying on French military preparations in Normandy.[16] The merchants were in demand because it was far easier for merchants – particularly merchants from the unaligned states of Italy – to move freely across national boundaries than it would have been for nationals of the belligerent states.[17] This difficulty of travelling through hostile territory was one of the factors that made it more difficult to establish an efficient diplomatic courier service.[18]

The main purpose of merchant despatches was obviously to provide information for the merchants themselves. Given the business sensitivity of so much of the information they retail, the cost of maintaining these courier services seems modest. Jacopo and Bartolomeo di Carocio degli Alberti and partners spent around 30 florins annually on the post between 1348 and 1350. Datini's firm in Avignon spent between 20 and 40 florins a year, and his Florence office a remarkably modest 13 florins. This was about the same as might be paid to a relatively junior member of staff as an annual salary.[19] As a proportion of annual outgoings it was probably well below what was expended on marine insurance. News too was insurance of a sort, and provided vital data on which to base business decisions. The difficulty was knowing what news to believe.

Lost in Transmission

The development of an international European business network had a transformative effect on access to news in the fourteenth and fifteenth centuries. The roots of this development lay in the emergence of major Italian consortia trading to every part of Europe. Trading in a wide range of commodities and luxury goods, companies like the Bardi and Peruzzi established branches throughout the region: in Bruges and London, Spain and the Levant. This branch system created an organic communications network. Frequent contact was necessary to exercise control over branch managers and prevent them making decisions that were not in the company's interest. In return one of the ways the managers could demonstrate their competence was to provide a steady flow of informed comment: on the safety of routes, the movement of exchanges and future trading opportunities.

Exposure in so many markets was not without its dangers. In the 1340s the Peruzzi and the Bardi had experienced a spectacular bankruptcy, when the failure of the English Crown to repay substantial loans left the Italians fatally exposed to their own creditors. The Italians had been lured into underwriting Edward III's ambitious schemes in France by the prospect of a dominant role in the English wool trade. The Florentines were only the latest of a series of Italian consortia to find that lending to the English Crown was a high-risk enterprise. But as each company failed, there was always another to take its place. In 1395 the Mannini advanced large sums to underwrite the cost of Richard II's marriage to the French king Charles VI's daughter, Isabella of Valois. When four years later he was forced to abdicate, they shared in his downfall. 'Because of the deed in England,' reported an unsympathetic rival, 'the said Mannini must needs give up their trade – and thus the world goes. Had there been no revolution in England, they might have become great, but no man ever allied himself with great lords, without losing his feathers.'[20] Yet there was always someone ready to try. Almost as soon as the Italians had news of Richard's deposition, and of his death the following year, they were speculating whether the usurper Henry of Lancaster was likely to take on Richard's young widow, or another wife: 'Whomsoever he may wed, there will be great feasting in England, and silken stuffs and jewels will go up in cost. Wherefore I would advise any who have fine jewels to send them here.'[21]

Here lay the paradox. Competition was natural and inevitable in the business world if fortunes were to be made. But cooperation in the sharing of information was also a necessity, when so much was uncertain and intelligence so hard to come by. Despite the impressive number of business letters that have come down to us, it is important to remember that they represent only a small fraction of what was written. The letters themselves express frequent anxieties about the difficulties of communication, and the uncertainties of the road:

Andrea sends you greetings. And you ought to know that the Sienese people who are here have despatched their letters through a common messenger after the last fair of Saint Ayoul. And I send you a bundle of letters through Balza, a carrier from Siena. If you did not receive them, do try again to get them. The messenger of the merchant guild has not yet come. May God send him to us with good news, for he has already taken too long.[22]

Greetings from Beaulieu. As I have written to you by other letters, I am surprised that after you left us here, we received no letter except the one that you sent from Nice. And were it not that I definitely think the fault is not yours (it is the fault, I believe, of those to whom you entrusted the delivery) I should say that you have entirely forgotten us. I am not writing anything more about this, except that you should be careful to whom you entrust letters, so that they are delivered to us.[23]

Many would no doubt sympathise with the despairing lament of a merchant in Paris writing back to Italy:

It seems as if we had been waiting a thousand years for news from you, for information about what is happening down there; later we shall not be so uneasy, but for Heaven's sake write often![24]

One strategy to ensure the post got through was to send duplicates. 'The Letter was sent on by chance and by two hands, following two different roads, so that you will be fairly sure to receive it.'[25] But this was expensive and cumbersome. Sifting through these letters brings home that many merchants did not make use of the formal courier services, either because they were not part of the consortia that ran them or because they could not afford them. Inevitably these business letters are part of a jigsaw with most of the pieces missing. We hear of transactions to be undertaken, but not how they turned out. And this points up one difference between business letters and the political news they contain. Political news provides context, describing events that have occurred and are likely to impact on trade. The business part of a letter is generally future-oriented, with plans, recommendations and instructions. It assumes knowledge of a context that does not need to be spelt out. The business letters are by and large intended to initiate action; the political comment to inform it.

Nevertheless, there were key similarities between the business discussion and the more general news included in these letters. The sharing of news was costly, and therefore precious. It relied on a network of friends and corre-spondents; it relied, most of all, on trust. Trust, and the trustworthiness of the person who offered the information, was a critical issue that would run through the history of news gathering for the next four centuries.

With so much at stake there were inevitably those who would attempt to steal a march on their competitors. 'If you engage in trade, and your letters arrive together with others,' wrote Paolo da Certaldo in a merchants' hand-book of the mid-fourteenth century,

> always keep in mind to read yours first before passing on the others. And if your letters advise you to buy or sell some merchandise at a profit, call a broker immediately and do what the letters advise, and then consign the other letters that arrived with yours. But don't consign them before having finished your own business.[26]

There were even couriers prepared to accept retainers from particular merchants in return for delivering the mail pouch to their favoured clients first.[27] That said, Paolo da Certaldo's well-known advice has probably received more attention than it deserves. His remarks on business ethics form part of a wry and cynical text which gives equally caustic advice on how Italian citizens should manage their spirited wives. His comments should be set against an equally strong tradition that commercially sensitive news should be freely shared; and much no doubt was, in the marketplace and in the taverns, when ships came in from far afield. In Emden, northwest Germany, where a new merchant community was established in the sixteenth century, the practice was that commercial letters from far-flung places were read aloud in the market square.[28] This would undoubtedly have been a tradition based on earlier German precedent, and the free sharing of information in many ways made far more sense. News about faraway events was precious, but difficult to verify. The quantity of rumour, travellers' tales and eyewitness accounts available in the marketplace therefore played a crucial role in making sense of what might be received in confidential letters. It was valuable to be ahead of the crowd, to buy up grain before it shot up in price on report of an impending dearth. But to act on a report that turned out to be false, or exaggerated, could be more disastrous than not to have acted at all.

It was a delicate balance, and no one wanted to go out on a limb. It was all very well to be first with the news – but how did one know whether it was true? The hope was that the dense network of connections in the merchant community would bring corroborative reports. Those most daring did not wait. Rumour on the Rialto could move prices on the Venice commodity market several points in a single day. Unscrupulous traders were suspected of deliberately spreading false reports so they could profit from market movements.

2.2 Albrecht Dürer, *The Little Courier*. Speed was of the essence for Europe's messenger services, as is dramatically captured in this woodcut.

So despite all the hazards, merchants were assiduous collectors of rumour. 'Keep me informed,' wrote Francesco Datini to a correspondent in Genoa in 1392, 'about spices and about everything related to our trade, especially all the rumours and all the news that you hear about the sea and other things. When you see anything that involves importing or exporting merchandise, let me know.'[29] Of course an unlucky or credulous choice could damage a reputation as well as ruin a speculation. In 1419 the Venetian diarist Antonio Morosini devoted some considerable time to compiling a long despatch of news for his nephew Biagio Dolfin, the Venetian consul in Alexandria. Morosini would have been less than pleased had he known that another nephew, Alban, had written to warn Biagio not to trust what he read:

> I have read a letter of my uncle Antonio, who gives you much news but also many lies, which were passed on to him. And so he writes you what he hears. But I advise you that you should not trust such gossip, which I am afraid, could cause him difficulties one day. So please, don't show or read in public [the parts of] these letters, which in your opinion should be kept discreet.[30]

This is all the more galling as it seems to have been unfair: Morosini's letter does not include anything that was not reported elsewhere. The whole issue of when rumour became news was a thorny one. It was up to each man's judgement to know what to believe, and when to act.

Much rested on the personal reputation of the individual making the report. The early medieval tradition that word of mouth was more to be trusted than a written report lingered on in some of the correspondence. 'Put Domenico on horseback and send him quickly by land, giving me news of what you have done' was the demand of one impatient merchant.[31] But most often this was simply impractical. Datini lived in constant fear of double-dealing (perhaps because his own practices with his partners were none too scrupulous). Merchants were perfectly aware that managers and brokers in far-flung places would be trying to line their own pockets. When contracts were drawn up with agents abroad, clauses were routinely added forbidding them from playing games of chance, reflecting an awareness that heavy gambling losses could lead to desperate attempts to cover debts by embezzlement.[32] These fears were perfectly understandable; but in the last resort trade could only function if merchants shared information. 'When you write to me, always inform me in full,' wrote an Italian trader in Damascus to an associate in Barcelona, 'how the situation is at your place and what you think of it, and about the departing ships destined to this region, and what their cargoes are. And I will do the same for you.' This man's philosophy might stand for the whole community: 'in this way the one hand washes the other'.[33] The business correspondence is full of plans and schemes, but also cautionary tales: ships lost at sea, goods stolen, a caravan loaded with precious cargo robbed by Arabs. Mediterranean piracy was an occupational hazard. Access to information could be the difference between prosperity and ruin. The development of Europe-wide enterprises was necessarily a matter of trust and reciprocity. In the last resort the Italians trusted their own trading apparatus, even if the human beings who formed its sinews sometimes fell short.

Venice

By the third decade of the fifteenth century, Venice had achieved a position of primacy among the Italian trading cities. It now played the pivotal role in three crucial areas of the international economy: the trade in cloth with London and Bruges, the trade in wool with Spain, and the exchange of cotton and spices with Egypt and the Levant. While much of the trade with northern Europe went via the circuitous sea route through the Mediterranean, the overland route to Germany offered an alternative. By this time merchants from the southern German cities were themselves active traders in the Venetian market. The system of government in the Republic was entirely orientated towards the protection of trade. The Senate would take charge of the composition and itinerary of the galley fleets that brought goods from the east and transported them on to Spain and London. It also intervened actively to prevent the creation of monopolies, thus protecting the livelihoods of the independent traders who were the lifeblood of Venetian commerce.

The Republic's growing economic power did not go uncontested. At the beginning of the 1430s Venice prevailed in a trial of strength with the Sultan of Egypt, defeating his attempts to establish a monopoly over the spice and cotton trade. War with the Duke of Milan meant that for several years Venetian sailors risked capture by the powerful Genoese fleet. Meanwhile, the emperor Sigismund, a bitter foe of the Republic, attempted, largely without success, to enforce an embargo on Venetian goods in Germany. All of this meant that the Republic's trade was particularly vulnerable to the vagaries of enemy action. Merchants had to follow every twist and turn in the conflicts if they were to avoid ruinous losses.

The instability of the times created opportunity as well as danger. Those who were prepared to take risks could maximise profit while the more cautious kept their ships in harbour. When peace was declared, previously idle capital flooded the market. In 1429 the price of pepper fell two points on rumours that the Sultan of Egypt had been deposed. War raised the price of pepper but depressed the price of cloth, making it more difficult to ship to the east; peace had the opposite effects.

A peculiarity of Venetian trade was that whereas bulk goods to northern Europe were transported in the galley fleets by sea, mail was despatched overland. This provided the opportunity for the agile merchant to influence the market while the goods were in transit. The following advice from Andrea Barbarigo is perhaps not untypical:

> You asked about pepper and I reply as follows. My opinion would be that you dispose of said pepper at the end of January or before, especially if you can sell at 13 d or more, although our Vittore thinks it should be worth 15 d. I advise you that it is believed that none will be sent to the west by the Catalans, and if the Florentines bring any it will be very late. Of the Genoese I have no knowledge. I do not think there will be much brought by the galleys [of Beirut and Alexandria] because the Soldan [Sultan] has sent to have it taken by his mercantile agent in Alexandria. When the fleet from that port does arrive, which will not be before February or some months later, I think pepper will be worth perhaps 45–50 ducats. All that I say above is to advise you of my opinion, but I wish you to sell my pepper according to your judgement, for cash, term, or barter, and I leave you freedom as to price, trusting you to do the best you can.[34]

As this shows, much was left to the judgement of the agent. Venetian traders, rather than establishing branch offices, tended to undertake new arrangements from voyage to voyage. Agents who were settled in Valencia, Bruges or Acre worked on commission. In the mid-fifteenth century letters from Bruges reached Venice in about twenty-five days. From Valencia, in northern Spain, they took about a month.

By the end of the fifteenth century both the speed of transit and the intensity of contacts had increased markedly. Venice was by this point the undisputed news hub of Europe. Correspondence and despatches arrived in the city in considerable numbers every day, and the most sensitive reports were relayed directly to the Senate. Here their arrival was meticulously noted by the young patrician Marin Sanudo, a long-serving member of the Venetian administration who aspired to be named the city's first official historian. In this he was to be disappointed, but the notes he accumulated in his diary provide the most precious evidence not only of the speed and volume of correspondence, but of its effect on the Venetian economy.[35]

From Sanudo's diary entries we see how directly political news impacted the price of commodities traded on the Venetian market. Venice was heavily dependent on imported grain; it was also re-exported to Germany in large quantities. The major source of imports was Sicily. Thus a report in 1497 that the harvest there was poorer than expected raised prices immediately.[36] The high-value trade in spices was particularly sensitive to changes in political fortunes in the Levant. In 1497 Sanudo noted reports from Alexandria of political turbulence in Egypt that made spice traders reluctant to sell, since they anticipated an interruption to supply that would force prices up. In this context the success of the Portuguese in opening up a new spice route to India around the Cape of Good Hope in 1501 was pregnant with consequences. The prospect that this would spoil the market to Flanders initially depressed prices in Venice. But then came news that the Portuguese had cornered the market, and there was little in Alexandria left to sell. The price of pepper in Venice rose from 75 to 95 ducats in four days.[37] When the Portuguese succeeded in repeating the ocean passage to India the following year, the significance of this feat was not lost on the European merchant community. The news was relayed to Venice from Lyon, Genoa and Bruges as well as from Lisbon. According to another contemporary diarist, the news of the Portuguese success caused greater consternation than any military defeat: 'everyone was stupefied; and this news was considered by informed people to be the worst ever received by the Venetian republic other than losing its freedom.'[38]

The money market and the market in marine insurance were even more volatile. The news that the Turkish corsair Kamali was at sea in 1501 and had taken a host of ships caused marine insurance rates to leap from 1.5 to 10 per cent.[39] With fortunes to be won or lost, those with money were prepared to pay to be first with the news. Also in 1501 the proprietors of the Venetian galleys destined for Beirut chartered a swift vessel to go ahead and advise the Arab traders that a richly laden fleet was on its way. The captain was to receive 850 ducats if he accomplished this voyage in eighteen days, but would lose 50 ducats for each two days of delay.[40] In the sixteenth century a sliding scale of this sort was built into the tariff for express courier services between Venice and Rome. A courier who managed the journey in under forty hours would be paid an impressive 40 ducats (equivalent to the annual salary of a minor administrative officer). If the message took four days to deliver, the fee was a quarter of this.[41]

With so much at stake, it is little surprise that the practice developed of annotating the outer wrapper of a letter with the time of despatch and arrival at each staging post on the route. The first known instance of timing dockets was recorded in the courier service established by Filippo Maria Visconti, Duke of Milan in the middle of the fifteenth century. The letters would be entrusted to mounted riders, sometimes with further scribbled invocations to emphasise the importance of the task: *Cito Cito Cito Cito volando dì et nocte senza perdere tempo* ('Haste, haste, haste, haste, fly by day and night, losing no time') was the insistent message recorded on a docket of the Milan courier master Tommaso Brasca on 6 February 1495.[42] Both this sort of annotation and the practice of recording staging times became standard in the imperial and national postal services of the sixteenth century.

An express courier was only used for news of exceptional importance or commercial sensitivity. What is extraordinary about the meticulous notes assembled by Sanudo is what they reveal about the sheer intensity of the news traffic arriving in Venice. The Venetian ambassador in Rome wrote every day, and couriers were despatched to Venice twice or three times a week. Intelligence from Naples, Lyon and London was almost as frequent. Several thousand of these incoming despatches were some time ago subjected to a systematic analysis by the French historian Pierre Sardella. He studied letters despatched to Venice from around forty different cities, noting, with the help of Sanudo's diary, the time of their despatch and arrival. For each place Sardella then calculated the longest time each letter took to reach Venice, the average and the shortest journey: this allowed him to create for each partner city a 'co-efficient of reliability' for the post between these places and Venice. By far the most reliable service was that between Venice and Brussels: letters arrived in Venice almost without fail ten days after despatch; note also the dramatic fall in transit time compared to Barbarigo's correspondence sixty years before. The post with London was slightly more variable because of the Channel crossing: correspondence that relied on long sea journeys, for example between Venice and Alexandria, could be very erratic.[43]

What Venice had discovered was that although the bulk of trade continued to be transported by sea, land communications were by far the more reliable. The hub of Europe's news networks was now the settled road and river routes linking the commercial cities of Germany, Italy and the Low Countries. This was a development of the utmost significance for the emergence of an international network of news.

The Eyes and Ears of Germany

Venice also enjoyed extremely efficient letter communications with the cities of southern Germany. However difficult it might be to haul bulky commerce over the Alpine passes, the post got through.

German merchants had played an important role in the European trade network since the twelfth century. Cologne was the northern gathering point of trade between inland Germany, the Low Countries and Italy. Merchants from northern Hanseatic cities such as Hamburg and Lübeck were also heavily involved in long-distance sea-trading.[44] The German merchants were the first formally incorporated national group in thirteenth-century Bruges. But it was the southern German cities that would emerge in the later Middle Ages as motors of the central European economy. Augsburg and Nuremberg were, by 1400, in the forefront of production of the luxury manufactures so much in demand in Europe's major markets: both cities specialised in the production of linen cloth and metalwork. Augsburg was the source of much of the best armour and a precocious centre of banking. Nuremberg, with its close connections to the mining regions of Saxony and Bohemia, specialised in ironwork and brass.

In the sixteenth century Augsburg would emerge as the critical nodal point in the European communications system. One hundred years before, this role had been played by Nuremberg. In the fourteenth and fifteenth centuries Nuremberg was the effective capital of the German Empire, a primacy recognised in the expectation that emperors would hold their first meeting of the German Estates, the Reichstag, in the city.[45] Nuremberg had the largest territory of any imperial free city. Its merchants had interests all over Europe, with particular concentrations in Spain, Italy and the Low Countries. The practice of merchant families sending their young men to serve apprenticeships in branch offices abroad persisted into the sixteenth century, as can be seen from the large numbers of letters that still survive in the archives from homesick and often misbehaving youngsters to their harassed parents.[46]

A cornerstone of Nuremberg's rise to greatness was its engagement in the financing of industrial ventures in the mines of Saxony. Nuremberg was Germany's gateway to the east, and the major firms had branch offices in Vienna, Prague and Krakow. The fact that its governing council was drawn from the wealthiest merchants ensured that the interests of business would always be well represented. A mirror of Nuremberg's economic power can be seen in the city's success in insisting that its merchants were exempted from tolls in many other German towns. Nuremberg's economic power was respected but also feared: the city fathers were fully aware that the interests of their city had to be defended against predators. That demanded, above all things, a steady flow of accurate information.

Nuremberg's status as an information hub derived partly from its geographic situation, at the confluence of twelve major roads. Martin Luther described the city as 'the eyes and ears of Germany', and it would play a critical role in spreading news of his quarrels with the papacy.[47] The role of the international merchant community as a source of information was widely recognised. In 1476 the minutes of the Town Council record a decision 'to seek advice from

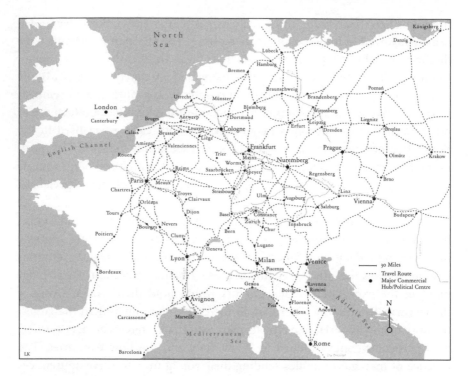

Map 2 Major European trade routes, c. 1500.

the merchants' and this would not have been unusual.[48] The steady Turkish advance through the Balkans in the fifteenth century threatened many areas where Nuremberg merchants had invested capital. When war seemed likely, the city merchants would entrust one of their number who had interests in the area with finding out what was afoot. Critical information was frequently shared with other German cities. In 1456 news of the war with the Turks was despatched onward to Nördlingen and Rothenburg. In 1474 when the merchants contacted a friendly source in Cologne for information, they in return forwarded news from Bohemia, Hungary and Poland.[49]

To service this far-flung information system the German towns and cities maintained a sophisticated courier network. A regular courier service was in operation between Augsburg and Nuremberg by 1350, and the first surviving city accounts for Nuremberg, which date from 1377, show that the city was already making use of paid messengers.[50] By the fifteenth century Nuremberg had a number of couriers on the city payroll. Notwithstanding the expense, the city made frequent use of their services: in the ten years between 1431 and 1440 Nuremberg sent out 438 messengers.[51] This period of intense activity coincided with the latter stages of the Hussite wars, and in such turbulent times it was vital that the merchant community be aware of the latest developments in case their goods were impounded – either where they were traded or in transit. The city fathers regarded the outlay on messengers as money well spent.

With these city courier services the south German cities had established a system that fell halfway between the traditional ad hoc system of merchant correspondence and the diplomatic networks beginning to be developed by Europe's leading princes. They were able to take advantage of the same synergy of interest we have observed in that other great merchant republic, Venice.

In the sixteenth century the network of German city courier services would be linked up to provide a regular weekly service as an adjunct and later rival to the imperial post. Because the imperial post followed the major trade routes between the Netherlands and Italy, the north/south trade axis through the Empire was not well served, and this is where the city post came into its own. But this was for the future. At the close of the Middle Ages the merchant posts had established an intense and permanent node of communication between Venice and southern Germany, linking two of Europe's most sophisticated merchant economies. In turn this established a second vital stream of information to mirror the route through the western Alps linking Italy with Paris and Bruges. Venice and Nuremberg, the two great trading centres of the age, had established an undoubted primacy as information hubs south and north of the Alps. It was no accident that these cities would also be pioneers in the new information age that dawned following the invention of printing.

CHAPTER 3

The First News Prints

IN the new commercial world of fourteenth- and fifteenth-century Europe, wealth brought many privileges. Men of power had long enjoyed the luxury of space: land on which to hunt; large and eye-catching villas on the main streets of Europe's richest cities. Now, thanks to international commerce, they were able to fill these houses with beautiful things. Their homes became the visible symbols of their wealth. They built gardens, wore fine clothes, and filled their rooms with exquisite objects: tapestries, sculpture, pictures and curiosities, the horn of a unicorn or precious stones. They also began to collect books. For the development of European intellectual culture the new vogue for books was highly significant. Until this point books were essentially a utilitarian tool of the professional writing classes. Books were accumulated only where they were used: in religious houses, by teachers in the new universities. Students might own one or two texts, often laboriously copied from dictation or from a rented master copy. It was only in the late fourteenth century that the building of a library became an important part of elite culture.

Books and learning played a critical role in the new culture of the Renaissance. Scholars placed the rediscovery of lost classical texts at the heart of an exciting new world of intellectual exploration and literary fashion.[1] Europe's major commercial hubs, in Italy, Germany and the Low Countries, became the centres of a new trade in the manufacture and decoration of books.

As long as each book had to be hand-copied from another manuscript, the pace of growth was limited by the availability of trained scribes. Inventive spirits in different parts of Europe began experimenting with ways to speed the process by mechanisation. The honour of having first mastered the craft of printing would go to a German, Johannes Gutenberg, the manufacturer of pilgrims' mirrors of a decade before.[2] In 1454 Gutenberg was able to exhibit at the Frankfurt Fair trial pages of his masterpiece, a Bible, that he would go on to produce in 180 identical copies. Europe's book-owning classes were not slow to understand the importance of what Gutenberg had achieved. Attempts to protect the secret of the new technology were unavailing. Soon craftsmen were introducing the new technique of book manufacture to all corners of Europe.[3]

The technological brilliance of print was indeed impressive, but the first generation of printers was remarkably conservative in the choice of books they brought to the market. The first printed books mirrored very closely the taste of established customers for manuscript books. Gutenberg's Bible was followed by psalters and liturgical texts. Italy's first printers published multiple editions of works by classical authors, the cornerstone of the humanist intellectual agenda. Standard legal texts of civil and canon law, medieval medical and scientific manuals, also became staples of the new market. These were on the whole big and expensive books. It took some time for printers to understand how this new invention might be used to exploit the market for news.

For this reason the news events of the late fifteenth century did not, on the whole, leave a substantial impact on the new medium of print. The fall of Constantinople in 1453 came just before Gutenberg had successfully unveiled his new invention. For the next thirty years printers would be largely focused on mastering the new disciplines of a marketplace suddenly awash with unprecedented numbers of books, not all of which found customers. News of the conflicts in France, England and the Low Countries, and the darkening clouds gathering over the eastern Mediterranean, was spread by largely traditional means: in correspondence, and by travellers. The fall of Negroponte in 1470 and the siege of Rhodes in 1480 were the first contemporary political events to find a significant echo in print: the threat of Turkish encroachment, here as later, stimulated a pan-European response. Printed copies of the Pope's appeal for coordinated action for the defence of Rhodes were widely circulated.[4] But these were ripples on the pond.

For as long as the new industry remained geared to the production of large books for traditional customers, the reporting of contemporary events would remain a subsidiary concern. The expansion of print into new markets proceeded by tentative steps. First, printers would learn the value of varying their output by publishing small items for volume sales (cheap print). Then they would make experimental use of print to share news of the discoveries of faraway continents in the age of exploration. But it was only in the early sixteenth century, a full seventy years after Gutenberg published his Bible, that the world experienced its first major media event, the German Reformation.

The Reformation catalysed a movement of powerful change that destroyed forever the unity of Western Christendom. It also alerted Europe's nascent printing industry to the potential of a whole new mass market for printed news of contemporary events. The news market would be changed for ever.

The Commerce of Devotion

In 1472 the first printers in Rome, Konrad Sweynheim and Arnold Pannartz, appealed to the Pope for help. Their publishing house stood on the brink of failure. Their printing shop, according to their piteous petition, was 'full of printed sheets, empty of necessities'.[5] They had to this point manufactured an impressive 20,000 copies of their printed texts: but they could not sell them. Theirs was not an unusual experience for the first generation of publishing pioneers. The first printers were guided in their choice of texts by their most enthusiastic customers. The universities wanted texts; scholars wanted the classical works admired by humanists. The result was that many of the first printers produced editions of the same books. It turned out they had given too little thought to how they would dispose of the copies. The market in manuscripts was close and intimate: the scribe usually knew the customer for whom he copied a text. Now printers faced the problem of disposing of hundreds of copies of identical texts to unknown buyers scattered around Europe. The failure to resolve these unanticipated problems of distribution and liquidity caused severe financial dislocation. As a result a large proportion of the first printers went bankrupt.

For the shrewdest among them, salvation lay in close cooperation with reliable institutional customers: the Church or State. In the last decades of the fifteenth century the rulers of a number of Europe's states began to experiment with the mechanisation of some of the routine procedures of government. The use of printing to publicise the decisions of officialdom would in due course become one of the most important aspects of the new information culture.[6] But for the first generation of printers the Church would be the new industry's most significant customer. Alongside the numerous prayer books, psalters and sermon collections, church institutions also began to contract printers to mechanise the production of certificates of indulgence.

One of the ironies of Luther's later criticism of indulgences was that they were not only hugely popular, but an early mainstay of the printing industry.[7] After several centuries of evolution the theology of indulgences reached its mature form in the fourteenth and fifteenth centuries.[8] In return for the performance of pious acts – participation in a pilgrimage, contribution to a Crusade or church building – the repentant Christian was offered the assurance of remission of sin. The practice was closely associated with the doctrine of purgatory, to the extent that the length of the remission, often forty days, was precisely quantified. The contribution was acknowledged with a receipt or certificate: initially on parchment or paper, and handwritten.

It was swiftly recognised that the labour of inscribing such certificates would be greatly reduced if the terms and details of the gift could be printed, leaving gaps for insertion of the name of the recipient and the sum donated. Certificates of indulgence soon became a ubiquitous feature of publishing in Germany. For printers, this was the ideal commission. The work was short, a few simple lines of text, easily set up and executed. Since the complete text was a single sheet, on one side of paper, it demanded no technical sophistication. Most crucially, a printed indulgence posed the printer none of the complex problems of distribution that shipwrecked so many early businesses. With indulgences the printer undertook the work as a commission from a single client, normally the bishop or a local church. It would be for the institution to distribute the copies: the printer would receive his full payment on delivery of the work.

The scale of this business was clearly immense. Of the 28,000 printed texts that have survived from the fifteenth century, the first age of print, around 2,500 were single-sheet items or broadsheets. Of these, a third were indulgences. Furthermore, indulgence certificates were printed in far larger editions than was normal. The earliest books were printed in editions of around 300, rising to 500 by the end of the fifteenth century. However, for indulgences we know of orders for 5,000, 20,000, even in one case for 200,000 copies.[9] This was work so lucrative that printers would often interrupt or put aside other orders to fulfil these commissions, as frustrated authors frequently complained. Gutenberg was one of many printers who undertook work of this sort, alongside more ambitious projects.[10]

This sort of ephemeral printing is particularly prone to the natural wastage that has caused so much early print to be lost. Some publications that have vanished altogether can only be documented from archival records. Taking all this into account, we can reliably estimate that by the end of the fifteenth century printers would have turned out as many as three to four million indulgence certificates. This was good work for printers, and they grabbed it like a lifeline.

The indulgence campaigns also gave rise to a host of associated works. One of Gutenberg's early publications was the so-called *Türkenkalendar*, a six-leaf pamphlet entitled *A Warning to Christendom against the Turks*.[11] Under the guise of a calendar for the year 1455, a series of verses exhort the Pope, Emperor and the German nation to arm for the fight against the common enemy. The following year Pope Calixtus III proclaimed a Bull exhorting the whole of Christendom to join the crusade, either in person or through

3.1 The trade in salvation. An indulgence published as part of Raymond Peraudi's third great German campaign, 1502.

monetary contributions. The German translation of this Bull was published as a fourteen-leaf pamphlet.[12]

These pamphlets had an important news function. Campaigns that raised money for international causes, such as the incessant calls for crusade against the encroaching Ottoman Empire, brought news of these faraway events to a wide public.[13] These publications, though generally originating in Italy, achieved a remarkable geographical range. The crusading writings of Cardinal Bessarion were among the first books published in France.[14] William Cousin's account of the siege of Rhodes was the first book published in Scandinavia (in 1480). Two years later, an explanation of the plenary indulgence decreed for the Turkish crusade was the very first book published in the Swedish language.[15]

The unchallenged superstar of this new financial evangelism was Cardinal Raymond Peraudi. An indefatigable preacher and pamphleteer, Peraudi led three major fund-raising campaigns in northern Europe between 1488 and 1503. His sermons were major events for the towns that received him, and the sums raised were divided between the Church and the local authorities according to a carefully laid-down formula. Peraudi's activities were supported in a blizzard of publications, in both broadsheet and pamphlet form.[16] The careful orchestration of information, exhortation and excitement has much in common with modern campaigning techniques.[17] Peraudi would arrive in a city with great pomp and circumstance. His visit was often preceded by publications announcing his impending arrival and the cause for which he preached. After he had roused the crowds to pious devotions, contributors would be provided with the indulgence certificate stipulating their donation and the promised remission. Those keen to learn more could buy locally printed copies of Peraudi's sermon.

Peraudi could not be everywhere, so in other places the campaign was led by appointed deputies. In Sweden it was headed by the Dutchman Anthonius Mast, who brought with him 20,000 letters of indulgence, of which 6,000 were taken on to Finland by Michael Poyaudi.[18] This was a carefully coordinated and highly sophisticated media campaign, designed to energise Christendom to a sense of shared responsibility for critical events in faraway lands. It was also a precocious demonstration of the potential impact of printing.

These events were intensely moving for those who witnessed a great preacher at work; for the history of publishing they are also deeply significant. For many of Europe's citizens the precious certificate of indulgence would be the first printed text they owned. In contrast to the rather conservative instincts of many early publishers, these fund-raising campaigns increased awareness in the industry of the possibilities of the new medium. The publishing opportunities surrounding the preaching of indulgences alerted many publishers for the first time to the value of cheap print. It was an important dry-run for the media storm that would engulf Germany a generation later with the coming of the Reformation.

New Worlds

On 18 February 1493 a small weather-beaten ship, the *Niña*, made landfall on one of the Portuguese islands of the Azores. On board was the Genoese adventurer Christopher Columbus, who had just completed the first successful voyage back and forth across the expanse of the Atlantic Ocean. The discovery of the Americas was one of the critical turning points in world history, and it took place just as Europe's public was beginning to explore the potential of printing as a news medium. In 1492, the same year that Columbus had set sail from Spain, a giant meteor fell near the Alsace village of Ensisheim. An enterprising poet, Sebastian Brant, had composed a verse description of the event. Several German publishers then printed this text, along with a bold woodcut representation of the meteor racing across the sky. This news broadsheet proved enormously popular, and several editions still survive.[19]

The discovery of the Americas was potentially of a whole different order. In the long term, if hopes were realised of large discoveries of gold and spices, it could transform the European economy. In the shorter term it pitted against each other the two great monarchies competing for domination of the trans-oceanic lands, Portugal and Castile-Aragon. A few years later the Portuguese would triumphantly conclude their own momentous feat of exploration, linking the Eastern spice lands with the European market by rounding the southern tip of Africa.

At the time, it must be said, this Portuguese expedition seemed to Europe's news markets the more significant story of the two. The true impact of Columbus's three great voyages emerged only gradually. Despite this, the response to Columbus offers a particularly interesting case study of a developing news event at a time when the news market was itself in a state of transition.

Even before the forced landfall in the Azores, Columbus was acutely aware that accounts of his voyage would have to be carefully managed. He had departed garlanded with the most expansive promises of rewards should he find, as he had promised, a westward passage to the Asian spice markets. As Admiral of the Ocean Seas he and his heirs were to be invested with hereditary dominion and a tenth of the profits emanating from the new discovered lands. His ships had crossed the ocean but what they had discovered was by no means clear. Columbus could not definitely confirm a route to Asia, nor offer any clear prospect of riches: the novelties he could display, parrots and native captives, might seem an insufficient surrogate for the gold and spices he had promised.

Even to make his report to Ferdinand and Isabella, Columbus had first to endure a second unwanted brush with the Portuguese. After extricating his crew, with some difficulty, from the Azores, Columbus's ship was forced to take refuge in the harbour of Lisbon. He was summoned to a potentially diffi-cult interview with the King of Portugal, a man who had previously turned down his offer of service, but would now have a very shrewd understanding of what his navigational feat might mean.

Before he attended this awkward rendezvous, Columbus had taken the precaution of sending a report of his discoveries to his royal patrons at Barcelona. He despatched a second copy from the Spanish port of Palos, near Cadiz, after his patched-up ship had been allowed to sail on – to his enormous relief – from the Portuguese capital. Both reports made their way successfully to Barcelona, where they had in fact already been anticipated by a messenger from Martin Pinzón, captain of the *Pinta*, which had been separated from the Admiral's ship in the storm that blew Columbus into the Azores. The *Pinta* made landfall in northern Spain, from where Pinzón sent word overland to the court, asking leave to come in person to tell the story of the voyage. This was refused: the sovereigns insisted this was the prerogative of Columbus. He was now summoned to Barcelona for what became a triumphant festival of celebration.

In the weeks following Columbus's meeting with Ferdinand and Isabella, further manuscript copies of his report circulated around the court. It was not long before one appeared in print, in a Spanish translation published in Barcelona. A copy of the original letter was printed almost simultaneously in Valladolid, and it was this Latin *Epistola de insulis nuper inventis* ('Letter from the islands recently discovered') that became the basis for a rapid flurry of reprints: in Rome, and north of the Alps at Basel, Paris and Antwerp. A paraphrase of this letter was also rendered into Italian by Giuliano Dati, and it too found an eager public, with three editions published before the end of the year.[20]

Columbus, for all his fantasies and delusions, was a remarkable man. He had charted, almost by instinct, what was to prove the most expeditious route for transatlantic sailing; he also proved a remarkably effective publicist. His account of this first voyage was a masterpiece of concise exposition, fitting neatly into an eight-page pamphlet. But the commercial success of *De insulis inventis* should not lead us to overestimate its influence in shaping contemporary perceptions of Columbus's discoveries. Even before the pamphlet was printed in Rome, sometime after 29 April 1493, news of the voyage had already made its way to at least seven different cities through manuscript reports.[21] These manuscript letters, and the earliest verbal reports, seem to be what weighed most heavily among opinion-formers. Columbus stuck doggedly to the view, at least in public, that the lands he had discovered were Asiatic; he had therefore fulfilled the terms of his contract and deserved his reward. Others were more sceptical. Among those who had the chance to converse with Columbus at court were two men who would themselves be influential in promoting the oceanic discoveries in their publications, Pietro Martire d'Anghiera and the young Bartolomé de Las Casas. At his Lisbon landfall Columbus had also made the acquaintance of Bartholomeu Dias, a veteran of the first Portuguese voyages around the Cape. These men were aware that Columbus had done something remarkable, but doubted that he had found a route to Asia. The formal response of his royal patrons reflected this emerging consensus: their greeting referred more ambiguously to 'Islands you have discovered in the Indies'.

Such doubts did not diminish enthusiasm for Columbus's announced plan for a return voyage. He had little difficulty in recruiting 1,500 volunteers, who in September 1493 embarked with a greatly enhanced fleet of seventeen ships. But the stakes were very high. The potential of the westward voyages pointed up the need for urgent resolution of the contesting claims of Spain and Portugal. News of an agreement, the treaty of Tordesillas, was conveyed to

Columbus in a letter from Queen Isabella in 1494 when he was already back in Hispaniola. The fact that other ships were already at this stage making the Atlantic passage independently also caused Columbus problems. It was now more difficult to manage news: reports of the increasingly chaotic state of the new settlements were soon being conveyed back to Spain by the disgruntled and the disillusioned. The scale of royal investment in the second and third voyages made the dawning recognition that Columbus's Asian fantasy had no foundation difficult to deal with. On his return in late 1496 from his second voyage, Columbus was subjected to a formal commission of inquiry; during the third voyage he was stripped of his powers and returned to Spain in 1500 in chains.

Despite these reverses many of the early enthusiasts kept faith. Pietro Martire d'Anghiera was an influential friend. His letter of November 1494 celebrating 'this Columbus, discovered of a new world' coined a usage that has remained current to this day. The term passed into general use, reinforced several years later when d'Anghiera published a highly influential account of the New World discoveries, *De orbis novo*. But the drama of the later voyages no longer had the same resonance in correspondence and print. In pragmatic mercantile circles the failure to discover the elusive western passage to Asia diminished interest in America. The news that the Portuguese had imported significant quantities of spice via the Cape route in 1499 and 1501 caused, as we have seen, far more turbulence in the financial and commodity markets.[22]

In 1502 the exploration of the Brazilian coast by Amerigo Vespucci provided definite proof of the discovery of a new continental land mass. Vespucci was also a gifted self-publicist. His description of this voyage, undertaken in the service of Portugal, was quickly published in several languages and multiple editions.[23] Interestingly, this was the first of the great travel narratives to find a large resonance in Germany, where it was published in German translation in at least eight different cities. This suggests a telling contrast with the earlier Columbus expeditions. Discussion of the first oceanic voyages focused very much on their political implications, hence the particular interest they excited in Italy, where the Spanish Pope Alexander VI was heavily involved in resolving the resulting jurisdictional quarrel between Spain and Portugal. The Portuguese Crown, despite being first with the news of Columbus's extraordinary feat, made no attempt to publicise it: it was hardly in their interest to do so. Ferdinand and Isabella, and Pope Alexander in Rome, on the other hand, actively promoted publicity of the expedition's success. North of the Alps there was a curious lack of resonance, despite the success of Columbus's first account. Here there was a certain ambivalence towards Spanish ambitions, reinforced by the emerging Habsburg connection with the Spanish Crown. The pronounced preference in France and Germany for news of Portuguese success (Portugal was a traditional French ally, as well as a counterweight to Spanish expansion) thus also has its political aspect.

Over the course of the sixteenth century publications about New World colonisation would multiply. As the full extent of the new Spanish possessions became clear, Europe's northern powers found themselves drawn inexorably into the unfolding Atlantic geopolitics. Taken on their own, the accounts of the first Columbus expedition provide an interesting snapshot of the news market at the end of the fifteenth century. To carry the first news to Spain and onwards to Italy, Columbus and his backers relied primarily on correspondence. In quantitative and qualitative terms this remained the most important and quickest form of super-regional news distribution. Correspondence provided precise, rapid information for those who needed to know. Letters had a limited distribution, but a high degree of reliability.[24] Print played a different role. Print allowed news to reach a broader public, those who could not expect to be in receipt of privileged information. Often what was presented as news was intended to serve the wider public debate that followed after significant events. This was the case with the publications that followed the fall of Negroponte (1470), one of the first news events to be widely discussed in print.[25] The disastrous loss of this key Venetian citadel in the eastern Mediterranean to the Turks provoked a flurry of print commentary, much of it in verse. But few readers of these works would have been learning the news for the first time. The plight of the garrison was well known, and news of their capitulation was swiftly disseminated from Venice around Italy, by letters and word of mouth. Here the publication of news pamphlets played a part in an acrimonious debate about political responsibility; they also allowed Italy's eager humanists to display their literary virtuosity on the subject of a contemporary tragedy.

At this early date print was a sporadic, occasional medium. It could not yet provide the constant flow of information necessary for those in positions of responsibility for whom critical decisions could depend on remaining fully informed. When Columbus arrived back from his first voyage, the full potential of print as a news medium was only just beginning to be recognised. That would await Europe's next resonant news event, the Protestant Reformation.

The Wittenberg Nightingale

There were many reasons why what became the Protestant Reformation should have come to nothing. Martin Luther was an unlikely revolutionary: a conservative middle-aged academic, who had made a distinguished career in the

Church. There seemed no reason for him not to esteem an institution that had nurtured and rewarded his talent; he certainly thought of himself as a devout Catholic. When his stubborn determination to hold to his controversial propositions on indulgences led him into irreconcilable confrontation with the church hierarchy, he found ranged against him the full might of Europe's most powerful institution. The Luther affair should have ended there, with the disgraced friar stripped of office and incarcerated, and quickly forgotten.

What saved Luther was publicity. When he formulated his ninety-five theses against indulgences, he sent copies to several potential disputation partners, including his local bishop, Albrecht, Elector of Mainz and Archbishop of Magdeburg. The theses soon found their way into print, and into the hands of a circle of interested intellectuals in Nuremberg and Augsburg.[26] From there news of Luther's angry denunciation of indulgences spread quickly around northern Europe. This was wholly unexpected. From any perspective Wittenberg, a small town tucked away in the northeastern reaches of the German Empire, was an unlikely focus for a major news event. Wittenberg was far removed from Germany's major communications network, and in the years that followed Luther would not always find it easy to keep up with the tidal wave of events unleashed by his protest. Both he and his friend Philip Melanchthon complained about the difficulty of getting news in Wittenberg.[27] If the papacy was slow to react, it was partly because the Church authorities in Rome could not conceive of anything of any significance emanating from such a backwater.

From the time that Luther's defiance became a public event, the torrent of publicity that accompanied each stage of the drama was quite unprecedented. News of Luther's developing critique of the Roman Church and the ominous steps taken to bring him to heel punctuate the correspondence of Europe's educated elite. Erasmus was fascinated by Luther, and initially inclined to sympathise with a man who seemed to share his withering contempt for some of the more debased and commercial aspects of the medieval Church.[28] But it was print that won Luther a wider audience, and ultimately ensured his survival. Luther made the first decisive move when he published – in German rather than the Latin of academic controversy – a sermon defending his criticism of indulgences.[29] By expanding debate beyond the closed circle of qualified theologians and engaging a wider public, Luther threw down the gauntlet to his Church critics. By 1518 he was Germany's most published author; by 1520–1, when the Pope finally pronounced his excommunication and the new Emperor Charles V endorsed this sentence, Luther was a publishing sensation. His writings were effecting a wholesale transformation at the heart of the European printing industry.

The Reformation was Europe's first mass-media news event. The quantity of books and pamphlets generated by interest in Luther's teaching was quite phenomenal. It has been estimated that between 1518 and 1526 something approaching eight million copies of religious tracts were placed on the market.[30] This was a very one-sided contest. Luther and his supporters were responsible for over 90 per cent of the works generated by the controversy.

The Reformation also provided a lifeline for a struggling industry. The bankruptcy of many of the first printers in the fifteenth century had brought about a substantial contraction in the numbers engaged in publishing printed books. By 1500 about two-thirds of Europe's books were being published in just a dozen cities, mostly major commercial centres like Venice, Augsburg and Paris. The industry was dominated by large firms with deep pockets, able to sustain the financial outlay (and raise the venture capital) to cope with the frequently long delays between publishing and selling large books. For the German publishers and booksellers who had previously struggled to make money from printed books, the Luther controversies offered a new way forward. For the books of the Reformation were different. Many of Luther's writings, and those of his supporters, were short. The vast proportion were published in German at a time when most books published for the international scholarly community were in Latin.

Short books, with a largely local market, which sold out quickly: these were the ideal product for small, less well capitalised print shops. As a result of the Reformation printing returned to, or was established for the first time in, over fifty German cities. Wittenberg itself became a major centre of print.[31]

The Reformation was also responsible for substantial changes to the design of books, changes that would be highly influential in the subsequent production of news pamphlets. Much of this design innovation emanated from Wittenberg itself. Here again Luther was lucky. His patron, Frederick the Wise, had succeeded in attracting to the city Lucas Cranach, one of Europe's most distinguished painters. Cranach was not only a fine painter, he was also an exceptionally shrewd businessman.[32] He established both a busy painting workshop and a business for the production of woodcut blocks, used to illustrate some of Wittenberg's earliest publications (including, rather ironically in the light of Luther's later criticism of indulgences, a glossy catalogue of Frederick's relic collection). Although Cranach would cheerfully fulfil commissions for Catholic clients to the end of his life, he was an early and sincere supporter of Luther. His Wittenberg workshop was soon playing an important role in the promotion of Luther's cause.

It is to Cranach that we owe the iconic images of Luther that marked the stages of his career from idealistic preacher to mature patriarch.[33] Thanks to the woodcut portraits taken from Cranach's sketches, Luther's was soon one of the best-known faces in Europe. Cranach's artfully presented portrait iconography of the solitary inspired man of God did much to build the mystique of Luther. In an age where few outside the ranks of the ruling classes would ever have had their portrait taken, this gave Luther a celebrity status that greatly enhanced his aura. It was as a celebrity that Luther was greeted and mobbed as he made his way through Germany to face the Emperor at the Diet of Worms in 1521. It was because Luther was a celebrity that the Emperor could not follow the private advice of his advisors, and deal with Luther as the Council of Constance had dealt with Jan Huss: that is, withdraw his safe conduct, arrest and execute the heretic.

Safely back in Wittenberg, Luther continued a frantic regime of writing, preaching and publishing. The work was shared around Wittenberg's growing band of publishers who, with the benefit of Cranach's woodcuts, achieved a remarkable degree of design coherence. All the Reformation pamphlets, or *Flugschriften* as they were called, were produced in the convenient quarto format (about 20 by 8 centimetres) used for most short works at the time. They were often as few as eight pages long, and seldom more than twenty. In the first years these pamphlets were austere and functional, but as Luther's fame spread, Germany's printers exploited their greatest asset with increasing confidence. Luther's name was carefully separated from the main title on the front: the title-page text was wrapped in an ornate woodcut frame. This was the major design contribution of Lucas Cranach's workshop, and it became the distinctive livery of the Wittenberg *Flugschriften*.[34] It served as a visual marker that would identify Luther's publications on a bookseller's stall. Many of Cranach's designs were eye-catchingly beautiful: works of art in miniature to honour the words of the man of God. The success of the Reformation pamphlets also helped printers and booksellers appreciate the commercial benefit of brand identity, a significant step towards the development of serial publication. Customers responded by binding the pamphlets together in an impromptu anthology, which is how many have survived today.

The *Neue Zeitung*

In the field of communication the Reformation was remarkable for a number of features, each in its own way a first: the manner in which a theological quarrel became a political event; the speed with which Luther attracted the support of a broad public; and the enthusiasm with which the printing industry exploited a commercial opportunity. In the outcome, the consequences for

Der zwey vnd
zwentzigste
Psalm Dauids
von dem leyden
Christi.
Deus meus/deus meus

Doct. Marti.
Luther.
Wittemberg.

3.2 Brand Luther. The maturing Luther pamphlet highlights the elements most critical to its sale.

the publishing industry were almost as profound as they were for the Western Church.

The Reformation brought about a large and sustained increase in the volume of books published in Germany. Eventually, however, the fires dimmed; the number of new titles dedicated to the Reformation controversies began to fall. This left a considerable gap in a greatly enlarged book market. The Reformation had created new classes of readers, men and women who had developed the habit of buying books for the first time. It had also greatly increased the number of printers working in Germany, including many in towns that had not previously been able to sustain a printing press. These men were inevitably eager to retain the new readers and sustain their new habit of investing precious income in books.

It is therefore no coincidence that the years when Reformation publishing fell from its peak witnessed a sharp rise in the numbers of other types of pamphlet literature. Among these was a new type of news-book: the *Neue Zeitung*.[35] This was not, as the title might suggest, a newspaper. Although *Zeitung* has now become the German word for 'newspaper', this is a change of sense from its use in the sixteenth century. *Zeitung* derives from an earlier Middle German word *zidung*, which is closest to the Dutch *tijding* or English 'tiding'. *Neue Zeitung* is therefore best translated as 'new tidings' or 'a new report'. Etymologically the word *Zeitung* on its own does not carry the same resonance of novelty or newness as the English word 'news' or the French *nouvelles*.

This raises the interesting issue of whether a report has to be of recent events in order for sixteenth-century readers to regard it as news. The answer seems to be that it very much depends on what is being reported. It was not unusual for news pamphlets to be re-published years, even decades after the events they described.[36] One interesting example is the rash of late fifteenth-century pamphlets (published between 1488 and 1500) celebrating the life and deeds of Vlad Dracula, the Impaler, who had died in 1476. These publications, stimulated by the contemporary concern at Turkish encroachment in eastern Europe, were really works of history dressed up as news pamphlets. Here a brutal warrior was reappropriated as a hero of Christian resistance to the Ottoman foe.[37] On other occasions news pamphlets do genuinely offer the first intimation of dramatic developments. Sometimes we are offered a 'new report' of an unfolding event: a siege, a campaign, or the meeting of a Council or Diet.

The *Neue Zeitungen* were comparatively brief texts, almost invariably continuous pieces of prose devoted to a single news report. This marks them out from the more varied digests of news presented in the merchant corre-spondence, or in the manuscript newsletters that would be the true ancestors of the newspaper.[38] This prose structure did, however, allow these news pamphlets to inform the public in some depth about the great issues of the moment. They first appear on the market in Germany in the first decade of the sixteenth century: the first *Neue Zeitung* that survives today dates from 1509.[39] They remain comparatively rare until at least the 1530s. In Germany the Luther affair had so overwhelmed interest in other types of news that printers had little reason to seek alternative markets. It was in the middle decades of the century that the news pamphlets first came into their own. In form and presentation the *Neue Zeitungen* were remarkably similar to the Reformation *Flugschriften*, from which they had clearly adopted important aspects of pres-entation. Almost without exception they were published in the quarto format favoured for German pamphlets, with a text of four or eight pages. Occasionally the front cover would be decorated with a woodcut illustration, usually a generic battle scene, seldom specially cut for the particular title. There was scarcely ever any further illustration in the text. These texts were not then costly to produce. A quarto of four or eight pages was a single day's work for even a relatively small print shop. An edition of five or six hundred copies could be out on the streets within a day or two of the printer obtaining the text.

The news pamphlets proved immensely popular, both with the buying public and with publishers. Printers could make good money for a very limited outlay. Pamphlets of this sort offered far quicker returns than more substantial books, especially as most of the copies printed could usually be disseminated locally. One can easily see why publishers were so eager to feed an appetite for news whetted by the vast increase in the volume of cheap print during the Reformation. We will never really know how many of these news pamphlets appeared on the market in the course of the sixteenth century. These little works were intended to be read, passed around and then discarded. Many titles have no doubt disappeared altogether, so it is quite remarkable that some four thousand of these

3.3 The *Neue Zeitung*. This is one of many examples that bring news of the war with the Ottoman Empire.

German news-books have survived. This represents a substantial proportion of the total output of German books during the sixteenth century.[40]

The news market, as one might expect, was strongest in the great commercial cities. Nuremberg, Augsburg, Strasbourg and Cologne were all established news hubs; but the predominance of these places was not absolute. The production of news pamphlets was remarkably dispersed, both around Germany and among the competing print shops of the major cities. It would be wrong to think that because pamphlets were cheap to produce, they were left to the smaller printing houses. Wealthier publishers were also keen to have a slice of this lucrative market, and in securing the latest texts they had a significant advantage. Many early news-books were based on letters or despatches addressed to the city magistrates. The city councillors were happy to see these reports placed in the hands of figures from the local printing establishment, who could be relied upon to publish sober, dispassionate and accurate versions, less likely to stir alarm and public agitation.

The overwhelming proportion of the *Neue Zeitungen* deal with high politics: usually, foreign affairs. The first surviving *Neue Zeitung*, of 1509, is a report of the Italian wars; the second, from 1510, reports the reconciliation of the French king and the Pope.[41] Over the century as a whole a large proportion of the news pamphlets published in Germany were devoted to chronicling the engagements and campaigns of the conflict with the Turks, on land and at sea.[42] The land war, in particular, was very close to home for the German city states; at various times the seemingly inexorable progress of Turkish arms threatened to envelop the eastern Habsburg kingdoms, markets in which the German merchants had important investments. Pamphlets that kept readers in touch with these events found an eager, if anxious audience.

This was by no means the whole of the news agenda. Printers also seized opportunities to share news of floods, earthquakes and destructive fires, celestial apparitions and notorious crimes. But these sorts of news events were not particularly common in the pamphlet literature. They found a more natural home in the ballad sheets and illustrated broadsheets that also play an increasing role in the news market of this period.[43] These were the genres of news sensations: in contrast the *Neue Zeitungen* were generally rather sober and restrained in tone. The title-pages took pains to emphasise that these reports came from authentic sources. Very often the title-pages declared that their text was 'received from a trustworthy person' or reproduced a letter sent from abroad 'to a good friend in Germany'.[44] Sometimes they reproduced verbatim a despatch written by a captain from the camp or scene of battle.[45] In this way the news pamphlets invoked the trust that reposed in correspondence as a confidential medium between two persons of repute, to bolster the credentials of publications that were now commercial and generally available. In keeping with these principles the news pamphlets are also generally careful to avoid any sensationalism. The titles are far more likely to emphasise that the despatch was 'reliable' or 'trustworthy' than shocking or astonishing. That sort of reporting was left to other parts of this increasingly sophisticated and diverse news market.

The market for news pamphlets was not confined to Germany. The Low Countries were another important news hub; a significant number of news pamphlets were also published in England, many of them, particularly in the last decades of the sixteenth century, verbatim translations of news from France or the Low Countries.[46] But news pamphlets were very much a phenomenon of northern Europe. It required really major events, such as the victory over the Turks at Lepanto in 1571, to stir Italian publishers to a significant output of news pamphlets; the Italian Peninsula, to this point the hub of the European news market, was in this respect beginning to diverge from the north European norm. The German pamphlets were unique in their success in establishing such clear brand identity. No other print tradition developed anything to match the *Neue Zeitungen*. These were the first publications in the new era of print to acknowledge on their title-pages that the bringing of news of current events was their primary purpose. They shared this news, often of faraway places and events, with a broad and expanding public – and at a modest price. They made possible the wide circulation of information that had previously only been available to a privileged few opinion-formers. In this respect alone the emergence of this new print genre represents an important moment in the development of a commercial market for news.

CHAPTER 4

State and Nation

THE rulers of medieval Europe devoted much time and effort to making their wishes known to their subjects and fellow citizens. As we have seen, this became an important part of the information culture of the age. Decrees and ordinances were made known by public reading; trusted lieutenants were informed by letter. With the invention of printing much thought was naturally given to how the new technology could be applied to simplify this task. In the compact city states of Italy, such a use of print may have seemed superfluous. Most citizens could be made aware of changes in law or regulation by proclamations in the marketplace or citizen gatherings. The larger nation states faced a different problem. Here it was likely that different instructions would have to be drafted for the governors and sheriffs of the disparate provinces. It was the restless mind of Maximilian I that helped inspire the first sustained experiments in the use of print for official purposes. The year 1486 witnessed the publication of several texts celebrating Maximilian's election as King of the Romans (confirming that he would succeed his father Frederick III as Emperor). Printers in seven different German cities took part in the publicity campaign.[1]

The press could serve the prince, but it could also bite. Maximilian received an object lesson in these dangers when, two years later, his attempt to impose his authority on his truculent subjects in the Netherlands ended in disaster. On 31 January 1488 he was stopped at the gates as he attempted to leave Bruges, and hustled away to the castle. There Maximilian was held until, under duress, he had conceded to the demands of the rebels. The humiliating treaty was promptly published in Ghent; only then was he released. Several gleeful accounts of his discomfiture were circulated in Germany.[2] The bruised but ever resilient Maximilian determined to make the printing press his own instrument. Over the next thirty years he made repeated use of print to publicise treaties, new legislation, meetings of the German Diet, instructions to officials and the raising of taxes. Under his father, all of this would have had to be done by handwritten circular letters. Maximilian achieved not only greater efficiency but far greater public awareness of the workings of government.

This inaugurated a new era in the exploitation of print. In the course of the sixteenth century the state became one of the most important patrons of the publishing industry. Official publications of one sort or another became a staple of the industry. In many provincial cities the demands of local and national government for printed ordinances and regulations helped maintain a local printing press that would otherwise scarcely have been viable.

The success of these experiments led to something altogether more ambitious. Could print be used, not only to inform, but to persuade? Could print become a powerful instrument for explaining policy and shaping public opinion? It was not long before Europe saw the first sustained campaigns of state-sponsored polemic. This was a development of huge significance for the history of the news.

Patriot Games

We can see that the propaganda potential of print had not been lost on Maximilian. Having been humiliated at Bruges, he was keen that sympathetic printers elsewhere in his dominions would laud his policies as well as circulate his instructions. The publication of treaties was always an opportunity to advertise the virtues of peace, and praise the wisdom and magnanimity of the great. But for the most systematic exploitation of the press by the state to mobilise public support we should look not to Germany or Italy, the two largest and most developed news markets of the Renaissance era, but to France. At the end of the fifteenth century France was a powerful state emerging from 150 years of chronic warfare and political division. At times during the Hundred Years War the portion of French territory acknowledging the authority of the king had shrunk to a rump in central France; after the battle of Agincourt in 1415, even Paris had briefly been occupied by the English. The expulsion of the English in 1453 was a turning point; thereafter the French Crown consolidated its territories through the incorporation of important fiefdoms in the west and south. By 1490 France was an exceptionally coherent and potentially wealthy state of some 12 million inhabitants.

To celebrate this new national awakening French kings were able to draw on some of the most gifted writers in Europe. The circle of poets and chroniclers who followed the court had already been put to good use in some precocious campaigns of political writing at the beginning of the fifteenth century.[3]

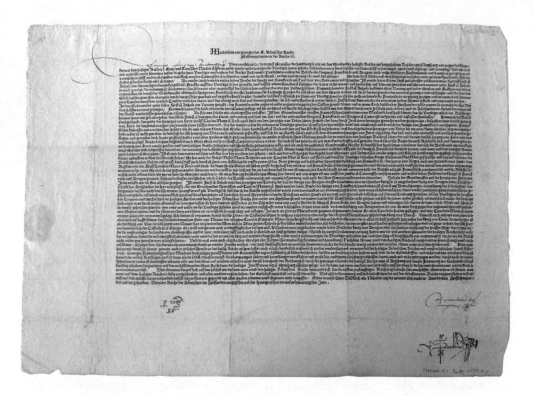

4.1 Print in the service of officialdom. In summoning a meeting of the German Estates, Maximilian gives a detailed account of recent events, including the battles of Verona and Vicenza.

This established habit of literary advocacy could easily be adjusted to the age of print. And here the French possessed a priceless weapon, because in Paris they had at their disposal one of the greatest and most sophisticated centres of early print culture. In the fifteenth century this had been orientated mostly towards the publication of scholarly and Latin books. Now it would be used to engage the French public in the Crown's ambitious plans for territorial conquest.

In seeking to exploit their new-found unity and strength, French eyes had turned inevitably to Italy. In 1494 the French claim to the kingdom of Naples led Charles VIII to embark on the first of a long series of military interventions that would, in the next sixty years, bring much tribulation to the Italian Peninsula, and ultimately little glory to France. From the beginning the military campaigns were accompanied by despatches home chronicling French progress and lauding their victories. A flurry of printed pamphlets shared news of the king's entry into Rome, his audience with the Pope, the conquest of Naples and Charles's coronation.[4] These were all short pamphlets of four or eight pages, sometimes embellished with an eye-catching title-page woodcut. Most were the work of Parisian printers, though a number seem also to have been published in Lyon, a natural intermediary point for returning news on the road to the capital.

The pamphlets of the Italian campaign were not absolutely the first of this genre to appear on the French market. In 1482 the treaty concluded between Louis XI (Charles VIII's father) and Maximilian had been published as a pamphlet.[5] The printing of treaties became a staple of official publications, if necessary with some judicious editing of the more controversial clauses to ensure a favourable reception. This was certainly the case with the Treaty of Étaples, concluded between Charles VIII and Henry VII of England in 1492. Rapid shifts of royal policy needed careful and sympathetic handling, and the French Crown could call on a number of distinguished writers to make the case for peace, or war, as the occasion demanded. In 1488 Robert Gaguin called for peace with England in his 'Passetemps d'oisiveté'; four years later Octavien de Saint-Gelais supported the renewal of war in a poem advising the foreign troops that they would be 'better off back in Wales drinking your beer'.[6]

Some of these effusions circulated in manuscript, others in print. Sometimes the propaganda effort overflowed onto the stage. We see some of the most imaginative use of regime-friendly propaganda during the reign of Louis XII, who in 1498 had rather unexpectedly inherited both the French throne and Charles VIII's claims in Italy. The outpouring of news pamphlets reached its high point with Louis's campaigns of 1507 and 1509, which brought about first the suppression of the rebellion of Genoa, then the humbling of Venice by the League of Cambrai.[7] Louis's success provoked a counter-alliance determined to limit French power, led by the irascible warrior-pope Julius II. The bitter and very personal feud that now erupted between Louis and Julius was accompanied by a sustained campaign of personal denigration. A wave of political treatises and poetry engaged, among others, the talents of Jean Lemaire de Belges, Guillaume Crétin and Jean Bouchet. A printed placard carried a caricature of the Pope lying prone beside an empty throne and surrounded by corpses; a early example of political caricature. Pierre Gringore, the most talented of contemporary playwrights, staged a newly written *sottie*, *Le jeu du prince des sotz et de mère Sotte* (*The Game of the Prince of Fools and his Idiot Mother*). Full of cutting ridicule of Julius, this was performed at Les Halles, the main marketplace of Paris, on Mardi Gras in 1512.[8]

If this was a treat for the citizens of the capital, it was printed pamphlets that ensured the widest possible circulation in the nation as a whole. In all we can enumerate at least four hundred news pamphlets published in French during the period of the Italian Wars (1494–1559).[9] The truly innovative character of this literature can best be appreciated if we contrast this French use of print with the public reaction to the French assault in Italy itself. The French descent into Italy was a cataclysm for the Italian states. The sophisticated mechanism of communication developed to keep the rulers of the Italian states abreast of events helped generate an ever-shifting pattern of alliance and antagonism between the rival powers. It offered little protection against a ruthless external foe. As the most vulnerable Italian cities marshalled inadequate defences, others sought to pursue their hopes of territorial gain by allying with the invader. The result was chaos.

The news networks of Renaissance Italy had been developed to serve the needs of a closed political and commercial elite. Now, in a time of crisis, the limitations of this culture were laid bare.[10] The division between the rulers and an alert, articulate people was nowhere more obvious than in Florence. The great city of the Medici had shown little enthusiasm for the printing press. Now it paid the price as the thunderous prophecies of Savonarola captured a rapturous audience, first for his preaching, then for subsequent printed versions. Florence's under-appreciated printers, starved of patronage, were naturally delighted to find a new audience.[11]

In Venice, Rome, Milan and elsewhere the writers of Italy turned away from demonstrations of polished humanist eloquence to an outpouring of vituperative political commentary. The poetry of the years of the French invasions is charged with a vivid savagery, as Italy's poets lamented the consequences of selfish and short-sighted political divisions, the hypocrisy of Church leaders, the vanity of princes, and the worthlessness of treaties and alliances. Little of this made its way into print; most was circulated in manuscript or posted anonymously in public places. From 1513, and the election of the Medici Pope, Leo X, this political poetry took on a pointedly personal tone. Leo and his successors, and indeed the entire college of cardinals, were denounced for a catalogue of vices.

Seen in the round this literature of denunciation makes clear the hopelessness of Italy's predicament. The contrast between the optimistic, celebratory literature orchestrated by the French Crown and the utterly negative and destructive tone of the Italian pasquinades (satiric verses) is very striking. The political poetry of Rome, though witty and carried along by a torrential energy, was inward-looking and parochial. It may well have been that Cardinal Armellini had a mistress, but would Rome have been better defended, and the Church better governed, had he been chaste? The smallness of these concerns and their mean-spirited nature made it difficult to see beyond this world of gossip, manoeuvres and tiny victories towards any real solution of Italy's predicament. This would be the fate that would await many satirists in the centuries that followed: the impotent glee of enraging the great, momentarily diverting, but ultimately changing nothing.

The Fog of War

The bitterness of these internecine conflicts in Italy and the conservative tradition of Italian letters made impossible the effective use of print such as we have seen in the case of France. The first to follow the French into the realms of political propaganda were not therefore the sophisticated Italians, but their Habsburg adversaries. With his election as Holy Roman Emperor in 1519, Charles V had fulfilled the elaborate dynastic plans of his grandfather Maximilian in the most spectacular way. France was encircled by a suffocating mass of Habsburg territories. The struggle for supremacy was fought in an exhausting sequence of campaigns and battles, a conflict that also had a profound echo in a coordinated effort to shape the news.

The ebb and flow of pamphlet warfare mirrored closely the rhythms of the conflict. French campaigning in Italy produced a flurry of publications in 1516 and 1528–9. On the imperial side the interconnected events of 1527–9, with the coronation of Ferdinand I as King of Hungary closely followed by the renewal of the French War, produced a comparable outpouring of news prints in the Netherlands. Here Antwerp was in precisely these years emerging as Europe's northern news hub, and a major centre of print. More than thirty printers there helped chronicle the Emperor's determined efforts to humble France.[12] Needless to say, both sides were keener to celebrate success than to acknowledge reverses. Charles V's loyal subjects would read of the king's great triumph at Tunis in 1535, but not of the catastrophe at Algiers six years later. It was the French who chose to publicise the scandal of the sack of Rome in 1527, laid waste by imperial troops under the French defector, the Duke of Bourbon. Netherlandish printers preferred to reserve comment until the Emperor's triumphant entry into Rome in 1536 provided them with a more palatable subject.

The climax of this polemical ping-pong came in the years 1542–4, a period of intense diplomacy concluded by simultaneous war in several theatres. In 1538 Charles V and the French King Francis I had been temporarily reconciled following a peace treaty painstakingly brokered by the Pope. Francis now faced the delicate task of explaining to the politically informed in his nation why a reviled adversary was to be welcomed to French territory as the Emperor journeyed from Italy to the Low Countries, feted in lavish civic receptions at every step. Once again the literary men did their duty: Clément Marot celebrated Charles as a new Julius Caesar, this time come to Gaul in peace. France's printers, meanwhile, offered fascinated accounts of the Emperor's reception in Orléans and Paris. By 1542, however, the fragile reconciliation was in tatters. The French declaration of war was published as a pamphlet in four French cities: Paris, Troyes, Lyon and Rouen.[13] The beginning of a provincial culture of printed news was a new development in these years. The recent discovery of a large cache of pamphlets published in Rouen between 1538 and 1544 allows us to reconstruct it in unexpected detail.[14] The Rouen pamphlets were very rudimentary works: all in a small octavo format, seldom more than four pages long. But they offered local readers in this important regional centre the opportunity to follow the progress of the struggle in surprising detail.

The Rouen pamphlets are especially valuable because they give us a rare glimpse of a news community beyond the privileged members of the political decision-makers and the informed citizenry of the capital. By the spring of 1544 the Emperor had led his forces deep into northern France. Yet even during these perilous months readers in Rouen were offered a stream of optimistic bulletins of minor imperial reverses. However misleading in terms of the general strategic situation, which was dire, Rouen readers consumed these pamphlets eagerly. The news of war sustained two separate printing houses there for six years. After peace was signed in September, they quickly faded away.

How effective were these intense and, it must be said, quite unprecedented attempts to marshal public opinion? In 1543 the English ambassador in Paris reported ominously that the French king's subjects 'murmureth marvellous, not only here but universally through his realm'.[15] But he was the representative of a hostile power, and hardly an unbiased witness. In fact, at this moment of profound crisis, the nation held together. Some of this at least can be ascribed to the concentrated printed propaganda of the period. An anonymous Parisian chronicler of the time, known usually as the Bourgeois of Paris, wrote a narrative of events compiled largely from documents in the public domain, making good use of these news pamphlets. He takes them very much at face value: his journal reveals a natural conformist, keen to understand royal policy in its own terms. Even in the case of those with more privileged access, the successful diffusion of the official patriotic view can be discerned in contemporary historical writings and literary works. Authors such as Jean Bouchet, who offers detailed and well-sourced accounts of the military campaigns, were firm in ascribing responsibility for the war to the king's enemies. Guillaume Paradin justified the war of 1542 as a consequence of the Emperor's treachery, even ascribing to Charles responsibility for the death of the Dauphin in 1536, 'poisoned by the Emperor's unheard of malice'. Echoes can even be found in Rabelais's *Gargantua and Pantagruel*, namely in the unflattering lampoon of Pichrochole, a ruler who sees himself as a new Alexander.

Attempts to present a positive view of royal policy and the events of war were generally well received: the French Crown faced a greater danger when it left a news vacuum, such as in the aftermath of the evident disaster at the battle of Pavia in 1525. The news of the defeat and the capture of Francis I were communicated to local administrators by private letter. The public, however, were told nothing. Not surprisingly, rumour filled the vacuum, leading another contemporary diarist to conclude that the defeat signalled 'the total loss and destruction of the kingdom'.[16]

In the Netherlands efforts to forge patriotic identity through a lively culture of news met with less success. The seventeen provinces brought together under Charles V had never been a nation; incorporation of the last independent territories was completed only in 1543, with the subjugation of the Duke of Gelderland. Each of the provinces carefully nurtured its own separate relationship with the Emperor, who was Count of Flanders, but Duke of Brabant, Lord of Holland, and so on. It was thus by no means straightforward to promote the perception of a common cause against a common enemy. This was particularly the case in the southern French-speaking lands, an extremely permeable border zone from which it was hardly possible to exclude contrary points of view. French Tournai engaged in a lively dialogue with Habsburg lands roundabout. When the city fell to the English in 1513, Henry VIII was unimpressed by what he described as its 'incorrigible and ill-conditioned people, making farces, ballads and songs about their neighbours'.[17]

Netherlanders were notoriously disinclined to help neighbouring communities, who might be commercial rivals, in time of war. The raising of funds and levies to pursue the war with France provided Emperor Charles with the opportunity to persuade his Low Countries subjects that they should recognise a common obligation to 'acquit themselves in the defence of their fatherland'.[18] But words alone could not create a sense of common identity where none had previously existed. Even ceremonial entries, the formal occasions in which a city celebrated its mutual obligations with the prince, could leave an unwanted legacy. The volumes that depicted the celebrations and tableaux for the entry into Antwerp of Charles's son Philip in 1549 were cited years later as evidence of inappropriate extravagance. The Netherlands came together as an entity most obviously in times of danger. The defeat of the enemy general Maarten van Roersum after his destructive incursion during the Emperor's war with the Duke of Gelderland in 1542 was celebrated throughout the territories. But the development of a true sense of nationhood would await the second half of the century when this national sentiment was turned against the Habsburgs: they were portrayed not as the protectors of Netherlandish liberties, but as the foreign oppressor.[19]

Times of warfare inevitably stirred strong emotions. In promoting mainly regime-friendly, patriotic news the publishers of news pamphlets mirrored the hopes and passions of their readers. Dispassionate analysis of the true disposition of forces was hardly to be expected, even had it been permitted. By this time most states in Europe had developed mechanisms for control of the press, aimed at preventing the publication or circulation of disapproved texts. Since the Protestant Reformation these systems of pre-publication inspection of copy (more theoretical than practical) had been reinforced by brutal penalties for any who challenged the local orthodoxy. Printers knew they had to tread carefully. But it would be wrong to ascribe the overwhelmingly loyalist tone of the news pamphlets primarily to censorship. Although the French press was carefully regulated, most printers cooperated readily in the output of patriotic literature. In the fog of war it became impossible to learn the true state of affairs by print alone. Those who needed more accurate information, merchants with consignments of goods on the road, for example, continued to guard their own confidential means of keeping in touch.

Of Tax and Chickens

The persistent warfare of the sixteenth century required a vast expansion of the apparatus of government. Armies grew larger, campaigns longer and defensive fortifications more elaborate. All of this required the development of a complex bureaucracy, and the raising of ever more cash. Whatever their theoretical aspirations to rule unquestioned under God, in practice Europe's rulers understood that the repeated demands for financial contributions from hard-pressed subjects required explanation and a measure of persuasion. This was a society still wedded to the historic principle that the king, like other great lords, should live from the income of his own lands. Although this had long ceased to be the case, it had not been replaced by a more practical recognition that subjects should surrender a regular portion of their income to underpin the apparatus of state. Aside from inevitable and resented duties on consumption, levies on property or income were always exceptional. The ruler had to make a case for burdening his subjects in this way.

This communication of the business of government made increasing use of print in the sixteenth century. These printed edicts, laws and proclamations were ostensibly intended to make citizens aware of new obligations and regulations, to raise money, to command obedience, and to warn against disorder. But they also had an important news function. To encourage the citizenry to contribute willingly to taxation, the state authorities often offered quite detailed explanations of why it had become necessary to impose fresh levies.

The same was true of the regulation of crime or commerce. Such statements of intent were often set out in the preamble to a printed edict, and these texts could offer a surprisingly frank account of the policy-making process.

In this way the making of law played an important role in spreading the news. News pamphlets may have been popular, but not many people outside the political and commercial elites would have been directly touched by the events they described. The law, in contrast, made demands on everyone. To be effective, laws had to be widely known. The problem was particularly acute in the national states of western Europe, where the king's command had to be made known to a dispersed population, most of whom would never, in their lifetime, see the fountainhead of this authority. In France the monarchy consciously used the taxation system to communicate justifications for its foreign-policy objectives. In the first half of the century, even though the Crown's right to levy taxation was in theory untrammelled, requests for additional levies were frequently accompanied by detailed explanation of why they were necessary. The 2.4 million livres of *taille* levied in 1517 was justified as the price of achieving peace; a similar sum raised in 1522 instanced the need for new artillery to resist the English invasion of Brittany.[20] In 1526, a time of manifest crisis after Pavia, the regent accompanied the request for additional funds with a careful justification of the policy decisions that had drawn the king so disastrously into Italy, while offering reassurances of her constant striving for peace.

Many of these communications were conveyed by the traditional means of manuscript circular letters to the provincial estates. Their authors took into their confidence a limited circle of the leaders of local society. For many of the population, information would have come from briefer demands for taxes sent down from the provincial capital. As the century wore on, however, an increasing number of royal edicts was rendered into print. Only 2 per cent of the royal acts of Francis I was printed, but by the time of his grandson Francis II (r. 1559–60) this proportion had risen to 20 per cent. In the troubled times of the French Wars of Religion the Crown made extensive use of print to promote religious peace. Over the course of the century royal edicts were published in more than five thousand editions.[21] Edicts published in Paris were spread into the provinces by a relay of local reprints.

In England, successive rulers faced the difficult task of reconciling a sometimes baffled population to the frequent adjustment of familiar patterns of worship. Henry VIII's repudiation of the Pope was translated into a full Protestant settlement in the reign of his son Edward VI (1547–53). With the succession of Mary in 1553 it was clear to the politically aware that Catholicism would be restored. This was effected by an Act of Parliament in 1554; but the process was begun by action taken to supress religious debate and unwanted demonstrations against the queen's policy.

Mary's wishes were set in hand by a proclamation of August 1553 forbidding religious controversy, and banning unlicensed plays or printing. The text progresses cautiously to the heart of the issue. It assured the reader that the queen, although compelled by conscience to follow her religion, had no intention of imposing her choice on her subjects unless such a measure was taken by common consent. It laments the disorder caused by religious dissent. Only after six hundred words (and remember, this was meant to be proclaimed aloud) does the proclamation arrive at the heart of the matter: all are forbidden 'to print any books, matter, ballad, rhyme, interlude [play], process or treatise, nor to play any interlude, except they have her Grace's special licence in writing for the same'.[22]

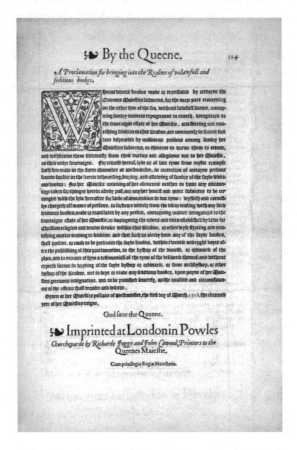

4.2 Elizabeth I. Proclamation for the bringing into the realm of unlawful and seditious books.

Printing was a London matter; but the staging of offensive plays could have a corrosive impact on obedience anywhere in the kingdom. The proclamation was therefore printed by the queen's printer for distribution. The local officials who received the copies would no doubt read it in detail, and convey its essence to local enforcement officers. It is difficult to envisage a text of this complexity making sense if it had only been communicated by the traditional means of being read out in public places. The circulation of printed texts thus played an increasingly essential part in the communication of public policy. Royal acts and proclamations were exhibited on posts or on boards in public places. It should be noted though that this proclamation, like many Tudor proclamations, was a single sheet printed on both sides; it would not have been particularly easy to read if affixed to a board. So, more practically, piles of them were made available for perusal in public buildings or shops. In April 1537 Adam Lewes, a schoolmaster of West Malling near Maidstone in Kent, went into a local shop 'where lay certain Actes concerning apparel, artillery and unlawful games'.[23]

In 1563 Queen Elizabeth faced an even more delicate task. Her bold attempt to wrest back a foothold on French soil through alliance with the French Huguenots had ended in disaster. The English expeditionary force, cooped up in Newhaven (Le Havre), had been struck by plague. The expedition's commander, the Earl of Warwick, had no choice but to make what terms he could to extricate the remnants of the garrison.[24] As the defeated army straggled home, the government issued a proclamation explaining that this reverse should be put down entirely to the visitation of sickness: the army had conducted itself nobly and with honour. The considerable sum of £17 was allocated to pay for messengers to carry the printed copies through the realm.[25] The Flemish agent in London saw this extraordinary acknowledgement of a foreign policy catastrophe as an attempt by the queen's chief advisor William Cecil to avoid the blame for what might have been a career-ending blunder.

These were responses to extraordinary events; the bulk of sixteenth-century legislation was far more mundane. Many written texts claimed, with much justification, that the regulations had been enacted on the prompting of interested citizens. The encroachment of government into an ever-widening range of functions regulating the economy and society was indeed partly stimulated by the appeals of interested parties. Very often these were powerful economic lobbies that wanted competition to be restrained, the regulation of apprenticeship enforced, or roads and bridges repaired.

The use of print in pursing these objectives has very largely been obscured by the very poor rates of survival of such printed ordinances. Everyday print

of this sort was not intended to be collected: the exhibited copies were generally left pinned up until rendered illegible by rain or covered up by other
notices. Sometimes they suffered greater indignities. In 1535 four men were
called before the magistrates at Coventry to answer the charge that they had
torn down proclamations posted in the marketplace, a manifest act of sedition
if proved. It turned out that they had been out drinking, and after relieving
themselves one of them had used the papers to 'wipe his tail with them'.[26]

Printed works of this sort were not really meant to survive so we are fortunate in the extraordinary passion for archiving of the Antwerp printer
Christophe Plantin. Although Plantin is famous for the publication of some of
the greatest books published in the Low Countries in this era, he also cheerfully undertook the publication of broadsheet ordinances for the local town
council; helpfully he also retained a copy of each one for his own records.[27]
Uniquely, then, in the case of Antwerp, we can follow the activities of a city
administration over a ten-year period in some detail.

Antwerp was one of Europe's greatest cities and these were turbulent times.
The city's decrees reflect the impact on city life of the revolt from Spain and
the re-conquest of 1585. Through all these great events a constant preoccupation is to ensure the food supply for the city's large population. Much attention is given to the proper regulation of markets. A not untypical edict
addressed the problem of irregularities in the poultry trade. It has come to our
attention, such an edict might begin, that traders are selling their chickens
away from the designated poultry market. It is therefore decreed that from
henceforth the following regulations shall apply: and so on, listing a rising
scale of penalties for persistent infringers.[28]

It is easy to pass over the importance of this sort of law-making; historians
very often have done, and students of communication have not noticed such
cases at all. But for many of Europe's citizens coming to market with a cartload
of produce, only to be turned away or have their goods or livestock confiscated,
this was the news that really mattered. With this sort of legislation we also detect
the beginnings of a news culture that touches on domestic affairs. This was an
aspect of news that had previously bubbled along as the domain of word-of-
mouth gossip, rather separate from the great events captured in international
correspondence and print. In the sixteenth century matters closer to home
began to impact on the news prints.

True Crime

Many of Europe's citizens would have witnessed an execution. This was part
of the ritual of community life: that malefactors be put to death in the places

where their crimes were committed.[29] Most were soon forgotten. Occasionally the details of a particularly heinous or curious crime might be noted by a diarist, or in correspondence. More usually, these cases have their only record in the proceedings of the legal jurisdiction that heard the cases and condemned them. But in the sixteenth century a new type of publication allowed a wider public to experience vicariously the horror or thrill of these villainous acts: the sensational broadsheets.

These illustrated broadsheets became a particular feature of German print culture in the sixteenth century. They are often beautifully designed and crafted. Invariably the top half of the sheet is given over to a woodcut illustration, usually specially cut, describing the event, which is then narrated in text below. Although eminently collectable, these illustrated news broadsheets survive only rarely. Passed around from hand to hand, or posted up on walls, they were often used to destruction. That so many are known today we owe largely to the collecting enthusiasm of one eccentric Swiss clergyman: Johann Jakob Wick.

Wick began collecting soon after his appointment to a position at Zurich Cathedral in 1557.[30] Here he would have worked closely with the leaders of the Zurich Church, Heinrich Bullinger and his successor Rudolf Gwalter. Both were important sources for Wick's collection: Bullinger in particular was at the centre of one of Europe's most developed networks of correspondence, and he willingly passed on to his colleague interesting nuggets of news. Wick began collecting in 1560. From then until his death in 1588 he filled one fat volume a year, with reports of great and startling events from Switzerland and beyond. Like all great collectors, Wick was eclectic in his sources. Sometimes he transcribed reports from letters or diplomatic despatches; he took a particular interest in the Huguenot struggle in France. His collection quickly became well known locally, to the extent that visitors would drop by and share notable events and marvels they had seen or heard reported. Wick would carefully transcribe these accounts, along with the texts from news pamphlets he had been loaned. In the scrapbooks many of these manuscript entries are beautifully illustrated with hand-coloured drawings. He would also insert printed items directly into the scrapbooks: a total of 500 pamphlets and 400 broadsheets were interspersed through the pages. An important source for Wick was the Zurich printer Christoph Froschauer, who would bring back material for Wick from the Frankfurt Fair. As a result, and in contrast to the more international character of the transcribed news reports, most of the printed broadsheets in the collection are from Germany.

These news broadsheets constitute an irreplaceable resource for the study of early crime reporting. Stylistically the woodcut illustrations fall into three

4.3 True crime. A graphic representation of the murder of a young woman by a German apprentice.

groups. Some, the smallest number, present a single dramatic moment in the narrative. An example is the tale of an apprentice who murdered a ten-year-old girl and dismembered the body. The woodcut shows the perpetrator surrounded by body parts: an arresting image, although crudely done.[31] More often the woodcut presented several scenes from the drama in a sequence that scrolls around the landscape from the crime scene to the place of execution. This format, well known from the Passion narratives of late medieval painting, was particularly well adapted to crime reporting, where the cruelty of the mode of execution was matched to the shocking nature of the crime. Several of these broadsheets show a notorious criminal being tortured on their way to the place of execution, there to be broken on the wheel.[32] A variation of this narrative form was to have the drama broken up into separate scenes, in the manner of a strip cartoon. One crime that we find represented in both ways is the shocking case of Blasius Endres, who, on discovering that his wife was stealing money from him, murdered her and their six young children.[33] These crimes were committed in Wangen, 150 kilometres north of Zurich. One of the broadsheets was printed in Lindau, the other in Augsburg, 150 kilometres further north. News of the most spectacular crimes spread widely, and also found its echo in the pamphlet literature.

The exemplary character of crime and punishment was not diminished by distance, nor particularly by time. The London printer Thomas Purfoot published in 1586 an account of a triple murder committed by a Frenchman in Rouen, the victims being an innkeeper, his wife and child.[34] Readers would be chilled at the predicament of a family slaughtered by a stranger in their home – it did not matter that in this case the events occurred abroad. The recitation of shocking and unnatural deeds, decorously clothed in a narrative of horror, discovery and signal justice, catered to many tastes, godly and ghoulish, and ensured a steady market for these sorts of news pamphlets.[35] In such cases cruel and exemplary punishment was seen as a necessary part of the fight between good and evil. The world was full of danger, and many lived a life of quiet desperation. In a society where only very limited resources were available to the state for preventative policing measures, it was widely believed that only the fear of a gruesome death could act as a deterrent. In the literature of crime, most of those apprehended went to their deaths sorrowful and repentant. To die a good death was an important part of the healing process.[36] In his diary Wick records the case of a young thief who went to the place of execution cracking jokes along the way. He died with the words, 'Lord Jesus, receive my soul'.[37]

This last case was not sufficiently memorable to merit publication. The broadsheets concentrated on the most arresting cases, such as the man who allegedly disguised himself as the Devil to commit his crimes.[38] Cases like this shaded easily into the wider literature of sensational and supernatural events that were the stock in trade of the news broadsheets. Publishers and woodcut artists turned out a steady diet of monstrous births, strange animals, unusual weather events and natural disasters.[39] Earthquakes and floods were chronicled with some care. By far the most popular with the buying public were tales of celestial apparitions. These could be meteors or comets, or the vision of an armed man, a flaming cross, or horsemen riding through the sky. Wick chronicled these events assiduously and without scepticism. Comets and other heavenly perturbations were widely interpreted as portents of future calamities. A spectacular showing of the Northern Lights in 1560 was associated with an extraordinary number of different events over the following decade. Wick possessed a magnificent, if not particularly authentic representation of the Aurora Borealis from a later manifestation.[40] In 1571 he transcribed into his notebooks an excerpt from a French pamphlet written by Nostradamus describing a comet seen in the sky over Langres. Wick returned to this page some time later to add a further sober reflection: 'I believe this apparition could be seen as a warning and presentment of the terrible murders that occurred the following year on St Bartholomew's day in Paris, and other places in France.'[41]

The news prints showed a particular fascination with the crimes of women. This was partly because they were exceptionally rare. A comprehensive survey of German legal documents for sixteenth-century Württemberg finds that only about 5 per cent of crimes concerned women.[42] Spectacular cases, such as the English pamphlet account of a woman who incited her lover to kill her husband, were thus all the more newsworthy. They also spoke to society's deepest fears of attacks on established social and gender hierarchies. Particularly shocking were crimes by women against their own children. One particularly wrenching broadsheet from 1551 illustrated the case of a woman who had murdered her four children before committing suicide.[43] In common with many of the broadsheets, the text narrative is in verse: the starving woman had seen no other way out of her predicament. Such a story spoke to the most dreadful anxieties of a society where many lived on the edge of subsistence, and where a sudden change of fortune, the death of a breadwinner, adverse weather, the incidence of war, could plunge them into destitution. Such anxieties help explain the popularity of a very different tale of providential deliverance, in which a starving family is saved by a shower of corn. This marvellous example of divine inspiration was the subject of several broadsheets and pamphlets, and even turned up in an English collection of *God's marvellous wonders* at the very end of the seventeenth century.[44] The morbid fascination with hailstorms and extreme weather also speaks to the same nagging anxieties about the food supply.

Most of the crime pamphlets and broadsheets were published without naming the author of the accompanying text. But where the author is known, a significant number were clergymen. This is less surprising than it might seem. Such dramatic narratives offered the opportunity for a living sermon: a story with a lesson to teach. Horrid crimes confirmed the ministers' theological sense of the utter depravity of human nature and the ceaseless activity of the Devil. The success of the 1551 broadsheet describing the murder of four children by a starving mother owed a great deal to the skilful writing of Burkard Waldis, a Lutheran pastor. Waldis was a prolific writer of fables, plays and anti-papal satire, and he was able to wring every drop of pathos from the terrible scene, as when the young son, cornered in the cellar, pleads for his life:

He said, 'O dearest mother mine
Spare me, I'll do whate'er you say:
I'll carry for you from today
The water the whole winter through.
O please don't kill me! Spare me do!'

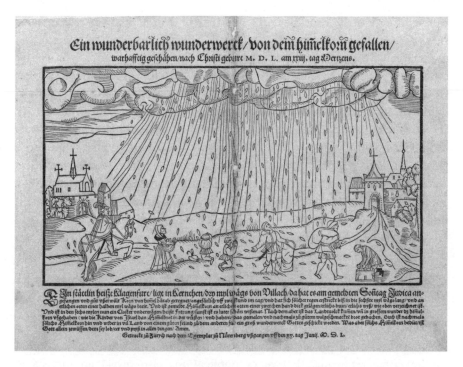

4.4 Raining corn. Johann Wick was equally keen on these tales of inspiring miracles.

But no plea helped, it was in vain;
The Devil did her will maintain
She struck him with the self-same dread
As if it were a cabbage head.[45]

This was a story that would tell itself. In other prose accounts the moral was
more overtly drawn. For pastor Johannes Füglin of Basel, the horrible murders
committed by a young weaver, Paul Schumacher, was a classic tale of descent
into vice, from Godless idleness into the clutches of the Devil. But it was also
part of a larger pattern of moral decay: 'In the shedding of human blood, such
shocking and horrifying cases have sometimes also occurred in the past, but
more and more in the present day.'[46]

It is no surprise that these sensational cases attracted the most attention in
print, sometimes far away from the location of the crime and long after it had
occurred. Waldis's broadsheet text was printed three times in 1551, and once
more over twenty years later. Given the common assumption, voiced systematically from the nineteenth century, that such sensationalism panders mostly

to the tastes of the lower classes, it is instructive to note that its status in early news reporting was far more respectable.[47] The authors were clergymen, the readers mostly members of comfortable burgher households. This is not inherently surprising. These were the sort of citizens who had most to fear from servants and apprentices who turned bad or greedy, and attacked their employers or vulnerable family members. Sixteenth- and seventeenth-century societies were inherently dangerous and risky; it required boldness and forti-tude to claw one's way through the multiple hazards to security and pros-perity. The irony is that the most avid consumers of these crime pamphlets were those who had achieved a measure of stability and material success. They served as a reminder that even in the most orderly households danger lurked unpredictably around every corner; the peace and order so painstakingly constructed could be overturned in an instant. The sixteenth century was not the only one in which crime was most feared and retribution most actively supported by those least likely to be directly affected.

Witches

It is perhaps not surprising, given the strong theological undertow exhibited in the crime reporting, that news publications also reveal an increasing concern with witchcraft. There can be no doubt that print played a large and malignant role in fuelling the witch-craze of the sixteenth and seventeenth centuries.[48] Up to this point Church leaders had retained a degree of sceptical distance from demands to pursue witchcraft prosecutions. The Austrian Inquisitor Henry Kramer, an early enthusiast of witch-hunting, had a chilly relationship with the local bishop, who threatened to expel him by force if he remained in the diocese. Kramer turned the tables by having his witch-hunting manual printed. Although the *Malleus Maleficarum* failed to win approval from university theologians, it was an instant publishing success.[49] The *Malleus Maleficarum* took its place in libraries as a handbook of persecu-tion; alongside a contemporary rival publication by Ulrich Molitor it estab-lished an important and popular new genre of learned publication.[50]

The manuals taught people how to search out and prosecute witches; news pamphlets enthusiastically reported the consequences. We can reconstruct in some detail the emergence of witch trials as news events through the noto-rious case of a woman who was executed after having set fire to the town of Schiltach in the Black Forest in 1533. An account of her trial appeared in print little more than a week later, to be reprinted in Leipzig, on the other side of Germany, within a few weeks. The case acquired its greatest notoriety when the Nuremberg publisher commissioned a woodcut from the artist Erhard

Schön, which was then issued as a broadsheet. Obviously the text had to be greatly simplified, but this only added to its sensational impact. It was this version that Wick obtained, years later, to paste into his scrapbooks.[51]

According to Christopher Froben, by this time the 'devil of Schiltach' had become proverbial throughout Germany. If this was so, it could only have been due to the success of the case as a media event. Not everyone approved. When in 1535 a Strasbourg printer applied for a licence to print another account of these events, the magistrates refused. At this point they were prepared to say of their illustrious and serious-minded city, 'We don't do devils.'[52] But the tide of history was running against them. The Protestant Reformation certainly intensified the sense of an intense conflict between God and the Devil; books describing the Devil and his cohorts poured off the presses, and filled the sermons of the Lutheran pastors. Predictably, the resulting trials and executions created work for the news prints.

Some intellectuals continued to call for restraint, led notably by the Dutch physician Johann Weyer.[53] But if the learned texts left room for doubt and qualifications, this was seldom true of the pamphlets, and even less so of the broadsheets. By the last quarter of the sixteenth century, news broadsheets were reporting mass executions of witches in various parts of Germany and Alsace. One described how the Devil had summoned an assembly of witches to the castle at Colmar, to which five hundred flew on cats or calves.[54] On this occasion over one hundred witches were executed. In such reports the notion of the suffering individual was wholly lost in the sensation conveyed of horrific threat and massive retribution. These pamphlets added yet one more layer of blood-curdling insecurity to the anxieties articulated in other tales of wonder, sensation and crime.

The sixteenth century had demonstrated that print could be a vital tool of state-building. Used with subtlety and care, the news prints allowed Europe's rulers to take the wider political nation into their confidence, and marshal patriotic loyalty to their dynastic ambitions. Printed ordinances enabled the state to extend the range of government functions, and make known to all levels of society the need for regulation or taxation. This was one of the most impressive and effective ways in which the culture of news was exploited for the shaping of society. But the people of Europe were far from passive recipients of this news. They had their own views; they could compare what was expressed officially in print with what they heard on the streets. Increasingly they developed their own news values, stoking a commercial market that could, if unrestrained, threaten the delicate order that the state had sought to promote. It was a harbinger of dangerous times.

CHAPTER 5

Confidential Correspondents

B Y the middle of the sixteenth century the development of printing had had a profound impact on the availability of news throughout Europe. Those who wished to keep abreast of current events now had access to a profusion of printed pamphlets and broadsheets. These news prints were among the cheapest books for sale, many retailing for a penny or its equivalent. For those privileged groups who had been the principal consumers of news in medieval Europe these developments were in many ways unsettling. In the old world, news had been essentially a private and intimate transaction, exchanged between trusted individuals. Because you knew your correspondent, you knew how to weigh up the value of his news: his reputation stood behind it.[1] But how could you say that of a news pamphlet published often by an unknown printer in a faraway place, and now spread promiscuously around the marketplace? News was now a commercial transaction. Did this not undermine the credit of the information? How could one know what to believe from these unknown anonymous correspondents? Were they exaggerating for effect, or just to make money?

Questions of this sort were particularly pertinent for the traditional clients of news in medieval society: Europe's rulers and merchants. They might study pamphlets to take the temperature of public debate, but they needed their own sources of news for more precise intelligence. For those in positions of power, the confidential despatch remained the touchstone of reliability. Among Europe's elites, the exchange of news continued to rely on tried and tested systems of information gathering: through conversation, observation, and, where all else failed, espionage. This tradition of news gathering was not superseded by the birth of commercial news print; indeed, in many ways the networks of confidential correspondence strengthened and intensified as postal networks improved and it became easier to maintain regular connections across national boundaries. Private citizens continued to rely on their friends to send them the news. In troubled times governments leaned heavily on their resident ambassadors for information and informed advice.

In the sixteenth century this yearning for swift and reliable information also led to the establishment of the first private news offices, dealing in confidential news on a subscription basis. These news agencies, with their commercially distributed manuscript news-sheets, are by far the least known of the communication media of the period. But these agencies would play an essential role in creating an international news network in the age before the newspaper. For two centuries their news-sheets, or *avvisi* as they were known, would be the touchstone of reliability for those who needed to keep abreast of events – and who could afford to pay the subscriptions.

Diplomats, of course, furnished their own confidential briefings and advice. The resident ambassador was meant to be able to separate the wheat from the chaff: to bring his experience to bear to distinguish rumour from fact, and offer his own sage judgement of the local political situation. But the ambassadors too were avid readers of the *avvisi*. Sometimes it seemed to their princely employers that they did little more than take the manuscript newsletters and prepare their own digest. A new news medium had been invented; and like the craft of diplomacy itself, its origins must be sought in Renaissance Italy.

The Business of Peace

The sixteenth century was the great age of Renaissance diplomacy. It had taken some time for a network of diplomatic representatives to become wideless spread throughout Europe. Although the Italian city states had been exchanging ambassadors since the fifteenth century, the larger kingdoms held to night back: at the accession of Francis I in 1515, France had only one resident ambassador. When he died in 1547, there were ten.[2] Ambassadors had become a major adornment of the Renaissance court, a vital symbol of their nations' status in the European state system. Usually drawn from the higher social echelons of their own country, the ambassadors would be expected to move easily among their peers, sharing courtesies and information. Their personalities, scheming and not infrequent struggles for precedence were the subject of much animated comment.

Fourteenth-century diplomatic theory envisaged an embassy as the response to a particular problem, to resolve an issue or conclude an alliance between two states, rather than as a permanent state of residency. In practice, the distinction was quickly dissolved. While a special embassy might be despatched to propose a diplomatic marriage, treaties or alliances could seldom be concluded so rapidly. Ambassadors rarely had full licence to close the inevitable gaps between the negotiating positions of the two parties. So an embassy might drag on, as the ambassador sought further instructions, often to the weary envoy's intense frustration.

The diplomatic despatch was in this respect an unintended by-product of this evolutionary process. 'The business of an ambassador,' as Bernard du Rosier emphasised repeatedly in his influential 'Short Treatise' (1436) on the

5.1 A diplomatic mission asks for the hand of the king's daughter in marriage.

office of diplomacy, 'is peace.'[3] 'The speedy completion of an ambassador's mission is in the interest of all.' Nowhere was it envisaged that these illustrious plenipotentiaries should become informed observers of the host state. But as time went by, and the web of negotiation between contesting powers became more intricate, the need for informed assessment of the mood, strength and true intentions of potential allies became ever more acute. Ambassadors were instructed to write home on a regular basis. The art of diplomacy had spawned a whole new medium: political commentary. This was the first real sustained attempt to add commentary and analysis to the raw data of news.

About the earliest generation of diplomatic despatches we are not well informed. Though in other respects precocious exponents of bureaucracy, the Italian states did not make provision for the systematic filing of incoming ambassadorial reports. The earliest examples have only survived because they made their way into family archives: the papers and despatches accumulated by an envoy abroad remained, just like ministerial papers, their own personal property, to be retained or disposed of as they thought best.[4] Venice legislated to ensure that all public papers in the possession of returning diplomats were surrendered to the state, but to little avail.[5] It was only in the 1490s that Venice began to assemble an archive. But what despatches they are: over the course of two centuries Italian ambassadors abroad offer a stream of shrewd and well-informed observations on the politics, customs and personalities of their hosts. Their reports range widely, from the immediate issues of the day, through gossip, strange occurrences, to more anthropological observations about the differences of national character, dress and behaviour. Tempered in the harsh schools of Italian politics, closely connected to the business elites from which they were sometimes drawn, pragmatic and thoughtful, Italian ambassadors were ideally suited to this new craft.

Diplomatic despatches were not, of course, public documents. They were intended only for a limited circle in the innermost councils of the state: this was news and analysis for a privileged elite. But some news did begin to leak out, through indiscretion or the vanity of the envoy. A semi-licensed form of publicity developed with the tradition of the *Relazione*, the final reflective despatch presented to the Venetian Senate on the conclusion of an embassy. The purpose of a *Relazione* was quite different from that of the regular despatch. Rather than reporting on the hubbub of everyday events, the ambassador now took stock: he offered his view on the character of the ruler and his principal advisors, the strengths and weaknesses of the state, the attitudes and sentiments of the people.[6] These reflections were presented orally, by men who relished the opportunity for a display of erudition. *Relazioni* were eagerly anticipated, not least for the calculated indiscretion. Who, of those present,

5.2 The reading of a despatch before the Doge of Venice and other members of the Signoria.

would not have marvelled at the impudence of ambassador Zaccaria Contarini's frank description in 1492 of Charles VIII of France:

> The Majesty of the King of France is twenty-two years of age, small and badly formed in his person, ugly of face, with eyes great and white and much more apt to see too little than enough, an aquiline nose, much larger and fatter than it ought to be, also fat lips, which he continually holds open, and he has some spasmodic movements of hand which appear very ugly, and he is slow in speech. According to my opinion, which could be quite wrong, I hold certainly that he is not worth very much either in body or in natural capacity.[7]

This was not kind; all the more so as this candid and rude assessment was very likely to filter back to France, souring relations and complicating the life of Contarini's unlucky successor as ambassador there. But among contemporaries such despatches were much admired. The anonymous French author of *Traité du gouvernement de Venise*, composed about 1500, noted with approval that newly appointed ambassadors would seek out in the archives the

5.3 Charles VIII of France.

Relazioni of their predecessors, in order to begin their missions well briefed.[8] These documents circulated widely among the senators, and many Venetian families kept copies of those which they believed brought them honour. With the passage of time copies were made and circulated outside the circles of those strictly entitled to see them; some copies changed hands for money. Towards the end of the sixteenth century the Venetian Senate finally acknowledged the public value of *Relazioni* and allowed a small number of them to appear in print. Presumably none of those chosen contained anything as wounding as Contarini's dissection of the young French king a century before.

Lying Abroad

In the development of international diplomacy a crucial figure was the shrewd and far-sighted Ferdinand, King of Aragon (r. 1479–1516). As ruler of Spain's Mediterranean kingdom he had a close interest in Italy at a time when French ambitions in the peninsula were transforming its politics. As co-ruler of Castile, through his wife Isabella, Ferdinand was the master of Europe's incipient superpower, Spain. His great strategic goal was to challenge the hegemony of France; his principal instrument, alliance backed by traditional dynastic marriages. In the pursuit of these goals Ferdinand established a web of permanent embassies: his was the first of Europe's nation states to do so. He even attempted to plant an embassy in France, largely to collect military intelligence. Such a legation, to a hostile power, would again have been a first, but Charles VIII was no fool and Ferdinand's envoy was soon sent packing.[9]

Ferdinand was not an easy man to please. The king sometimes neglected to write to his ambassadors for long periods, and often kept them in ignorance of his plans. His reciprocal demands for regular information were made without concern for the logistical obstacles. His long-suffering London envoy, Dr de Puebla, calculated that to send news to Ferdinand daily, as the king had requested, would require a relay of sixty couriers; in fact de Puebla had two, and could not afford to pay those. Ferdinand was also careless with paperwork, and prone to leave unsorted chests of papers in remote castles. But like Emperor Maximilian, his irrepressible contemporary, Ferdinand was an innovator. He left his ambassadors in place long enough for them to become real experts: nine years was the norm, and de Puebla was in London for most of the last twenty years of his life. As a result, Ferdinand bequeathed to his grandson Charles V a Spanish diplomatic corps that remained an established fact of European politics for the rest of the century.

A case study in suave and effective diplomatic service is provided by Eustace Chapuys, long-term ambassador for the Emperor Charles at the court of King Henry VIII.[10] Chapuys arrived in September 1529 in unpromising circumstances. Henry VIII had by now made unmistakably clear his determination to proceed with divorcing Katherine of Aragon. The queen, previously a valuable source of informed advice for the Spanish envoys, was no longer available for consultation; and the ambassador could scarcely in all conscience conceal his master's appalled opposition to Henry's policies. But over the course of sixteen years Chapuys gradually created a dense and subtle network of information to pepper the shrewd and well-sourced reports that have been such a treasure trove for historians. His first step was to take into his service several members of Katherine's household, including her gentleman usher, Juan de Montoya, who now became his private secretary. Young men of breeding, who could circulate unobtrusively at court, were recruited from France and Flanders. Although Chapuys did not speak English himself, he insisted that these young men should learn the language; the taciturn valet who accompanied him everywhere (Chapuys suffered from gout) was also a talented linguist. Through these agents Chapuys heard much of value that should not have been said in his presence. He was also at pains to lavish care and hospitality on the international merchant community, the source of a great deal of valuable information about currency movements, and on the incipient Lutheran movement (Chapuys had his friends among the German merchants too). Some information was paid for. It was a major coup to turn the French ambassador's principal secretary, who for eighteen months made available to

Chapuys Marillac's private correspondence, and Chapuys also received regular reports from one of Anne Boleyn's maids. But most of what he reported was freely given, from the merchants 'who visit me daily': the gossip of informed but often lonely men far from home, exchanged for hospitality and good fellowship.

A Spaniard in Rome

In the fourteenth and fifteenth centuries Rome had been the inadvertent laboratory of the new diplomacy. A common desire to exploit the resources of the Catholic Church made it necessary for Europe's rulers to send frequent emissaries to Rome requesting the confirmation of nominees in ecclesiastical office and other favours. Forced to linger by the slow pace of papal business, they became, in effect, ambassadors. Even in the sixteenth century Rome lost none of its importance as a centre of business, politics and news. Its centrality in the political calculations of the Spanish Habsburgs is indicated by the fact that the Roman ambassador was always paid the largest salary (though this, in common with all ambassadorial remuneration, never covered expenses).[11]

Although the Habsburgs had largely succeeded in establishing supremacy in the Italian Peninsula in the sixteenth century, vanquishing French competition, their ambassadors were ever vigilant. Their reports suggest anxiety more than confidence, and an overwhelming sense of the volatility of Italian politics. The case was well put by Miguel Mai, imperial ambassador to Rome, in a despatch to Charles V in 1530:

> As Rome is the vortex for all the world's affairs, and the Italians catch fire at the least spark, those who are partisan and even more those who have been ruined [by recent events] are stirring up trouble here, because they always want novelties.[12]

Note that this was written only months after the great triumph of Charles V's coronation at Bologna, when imperial power was at its apparent height. Spanish ambassadors returned again and again to the Italian thirst for novelty (*novedades*) that made them such fickle allies, and here they made no distinction between Rome, Venice and Florence. Spain, of course, wanted the opposite, quiescent allies who appreciated the virtues of Spanish hegemony. In this they were constantly disappointed.

Within the colonies of diplomatic representatives that gathered in Rome, Venice and elsewhere, we can detect two contrasting strategies for diplomatic representation. England, admittedly one of the minor players, made great use of Italian nationals, rather in the pattern of today's consular representatives.[13]

Charles V, and Philip II after him, always appointed Spanish noblemen. There were advantages to both strategies. The native Italians could move smoothly among the indigenous noble and merchant communities, and doubts as to their loyalty to the foreign power they served seem largely to have been unfair. The Spanish ambassadors represented their masters with energy and passion, but sometimes failed to appreciate why Italians did not accept the *pax Hispanica* as the natural order. They also frequently felt disliked and frozen out of the gossip and exchange of information that were the essential lubricants of diplomatic life. But as members of the highest caste of Spanish society they were adept at reading the implications attached, for instance, to the welcome given to the emissary of a rival power.[14] This was an age in which shifts in policy were often signified by public gestures: affection shown to a nobleman restored to favour, a visiting prince or a likely suitor; slights to those whose fortunes were on the wane. None of this escaped the eye of the astute diplomat, and news of this sort filled reams of ambassadorial despatches.

Papal elections were among the great news events of the sixteenth century, marking as they did the potential for major shifts in policy and alliances. Since they were so different from the hereditary succession of nation states, papal elections were difficult to plan for, though ambassadors were obliged to try. The characters and loyalties of the potential popes among the cardinals were the subject of obsessive diplomatic interest: Spanish ambassadors sent back to Spain copious dossiers detailing the characters, wealth, ambitions and – crucially – state of health of the significant figures. A series of profiles of over fifty cardinals compiled by ambassador Luis de Requeséns in 1565 ran to forty-eight pages.[15]

Ambassadors were well aware that the election of a pro or anti-imperial Pope could either consolidate or threaten Spanish power in the peninsula. Every election was hotly contested, as France, in particular, seized the opportunity to reverse by diplomacy the consequences of successive battlefield defeats. The resident ambassador bore much of the burden of this warfare of whispers and insincere promises, but this sort of multi-dimensional chess was deeply unpredictable. News of the election of Giovanni Maria del Monte (Julius III) in 1550 was greeted with joy in Paris, since he had been a prominent name on Charles V's blacklist.[16] In fact he proved a good friend to Habsburg pretensions until the two fell out over the war of Parma in 1551. But this was as nothing to the disaster of the election of the Neapolitan Gian Pietro Carafa (Paul IV) in 1555, whose hatred of Spanish domination of his homeland was deep and unshakable. Any hope of rapprochement probably died the following year when the Spanish ambassador, finding himself unrecognised by the guard at the city gate, battered down the door to force an entry.[17]

Despite Spain's domination of the Italian Peninsula, this was a difficult posting and many ambassadorial careers ended in failure. Both of Philip II's first two ambassadors left in high dudgeon having antagonised the Pope. Spanish emissaries found the shifting, multi-polar politics of Venice equally difficult to fathom. Diplomacy was a new trade, requiring discreet charm and subtle skill. Not all ambassadors realised that if they became the story the game was probably lost.

Espionage

As these examples suggest, the development of a network of permanent diplomatic representation was not always a force for harmony. The high-minded principles enunciated by Bernard du Rosier in 1436 had been replaced by more pragmatic nostrums. The Venetian scholar-diplomat Ermolao Barbaro, writing in 1490, set out the new doctrine with brutal clarity. 'The first duty of an ambassador is exactly the same as that of any other servant of government, that is, to do, say, advise and think whatever may best serve the preservation and aggrandizement of his own state.'[18] The tortured conflicts of the Reformation era added further layers of peril and distrust to international relations. Diplomats of the major powers had to ply their trade in an atmosphere of increasing distrust and hostility. Previously routine connections and hospitality became potentially compromising for citizens of the host country. 'It is impossible for me to find out anything certain at present here,' reported the Count of Feria, Philip II's first ambassador to Queen Elizabeth. 'Nobody wants to talk to me; people flee from me as if I were the devil.'[19]

These complications added new and testing responsibilities to the envoy's tasks. The urgent search for information required increasing recourse to clandestine contacts and espionage. In the age of confessional conflict disaffected subjects prepared to share their schemes with foreign agents were not difficult to find. But these connections did not always lead an ambassador towards sober or dispassionate judgements. It was dangerous to be swayed by easy if somewhat desperate accounts of the strength of opposition, and passionate if treasonable offers of assistance. Sixteenth-century governments had many opportunities to experience the undoubted truth that there is nothing so poisonous to intelligence gathering as the wishful thinking of the disenchanted and dispossessed. Captured Spaniards from the Armada fleet in 1588 revealed that they had been led to expect that between a third and one half of the English population was ready to support the invasion.[20] This was a total fantasy: Spanish ambassadors proved all too credulous in their dealings with English Catholics, and Protestant English policymakers made the same mistake with French Huguenot émigrés. English ambassadors in Spain faced a frosty reception, but at least there were no Spanish Protestants to lead them astray.

In these highly charged times the stakes were high, and it became increasingly difficult to assess the quality of information received. It is always possible in retrospect to isolate nuggets of truth in a blizzard of contradictory intelligence reports, and marvel that they were not acted upon. At the time it is never so obvious. The English government already possessed by 1586 an exact logistical plan of the proposed Spanish invasion of England. But even as the Armada prepared to set sail two years later, in late May 1588, they continued to doubt its intended destination. Admittedly they were not helped by confident predictions conveyed by the English ambassador in Paris, Sir Edward Stafford, that the Spanish fleet was to be directed to Algiers, or the Indies (this he reported as late as June). The English government were not to know that this supremely well-placed source was in the pay of Spain, and deliberately sowing disinformation.[21]

Even if an agent received valuable information, it could be extremely difficult to convey it back home. Their hosts knew full well who the ambassadors had been meeting and wanted to know what they had written. Diplomatic despatches became a legitimate target. Cardinal Wolsey would intercept diplomatic correspondence on the most spurious of pretexts, as did Cardinal Gattinara on behalf of Charles V. Later ministers contrived sophisticated ways of reading outgoing despatches and then resealing them undetected. To secure the safe passage of their reports, ambassadors increasingly made use of ciphers.[22] On the whole these were not very effective ways of protecting despatches. Most embassies used simple systems of substituting a numeral or arbitrary symbol for each letter or short word: anything more complex proved too cumbersome or resulted in messages becoming hopelessly scrambled. Ambassadors tended to undermine the system by using the same cipher for years on end, such as Chapuys for instance during his entire embassy (1529–45). Although the Spanish Embassy in Prague had several ciphers at its disposal, the ambassador used the same one for the whole period between 1581 and 1608. Europe's major capitals all possessed the key.

Almost all ambassadors maintained a network of spies and informers. Some were valuable sources; others deluded fantasists or light-fingered opportunists who deftly played off one intelligence service against another.[23] The best form of intelligence was often obtained by a simple cash transaction with a relatively junior member of the burgeoning state bureaucracies. For a fee a clerk or secretary could often make copies of incoming letters. Several of the letters included with the Urbino collection of newsletters were obtained in this way.[24]

Given the casual nature of fifteenth- and sixteenth-century record-keeping, this was neither difficult nor dangerous. The English agent in Venice had a budget of £40 for bribes which he mostly employed to buy copies of letters directed to rival diplomats. Even in Spain, the postmaster's office proved susceptible to English gold. A report to William Cecil, Lord Burghley, in 1598 included the remarkably matter-of-fact observation from his Spanish agent:

> Postmasters in Spain weigh out the letters to their servants, and are easily corrupted for 28 ducats a month: the one at Madrid, Pedro Martinez, let me have all of Cressold's and Englefield's letters, returning such as I did not care to keep.[25]

The burgeoning commercial news services of these years would also make increasing use of paid contacts among the low-paid clerks and officials who necessarily had sight of sensitive material.

No amount of sophisticated intelligence was of much use, however, if the information was poor. The embittered confessional politics of the second half of the sixteenth century represented a difficult time for Renaissance diplomacy. The permanent state of enmity that engulfed Europe's leading powers made the maintenance of traditional diplomatic relations virtually impossible. Ambassadors were frequently being withdrawn or expelled. Nothing better symbolises this deterioration than the colourful career of Bernardino de Mendoza, one-time Spanish ambassador to England. Expelled by Queen Elizabeth in 1584 for his shameless orchestration of a plot to have her assassinated, Mendoza was then sent to France with the explicit task of organising the opposition of the Catholic League to King Henry III. After the French king's assassination in 1589, Mendoza ended his diplomatic career, sword in hand, leading the resistance of the French capital to their new king, Henry of Navarre.[26]

Strange times indeed for the craft of diplomacy. It was clear that men of this temper could no longer provide the dispassionate advice necessary for decision-making. A different source of informed confidential advice was required. In the sixteenth century this emerged in the form of a new commercial manuscript news service: the *avvisi*.

The First News Agencies

In the years around 1590 the Italian city of Lucca was looking to find a new source of confidential information in Rome.[27] A correspondent there recommended that they employ Giovanni Poli: he was said to be far and away the best, and that there was not a single Italian ruler who did not have him under contract. Poli was also a careful man, both savvy and discreet. He knew that the reputation of his business depended not only on the quality of his product, but also on the cultivation of a certain mystique. So he developed a particular way of conducting business. He would rise early in the morning to write his reports. Then he would carry them personally across the city to deliver them to the post. This way he would ensure that they could not be tampered with en route; and Rome would see a master craftsman going about his business.

Poli was a *novellante*, one of a new breed of news-gathering scribes who offered a commercial news service to subscribing customers. The clients were invariably rich and powerful men from the governing or commercial classes, for the service was not cheap. (Lucca, incidentally, accepted the recommendation to engage Poli, and remained a subscriber to his newsletter for almost thirty years.) To succeed, *novellanti* had to earn a reputation for the quality of their information and the range of their sources. This was certainly the case with Poli: the despatches from the Spanish ambassador in Rome were said to be nothing much more than Poli's reports rendered into Spanish. Poli was at the top of his trade, which was why his weekly perambulation through the busy streets of Rome became part of the folklore of this remarkable city.

Poli represented a new twist in the development of an ever more diverse sixteenth-century news market.[28] The craft of the *novellanti* was incubated in the twin cities of Rome and Venice, the European centres of commercial news and political gossip. The roots of the new medium can be traced back to the commercial correspondence of medieval times. A fascinating despatch survives from the year 1303, sent by members of the Ricciardi company of Lucca to their representatives in London.[29] The letter offers a long digest of news from Lucca and the Italian Peninsula, along with news from France. For the wealth of incidental detail this can be compared with the despatch prepared, a century later, by Antonio Morosini for his nephew serving as the Venetian consul in Alexandria.[30] These digests of political information, rare for their detail, are a reminder that it was as important to keep far-flung agents abreast of events at home as it was for them to send back intelligence from their postings.

In these despatches political news was generally mixed with instructions and information about essential commercial transactions. The emergence of the manuscript newsletter as a separate entity took a step forward through the initiatives of two well-connected Italians, Giovanni Sabadino degli Arienti and Benedetto Dei. The two men, who developed a close friendship towards the end of Dei's life, had arrived at their vocation as purveyors of news through rather different routes. For Arienti, his interest in news was almost an accidental by-product of the conventional search for patronage through literary endeavour. In the course of this literary life he moved into the circle of Ercole d'Este, Duke of Ferrara; Arienti would later be a valued correspondent of Ercole's daughter, Isabella, after her marriage to Francesco Gonzaga of Mantua.[31] Both appreciated his regular and extensive compilations of news. Based in Bologna, Arienti was well placed to cull news from travellers on the road to Florence and Rome. He also maintained an extensive web of correspondents. One of these was the indefatigable Benedetto Dei. Dei's activities as a news correspondent were the culmination of an eventful life that had taken him to France, England and Germany, and had involved extensive travels in Asia and Africa. He returned to Florence in 1468 after several years' residence in Constantinople. Clubbable and gregarious, Dei used the web of connections developed during these years to build an unrivalled reputation as a source of news. Between 1470 and 1480 he adopted the practice of issuing regular bulletins which, for the first time, deviated from the customary epistolary style to create a new form of writing. One surviving letter, from 1478, offers fifty short items. Each is a single sentence with a dateline indicating the source of the report:

> I have news from Genoa that the Doge has knighted Batistino and sent away the [families of] Adorni and Raonesi.
> I have news from Lyon, the trade fair has been very very good; a lot of textiles have been sold and a good deal of money gained too.
> I have news from France that nine ambassadors are coming to Italy with 200 horse to make peace for everyone.[32]

Dei's correspondence with Arienti offers numerous examples of how his news was gathered. Arienti frequently forwarded mail to Dei from Bologna, re-directing it to the Medici bank in Florence where Dei received correspondence. Much of Dei's detailed information from France came from Medici contacts, particularly Francesco Sassetti of the Medici bank in Lyon.[33] Spanish news came from merchants resident in Florence. Dei traded particularly on his unrivalled contacts in the Ottoman Empire and at the court of the Sultan of Egypt; he boasted of his ability to send regularly every Saturday 'the news from Asia and from Africa and from Europe always'. This was a very significant remark, for it indicates that Dei was the first to conceive of his news bulletins as a weekly service. Whereas Arienti, in the medieval and Renaissance fashion, hoped to curry princely favour through his news digests, Dei expected and received regular payments for his bulletins. In the last years of his life Dei held a unique position at the centre of a web of news gathering. A letter from an admiring correspondent in Cortona in 1490 assured him that his letters were eagerly awaited: as soon as they arrived they were immediately copied many times over.[34]

It is clear from this that Dei had not yet developed the most effective commercial model. To maximise income the news correspondent had to supervise personally the processes of replication and distribution. In the next few decades the *avviso* gradually developed into its mature form. The *avvisi* of the sixteenth century generally consisted of one or two sheets of paper folded once, to make the equivalent of a quarto pamphlet of four or eight pages. These were filled with a sequence of reports, each consisting of a short paragraph of two or three sentences. They began in the style that Dei had pioneered with a dateline: 'News from Venice, 24 March 1570'; 'In a letter from Constantinople it is reported'. The paragraph then summarised the news reported from that place. So under 'news from Rome' would be listed all the news emanating from Roman sources, even if it related to places far away. It would be followed by news gathered from Venice, France, Constantinople, from the Low Countries and England. This style of presentation was maintained largely unchanged in manuscript news services into the eighteenth century; it also proved deeply influential in shaping the first printed news serials. The newspapers of the early seventeenth century would in this respect owe far more to the conventions and news values of the *avvisi* than to the very different style of the printed news pamphlets.

The places from which news was gathered were a largely unvarying list of key news hubs: in the case of transalpine locations, generally major commercial centres well served by the continental postal services. The tradition was that the news should be transmitted in crisp sentences with little by way of commentary or analysis. The emphasis was on providing the maximum information; the merchants and members of the governing classes who were the major clients of the *novellanti* could draw their own conclusions. Thus the *avvisi* were very different from diplomatic despatches, where the information supplied would be shaped by the known political priorities of the ambassador's home state. The *avvisi*, in contrast, affected an air of studied neutrality. Although this could sometimes be deceiving, it did permit commercial newsmen to develop a wide circle of clients among the leaders of Italy's often feuding states. The *avvisi* were neither tailored to nor adapted for individual clients. In the newsletters supplied to the Duke of Urbino from Rome after 1565 he would regularly receive news of his own activities – at least as they were reported in the eternal city.[35]

A further unvarying convention was that the newsletters were unsigned. This may seem rather odd to us, since the *novellanti* certainly wished to advertise their skills and broaden the circle of their clients. The best, like Poli and the Venetians Hieronimo Acconzaicco and Pompeo Roma, became well-known figures. The tradition of anonymity has more to do with a conscious attempt to differentiate between fact, as reported, and opinion. Unverified reports were clearly indicated as such: 'it is said . . .'; 'it is reported from Lyon'.

The two major drivers in the development of commercial news agencies were Rome and Venice. It is not difficult to see why these cities were so influential. Venice was the commercial metropolis of the region, with the most highly developed diplomatic networks, territories and trade in the eastern Mediterranean and the Levant. Since Venice was also a nodal point in European postal and diplomatic communications, the well informed could rely on hearing news from Paris, Lyon, Brussels and Spain, as well as from the imperial capitals of Vienna and Innsbruck. The Rialto was Europe's premier hub of commercial information exchange and gossip. When Salanio initiated a conversation in *The Merchant of Venice* with the greeting, 'Now, what news on the Rialto?', Shakespeare could expect a knowing chuckle from London playgoers.[36]

Rome for its part was the critical centre of political and ecclesiastical power. The need for papal approval of benefices made Rome a constant place of intrigue and the destination of numerous diplomatic missions. The continual inflow of Church revenues also made it a major centre of banking: a survey of 1550 enumerated fifty-one banking firms active in the city.[37] In the second half of the sixteenth century an activist papacy, energetically promoting war against the Turk and Protestant heretics, commanded the attention of all Europe.

The different character of the two cities was reflected in a palpably different tone of the news reports circulated by their respective *novellanti*. In Rome the *avvisi* tended to be more gossipy, offering detailed reports of the manoeuvres of the Curia and ambitious cardinals. The most sophisticated news writers even attempted to develop a two-tier news service, distinguishing an ordinary bulletin from a premium service of confidential news for favoured clients. This was all well and good so long as the two did not get confused, as was the case with one Roman news writer whose secret sheet critical of the papal household was soon in the hands of the Pope. The odd mishap apart, the Roman *novellanti* were happy to cultivate a reputation for being able to penetrate the most secret counsels of this city of schemes. A newly appointed aide to the court of one cardinal was strictly enjoined to have no contact with the news writers. They could, he was warned, 'take the egg out of a chicken's body, let along the secret out of a youth's mouth'.[38]

As can be seen from these two examples, although Italian news writers provided what was increasingly regarded as an indispensable service, they were

not universally well regarded. In the second half of the sixteenth century successive popes took strong action to set limits to their activities. In 1570 Pius V
announced that he would energetically pursue the authors of defamatory broadsheets. Soon after this the writer Niccolò Franco was arrested, tried and executed.
In 1572 an edict was promulgated against *avvisi*:

> Let nobody dare or presume to compose, dictate, write, copy, keep or
> transmit to anyone libellous writings or letters of advice, called in the vernac-
> ular 'lettere di avisi', containing abuse, insults or personal attacks on
> anyone's reputation and honour, or any writing that discusses future
> events.[39]

The prohibitions were renewed by an edict of Sixtus V in 1586, and these years
saw sporadic efforts to see them enforced. In 1581 one writer was given a life
sentence for allegedly spreading rumours of the Pope's health. In 1587 a man
described as the 'head of a sect of gazetteers' was executed for leaking confidential information. The actions against the news writers seem to have been
particularly severe in Rome because their activities became conflated in the
popes' minds with the scurrilous writings of those who posted around the city
the libellous satirical verses known as pasquinades. These were unrestrained
and wilfully defamatory hits at those in power. Because they were posted up
anonymously (many on the ancient statue nicknamed 'Pasquino', from which
the name is derived), their authors were seldom discovered.[40] The authors of
the news-sheets, many of whom ran a large scribal office employing numerous
clerks, were easier targets.

   Although many of the pasquinades were bitingly topical, the confusion of
the two forms was unfair. The *avvisi* could be cynical, but with rare exceptions
were not openly offensive. Their value lay in their reliability as news; the
writers could not exaggerate for effect, nor indulge in wishful thinking. In the
clear distance between the *avvisi* and polemical writing lay their marketability.
They would demonstrate their maturity as a news form during the Armada
campaign of 1588, when they remained calmly sceptical of early reports of a
Spanish victory, a victory that was of course fervently desired in Rome.[41] The
fiercest antagonism to the news writers tended to be at times when those in
authority had an interest in preventing news circulating, often of course when
it was bad.

   In time, the intermittent threat of retributive action did have its effect on the
tone of *avvisi*. The Roman *avvisi* became more monotonous, and certainly
more cautious, with the passing of years.[42] For all that, they remained an absolutely essential part of the news network for those in official positions, and

increasingly for a wider public as well. A highly suggestive edict of 1590 prohib-
ited preachers from referring to newsletters in their sermons, the clear infer-
ence being that the city clergy were among their readers.[43] The manuscript
news-books continued to be the dominant form of news publication in Italy
throughout the seventeenth century, long after the arrival of newspapers.
Venetian merchants still relied on the *avvisi* for information likely to move the
sensitive financial markets. In Rome, *avvisi* played a crucial role in the rampant
betting market.[44] But whereas in the sixteenth century *avvisi* had been at the
forefront of news culture, in the seventeenth century this became less and less
the case. An admirer of Rome in 1637 could still boast that 'this was the place
where all of the news of the world is found'. But a perusal of the *avvisi* would
have told him that this was no longer the case. The world was moving on. The
focus of events and the shapers of Europe's politics were now to be found in the
north – as was the gravitational pull of Europe's news culture.

The Fugger Newsletter

The steady growth of a commercial news market in Italy could not go un-
noticed north of the Alps. Given the close business ties between Germany, the
Netherlands and the Italian Peninsula, it was inevitable that the manuscript
newsletters would soon be in demand elsewhere. At first, German clients
simply availed themselves of the services of the established Roman, and particularly Venetian, *novellanti*. But by the last quarter of the sixteenth century
professional news agencies were becoming a feature of the northern news
market as well. These were situated, first and foremost, in the leading commercial centres, Antwerp, Cologne and especially Augsburg. The south German
city enjoyed a unique position, a major commercial metropolis that was also a
principal hub of the northern European information network. Augsburg was
the junction of the postal service between Venice and northern Europe, and
between the imperial capitals of Vienna and Brussels: it was the only one of the
major German cities to be an integral part of the imperial postal route.[45]

The first northern clients of the manuscript newsletters were mostly the
princes and officials of the German court. Theirs at least are the collections
that have survived: the strong bias towards commercial and political news in
the surviving copies, however, hints strongly at a lively market among the
patrician merchants of the south German cities. The largest surviving collection was that compiled by the merchant and banking family, the Fuggers of
Augsburg.[46] The Fuggers had profited massively from their close association
with the Habsburgs in the first half of the sixteenth century. In later decades
their commitment to Philip II left them more exposed and imperilled. To

protect their far-flung business interests the Fuggers built the most extraordinary news information service of the age.

To get the measure of this global news service we need to turn to twenty-seven neatly bound volumes that survive today in the National Library in Vienna.[47] Each volume contains hundreds of items: issue after issue of the manuscript newsletters. The first volume in Vienna dates from 1569, but the Fugger news service seems to pre-date this. The Vatican archive in Rome has a set of earlier volumes dating from 1554, which had been the property of Ulrich Fugger. These had been presented by the family to the University of Heidelberg, before making their way to Rome when that wonderful library was plundered by Catholic armies during the Thirty Years War.[48]

The Vienna volumes comprise the archive of two brothers of a younger generation, Philip Eduard and Octavian Secundus, who took control of the interests of their father Georg after his unexpected death in 1569. Happily the young men could call upon a network of long-established commercial partners in every corner of Europe. It was David Ott, an Innsbruck merchant based in Venice, who put them in touch with two of the most reputable Venetian *novellanti*, the aforementioned Hieronimo Acconzaicco and Pompeo Roma, who provided a weekly service at the cost, in 1585 and 1586, of 113 florins. Ott had previously recommended Accozaioco to Hans Fugger, son of Anton, though with less success. In 1577 Hans complained to Ott that Accozaioco sent only rubbish: 'all hot air and nothings'. He asked Ott to contract Juan Donato instead, since he had a better reputation.[49] In fact, Accozaioco was still writing for the Fuggers two years later. The Venetian *avvisi* in the Vienna archive were despatched, and presumably read, in their original Italian.

This was a straightforward commercial transaction. From elsewhere in northern Europe the Fuggers received not only regular packages containing the local news-sheets, but a digest prepared by their local agent. The managers of the Fugger branch offices were persons of considerable standing in their own right, usually highly educated men from leading German patrician families. It fell to them not only to sift the reports for the most reliable news, but to see that those in Dutch were translated into German. The news writers frequently mentioned news reports they chose not to pass on, because they found them doubtful. 'Although I have read other particulars, these are the ones that seem to me to be the best,' wrote Christoph Winkelhofer, passing on news from Vienna.[50] The newsletters archived by the Fuggers are not much concerned with the everyday staples of the news broadsheets: sensations, prophecies and wondrous tales. For these serious men, 'worthy of writing' meant political and economic news.

In 1586 the brothers Philip Eduard and Octavian Secundus entered into a partnership which contracted with Philip II for a five-year import licence of the Asian pepper trade. (This Portuguese monopoly had fallen to Spain since Philip's contested occupation of Portugal in 1580.) It was a risky new venture that required an expansion of the news service to include more regular reports from the Iberian Peninsula. The Welser factor in Lisbon took charge of arranging reports from the erstwhile Portuguese capital; a succession of agents in Spain organised compilations of news from Seville, Valladolid and Madrid. The development of the Asian trade also brought the first news reports direct from India. Many of these despatches from trusted agents consist of something rather different from the commercial newsletters of Venice. Here the local Fugger agents acted as a filter, applying their judgement to gauge the veracity of the reports they assembled, before they passed them on. But they also made sure that the originals, the raw data, made their way to Vienna. Even the most fanciful and speculative reports were useful in gauging the temper of the times.

Once they arrived in Vienna the Fugger brothers were generous in sharing the information that poured into their headquarters with every post. Weekly digests were prepared for both the Duke of Bavaria and Archduke Ferdinand of Tyrol.[51] Philip Eduard and Octavian Secundus even apparently allowed some of their news reports to be printed, especially the drawings which many of their correspondents included with their despatches. In 1585 the brothers contracted the Augsburg engraver Hans Schultes to make an illustrated broadsheet of a watercolour sent to them of the fortifications constructed by the Duke of Parma for the siege of Antwerp, the climax of his successful campaign of reconquest in Flanders and Brabant.[52] This publication seems to have been extremely successful: these sorts of military diagrams had been an important vogue in the news market since the siege of Malta in 1565.[53] They allowed a dispersed public to follow the progress of these long drawn-out military engagements in some detail.

The Fugger news archive was a private resource, created as an adjunct to one of Europe's greatest business empires. But it was not long before the enormous opportunities of news gathering stimulated the growth of commercial news agencies in imitation of the Venetian *novellanti*. The Fuggers may well have employed one of the first independent entrepreneurs in Augsburg, Jeremias Crasser, to prepare digests of incoming despatches. But it was another Augsburg man, Albrecht Reiffenstein, who made this extraordinary proposition to Duke August of Saxony in 1579:

I know you maintain people in Venice, Cologne, Antwerp and Vienna, who send you all the news from there. But the post brings to Augsburg from Italy,

France, Spain and Portugal and the Imperial Court all the news reports from the whole of Christendom, from which I make reports for the leading Lords. Because I was born as your subject, I will do the same for you on a weekly basis, and send it to Nuremberg and then to Leipzig, so you can be as well informed as any other prince in Germany.[54]

This suggests an extraordinarily developed network of commercial news men. Certainly within a few years news writers were prospering in Hamburg, Cologne, Frankfurt, Prague, Vienna and Leipzig. Duke August, incidentally, accepted Reiffenstein's proposition by return of post. Four years later he had contracted another man, Philip Bray, to provide news from France and the Low Countries. Bray was to be paid the enormous sum of 100 florins every quarter. His newsletter would be sent by courier to August by way of Nuremberg and Dresden.

These transactions demonstrate the astounding value that the political and business leaders of Germany placed on reliable news. In difficult times – and these were particularly troubled years – it was necessary for those in positions of authority to have access to the swiftest and most accurate information. The local Fugger agents played a role that was similar to that of the ambassadors serving Europe's crowned heads, gathering up, listening, sifting and passing on their best judgement of what was to be believed. But they also passed on as many of the different news reports as they could gather together. An important regional ruler like August of Saxony wanted both the reports of his own agents and those of the commercial news men.

The commercial manuscript newsletter proved remarkably enduring. The news writers survived the hostility of sixteenth-century popes and the arrival of the first printed newspapers. In the seventeenth century the manuscript news services even moved into new territories, with the establishment of the first news agencies in London.[55] Through all the pamphlet storms and techno-logical change of the seventeenth and even eighteenth centuries the newsletters lived on with the same orderly progression of neat paragraphs: 'It is reported from Vienna', 'News from Granada', 'It is said on the Bourse'. Well-sourced, dispassionate and reassuringly expensive, the manuscript newsletters were a distinctive and now almost wholly forgotten part of the news world. For two centuries Europe's opinion-formers would not be without them.

CHAPTER 6

Marketplace and Tavern

THE manuscript news agencies were the tools of the privileged. The expense of commercial manuscript news was in this sense no disadvantage: rather, expense offered the reassurance of authority that men of power looked for in a well-informed source. Those without access to these services could still learn much from printed news pamphlets, a more promiscuous and boisterous medium, and one that now played an increasingly confident role in sharing news of current events with a wide reading public. But there was a third strand to early modern news culture that should not be ignored: news passed by word of mouth.

The full potency of this verbal news culture was first demonstrated in England in the years after the Reformation. In the 1530s the introduction of the new worship service and dissolution of the monasteries caused widespread unease and some outright opposition. The task of seeing that this did not get out of hand fell to Thomas Cromwell, Henry VIII's loyal minister and the primary architect of the new Protestant regime. Cromwell was nothing if not thorough. In these difficult and troubled years the Chief Secretary and his agents embarked on a sustained campaign to winkle out dissent and to punish the guilty.[1] Many of those caught in his net were barely literate and not very articulate. But they had strong views to express. Denis Jones, a smith from London, was one who passed on the news he had gleaned in the capital when he stopped by the Bear Inn in Reading. Some time before he had been drinking with a group of neighbours from the Isle of Wight when a pedlar came in and told them 'that he heard at London that Queen Anne was put to death and boiled in lead'. Others gave garbled accounts of royal legislation and shared rumours of the king's death. When in March 1535 Adam Fermour of Walden in Essex returned home after a trip to the capital, he faced the inevitable question, 'What news?' His neighbours had no trouble remembering his chilling reply. 'By God's blood, evil news! For the king will make such laws that if a man die his wife and children shall go a-begging.'[2] This was politically dangerous indeed, and it is no wonder that the government took such strong action. But what comes through most forcibly in these reports is the ubiquity of travellers as vectors of information, and inns as places where it was heard and reported. Even in a country like England, where printing was entirely confined to the capital, news could travel fast, if not always accurately.

Pre-industrial society was still to a very large extent an oral culture. It was not just that many men and women could not read, though this was certainly true. Rather the whole process of social organisation and decision-making was organised around an inherited tradition of communal activity, verbal expression and face-to-face contact. Governments across Europe could make war, pass laws and raise taxes, as they did with increasing confidence and frequency. But these decisions still had to be explained to an active and interested citizenry. A wide measure of public consent had to be obtained, because laws could not otherwise easily be enforced. States lacked the power for sustained coercion of their own citizens: there were no standing armies and only the most rudimentary police forces.

Even in less urgent times early modern societies were characterised by an insatiable curiosity: news of neighbours, friends, the mighty, great events and catastrophes, all added spice to the humdrum and leavened the hard realities of everyday existence. The principal locations for this social interaction were the marketplace and the tavern. These were the universal gathering places of early modern society. They brought together travellers and residents, the literate and illiterate, members of different social classes, and, to an extent, men and women. These were the kingdoms of the spoken word of news.

To Market

The marketplace was the central site of information exchange across European society. In the routine of everyday life, long-distance travel and trade were unusual. Most of the essentials of life could be obtained locally: in the village, or from the local market. Since medieval times market towns had developed as a natural network about 30 miles apart. Most villages would be not more than 15 miles from a market town: a stiff day's journey there and back for a mounted rider or a farmer with his oxen and cart.[3] This normative sense of a day's journey was, as we have seen, strongly influential in the construction of the European road system, with its network of inns and lodging, and the postal system.

Entertainment and variety were offered by those who visited from farther afield: entertainers, quack doctors and tooth-pullers, and long-distance travellers. These played an important role in the network of news. Often, in contrast to the authoritative news bearers we have encountered in previous chapters, they were men and women of low social status. Alice Bennet, a poor woman from Oxfordshire, was described as one who 'goeth abroad to sell soap and candles from town to town to get her living and she useth to carry tales between neighbours'.[4] There were fitful attempts to control such tattle, but they were bound to fail. In England any traveller arriving from the capital was regarded as an authority and likely to face the question, 'What news from London?' Some information could be gleaned from the boatmen who rowed across the Thames, other news from the ubiquitous taverns. Harry Shadwell had heard various rumours in 1569 about the Duke of Alva in the Netherlands, and an alarming tale that ten thousand Scots had joined the Rising of the Northern Earls. William Frauncis returned to Essex with the rumour that 'there was one in the Tower which sayeth he is King Edward'.[5] Travelling tradesmen could also bring the occasional letter to friends and family in the provinces, as in the case of the London apprentice who in 1619 sent back to his parents in Wigan, Lancashire, the following breathless despatch:

> I have but little but that there is like to be a great changing in England. Many strange wonders about London. There is a hand and a sword risen out of the ground at a town called Newmarket, where the King is, and stands striking at him. And the King went to see it and ever since he hath kept his chamber and cannot tell what it means: and other strange things which now I will not speak of.[6]

Given that the news vouchsafed is complete nonsense, one can only wonder what might have been the quality of the 'other strange things'. But we can sense the excitement of the new-minted Londoner happy to be in the thick of things – and not averse to tantalising his distant parents with his unaccustomed superiority in the news market, however illusory.

The marketplace was the major public space at the heart of any community. It gathered residents, folk from the surrounding villages, and travellers who came to buy and sell. Market towns were also frequently the seats of local government, and of other powerful organisations such as town corporations and guilds. At irregular intervals market towns would also be the seats of the local law courts, or assizes. Early modern justice was swift, and those who came to trade might also see justice done. Bakers who sold underweight bread, fraudsters, prostitutes or vagabonds would frequently be punished, by ridicule or corporal punishment, in the market square. This was also sometimes the place of execution, though sentence was often conducted in some other large open space away from the main trading area. Executions were invariably a public spectacle. To modern eyes this appears cruel and voyeuristic. But the ritualised quality of such public punishment was essential to the early modern sense of community.[7] Justice was a communal process, and execution a ritual act of expulsion. So although the onlookers might sometimes pity the prisoners in their terrifying last moments, they undoubtedly approved the process of the law. They would carry the news away with them, along with their purchases.

It is sometimes suggested that the news value of the more sensational cases was eagerly exploited by nimble publicists, who would move through the crowd selling accounts of the crimes and the prisoners' deathbed confessions. This seems improbable, at least in the sixteenth century. As we have seen, such accounts of notorious crimes circulated widely, and for long after the event.[8] Their pedagogic value, and capacity to titillate, was not closely linked to the place where the crime or execution took place. In England such a market for news would have been impossible in any case, since there was virtually no printing outside London.[9] These were news events experienced for the most part by eyewitnesses and shared by word of mouth. The corpse left to rot on the gibbet would serve as a reminder to those who came by later.

Visitors to the market could also see news being made. Authorities took advantage of the presence of a crowd to announce the latest regulations, or pass on news of recent legislation. In major cities, where the market was a permanent event, these proclamations might happen any day. In France and elsewhere the public announcement of the latest royal decree was attended by an elaborate ceremony. The royal herald would appear accompanied by a trumpeter to gain attention. Once the crowd had been silenced, he would declaim the king's announcement before moving on to the next main thoroughfare. In Paris there was a fixed itinerary to be used on such occasions. The new decree was then carried by courier to the main provincial towns, where the municipal authorities were obliged to repeat the ceremony.

It is hard to know how much the witnesses of these solemn ceremonies would have taken in. Presumably the trumpeter (in other places the ringing of a bell) would have secured reasonable attention; but the general hubbub, the clucking and bellowing of live animals, and the coming and going of impatient shoppers would have made the reading difficult to hear. Proclamations could also be long, and couched in formal legal language, complex and intricate. The announcement would therefore also subsequently be posted up, usually in many copies, which more and more frequently would be printed texts. These would be pinned up in prominent public places, in the marketplace, on the church door, in the toll booth. The public reading served as much as intimation that something important was afoot, and the citizenry should acquaint themselves with the details. These could be passed by readers to other interested parties, ideally with reasonable accuracy. For those with a professional need to know, a printed text, sometimes a broadsheet and sometimes a pamphlet, became an increasingly important adjunct to these public readings. Even so, the process of law enforcement always began with a spectacle, or announcement, in public open space.

The marketplace was volatile: a powder keg as well as a place of exchange. In times of dearth high prices or empty stalls offered a tangible demonstration of the authorities' need to take steps to ameliorate the crisis. The gathering of disenchanted citizens provided a fertile environment for the spreading of rumour, misinformation and discontent. In such situations the power of early modern government was limited. These were not police states: most cities could afford only a handful of bailiffs or guards, and the presence of other armed men, troops or a noble retinue, was usually highly unwelcome. The maintenance of law required a tacit public consent and, if this was withdrawn, there was little the magistrates could do but ride out the storm. In such circumstances news, spread by rumour, mishearing and misunderstanding, was a poison. Its toxic quality was only exacerbated by the ubiquity of strong drink.

Singing the News

The market was an essential cog in the early modern information network. Its place at the heart of village life can be judged by its importance in folk tales: country people went to market to sell their wares, but also to be duped and cheated by the sly rogues who lay in wait. The market was too the locus operandi of the most marginal figures in the world of news, the itinerant pedlars.[10] In some European cultures these were known as 'news singers' because they would literally sing out their wares. Their songs were often contemporary events turned into ballads.

This is the one part of the early modern news world that has no clear equivalent today. In the Europe of the sixteenth century, however, singing played an important role in mediating news events to a largely illiterate public. The news singers, sometimes blind and often accompanied by children, would sing out their wares, then offer printed versions for sale. In Spain the writers of ballads would sometimes teach them to a group of blind pedlars before sending them out on the roads. The pedlars displayed their wares on a wooden framework strung with cord, rather like a clothes line; in consequence these publications are sometimes known as 'cord literature'.[11] Broadsheet ballads were clearly printed in enormous quantities, as we can see from the thousands of copies listed in the inventories of booksellers' stock, and ballad pamphlets

6.1 An early song broadsheet. Note that, although this song text was conspicuously well printed, there is no musical notation. Published in 1512, it relates the French victory at Dôle in an earlier war.

were also popular. Samuel Pepys bought a whole bundle when he visited Spain from Tangiers in 1683.[12] Most likely, though, with the Inquisition keeping a close eye on the print industry, Spanish ballad singers would usually have steered clear of the more dangerous contemporary news topics.[13]

This was not the case elsewhere in Europe, where topicality was a major selling point. Although the sellers were among Europe's most marginal groups, and could be brutally treated by the local authorities, the trade was lucrative. In 1566 a travelling pedlar in the Low Countries had a printer in Overijssel run off one thousand copies of a sheet containing three popular political songs. He paid one guilder for the whole batch. Even if he sold them for the smallest coin then in circulation, he would have made a handsome profit.[14] The trade in song-sheets was also welcomed by more established members of the trade, such as the Oxford bookseller John Dorne: in 1520 he sold over two hundred broadsheet ballads in forty separate transactions. He charged a standard halfpenny a sheet, though there were discounts available for customers who bought more than six.[15] In Italy the printed versions of performed songs tended to be short pamphlets rather than broadsheets; here, it is suggested, pedlars might take the edition from the printer in instalments, taking more copies as the cash came in.[16] The most successful public singers moved far beyond these humble beginnings. The famous blind singer of Forlì, Cristoforo Scanello, owned his own house and was able to invest two hundred *scudi* in having his son trained for a commercial career. Another well-known and versatile balladeer, Ippolito Ferrarese, was able to build on his fame as a performer by publishing his own compositions.[17]

In Italy, in particular, the street singer was deeply rooted in the culture of the urban commune. In the thirteenth century cities had employed singers to perform at public ceremonies. This official encouragement prepared the way for an increasingly overt political repertoire in the sixteenth century. The crisis in Italian politics with the French invasions after 1494 provoked a flood of sung commentary. In 1509, the height of the danger for Venice, a local chronicler complained that throughout Italy anti-Venetian verses were being sung, recited and sold on the piazzas 'by the work of charlatans, who make a living from this'.[18] Some of this was deliberately orchestrated by the Pope, Julius II, a determined and deadly foe of Venice and a statesman who took an active role in promoting political propaganda. Many of these songs were very cheap: 'so that you can buy it, it will cost you only three pennies', as was stated in one song celebrating the might of Venice's opponents. Some texts, indeed, were distributed free of charge, as was the case with the propagandistic poetical works showered down from windows and distributed on the piazza when the papal legate made his formal entry into Bologna in 1510.[19]

These songs were clearly intended not only to entertain but also to inform. The anonymous author of a poem about the battle of Ravenna in 1512 told his audience that his principal intention in composing the work was 'not because you would take pleasure from it, but so that you might have some indication of this event'. Events moved fast in this conflict of swift marches and topsy-turvy alliances, and the singers were obliged to respond. A song composed to celebrate the naval battle between the Ferraresi and the Venetians, which took place on 22 December 1509, was already in print by 8 January 1510. A singer who published a song about the battle of Agnadello in 1509 claimed to have composed and given it to the press within two days.[20] A French example from a later date has a song celebrating the Huguenot victory in Lyon in 1562 on the streets the very same day.[21]

Singing was an important part of the festive culture of the day. The most popular of these political songs were those that captured a public mood of celebration, usually with new words set to a familiar tune (compositions known as *contrafacta*). But singing also offered a means to process bad news. A local publisher would not, on the whole, wish to test the patience of the local authorities by publishing a prose account of a crushing defeat: such adverse news was usually left to pass by word of mouth. A poignant lament, on the other hand, could catch the mood of the moment, without calling down retribution. But even here, care was required. The Venetian Senate was certainly aware of the potential dangers of free circulation of political songs at a time of crisis. In 1509 they intervened to remove from sale a song critical of the Holy Roman Emperor, Maximilian I, an erstwhile foe but now an ally (it is possible the vendor had just not kept up with the turn of events). The Senate continued, however, to encourage the sale of songs against the Ferraresi.

This period of frenetic activity seems to have been the high-water mark of the political song in Italy. At this moment street singing lay truly on the front line of communication.[22] As the century wore on, Italian street singers seem to have withdrawn to safer topical ground. They would celebrate the withdrawal of an unpopular tax, or report a tumbled-down bridge. This may partly have been self-censorship, but it also reflected a more hostile political climate. In the second half of the sixteenth century Italian authorities intervened to bring order to the piazza. The regulation of public space was partly prompted by Counter-Reformation disapproval of anything that besmirched the dignity of public religion (and many of the songs were scarcely disguised satires of religious tunes). But the new restrictions may also be seen as a concerted attempt to draw in the boundaries of popular politics, particularly when set alongside the brutal assault on the writers of the pasquinades and the regulation around manuscript *avvisi*.[23] However, at least as regards street singers, this effort at regulation seems largely to have failed. As members of a marginal social group, professionally peripatetic, the news singers had far less to lose than established printers and the owners of news agencies. When in 1585 Tommaso Garzoni published his encyclopaedia of the professions, the street singer occupied a prominent place. Far from being banished by hostile regulation, they had 'grown like a weed, in such a way that, through every city, through every land, through every square, nothing is seen other than charlatans or street singers'.[24]

Germany too had a lively musical tradition which could be put to use in the service of popular politics. Martin Luther was a passionate musician and composer of hymns: some of his compositions are still staples of the repertoire. Because the tunes were soon so strikingly familiar, they were obvious candidates for reuse in a more overtly political context (later French Calvinists would use the tunes of the psalms in exactly the same way).[25] The high point of political song in Germany came in the wake of the Protestant defeat in the Schmalkaldic War (1546–7). The victorious Charles V now attempted, by way of the Augsburg Interim, to enforce a partial restoration of traditional Catholic practices and beliefs. Although the settlement was reluctantly accepted by some Protestant cities and theologians, including Philip Melanchthon, much of Lutheran Germany stood firm. Led by the free city of Magdeburg in a heroic four-year resistance, Lutherans vented their anguish in a storm of pamphlets and songs.[26] A diligent search of printed and manuscript sources has revealed a remarkable number of songs about the Interim.[27] Most of their composers were educated men; this was not, initially at least, the music of the streets. But it clearly became so. The disapproving Catholic chronicler of Magdeburg recalled:

> The Interim teaching in itself has been treated quite disgracefully and contemptuously. People played 'Interim' on gaming boards, cursed it, and sang about it as follows: Blessed is he who can trust in God and does not approve of the Interim, for it has a fool behind it.[28]

Luther had shown the way with a clever satirical song, 'Ach du arger Heinz', attacking the resolutely Catholic Heinrich of Braunschweig. This was to be sung to the tune, 'O du armer Judas'. Here the resonance of the title added a further layer of insult, as well as providing a familiar tune.[29]

When exhaustion and military stalemate forced Charles V to compromise, the liberties of Germany Lutheranism were restored. Magdeburg surrendered to Charles's then ally, Maurice of Saxony, on remarkably generous terms. But Maurice made one exception to this leniency: he required that the minister Erasmus Alber be banished from the city. Alber's contribution to the published literature of the resistance, consisting almost entirely of hymns and satirical songs, had clearly hit home. Maurice insisted that because Alber had attacked him 'coarsely in public and in private writings, with rhymes and with drawings he must be got rid of. Even a peasant would not bear such an attack lightly.'[30]

Remembering how they had harnessed the power of song so successfully, the Lutheran states were all the more determined that it would not be employed against them. Several cities took action to control or ban the *Marktsänger* and *Gassensänger*, as the singers were known (because they sang in the marketplace or alleyways). As early as 1522, Augsburg had required its printers to take an oath that they would not print any disgraceful book, song or rhyme. When the city finally instituted reform in 1534, the new discipline ordinance specified carefully that it was illegal, not only to print offensive

6.2 Fighting back in verse. One of the many musical works satirising the Augsburg Interim.

books, songs and rhymes, but also to write, sell, buy, sing, read or post them; or, indeed to bring them to the light of day in any way.[31]

In Germany the control of opinion necessarily worked rather differently from the centralised nation states of western Europe. Most German towns, in principle, established a process for the pre-publication inspection of books and pamphlets. But this would have been far too time-consuming in practice: the designated censors, usually civic officials rather than clergymen, were far too busy with other duties. In any case much of the printed material in circulation would not have been printed within the local jurisdiction. So most German authorities essentially relied on self-regulation, encouraged by harsh punishments when they learned of a particularly malicious or politically dangerous public utterance.

If we examine the management of opinion in one particularly important jurisdiction – the great imperial city of Augsburg – it is striking how often these interventions were prompted not by print but by seditious singing. In 1553 a bookseller got into trouble when he passed around a tavern a song mocking Charles V's recent humiliation at the siege of Metz. If the bookseller was attempting to road-test a potential song pamphlet, the strategy backfired badly, as most of the drinkers were too shocked to want anything to do with it; further attempts to have the song copied led to his arrest and interrogation.[32] Here the city council could rely on the support of local people in enforcing reasonable standards of decorum.

In the last years of the sixteenth century this social consensus became increasingly frayed, as Lutherans reacted with mounting alarm to the resurgence of Catholicism. The expulsion in 1584 of Augsburg's popular Lutheran minister during the controversy following the imposition of the new Gregorian calendar led to a barrage of songs critical of the city council and supportive of the exiled clergy.[33] Some were printed but others circulated widely in manuscript copies, or by word of mouth. These were tough times economically, and discontented weavers became heavily involved in the agitation. Abraham Schädlin confessed that he had written 'Wo es Gott nit mit Augspurg helt' ('When God does not stand by Augsburg'), a political song based on the Lutheran psalm 'Wo Gott der Herr nicht bei uns hält' (taken from Psalm 124, 'If the Lord had not been on our side'). Because Schädlin had turned himself in, he was treated leniently. Jonas Losch was not so lucky, and two extended interrogations under torture extracted the story of a song he had adapted from a printed original and then sung on the streets. These interrogations (still preserved in the Augsburg town archives) reveal a busy world of singing and cheap print.[34] Losch made extra money singing at weddings before turning to politics; the printer Hans Schultes sold 1,500 copies of an image of the expelled minister Georg Müller; two women caught up in the agitation made money selling on the copies. The intersection of political dissent with this lively culture of singing and pub-going was a potential powder keg, and the Augsburg authorities clamped down hard.

The newly resurgent religious orders, the Capuchins and Jesuits, became particular targets for Lutheran anger. 'A new song about the Capuchins', circulating in Augsburg around 1600, alleged the alms they collected went to fund liaisons with prostitutes. It was sung, rather indecorously, to the tune of the Lutheran hymn 'Lord keep us steadfast in thy word'.[35] The following year Jacob Hötsch was prosecuted for singing defamatory songs about the Jesuits. This followed a neighbourhood contretemps, in which a Catholic boy punched a Lutheran girl for singing a song about Hell being full of priests.

The Council tried doggedly, but in vain, to restrain this inter-communal anger. In the difficult years before the Thirty Years War these provocative compositions had the potential to destroy the fragile public peace. In 1618, on the very eve of the fighting, the Council ordered its officers to root out the news-sheets and songs circulating in the city. This seems to have been precipitated by the discovery and confiscation of an illustrated news ballad, *A True new News Report from Bohemia on the siege, taking and conquest of the Catholic city of Pilsen*.[36] This was not, by any means, an objective piece of reporting. According to the song, the revolt in Bohemia was entirely due to the machinations of the Jesuits, the 'spawn of vipers', acting at the Pope's instigation. In bi-confessional Augsburg this went far beyond what would be tolerated in news reports. But despite its vigilance, the Council found it almost impossible to control what circulated largely by word of mouth. Print provided the smoking gun that led directly to the responsible printer. Seditious singing disappeared on the wind. To a frightened, angry and increasingly alienated religious minority, it was a potent weapon indeed.

The second half of the sixteenth century was also the first great age of the English street ballad.[37] It has been estimated that by 1600 over four million printed song broadsheets were in circulation. This was the visible remains of a vast and participatory culture of song; and although the printing of broadsheets implies interest among the literate, their appeal was not limited to those who could read. In 1595 the minister Nicholas Bownde noted people who 'though they cannot read themselves, nor any of theirs, yet will have many ballads set up in their houses, that so they might learn them, as they shall have occasion'.[38] Those who could not read might still remember the tunes, and memorise the new words. Exasperated ministers noted the speed with which their congregations committed ballads to memory, contrasting this with their inability to retain knowledge of Scripture. According to Bownde, at every market or fair one or two persons could be observed 'singing or selling of ballads'.[39]

The ballads covered a wide range. The ever diligent Samuel Pepys organised his very considerable collection according to his own patent, though very logical, classification scheme. 'States and Times' (that is, politics and current affairs) made up about 10 per cent – a good deal less than 'Love – Pleasant' or even 'Love – Unfortunate'. One may speculate, however, that political songs were far more likely to circulate only by word of mouth. Occasionally we have evidence of this, when pointed adaptations of popular songs turned up in libel cases. It was far more difficult to commit to print political satire than rollicking humorous tales or pious devotional ballads. Only in times when the political controls were seriously loosened were political ballads printed in large numbers. In France Pierre de L'Estoile heard and then transcribed from memory a good number of political songs circulating in Paris during the 1590s.[40] None of them survives in print. This was an angry time in French politics. The capital city, a stronghold of the Catholic League, seethed with indignation at the treachery of Henry III, the murderer of their hero the Duke of Guise. When the king was assassinated in turn, in 1589, Paris reacted in revulsion at the prospect of a Huguenot successor. The city's printers erupted with a tumult of vitriolic prose; so it is interesting that, even at a time when it was safe to print opposition pamphlets, scurrilous verse still circulated largely by word of mouth. L'Estoile, whose sympathies were privately royalist, kept his head down. Joining a circle copying loyalist tracts and circulating them in manuscript was already, in the circumstances, quite courageous.

The balladeer was a potent force in the sixteenth-century communications network. Part of the great Pepys collection came from another early enthusiast, John Selden, and Pepys transcribed into the first volume an observation of Selden's on the importance of ballads (which he equated with 'libels'). 'Though some make slight of libels, yet you may see by them how the wind sits. More solid things do not show the complexion of the times as well as ballads and libels.'[41]

Singing ballads was a powerful part of information culture, and it made a good living for many on the very margins of respectable craft society. But not everyone made a good balladeer. You needed a strong constitution, a voice to make yourself heard above the crowd, and a certain charisma. The irrepressible reverend Richard Corbet, finding that a travelling pedlar was struggling to make an impact in the marketplace at Abingdon, sprang to his rescue, to good effect: 'and being a handsome man, and had a rare full voice, he at once sold a great many, and had a great audience'.[42] It is to be doubted that without this unexpected clerical support the timid ballad seller would have lasted long in the business. We should leave the last word to one Thomas Spickenell, 'sometimes apprentice to a bookbinder, after a vagrant peddler, then a ballad singer and seller, and now a minister & Alehouse keeper in Maldon'.[43] Spickenell had completed the grand slam of sixteenth-century communication media, from the book trade to singing, to the church and the alehouse: where we will now follow.

Bald Talk about Great Lords

Taverns were a ubiquitous part of early modern society. It has been estimated that in England alone there were twenty thousand drinking establishments: about one for every twenty adult males in the population.[44] It is unlikely continental Europe was any less well served. Aside from the church, with which the tavern coexisted in a relationship of undisguised competition, this was the quintessential gathering place of early modern society. It was a volatile environment in which to share the news.

Like other social institutions, inns and taverns ranged widely, from large, wealthy and well-founded businesses to low dives, little more than the dingy front room of a village house. At the top end of the spectrum the inn occupied an important place in the network of international communication. In the four-teenth century innkeepers, in addition to providing food and accommodation, played an important role in the provision of banking services for the interna-tional merchant community. Many money brokers set themselves up as innkeepers, and many innkeepers acted as brokers.[45] In provincial towns the largest inns, particularly those that ringed the market square, often provided space for merchants to conduct business. Some became a semi-permanent loca-tion for trade in specific commodities.[46]

The development of the transcontinental road network offered further opportunities for the canny entrepreneur. The medieval itineraries guiding the traveller on long-distance routes marked the stage between each major habitation with a wayside inn. In the sixteenth century many of these places became posting stations, responsible for providing accommodation and relays of fresh horses for couriers. In many locations the postmaster was the most substantial innkeeper of the town.

6.3 A German pedlar advertises his wares. Note the copy of a *Neue Zeitung* prominently displayed.

The keepers of these elite posting houses, with their constant passing trade of well-heeled travellers, made it their business to remain well informed, as did most innkeepers. The peripatetic Anabaptist Ambrosius Stitelmeir would always call in at the tavern to discover whether the local minister preached in accordance with the Gospel.[47] Innkeepers were a natural source of advice for travellers planning the next stage of a journey, or wanting information about local conditions. Pilgrim manuals recommended particular hostelries and particular hosts, such as Peter von Fryberg, the 'German host' in Geneva, who was willing 'to help you in all matters'. Such a trade was very lucrative. When the pilgrim Hans van Haldheim decided to seek out a famous holy man at Bern, he directed himself to the publican of the Bell Inn. The publican willingly told him how to secure an audience with the reclusive sage, and offered a horse for the journey: 'My good Lord, you do not have to go on foot, for I will lend you a grey stallion. I have three horses standing in my stable, and you can choose whichever you like.'[48]

These were the aristocrats of the industry: they made it their business to keep themselves informed, and they had plentiful opportunity to do so. In places where there were no suitable buildings such inns might serve as impromptu law courts, or even for the formal welcome of visiting dignitaries. But such high-class establishments did not describe the normal run of sixteenth-century tavern. These were raucous places, full of noise: boisterous, smelly and frequently violent. People came to let off steam, to celebrate with friends, and to forget the cares of a harsh and punishing life.

These more humble places were also important hubs of communication. Patrons would discuss the issues of the day, pass on rumours and sing together. It was expected that strangers would join the conversation: the solitary traveller who sat alone was often an object of suspicion, and in many places regulations obliged innkeepers to report the names of strangers who took rooms for the night. Even dingy village taverns provided the opportunity for travelling players and musicians to offer impromptu entertainment.

An environment in which friends met strangers, fuelled by alcohol, could be turbulent: profanity and insults led to fighting and assaults. In a wide-ranging survey of data taken from different parts of Europe, around one third of complaints dealt with by secular and ecclesiastical courts were directly linked to taverns.[49] But taverns were also the location of serious political discussion and the singing of hymns and psalms. In the early days of the Reformation evangelical groups passed word of particular taverns where it was safe to congregate.[50] In towns with no bookshop inns became distribution points for evangelical pamphlets. In the German Peasants' War of 1524–5 taverns played a particularly important role in the spread of the movement, as news of the extent of the insurrection flashed around the Empire.[51]

The German Peasants' War was not just a revolt of the countryside: the social gospel also had obvious relevance to the aspirations of the urban poor.[52] As news of the revolt spread, municipal authorities were particularly alarmed at the thought that their own populations might join the insurrection. A particularly well-documented case arises from the investigation undertaken to winkle out supporters of the rebellion in the German town of Nördlingen. Because of its situation in the area of greatest peasant agitation, Nördlingen was in the eye of the storm, and at an assembly in 1525 sympathetic citizens had asked that the town declare its support for the rebellion. The peasants' supporters had not carried the majority, but the town was still on a state of high alert when on 8 May a member of the night watch, Hans Trumer, was arrested for singing a seditious song. The song was the work of a local weaver, Contz Anahans, and it seems to have been circulating in the town since the events of April. It was certainly incendiary:

> A vulture has soared on high
> Over the Hegau near the Black Forest
> And has raised a brood of offspring
> The peasants everywhere
> They have become rebellious
> In the German nation
> And made an organization of their own
> Perhaps they will succeed.[53]

There was much more: another nine verses. The interrogation of Trumer and his accomplices allowed the city council to reconstruct in some detail the process by which the song had passed into common knowledge. It was sung at the inn run by Balthasar Fend, one of the leaders of the April commotion. Anton Furner, a member of the council, heard of it and asked Anahans to sing it at his house. It was then sung at another inn. By May it was so familiar that even the drunken Hans Trumer could remember the words. It is pertinent to note that Nördlingen at this time had no printing press. Contz Anahans's call to arms could only circulate by word of mouth.

The city council clamped down hard. Those involved were interrogated under torture. The innkeeper Fend was executed. Without such severity it is highly unlikely we would possess this forensic reconstruction of how news spread, and how a potential insurrection was fomented. In more normal times, when asked to name names, most people caught up in an act of group violence struggled to remember particulars. The famous early modern memory, a cornerstone of information culture, was replaced by fumbling and incoherence. This was a very sensible defence strategy. The early modern justice system relied to a very large extent on confessions for convictions, so those under interrogation were understandably reluctant to engage in potentially lethal acts of self-incrimination. Faced with such self-deprecating forgetfulness, few magistrates were sufficiently dogged to persist in the face of conflicting or incomplete evidence. The bureaucracy of justice was at this point simply not up to the task. The Spanish Inquisition, defending the purity of faith, was a rare exception. In the patient investigations of the Inquisition many words that had been spoken in anger or due to drink were repented at length.[54]

The German Peasants' War was a time of particular tension, when the Reformation and German society entered uncharted waters. But as the place where groups most regularly gathered to enjoy the loosening of normal social restraints, the tavern provided obvious opportunities for potentially subversive conversation. 'Do you want to hear bald talk about great Lords, princes and powerful men? Just go to a tavern.' This was the resigned conclusion of one critic of tavern culture in 1610.[55] As time passed, innkeepers exploited the potential of their premises as hubs of communication more systematically, posting printed broadsheets on the walls and, in the seventeenth century, providing newspapers. In some German jurisdictions it was legally required that inns display printed copies of local ordinances.[56] Numerous pictorial representations of the seventeenth century show the inn as a place of communal reading, with the country dullards crowding open-mouthed around the literate neighbour who carefully picks out the news. These were fairly stock representations of country folk, intended for the mocking amusement of the sophisticated bourgeois. But they must certainly have possessed a grain of truth.

Most of what passed in ale-house conversations is lost to history. But enough has been preserved to make clear that sixteenth-century governments were well aware that tavern conversation had a dangerous potential to incite and inflame. The careful steps taken by Thomas Cromwell to police information during the most anxious years of the Henrician Reformation provide us with many examples of the inflammatory potential of the spoken word. In the poisoned atmosphere of the 1530s many citizens were happy to imagine not only the fall of Anne Boleyn but the death of Henry VIII. A rash of false reports led the Henrician government to take firm action to ban any seditious prophecy. It was clear that at least some of these malicious stories were deliberately planted, often by leaders of local society who opposed the king's policies. In December 1537 parishioners from Muston in the East Riding went to York to accuse their vicar, John Dobson, of spreading such prophecies in the village, repeating them 'both in the church porch and the alehouse'.[57] But it was not easy for the government to get their message across. In troubled times people were particularly prone to panicked and incendiary interpretations of newly published laws. Lewis Herbert, returning home from London to Wales, stopped off at the Sign of the Lamb in Abingdon. Faced with the inevitable 'What news at London?', Lewis had something sensational to share. 'There was a cry at the cross in Cheapside,' he told his audience, 'that no unlawful games should be used, and that angel nobles should go for 8s and cross groats for 5d apiece' (the angel was originally 6s 8d and the groat 4d).[58] There was nothing more likely to disturb his audience than an unverified account of the manipulation of the currency.

It was no wonder in the circumstances that the English government took repeated if largely unsuccessful action to prohibit the spreading of rumour and false reports. The Henrician treason legislation made it an offence to act, write or speak in a manner tending to the overthrow of royal authority. The act of 1532 was progressively extended in scope by those of 1534, 1552, 1554, 1571 and 1585, that is, in the reign of every Tudor monarch of whatever religious persuasion. In laws inherited from the medieval period it was already an offence to utter words considered seditious, and this too was reinforced by new legislation in the Tudor period.[59] Rulers comforted themselves that such measures were necessary, because the people were by nature credulous and easily led. 'How ready vulgar people are to be abused by such and are disposed to disperse seditious rumours thereby to procure troubles and motions,' as Queen Elizabeth put it in a letter to the Earl of Shrewsbury in 1565.[60] In many respects this was unfair. The common people were often rather shrewd judges in the essentials of a case. Historians would now generally accept that the common voice, which despised Anne Boleyn and stoutly maintained the rights of Katherine of Aragon, understood the cause of the revolution in the English Church rather better than those in the political nation who insisted on the purity of the king's religious motives. And the people had plentiful opportunities to keep themselves informed. Everyone agreed that if the English people had one characteristic, it was a passion for news. The Italian observer and language teacher John Florio noted that an enquiry after the news was always 'the first question of an Englishman'.[61] To help travellers abroad, the editors of language primers took to including instructions on how to ask for news in their imagined dialogues. Thus Claude Holyband in the French Littelton: 'What news have you? How goeth all in this city?', along with some conciliating replies: 'Surely I know nothing. All goeth well. Great cheer he that hath money.' The dialogue was called 'of the inn' and the French translation of these conversational sallies was given on the opposite page.[62]

From the Pulpit

Not everyone observed this passion for news with enthusiasm. The minister George Widley was far less indulgent. His sour view of his parishioners was that 'if any question shall be put concerning religion, they grow as mute as fishes'. But not so for news: 'they rehearse and tell nothing but gossips' tales, and news, that love to have their tongues to run through the world, and meddling in other man's matters'.[63] This frustration was widely shared in the preaching ministry; but it should not obscure the fact that the pulpit was itself an important conduit for news. One day a week the minister owned the public platform, with the opportunity to put aside the disorderly hubbub of the streets, and impose some sort of meaning on everyday events.

In the sixteenth century, and particularly in Protestant northern Europe, the sermon became an important part of the weekly round. This was a new development: for medieval Christianity, the sermon had been a part of public festival culture, but a sporadic one.[64] On such occasions a sermon would often be delivered by a visitor, for example a travelling mendicant monk. The best preachers were great masters of theatre, not least the theatre of suspense. News of their coming to the neighbourhood would be eagerly passed around the marketplace; their arrival would be impossible to miss, since the most celebrated preachers picked up a considerable caravan of followers in the course of their travels, trailing them from place to place. To prevent the sermon becoming an undignified scrum, senior clerics would negotiate their arrival in advance. This was the case with the great master of the indulgence campaign, Raymond Peraudi, whose appearances were carefully orchestrated in a flurry of printed pamphlets.[65] So at this level a sermon was always news, and as often as not it was preached in the town's most prominent public space. This tradition finds its memorial in the external stone pulpits built into the walls of a number of European churches, precisely to facilitate such outdoor preaching.

The great achievement of the Protestant Reformation was to make the sermon an integral part of the service of worship.[66] This brought the sermon indoors; it also passed responsibility for preaching to the clergy in general, rather than a small cadre of preaching specialists. This had advantages and disadvantages. For parishioners the weekly act of worship became more participatory and comprehensible. Rather than being mere observers of a Mass conducted in Latin, they now sang, recited prayers and listened. They became a more informed but also a more demanding audience. For the minister was required not simply to intone the liturgy and perform the Mass: he was expected to expound the word of God.

In the first years of the Reformation, preaching was itself the event. The first inkling that many congregations would have that a change in their religious practice was imminent was when their priest, often more austerely dressed than usual, mounted the pulpit to proclaim his allegiance to 'the pure Gospel'. These conversion events were essential to the survival of Luther's movement. No major city in Germany adhered to the Reformation without the support of a prominent local minister, sometimes leading a local evangelical movement in bold defiance of still reluctant magistrates. As the Reformation became entrenched, the ministers became essentially agents of the state, their pulpits a conduit for official policy. As salaried officials they were expected to support magisterial efforts to promote good order, preaching obedience and reproving vice. Thus religion and politics became inextricably intertwined.

The leading figures of the new Protestant movement were all inspirational and indefatigable preachers. Martin Luther combined his duties as a professor at Wittenberg University with a position as minister of the (only) parish church in Wittenberg; his skills as a preacher were honed years before he fell out with the Pope. During a long career he preached more than six thousand sermons.[67] John Calvin, the reformer of Geneva, would preach three times a week: cerebral, forensic biblical sermons, unstinting in their denunciation of vice. So celebrated was his mastery of the art of preaching that travellers made a point of stopping off at Geneva to hear him.[68] Determined that nothing should be lost, disciples paid for each sermon to be transcribed for posterity. Calvin disapproved – he made a clear distinction between his academic lectures and these extempore performances – but it is largely thanks to these transcriptions that we can hear the authentic voice of the master, without the mediation of print. Calvin did not spare his audience. Frequently he would turn from the word of Scripture to the discontents of the present day: those reluctant to abandon familiar religious practice, those guilty of sharp dealing in their business.[69] Members of the congregation often left feeling bruised and put upon; a resentment compounded when they had to endure the taunts of those who had enjoyed Calvin's well-aimed shafts landing elsewhere. Several times this led to scuffles outside the church door, an unseemly end to worship that the magistrates had to resolve.[70]

This was raw politics, and the Church was not above using sermons for purely political purposes. In 1546 Martin Luther, father of the Protestant Reformation but to Catholics a notorious apostate, lay dying. For Catholics this was an eagerly awaited moment of truth: would the Devil come and claim him? So it was vitally important for the Reformation that Luther died well, peacefully. His principal lieutenants crowded around the bedside to witness his passing, and when he had slipped away without incident they publicised the dignified manner of his death in widely circulated sermons.[71]

As the Protestant movement became entrenched, the burden of religious instruction was shared by many thousands of preaching ministers. This was a heavy responsibility, and many did not fulfil it. Faced with a dull or incompetent preacher, religious enthusiasts went to other churches to hear more accomplished practitioners. Those who remained sometimes struggled to stay awake. Preachers often claimed that their congregations were disrespectfully inattentive, but this was not always the case. When in a sermon the English minister Nicholas Day made what seemed like an astonishingly indiscreet denunciation of the English expedition to La Rochelle in 1627, he was reported by three members of his congregation; one of whom, as it turned out, had taken detailed notes.[72]

The accused minister talked himself out of this indiscretion, but the incident demonstrates vividly the power of the pulpit to shape and disturb local opinion. This was partly because local pastors were more likely to stray into the delicate territory of domestic politics than were the published news media. In this particular regard published sermons are a poor guide to what was said, since they were often stripped back to their theological essentials, with the potentially contentious topical references removed.[73] This can tend to disguise their potency as a mode of topical debate. But the state authorities were not deceived. Not only did they keep a close ear out for what was said; they also took care to sponsor sermons that promoted the official line on the issues of the day. In England sermons at court and at Paul's Cross in the City of London were both occasions for the explanation of official policy, and the opportunity for the young and ambitious to make themselves known.[74] Indeed, some serious sermon-goers disapproved of the preaching at Paul's Cross, on the grounds that those who attended were attracted more by the hope of news and novelty than by serious theological intent.[75] Political sermons by prominent preachers were an important arm of policy. In Italy Francesco Visdomini preached two widely circulated sermons, one to celebrate England's reconciliation with Rome in 1555 under Mary Tudor, the other almost four years later to reflect the sobering consequences of her death in 1558.[76]

These examples help place the sermon in the range of oral media discussed in this chapter. Unlike market gossip and tavern talk, sermons were unlikely to be a primary conduit of news. Few of those ranged in the pews would have been receiving their first intimation of events as they listened to a sermon. Where the sermon could play a crucial role was in shaping interpretation. This was all the more potent in an age when tidings good and bad were interpreted within a theological framework. Ministers could help their parishioners understand changes of government and worship practice, declarations of war and peace, natural disaster and human catastrophe. Preaching could help regulate a society easily disturbed by rumour and ill-tidings. The role of preaching as medicine for troubled souls was all the more effective because the sermon shared several critical characteristics with the other principal forms of oral news dissemination. Like the swirling, disorderly market gossip it sought to regulate, effective preaching appealed to the emotions as well as the intellect. The best preachers were passionate and engaged as well as learned. The primacy of preaching in the service of worship also represented an acknowledgement that learning was a communal process – here led not by drink-fuelled rumour but by an informed and respected leader of the local community. It was for these reasons that many exponents of preaching argued that the private reading of the Scriptures was no alternative to hearing sermons, an interesting shift from Luther's initial uncompromising emphasis on the primacy of Scripture.[77] It also seems to be the case – and this is something that we will observe later about the market for newspapers – that people did not necessarily need to understand everything they heard (in the case of newspapers, read) to appreciate its worth.[78] Those who sat through many hours of abstruse, repetitive, and no doubt often poorly delivered sermons seem nevertheless to have valued the experience. It was, at the very least, a sign that the Church took the salvation of their souls very seriously.

By bringing the sermon into the regular round of the weekly service, Protestantism had created a powerful new mechanism of communication – but also a potential new focus for dissent. This was why the new religious regimes devoted so much attention to the regulation of the clergy, and why the clergy collectively exercised such power. The result was an emerging and widely acknowledged convergence of interest. The state required from the clergy obedience and support for government policy. In return the state supported clerical efforts to create a godly people and maintain a well-regulated Sabbath. Thus while ministers were regaling their congregations on a Sunday, many European cities employed officers charged with patrolling the streets, ensuring that shops or taverns did no business; and absentees from church were not permitted to engage in sports or other disapproved distractions.[79] On Sunday ministers were to have the monopoly of public communication. But they were perfectly aware that this was but a brief respite from the cacophony of the working week, when gossip, singing and the mundane networks of everyday communication would reign supreme. This, they knew, they were powerless to control.

CHAPTER 7

Triumph and Tragedy

O N 19 October 1571 a single ship eased cautiously into the harbour at Venice. Earlier in the autumn a combined Christian fleet had sailed eastward to confront the galleys of the Ottoman Empire. Nothing had been heard since. Those who now saw the *Angelo Gabriele* were at first appalled. The men on board appeared to be wearing Turkish garb, so the Venetians feared the worst. It was only when they realised these were clothes captured from the defeated Turkish fleet that they began to feel hope. The ship's captain then stepped ashore and confirmed the glad tidings: the Christian fleet had won a crushing victory. As the bells rang out, men ran through the streets shouting, 'Victory, victory.' The crew were escorted in triumph to St Mark's Cathedral to give thanks.[1]

Thus Christian Europe heard the first news of the battle of Lepanto. It was an extraordinary feat of arms; even on a continent now bitterly divided between competing faiths, the victory was greeted with universal acclamation. The news of the battle spread swiftly throughout Europe: celebration was sustained and heartfelt.

The battle of Lepanto was the first of several major news events which, for different reasons, engaged the attention of the whole of Europe. The intricate network of communication that had been building since the onset of print had reached its first stage of maturity: the aftermath of Lepanto is remarkable both for the speed with which the news was passed around the continent and the sophistication of the media reaction. The same may be said of two other seminal moments from this troubled and turbulent era. Whereas the victory of Lepanto was greeted with near universal rejoicing, news of the St Bartholomew's Day Massacre reignited the full bitterness of the conflict between Europe's divided confessions. The defeat of the Spanish Armada over a decade later, in 1588, was the tense and drawn-out denouement of these fundamental religious and political conflicts. These were three very different events in terms of news. The battle of Lepanto provided a rare moment of optimism in the prolonged and anxious period of warfare between the forces of Christianity and their perpetual foe, the Ottoman Empire. This was news anxiously awaited. In contrast the St Bartholomew's Day Massacre came as a thunderbolt that transfixed and divided European opinion. The climax of this new era of religious bitterness and hatred was experienced in the shape of the Spanish Armada, an agonisingly slow burner played out in maritime conditions particularly challenging for news reporting.

All of these events provoked a profound response from Europe's increasingly anxious and divided peoples, demonstrating the extent to which the various channels of news had now merged and intertwined as the consequences of faraway events became matters of real and present urgency. Those telling the news reflected the strong emotions of their audience: the need to be informed or consoled, the desire for reassurance or the urge for exuberant celebration. This was a new world, in which expanding horizons revealed a sense of more imminent peril.

Lepanto

The battle of Lepanto was the consequence of a clash of cultures that had persisted, without hope of resolution, since the fall of Constantinople in 1453. By extinguishing Byzantium the Ottoman Empire had announced its arrival as the dominant power in the eastern Mediterranean. An inescapable partner in matters of trade, since the Turks now controlled access to the spice market of the Levant, each successive sultan posed a potent challenge to Venetian power in the Mediterranean and Aegean Seas. Meanwhile Turkish armies gradually advanced through the remnants of Byzantine lands in the Balkans to the borders of Habsburg Austria. Print had come just too late to record the fall of Constantinople, but the successive stages of this advance were each marked by a flurry of news pamphlets: the fall of Negroponte in 1470, which coincided with the beginnings of print in Rome and Venice; the siege of Rhodes in 1480; the shattering, calamitous reverse at Mohács in 1526 where the destruction of the Hungarian nobility resulted in the partial occupation of this ancient Christian kingdom, and brought Turkish power into the heart of Europe. All of these events were followed with fascination in Europe's western lands.[2] With the death of Hungary's young king Louis at Mohács, the remnants of the kingdom passed into Habsburg hands; this was welcomed as a bulwark of Europe's defence. Attempts to form a common front brought forth fine exhortations to a new crusade. These events too were widely reported in the news press.

7.1 A broadsheet portrait of Ibrahim Pascha. The fascination with the Turkish Empire was an enduring feature of sixteenth-century news culture.

We have already had occasion to acknowledge Christopher Columbus's letter announcing his New World discoveries as a highly effective and precocious piece of news management.[3] Over the course of the next century Europe's reading public would digest the importance of the explorations and conquest of new continents. So it bears repeating that for contemporaries – and quite distinct from our own historical perception – the interest in the Americas was always dwarfed by the incessant, recurrent fear of Turkish conquest.[4]

And so it went on. The siege of Vienna (1529), the capture of Tunis (1535), the disasters at Algiers (1541) and Djerba (1560), all were significant news events. A new chapter opened with the siege of Malta in 1565. Confronting a heroic resistance from the Knights of St John, the sultan's army was eventually forced into retreat. The European news community could follow these events not only in a burst of celebratory pamphlets, but in detailed maps of Malta's fortifications, progressively updated during the stages of the siege.[5] The relief of Malta proved to be only a temporary respite. Five years later, in 1570, Cyprus was attacked by an overwhelming Turkish force, and despite heroic resistance its Venetian garrison was eventually overcome. This disaster was widely attributed to the failure of the Christian powers to mount an effective relief effort. The Lepanto campaign reflected, at last, a determination to put aside selfish differences, and make common cause. The Christian fleet, sponsored by Venice, Spain and the Pope, set sail eastward on 16 September 1571. The Turkish fleet was discovered in the Gulf of Lepanto on 7 October and battle was joined. Although the forces were fairly evenly matched (208 galleys on the Christian side against 230 in the Turkish fleet), the Holy League's victory was overwhelming.

The arrival of the *Angelo Gabriele* in Venice set off weeks of riotous celebration. Church bells rang out and fireworks were discharged for three days. Mass was celebrated in San Marco by the Spanish ambassador in the presence of the Doge and Senate, followed by a procession headed by the Doge himself carrying the basilica's most precious crucifix. After these official thanksgiving events, different parts of the community, led by the German merchants, staged their own events. These in turn necessitated more feasting, more processions and more fireworks.

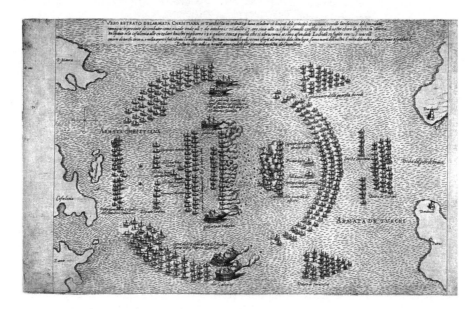

7.2 Engraved Italian depiction of the opposing fleets at Lepanto.

While this was going on, news of the victory was despatched to the capitals of Europe's nation states, carried by couriers and the news writers. The news had reached Lyon by 25 October, and Brussels five days later. A courier from Venice brought the news to Madrid on 31 October. The Venetian ambassador hurried to tell Philip II, and found him in his chapel. When he explained his business he was immediately admitted. 'The King's joy at receiving the news was extraordinary,' the ambassador reported with some satisfaction. 'In that very moment he ordered a Te Deum sung.'[6] The king kept the ambassador by his side for most of the day, and insisted he accompany him at the solemn procession of thanksgiving. The official messenger sent by the fleet commander, Don John, arrived only on 22 November, by this time thoroughly upstaged. Nevertheless, the king questioned him eagerly. The extent to which this news overcame Philip's distaste for meetings (he much preferred written communications) betrays the depths of his joyful relief.[7]

Even before the last fireworks had been exploded, the Christian victory had begun to be celebrated in print. In Venice the first wave of pamphlets offered accounts of the celebrations, and were presumably bought as mementos by those who had witnessed or participated in these events.[8] Thereafter such reports turned to reconstructing the heroic tale of victory. Many of these short pamphlets were despatched abroad along with the manuscript *avvisi*: around fifty Venetian editions found their way in this manner into the Fugger archive.[9] A number of the news prints adopted the *avviso* title of the manuscript newsletters, though not all of them adopted the same dispassionate style. The *Aviso to Sultan Selin, of the rout of his fleet and the death of his captains* was not the reproduction of an *avviso*, but a jeering piece of triumphalism.[10]

The news narratives were then reinforced by a third wave of publications, celebrating the Christian triumph in verse. The victory inspired an astonishing outburst of creative energy in Italian literary circles, with at least thirty named authors contributing songs or poems.[11] Almost all of these works were published as short, cheap pamphlets: this was a chance to seize the moment and cash in, for both author and publisher.

The newsletters found a substantial echo in the international press. In Paris, Jean Dallier published a newsletter penned in Venice on 19 October, the very day the news of victory had arrived, together with a letter from Charles IX ordering the bishop of Paris to organise an official thanksgiving. Further accounts of the battle were published by four other Paris printers as well as in Lyon and Rouen.[12] The first English pamphlets were translated copies of these Paris imprints.[13] German news pamphlets were published in Augsburg, Vienna and at least five other cities.[14] One enterprising Augsburg printer had a woodcut view of the battle (clearly based on an Italian original) made to accompany a broadsheet description of the events.[15] German printers also produced their share of celebratory songs, to match those of the Italians. The celebration was heartfelt and generous. Few at this point paused to reflect what might be the consequences of this extraordinary vindication of Spanish military might. This was that rare news event which created, for a fleeting moment, a shared community of celebration that overrode all considerations of partisan advantage. It would not be repeated in the difficult years that followed.

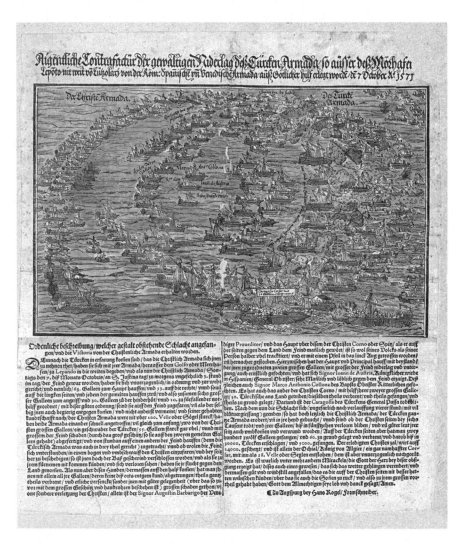

7.3 A German news broadsheet, with an account of the battle of Lepanto. The debt to the Italian model is obvious, though this makes for a more dramatic rendition.

Massacre

The victory of Lepanto represented a rare moment of unity in Europe's divided Christendom. A year later the fragility of this sentiment was laid bare in an event so shocking that it seared the consciousness of Protestant Europe for two centuries. It began with a wedding, intended to reconcile France's feuding religious parties. It ended with over five thousand dead in an unbridled orgy of killing that put beyond hope any prospect of religious reconciliation.

On 22 August 1572 the leader of France's Huguenots, Admiral Gaspard de Coligny, was shot and wounded by a concealed gunman as he rode through Paris. The young king, Charles IX, who was personally close to Coligny, sent guards and his personal physician to attend to the wounded man. It was clear that Coligny would live, but the mood turned ugly as the Protestant nobility, crammed into the city for the marriage of their titular lord, Henry of Navarre, called angrily for retribution. In a heated late-night meeting of the Privy Council the king was persuaded that only a pre-emptive strike could thwart a Protestant insurrection. Early on the morning of 24 August the Catholic champion, the Duke of Guise, was despatched to see to the murder of the injured Coligny. What followed was probably at least partly unintended. As the remains of the admiral's corpse were hauled through the streets, the Catholic nobility, city militia and population of Paris began settling scores. First the noble Huguenot leadership, then other prominent Calvinists and finally ordinary men and women of the congregations were hunted down and killed. News of the massacre sparked copycat events in other French cities: in Lyon, Rouen, Orléans and Bourges. Those who did not die recanted or fled. The Huguenot movement in northern France was effectively destroyed.[16]

St Bartholomew's Day, 24 August 1572, was for Protestants a day that would live in infamy; indeed, they ensured that it would, by a carefully nurtured campaign of remembrance that put the piteous human drama at the heart of a tale of treachery, bad faith and deceit.[17] The news of the massacre spread rapidly through Europe. In the Protestant states the reaction was one of stunned disbelief at the scale of the calamity, followed by searing anger and revulsion. The first news of the Parisian massacre reached Geneva, the fountainhead of French Calvinism, on Friday 29 August, brought by merchant travellers from Savoy. The following Sunday, Théodore Beza and his colleagues announced the sombre news in their sermons. Beza, Calvin's successor in Geneva, seems at this point to have been in a state of shock. In a brief letter of 1 September written to his opposite number in Zurich, Heinrich Bullinger, he spoke in apocalyptic terms. Three hundred thousand co-religionists in France stood in imminent danger, as did those sheltering in Geneva: this might, he warned his friend, be the last time he would be able to write. 'For it is abundantly clear that these massacres are the unfolding of a universal conspiracy. Assassins are seeking to kill me, and I contemplate death more than life.'[18] This was an exaggeration born of shock and despair. But the fear that the attacks in France heralded a universal conspiracy to settle with Protestantism once and for all spread very quickly in Protestant Europe. On 4 September the Genevan city council, which had acted with admirable speed in sharing the news with Swiss allies, wrote in far more emotional tones to the Count Palatine, a key German friend of the Reformed religion:

> The whole of France is bathed in the blood of innocent people and covered with dead bodies. The air is filled with the cries and groans of nobles and commoners, women and children, slaughtered by the hundreds without mercy.[19]

By this time the beginnings of what became a flood of refugees were arriving at Geneva's gates. As of 4 September Beza had pieced together a remarkably accurate narrative of Coligny's death.[20] But despite the availability of eyewitness reports, wild rumours continued to circulate. Refugees from Lyon reported that three thousand Protestants had been killed in the city. It was widely thought that Henry of Navarre and the young Prince of Condé had been put to death: in fact they had been spirited away for their own safety. Beza reported to his correspondents that a French fleet had been gathered at Bordeaux for the subjugation of England; a week later he had heard talk of a parallel plot to assassinate Queen Elizabeth. The tales of horror were leavened only by the arrival in Geneva of some friends previously thought lost. The French jurist and political thinker François Hotman had escaped from Bourges and walked to Geneva. The following day he shared his belief that 'fifty thousand people have been slaughtered in France in the space of eight or ten days'.[21] Traumatised refugees only added to the sense of despair that seems at this time to have overcome the normally resilient Genevan pastors. Only the urgent requirement to attend to the physical needs of the new arrivals helped shake Beza from a torpor in which he longed for death and martyrdom.

Among the appalled eyewitnesses to the events in Paris was the English ambassador Francis Walsingham, later Queen Elizabeth's principal secretary and de facto head of intelligence. The English residence was some way from the epicentre of the violence, but Walsingham was soon aware of what was afoot, first from the sound of gunfire, then from the stream of terrified refugees seeking sanctuary in the embassy.[22] Conscious that some Englishmen were among the dead, it was only on 26 August that Walsingham dared venture out, and the following day before he despatched a messenger back to England. He thought it best not to entrust his thoughts to paper, and instead left the courier to make a verbal report. In fact, by the time this rider had made his way across the Channel, the massacre was common knowledge in London, brought by returning merchants and the first refugees. The condemnation of the French Crown, so recently welcomed as allies in the fight against Spain, was swift and universal. The French ambassador Fénélon was obliged to report:

> It is incredible how the confused rumours which began to come in on 27 August of the events in Paris have stirred the hearts of the English, who, having heretofore shown a marvellous affection for France, have suddenly turned to extreme indignation and a marvellous hatred against the French. . . . Even when the matter has been explained, they are no more moderate, holding that it was the Pope and the King of Spain who kindled the fire in France and that there is something evil afoot from all three of them against England.[23]

It was not until 8 September that the ambassador had the chance to put the French government's perspective in a frosty interview with Queen Elizabeth, and subsequently before the sceptical Privy Council. By this point English opinion was immovable. 'As to the Ambassador's negotiation with us here,' wrote William Cecil, Lord Burghley, 'to seek to persuade us that the King was forced for safety of his own life to cause the execution to be done as it was, you may imagine how hard a thing it is to us to be so persuaded against all our natural senses.'[24] The Council was under strong pressure to strike back by the first available means. Among the recommended actions forwarded to Burghley by the bishop of London was 'Forthwith to cut off the Scottish Queen's head'. Mary, Queen of Scots had been an awkward English prisoner for several years, and a natural focus for Catholic disaffection. More sober counsels prevailed. There was little to be gained by severing all connections with France, when it was widely believed that Spain had been instrumental in orchestrating the massacres. Such suspicions only hardened when Protestants became aware of the glee that had greeted news of the massacres in Spain and Rome.

The first news arrived in Rome on 2 September, brought by a special courier from Lyon. The messenger carried two letters, both written by the governor of Lyon's secretary: one was addressed to a local French contact, the other to the Pope. The news was passed to leading members of the French diplomatic community, who now accompanied the Cardinal of Lorraine to share the glory of the tidings with Pope Gregory. 'What is the news,' Lorraine is said to have asked the Pope, 'that your highness desires above all others?' 'For the exaltation of the Catholic faith, the extermination of the Huguenots' was the Pope's reply. This provided the cue for Lorraine's triumphant climax: 'It is precisely that that we can now announce to you for the glory of God and the majesty of the Holy Church.'[25]

At this point the French ambassador counselled Pope Gregory against premature effusions of public joy. He should rather wait for official confirmation, which arrived on 5 September, in letters borne by special couriers from the French king, and the papal nuncio in Paris, Antonio Maria Salviati. The nuncio's courier brought a detailed despatch, written on 27 August, along with a duplicate of a first hurried report from the day of the massacre itself. The original of this first letter had been entrusted to the French king's messenger, and thus arrived a couple of hours after the duplicate. The other despatches carried by the king's envoy allow us to reconstruct the rapid evolution of the official explanation of the massacre. Charles IX's first despatch, written on 24 August, presents the massacre as the unhappy consequence of the long feud between Coligny and Guise. By 26 August, however, the decision had been made to accept full responsibility: the massacre was now presented as an extra-judicial execution designed to pre-empt an imminent Protestant attack. For Pope Gregory, the cause or motivation was not, at this point, the principal issue at stake. The nuncio's account was read aloud to the assembled cardinals, and Gregory ordered a solemn *Te Deum* to be sung in celebration.

From this point news about the massacres in France was conveyed to Rome in a flood of bulletins from diverse sources. The papal nuncios in Venice, Vienna, Madrid, Turin and Florence added their reflections to those of Salviati in Paris. Most offered important observations on the political fallout; the nuncio in Florence was able in addition to offer a digest of the *avvisi* and other reports passing through this crucial information crossroads. In addition papal officials had access to a series of commercial newsletters despatched from Paris and Lyon from 24 August onwards. These provided both a developing picture of the true extent of the killing and reports of the speculation in France as to the causes. The Lyon *avviso* of 8 September mentioned 5,000 dead in the capital, 1,200 in Orléans and 500 in Lyon. Most other reports put the number of victims in Paris at around 2,000.[26] It should be noted that the prevailing estimates in the commercial newsletters were much closer to the truth than the overheated rumours circulating in the Protestant cities.

The first firm news reached Madrid only on 6 September. King Philip, then residing at the monastery of St Jerónimo, called over a secretary to have him translate a French account of the disposal of the Huguenot grandees. Shortly thereafter letters arrived from the Spanish ambassador in Paris, and a personal communication from Catherine of Medici written on 25 August. For Philip this was indeed a bounteous gift from a loving God. The looming threat of a French intervention in support of his Netherlandish rebels disappeared at a stroke. On 7 September he summoned the French ambassador St Gouard to witness his joy. In the ambassador's subsequent report of the audience, Philip 'began to laugh, with signs of extreme pleasure and satisfaction. He said he had to admit that he owed his Low Countries of Flanders to your Majesty.' Philip was in similar celebratory mood in his reply to his own ambassador in Paris. 'I had one of the greatest moments of satisfaction that I have had in all my life, and will have yet another if you continue writing to me of what is happening in the other parts of that realm. If things go as they did today, it will set the seal on the whole business.'[27] Even the normally restrained Duke of Alva, writing from the Netherlands, caught the mood:

> The events in Paris and France are wonderful, and truly show that God has been pleased to change and rearrange matters in the way that He knows will favour the conservation of the true church and advance His holy service and His glory. And, besides all that, in the present situation these events could not have come at a better time for the affairs of the King our Lord, for which we cannot sufficiently thank God's goodness.[28]

It is noticeable that the Catholic reaction, in both Madrid and Rome, concentrates almost exclusively on the decapitation of the Huguenot leadership: the scale of the subsequent killings concerned them hardly at all. The solitary exception on the Catholic side was the Emperor Maximilian, who, living among Protestants in the Empire, faced a more delicate political canvas. German Lutherans fully shared the horror of their Calvinist co-religionists, and Maximilian had to take strenuous steps to deny that he shared in the responsibility for the widely rumoured international Catholic conspiracy.[29] This disjunction, between a Catholic concentration on the political aspect and Protestant horror at the scale of the subsequent violence, was critical in shaping the ensuing narrative of events. Given the amount of time historians have devoted to reconstructing the train of events that led to the massacre, it is notable that contemporaries were almost unanimous in concluding that the destruction of the Huguenot nobility represented a deliberate act of policy. The Spanish ambassador was in no doubt that the strike against the Huguenot leadership was the responsibility of King Charles and Catherine of Medici; the papal nuncio reported in similar terms. The commercial newsletters from Paris and Lyon concurred in affirming the king's responsibility. The royal proclamation issued by Charles explaining that he had felt obliged to take action by the evidence of imminent treachery seemed to settle the issue.[30]

7.4 The military aftermath of St Bartholomew. A Parisian broadsheet view of the fortifications of the Protestant stronghold of La Rochelle, under close siege by the royal army.

That might have been the case had it not been widely suspected that the events of the summer were the result of a long-gestated plot, through which the too trusting Coligny and the Huguenot nobility had been lured to congregate in Paris. The Paris *avviso* of 27 August reported that the decision to eliminate the Huguenots had been taken by the king nine months previously, in conference with the Queen Mother, and at the instigation of the Duke of Guise.[31] The Cardinal of Lorraine added fuel to the fire by speaking in Rome of a shadowy Protestant plot, and indicating that the French court had formulated plans in advance to neutralise the threat. The theme of premeditation found its most developed articulation in a work of the papal courtier Camillo Capilupi, who penned a letter, ostensibly to his brother, setting out a plan to eliminate the Huguenots going back to 1570. The letter, which was published as a pamphlet under the striking title, *The Stratagem of Charles IX against the Huguenots*, cited several documents that purported to show Catherine and the king revealing their preparations to key contacts, including the Venetian ambassador. Although Capilupi, like all the Catholic observers who discussed the massacre, had nothing but praise for the French king, his tract was a propaganda windfall for the Calvinists, who made swift arrangements to have it republished in Geneva with a French translation.[32]

This was one of a succession of pamphlets rolling off the French Protestant presses that execrated the French court for their scheming perfidy, their abuse of the honourable Coligny, their bad faith and cruelty. As French armies gathered to finish by military force what the massacre had begun, a new generation of writings called openly for resistance, articulating a novel vision of contractual monarchy in which the rights of abused citizens might lead ultimately to the deposition of a tyrannical ruler.[33] But nothing spoke louder than the events themselves. By far the most influential writings of the day were the simple narratives of events: of the trusting, noble Coligny who greeted his killers from his bed, and the numerous men, women and children who had met death with courage and faith.[34] To Philip II this was irrelevant collateral damage from an essentially political event. In the Protestant consciousness these ordinary victims were the heart of the story. And it was a story that persuaded Protestant Europe of the unbridgeable gulf that now separated Catholics and Protestants.

Grand Designs

The conflict between Europe's warring religions reached its climax with the Armada campaign of 1588, Philip II's grand design. The fleet despatched for the invasion of England was intended to resolve a whole complex of

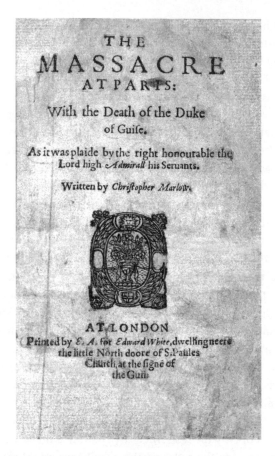

THE
MASSACRE
AT PARIS:

With the Death of the Duke
of Guise.

As it was plaide by the right honourable the
Lord high *Admirall* his Seruants.

Written by *Christopher Marlow*.

AT LONDON
Printed by *E. A.* for *Edward White*, dwelling neere
the little North doore of S. Paules
Church, at the signe of
the Gun.

7.5 A day that would live in infamy. Twenty years later Christopher Marlowe scored a
success on the London stage with this stage version of the massacre, nicely timed to take
advantage of a new crisis in French affairs.

interrelated problems. After twenty years the Revolt of the Netherlands was
no closer to resolution; indeed, since 1585 the intervention of English troops
had slowed the Spanish advance and seemed to point to a costly military stalemate. Philip II was finally convinced that only if England were eliminated
from the conflict could the Dutch rebels be brought to book. The incorporation of the Portuguese Crown in 1580 with its precious ocean-going fleet
made a seaborne invasion possible; Philip's alliance with the Catholic League
in France neutralised any possible hostile action by the French king. All that
was now required was a fair wind to speed the Spanish fleet through the
Channel, a successful juncture with the Duke of Parma's troops in Flanders,
and the rising of English Catholics that Philip had been promised by enthusiastic exiles and his own London agents.

It was impossible for an enterprise on this scale to be kept secret. The English knew what Philip had in store from at least 1586; indeed, a successful sortie into the port of Cadiz in April 1587 helped disrupt preparations sufficiently to force him to postpone the campaign for a year. But once the Armada set sail, Europe entered a period of anxious waiting. While the fleet made its way north, information centres across the continent experienced the equivalent of a news blackout: such snippets as were picked up by passing vessels and returning seamen often turned out to be wildly inaccurate. Even from the point at which the Spanish flotilla was sighted in the Channel, it would be several weeks before its success or failure would be determined. The Armada campaign was thus quite different from the joyful announcement of the distant victory of Lepanto, or the thunderclap of St Bartholomew. This was a rolling news event which occupied most of an anxious summer, where hard news was scarce, and rumour, uncertain reports and speculation filled the vacuum.

The Armada that left Lisbon at the end of May soon encountered foul weather, and was forced to take refuge in the north Spanish port of Corunna. It set out again only on 21 July. The decisive action against the English took place on 7 and 8 August. Having kept his fleet intact on the passage through the Channel, Admiral Medina Sidonia anchored off Calais to await the juncture with Parma's army. It was here that the English fleet made its move, sending in fireships to force the Spanish ships to scatter. Driven north by strong winds, the Armada headed ever further from the proposed invasion rendezvous. By the end of August there was no hope of a return. The remains of the once proud fleet were left to make a straggling passage around Ireland and back to Spain.[35]

For those far from the action this was a long drawn-out summer of waiting. Nowhere was news more anxiously awaited than in Rome. Pope Sixtus V had committed himself heavily to Spanish success, promising Philip a contribution of one million ducats once Spanish troops disembarked on English soil. These were difficult times for newsmen. It was clear how ardently Rome desired to hear good news. Spanish agents in the city were keen to announce the victory that would induce the Pope to release the promised subsidy. The Spanish postmaster, Antonio de Tassis, was heavily engaged in promoting every positive rumour. The *avviso* of 13 August reported that Tassis had wagered heavily that he would have good news by 20 August: a rumour deliberately planted to sway the markets. The snippets picked up by the merchant networks could also be misleading. Back in July Agostino Pinelli had been exhibiting in Rome letters from Lyon reporting that the Catholic army had arrived in Scotland, and was disembarking there. In August, following further news of an English defeat, the Duke of Parma was obliged to send word that no such report had been received in Antwerp.[36]

The commercial *avvisi* in Rome acquitted themselves well in the Armada campaign. They reported the rumours of Spanish success, but noted that these were unconfirmed reports requiring corroboration. On 16 July the Pinelli bankers received word from France announcing a Spanish triumph, but, noted the *avviso*, 'because there is such great desire to believe in a victory it is necessary to wait for confirmation'. The *avviso* of 26 July reported further glad tidings from Cologne, but also that none of the other couriers had word of it. On 22 August a special courier of the Duke of Savoy arrived in Rome with news of an English defeat, 'but this will remain in doubt until it is confirmed by other couriers'.[37]

The patent scepticism and professionalism of the Rome *avvisi* did not prevent news of the Spanish victory being widely celebrated in Catholic Europe. A large part of the responsibility for this rests with the Spanish ambassador in Paris, Bernardino de Mendoza, who received and then circulated a sequence of highly misleading reports.[38] At the end of July news reached Paris of the battle off the Isle of Wight: fifteen English ships were said to have been sunk. Mendoza sent this news straight to Madrid and made arrangements for an account of the Spanish victory to be published in Paris.[39] The English ambassador Sir Edward Stafford countered with his own chronology of events, laying out the course of the battle until the decisive engagement of 8 August. This too was published in French, though no reputable Paris printer was prepared to put his name to it.[40] Mendoza was unimpressed. 'The English ambassador here had some fancy news printed, stating that the English had been victorious,' he informed King Philip, 'but the people would not allow it to be sold, as they say it is all lies.'[41] Instead Mendoza chose to share with Philip a more optimistic report that Medina Sidonia had worsted and captured Sir Francis Drake. Mendoza's first report arrived in Madrid on 18 August. When the second came on 26 August, Philip was prepared to declare victory. Uncharacteristically, he had it announced by a printed broadsheet. A local English agent reported that the news was greeted with wild public rejoicing.

Elsewhere it was the same story. On 17 August the Senate of Venice voted to convey their congratulations to King Philip on his great victory. On 20 August in Prague the Spanish ambassador ordered a *Te deum* to be sung in celebration. But just then a report came in with contradictory news. In Rome it was left to the *avvisi* to prick the bubble of wishful thinking, as the true extent of the Spanish defeat emerged, beyond the capacity of even the most optimistic to wish away.

What of the protagonists? England, its treasury badly depleted after three years of warfare in the Netherlands, had staked everything on the success of the navy. The county levies had been raised and drilled, but few had exercised with live firearms. Although the English government was now finally appraised of the essential pivot of Philip's grand design, the juncture of the Armada with Parma's army of the Netherlands, the precise point where the enemy's main force would land was still unknown. Elizabeth believed they would attack through Essex, or sail up the Thames: the county forces were instructed to muster at Brentwood. For all the money spent on Walsingham's intelligence service, around 5 per cent of the Crown's annual revenues, it had not been able to determine that the invasion force was aimed at Kent.[42]

Certainly it was a close-run thing. By driving the Armada away from Calais before Parma's troops could embark, the English navy had exploited the weakest point in Philip's plan. By the time Elizabeth travelled downriver to address her forces gathered at Tilbury in Essex (where they would have been badly wrong-footed had the invasion taken place), the Armada had already passed the Firth of Forth, heading away from England. Elizabeth might have had 'the heart of an Englishman', but thankfully the military skills of those who heard the Tilbury speech were not to be tested.

In Spain the full scale of the disaster became clear only gradually. A defensive despatch from Parma, admitting that the juncture with the Armada fleet had not taken place, arrived in Madrid on 31 August. Four days later a courier from France brought news of the fleet's flight northwards. Not surprisingly, there was little appetite in the king's inner circle to convey this news to Philip. The choice fell on Mateo Vásquez, but even he preferred to make the communication in writing, sending in to Philip an oblique and rather tactless letter which wrapped the news in a convoluted comparison with Louis IX of France, the sainted king who had nevertheless led his troops to disaster.[43] For the Spanish Crown the autumn months were grim, as the tattered remnants of the fleet limped home and ships were confirmed lost. The expedition had cost Spain 15,000 men and around 10 million ducats. Most of all it had cost Philip his reputation as the invincible master of the world's most feared military power. The tectonic plates had shifted, and Philip II's carefully constructed masterplan swiftly disintegrated. The French king Henry III was now emboldened to turn on his persecutors in the Catholic League, and take desperate action to restore his authority. The Duke of Guise and his brother the Cardinal were summoned to the royal palace at Blois, and there done to death by the king's guards.[44] The news of their hero's assassination stunned and then enraged Catholic opinion. In France the Catholic League rose in revolt. In foreign capitals governments had to assess what now would be the fate of France, its beleaguered king, and the patient Protestant heir, Henry of Navarre.

This was a news event to rival even the defeat of the Armada. Guise was assassinated on 23 December 1588. The news was known in Rome on

4 January 1589.[45] The following *avviso*, describing how the news was received, reflects the universal recognition that something of European significance had occurred at Blois:

> 7 January. On Wednesday at 10 pm a courier arrived from Blois for the Cardinal Joyeuse, an hour later another from the Duke of Savoy to his ambassador, then a third towards midnight from the Grand Duke of Tuscany with a dispatch from France signed by H. Rucellai. Finally on Thursday a fourth courier arrived for the French Ambassador from the most Christian King. All had the same news: the death of the Duke of Guise.[46]

The outraged Pope now excommunicated Henry III, who had little option but to make common cause with Navarre in an attempt to restore his crumbling authority. On 2 August Henry was himself assassinated. The news reached Rome on 16 August, and was reported in the *avviso* of 23 August. Henry's death was a catastrophe for a number of Rome bankers who were heavily exposed by their lending to the French king. They attempted to cast doubt on the reports. The envoy of the Duke of Urbino therefore sought corroboration, as was his custom, from the Spanish ambassador. The duke's copy of the *avviso* of 30 August is carefully annotated in the ambassador's own hand:

> The King of France is dead, exactly as people have said. Today there arrived two couriers, one sent by the Bonvisi of Lyon with letters of the 20th, another from Nancy with two letters, from that town of 17th and from Paris dated 8 August. There can be no doubt.[47]

In the wake of the Guise assassination the League had occupied both Paris and Lyon, principal news hubs en route from northern Europe to Rome. Navarre responded by sending his own messengers to Rome, to build his case for an amelioration of the perpetual excommunication proclaimed against him.[48] By the middle months of 1589 Rome was receiving news from both sides by special courier almost every day. In such highly charged times statesmen were all too aware that the news could be manipulated or become distorted. The *avvisi* reflected this caution for their customers. Momentous news required confirmation, as was frequently emphasised in the way it was reported:

> 22 September 1590. As we hear from Venice, Turin, Lyon, Augsburg, Innsbruck and elsewhere, a battle took place on 27 August between Parma and Navarre, and 15,000 are thought to have been killed. The Pope has the

same report from his Nuncio in Venice, while the Spanish Ambassador has received letters from Parma's camp dated 28 August.[49]

To the victor, the spoils. The defeat of the Spanish Armada provided the opportunity for a great wave of celebratory pamphleteering, in England, the Netherlands and Germany.[50] The vanquished licked their wounds in silence. The presses of Italy, so busy after Lepanto, had little to offer. France was mostly consumed by its own affairs, though the Parisian press did briefly rouse itself to report a Spanish victory off the Orkney Islands as the returning fleet made its long and tortuous way home.[51] This again seems to have been largely wishful thinking, though similar reports were clearly circulating in Antwerp.[52]

England had been badly shaken by the events of the summer. Preachers spreading blood-curdling rumours that the Spanish planned to kill every man between seven and seventy might have encouraged desperate resistance, or they might have caused morale to collapse altogether. Calls for repentance mixed with invocations of divine favour also risked drawing attention to the ramshackle nature of military preparations. When the Armada achieved its rendezvous with Parma without substantial loss, some began to criticise the admiral's apparent lack of boldness in handling his fleet. But as the scale of the victory became known, all was forgiven. Queen Elizabeth's speech at Tilbury was witnessed by a number of aspiring authors keen to perpetuate its memory. Two agile and enterprising entrepreneurs returned to London and registered ballads celebrating the speech the very next day. These Tilbury ballads were part of a cascade of cheap print as London's often under-employed printers cashed in on the mood of national celebration.[53] James Aske, whose *Elizabetha Triumphans* was an altogether more ambitious literary work, at one point despaired of seeing it printed at all, because 'of the commonness of ballads'. With the danger now past it was time to mock recent fears. It was widely reported that on board the captured Spanish ships had been found large numbers of whips and leg-irons, clearly to enslave and torment the conquered nation. This was cheerfully satirised in a blood-curdling ballad illustrated with woodcuts of the whips.[54]

One of the most subtle pieces of government-sponsored propaganda was an English version of the Spanish pamphlet listing the ships, munitions and men of the Armada.[55] The original, printed at the time of the fleet's embarkation in Lisbon, had been republished in French by Mendoza during the summer.[56] Now England threw back in his face the battle array of the 'invincible' fleet, vanquished by England's mariners and God's will. All told, we can detect a new confidence, wit and polemical flair in the English pamphlet literature of

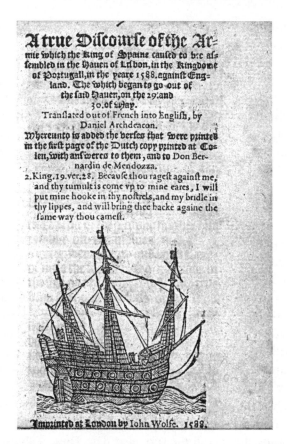

A true Discourse of the Ar=
mie which the King of Spaine caused to bee as=
sembled in the Hauen of Lisbon, in the Kingdome
of Portugall, in the yeare 1588. against Eng=
land. The which began to go out of
the said Hauen, on the 29. and
30. of May.
Translated out of French into English, by
Daniel Archdeacon.
Whereunto is added the verses that were printed
in the first page of the Dutch copy printed at Co=
len, with answeres to them, and to Don Ber-
nardin de Mendozza.
2. King. 19. ver. 28. Because thou ragest against me,
and thy tumult is come vp to mine eares, I will
put mine hooke in thy nostrels, and my bridle in
thy lippes, and will bring thee backe againe the
same way thou camest.

Imprinted at London by Iohn Wolfe. 1588.

7.6 The might of the Spanish fleet. After its defeat this enumeration of the vessels and
their armament was a celebration of English naval prowess.

these years, epitomised by *A pack of Spanish lies*, a typographically subtle piece
that presented the Spanish claims of the summer, in a ponderous Gothic type,
alongside a corrected narrative in sprightly Roman.[57] We are the future now,
it seemed to say: thus was false news held up to ridicule. At the beginning of a
decade when news of continental wars would consume the London press,
England's printers were taking significant steps towards the development of
the fully fledged news market that had hitherto eluded them.

The Spider's Web

The common thread in all three of these instances is the Spanish king, Philip
II. He had organised and financed the expedition that had ended with the

victory of Lepanto. He was widely suspected of being the evil genius behind the massacre of 1572, particularly (but not exclusively) in Protestant Europe. The Armada of 1588 was to have been the crowning enterprise of his grand design, to save Europe for Catholicism and put his enemies – in England, France and the Low Countries – to flight. Its failure dashed these hopes and condemned Europe to a brutal decade of attritional warfare.

Philip ruled Spain at the height of its powers. It was Europe's military superpower, its armies paid by the seemingly inexhaustible bullion extracted from the silver mines of Potosí (now in Bolivia) in the viceroyalty of Peru. From 1580 Philip also had at his disposal the resources of Portugal, and especially its deep-water fleet. No wonder that Spanish plans and ambitions were the constant concern of international diplomacy and the European news market. Yet Philip himself remained a rather mysterious presence, or, more correctly, absence, inscrutable and seldom seen. From the time of his return to Spain from the Netherlands in 1559 he never again left the peninsula. He spent the later decades of his reign at the newly built monastery palace El Escorial, deliberately remote from Spain's major towns. From here he attempted to manage a foreign policy of sustained and unprecedented ambition.

It is worth concluding our survey of the effectiveness of Europe's sixteenth-century news networks by contemplating the events of this period from Philip's perspective. For all Spain's military might, it remained during Philip's reign, as it had been in the previous two centuries, somewhat remote from the main European highways. The correspondence of medieval merchants had been mostly with the Mediterranean ports (especially Barcelona) not the Castilian interior. The rising power of Seville was, like Lisbon, orientated towards the Atlantic rather than main European trade routes. When Philip decided on Madrid as the main base of his operations, this required significant adjustments to the postal infrastructure. In 1560 a new 'ordinary' post was established between Madrid and Brussels. This passed by Burgos and Lesperon, and then through France via Poitiers, Orléans and Paris. When the king moved residence, in what became an increasingly fixed annual routine, the central administration remained in Madrid. Documents were brought to him in the Escorial or elsewhere by daily courier. The establishment of the ordinary post led to a great increase in the volume of mail and a commensurate reduction of cost; but it also meant that a great deal of routine diplomatic traffic was reaching Madrid by non-secure routes. This, and the normal hazards of postal communication, encouraged Spanish diplomats to adopt the prudent practice of sending duplicates of important despatches. On 15 August 1592 the king's ambassador in Savoy wrote to inform him:

On the second of this month I dispatched a letter to Your Majesty on a frigate from Barcelona whose owner is named Bernardino Morel and I included the copy of the dispatches of the 8, 10, 17 and 21 July and in view of the good prevailing weather I trust that they will have arrived so long as no ship has cut them off.[58]

This of course meant that Madrid frequently received several copies of the same despatch.

Direct communication with Madrid was only one part of the vast official correspondence maintained by Philip's agents abroad. The instructions communicated to a new ambassador in Paris in 1580 required him in addition to maintain correspondence with the governors of Milan and Flanders, the viceroy of Naples and ambassadors in Rome, Venice and Germany. Communication with some of the most distant outposts was especially challenging. Post from the imperial court at Prague could take up to five months to arrive in Spain, and sometimes was lost altogether.[59] Even an arterial route like the sea lanes between Naples and the Iberian Peninsula only operated for part of the year: between 15 November and 15 March the galley fleet was laid up because of the difficult and stormy conditions of the Mediterranean in winter. Post then had to be carried along the circuitous landward route via Genoa and Barcelona.

Maintaining efficient contact with his network of ambassadors, agents and allies was for Philip both complex and expensive, even in the best of times. But these times were far from normal, thanks, not least, to the incessant warfare stimulated by his own policies. The quality of the postal network clearly deteriorated in the second half of the sixteenth century.[60] Delays multiplied and the security of the post was frequently compromised. Most urgent was the interruption to the post caused by the wars in France. The arterial route between Barcelona and Italy passed through southern France to Lyon. By 1562 two of the crucial staging posts on this route, Montpellier and Nîmes, were in Huguenot hands, and couriers were frequently searched or robbed on the journey. On the northern route to Brussels the heavily wooded area around Poitiers was notorious for brigandage. In 1568 a Spanish royal courier was waylaid and murdered, and attempts to retrieve the diplomatic pouch were unsuccessful. It was soon recognised that the French transit routes were too hazardous. But avoiding France involved either a circuitous journey along the imperial post roads through the Empire, or using ships through the English Channel, where Spanish vessels faced increasing hazards from Calvinist privateers operating out of English ports or La Rochelle.

In Brussels, the Duke of Parma faced particular problems in communicating with Philip II in time of war. On one occasion in 1590 he sent five copies of one despatch to ensure its arrival. Sometimes, it must be admitted, these logistical difficulties could be used to advantage. When Parma was asked in December 1585 to prepare an operational plan for the invasion of England, he took until April 1586 to reply. He then chose to send his report by the longest possible route, via Luxembourg and Italy, with the result that it arrived in Madrid on 20 July. This, as Parma was clearly aware, rendered a campaign that year impossible, and allowed him to keep his army intact for the war against the Dutch for another fighting season.[61] The vagaries of the post also spared the Venetian ambassador in Madrid embarrassment during Armada year. As we have seen, on 17 August the Venetian Senate voted to offer Philip congratulations on his famous victory. Happily these instructions arrived in Madrid only on 2 October, by which time the scale of the catastrophe was becoming clear. The ambassador thought it best to ignore the despatch.

The information network constructed by Philip was on paper impressive. But in practice the logistical difficulties under which it operated meant that a vastly increased volume of communication was combined with decreased efficiency: Philip was being drowned in stale news. These difficulties were compounded by the manner in which he chose to conduct business. Philip developed a style of government that deviated sharply from the accepted conduct of princes. At all points possible he avoided meetings. Papers were brought to him, and he considered them in private. This had a certain rationality: there were so many people wanting the king's ear, including the large residential diplomatic corps, that even to meet ambassadors on a regular basis would have been inordinately time consuming.[62] Some accommodated themselves to the king's preferences. The French ambassador Fourquevaux, instructed to seek an audience, instead sent a letter. 'I know that I would please him more if I communicated with him by letter,' he explained to Charles IX, because 'he prefers ambassadors to deal with him by letter rather than in person while he resides in his country houses.'[63] Others, including the papal nuncio, who had been unable to secure an audience for four months, proved less understanding.

Nothing could disguise that this was completely at variance with the normal traditions of court life, and many of King Philip's subjects expressed their disapproval. 'God did not send your Majesty and all other kings to spend their time on earth so that they could hide themselves away reading and writing,' wrote the king's almoner, with alarmingly frank courage. He went on to denounce 'the manner of transacting business adopted by Your Majesty, being permanently seated at your papers in order to have a better reason to escape from people'.[64]

Philip was not a recluse. He understood the value of showing himself to his people, and on such occasions the population responded with enthusiasm. He

seems simply to have felt that the business of government could most effectively be conducted by reading. Theoretically his father Charles V had established a highly efficient system to sort and order the papers that flowed into
the chancery. Councils were named to deal with the affairs of each province,
and separately with war, finance and forestry. But Philip still insisted on
taking all decisions himself. He rarely attended Council meetings, and was
disinclined to join discussions between his advisors. High-ranking officials
were not encouraged to return to Spain for debriefing between postings.
Philip therefore chose to forgo important opportunities for detailed conversations with informed experts and advisors. He also completely discontinued
the common practice of sending trusted messengers with oral instructions: all
was set down in writing.

The Council system did not succeed in establishing limits on the amount of
paper that flowed across the king's desk. Philip would read anything that came
his way, even from individuals who had bypassed the system to send him a
paper: the original master plan for the Armada expedition came from one
such unofficial source (the inquisitor and amateur strategist Bernardino de
Escalante). It was not unusual for Philip to receive a thousand petitions a
month. Some days he signed four hundred letters, all of which he read and
often sent back for revision.

For forty years Philip attempted, as one awestruck English observer put it, to
govern the world with his pen and his purse. But was such a system possible in
the communications environment of sixteenth-century Europe? Even if Philip
responded to an urgent communication from the Viceroy of Naples on the day
it arrived, this still involved a round trip of six weeks, if the system worked
perfectly. Communication with the outlying territories of the Empire, in the
Americas and Asia, took far longer. These difficulties were compounded by the
time Philip took to arrive at decisions. Officials grumbled about the time they
were kept in limbo, waiting for the king's commands. 'If we have to wait for
death,' they quipped, 'let us hope that it comes from Spain, for then it would
never arrive.'[65] Sometimes the delay was itself policy, as when Philip attempted
to spin out a response to a developing crisis in the Netherlands until he had
resolved the urgent conflict in the Mediterranean with the Turkish assault on
Malta. But by failing to take his governor in the Netherlands, Margaret of
Parma, into his confidence, Philip precipitated a new disaster. Despairing of a
response, Margaret was forced to take the initiative and declare a limited
suspension of religious persecution. When the king's instructions eventually
arrived, ordering that persecution be maintained, the repudiation of previous
concessions led to a far greater explosion of anger.[66] Margaret was left humiliated and discredited, her authority effectively destroyed.

The limitations of Philip's system were fully exposed when his attempts to resolve the complex politics of northern Europe from his desk in Spain collapsed in ruins. Three years of continual correspondence with the Duke of Parma in the Netherlands had failed to devise an invasion plan for England that could succeed. During this time Philip changed his mind constantly, at different times favouring a direct assault from the Low Countries and a landing in the Isle of Wight or Ireland. Even in August 1588 the bureaucrat king was attempting to guide the course of the battle (in fact already over) by insisting that his instructions were meticulously followed. The final act came when orders were drafted for Medina Sidonia to land in Scotland and ally with the local Catholics. But it was now mid-September, and the remnants of the invincible Armada were at this point approaching the Spanish coast. This was the fantasy of a defeated, exhausted man.

PART TWO

MERCURY RISING

CHAPTER 8

Speeding the Posts

Iт used to be said that the three centuries before 1800 saw no fundamental change in communication infrastructure, certainly nothing that could be described as a technological revolution. These were the times when sailors faced and overcame the challenge of ocean voyages, itself no mean feat and one based on small, incremental changes in the design of ships, sails and navigational instruments. Land transportation could register no equivalent landmarks. Europe's roads remained difficult and dangerous: there is some evidence that they may actually have deteriorated since the High Middle Ages. Travellers remained as before dependent on horses, carts and haulage for the movement of people and goods. Transportation by water, around Europe's waterways, depended as always on wind and tides, and the backbreaking work of oarsmen.

Yet if much of the communication infrastructure of Europe was familiar and unchanging, the beginning of the seventeenth century did witness a step change so decisive as to amount, if not to a revolution, then certainly to a new beginning. This has escaped the view of most historians because it was an organisational shift, rather than a technological one. It was not like the introduction of gunpowder or printing: rather it required the application of bureaucratic intelligence to existing systems. Its impact was, however, as dramatic as many of those developments to which we attach the label 'revolution'.

The change in question was the wholesale transformation of the international postal service. In a few decades from the beginning of the seventeenth century, communication by post became quicker, cheaper and more frequent. The network of places linked by the post became dense and more intricate. For the provision of news this was a vital transformation. It made possible the frequent, rapid and reliable delivery of news necessary for the next crucial media innovation: the invention of the newspaper.

The first newspaper was established in Strasbourg in 1605.[1] It was the creation of a stationer who already had his own regular manuscript newsletter.
The introduction of a weekly printed serial represented merely the mechanisation of an existing commercial process: the printed sheets, containing much
the same news, gave Johann Carolus the opportunity to expand his client base
for minimal extra cost. It was an experiment that carried little risk, and it
seems to have been successful. Soon Carolus's *Relation aller Fürnemmen und
gedenckwürdigen Historien* was being imitated in other German towns and in
the Low Countries.

The newspaper did not, however, meet with a universal welcome. Italy, the
centre of the most intense network of commercial manuscript *avvisi*, did not
take to the printed news-sheets. The world of news divided in two, between a
north soon densely populated by a network of printed weekly news-sheets,
and a south where they held no appeal. The centre of the European news
network was to move north: much of the innovation of future centuries would
be in the northern lands.

This media transformation followed directly from the reorganisation of the
postal services initiated at the beginning of the seventeenth century. These
developments were not uncontested: many vested interests were bound up in
the ad hoc systems that had served the provision of news, more or less
adequately, over the previous hundred years. It required a great deal of determination, and some ruthlessness, to drive through the changes necessary to
draw together the various systems into an integrated whole. This was the great
achievement of the imperial postmasters, the family Taxis (or Tassis as they
were known in Italy and Spain), who had now held these responsibilities for
over one hundred years. Theirs is one of the great unsung achievements of
European civilisation.

At the Sign of Mercury

The spine of the new postal network established in the seventeenth century
was the imperial post created by the Emperor Maximilian one hundred years
before. Intended originally to link his dominions in the Netherlands and
Austria, the system was in due course expanded to take in the extensive new
dominions encompassed by the inheritance of Charles V. His reign was the
first golden age of the imperial post. Regular, reliable and freely available to
those who could pay the tariffs, it became a mainstay of diplomatic and
merchant communication. The Fugger family in Augsburg scored a significant coup when they negotiated privileged access to the postal system, an
access later extended to a wide variety of paying clients; the family's carefully

nurtured connection with the imperial postmasters was a cornerstone of their European trade network. The smooth functioning of the imperial system can be contrasted with the halting development of the post in two nation states outside the Habsburg orbit, France and England.[2]

While Maximilian's initiative of 1490 had shown the way, the two crucial stages in the early development of the European postal network were the contracts with the Taxis family in 1505 and 1516.[3] These agreements set the structure of the future imperial network in three critical ways: they established fixed contractual obligations for the delivery of post within a specified time; they extended the postal network to Italy and Spain; and they confirmed the position of the Taxis at the heart of the system. The treaty of 1505 granted the Taxis a fixed annual salary. The treaty of 1516, with the future Emperor Charles V, guaranteed that they would enjoy a monopoly on all postal transactions along the post roads. This, together with the right to take letters for private clients, made the Taxis rich.

It also gave them the confidence to invest in further improvements to the system. The distance between postal stations was steadily reduced: from 38 kilometres under the original scheme to 30 kilometres in 1505. In the second half of the sixteenth century the intervals were reduced further, to three German *Meilen* or 22 kilometres.[4] The treaty of 1516 established a new route from Antwerp via Innsbruck to Rome and Naples, linking these two great European trade centres (and news markets) to the imperial post. The contract envisaged that the new route would speed the post from Antwerp to Rome in 252 hours, or 10 ½ days. It was astonishingly ambitious, yet all the signs, from surviving docketed letters, are that the timetable was adhered to.

Such a system required an elaborate and expensive infrastructure and a constant attention to its day-to-day administration. This was the great achievement of the Taxis. The family spawned an extraordinary number of gifted executives. Over successive generations they proved to be energetic, robust and (especially in the sixteenth century) long lived. By the third decade of the sixteenth century there were members of the family serving as postmasters in Innsbruck, Augsburg, Brussels and Spain. Raimond de Taxis accompanied Charles V on many of his journeys, including to Tunis. Another branch of the clan provided successive masters of the papal post in Rome.[5] Secure in the confidence of the imperial family, the Taxis were able to introduce further important structural changes. The establishment of a secure route between Trento and Bologna closed a notorious gap in the Italian postal network and led to a significant fall in transit times between Vienna and Rome. Postmasters began to invest in the construction of purpose-built postal stations, rather than simply making use of the best available inn. And in the 1530s the Taxis

introduced the 'ordinary' post. Rather than sending despatches when required
by the imperial administration, or when a sufficient volume of letters had
accumulated, the main route now had a fixed service, publicly advertised,
leaving on a particular day of the week. This was a critical development for
both business and news: it established the rhythms of the postal week that so
stamped its imprint on the weekly manuscript news service, and later on the
printed weekly newspapers. Indeed, the sixteenth-century *novellanti* could
not have offered clients their service without the promise of a fixed weekly
post. The 'ordinary' principle introduced on the Flanders–German route was
soon extended to Italy, with the establishment of an ordinary post between
Rome and Venice in 1541.[6]

The expansion of the imperial post during the reign of Charles V created
the potential for a European postal network. The liveried messengers with
their staffs crowned by a flying Mercury, and the post horn to advertise their
coming, would have become an increasingly familiar sight and sound. For
those engaged in commerce the day of the arrival of the post became the pivot
of the business week. Crowds would congregate at the post-house, 'at the sign
of Mercury', to await the courier's arrival. The Taxis also now moved towards
the advertisement of fixed rates for the carriage of letters or parcels along
specified lengths of the route. The tariffs were fixed, as today, dependent on
the size and weight of the letter. Given the volume of business now being
conducted, these rates were increasingly affordable.[7]

Impressive though this was, the Taxis' imperial service was still some way
short of offering a fully functioning and integrated European postal network.
In France the ambitious system laid out by Louis XI in the fifteenth century
had largely fallen into decay. Paris and Blois were served by couriers on the
imperial routes, and Lyon was a major postal hub between Spain and
Germany; but the restrictions of the French royal system left many parts of the
kingdom unserved.

The reform of the French royal post was taken in hand in the brief reign of
Francis II (1559–60).[8] This was another period of internal political tension, a
time of intense partisan agitation before the outbreak of the French wars
of religion. The new decree introduced several postal routes, radiating out
from Paris to the kingdom's frontiers, with two important lateral routes
from Lyon to Marseille and Blois to Nantes. The arterial road from Paris
to Bordeaux and onward to the Spanish frontier had fifty-three stages.
The decree stipulated payments including stipends for twelve ferrymen: a
reminder that not even all main roads were continuously linked by bridges,
even at this point. Whether the reorganised French system worked in practice
is also to be doubted. Within years France had been plunged into turmoil by

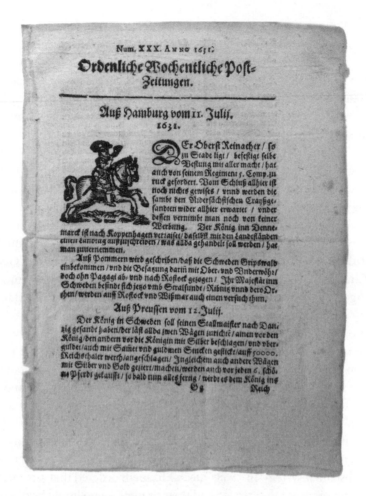

8.1 The postman, as represented in an early German newspaper.

the outbreak of the Huguenot rebellion. Fighting continued intermittently for forty years, rendering the already notorious French road system even more perilous.

In England, rather as in France, the need for the improvement of the postal service was most acutely felt in times of emergency.[9] When Henry VIII crossed the Channel for his first campaign in France (1513), he was accompanied by his master of the posts, Sir Brian Tuke, and fourteen messengers. But in the sixteenth century, as before, the main onus of ensuring the distribution of the post was placed on local agents, principally the king's sheriffs. The costs of maintaining the postal relays fell on the towns along the mail routes. It is interesting to contrast the vague nature of Tuke's instructions, as laid out in a letter to Thomas Cromwell in 1533, with the vastly more ambitious imperial system in continental Europe. 'The king's pleasure,' Tuke wrote,

> is that the posts be better appointed, and laid in all places most expedient; with the commandment to all townships in all places, on pain of life, to be in such readiness, and to make such provision of horses at all times, as no tract or loss of time be had in that behalf.[10]

The English municipalities no doubt bore these burdens patiently, but the effeciency of the postal system had in effect been subcontracted to a host of subsidiary authorities of widely varying capabilities. Nevertheless, this was the way in which the English Crown conducted its business. An instruction preserved in the town archives of Southampton ordered the municipal authorities in 1500 'to see the letters enclosed conveyed to Jersey and Guernsey [the Channel Islands, off the coast of France] by the next convenient messenger'.[11] The Crown also made generous use of the post maintained by the City of London.

Those towns that lay along the road to the north were particularly burdened. In times of genuine crisis a special effort was called for. During the northern revolt in 1536 the mayors of Huntingdon, Stamford and Lincoln were required to appoint 'an able man well horsed' to be available night and day to carry letters from the king and Privy Council. But in more normal times municipal authorities found the expense hard to bear. The Council's attempt to keep the rate paid for post horses at the largely nominal penny a mile caused great resentment, but the resources were simply not available for a more substantial system. In 1568 Queen Elizabeth ordered that any local post-masters not prepared to serve for half their present wage should be discharged. The attempt to adopt some of the continental practices – the notation on letters of the times of despatch and arrival at intermediary stages on the route and other exhortations to haste, for instance – were only fitfully successful. Notwithstanding the urgent 'For life, For Life' on the package, letters had still taken nine days to reach Calais, complained a rather testy Lord Wharton in 1548. The use of the gallows sign to signal urgency also backfired when the treasurer of the northern garrison, clearly mistaking its meaning, took offence and wrote a pained letter of protest.[12]

The Tudor Crown recognised a need to maintain on a permanent basis only the arterial roads to the Channel at Dover and to Scotland. In times of military necessity, postal relays were established to Holyhead or Milford Haven (that is, towards Ireland) or to Plymouth, to shadow potential dangers in the English Channel. Otherwise the distribution of official mail worked much as in medieval times, with royal messengers carrying writs to county sheriffs, who would take responsibility for distributing them locally.

The postal systems of France and England also differed from the imperial system in that the Crown maintained them for the exclusive use of official business. This meant that potential private or commercial customers had to shift for themselves. By far the most developed and efficient private postal system was that set up by the foreign merchant community in London, the Merchant Strangers. This linked the English capital with the imperial postal network, and with a second route through France via Rouen and Paris. From London the merchant post also carried letters down to the English ports: to Plymouth and Exeter in the West Country, to Norwich, Colchester and Harwich in East Anglia.

The Italian Corsini family, which established a base in London during Elizabeth's reign, achieved a remarkably regular connection with their agents in these coastal towns and with correspondents abroad.[13] The volume carried by these merchant posts kept the rates low, and the English Merchant Adventurers could also rely on the constant passage of ships between London and their staple markets abroad. For private citizens not enrolled in these two associations secure connections were much more difficult to achieve, and more expensive.

The failure of ambition implied by these parallel systems was an impoverishment of the network as a whole. Deprived of this additional lucrative business, the postmasters of the royal post had little incentive to invest to improve the system. For much of the sixteenth century, therefore, France and England remained essentially outside the European postal network. The provision of news for these places, in consequence, always required a greater effort and the use of merchant posts. In these respects the merchant metropolis of Lyon, strategically situated halfway between Paris and the German trading regions, played a crucial role. The density of commerce between Antwerp and London helped speed communications across the Channel. But even here the English Crown made life more difficult for those anxious for news by imposing stricter controls on the foreign merchant posts in the last decades of the sixteenth century.

The other major drawback to the imperial system was that it made little provision for the German cities. This, it must be said, was partly through their own choice. Having fought so hard to establish their jurisdictional independence, the imperial cities were extremely reluctant to admit a Habsburg institution within their walls.[14] They also refused under any circumstances to open the city gates at night, and the imperial post ran continuously round the clock. There was, too, the not insignificant matter that during the course of the Reformation most of the imperial cities had adhered to Protestantism. The imperial post was very much a Catholic institution, and the Taxis postmasters proved unwavering in their allegiance. In consequence the only imperial city that formed part of the Habsburg postal network was Augsburg. Speyer, though it lay at a strategic juncture on the route, refused to admit a post office. Even the splendid new post office at Augsburg in 1549 was built outside the city walls. Apart from Augsburg the German postal stations had perforce to be placed in relatively small settlements, like Rheinhausen, the crucial Rhine crossing just a few miles from Speyer.

The merchant communities of the German cities were the major victims of this ideological purity. The Fugger and Welser of Augsburg were able to make full and profitable use of the post; in fact the Fugger system of agents, which reached its highest state of development during these years, is virtually inconceivable without their access to the imperial post.[15] Alongside substantial sums for letters sent through the post, the Fugger accounts also record generous gifts to the Taxis postmasters, with whom they were on friendly terms.[16] In the other German cities the merchants were obliged to carry their post to the nearest imperial post station. In the case of Frankfurt, this would have been Rheinhausen, over 120 kilometres distant. This was a critical liability both for the German cities and for the European international commercial system. It even began to distort German political life. Speyer and Augsburg were increasingly chosen for meetings of the imperial Diet specifically because they were close to the main postal routes.

Crisis

In 1889 workmen clearing an administrative building in Frankfurt made a remarkable discovery. Tucked away in an unassuming sack was a large cache of letters written three hundred years previously, in the year 1585: the sack contained a total of 272 items of post. This, it turned out, was the remnant of two or more mail sacks from the imperial postal service. Somewhere north of Rheinhausen the mail had been intercepted. The most politically sensitive letters had been removed, and the remainder, routine business and family transactions, discarded. Swept into a bundle and stored in the corner of some office, somehow they had survived the next three hundred years to emerge as a mute witness to the late sixteenth-century postal system, its vitality and its dangers.[17]

The surviving letters, now a prized possession of the Frankfurt Museum of Telecommunications, offer a fascinating snapshot of the European news network, almost a century after the imperial postal couriers had first begun to make their way along the trans-continental highways. The discarded mail linked merchants and other correspondents in twenty different Italian cities

with friends and business partners in Cologne, Liège and numerous places in
the Low Countries (the messengers had clearly been travelling north). The
overwhelming majority of the surviving letters are from Italian merchants to
their business partners in northern Europe, mostly in Antwerp and Cologne.
Particularly striking is the number of Italian names among the addressees:
trans-continental trade still relied to a large extent on connections between
Italian merchants and members of the extended family settled (often long
settled) in northern Europe. A significant number of the letters was destined
for friends in Antwerp, even though the city was under close siege from the
army of the Duke of Parma. Another group of letters was destined for soldiers
in the besieging armies.

The letters contain details of transactions in an impressive variety of
commodities, a testimony both to the continuing vitality of international
trade and to the role of the imperial post in sustaining it.[18] Except for one
thing: these letters never got through. These postal deliveries fell victim to the
political turbulence then raging in Germany, specifically the warfare that had
erupted (1583–8) when the Archbishop of Cologne attempted to convert his
domain to Protestantism. Nor was this an isolated example: the imperial
postal system, functioning so efficiently up to the abdication of Charles V in
1555, ran into serious difficulties in the second half of the century, partly as an
inevitable consequence of these troubled times. The protracted military and
political conflict unleashed by the Revolt of the Netherlands badly disrupted
the northern end of the postal system.

The Low Countries experienced serious fighting in 1566, 1568, 1572–4 and
1579–85. The attempt to flush out the Dutch Protestant minority also stimulated widespread emigration among the merchant and artisan communities,
leading to the creation of a new type of postal service: a clandestine courier
service operated by the exiles themselves to keep in touch with family
members they had left behind. Unusually, we know a great deal about the
functioning of this Protestant underground thanks to the interception of one
consignment before delivery: letters were discovered in the false bottom of a
basket of vegetables close to the villages where they had been gathered up
before transportation to England.[19] If this consignment failed to get through,
others clearly did: the letters speak of regular communication, and they have
an unhurried sense of routine, even if many express a moving sense of loss at
the separation from husbands and fathers now forced to live abroad.[20]

Such a service could be remarkably efficient in speeding letters to their
destination in just a few days. The dense merchant traffic that linked Antwerp,
England and the north German ports provided the perfect cover. The landward connections down the Rhine were more problematic, passing as they did

through lands often disrupted by campaigning armies: these, of course, were the vital arteries of the imperial post. The sack of Antwerp by mutinous Spanish troops in 1576 was also a hammer blow to the northern trade emporium, by this point a critical node in Europe's commercial network. As noted, the war of the Archbishopric of Cologne was another highly disruptive conflict at a critical node of the northern postal network.

The French Wars of Religion also had a significant impact on the imperial postal system, particularly on those routes that linked Italy and southern Germany to the Iberian Peninsula. We have seen already how critically the vulnerability of this road system through southern France impeded Philip II's communications with Rome and Vienna.[21] The Fuggers, too, frequently expressed their frustration at the difficulty of maintaining correspondence with Spain. On 26 April 1587 the Fugger agent in Portugal was obliged to report that the ordinary post from Lisbon had been waylaid near Bordeaux, and the letters rifled.[22] In the following decade the Fuggers were grimly aware that all their Spanish letters were being routinely opened in France. Eventually they felt they had no choice but to instruct their agents to send all correspondence by the sea route to Genoa, or even the circuitous northern route via Flanders.

The Taxis also had their difficulties in these years. The division of the Habsburg inheritance between Spain and Austria compromised their existing contracts as imperial postmasters, and led to legal and jurisdictional problems. The imperial post had to this point been paid for by the Netherlandish treasury, underwritten by Spanish subventions. When Philip II inherited the Netherlands, the service became de facto Spanish. This in itself was sufficient to alarm the German postmasters, since a number of those appointed to man the local stations were Protestants. In 1566 two members of the Taxis clan, Leonhard the general postmaster, and Seraphin, postmaster of Augsburg and Rheinhausen, actually embarked on litigation with each other to resolve a dispute over the division of fees along the Netherlandish/German road.[23] That the payment of the postmasters' salaries depended on Spanish subventions became increasingly critical when the Spanish treasury ran out of money. Spanish bankruptcy meant that salaries went unpaid. The system began to creak. In 1568 Cardinal Granvelle was already complaining of stoppages and major delays. A decade later the German postmasters could stand it no more; in 1579 they went on strike.

For the German Lutherans the patent inadequacies of the imperial postal service in this period represented something of an opportunity. The leading princes established their own messenger relays. In 1563 Philip of Hessen and August of Saxony joined together to sponsor a courier service to keep them in touch with William of Orange, a vital ally in the Netherlands.[24] Later Württemberg and Brandenburg-Prussia would be brought into the network, though it remained essentially a private system of communication between the German Protestant courts, not open to the public.

For the imperial cities, the motivation was more commercial than political. For some time a single arterial network that privileged official government mail had not suited their needs particularly well. In 1571 the merchants of Nuremberg petitioned for the establishment of a direct link with Antwerp via Frankfurt and Cologne. The following year Frankfurt established its own weekly postal service to Leipzig. These *Ordinari-Boten* were the descendants of the fifteenth-century city messengers. The difference was that the system would, like the imperial post, be open to all, and would follow a regular published timetable.

The 1570s witnessed the establishment of a dense network of these city courier services throughout Germany.[25] The northern city of Hamburg had previously laboured under a significant disadvantage through its distance from the main postal routes.[26] Now, starting in 1570, the city created a whole postal network of its own, with weekly services to Amsterdam, Leipzig, Bremen, Emden, Cologne and Danzig. The influence of the Netherlandish Protestant diaspora is evident in the choice of routes, since many of these cities (Hamburg included) had significant colonies of exiled Dutch merchants. Even in privileged Augsburg the merchants saw which way the wind was blowing. In 1577 they established their own independent merchant post to Antwerp via Cologne.[27]

The Augsburg postmaster, Seraphin von Taxis, was understandably furious at this apostasy, but while the imperial post was in chaos there was little he could do. This same year the general postmaster Leonhard was forced to flee Brussels to avoid being imprisoned by the Dutch rebels. The situation could not go on, and in the last two decades of the sixteenth century the Emperor himself intervened to take matters in hand.

Regeneration

The reform of the post became the rather unlikely crusade of Emperor Rudolph II, who had succeeded his father Maximilian II as ruler in the Habsburg dominions in 1576. In his last years Rudolph would become a tragic figure, self-exiled to his castle in Prague with his ever-expanding collection of curiosities. But even Rudolph could see that the brewing crisis of religion in the imperial lands required closer coordination of imperial Habsburg policy. The result, in 1597, was a milestone edict reforming the imperial post.[28] This mandate proclaimed the reunification of the Spanish and imperial systems and simultaneously announced stern measures against unauthorised competition. If this had the urban courier services in its sights, it was bound to remain a dead letter while the imperial postal routes provided no service for the major German cities. In 1598 therefore the imperial post took a major step forward with the establishment of an imperial post office in Frankfurt, with a branch line linking Germany's main commercial marketplace to the existing network. An entirely new post road then connected Frankfurt directly with the Netherlands via Cologne. After protracted negotiations a new east–west service was created between Cologne and Prague, via Frankfurt and Nuremberg. Finally a direct service between Cologne and Hamburg, and between Frankfurt and Leipzig, brought the principal cities of the north and east into the system.[29]

8.2 The postal service between Paris and Antwerp, five times a month in both directions. This was a vital lateral route, connecting two major news hubs and through them the Low Countries and provincial France.

All this was not achieved without a certain amount of bad blood. Having invested in their own regular courier services, the German cities did not take lightly to their prohibition. An arrest of city couriers on the road between Frankfurt and Cologne led to a collective protest to the Emperor.[30] But the imperial post had one critical advantage. The new imperial routes were set up with the same sequence of relays as the main imperial line. The city courier services, in contrast, had no intermediary stages for changes of horses: the couriers rode the whole length of the route. In direct competition the imperial service could often deliver the mail on the longer journeys in half the time. As tempers cooled, the German city councils recognised the benefits of the imperial system and the independent German courier services gradually withered away.

By 1620, at the conclusion of these developments, the German Empire had been provided with a postal system of unparalleled efficiency and sophistication. The single arterial route between Brussels and Vienna had been replaced by an intricate network of services centred on Germany's new postal capital, Frankfurt. Taken together with simultaneous renovations in the English and French systems, the revitalised imperial post made possible a new era in the history of communication.

The new imperial postal network reached its completion just as the long period of peace enjoyed by Germany since 1555 was about to come to an end. In 1618, two years after the announcement of the new Frankfurt–Leipzig line, the Defenestration of Prague began the tragic sequence of events that made Germany the new battlefield of international politics. The Thirty Years War brought death and destruction to large areas of Germany, as foreign and mercenary armies criss-crossed the Continent. The conflict caused terrible damage to the Germany economy, and ended for ever German supremacy in parts of the European book trade. But one perverse consequence was to give new impetus to the development of an effective international postal network. The involvement of so many foreign powers in the German conflict meant that all Europe's capitals felt the need for swift, reliable information. Several took steps to improve their own internal communications, and to link these systems to the central European postal network. In France the royal postal monopoly was strengthened, and the network of postal stations expanded in 1622 to take in the southern cities of Bordeaux and Toulouse, and also Dijon, close to the potential battlefields in the east. In this same year Lamoral von Taxis established a courier service between Antwerp and London. This was followed, a decade later, by a treaty between the Brussels postmaster and the English postmaster general.[31]

Danish and Swedish interests in Germany also stimulated an improvement in the information network.[32] In 1624 Christian IV of Denmark set up his own

1. Excellentiſſimus Comes a latere Schaldis Hemiſſem ingreditur, ubi ſeſto tubarum clangore, læta tormentorum exploſione, atque unanimi applaudentium incolarum latitia, inſigni comitatu excipitur

8.3 The profits of a postal monopoly. Part of a series of four prints commemorating a visit by the Imperial Postmaster-General, the Count Thurn and Taxis, to the Postmaster of the Netherlands. The size of the retinue is impressive.

postal system, based on Copenhagen, with a branch office in Hamburg. Four years later the Swedes extended this network with their own connection between Hamburg and Helsingör. The Swedish invasion of Germany in 1630 briefly resulted in the creation of an alternative postal network centred on Frankfurt, with 9 routes and 122 posts.[33] While this soon collapsed after the Swedish defeat at Nördlingen in 1634, a more enduringly significant development was the establishment of a direct route between Paris and Vienna, via Strasbourg, finally cutting out the long diversion through Brussels that had so limited French access to the international post.

With this development, the European postal network was fundamentally complete. The only further innovation that would be introduced, really until the coming of the railways and the penny post, was the substitution of a coach service in place of the postal riders.[34] The postal coaches increased the volume of mail that could be carried, and created the possibility for travellers to avail themselves of the service. In the sixteenth century merchants and messengers who had ridden post had to be able to ride at the speed of the postal riders. This was an expensive service and only men who rode well could consider it. The postal coaches were a different matter; from the mid-seventeenth century, when coaches started to appear on short stretches of the German roads, a far wider cross section of travellers could avail themselves of the opportunity to travel in comfort. No longer did a traveller have to furnish their own wagon, ensure that the horses were strong and sound, and check that the driver was equipped to make what repairs were necessary on the journey: all that would be taken care of. Regular timetables meant that travellers could plan a journey with the reasonable assurance of timely arrival. The extra carrying capacity was especially important for the distribution of bulky mail items, such as newspapers. Within a few decades of their establishment the mail coaches came to bear the major burden of the timely distribution of printed news.

The developments we have witnessed in this chapter represent a remarkable advance in European communications. The previous centuries had seen slow incremental changes in the rates of travel, accompanied by an increase in the volume of correspondence between those with sufficient funds to create their own network of communications. The best news was available only to those who could make the considerable investment necessary for what were essentially private networks, official or commercial. The coming of print in the sixteenth century had brought with it a substantial transformation in the reader community, and ingenious innovation in printed news: though much of this news was not particularly fresh, or, indeed, time specific. All of this changed within two decades of fierce innovation at the turn of the seventeenth century. At their end all of Europe's major commercial centres were closely linked in a dense web of public postal services. News could now be passed along reliable channels, at modest cost, with far greater regularity. It is no surprise, therefore, that the next significant development in the commercial exploitation of this news should take place here, in the commercial hubs of Germany and northern Europe. This development, closely connected with the expansion of the postal service, was the birth of the newspapers.

CHAPTER 9

The First Newspapers

Iᴎ the year 1605 a young book dealer named Johann Carolus appeared before the Strasbourg city council with an unusual request. Besides his bookselling Carolus had recently also developed a lucrative sideline, producing a weekly manuscript newsletter. By this date, as we have seen, the manuscript newsletter had become the cornerstone of the information market for Europe's elites. From its early days in Rome and Venice, the production of manuscript newsletters had now spread across Germany, and from Augsburg and Nuremberg to Brussels and Antwerp in the Low Countries. Strasbourg, situated close to the crucial Rhine crossing serving the imperial post service at Rheinhausen, was extremely well placed for such a venture. Carolus could be sure of a steady supply of news from the imperial postmaster and the constant passage of commercial traffic. And in a busy city like Strasbourg he would not have been short of customers.

His enterprise clearly prospered; by 1605 Carolus was in the position to diversify further by buying a print shop. He now conceived a plan to mechanise his existing trade in manuscript newsletters by producing a printed version. In a neat echo of Gutenberg and the invention of print one hundred and fifty years before, this was a logical response to a situation where increasing demand was straining the capacity of existing technology to deliver adequate quantities. But the investment costs, not least in buying his printing press, had stretched Carolus's resources, so now he turned to the city council for help. He told them that he had already produced twelve issues of his printed newsletter. But he obviously feared that if it proved successful others would try to copy him and wipe out his profits. So he asked the council to grant him a privilege – that is, a monopoly – on the sale of printed newsletters.[1] This was not unreasonable. Any entrepreneur who believed he had pioneered a new industrial or manufacturing process would seek protection against interlopers copying his innovation, and such privileges were common in the book world.[2] Carolus had good reason to hope that members of the Strasbourg city council, who made up a large part of his client base, would be sympathetic.

For an event of such momentous consequences Carolus's intentions were surprisingly modest. He merely sought a way to simplify a process that currently involved writing by hand an increasing number of copies, and thus to speed production. The output itself would not be essentially different: still the same sequence of bald news items familiar from his manuscript news service. But from this modest, rather tentative transaction emerged a new form of communication that would in due course transform the European news market: Carolus had invented the newspaper.

The Rise of the North

If Carolus did begin publishing his newspaper, the Strasbourg *Relation*, in 1605, the earliest issues are unfortunately all lost: the first surviving copies date from 1609.[3] For this reason many older histories of the newspaper will time its beginnings from this later date; it is only relatively recently that the full significance of the discovery in the Strasbourg archive of Carolus's petition to the city council has been appreciated.[4] That four complete years of the earliest issues have simply disappeared is not at all surprising. It is very rare to find a complete run of the earliest newspapers, and many are known only from a handful of stray copies: sometimes only a single issue survives to attest to a newspaper's existence.[5]

We can nevertheless be reasonably certain that Carolus did begin production in 1605. His petition to the council after all speaks of twelve issues already published. When we look at the first surviving copies from 1609, we see that these are certainly faithful to his stated intention that the newsprint would simply be a mechanised version of the handwritten newspaper. Individual issues have no title-heading: the title is given only in the printed title-page supplied to subscribers so that they could bind together the year's weekly issues. Instead the news begins, rather like the *avvisi*, at the top of the first page. In every respect the familiar pattern of the *avvisi* is retained: a sequence of news reports gathered by their place of origin and dated according to their date of despatch: 'From Rome, 27 December'; 'From Vienna, 31 December & 2 January'; 'From Venice, 2 January'. The order reflects the sequence in which the posts from these various stations arrived in Strasbourg. The contents were almost exclusively the same dry political, military and diplomatic reports that had dominated the *avvisi*.

In this respect the Strasbourg *Relation* set the tone for all the earliest German newspapers. Sticking closely to the model of the manuscript news-letter, the news-sheets adopted none of the features that made news pamphlets attractive to potential purchasers. There were no headlines and no illustrations. There was little exposition or explanation and none of the passionate advocacy or debate that characterised news pamphlets; indeed, there was little editorial comment of any sort. The newspapers also adopted none of the typographical features that helped pamphlet readers find their way through the text. There were no marginalia: in fact the only concession to legibility was an occasional line-break between reports. Although the news-sheets were soon being produced in very considerable numbers – a weekly edition of several hundred was not unusual – they made no allowances for the fact that new readers might not be so well versed in international political affairs as the narrow circle of courtiers and officials who had read the manuscript news-letters.[6] If readers did not know who the Cardinal Pontini recently arrived in Ravenna was (or even the whereabouts of Ravenna), the newsletters made no effort to explain.

For all that the new genre proved exceptionally popular. The Strasbourg *Relation* was joined in 1609 by a second German weekly, the Wolfenbüttel *Aviso*. This did introduce one notable innovation, a title-page, bearing a fine woodcut with a winged Mercury soaring over a landscape populated by busy news-bearers. This gave the Wolfenbüttel paper more of the appearance of a news pamphlet, but greatly reduced the space for news. Since the back of the title-page would also be blank, this left only six pages of an eight-page pamphlet for text. In the Wolfenbüttel case this was probably not crucial, since publication was almost certainly subsidised by the Duke of Wolfenbüttel-Braunschweig, a notable news addict. But this was less suitable for purely commercial ventures, which mostly followed the Strasbourg model of beginning the text immediately below the title-heading. All retained the quarto form familiar from the German news pamphlets and indeed the manuscript newsletters.

The new genre of news publication spread through the German lands very quickly. A weekly paper was established in Basel in 1610, and shortly thereafter in Frankfurt, Berlin and Hamburg. The outbreak of the Thirty Years War in 1618 stimulated a new wave of weekly papers, and a dozen new titles were published after the Swedish invasion of 1630. In the following decade a number of established papers, responding to the quickening of interest in public affairs, began to publish more than one issue in a weekly cycle. Generally these papers appeared two or three times a week, though in 1650 the Leipzig *Einkommende Zeitungen* ventured an issue every weekday. Print runs also increased rapidly. In 1620 the *Frankfurter Postzeitung* was published in an edition of 450; the Hamburg *Wochentliche Zeitung* may have printed as many as 1,500 copies. This was exceptional; the average print run was probably in the region of 350 to 400.[7] All told we can document the existence of around 200 titles published in Germany by the end of the seventeenth century: a total of some 70,000 surviving issues. Taking into account those that have been lost, this indicates a total output of around 70 million copies. With extraordinary rapidity a large proportion of the literate population of Germany would have had access to this new type of reading, particularly if we consider that these 200 newspapers were spread around eighty different places of publication. In the development of this new market the most significant steps were the establishment of newspapers in the two premier northern commercial centres of Frankfurt and Hamburg. The *Frankfurter Postzeitung*, founded in 1615, was the work of the remarkable Johann von den Birghden, the imperial postmaster.[8] It was von den Birghden who had been responsible for extending the imperial post network into northern and eastern Germany, notably with the establishment of the crucial arterial route between Frankfurt and Hamburg. The newspaper was very much a by-product of this activity. Sadly von den Birghden did not bring to publishing the same conceptual genius and attention to detail that characterised his work with the post roads: his newspaper is as conventional and undistinguished as the other earliest papers. He was, however, the first to call attention to the close connection between the post and the news in the title of his paper. Its contemporary success and wide distribution can be attested by its survival in almost thirty separate libraries and archives.[9]

The situation in Hamburg was rather different. This great commercial city in northern Germany was rather remote from the principal news arteries running along the imperial post route from Italy to the Low Countries. Necessarily the city had relied on its own messenger services, established since the medieval period, and by the sixteenth century a regular network of courier services connected the Hanseatic port with trading partners in the Baltic, the Low Countries and England. The founder of the first Hamburg newspaper, Johann Meyer, was heavily involved in the long-distance freight trade. Drawing on the connections developed from this business, Meyer had created a manuscript news service; rather like Carolus in Strasbourg, the establishment of his *Wöchentliche Zeitung auss mehrerley örther* was an attempt to mechanise this existing business. The potential for growth was, however, far greater in Hamburg, a great regional centre of trade and news, and Meyer's venture was very successful. The profits to be made soon sparked controversy with others in the Hamburg book world. In 1630 a consortium of booksellers

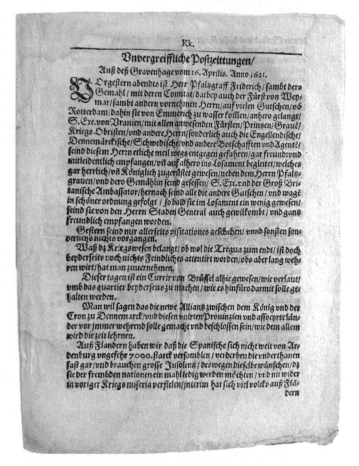

9.1 An early issue of the *Frankfurter Postzeitung*. The newspaper offers a good coverage
of news from northern Europe, especially the Low Countries.

and bookbinders challenged Meyer's right to sell the paper directly to his
customers. After submissions from both sides the city council determined that
Meyer could sell his paper retail for the first three days of the week; thereafter
it was to be made available to local booksellers in batches of one hundred for
9 pfennig per copy.[10]

Hamburg soon established a role as the supplier of news for the whole of
northern Germany; other regional papers were essentially reprints of texts
supplied from Hamburg, a fact explicitly acknowledged in the title of the first
Rostock paper, the rather confusingly named *Wöchentliche Newe Hambürger
Zeitung*.[11] Hamburg was also the first city in Germany where the potential
profits of newspaper publishing led to serious rivalry between competing
papers. In 1630 Meyer faced not only complaints from the local booksellers

but the emergence of a potentially serious challenge from a new imperial post-master, Hans Jakob Kleinhaus. This was at the height of imperial military success in the Thirty Years War and in setting up his own paper, the *Postzeitung*, Kleinhaus seemed determined to put Meyer out of business.[12] The dispute rumbled on until Meyer's death in 1634 when his paper was inherited by his redoubtable widow, Ilsabe. Her determination to maintain her livelihood found a sympathetic hearing with the city magistrates. In 1637 the council brokered a settlement. The postmaster's insistent claim to a monopoly of the press in Hamburg was refuted, but his exclusive use of the title *Postzeitung* was upheld. Still, Ilsabe was not yet finished. In this era it was common (and thoroughly inconvenient for students of the press) for proprie-tors to refresh the name of their papers quite frequently. If they moved to twice-weekly publication they would also often give the mid-week edition a separate title.[13] Ilsabe Meyer took to shadowing the changing title of the impe-rial paper to blur the distinction between them. When the postmaster renamed his paper the *Priviligierte Ordentliche Post Zeitung*, hers became the *Ordentliche Zeitung*.

Such commercial skulduggery reflected a perception at least that there was money to be made in newspapers. As Germany became for an extended period in the seventeenth century the fulcrum of European politics, the circles of those who felt they needed to keep abreast of the news grew ever wider. The urgency of events made for rich pickings in Germany's dispersed and dispa-rate reading communities. It was far easier to start a new paper, repeating news passed along the postal routes, than it was to import papers published elsewhere. But the elastic market and easy profits also served to reinforce the conservatism of the genre. The German newspapers of the later seventeenth century were remarkably little different in content or design from the earliest ventures. It would be in other parts of Europe that the most significant exper-iments of design and composition were seen.

The explosion of news print was, for all that, highly significant for the development of the European news market. It marked a very significant reori-entation of the European news world towards northern Europe. Up to this point the exchange of news had been dominated by the connection between the Mediterranean and the Low Countries, linked by the arterial route of the imperial post road. But the most important centres of newspaper production in Germany were far removed from the old imperial postal route: Augsburg, the German axis of the imperial postal network, spurned the newspaper revo-lution. Elsewhere in Europe, too, it was the northern powers that eagerly embraced the new invention. The centre of gravity of European information exchange had shifted decisively.

Stop Press

The first newspaper to be published outside Germany appeared in Amsterdam in 1618. Here, too, the industry would develop very rapidly.[14] In this period the newly independent Dutch provinces were concluding their swift progress to the first rank of European powers: Amsterdam would be the dynamic heart of this new economy. The city now inherited the economic and political hegemony enjoyed in the previous century by Antwerp and Brussels (which remained under Habsburg rule). Within two decades Amsterdam had also established a clear supremacy as the centre of the west European news market.

The first Dutch newspaper was a comparatively modest affair: a single broadsheet printed on one side only, with the news in two columns. In design terms this represented a significant departure from the German pamphlet form, though the news included in Jan van Hilten's *Courante uyt Italien en Duytsland* would have been utterly familiar. As in the German prototypes each sequence of reports was announced by a heading indicating the place of origin and date of the despatch: 'From Venice, 1 June'; 'from Prague, 2 ditto'; 'from Cologne, 11 ditto'. The issue concluded with a brief digest of news gathered from The Hague (here dated 13 June); presumably the sheet was published the next day.[15]

Van Hilten's concept proved extremely influential: the broadsheet in two columns became the prescriptive form for early newspapers in the Dutch Republic. In 1620 the mounting quantity of news obliged van Hilten to extend over to the reverse side of the sheet, but this generally proved sufficient. By this point he already faced competition. In the lively and loosely regulated book world of the United Provinces there was no question of a monopoly; already by 1619 Broer Jansz had set up his *Tijdinghen uyt verscheyde Quartieren* (*Tidings from Various Quarters*). Jansz was an experienced printer who had dabbled in contemporary history; he was also well connected, as he emphasised by styling himself 'couventier' to the Prince of Orange in the first surviving issue of his paper. For ten years van Hilten and Jansz shared the market. It was clearly lucrative; by 1632 van Hilten found it necessary to set up simultaneously on two presses to double the print run. In this way he could print more copies without extending printing time by a day, and thus risk missing the latest news.[16]

Late-arriving news was a perennial problem for publishers. However early on the day of publication they roused their workmen, it still took several hours to print several hundred copies, one pull at a time, and then the sheets needed some time to dry before the reverse leaf could be printed. The problem was only exacerbated as print runs grew larger. So when news came very late, van Hilten would stop the press and rearrange the text, deleting a story of lesser

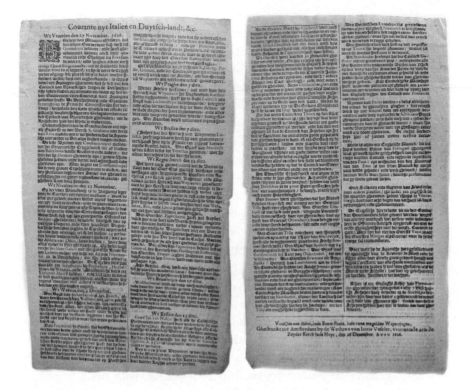

9.2 The first newspaper in the Netherlands. Unlike the German prototypes, both Amsterdam news men adopted a broadsheet format.

importance. If the new report required more space, he would either make further small adjustments or set the new text in smaller type.[17] Thus was the principle of 'stop press' invented.

From Amsterdam it was perfectly possible to distribute news-sheets over the whole of Holland, using the province's extremely efficient canal-boat network. Not surprisingly, though, other printers in the United Provinces were equally keen to take a share in the market. In 1623 a paper was established in Delft. This, however, was not what it seemed. A comparison of a weekly issue of the Delft news-sheet of 10 May 1623 with that of Broer Jansz two days before shows that 90 per cent of the Delft reports were lifted unaltered from the Amsterdam paper.[18] The first truly independent enterprise outside Amsterdam was established at Arnhem, near the German border. Here the local printer was encouraged to start a paper by the town council, who obligingly resolved to cancel their subscription for a manuscript news-service from Cologne and instead paid Jan Janssen 20 gulden a year to print one. This was generous. Janssen rose to the challenge and his was the first newspaper in the Netherlands to be printed with sequential numbering.

In Amsterdam the rage for news showed no sign of abating. By the 1640s the city sustained no fewer than nine competing titles: a news aficionado could find fresh news available on four days of every week.[19] Such competition encouraged a degree of innovation. The Dutch papers were the first to include advertisements. The Amsterdam papers also included, as the last substantial report before the advertising material, a section of news furnished locally. This was not in any genuine sense domestic news: rather it gathered up news from France, England and, from 1621, news from the front in the renewed conflict with Spain. This was relayed in a curiously dispassionate tone; there was little sign of the political debate raging in the contemporary pamphlet literature. This reluctance to be drawn into domestic politics was entirely typical of the early newspapers. Parochial affairs intruded only in the advertisements and public notices inserted by the municipality: the promise of reward for the return of stolen goods, the description of a wanted criminal. Here, for the first time, the newspapers descended truly to the level of the local.[20]

While the Amsterdam papers thus made tentative steps towards the accommodation of a broader range of materials, the larger proportion of space was devoted to the usual diet of battles, treaties and diplomatic manoeuvres.[21] The ordering of materials followed a traditional sequence, with news from Italy preceding news from the Empire and elsewhere. In this respect the Dutch folio sheets followed the German prototypes in sticking close to the template of the manuscript newsletter. For true innovation, which offered an attractive alternative vision of the future of news publication, we need to call in at the shop of a little-known figure from the southern Netherlands, Abraham Verhoeven.

Tabloid Values

Before he plunged into the market for current affairs Verhoeven had eked out an existence on the margins of the Antwerp book world.[22] While the firm of Plantin occupied its palatial buildings on the Vrijdagmarkt, Verhoeven sold his more modest merchandise, pamphlets, almanacs and prayer cards, from a shop in the Lombardenvest, a part of town inhabited by pawnbrokers and other small businesses. What propelled Verhoeven into the front rank of Antwerp's affairs was his attempt to exploit the heightened interest in current affairs in the early years of the Thirty Years War by creating a new topical serial devoted to publicising German and other international events.

Verhoeven was born into the trade; his father was a cutter of prints, who for three years worked in the Plantin workshop colouring engravings before they went on sale. After a long apprenticeship Abraham got his first major break as an independent artisan in 1605, when he offered on the market an illustrated print of the battle of Ekeren, a decisive victory for the southern Netherlandish forces over the marauding Dutch.[23] Verhoeven seems then to have survived mostly on jobbing work until 1617. In that year we see the beginnings of something more systematic and ambitious, with the publication of a sequence of pamphlets that combined a digest of topical news with a rudimentary illustration.

By now Verhoeven had developed the concept that would give him a dominant place in the Antwerp news market. It would blend his new activity as a publisher of news pamphlets with his established expertise as an engraver. But he was determined not to be undermined by competitors, or imitators: like Carolus in Strasbourg before him, Verhoeven appealed to the authorities for a privilege (or monopoly). On 28 January 1620 this was granted; Verhoeven was to have the exclusive right to publish news-books in Antwerp, or, as the privilege expressed it, 'all the victories, sieges, captures and castles accomplished by his Imperial Majesty in Germany, Bohemia and other provinces in the Empire'.[24]

This, in a nutshell, encapsulated Verhoeven's mission. His *Nieuwe Tijdinghen* would be a deliberate departure from the sober, neutral tone of the Amsterdam and German newspapers: essentially a propaganda vehicle for the local Habsburg regime. Verhoeven offered his readers up to three eight-page pamphlets a week: a torrent of wickedly committed, exultant reports of imperial victories and Protestant humiliations. These were not the sober miscellanies that German readers would expect for their weekly subscription. Verhoeven's pamphlets very often gave the whole issue to a single extended report, in the old pamphlet style.

It took Verhoeven a little time to arrive at a product with which he was entirely satisfied. In the early years we can see him experimenting with the best means of luring and keeping his audience. In 1620, the year he received his privilege, Verhoeven issued 116 news pamphlets: this year, we must assume, marked the beginning of his subscription service. But it was only in 1621 that he decided to make the pamphlets part of a numbered sequence, and to incorporate this numbering into the top of the title-page. By this time, too, Verhoeven had established the distinctive character of his news serials. They were distinguished, firstly, by a great deal more stylistic variety than the Dutch and German newspapers. Some issues of the *Nieuwe Tijdinghen* were, like other newspapers, given over to a miscellany of small items. Others were entirely occupied by a single despatch, or a couple of songs celebrating some imperial triumph. Publishing three times a week gave Verhoeven considerable freedom to entertain as well as inform his subscribers, but over the week they would probably have got much the same amount of news as subscribers to the Amsterdam papers. By giving up space for a title-page, and often repeating in full the privilege on the back page, Verhoeven greatly restricted the space for actual news: in any one issue the whole text would not exceed around 1,200 words. It was short, lively and easily digested.

Verhoeven's most distinctive innovation in the new world of newspapers was the illustrated title-page. The title for the issue of 16 December 1620, inevitably focusing on the events of the Thirty Years War, reads: 'News from Vienna and Prague, with the number of the principal gentlemen fallen in the battle'. The illustration bears the explanatory rubric, 'The fort of the Star where the battle was fought'. The sub-heading drives home the message of this Catholic victory: 'Frederik V has been driven away'.[25]

But for the heading declaring this to be part of a serial, it could have been one of the Antwerp news pamphlets published fifty years before, with its descriptive title, sub-title and jaunty woodcut. The title picked out the story most likely to interest readers – the origins of the headline – but this would not necessarily be the first report in the text, nor indeed the story that occupied most space. Thus the headline of issue 112 of 1621 focused on the burial of the recently slain imperial General Busquoy.[26] But readers would have discovered this only as a small report on page seven. The issue begins with a despatch from Rome, and proceeds through an earlier report from Vienna, then Wesel, Cologne and Cleves, before arriving at the Vienna despatch dealing with Busquoy. Nor was the woodcut illustration a particularly clear steer to the most important contents. In this case the illustration was a generic bastion fortress rather than a portrait of Busquoy (although Verhoeven had a variety of such portraits that he used many times).

Verhoeven was learning his trade as he went along, and keeping up a hectic pace. Happily, as his paper was an official venture Verhoeven could rely on a great deal of help. The well-known Catholic polemicist Richard Verstegen wrote for him often; the leading Catholic clerics of Antwerp were supportive.[27] Each issue carried the imprimatur of the local censor. For ten years Verhoeven kept up a relentless schedule of publication. There were a remarkable 192 numbered issues of the *Nieuwe Tijdinghen* in 1621, and 182 in 1622. Between 1623 and 1627 only once did the number fall below 140. These totals also do not take into account that demand for the paper often required Verhoeven to reprint certain issues: careful examination of individual numbers reveals small differences suggesting that the printer was frequently required to run off extra copies to meet demand.[28]

While the imperial cause prospered, so did Verhoeven. Yet in 1629 he suspended his pamphlet news serial, resuming a few months later with a more

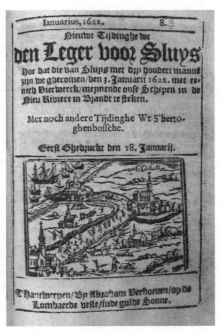

9.3 Verhoeven's *New Tidings*. The popularity of his serial news pamphlets was such that Verhoeven was frequently, as here, forced to reprint individual issues.

conventional weekly newspaper. What had precipitated this change is not certain. Perhaps demand was falling as the tide of war began to turn against the Catholic forces; and the Antwerp authorities were becoming tetchy. In February of that year the Council of Brabant instructed Verhoeven to desist from his 'daily' publication 'of various gazettes or news reports most incorrect and without prior proper visitation', a charge as unfair as it was inaccurate, given Verhoeven's almost slavish adherence to the Catholic and imperial cause.[29]

Perhaps Verhoeven himself was worn down by the relentless schedule of publication. Most early modern serials that relied on a single charismatic voice for success were of short duration, and by lasting a decade Verhoeven had outlived most such enterprises. It is certainly the case that the issues of the *Nieuwe Tijdinghen* were beginning to look a little tired. The woodcuts that Verhoeven had prepared for the first issues had now been used and reused many times over. And Verhoeven was running short of money. In 1623 he had written to the Antwerp city council to remind them that payment for their block order of 24 copies was seriously in arrears: he asked for 145 gulden to

clear the debt, but received only 50. In truth, Verhoeven never seems to have
been a particularly effective business manager. In 1625 he came into property
from his parents, but in the same year his wife fell ill, and her prolonged period
of invalidity, before she died in 1632, was a further drain on his resources.

So in 1629 Verhoeven announced the end of his *Nieuwe Tijdinghen*. A
month or so later he launched a weekly news pamphlet, the *Wekelijcke
Tijdinghe*. This was the response of a scared or defeated man. After the innovation, variety and energy of the *Nieuwe Tijdinghen*, this new enterprise was
merely a pallid imitation of the German and Dutch papers, a single sheet
folded once to make four pages with the same sequence of sober news reports.
But if Verhoeven thought this reversion to the norm would rescue his
fortunes, he was sadly misguided. The *Wekelijcke Tijdinghe* lasted less than
two years, its successor the two-page *Courante* only another two. In 1634
Verhoeven sold his business, and the paper, to his second son Isaac. The last
years of his life were miserable indeed: forced to live in rented accommodation, eking out a living as a day labourer in his son's workshop.

Verhoeven's vision, of a serial publication that combined the business
model of a newspaper with the familiar excitement and style of news
pamphlets, was by far the most interesting experiment of this transitional age
of news reporting. But it was not widely imitated. It would be two centuries
before the mixture of news, comment and blatant partisanship that characterised Verhoeven's work would make the leap from occasional pamphlets to the
newspapers. His tabloid values proved to be ahead of their time.

A Staple of News

By the last decades of the sixteenth century English readers had developed a
strong taste for news. As the country was drawn ever deeper into continental
warfare after the Armada campaign, London printers found a ready market
for translations of French and Dutch accounts of the wars.[30] In the first years
of the new century policymakers and gentry customers could also avail themselves of the first regular manuscript news services, edited by London
newsmen from continental sources.[31] The growing public interest in current
affairs was not viewed with any great warmth by the recently imported
Scottish king, James VI and I. The latter half of his reign, in particular, was a
difficult time for English foreign policy. The gathering storm in Germany
inspired widespread public enthusiasm for the Protestant cause. The cautious
king, unwilling to be stampeded into military action, had no wish that this
enthusiasm should be fuelled by incessant printed reports of the unfolding
situation. A proclamation of 1620 warned pointedly against 'excess of lavish

and licentious speech in matters of state'. Duly warned, the generally docile and submissive London printers drastically reduced their production of news pamphlets dealing with continental affairs.

It is therefore no surprise that the first serial news publication in English was published not in London but in Amsterdam. In December 1620 the enterprising Pieter van den Keere published the *Courant out of Italy, Germany etc.* This was a straightforward translation of the Dutch edition, published in the same single-sheet format.[32] It was sufficiently successful for van den Keere to maintain publication for the best part of a year. Success brought imitation: by 1621 several of these single-sheet 'corantos' were in circulation. The most successful, though prudently attributed to the Amsterdam firm of Broer Jansz, may actually have been printed in London, and from September 1621 the London publisher Nathaniel Butter was openly advertising his responsibility for what was in effect a continuation of van den Keere's series.[33] Several other London printers also re-entered the market with unnumbered pamphlet news-books.[34]

Rather than tolerate an unregulated free-for-all, the English authorities resorted to their preferred means of control: establishing a monopoly. This was awarded to Butter and Nicolas Bourne, who were now permitted to publish a weekly news-book provided it was submitted for prior inspection. The publishers would not be permitted to publish any domestic news or comment on English affairs. What was intended was a dry and fairly literal translation of the reports inherited from the continental newspapers.

While they accepted these conditions in order to kill off competition, Butter and Bourne soon demonstrated that they would bring to their task a keen commercial spirit. Butter was an old hand with printed news: news pamphlets, many of them with tales of sensational domestic murders, had made up a large part of the output of the print shop he had inherited from his father. Immediately Butter and Bourne converted their news-book back from the single sheet of the Amsterdam translations to the familiar pamphlet form.[35] Rather than follow the practice of the German newspapers, where the news followed immediately after the heading on the title-page, the English editors chose to imitate Verhoeven's Antwerp style (or that of their own earlier news pamphlets) where the title-page was occupied with a description of the contents.[36] Deprived of the opportunity to decorate their pamphlets with an expressive woodcut (this was not something that could easily have been furnished in London), Butter and Bourne instead allowed their title-page description of contents to stray down the whole page. Since this militated against a standard title, only the provision of a date and numbering reminded the reader that these were part of a serial.

Nor were Butter and Bourne prepared to replicate slavishly the contents of the continental news-books. At some point around 1622 they engaged the services of an editor, Captain Thomas Gainsford. Gainsford was the classic English adventurer. Driven by debt into military service, he had travelled extensively on the continent, ending with a period in the service of Maurice of Nassau. Like Nathanial Butter he was a passionate advocate of the Protestant cause. Returning finally to England, Gainsford embarked on a somewhat unlikely literary career, specialising in works of popular history. Butter, the publisher of at least one of these volumes, clearly thought of him as the man to add spice and zest to the rather lifeless reports inherited from the continental news-books.[37] In this Gainsford succeeded magnificently. The reports of troop movements and diplomatic manoeuvres were knitted together into a coherent narrative. Sometimes Gainsford would address the 'Gentle reader' directly, assuring him of the veracity of the reports and defending himself against any taint of partiality. These murmurings must have stung, for Gainsford was eventually moved to a spirited defence:

> Gentle readers, how comes it then to pass that nothing can please you? If we afford you plain stuff, you complain ... it is nonsense; if we add some [embellishment], then you are curious to examine the method and coherence, and are forward in saying the sentences are not well adapted.[38]

Nor could Gainsford concoct news if none were to be had. Readers must not be greedy, not 'look for fighting every day, nor taking of towns; but as they happen you shall know'[39].

Butter and Bourne faced one problem that did not impact on the continental news men: the English Channel. If the wind was adverse, or the sea shrouded in fog, the news reports could not get through, and the English news-books had nothing to report. So the English news-books do not observe the strict periodicity of their continental peers: a weekly issue was the clear intention, but the London paper had no regular day of publication. Even so it seems to have been widely read in London and distributed to the country by the regular London carrier services. Gentlemen readers took to enclosing corantos in their correspondence with friends.[40] Even the purveyors of the subscription manuscript news services recommended that their moneyed clients also read the printed sheets. John Pory put it rather loftily in a letter to John Scudamore: 'The reason [sic] why I would have your lordship read all corantos are, first, because it is a shame for a man of quality to be ignorant of that which the vulgar know.'[41] It is interesting that Pory did not regard the new printed medium as any sort of threat to his superior bespoke service; as on the continent, the two subsisted together.

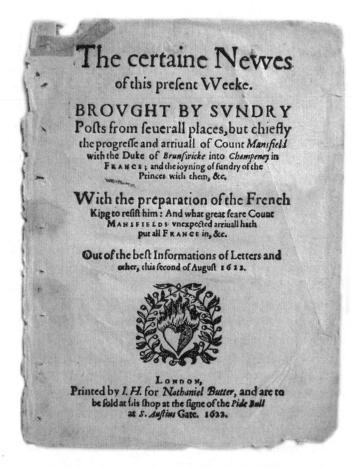

The certaine Newes
of this present Weeke.

BROVGHT BY SVNDRY
Posts from seuerall places, but chiefly
the progresse and arriuall of Count *Mansfield*
with the Duke of *Brunswicke* into *Champeney* in
FRANCE; and the ioyning of sundry of the
Princes with them, &c.

With the preparation of the French
King to resist him : And what great feare Count
MANSFIELDS vnexpected arriuall hath
put all FRANCE in, &c.

Out of the best Informations of Letters and
other, this second of August 1622.

LONDON,
Printed by *I. H.* for *Nathaniel Butter,* and are to
be sold at his shop at the signe of the *Pide Bull*
at *S. Austins* Gate. 1622.

9.4 Butter's news serial. Only later in this year did Butter begin to number the series.

Thomas Gainsford died in 1624 and was not replaced. Without him the news-books struggled to maintain their appeal. The printers adopted the non de plume *Mercurius Britannicus*, and gave their news-books a title that most usually began *The continuation of our weekly news*; but by this date the news for a predominantly Protestant audience was unremittingly bad, and this may have damaged sales. In 1625 Butter made a memorable appearance in Ben Jonson's *A Staple of News*, a brilliant satire on the craze for current affairs. Jonson's darts hit the mark, but he was, if anything, unlucky with his date. Not only was the craze declining, the play also pre-dated by a couple of years the most remarkable episode of the early history of English newspapers: an attempt to corral the newspaper trade as a propaganda vehicle for the Duke of Buckingham's assault on La Rochelle.

Heroes and Villains

In 1627 the Duke of Buckingham's public reputation was in sharp decline. Previously feted for his perceived role in saving the young Prince Charles from a Spanish marriage, when Charles became king in 1625 Buckingham became the whipping boy for every discontent. As the war with Spain teetered towards disaster, Parliament made a formal complaint against his influence. The favourite was fast becoming a national laughing stock. A group of fiddlers toured the country with a song of ironic praise for the duke, lauding his achievements: 'let us sing all of this noble duke's praise, and pray for the length of his life and his days'. The audience then joined in the chorus of refutation: 'the clean contrary way, O the clean contrary way'.[42]

Buckingham opted for decisive action: almost incredibly the regime responded to the failure of war with Spain by precipitating a simultaneous conflict with Europe's other great power, France. An expedition would be sent to assist the French Protestant minority at La Rochelle; Buckingham would lead it in person.

Buckingham was no general, but he did have a quite precocious view of public relations. Some years before, Thomas Locke and John Pory, both purveyors of manuscript news services, had suggested that the government capitalise on the appetite for news by creating their own paper. Their petition set out three potential benefits; it is a perceptive and prescient document. In times of crisis, they argued, a newspaper could help mould and direct public opinion; in more sober times newspapers could circulate the official viewpoint; thirdly, newspapers could raise morale and train the people to a habit of obedience. It was a remarkably forthright view of the benefits of a controlled press.[43]

At the time this went unheeded, and Butter and Bourne received the privilege, with uncertain results from the government's perspective. Now Buckingham resolved to do better. When the fleet sailed for La Rochelle, he could exercise complete control over reporting from the front; his despatches were sent back to London, and placed in the hands of a cooperative bookseller. The first issue of this new *Journal* cast the duke in a heroic mode, and clearly resonated with the public. A second was planned, but first the Privy Council had to deal with Butter and Bourne. This proved easy enough; the news-book printers had been slack in presenting their texts for censorship, and this provided the justification for hauling Butter off to prison. He was soon released but suitably warned, and *The continuation of the weekly news* henceforth confined its reports from La Rochelle to the tersest notes. This left the field clear for Thomas Walkley, Buckingham's instrument.

This exercise in war propaganda has received little attention, though it deserves more.[44] The progress of the expedition was charted in successive issues of the *Journal* that ran from August to November. The avid reader could hardly fail to be impressed by the swift progress of England's previously untrained forces, under the decisive yet chivalrous leadership of Buckingham. Casualties were light, and those who did fall victim to the unfamiliar temptations of the local wine were assured of expert medical attention. Buckingham, like Henry V before Harfleur, was everywhere. On the day of the landing 'the L. General was up and ready by three of the clock'. After a hard day's fighting he 'spent every evening visiting those that were hurt on our side'.[45] Even Buckingham's numerous critics at home began to revise their opinions of him.

In the short term these carefully prepared despatches could not have been more successful. But ultimately they could not disguise the military catastrophe that was unfolding on the Île de Ré, the fortified island that held the key to the assault on La Rochelle. The citadel held by the French could not be breached. Through strategic bungling half the troops involved in the final assault were cut off and mercilessly slaughtered. As the bedraggled survivors stumbled back to England, a shocked Privy Council imposed a news blackout on casualties; but the number of gentlemen who did not return told its own story. Buckingham had used the media so brilliantly to raise expectations of victory that the impact on his reputation of a surprise defeat was all the more calamitous. A year later he would be assassinated by one of the men he had led to disaster.

The chequered early history of the English newspapers had one final act. After the collapse of Walkley's *Journal*, Butter and Bourne were left to resume their monopoly. For a time, the news-books prospered. The Swedish intervention in the Thirty Years War had rekindled Protestant hopes, and placed ever greater scrutiny on the veracity of the reports received in this most turbulent era. Many, perhaps remembering the Île de Ré fiasco, may have prayed with the Reverend Christopher Foster:

to inspire the Coranto-makers with the spirit of truth, that one may know when to praise thy blessed and glorious name and when to pray unto thee. For we often praise and laud thy holy name for the King of Sweden's victories, and afterwards we hear that there is no such thing. And we oftentimes pray unto thee to relieve that same King in his distress, and we likewise hear that there is no such cause.[46]

For a time the news from Germany offered hope to Protestant hearts; too much, indeed, for the rather different spirit of Charles I. In 1632, following a complaint from the Spanish ambassador, the government instructed Butter and Bourne to cease publishing. Butter, a newsman through and through, remained in the market with works of contemporary history that were thinly disguised hymns to the Protestant cause.[47] Bourne, more wisely, diversified into other ventures. When the prohibition was relaxed in 1638, the revived corantos were soon overtaken by news-books devoted to domestic politics. Bourne, the businessman, was in due course elected master of the Stationers' Company, and prospered. Butter, the frustrated newsman, died a pauper.

Two Machiavellian Statesmen

For twenty years England made a lively and potentially innovative contribution to the early history of the newspaper. By the time English production revived in the years before the Civil Wars a dense network of serial publications extended from London through the Low Countries and across the German-speaking lands to Danzig, Prague and Vienna. Elsewhere in Europe serial publication did not enjoy the same success. The early newspapers were a geographically circumscribed phenomenon. Spain was a latecomer to the market in serial news publications, and this was true also of two of the three largest markets for print, France and Italy. In the case of Italy this was all the more striking as the peninsula had been the fulcrum of the European news network since the Middle Ages. In France the suppression of a market for news was a conscious act of state on the part of the most potent statesman of the age, Cardinal Richelieu.

Richelieu had no reason to love the press. His had been a backstairs career; a steady rise to eminence through carefully cultivated royal favour. His political apprenticeship had coincided with the turbulent minority of Louis XIII, a brutal struggle for power between the Queen Mother and successive favourites. This feuding at court spilled out into the streets in a torrent of frantic pamphleteering that reached its peak in the years between the summons of the Estates General in 1614 (the last meeting of this national assembly before the French Revolution) and the assassination of the hated favourite Concini three years later. Over a thousand political pamphlets were published in these years, many boldly contemptuous of those who struggled for supremacy at court.[48] The passions unleashed were truly terrifying in a nation apparently teetering on the brink of the resumption of the civil war that had scarred the country in the sixteenth century. Richelieu's first years in power were dominated by the last great Huguenot rebellion, finally resolved when the Protestant citadel of La Rochelle was reduced to obedience (the campaign in which Buckingham's intervention had proved so ineffective).

Richelieu was a keen student of the press. In his early career he had followed the political campaigning that accompanied the Estates General, and he ensured that the triumph of La Rochelle was marked by an intense flurry of laudatory pamphlets celebrating the Catholic victory.[49] Thus when the first weekly newspapers appeared in 1631, Richelieu was quick to see the benefit of bringing them within his orbit. These were not strictly speaking the first weekly news-sheets to be published in French. As in the English case, the Amsterdam news men had tried their hand with a French translation of the Dutch *Courante*, but it had lasted only a few issues.[50] When this paper folded it would be ten years before another French-language newspaper was established, this time in Paris. The *Nouvelles ordinaires des divers endroits* was the work of three experienced Paris bookmen, who sensibly employed a German, Louis Epstin, to shape the new venture.[51] It clearly found a ready audience, and this in turn encouraged competition. On 30 May 1631 there appeared the first edition of the Paris *Gazette*, the work of a man well known in Paris, though not in the printing fraternity: Théophraste Renaudot.

Renaudot was a rather unlikely newsman.[52] Born into a Protestant family in 1586, he was a star student at the famous medical faculty at Montpellier, attaining his doctorate at the age of twenty. Returning to his home town Loudun, in 1611 he was introduced to the local bishop, Armand de Richelieu. Renaudot immediately gravitated into Richelieu's circle. Appointed a royal physician in 1612, he followed Richelieu to Paris, converted to Catholicism, and was appointed to manage and reform the provision of poor relief in the capital. Well connected among the Parisian intellectual community, Renaudot had little experience as a printer. But when he tried his hand at a weekly news-sheet, sparking outraged protests from the publishers of the *Nouvelles ordinaires*, Richelieu saw the opportunity to take the nascent newspapers under his control. On 11 November 1631, by Crown decree, it was confirmed that Renaudot should have the exclusive right to print, sell and distribute newspapers within the kingdom.[53]

Renaudot moved quickly to press home his advantage. Epstin was induced to leave the Paris consortium to work for him; Renaudot even stole the title and published his own *Nouvelles ordinaires* as a supplement to the weekly *Gazette*. His competitors did not give up without a fight. They protested to the king that Renaudot's *Gazette* was little more than a translation of news gathered from foreign news-sheets. The *Gazette* may indeed have been professionally unadventurous, but at this point this was exactly what Richelieu wanted. In 1633 and 1635 Renaudot's exclusive privilege was confirmed, with ever harsher penalties for breach. The Paris consortium gave way.

The *Gazette* appeared every Saturday. Using three presses, Renaudot could publish an edition of 1,200 copies in a day, no mean feat since with the addition of the *Nouvelles ordinaires* the *Gazette* ran to twelve or more quarto pages. Although foreign despatches remained a mainstay, Renaudot began to offer in addition increasingly detailed reports of the king's activities, from Paris, Versailles or St Germain. It was here that the *Gazette* deviated most profoundly from the European norm, for in contrast to the dry detail of the foreign despatches, the news from court adopted a tone of worshipful adulation. Renaudot's glorification of the king was unrestrained and unremitting: France was blessed with a ruler of rare gentility, talent, courage and humanity. This catalogue of all the virtues extended of course to artistic talents: he performed at ballet 'with the delight inseparable from all the activities to which His Majesty applied himself'.[54]

The reality was that Louis XIII was never robust; the steady deterioration of his health in 1642, well known at court, was not touched upon in the *Gazette*. The same gushing deference was of course extended to Richelieu, to whom Renaudot exhibited unstinting loyalty. When Richelieu appeared before the

9.5 The Paris *Gazette*. Despite his previous lack of experience in the industry, Renaudot brought to the enterprise considerable flair and design sense. The *Nouvelles ordinaires* specialised in news from the Empire.

Parlement of Paris in 1634 to deal with the difficult issue of the king's brother's marriage, Renaudot was on hand to record his persuasive skills:

> His Eminence's unequalled eloquence, and the perfect knowledge he had of this material made the discourse so easy for him, that he spoke for nearly an hour. During which time one had never seen such attention, with the eyes of the entire assembly steadily fixed upon him, their ears set upon every word, and their bodies immobile, these were certain signs: as their unanimous applause was so far from any suspicion of flattery, it was their state of rapture which made him so able to gain the hearts of the entire audience.[55]

Beyond these oblations to power, and assured of the Cardinal's trust, Renaudot also found room in the *Gazette* for a wide variety of reports from abroad. After 1635 despatches from Germany took up increasing space, and Renaudot also kept his readers fully acquainted with the developing crisis in the English monarchy. The contrast with the stability of the French Crown was implicit, but helpful.

In such turbulent times the desire to be informed extended well beyond the metropolitan elite of Paris, and the *Gazette* was soon being pirated in provincial markets: in Rouen from 1631 and from 1633 in Aix-en-Provence. Rather than engage in costly litigation, or supply the market himself from Paris, Renaudot found a novel solution: he franchised the text of the *Gazette* to licensed provincial printers.[56] In return for a fee they published their own editions. Thus regional editions of the *Gazette* were established in Rouen, Lyon and Bordeaux. From these places copies could reach every corner of the kingdom. The accounts of a Grenoble bookseller, for instance, record him sending copies to clients in Die, Valence, Gap, Nîmes and Besançon. The voice of the court was heard throughout the kingdom.

This was shrewd as well as lucrative. By this system Renaudot ensured that none of the printers in the south of France, far removed from the close supervision possible in Paris, would be willing to chance their arm with their own newspapers. Thus it came to pass that a kingdom of close to 20 million inhabitants, with more than thirty established centres of printing, subsisted on a single weekly newspaper. So it would remain until the great rebellion of mid-century, the Fronde, temporarily suspended royal authority, and provoked a new storm of public debate.

The Fronde was, in essence, a shriek of pain by two groups who resented their exclusion from power during the minority of Louis XIV: the nobility and the Paris legal establishment. They focused their discontents on the minister who had smoothly adopted the mantle of Richelieu, Cardinal Mazarin. The campaign against him was conducted very largely in print, in a deluge of pamphlets; as many as 5,000 in the three years of the conflict, including 3,000 in the year 1649 alone.[57] No wonder one of these titles offered ironic thanks to Mazarin for making so much work for printers: 'Your life is an inexhaustible subject for authors, and indefatigable for printers. . . . Half of Paris is either printing or selling these books, the other half is writing them.'[58] These pamphlets had everything: wit, oratory, passion, even a talking horse.[59] Yet even while, in this moment of crisis, printers reached for the pamphlet, the traditional safety valve of major news events, they were still keen to appropriate for these works the new nomenclature of the periodical press. Thus there was a flurry of pamphlet *Couriers* and *Journals*, the odd *Mercury*, and even one optimistically titled *Disinterested Gazetteer*.[60] Small hope of that. Like all the rest, this title was an excoriating denunciation of Mazarin and all his works:

> Aristotle tells us that some are good by nature, some by doctrine, and some by custom. Cardinal Mazarin demonstrates that he is of a fourth type, since he could only be good by a miracle.[61]

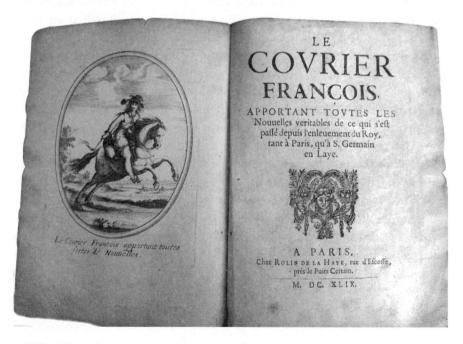

9.6 The *Courier françois*, which flourished briefly during Renaudot's exile from Paris.

Amongst this pamphlet fury there was one attempt to establish a genuine serial to replace the suspended *Gazette*. Renaudot, no doubt with some reluctance, had been forced to follow the king to St Germain, leaving an opportunity for some enterprising Parisian printer to fill this gap in the market. The result was the *Courier françois*, which went through twelve issues in 1649, and several reprints.[62] It was once thought that this was the work of Renaudot's two sons, left behind in Paris by the gazetteer to continue his business. This seems unlikely. Even in the slippery world of news publishing it is improbable that a man who had benefited so freely from royal patronage would have attempted to serve both the king and his opponents simultaneously.[63] In any case as soon as Paris was restored to royal control Renaudot moved to suppress the new rival. This tussle also found its echo in the pamphlet literature, in a piquant booklet entitled *The commerce of news re-established, or the Courier suppressed by the Gazette*.[64] Not everyone in the Paris trade was pleased; but Renaudot retained the king's confidence, and that was decisive. The *Gazette* re-emerged, with its monopoly intact, to chronicle the foreign triumphs of France's armies in the reign of Louis XIV.[65]

The logic of monopoly seems also to have attracted another powerful mind, Paolo Sarpi in Venice. In the early years of the seventeenth century Sarpi had built a reputation as a gifted writer, notably as a defender of the city against Cardinal Bellarmine in the Interdict Controversy of 1606–7.[66] Reflecting on these events a decade later, and aware of the growing market for printed news in other parts of Europe, Sarpi at first believed that Venice should grasp the nettle and make its own case to an informed public. The best strategy, he argued, was to create one's own narrative of events, and thus crowd out false or unhelpful intelligence. But this raised the danger that any information in the hands of the subject could lead them to develop their own opinions on political affairs. When the subject becomes politically informed,

> He gradually begins to judge the prince's actions; he becomes so accustomed to this communication that he believes it is due him, and when it is not given, he sees a false significance or else perceives an affront and conceives hatred.[67]

All in all, this was best avoided. 'Everyone confesses,' was Sarpi's reluctant conclusion, 'that the true way of ruling the subject is to keep him ignorant of and reverent towards public affairs.'[68]

Sarpi was remarkably frank, but the sentiments he expresses here seem to have been the prevailing view in Italy's largest cities. Neither Rome nor Venice, the two great centres of European news publication, produced newspapers. The first experiments in serial publication were in much smaller places and started remarkably late. Newspapers were established in the 1640s in Genoa, Naples, Bologna and Florence. As was the case in Germany, they were often the work of men who ran an existing manuscript news service, or of printers whose output included news pamphlets. None seems to have achieved great success. The early Italian newspapers have none of the typographical boldness and clarity we associate with early Italian printing. The first Bologna paper offered a cramped digest of news on a single folded sheet of cheap paper. As late as 1689 the newspaper of Mantua had a print run of only 200 copies, and, even so, 'there are always some left over that are not sold, but instead are given gratis to the chancery, to the ministers, and to others'.[69]

Why did the Italians not embrace the newspaper more warmly? The answer lies partly in the continuing success of existing news media. Crises in the peninsula, such as the Interdict Controversy and the revolt in Naples, could stir up a storm: Italian printers could certainly respond to great events. But for the everyday of political life and court intrigue the manuscript newsletters retained the loyalty of their subscribers. In Rome and Venice, communities that lived on gossip and private intelligence, a confidential news service remained an absolute necessity. The manuscript newsletter possessed a subtlety and flexibility lost in a public printed document. Throughout the seventeenth century Italian newsletter writers retained the distinction between their normal manuscript service and 'secret' sheets they would provide to especially favoured customers. These offered comment on prominent public figures with a frank and brutal disregard for the reputations of the great that would have landed any printer in prison, or worse. It was also relevant that both Rome and Venice were magnets for ambitious young men of talent and education. This created a pool of cheap scribal labour that allowed news writers to build workshops of considerable size. If these writers were well informed, the profits to be made from a confidential news service outran that possible from a printed newspaper many times over.[70]

The sheer triviality of these breathless reports was occasionally remarked upon. 'You who after silly tales are lusting, anxious to hear rumours and reports, quickly, run and look at the gazettes, and see if the news is good, fine or disgusting': so wrote one jaundiced Paduan pamphleteer.[71] But whatever the protestations of the fastidious, gossip remained the lifeblood of Italian politics, and news not fit to print was the most valuable of all. Then, as now, those in the thick of it took these tiny hints of shifting power with deadly seriousness. Who was up, who was down, who had snubbed whom; was the Cardinal's leaving Rome to take the waters a genuine sign of ill health, or a pretext to hide his disgrace? Of such was political life in Machiavelli's homeland. Perhaps, for those who cared, it disguised the unpalatable fact that real power had shifted to elsewhere in Europe.

The first age of the newspaper was a period of profound but constrained experimentation. The new invention flourished in a comparatively small part of the European land mass and, even here, the dry and rather routine reporting of faraway events does little to quicken the blood of a modern reader. We can find some interest in the different solutions to the design and practical problems of serial publication, but, this apart, what had been achieved by the first tentative steps in the creation of a regular printed news service? Here, examining the short, often rather grubby surviving issues, it is easy to be too dismissive. Contemporaries certainly valued them very highly. We should not belittle the English squire, or the citizen of Amsterdam or Dresden, poring over their paper, trying to make sense of the shifting kaleidoscope of faraway events. No doubt perusal of the weekly newspaper required frequent recourse to an atlas, another increasingly necessary adornment of a well-stocked library. Undoubtedly it was by no means easy to determine whether the clipped reports of campaigns and manoeuvres brought news that was good, bad, or even very interesting. But if much news was ill-digested, there is no doubt that by placing it in so many hands the newspapers of the seventeenth century achieved a double broadening of political consciousness: they increased the numbers of the politically aware, and they expanded their worldview. Newspapers also began to build in their readers a habit of news. Great events would still unleash a storm of pamphlets, full of engaged advocacy, but in quieter times readers came to value the steady miscellany of information that arrived with the newspaper. For many in the seventeenth century, and for the price of two pence a week, it was an affordable habit. In the years ahead, it would increasingly become an addiction.

CHAPTER 10

War and Rebellion

I N 1618 the edgy, brooding truce that had kept the peace in central Europe
for over seventy years stood on the brink of collapse. A resurgent Catholic
activism had caused Protestants to fear that the liberties guaranteed by the
Peace of Augsburg in 1555 would not be long maintained. The prospect that
the Emperor Matthias would be succeeded by his much more militant cousin
Ferdinand stirred anxiety in the Habsburg lands, particularly in Bohemia
where Protestants were a long-standing majority. The crisis came to a head in
Prague on 23 May 1618, when Protestant deputies from the Czech Estates
confronted loyal imperial regents. After angry exchanges two prominent
imperial officials were hustled to a high window of the castle and hurled
through it. Their unfortunate secretary was tossed after them.

Miraculously, all three survived the sixty-foot drop. The victims landed on
a pile of refuse and were able to stagger away, largely uninjured. For the
Protestants of Bohemia this unexpected denouement was an ominous portent
of ill-fortune. For the Emperor's supporters, on the other hand, the survival of
the defenestrated officials offered a remarkable propaganda coup. News of
their escape circulated swiftly around Europe, though presumably not
everyone believed the excited accounts of reported bystanders who claimed
that they had seen the Virgin Mary intervene to cushion the fall.[1] The victims
themselves were grateful enough for the providential dung-heap.

The defenestration of Prague would usher in thirty years of warfare that in
due course drew in almost all of Europe's major powers. It was immensely
destructive for Germany, and led to permanent shifts in the European power
structure. It was also the first European conflict to be fought in the full glare of
the new news media. The Thirty Years War erupted only a few years after the
introduction of the new postal routes linking northern Europe to the imperial
system, and the establishment of the first newspapers. It would be a remarkable

test for the capacity of the new communications network to provide news and analysis to Europe's anxious and suffering peoples. These developments, of course, were not confined to Germany. By the time Protestant and Catholic powers were finally brought to the negotiating table, new conflicts, the Fronde in France and the British Civil Wars, were testing the capacities of the new media to incubate opposition and marshal opinion. This was an age in which news media sought a wider public, and where a wider public was desperate for news. The impact would be profound and long-lasting.

From Prague

In the years after 1618 those waiting anxiously in Europe's capital cities for news of events in Germany would have many occasions to praise the industry of Johann von den Birghden, the imperial postmaster of the newly established station at Frankfurt. For it was von den Birghden who had personally ridden to Prague to see to the placement of the postal stations that connected the imperial capital to the German postal network and thus linked up the rest of Europe, through Frankfurt, to the tumultuous events in Bohemia.[2] With the defenestration of Prague the Bohemian Revolt had passed the point of no return. By throwing off Habsburg allegiance and electing the Protestant Frederick of the Palatinate as King of Bohemia in place of the deceased Matthias (August 1619), the Protestant Estates ensured that only military conflict would settle the issue. These extraordinary events provoked the customary rash of celebratory or disapproving pamphlets: many offered a remarkably serious and measured response to the constitutional crisis in the Empire, which had now entered uncharted waters.[3] The war was also the first test of the new weekly newspapers. Since 1605 the printed news-sheets had been set up in at least half a dozen towns, and this would double in the first years of the struggle.

One of the first reports of the defenestration of Prague appeared in the *Frankfurter Postzeitung*. Citing a despatch from Prague dated 29 May (six days after the event), the paper accurately reported that all three victims had survived, but was mistaken as to their names.[4] The next issue of this paper does not survive, so we cannot tell whether it published a correction. Although mistaken in some of the particulars, the sober tone of the reporting is utterly characteristic. Correspondents wrote as they would for their fellow diplomats and officials. They made no concessions to the fact that these reports might, through the newspapers, reach a wider public: they felt no duty to explain, to sketch the background, or introduce the persons named. The journalistic instinct to popularise and enliven reports of current events that we have witnessed in the sixteenth-century pamphlet literature is entirely absent.

The German newspapers of these years also carried reports from both sides of the developing conflict, with little attempt to differentiate or slant them towards the likely allegiances of their readers. In the circumstances of an increasingly bitter and bloody conflict such an unpartisan spirit could not endure. In 1620 readers in Hamburg, Frankfurt or Berlin could read reports from Prague and Vienna that would, in the case of the Bohemian despatches, speak of 'our King Frederick' or 'the enemy', whereas the Viennese despatches in the same issue offered a loyally imperial perspective.[5] An even more clearly differentiated market emerged with the establishment in 1622 and 1623 of newspapers in the confessional citadels of Vienna and Zurich. The first generation of German newspapers had all been established in the cities of north and central Germany. Thanks to the efficiency of the new postal routes, news entrepreneurs in these cities had access to a full range of reports from all the main stations of European politics. In contrast Matthias Formica, the founder of the first newspaper in Vienna, had no correspondents in Protestant areas: he would hardly have been able to print in the Habsburg capital their eager accounts of the usurpation of the Bohemian Crown in any case.[6] The Zurich newspaper also developed into a highly partisan organ on the Protestant side. But even that paper could do little to disguise the scale of the calamity that was unfolding. Disappointed in his hopes of support from other major Protestant powers, the newly elected King of Bohemia, Frederick of the Palatinate, was swiftly deposed by one Catholic army, while another laid waste to his Rhineland territories.

Faced by this rampant Catholic power, publications elsewhere in Germany also began to choose their words more carefully. This was not, it should be said, the result of any aggressive action by their own local rulers. In 1628 the city council of Berlin examined the printer of its own local paper after some grumbling from Vienna about the nature of its reporting. The printer protested that he simply published incoming reports as he received them, without altering a single word. This statement of general practice was accepted as reasonable, and no further action was taken.[7]

Merely to keep abreast of the extraordinary events of these years was a sufficient challenge for the first printed news-sheets, which seldom, even with the most dramatic news from the battle-front, deviated from the established format of four or eight closely written pages of sequential reports from the leading news centres. As the Catholic forces moved to consolidate their battlefield victories, with the deposition of Frederick and the investiture of Maximilian of Bavaria with his former Electoral title, even the pamphlet literature struggled to find an adequate response. Anxious commentary on the constitutional implications of the erosion of liberties guaranteed by the Confession of Augsburg did little to deter the Emperor from pressing home his advantage. For a true expression of the passion and confessional fury of these years we need to turn to another news medium: the resurgent trade in illustrated broadsheets.[8]

10.1 The Bohemian war, here described in sequential illustrations.

Lampooning the Winter King

In the sixteenth century broadsheets had tended to avoid political subjects: their major function was as a vehicle for the spreading of sensational news: lurid crimes, misbirths, miraculous apparitions and the like.[9] The sole exception was their role as a polemical tool in the Reformation conflicts. As this might imply, in the sixteenth century the polemical broadsheet had largely been a Protestant medium.[10] The major centres of woodcut production were in cities, like Nuremberg and Augsburg, where the evangelical movement had made an early impact, and Martin Luther's followers soon employed the skills of these artists to build support for the new movement and heap ridicule on the Pope. Just before the outbreak of the Thirty Years War the first centenary of the Reformation had prompted a new wave of pious images of Luther and other fathers of the Reformation.[11]

Now, in the early seventeenth century, stimulated by the potent political events in Germany, the broadsheet would demonstrate its full potential as an instrument of political propaganda. This was the golden age of the illustrated broadsheet: in place of the woodcuts of the sixteenth century, publishers made increasing use of copperplate engraving, which allowed for greater fineness of detail.[12] Later in the century, as the market declined somewhat, the woodcut would return as more sophisticated customers abandoned the broadsheet. But in the period of the Thirty Years War political broadsheets found an eager audience among precisely the same sophisticated urban clientele who were fuelling the growth of the newspaper.

In the first years of the Bohemian conflict printers in the Protestant cities cheered their customers by teasing and goading the Jesuits, newly expelled from Bohemian lands.[13] The Jesuits were widely blamed on the Protestant side for the new militancy among the Catholic leaders, and they remained a target for Protestant antipathy throughout the war. The woodcut artists also developed a neat allegory with Frederick, the new Protestant hero, tending and healing the Bohemian lion, wounded as it fought its way clear of the Habsburg thicket: a rather charming re-imagining of the well-known tale of St Jerome with the lion, presented here in an evocative strip cartoon.[14]

All this changed in the most dramatic fashion with the Protestant defeat at the battle of the White Mountain (8 November 1620). The humiliation of the Protestant armies, followed by the ignominious flight from Bohemia of Frederick, now contemptuously dubbed the 'Winter King', represented a complete reversal of fortune, and Catholic writers were quick to drive the message home. Celebrations of the Catholic heroes were accompanied by an outpouring of scorn for the Protestant leaders. A particularly popular cartoon shows a post boy riding through Europe seeking the missing Winter King; the woodcut, accompanied as ever by mocking verses, shows the perambulation as a sort of primitive snakes and ladders board.[15] The motif of the Bohemian lion is now reversed: caught in the act of assaulting the imperial eagle, it is mauled by the Bavarian bear, a reference to the leading role of Maximilian of Bavaria as Catholic champion.[16] This was a true cartoon, in that it scarcely needed the accompanying verses to make its point: indeed, a number of editions were published with no text at all. Another delightful cartoon showed the Protestant leaders gathered round a table in pointless inactivity while the Marquis of Spinola systematically reduced the Rhineland strongholds in Frederick's former Palatinate.[17]

Like many cartoons this was not an unfair statement of political reality. Concerned at their own individual vulnerability and divided by confessional and dynastic rivalries, the Protestant princes did little to contest the inexorable Catholic advance. Their own presses could offer little to raise the spirits, beyond a few sour and superior remarks about the quantities of useless print in circulation.[18] In 1621 the city of Nuremberg stripped the previously favoured engraver Peter Isselberg of his citizenship when he was unwise enough to publish in this Protestant citadel a polemical broadsheet against the Winter King, but such vindictiveness could do little to stem the tide.[19] The desire to blame the messenger is evident also in the first of a long series of lampoons against news-writers, accused of satisfying a gullible, news-hungry public with false reports. True or false, the news for the Protestant cause was unremittingly bad. A decade of military disaster came to a calamitous climax when in 1631 the armies of the imperial general Count Tilly stormed the city of Magdeburg and put it to the sword. A staggering 85 per cent of the population of this iconic Protestant citadel (the heartland of resistance to the Emperor a century before) lost their lives in the sack and ensuing fire.

The horror of Magdeburg shook even the weekly news-sheets out of their customary dispassionate detachment.[20] Newspapers on different sides of the confessional divide took contrasting perspectives. The Munich *Mercurii Ordinari Zeitung* offered a pious celebration of the Catholic victory. According to their report, probably derived from sources close to Tilly, the calamitous fire had been started by the Swedish troops defending the city, determined to deprive Tilly's troops of their plunder.[21] On the Protestant side the full horrors of the sack were captured by a highly rhetorical report from the Stettin *Reichs-Zeitungen*:

The heat was such that the inhabitants lost their courage, and there arose a screaming and lamentation so terrible that it defies description. To save their children from the enemy mothers threw them into the flames and then hurled themselves into the fire.[22]

Other heart-rending personal tragedies were told and retold in a cascade of publications, mostly, it must be said, published in Protestant cities. Catholic presses were relatively subdued; the scale of the civilian casualties seems to have diminished any triumphalism. Such a catastrophe proved also, perhaps happily, beyond the powers of the woodcut artists. Representations of the city's destruction were mostly conventional topographical battle scenes. Only a few cartoons make rather coy and inadequate reference to Tilly's rough wooing of a (fully clothed) maiden Magdeburg.[23] It was left once again to the pamphlet literature to tell the full gruesome story and draw the appropriate morals: for many Protestants, this was not only a tale of Catholic barbarity, but also a warning that only repentance and obedience to God's will would turn away His wrath.[24]

The Lion of the North

The German Protestant cause was by 1630 in a desperate position: the prospect of a reversal of fortune seemed hopelessly remote. Thus when the Swedish King Gustavus Adolphus offered himself as a new champion, the punch-drunk German princes initially held back. It is hard to blame them: the previous intervention by a Lutheran monarch, Christian IV of Denmark in 1625, had resulted in total fiasco, with the occupation of most of his lands by Catholic troops and the potential establishment of Albrecht von Wallenstein as the ruler of a new Habsburg satellite state in northern Germany. So when Gustavus Adolphus landed at Peenemünde in July 1630, even the carefully orchestrated symbolism of his arrival on the hundredth anniversary of the Confession of Augsburg could not persuade the German princes to risk another tilt against the might of Habsburg arms.[25] John George, Elector of Saxony, the pivotal leader of German Lutheranism, was especially reserved. It was only when Tilly turned from the destruction of Magdeburg to invade Saxon lands that John George was forced to embrace the Swedish alliance. The result was a crushing Swedish victory at Breitenfeld (17 September 1631). Within months the Swedish armies had occupied much of Germany.

Swedish military success had a transformative effect on the German news world. The shock of Breitenfeld, the first significant Protestant battlefield victory of the entire conflict, led to a predictably ecstatic outpouring of celebratory literature on the Protestant side. Many woodcuts were published of the

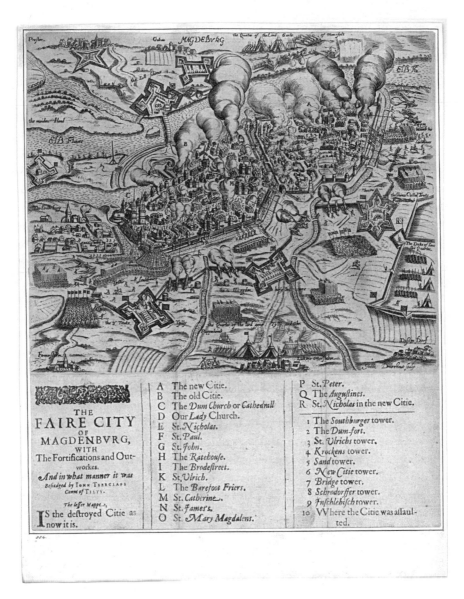

The legend of the map reads:

MAGDEBVRG

THE
FAIRE CITY
OF
MAGDENBVRG,
WITH
The Fortifications and Out-
workes.
And in what manner it was
Besieaged by IOHN TZERCLAES
Conte of TILLY.

The lesser Mappe,
IS the destroyed Citie as
now it is.

A The new Citie.
B The old Citie.
C The *Dum Church* or *Cathedrall*
D Our *Lady* Church.
E St. *Nicholas.*
F St. *Paul.*
G St. *John.*
H The *Ratehouse.*
I The *Brodestreet.*
K St. *Ulrich.*
L The *Barefoot Friers.*
M St. *Catherine.*
N St. *James's.*
O St. *Mary Magdalens.*

P St. *Peter.*
Q The *Augustines.*
R St. *Nicholas* in the new Citie.

1 The *Southburger* tower.
2 The *Dum-fort.*
3 St. *Ulrichs* tower.
4 *Krockens* tower.
5 *Sand* tower.
6 *New Citie* tower.
7 *Bridge* tower.
8 *Schrodorffer* tower.
9 *Infchlebifch* tower.
10 Where the Citie was assaul-
   ted.

10.2 The tragedy of Magdeburg.

battle, and the most popular illustrative response made ironic reference to the purported reply of John George when Tilly demanded right of entry to Saxon lands prior to his invasion. 'I perceive that the Saxon confectionery, which has been so long kept back, is at length to be set upon the table. But as is usual to mix it with nuts and garnish of all kinds, take care of your teeth.' Now a sequence of mocking cartoons pictured a bloated Tilly trying with evident discomfort to digest the German sweetmeats.[26] Other cartoons mocked Catholic confidence before Breitenfeld with a pair of woodcuts that show, first, a post messenger bringing news of a Catholic victory, before in the second the same messenger, now limping and wounded, reveals the true state of affairs.[27]

The Swedish victory was transformative also in the sense that by their control of most of the German land mass the Swedes also controlled the news network. The Thurn and Taxis imperial postal service was now hopelessly disrupted. The arterial route between Brussels and Vienna could only be maintained by a long southward diversion to avoid enemy-controlled territory. Gustavus Adolphus filled the gap by establishing his own postal service, based on Frankfurt. To run it he recruited the erstwhile Frankfurt postmaster Johann von den Birghden, whose position had fallen victim to the increased confessional tensions of the late 1620s. In 1628 von den Birghden had been dismissed on the spurious grounds that his weekly newspaper had been filled with false reports prejudicial to the imperial cause.[28] His career in ruins, there was no reason for von den Birghden not to throw in his lot with Gustavus. Within a few months this remarkable man had restored the postal routes to Hamburg and Leipzig, and established two new itineraries. One led to Venice through safely Protestant Zurich; the other via Metz to Paris, to keep Gustavus in contact with his nervous and wily ally Cardinal Richelieu.[29]

The period of Swedish dominance of German affairs was short-lived. In the spring of 1632 Gustavus resumed his apparently inexorable conquests, pressing deep into Bavaria and occupying Munich. Protestant allies were regaled with many exuberant cartoons featuring a rampant lion chasing a now chastened Bavarian bear.[30] A popular woodcut showed Gustavus surrounded by topographical views of the cities conquered by the Swedes: this went through many editions, as it had to be so frequently updated.[31] A popular scatological alternative showed a bloated Catholic priest, forced to regurgitate the fallen cities back into Protestant hands.[32] This year, 1632, represents the absolute high point of German political broadsheet production. A total of 350 recorded items are known, many of which survive in numerous copies. This is unusual for such ephemeral material, and is a sure indication that they were assiduously collected at the time they were first published.[33]

The rising tensions between Gustavus and his Protestant allies remain unexpressed in the Protestant broadsheets, which instead continue to heap ridicule on the hapless Tilly. But when the armies next faced each other, at Lützen in November 1632, the Swedish victory was bought at a high price: Gustavus Adolphus, the Lion of the North, was fatally wounded. Initial reports in the newspapers reflect the complexity of this bloody and indecisive

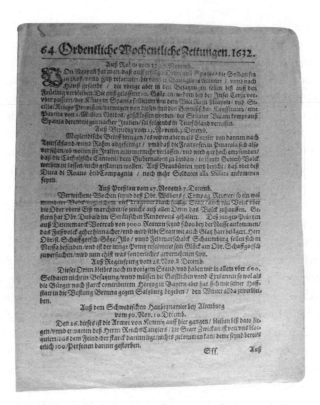

10.3 Von den Birghden in the service of the Swedes. Aside from the new postal routes, von den Birghden also resumed his newspaper. Note here the prominence of news from the Swedish headquarters.

engagement. Even when the outcome was known the Protestant papers were extremely reluctant to acknowledge that their champion had fallen. The confusion of the moment is captured by a Silesian paper which in eight pages carries three reports of the battle, printed in the order they came to hand. The first states quite correctly that Gustavus is dead; the second qualifies this with doubts; and the third, on the final page, declares that he is still alive and continuing the campaign against the remnants of Wallenstein's army.[34] Like a surreal modernist film where the narrative unfolds in reverse, these reports encapsulate the difficulties that still attended contemporary news gathering, particularly from the war zone.

The death of Gustavus Adolphus did not end Swedish involvement in the war. Management of the Swedish armies passed to Axel Oxenstierna, the administrative genius behind the logistical triumph of Swedish arms, and he successfully steadied the ship. But Swedish policy increasingly stressed dynastic and strategic priorities rather than the Messianic mission that had fuelled the cult of Gustavus. Even after the catastrophic defeat of Nördlingen in 1634 the Swedes fought doggedly on to preserve a north German territory to bolster their aspirations to hegemony in the Baltic. The clarity of purpose that had characterised the conflict in the years 1630–2 now disappeared. In 1634 news publications recorded without regret the assassination of Wallenstein, an increasingly uncontrollable free agent put to death on the orders of his former imperial master. In 1635 France declared war on Spain, a conflict that would be pursued very largely in a campaign for Rhineland security. Catholic fought Catholic and increasingly Protestant fought Protestant: at the battle of Wittstock (4 October 1636), the great Swedish victory that arrested their decline in influence, their beaten opponents included the forces of Lutheran Saxony.

It was no surprise that an exhausted public yearned for peace. The ravaged German territories were precipitated into an extended economic decline. The printing industry and the news networks were both badly affected by the economic disruption. Production of political broadsheets declined rapidly, but enough remained to record the progressive disengagement of the German states from the wars on their territory. In 1635 the Lutheran states made peace with the Emperor. In 1643 the foreign powers were persuaded to join them in negotiations to end the war and resolve outstanding territorial claims.

The process of peace-making was agonisingly slow. Protestant and Catholic would not sit down together, so the Catholics met at Münster, and the Protestants at Osnabrück. Questions of precedence and procedure consumed most of the first year, a maddening overture perfectly satirised by a brilliant cartoon which shows the plenipotentiaries as dancers, manoeuvring for a better position.[35] To facilitate the negotiations and consultation with absent principals, several new postal networks were established. The imperial postal service, successfully restored after the Swedish defeat at Nördlingen, established direct lines between Münster and Linz, and between Münster and Brussels. This was the achievement of the redoubtable Alexandrine de Rye, widow of Leonhard von Taxis, who had taken over the management of the imperial post after her husband's unexpected death in 1628.[36] She ran the post for eighteen years, presiding over a restoration of the family fortunes which ensured that the Taxis would continue in possession of the postal privilege until their replacement by the Reichspost in the nineteenth century. Several of the other powers represented, including the Dutch United Provinces and Brandenburg, established their own direct courier service to Osnabrück. At last, in 1648, sufficient progress had been made to declare peace.

The Peace of Westphalia brought to an end thirty years of an immensely destructive conflict. The repeated incursions of even more disorderly armies had taken a terrible toll on the fabric of German life. Some regions had lost over half their population, and would take generations to recover. So it seems strange to celebrate the extraordinary creative energies of the German news media in these years. Seventeenth-century Germany did not produce a Dürer or a Cranach, but its publishing entrepreneurs conjured from the tribulation what was, with the political broadsheet, a substantially new news medium.

For all that, the story told by these illustrated prints would be a very partial one. The execration of Tilly can be contrasted with an almost total neglect of Wallenstein. Whereas Gustavus Adolphus is celebrated in literally hundreds of prints, to go by the political broadsheets the Danish incursion of 1625 need hardly have taken place; the same could be said, very largely, of the French intervention after 1635.

How can one explain these disparities? The explanation must be that broadsheets play a particular role in news culture. They do not warn of a looming or present danger, as was certainly the case, for instance, with contemporary pamphlets. The pamphlet writers expressed their outrage at Frederick's acceptance of the Bohemian Crown; the cartoonists joined the fray only when he was ignominiously defeated. On the other side Tilly became the object of mockery only when he was humbled, not when his forces were victorious; the chorus of praise for Gustavus was unleashed only when he had won his first victory. Cartoonists, it seemed, prospered by sharing with their purchasers the moment of relief after the danger was past. Seventeenth-century satirists were by and large wise after the event: they restrict their praise or opprobrium to what has already happened and is already known.

In this respect the political broadsheets make a psychologically complex contribution to the media of news: never in the front line of criticism, always cheering from a safe distance. Whereas pamphleteers often took risks to espouse a cause, political broadsheets liked nothing more than to pummel a political figure already destroyed by events; and that, judging by the evidence of the broadsheets' popularity, also appears to have coincided with the preferences of their readers.

The Dam Bursts

If the first rule of politics is that you should be lucky in your enemies, then nowhere was this more triumphantly vindicated than for the initially small band who found themselves in opposition to the Stuart kings of England. While James VI of Scotland had been grudgingly accepted as the least bad solution to the question of succession after the death of Queen Elizabeth, his son Charles was almost preternaturally devoid of political skill. From his search for a Catholic wife to his assault on the traditions of Parliament and the Church of England, the policies of Charles I seemed designed to coalesce a truculent but generally obedient people into defiance. A man whose idea of public relations was to commission a new portrait by Van Dyck, Charles naturally totally missed the significance of the new news media. First he confirmed the right to produce newspapers as a monopoly; then he banned them altogether; then he restored them just in time (1638) for them to be a pillar of the opposition gathering against him.[37] Since the king also punctiliously upheld the prerogatives of the Stationers' Company of London against provincial interlopers, he also ensured that his rebellious capital would start the war with a near monopoly of the printed word.

In England the Civil Wars marked a long-delayed coming of age for the printing industry. For much of the sixteenth century the market was simply too small to sustain more than a modest and rather conservative range of titles, particularly as English readers continued to look to European imports for scholarly books in Latin. English printers were tied to the vernacular trade and dependent on the Crown for much of their work; the industry was almost entirely confined to London. Although Londoners shared in the general European thirst for news, much of it initially came in the form of translations of pamphlets first published in French or Dutch. In the 1620s London joined the European fashion for weekly news-sheets, and manuscript news services established a foothold. But it was only in the 1640s that the English press came into its own.

If Butter and Bourne imagined that the restoration of their corantos monopoly in 1638 would recover their fortunes, they were to be disappointed. Events had moved on. Their diet of despatches from the continental wars no longer met the public's expectations: readers had more urgent domestic concerns. The attempt to impose an Anglican settlement on the reluctant Scots brought the first armed confrontation and further isolated King Charles from a perplexed and anxious political nation. In 1640 all eyes were on Westminster, where the king's reluctant recall of Parliament catalysed the nation's discontents. The urgency of constitutional debate led to the production of a new type of serial publication, the rather misleadingly entitled 'diurnal' (or daily). These offered a weekly summary of events in Parliament with an account of each day's business. These diurnals were circulating in manuscript throughout 1640, but it was only in November 1641 that the first was published as a printed serial newsletter.[38] The diurnals struck an immediate chord with the reading public, and by the end of 1642 more than twenty independent publications had been published using *Diurnal*, or some variation, in their title.[39] The most successful and enduring was the *Perfect Diurnall of the passages in Parliament* of Samuel Pecke, an experienced editor of manu-script news-sheets and a pioneer of the new trend towards domestic news.

This resumption of serial news was significant, but not a major constituent cause of the unfolding political drama. The diurnals appeared in print only towards the end of 1641, the year that put the conflict between king and Parliament beyond peaceful resolution. Here, as in earlier conflicts, it was pamphlets that drove forward the political debate. The decisive years before the outbreak of the Civil War were accompanied by a torrent of publications. The output of the press grew almost fourfold between 1639 and 1641, and reached its peak in 1642 with almost four thousand published works.[40] Most of this increase can be accounted for by political pamphlets. We can chart the dramatic events of the crisis of 1641 through successive pamphlet surges: the trial of the Earl of Strafford; the attack on Archbishop Laud; the fear of Catholic plots.[41] The Irish rebellion stimulated a rash of hard-hitting publications, some with illustrations graphically describing the torments suffered by the Protestant settlers.[42] The feverish, vituperative tone of this literature reached new heights, for England at least. The pitiless hatred directed towards Strafford and Laud, the gloating descriptions of Strafford's descent into Hell, were matched by an increasingly martial tone in the calls for the defence of true religion. Though the fighting was only irrevocably joined when the armies squared up at Edgehill in 1642, the shedding of blood had been eagerly anticipated many times over in the angry, vengeful and virulently sectarian pamphlets of the previous year.

In contrast to the tone of the pamphlet literature, the diurnals may seem rather staid and cautious; nevertheless they represent a quiet revolution in the European news world.[43] For this was the first time that regular serial publications had been devoted primarily to domestic events. Secure in their command of England's only substantial print centre, Parliament embarked on a conscious effort to engage the political nation. Parliamentarians had imbibed the insight of Paolo Sarpi, that the informed subject 'gradually begins to judge the prince's actions', but had drawn the opposite conclusion: that this was desirable. In the years to come, Parliament would make conscious and effective use of its command of the London press, ensuring that its acts and proclamations were known in all parts of the kingdom under its military control.[44]

For royalists this posed a challenge almost as daunting as the military conflict. Having withdrawn from his rebellious capital in January 1642, Charles I finally recognised that a more active policy of public engagement was necessary if he was to challenge the overwhelmingly hostile use of print. The establishment of a press in cities loyal to the king did something to redress the balance, leading in 1643 to the foundation of a weekly news journal devoted explicitly to the royalist cause: the *Mercurius Aulicus*.

This, again, was an important moment in the history of newspapers: the beginnings of advocacy journalism.[45] To this point the periodical press had struggled to demonstrate its relevance to the conflict. Although 1642 had seen a rash of new titles, most had ceased publication by the end of the year. This set the pattern for the period as a whole. More than three hundred ostensibly serial publications were founded between 1641 and 1655, but the vast majority (84 per cent) published only one issue, or a handful of issues.[46] This makes the point that contrary to what we might imagine from this great burst of creative energy, these were not optimum conditions for the publication of newspapers. Papers needed stability: to build a subscription list it was always best to avoid giving offence, which risks providing the authorities with a pretext to close the publication down. This was hardly the temper of the times in these turbulent decades. News serials, with the address of the seller prominently displayed, were sitting ducks for retribution. Pamphlets, on the other hand, could be published anonymously, and increasing numbers were.

The *Mercurius Aulicus* was very different.[47] It offered a serial commentary on events, abandoning the clipped sequence of brief reports characteristic of news reporting to this point in favour of longer essays scorning and goading the king's enemies. The ammunition for many of its articles was drawn from other news-books. When it came to the actual reporting of events the journal frequently fell short. The calamitous royalist defeat at Marston Moor, which opened the way for Parliament's eventual military triumph, was first reported as a victory: 'Great newes' from York proclaimed the *Mercurius Aulicus* in its issue of 6 July 1644. It had received 'certain intelligence that the rebels are absolutely routed'. The following week it was forced into a humiliating retraction, albeit with the grumpy accusation that the Parliamentarians had deliberately held back the true report.[48]

At another level, though, the *Mercurius Aulicus* was very successful. It certainly did a great deal to stiffen the sinews of the king's supporters, and irritate his enemies. When a consignment of five hundred copies was intercepted by Parliamentary forces, this was reported almost like a military victory. In the summer of 1643 Parliament set up its own advocacy serial, the *Mercurius Britanicus*, explicitly to counter the influence of *Mercurius Aulicus*.[49] This journal also had the distinction of launching one of the seventeenth century's most remarkable journalistic careers.

Marchamont Nedham was a naturally gifted writer.[50] His combination of impassioned advocacy, biting wit and an easy, flowing literary style was exactly right for these troubled times. For successive issues he went head to head with *Mercurius Aulicus* and landed some heavy blows. A natural risk-taker, Nedham was bold and outspoken, and occasionally he strayed over the limits of what was permissible even in this extraordinary period. In 1645, after the king's defeat at Naseby, he fabricated a jocular 'Wanted' notice which made a crude reference to Charles's stutter.[51] Parliament took action, sending both the printer and the censor, who should have spotted this, to prison. Nedham was let off with a reprimand, a clear recognition of how valuable he was perceived to be to the Parliamentary cause. The *Mercurius Britanicus* was soon back in business, having missed only a single issue.

10.4 The arraignment of *Mercurius Aulicus*. This piece of Parliamentary wish fulfilment, with Sir John Birkenhead in the pillory, demonstrated the extent to which the king's propaganda vehicle had hit home.

This incident may have given Nedham too elevated a sense of his own importance, because the following year he was in trouble again, this time for an editorial describing Charles as a tyrant. He went to prison, but incarcerating Nedham for a symbolic fortnight did not have the desired effect. Tiring of his old employers, Nedham now made his apologies not to Parliament, but to the king; and Charles, incredibly, hired him to write for royalist publications. In the well-named *Mercurius Pragmaticus*, this versatile journalist now denounced Parliament and its Scottish allies for their conspiracy against the monarchy, and excoriated those pressing towards the rebellion's astonishing conclusion: the trial and execution of the king.[52]

The execution of King Charles I in January 1649 sent shock waves around the European news world. The reading publics of Germany, Holland and France were fascinated that the new citizen masters of England could bring their quarrels to such a conclusion. Continental readers hungered after details

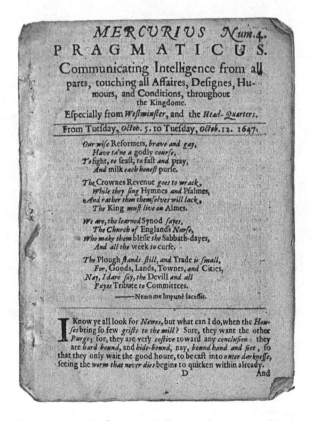

10.5 *Mercurius Pragmaticus*. Marchamont Nedham in the service of the king.

and explanations.[53] Pamphlets and above all illustrations of the execution were printed and reprinted in many countries.[54] In England itself the situation was very different. The century's most extraordinary news event produced a comparatively subdued response. This was partly because the defenders of England's ancient liberties ensured that this should be so. In February the House of Commons, reduced to a Rump by Pride's Purge of the previous year, responded furiously to pamphlets distancing their previous Presbyterian allies from the execution. An Act for the better regulation of printing imposed draconian financial penalties on those who 'shall presume to make, write, print, publish, sell or utter, or cause to be made, printed or uttered, any scandalous or libelous books, pamphlets, papers or pictures whatsoever'. Such regulations were not new: Parliament had already passed censorship measures in 1642, 1643 and 1647.[55] What is most striking is the new emphasis on regulating visual imagery, no doubt inspired by the awareness that there was no more striking image than that of a decapitated king. What Parliament could not control was the extraordinary popularity of the *Eikon basilike. The pourtraicture of his sacred majestie in his solitudes and sufferings*.[56] This purported to be the king's own account of events since 1640, interspersed with his prayers and meditations. It was a publishing sensation, with thirty-five English and twenty-five continental editions in its first year alone. At last, if rather too late, the Royalists had discovered the secret of successful propaganda.

The Parliamentary authorities had at least succeeded in tracking down Nedham, who in June 1649 was consigned to Newgate Prison. This provided the opportunity for deep, if uncomfortable, reflection, and in 1650 Nedham re-emerged into the public eye to announce his conversion to republicanism.[57] The Council of State had clearly got his measure. In May they determined his future journalistic efforts should be rewarded with a salary of 100 pounds a year. Thus encouraged, Nedham presented the prospectus for a new newsbook, the *Mercurius Politicus*. The flippant, ironical tone of his previous editorials would be replaced by serious essays extolling the virtues of the Republic. Nedham worked closely with John Thurloe, head of the Republic's office of intelligence, whose incoming mails provided an excellent source of foreign news. This took on a renewed importance when England descended into open warfare with the Dutch Republic (1652–4), events that were reported much more fully than Cromwell's final exasperated dismissal of the Rump Parliament (April 1653). When in 1655 the Cromwell regime closed down all but two of the London papers, both the survivors, *Mercurius Politicus* and its midweek stable-mate, *The Publick Intelligencer*, were being run by Nedham.[58] With an effective monopoly on sales and advertising revenues, Nedham was well on the way to becoming a rich man.

Nedham's frequent intellectual conversions and brazen exchange of loyalties have been harshly treated by historians. But these were strange times, and contemporaries who contemplated the deluge of print recognised them as such. It was a significant moment of transformation in the English news industry. The serials, pamphlets and official publications; the hiring of professional writers and sympathetic printers; the manipulation, suppression and embroidering of news; the censorship, controls and punishment of dissidence; all of this reflected a recognition that an unusually engaged public had to be cajoled and persuaded. But no one for a moment thought that this would go on indefinitely. All of those involved recognised this engagement with the public as a facet of an emergency, to be regretted rather than celebrated.

Cromwell's steely suppression of opposition voices might have seemed hypocritical, and was certainly denounced as such by Royalists and disillusioned former allies. But most would have grudgingly acknowledged that they would also have celebrated victory by stilling the cacophonous voices stirred up by the Civil War. Certainly the restored monarchy thought as much. The kingdom's liberation from Republicanism in 1660 was followed by a swift crackdown on the press. The chaotic year and more between Cromwell's death in 1658 and the return of Charles II witnessed a steady revival of polemical literature, this time increasingly dominated by supporters of monarchy. An expiring, exhausted regime had few friends; the merciless press that had once hunted Strafford and Laud now found new fiends on which to unload its venom, and atone for their own guilt. These new scapegoats were the regicides, those who had signed the death warrant of the now sainted king: in the autumn of 1660 those excluded from the new king's gracious pardon were hauled to a grisly execution, hounded and mocked by the popular prints. The public desire for news had found a voice, but not yet a sense of humanity.

Printed Pandemonium

The Dutch Republic was the phenomenon of the seventeenth century. Even its enemies, and they were many, could only marvel that a small province, almost destroyed by the struggle for independence in the sixteenth century, could have been transformed into Europe's most prosperous state: and all this without a king.[59] The rebellion begun in 1566 was only formally concluded in 1648, when Philip of Spain finally conceded that the northern part of his empire was irrecoverable. By this time, and despite a near constant state of war, the young Republic had turned itself into Europe's most advanced economy. It was the Continent's leading centre of international trade, home to the most sophisticated market in stocks, banking and insurance. It was

Europe's leading shipbuilding centre. Inevitably, it was also a major hub of news.

The new Republic had eagerly embraced the opportunities of the periodical press. By the 1640s Amsterdam had ten weekly newspapers published on four different days of the week.[60] The young Republic also took a keen interest in the affairs of its neighbours. The English dispute between king and Parliament was closely followed in Holland, with numerous translations of republican and royalist polemic made available to a new audience in Dutch translation.[61] Like much of the economy the printing industry fed off the easy availability of investment capital, and the unusual difficulty of imposing restraint: a publication forbidden in one city could usually be put to the press in another of Holland's towns.

All of this feverish economic activity came at a price. The economy was prone to extravagant fluctuations as surplus capital sought an outlet. The most famous example of this was the tulipmania of 1632, the first major economic crisis of the newspaper age.[62] The ruthless treatment of business rivals, exhibited here and in foreign trade, sat uneasily with the pious tone of public life. Religious solidarity cut little ice where there were markets to be protected. The Dutch were notoriously brutal colonists, and fickle allies. In 1672 all of these chickens came home to roost. Brilliant, opulent, ruthless and self-righteous, the young state suddenly found itself utterly without friends.

The crisis that engulfed the Dutch Republic unfolded very quickly. In March 1672 Louis XIV concluded the military alliances that left the Republic isolated and encircled. Lingering hopes of English friendship were dashed when the English navy attacked the returning Levantine fleet. In April France and England declared war. Despite a desperate but indecisive victory over the English at Solebay off the coast of Suffolk on 7 June, the inadequate Dutch land forces were swiftly overrun by Louis XIV's regiments, Europe's most professional army. Soon the landward provinces were in French hands, and Utrecht surrendered without a fight. The very survival of the nation was once more in doubt.

The collapse of Dutch military forces and the advancing French armies set off a tidal wave of popular fury. In July the republican regents of Holland, divided between defeatism and those who wished to fight on, bowed to popular pressure to install William of Orange as Stadtholder of Holland. The enemies of the discredited republican regime now took their revenge. On 4 August the Grand Pensionary, Jan de Witt, who had been wounded by a knife attack on 21 June, resigned his office. Three weeks later he and his brother Cornelis were set upon in The Hague, beaten, stabbed and shot to death. Their bodies were then dragged to the public scaffold, mutilated and dismembered.

Nothing like this had ever before been witnessed in Holland. The public lynching of two of the Republic's leading citizens was a drastic repudiation not just of their regime, but of the civilised values that had characterised this pros- perous bourgeois society. The critical moments of the drama could soon be relived in the dramatic sequence of engravings by Romeyn de Hooghe, a sympathetic witness to the brothers' violent end.[63] These ghastly events and their aftermath also stimulated a torrent of pamphlet literature. The most recent scholarly study of the print history of these episodes enumerates 1,605 pamphlets, of which 996 were original writings, and only 609 reprints.[64] Most of these were crowded into a very short period of intense activity between April and August 1672. The campaign engaged a remarkable range of authors, and a wide cross section of the publishing industry. Eighty-six different printing houses were involved in Amsterdam alone. This was not a campaign shaped by rival Orangist and regent factions. Rather, what we see is a highly literate, politically active citizenry responding to unusual events in a situation where the already lax censorship of the Dutch Republic was completely unhinged.

This was a political crisis fought out on the streets and in print: but the relevant print medium was the political pamphlet rather than the newspapers. There were several reasons for this, and this case study, like those above, serves as a sobering verdict on the early newspapers' real impact on public affairs. Firstly, fifty years after their first introduction, newspapers were still not geared to the production of domestic news. This was partly due to the heavy weight of tradition with its roots in the manuscript news service, but this was not always the case: the news-sheets re-established in England in the 1640s played a noisy and partisan role in the political debates of the Civil War and Interregnum. The real reasons newspapers played such a modest role in domestic political debate on the Continent were largely structural. The fixity of form gave little flexibility to respond adequately to great events. The unvarying sequence of reports from abroad left little room for commentary. This suited both producers and regulating authorities for a number of reasons. Foreign news provided sufficient copy to satisfy their customers and fill their pages. It also minimised risk. The publishers of newspapers were naturally inclined to caution and stylistic conservatism, partly because those in authority were their best customers, partly because any overbold diversion into commen- tary could lead to retribution. The publisher of a serial had always to think of the next number. He could be sure his text would be carefully read, given the nature of the client base. If he caused offence, he was a sitting target. The only safe strategy was a position of strict political neutrality. That way, when the storm abated, the newsman hoped still to be cranking out his weekly digest, safe from the fear of retribution.

For all of these reasons a pamphleteer could be far more adventurous than a newspaper proprietor. A pamphleteer could take risks, could be funny, abusive and outspoken, and cash in on the public mood. If things changed – if he had misread the political runes or boldly swum against the tide – he could move on. Many political pamphlets were in any case published anonymously, whereas a newspaper, frequently sold out of the printer's shop, had to be published with an address, so that potential purchasers could find it and subscribers knew where to send their payments.

By the middle decades of the seventeenth century, newspapers had established an important role in the political education of a diverse readership. But they were always likely to be overwhelmed by truly extraordinary events, such as those in the Dutch Republic in 1672. Quick-moving events could not necessarily be accommodated by the fixed weekly schedule of publication, and raised passions that demanded wordy advocacy, of the sort that could not easily fit within the confines of a subscription news-sheet. In much the same way the weekly news-sheets played little part in the Fronde, the enormous upheaval of revolt and political protest that swept away the press regime constructed by Richelieu, and, temporarily, his newspaper instrument, the *Gazette*. As in the Netherlands, during the Fronde it was pamphlets – the notorious *Mazarinades* – that bore the major burden of articulating the ideology of protest.[65] Only in England had the Civil War pointed the way towards a more active political role for the serial press. And it would be here, in the succeeding half century, that the newspaper would take its most giant strides towards the centre of the political stage.

CHAPTER 11

Storm in a Coffee Cup

So we return to Daniel Defoe, whom we left many pages ago scribbling away at his *Review*. After many failed ventures and several public humiliations – including bankruptcy and a spell in the pillory – this was make or break for Defoe. So he wrote and wrote, for anyone who would pay; and in the febrile period between the deposition of James II in 1688 and the contested Hanoverian succession there were plenty who would. In 1707 he spent a whole year in Scotland seeking to persuade the Scots that the abolition of their Parliament would bring nothing but good.[1] Journalism and advocacy were becoming inextricably blurred.

These were turbulent times and in the latter half of the twentieth century they would pique the interest of a distinguished German sociologist, Jürgen Habermas.[2] Habermas fixed his gaze on Defoe's London, and in particular its coffee shops. Coffee had been introduced into Europe very recently, and nowhere with greater éclat than in England, where coffee drinking became all the rage. Within a very few years there were scores of coffee houses, where the reasonably prosperous came to be seen, to converse, gossip and exchange news.[3] Observing these seething, cheerful houses of commerce and communication, Habermas discerned a new type of popular engagement, something he described as a public sphere: an articulate, engaged political class with the freedom and leisure to participate in political debate. Defoe, as we have seen, thought much the same. For him, too, this was a crucial moment in the birth of political opinion.

Seen in the longer perspective the claim to an entirely new form of participatory politics seems less plausible. We have uncovered plentiful evidence of the thirst for news in the centuries before coffee, and the birth of a lively market to slake this thirst. Defoe was of course also performing the salesman's eternal trick, of spicing the dish for new customers. But even setting this aside, was he perhaps right? Was there something genuinely new incubated in the coffee culture of the late seventeenth century that amounts to a step change in the history of news?

Creatures of the Sun

At this point it is worth remembering that London, though a growing metropolis, still occupied a somewhat peripheral role in Europe's news networks. We need to find out whether the new news environment envisaged in England can also be discerned elsewhere. What, for instance, of France, Europe's largest state and greatest military power? Here, in contrast, we observe the persistence of a remarkably controlled and supine press. The Fronde, the great rebellion of mid-century, had only briefly banished the carefully constructed news apparatus of Richelieu and Mazarin. The rebels had failed to find common cause, and their demands proved too amorphous and confused. Gradually, painfully, royal authority was restored, and by 1652 Mazarin had returned, ruling now on behalf of an adolescent who aspired to greatness, Louis XIV.

The age of the Sun King would not be a great age of the newspaper. The restoration of order required a restoration of Renaudot's monopoly; the *Gazette* resumed publication.[4] As the young king grew to adulthood, the kingdom would gradually be trained to accept a new type of royal self-image.

11.1 A coffee house.

In 1654, Louis, now fifteen, formally entered into his majority with a solemn coronation at Reims. When Mazarin died seven years later, Louis made clear that he would now rule without a first minister. In the cult of monarchy that was now constructed around Louis, the power and majesty of the king were proclaimed by a systematic exploitation of a wide range of cultural resources.[5] The galaxy of talented artists, writers and playwrights assembled by Nicolas Fouquet, Mazarin's right-hand man, was transferred to the service of the king. Louis's praises were sung in prose and verse, in French and Latin. The theatre celebrated a new Alexander, and sermons encouraged comparison with the sainted founder of the French monarchy, St Louis. At Fontainebleau, and later at his new palace of Versailles, Louis lived at the centre of an increasingly ornate and carefully choreographed ceremonial, where access to the king's presence was the climax of an ascending hierarchy of privilege.

The culture of Versailles fascinated contemporaries, and it has shaped the image of the Sun King then and since. But only a tiny proportion of the population would attend the king at court, see his portrait, or enjoy the sycophantic outpourings of court poets and theatrical performances. Carrying the king's image out into the provinces – where, despite the cultural supremacy of Paris, 95 per cent of the population still lived – was a more difficult task, and one to which the regime gave only fitful attention.

In the early years of the king's maturity, when Louis's armies carried all before them, victories became the occasion for national celebration. Royal officials were mobilised to sponsor spectacles, feasts and public events that echoed those occurring in the capital. But there would not always be victories; the first flush of success had already faded when Louis's ministers gave instructions for a large equestrian statue of the king to be placed in the public square of all France's main cities. This attempt to bring some of the grand architectural majesty of the new kingship to the furthest reaches of the kingdom met with a mixed response. Several less than grateful communities successfully combined loud protestations of dutiful obedience with ingenious procrastination to delay erection of the statues for many years.[6]

Cities like Bordeaux, Toulouse and Lyon were sophisticated communities in their own right. If they were to be fully engaged in the cult of the king, this could only be achieved through the medium of print. In the second half of Louis's reign a conscious effort was made to bring an ever larger number of France's provincial cities into the orbit of the national press. The system developed by Renaudot under Richelieu, franchising reprints of the *Gazette* for local production, was greatly expanded. In addition to the established local editions at Lyon, Rouen, Bordeaux and Tours, a further sixteen cities published editions of the *Gazette* between 1683 and 1699; the War of the Spanish Succession between

1701 and 1714 brought a dozen more into the network.[7] In each case a copy of the Parisian edition was carried down the postal routes to the licensed local bookseller; the day of publication depended on the efficiency of the post. Thus the *Gazette* published each Saturday in Paris could appear on Sunday in parts of the Paris basin, but only on the following Thursday in Bordeaux, Lyon and La Rochelle.[8]

This remarkable system was unique in Europe. In no other state was a monopoly preserved for a single official paper published and reproduced in up to thirty different locations. Through all of this time the *Gazette* remained a faithful mouthpiece of official policy. The heirs of Renaudot (the privilege would remain in the family until long into the eighteenth century) were not about to risk their valuable franchise by courting official displeasure. So the dry, factual tone of the foreign despatches, which continued to occupy much of their column centimetres, would be varied only to laud the king and all his doings. In the sensitive years after Mazarin's death the *Gazette* took pains to call attention to the king's diligence in the performance of his duties. Even when Louis went hunting, this was presented as a well-earned respite from a life of ceaseless toil: 'the care which his majesty takes always with affairs of state, with a marvellous assiduousness'. When Louis led his armies in the field, the *Gazette*'s admiration reached a new crescendo. 'See how victory and glory take pleasure to load their crowns on the head of our magnanimous king' was the *Gazette*'s triumphant reaction to the campaign in Holland in 1672.[9] Louis took with him on campaign not only his court ladies, but artists and writers who could, in their different ways, do justice to the greatness of his deeds. The dramatist Jean Racine, Louis's historiographer royal, was one who doubled as a war reporter, sending back despatches from the siege of Namur in 1687. The tone of the despatches that resulted can be judged by this extract from the *Gazette*, reporting the siege of Maastricht in 1673:

> Continue to follow in the footsteps of the greatest monarch in the world! See the wisdom with which he gives his orders, the energy with which he goes to where his presence is necessary, the indefatigability with which he works day and night and the steadfastness of soul with which he confronts dangers. Enter, with his majesty, into the trenches and follow him in his most martial actions where the most self-assured tremble before his intrepidness.

The editors prided themselves that such a lifelike description might even stimulate anxiety in some of their more imaginative readers, as if they were on the field of battle with their king. They were to be reassured: 'Have no fear you will not be any less safe from peril than you were previously and you will not witness all these objects of everlasting admiration elsewhere than in the present continuation of the journal of this famous siege.'[10]

The *Gazette* was a remarkable initiative, but its success in moulding French opinion was probably quite limited. Only a relatively small number would have read these effusions. Figures for print runs are, as ever, elusive, but it is thought that the four provincial editions in 1670 comprised in total only 2,500 weekly copies. By 1700 the twenty-two editions, serving smaller areas, published together around 7,000 copies. Taking into account the larger Paris edition, this suggests a total output of around 4,000 weekly copies in 1670, and around 9,000 at the later date: and this was the sole newspaper serving a large population of around 20 million inhabitants.[11] The contrast with the more diverse news markets of England, Holland and Germany is instructive.

The *Gazette*'s role as a willing mouthpiece for Crown policy made for testing times during the latter years of Louis's reign, when the tide of warfare turned inexorably against the king. In the War of the Spanish Succession a brutal series of defeats from Blenheim (1704) to Malplaquet (1709) shattered the aura of Europe's most professional army. Little of this appeared in the *Gazette*. By this time the various branches of the French bureaucracy were monitoring the paper with some care. In 1708 the editors were rebuked for describing the campaigns in the Caribbean in too much detail. In times of war, they were bluntly informed, 'it is not good that the public should be so well informed'.[12] But public interest, and anxiety, could not be quelled by silence. The gap was inevitably filled by the ubiquitous manuscript newsletters: as the *Gazette* became more reticent, these became the single most important source of military and diplomatic news.[13] Supplied with reliable intelligence by the clerks of the royal postal service and circulated around the coffee houses, these newsletters were almost impossible to control. The government's irritation found expression in an ordinance of 1705 prohibiting the writing and distribution of such newsletters, an order renewed on an annual basis for several years; a sure sign that the prohibition, although given 'by express order of the king', was having no effect.[14] The arrest and interrogation of several *novellistes* in 1706 turned the spotlight on the clerks of the Paris post office, thirty of whom were taken into custody. Their testimony revealed that the news writers had a well-developed system of information exchange between the Paris and Lyon post offices, and a client list that included some of the most powerful in the land.

The royal monopoly of news was also challenged by French-language newspapers published abroad. This was a problem entirely of the government's own making. In addition to upholding the *Gazette* monopoly, royal officials had also consistently favoured the major Paris publishing houses when awarding permission to publish books. This was especially disastrous for the well-established provincial publishing industries in Rouen and Lyon, which contracted sharply.[15] The result was inevitably to alienate publishers and booksellers in these crucial cities. With nothing to lose, Rouen developed considerable notoriety as a centre of production of disrespectful libels; Lyon, meanwhile, became a major distribution centre for the foreign gazettes.

The best known of the foreign papers was the *Gazette de Leyde*.[16] Established in 1677, the *Gazette* was one of a dozen French-language newspapers published in Leiden, Amsterdam and The Hague during the reign of Louis XIV. In the eighteenth century the Leiden paper would become the European paper of record, read by statesmen throughout the Continent.[17] But in its earliest incarnation its purpose was more partisan, to bring to a French-reading audience an alternative view of Louis as a power-hungry despot who would only be satisfied when Europe's kingdoms lay prostrate at his feet. Where Dutch armies had so conspicuously failed in 1672, now printed propaganda, alongside diplomacy, played a critical role in the creation of a European alliance to contain and, ultimately, humiliate the French king.

French ministers did their best to turn the tide. But it would have escaped no one's notice that the victories for which the king would order a *Te Deum* were often no more than minor skirmishes, whereas the defeats passed over in silence were utterly calamitous. Louis's enemies scented blood. When peace talks were opened in 1709 (ignored by the Paris *Gazette*) the allies would only bring hostilities to a close if Louis joined them in armed action to depose his grandson, Philip, from the throne of Spain. Louis would be forced to choose between his dynastic honour and peace for his shattered country. In these desperate times the king's ministers reluctantly conceded that the insistent attacks from abroad required an answer. When French armies had commanded the field, foreign minister Simon Arnauld de Pomponne could dismiss 'the million screaming tracts' that had roused France's enemies abroad as of no account.[18] Now it fell to Torcy, nephew of the illustrious Jean-Baptiste Colbert, to answer them. Torcy had cut his teeth with a series of pamphlets published secretly in Paris under the collective title *Lettres d'un Suisse à un François*. Purportedly the work of a politically engaged but neutral Swiss, these essays were in fact the work of Torcy's client Jean de La Chapelle. Their purpose was to drive a wedge into the allied alliance by warning the German states of the dangers of placing themselves in the protective embrace of the Habsburg Empire.

The *Lettres d'un Suisse* were a considerable literary success, but by 1709 even Torcy was forced to concede that their continuation now served no useful purpose. For, as he admitted to a correspondent in Italy, 'I would very much like to be able to soothe [your pains] with some good news, but unfortunately the greater part of what our enemies are circulating is true.'[19] Now the French Crown faced the difficult task of explaining why the hopes of peace (of which many must have been aware from the imported Dutch papers) would be dashed: the war must go on to rescue the king's honour and uphold his obligations to Philip of Spain. In these desperate times Louis spoke to his people directly, in a circular letter ostensibly addressed to the governors of the provinces. Printed in numerous editions, this frank and moving exposition achieved a massive circulation. It marked a sea change in the propaganda priorities of the king. For as Joachim Legrand, a gifted pamphlet writer of these later years, put it to Torcy:

> It is not enough that the actions of kings be always accompanied by justice and reason. Their subjects must also be convinced of it, particularly when wars are undertaken which, although just and necessary, nearly always bring so much misery in their wake.[20]

The king's address helped rally the French nation for a last desperate effort; certainly the allies were taken aback by the recovery of French morale, and realised that they had overplayed their hand. The first signs of a weakening of English resolution led to a new onslaught of Torcy's propaganda effort, ably seconded by Legrand. In the end it was probably Philip of Spain's victory over his Habsburg challenger that proved most decisive in ending the war, but the emissaries did not operate in a vacuum. The groundwork for the peace treaty signed at Utrecht in 1713 had been carefully laid by a torrent of pamphlets, in large measure orchestrated by the contending parties, but never wholly under their control.

Restorations

In England following the Restoration of 1660, Louis XIV had one fervent, if for the time being secret admirer: the king, Charles II. Skilfully riding a tide of popular sentiment exhausted by the austerities and hypocrisies of the Republic, Charles displayed a charm and public optimism that caught the mood of the moment. Beneath this appealing persona, however, Charles was deeply scarred by the long years of deprivation and humiliations abroad. If he conquered, to an extent, the natural instinct for revenge, he still aspired to rule, and to prevail, against the whirlwind of conflicting expectations aroused by his return. For this, he required a complaisant press. This opened the way for a fascinating conflict between a devious and stubborn monarch and a publishing community anticipating a return to the vigorous exchange of opinions that had preceded the sour austerities of Cromwell's personal rule.[21]

The newspapers inherited from the Commonwealth were soon put into reliable hands. Marchamont Nedham was too associated with Cromwell to hope for further employment, and prudently departed for Holland. But Henry Muddiman, a schoolmaster turned journalist who had attached himself to the architect of the Restoration, General George Monck, successfully contrived a change of allegiance alongside his patron. His *Parliamentary Intelligencer* was continued, though tactfully renamed *The Kingdom's Intelligencer*.[22] Despite these promising beginnings it did not take long for Charles's view of the press to be made manifest. In June 1662 Parliament passed the Licensing Act, requiring all printed books to receive prior authorisation. The upholding of these regulations was placed in the hands of Sir Roger L'Estrange, appointed to the new post of Surveyor of the Press.[23]

L'Estrange was a rather unusual newspaper man in that he believed that in a well-ordered world newspapers should not exist at all. This uncompromising viewpoint was trenchantly expressed when, in 1663, he was granted a monopoly of news publishing. The first issue of the re-launched *Intelligencer* contained the following statement of his journalistic philosophy:

> Supposing the press to be in order, the people in their right wits, and news or no news to be the question, a Public Mercury should never have my vote, because I think it makes the multitude too familiar with the actions and counsels of their superiors, too pragmatical and censorious, and gives them not only an itch but a kind of colourable right and license to be meddling with the government.

These, though, were not normal times. If a paper were necessary, at least it could be put to good use, for nothing, at this instant, 'more imports his Majesty's service and the public, than to redeem the public from their former mistakes'.[24]

Muddiman was initially retained on a salary to assist in the production of the new paper, but working for L'Estrange could hardly have been a pleasure. More and more of Muddiman's energies were instead devoted to the production of a manuscript newsletter, which he provided as a confidential service for favoured clients and public officials. For this purpose he was attached to the office of the Secretary of State, where his operation fell under the wistful gaze of an ambitious young under-secretary, Joseph Williamson. Williamson saw in the exploitation of the official communications flowing into the Secretary's office the chance to place himself at the heart of the news operation. But first he had to remove L'Estrange. The opportunity arose in 1665, when plague drove the court, accompanied by Williamson and Muddiman, to the sanctuary of Oxford. Marooned in London and shorn of his professional assistant, L'Estrange's incompetence as a newsman was laid bare. Williamson easily persuaded his superiors to strip L'Estrange of his publishing responsibilities in return for a generous pension. His news publications would be shut down, to be replaced by a single official paper: the *Oxford*, later *The London Gazette*.[25]

For the next fourteen years the *Gazette* would be the only paper published in England. Williamson's concept drew on several contemporary and historical models: Nedham's monopoly of news under Cromwell was one; the Paris *Gazette* was the obvious source of the title. But in contrast to these two, *The London Gazette* was not published in pamphlet form; instead it reverted to the broadsheet style of the earliest Dutch papers. From its first issue the *Gazette* would be a single sheet, printed front and back, with the text in two columns.

11.2 *The London Gazette.*

And whereas the Paris paper was a private monopoly, *The London Gazette* would be edited from within the office of the Secretaries of State, its text chosen from incoming newsletters and foreign newspapers. The actual editorial work was performed by civil servants, often quite junior members of the Secretary's staff. Williamson and Muddiman, meanwhile, devoted themselves to their real prize: the confidential manuscript news.[26]

The London Gazette was therefore a curious sort of newspaper. It quickly developed a wide circulation, its twice-weekly issues (sold for one penny) snapped up by the inhabitants of the news-hungry capital. In principle it should have been well informed and authoritative. Its editors sat at the centre of a considerable network of information. Their office received regular reports both from agents abroad (including consuls settled in many strategic ports) and from correspondents all over England. But very little of this domestic news appeared in the *Gazette*. This was a quite conscious policy of Williamson and Muddiman. To an extent they shared the prejudices of L'Estrange, that the public should not be kept abreast of public matters. One of the first acts of the new regime had been to decree that the votes of the House of Commons should no longer be reported. This was a touchstone issue for proponents and critics of a free press in England and in consequence a reliable barometer of attitudes towards public opinion. The *Gazette* was therefore largely filled with foreign news, in the best tradition of its Paris cognate, and the early corantos. Domestic news was kept for the confidential newsletters, circulated to a carefully defined circle of public officials: the county lieutenants, postmasters and members of the Privy Council. In return for a free copy the postmasters and customs officials were required to write regularly with their own news.[27] Other recipients paid a subscription, which underwrote the costs of the copy office.

The official manuscript newsletters were also sent to select newsmen abroad in return for their news services. They used the English news contained in the newsletters for the basis of their newspapers, with the rather bizarre result that the readers of a Dutch newspaper like the *Oprechte Haerlemse Dingsdaegse Courant* could read more English domestic news than was available to English subscribers of *The London Gazette*.

The *Gazette*, in this way, provided its readers with a very partial view of affairs, mostly confined to foreign news. But its sources of information were very good: text was abstracted from a range of continental newspapers and the manuscript news-books provided by continental newsmen as part of their exchange agreement. The *Gazette* was therefore reliable, and as informative as the government wished it to be. But apart from official communications, a reprinted proclamation or court circular, it said little or nothing about the pulsating politics of the day.

11.3 *Oprechte Haerlemse Dingsdaegse Courant.* As this issue reveals, its readers would have been very well informed about English domestic politics.

Coffee

The public enthusiasm that had greeted the Restoration turned to discontent with remarkable rapidity. Twice in rapid succession England found itself back at war with the Dutch. The Second Dutch War, between 1665 and 1667, led to a ragged and humiliating defeat; the Third, from 1672 to 1674, raised widespread public unease at Charles II's alliance with Louis XIV against a fellow Protestant nation. Public anxiety focused increasingly on the king's brother James, Duke of York; his evasive and truculent response to the Test Act in 1673 confirmed what the political nation had long suspected: that the heir to the throne was a Catholic. The political crisis was brought to a head in 1678 when the murder of Sir Edmund Berry Godfrey, a firm Parliamentary defender of Protestantism, seemed to lend some plausibility to shocking allegations of a Popish plot to assassinate Charles and install James in his stead.[28]

The Godfrey murder made a popular hero of Titus Oates, the opportunist charlatan who had first concocted the plot. Parliament now brought forward a formal bill to exclude James from the succession. Rather than allow this, Charles first prorogued, then dissolved Parliament altogether.

11.4 The Popish plot. Scenes from the murder of Sir Edmund Berry Godfrey.

An unintended victim of this crisis was the Licensing Act, which had been due for renewal and now lapsed. The collapse of the *Gazette*'s monopoly led to a flurry of new publications, many of them openly hostile to the court, and supportive of James's exclusion. Aware that in the circumstances Parliament would hardly sanction the return of licensing, the king struck back through the courts, obtaining a judgment that 'His Majesty may by law prohibit the printing and publishing of all News-Books and Pamphlets of news whatsoever, not licensed by his Majesty's authority, as manifestly tending to the breach of the peace, and disturbance of the kingdom'.[29] A proclamation to this effect brought some temporary respite, but by 1681, as the Exclusion Crisis reached its Parliamentary climax, London newsmen were no longer sufficiently intimidated by the fear of retribution to abstain from publication. This year and 1682 saw a wave of new, mostly short-lived London papers. It was only in the summer of this year, as the king at last succeeded in re-establishing control, that the opposition papers were suppressed. When, in 1685, James II succeeded to the throne, the Licensing Act was restored, and with it the *Gazette*'s exclusive privilege.

The Exclusion Crisis proved a false dawn for English newspapers. The public hysteria over the Popish plot was in fact at its most intense when the Licensing Act and *Gazette* monopoly were still in force; and the *Gazette*, with its stolid diet of largely foreign news, had certainly done nothing to feed public concerns. Yet something was clearly afoot. A genuine groundswell of public anxiety combined with the emergence in the political nation of what amounted to an organised political faction bent on opposing the king's will through Parliamentary action. In these years we can detect the origins of the combinations that became, through the dramas of the Glorious Revolution and the Hanoverian Succession, organised political parties, the Whigs and Tories. How was this debate conducted?

Jürgen Habermas was not the first to point the finger at the London coffee houses. Although the first of London's coffee shops had opened only in 1652, by 1670 they were a well-established institution, each with their own character and particular clientele.[30] Here men of business came to drink a dish of coffee, converse and hear the latest news. Proprietors were careful to ensure that they supplied their patrons with the current news-sheets: the *Gazette* certainly, but also occasional pamphlets of current affairs, and commercial manuscript newsletters. Henry Muddiman had built a lucrative commercial service alongside his official despatches, but he was not alone. In the 1670s opposition writers, notably the notorious Whig newsman Giles Hancock, created their own networks of clients. The manuscript newsletters successfully supplied the appetite for news left unsatisfied by the austere policies of the *Gazette*; pamphlets, rumour and private correspondence did the rest.

As opposition began to make itself felt in the 1670s, Charles II's ministers were all too aware of the role that coffee houses played in the circulation of information. During the Third Dutch War the French alliance was openly condemned. When the king's brother James took a Catholic wife, the coffee houses were a ferment of rumour as she made her way towards England. As Joseph Williamson remarked with some exasperation, 'every car-man and porter is now a statesman; and indeed the coffee-houses are good for nothing else'. 'It was not thus,' he added with some nostalgia, 'when we drank nothing but sack and claret, or English beer and ale. These sober clubs produce nothing but scandalous and censorious discourses, and at these nobody is spared.'[31]

The king had had his eye on the coffee shops for some time. The appearance of a controversial pamphlet in 1675 alleging a plot to reintroduce Catholicism resulted in a search of the London coffee houses for copies. In December the Privy Council finally gave way to the king's desire that they should be closed altogether. This provoked an immediate outcry; sustained lobbying led first to a delay in implementation, then a grudging acceptance that licensed houses might remain open, on a pledge of future good behaviour.[32] These pledges were unlikely to be met. As the crisis unfolded different coffee houses became known as centres of Whig or loyalist sentiment.

The flow of information was further improved by the introduction in London of a penny postal service, several centuries before the more celebrated national institution devised by Rowland Hill.[33] This London post was the brainwave of a customs official, William Dockwra. Though the national post had been somewhat improved during the Commonwealth, it was widely acknowledged that the expanding metropolis was ill-served. It was also generally (and correctly) surmised that the royal post functioned more as a source of revenue and intelligence than as a service to commerce (letters were routinely opened before delivery).[34] Dockwra now proposed a network of receiving stations from which post was collected hourly. Letters intended for the Post Office were taken straight there; those with London addresses were relayed to five sorting stations for immediate delivery. The system was remarkably successful, and openly supported by the London Whigs, who appreciated a service that bypassed the inspections performed by the postal clerks. For the same reason the service was resented at court and as soon as the Exclusion Crisis was passed, James, Duke of York, intervened to force closure of Dockwra's service. He was, however, shrewd enough to Recognise a commercial need, so just four days later he announced a new London district post which in effect replicated Dockwra's innovation.

In the last resort Charles II was also canny enough to appreciate that the suppression of information offered no solution to political conflict: the court would have to make its own case. Sir Roger L'Estrange was recalled to the colours and given his head. L'Estrange was responsible for two remarkably successful serial publications, not papers in the true sense, but opinion pieces presented in dialogue form. The first, *Heraclitus Ridens*, proclaimed its purpose, with L'Estrange's usual winning sensitivity, in its very first issue. Its aim was

> [t]o prevent mistakes and false news, and to give you a true information of the state of things, and advance your understanding above the common rate of Coffee-House statesmen who think themselves wiser than the Privy Council, or the sages of the law.[35]

It was joined two months later by *The Observator in Question and Answer*, which L'Estrange continued until March 1687. This was forthright and surprisingly witty. In 931 consecutive issues L'Estrange rained abuse on the Whigs and all their doings. L'Estrange's conversion to the principle of engaging with public opinion was complete, or as he put it more succinctly himself, ''Tis the press that has made 'um mad, and the press must set 'em right again.'[36] Although not really a paper, the *Observator* imitated the *Gazette* in its layout: a folio half-sheet, printed in two columns, on both sides. Like the *Gazette* it sold for a penny.

The success of this royalist counter-attack makes the point that, for all the hubbub of the rapidly maturing information market, pamphlets still played a dominant role in the discussion of public affairs. Between 1679 and 1681 the volume of pamphlets in circulation reached astonishing levels: estimates based on surviving print runs indicate that as many as 5 to 10 million copies may have been printed in these three years.[37] Whereas some were substantial works, pamphleteers had now seized the point that less is more or, as one contemporary put it, 'two sheets' (that would be eight pages) 'is enough in all reason for a dose for the strongest constitution, and one [sheet] for the weaker'.[38] Many of these little pamphlets sold for as little as one penny, the cost of the *Gazette*. In London, particularly, where a large proportion of the population could read, a broad cross section of the people could now engage with public debate – even in an age when the newspaper trade was carefully controlled.

Intemperate Freedom

The Revolution of 1688 was not a newspaper event. In the weeks following the landing of the Prince of Orange's Dutch fleet in Devon on 5 November, information was scarce. The *Gazette* carried a brief report of the Prince's landing on 8 November, but offered little further commentary as King James's authority ebbed away. In December the dam broke: as fear of prosecution receded, a number of London publishers chanced their arm. After all, as the new *London Courant* put it with some justice:

> It having been observed, that the greater the itch of curiosity after news hath been here of late, the less has the humour been gratified. Insomuch, that a modest enquiry where his Majesty, or his Royal Highness the Prince of Orange was, or what they were doing, could scarce be resolved, till the news had been exported and imported in a foreign news-letter.[39]

None of these opportunist ventures long survived the arrival of William in London and his prudential proclamation (gleefully published in *The London Gazette*) banning 'false, scandalous and seditious books, papers of news, and pamphlets, daily printed and dispersed, containing idle and mistaken relations of what passes'. The Licensing Act was in fact retained until 1695, but by that time the realisation was dawning that the *Gazette* monopoly had run its course. With the regime now more secure, the Act was allowed to lapse and other newspapers could try their hand.

The final removal of the Licensing Act inaugurated a remarkable era in the history of the English newspaper. A number of new papers were launched in 1695, including three that were to prove enduring: *The Post Boy, The Flying Post* and *The Post Man*. The use of the word 'post' in all of these titles reflects an aspiration to serve more than a London audience. London papers would, with increasing regularity, be circulated to readers outside the capital with the postal coaches and carriers. The year 1696 saw the launch of the first evening paper, Ichabod Dawks's *News-Letter*, and in 1702 London had its first daily, *The Daily Courant*. This, though, proved very much the exception. The norm was the thrice-weekly publication *of The Flying Post* and others (the *Gazette* also moved from twice to thrice-weekly publication in 1709). *The Daily Courant* would close in 1735, and the real age of the daily still lay some way ahead.

Nevertheless, the growth of the newspaper industry was truly astonishing. By 1704 London had nine newspapers, turning out 44,000 copies a week. In 1709 at least eighteen periodicals appeared weekly or more frequently: a total of fifty-five issues in each weekly cycle. By 1712 it has been estimated that a total of 70,000 copies of newspapers were published every week: this for a total national population of around six million.[40] Seen in this perspective, the total inadequacy of the 9,000 copies of the Paris *Gazette* available to serve a French population of 20 million makes a stark contrast.

This era also witnessed the establishment of the first newspapers outside London.[41] Between 1700 and 1702 papers were established in Exeter, Norwich and Bristol. The difficulty of fixing an exact date of foundation results from the fact that in none of these three cases does the first issue survive – the earliest date of publication has to be surmised by counting back from a much later copy, and assuming regular weekly publication. All of these places were, significantly, located on main roads and at considerable distance from London. Publishers had to be assured of a sufficient captive audience to sustain their venture, but London was still the source of the overwhelming proportion of the news that filled their pages. This was equally the case for the next rash of newspaper foundations, at Worcester, Stamford, Newcastle, Nottingham and Liverpool. Much of their news was lifted directly from the London papers. Other items were provided by subscription newsletters, or by London correspondents. The predominance of foreign news characteristic of the London papers was thus largely replicated, though gradually leavened by other occurrences of interest to a local audience. Some of this was provided by local readers, whose correspondence offered a running commentary on the papers' qualities and derelictions. If all else failed, the editor took a literary turn. 'We hope, in the present scarcity of news, the following poems will not be unacceptable to our readers,' offered the editors of the *Gloucester Journal*, optimistically.[42] Sometimes it was simply necessary to admit defeat, as in one issue of *The British Spy, or Derby Postman*:

> When the mails fail us, and the people so unactive at home, when great folks are so ill-natured as neither to marry nor die, nor beget children, we are upon the search for that scarce commodity call'd wit, which, 'tis well known, is in these days as hard to come in any week (especially in Derby) as intelligence.[43]

Despite this occasional hiccup, the provincial press took off in the eighteenth century. Around 150 titles were ventured in sixty different towns, and while not all succeeded, some continued for many years. This longevity was equally a feature of the London press. Whereas in the first serial boom of the mid-seventeenth century most titles had failed after a few issues, the newspaper revival of the early eighteenth century reversed these polarities: some spluttered and died, but many endured and made their publishers a very good living.

These were, in many respects, propitious times for the expanding newspaper market. England was in the middle of an extended economic boom. Rising prosperity meant that many more households had the disposable income for luxuries like papers. The long period of continental warfare that dominated the reign of Queen Anne engaged the interest of a wide public, and provided a series of military victories on which the papers could feast. The Duke of Marlborough's despatch from the battlefield of Blenheim in 1704 was published in full in *The Daily Courant*, and *The Flying Post* followed up with a gleeful translation of the report from the Paris *Gazette*, which somehow seemed to imply that the French had emerged victorious. So that their readers were left in no doubt, this was accompanied by two intercepted letters from French officers that candidly confessed the true state of affairs.[44]

As these examples suggest, the newspapers of the early eighteenth century remained dominated by foreign news. The domestic stories that made it into the London papers often reflected a rather patronising attitude to provincial society, with reports of crime, extreme weather and the sort of celestial apparitions that sophisticated Londoners now affected to treat with scepticism.[45] The papers continued to eschew overt editorialising. In this they followed *The Daily Courant*, where, in its first edition, the editor averred that he would publish no comments or conjectures of his own, 'supposing other people to have sense enough to make reflections for themselves'.[46]

The treatment of domestic political issues remained extremely circumspect. As the War of the Spanish Succession ground on and the political battle became more intense, with the looming prospect of a contested succession after the death of Queen Anne, it was once again pamphlets and the new pamphlet series such as Defoe's *Review* that bore the main burden of political debate. The key political writings of this period sold in fantastic numbers: Defoe's satirical poem 'The True Born Englishman' 80,000 copies; Richard Steele's *The Crisis* 40,000; Henry Sacheverell's notorious sermon, *The Perils of False Brethren*, as many as 100,000.[47] Helping to insulate the newspapers from more virulent criticism was the fact that opinion pieces like Defoe's *New Review* were so recognisably different, whole pamphlets devoted to a single essay, notwithstanding that they shared with the newspaper a serial form.

The long continental war was undoubtedly good for newspaper circulation, but its last years witnessed a new crisis. Because they were aware that the peace would be controversial, and opposition politicians likely to make trouble, the administration set out to muzzle the press. The chosen instrument was not a new Licensing Act but a tax, the Stamp Act (1712). Papers could only be published on stamped paper, supplied from the revenue warehouse in London, at the cost of one half penny a sheet. Industry observers feared a general collapse of newspapers, particularly outside London where editors faced the additional logistical burden of sending to the capital for supplies of the stamped paper. So it says a great deal for the maturity of the market that whereas a few papers did go under, most survived. Some proved ingenious in shifting shape to minimise their tax burden (the Act had not specified the size of sheets, nor anticipated a paper made from one and a half sheets).[48] Others simply passed on the tax to their customers, who paid. Rather than attempting to subdue the press, the next generation of ministers would take a more pragmatic response and buy the papers. This way, under a compliant editor, they could become a mouthpiece for the regime. The newspapers, moving on from their dull but dependable recitation of foreign despatches, would no longer offer a respite from the advocacy journalism pioneered in the work of Defoe, Swift and L'Estrange. In the age of Walpole, the two would merge.

PART THREE

ENLIGHTENMENT?

CHAPTER 12

The Search for Truth

O N 4 June 1561 the steeple of St Paul's Cathedral, the largest church in
England, was struck by lightning. It caught fire, and collapsed into the
roof of the church: this, too, could not be saved. Such a calamitous event at the
heart of the metropolis stirred even the relatively conservative English print
industry into action; since the stalls of many booksellers were located in
St Paul's yard, they would probably have been among the horrified eyewitnesses. Within days an atmospheric pamphlet account was circulating on the
streets, recounting the heroic efforts of London citizens, led by the Lord
Mayor, to save the church: 'there were above five hundred persons that
laboured in carrying and filling water. Divers substantial citizens took pains
as if they were labourers.'[1] Even these well-born auxiliaries could not save
St Paul's; the church was wholly ruined. Distraught Londoners were soon
offering explanations. 'Some say it was the negligence of plumbers; others
suspect that it was by some wicked practice of wild fire or gunpowder. Some
suspect conjurors and sorcerers.' The *True report* offered more sober counsels.
'The true cause, as it seemeth, was the tempest, by God's sufferance.'[2]

This final qualification was significant, for in all the uncertainties of life our
ancestors sought evidence of divine purpose. This was equally true of what we
would think of as natural phenomena (thunder, flood or earthquakes) as of
man-made disasters (fires, battles or crime). They dutifully gave thanks for
God's blessings, and trembled at evidence of God's displeasure. The calamity
at the headquarters of the new Elizabethan Church, so soon after the restoration of Protestantism, naturally attracted conflicting interpretations. To a
Catholic writer, the bolt of lightning was quite evidently a sign of God's wrath
at the abolition of the Mass. This could not go unanswered, and one of the
newly appointed bishops was swiftly put up to parry this charge. Bishop
Pilkington agreed that the destruction was a potent sign from God, but rather

it urged God's people to repentance and swifter reform: 'He exhorted his audience to take this as a general warning . . . of some greater plague to follow if
amendment of life in all estates did not ensue.'[3]

It was a fundamental belief of all Christian societies, Protestant or Catholic,
that evil deeds would not go unpunished: neither those of others nor your
own. The law was strictly enforced, and grim penalties were widely approved.
But only God could see into men's hearts. Where the law failed, early modern
people were happy to see God's hand at work to ensure that those guilty of evil
deeds were brought to book. At the time that the steeple of St Paul's was struck
by lightning, John Foxe was working towards publication of his massive
chronicle of the lives of the English Protestant martyrs. Although these stories
were dramatic enough, Foxe also found room to chronicle the many instances
of misfortune that had struck down those who had denounced or condemned
these victims. This was a popular theme, as was the retribution that befell
those who abandoned the true faith. One of the most widely circulated
pamphlets of the sixteenth century was the tale of Francesco Spiera, an Italian
who had first adhered to the Gospel and then returned to Catholicism. He
died heartbroken. This moral tale achieved an enormous circulation in several
languages, and was still being published a century later.[4] Among its admirers
was the seventeenth-century London puritan Nehemiah Wallington, who
collected from his circle of acquaintance and reading of news-books a whole
series of 'notable judgements of God' on those who transgressed his laws and
paid the price.[5]

When fire from heaven struck the greatest of God's houses, such an event
was obviously pregnant with meaning. News readers wanted to know not just
what had occurred, but what it portended for the future. In this way the news
world united past, present and future; and the truth had many layers.

Through a Glass Darkly

The news world of the sixteenth and seventeenth centuries was full of
portents. Comets, celestial apparitions, freaks of nature and natural disasters:
all were regarded as harbingers of great events. While news men passed on
news of strange and marvellous happenings, astrologers scanned the skies for
meaning. The passage of a comet was regarded as particularly portentous,
since it was widely believed to prophesy the death of some great ruler.
Naturally Europe's princes maintained a close if nervous interest. This was in
one sense good news for the Continent's most celebrated cosmographers,
since its rulers wanted to have them close by to offer their interpretations at
first hand. The tactful conduct of these duties secured several distinguished

scholars, such as Tycho Brahe and Peter Apian, valuable royal support for their scientific work.

Others less doubtfully wise also profited. The slyly opaque prophecies of Michel de Nostradamus secured him a comfortable billet as prognosticator to Catherine of Medici, and made him one of Europe's most published authors.[6] The subtle genius of prophecies simultaneously portentous and utterly ambiguous has ensured Nostradamus a following through the ages, but in his own time they hit home. When for 1560 he predicted misery, calamity and trouble, particularly for the clergy, this was taken particularly hard in England. Some were convinced by the astrologer that the world would come to an end twenty days after Elizabeth adopted her title as Supreme Governor of the Church. Strange premonitions reached into the heart of the Elizabethan establishment; so much so that when Matthew Parker warned William Cecil that he did not wish to be Archbishop of Canterbury, he was forced to assure him this was not because of the prophecies: 'I pray you think not that the prognostication of Mr Michael Nostredame reigns in my head.'[7] The Privy Council were sufficiently alarmed to attempt to suppress the astrologer's prophecies altogether. In 1562 twenty separate booksellers were fined for selling one of Nostradamus's works. Yet his writings were only the most visible aspect of a vast market in calendars and almanacs, which combined lists of festivals and fairs with astronomical charts and some predictions of future events.[8] Excerpts from such works were still being used as fillers in the newspaper press in the eighteenth century.

Heavenly apparitions were a staple of all parts of the news market. Comets and unusual conjunctions of the heavenly bodies were widely reported in news pamphlets, but it was illustrated broadsheets that most adequately conveyed the full drama of these events. The German poet Sebastian Brant had shown the way with his dramatic (and highly political) celebration of the Ensisheim meteorite in 1492, and as the capacities of the press expanded in the later sixteenth century this form of broadsheet news became extremely popular.[9] The comet of 1577 was recorded in at least four separate broadsheets, and others plotted the appearance of shooting stars, darkness at noon, the simultaneous appearance of sun and moon, or multiple suns.[10] Some of these observations may be attributed to the application of an untutored imagination to recognisable natural phenomena, like the description of the Aurora Borealis (Northern Lights) in 1580 and 1590.[11] But what are we to make of the relatively frequent accounts of animals, riding horsemen or monstrous beasts seen galloping across the skies? Armed soldiers were frequently reported among these celestial wonders: sometimes whole armies. It is little surprise that such accounts became frequent during times of warfare, in Germany during the conflict between Charles V and the Schmalkaldic League and during the War of Cologne (1583–8).[12] But this was not a phenomenon confined to the sixteenth century. In Denmark in 1628, at a time when much of the kingdom had recently been occupied by Wallenstein's imperial troops, the inhabitants of Sønderborg were transfixed by the sight of two great armies in the sky. The battle waged for several hours and was purportedly witnessed by hundreds of people. They took comfort in the fact that the army of the north emerged victorious, which they took to be a sign that they would eventually be free of the occupying force.[13] Almost twenty years later the Protestant wood-turner Nehemiah Wallington recorded something very similar, reported 'by credible persons certified from Hull': the appearance 'visibly in the air' of two armies of foot soldiers, 'which charged each other with much fierceness'.[14] Strange times indeed.

The same potent combination of observation and imagination can be observed in the astonishing interest shown in what were known, in the unforgiving terminology of the time, as monstrous births.[15] Conjoined twins were a fascination of the age, and were captured in images often of great anatomical precision. We are likely to give less credence to reports, chronicled with equal earnestness, that a woman had given birth to a cat. But these reports were treated with the utmost seriousness by sixteenth-century authorities, not least because they were thought to portend shocking and evil consequences. No less an authority than Martin Luther achieved an enormous success with the so-called monk calf, a tonsured half-beast he presented as an allegory of the corruptions of the Catholic priesthood.[16]

The birth of conjoined twins was universally accepted as a judgment on the sins of the parents. As a broadside of 1565 argued, the 'monstrous and unnatural shapes of these children are not only for us to gaze and wonder at'. The births of such children 'are lessons and schoolings to us all who daily offend ... no less wicked, yea many times more than the parents of such misformed' children.[17] And when, in 1569, the English Privy Council received reports of the woman who had given birth to a cat, they ordered one of their number, the Earl of Huntingdon, to investigate. Huntingdon was shortly able to send Archbishop Grindal a detailed transcript of the alleged mother's interrogation, complete with an illustration of the cat.[18] Having reviewed the evidence Grindal decided that this was a hoax, though it was never really established why it had been perpetrated. What is clear is that the event was not regarded as necessarily fantastical; a considerable amount of time was expended by senior officials in flushing out the truth.

This is the part of the sixteenth- and seventeenth-century news world that must seem to us most foreign. We are hard put to believe that women gave birth

12.1 The comet of 1577. A frequent subject for representation, and feverish interpretation.

to animals, or that the inhabitants of Sussex had been terrified by a dragon; yet such reports were published in pamphlets and newspapers right up to the eighteenth century.[19] Sudden calamities and afflictions prompted particular reflection: in this era all news had a moral shape. Victims of misfortune, particularly collective misfortune, were always invited to look to themselves for causes.

The sense that calamitous events represented the working out of God's purpose was still unflinchingly believed throughout this period. We see it in the Protestant reporting of the sack of Magdeburg, which highlighted both the horror and the need for God's people to turn back to Him with a humble spirit.[20] Incidences of plague, a recurring terror of these centuries, prompted a similar call for amendment of life. This was an affliction that seemed to defy both treatment and cure, striking indifferently at rich and poor. A stunned sense of powerlessness is as evident in pamphlets written at the time of the London plague in 1665 as it had been a century before. Plague was, in the Dutch expression, God's gift, beyond the fathoming of medical science.[21]

The plague was beginning to recede when in 1666 London was consumed by a devastating fire. In this case renewed reflections on God's dreadful justice were mixed with more prosaic analysis: rumours quickly circulated that the fire had been deliberately started by the Catholics.[22] This shift in emphasis, certainly encouraged by the increased level of news reporting, marks a trend towards a more rationalistic turn to the reporting of natural and man-made disasters. It coincides with the increased dissemination of empirical observation in the natural sciences. Scholars were encouraged, and encouraged each other, to gather and interpret empirical evidence, and be less respectful of inherited wisdom; as science advanced, so God's domain would contract.[23] Applied to the world of news reporting this shift in emphasis certainly had a darker side. For as news men gradually abandoned the pious calls for self-amendment, they focused instead on a new avenue of causality: if they were not to blame themselves, then blame must lie elsewhere. A ravenous news press fed and encouraged the search for scapegoats, and a heightened adversarial tone to political debate. In this respect, at least, news reporting became recognisably more modern.

News Well Buttered

The question of how much credit should be given to news reports was of course as old as news itself. It underlay all the calculations of rulers of medieval societies, as they weighed the value of the limited and incomplete sources of information at their disposal. But at least in earlier generations these problems had been relatively well defined: How much could one trust a messenger? Was the bringer of news an interested party? How much weight to put on a rumour? Necessarily, until recipients of news could obtain corroboration, much consideration was given to the credit of the bearer, who might be a trusted subordinate, a well-informed source who had provided good information before, or a correspondent whose integrity guaranteed straight dealing.

News reposed on the same bedrock of trust and honour that in principle underpinned all relationships among those of a certain social standing.[24]

This comparatively intimate circle of news exchange was significantly disrupted by the birth of a commercial news market. The market for news spread beyond those for whom it was a professional necessity to be informed, to new, more naïve and inexperienced consumers. The intensification of pamphlet publication and the first generation of newspapers also coincided with a series of complex international conflicts which generated a large but dispersed audience eager for the latest intelligence. It was inevitable that this new hunger for news and the commercial pressures to satisfy it led to the reporting of much that could not be verified, and some downright invention. In 1624 the young dramatist James Shirley wrote scathingly of the trade in fabricated tales from the battlefield, penned by men who had never been near the front. 'They will write you a battle in any part of Europe at an hour's warning, and yet never set foot out of a tavern.'[25] If there was money to be made, Shirley implied, the newspapers would print it.

This was not altogether fair. Shirley's observations were made at the height of the Thirty Years War, a critical but difficult era for news reporting. People all over Europe were desperate for the latest intelligence; but as we have seen the destruction caused by the fighting created severe disruption to the channels of information flow. Partisan hopes and fears made for additional distortions. The new generation of serials during the English Civil War faced similar problems with their domestic reporting, as William Collings, editor of the *Kingdom's Weekly Intelligencer*, wearily acknowledged in 1644. 'There were never more pretenders to the truth than in this age, nor ever fewer that obtained it.'[26]

As this example makes clear, news men were very conscious of the difficulties they faced in getting true reports. Thomas Gainsford was one of several who used his columns to urge readers to be less impatient: news could not be printed if there were none to be had. News men had no wish to be bounced into publishing information that turned out not to be true, not least because their livelihood depended on a reputation for reliability. William Watts was badly wrong-footed when after the battle of Breitenfeld in 1631 he reported the death of the Catholic general Tilly, and held to this even when reports emerged to the contrary. We can appreciate, though, that his reasoning did reflect a careful attempt to balance conflicting information. Watts just guessed wrong:

> Indifferent reader, we promised you (in the front of our last Aviso) the death and internment of Monsieur Tilly, which we now perform: notwithstanding the last Antwerpian post hath rumoured the contrary, against which you may balance each other, and accordingly believe. Only we will propose one question

12.2 Unquiet skies. Here Butter has both armies battling in the sky and clouds dripping blood. A strange apparition indeed.

unto all gainsayers, let them demonstrate where Tilly is, and that great formidable army which he has raised, and we will all be of the Catholic faith.[27]

In fact, instances where a news man would go out on a limb with an unconfirmed rumour were rare (and there is no evidence that Watts followed through on his pledge to turn Catholic). Seventeenth-century newspapers were on the whole characterised more by caution than risk-taking. Many news men were at pains to point out when foreign news was as yet unverified. Gainsford's judicious formula could stand for many: 'I would rather write true tidings only to be rumoured, when I am not full sure of them, than to write false tidings to be true, which will afterwards prove otherwise.'[28]

This professionalism was seldom credited by the critics of news men. Much of the criticism of newspapers, it must be said, emanated from privileged members of existing circles of news exchange, like James Shirley, and the proprietors of manuscript news services who had a financial interest in emphasising the superiority of their own sources. The ridicule heaped on the newspapers and their readers also reflected a decree of social contempt for neophyte consumers. Nowhere was this more evident than on the London stage, where dramatists made the newspapers a regular butt of their humour. The unfortunate Nathaniel Butter came in for particular ridicule, as his name proved an irresistible target for puns. In *A Game of Chess*, Thomas Middleton made great play of Butter, presumably knowing that for his audiences Butter was the public face of news. Abraham Holland concluded a more general assault on the news men with a memorable couplet:

To see such Butter every week besmear
Each public post and church door![29]

The news men's principal persecutor was Ben Jonson, the first to make the newspaper press the subject of their own play, *A Staple of News*. Here the target was as much the credulous purchasers of news as the news men, like the countrywoman whom Jonson imagines wandering into the staple office to ask for 'any news, a groat's worth'.[30] Such simpletons, he implied, were easily manipulated. The criticism was probably wide of the mark. Although in principle a single issue of the news serial was well affordable for many of very limited income, these were not the typical consumers of news serials. The news men aimed their productions at a subscription market: and subscribers were likely to have been wealthier (a shilling a month was a significant outlay) and more sophisticated readers; they would need to be, to make sense of the elliptical, staccato reports that were the newspaper style.

One should also keep in mind that sceptical commentators usually had an axe to grind, and the London playwrights were no exception. To some extent the newspapers threatened the theatre's role in contemporary news commentary. Ben Jonson was a representative of the established media, enjoying the access of the privileged to information and backstairs gossip. He had smoothly mastered the theatre's arch references to contemporary events for an informed and knowing clientele. He also disapproved of the news-papers' editorial line: he was no supporter of the policy of intervention in the Thirty Years War. He resented the papers' political role, which by raising consciousness of the plight of Protestants abroad piled pressure on the reluc-tant king to intervene.

So Jonson, like many representatives of the established media, was never likely to give the newspapers a fair hearing. Even so, his criticism does reflect a wider dissatisfaction with the serial form itself – and here there were fair points to be made.[31] Until this point the pamphlet had been the normative printed form of news delivery. Although news pamphlets and serials shared many points of similarity (the serials were closely modelled on the pamphlets in physical terms), their relationship with the potential audience was funda-mentally different. Non-serial pamphlets were very much superior as conduits of information. Because they only appeared when there were important events to publicise, they did not have to deal with uncertain or unresolved issues: they were published after the event. On the whole they had much more space (on average four times as much text as early newspapers) and dealt with a single issue rather than the newspapers' frantic miscellany. Because non-serial pamphlets were one-off publications they did not assume prior knowledge; they took time to explain context and consequences. The news events recorded in pamphlets often preserved their interest for some time. Many were published or reprinted a long while after the events described. They did not need to be rushed out; they left time for reflection and judgement.

The news serials were invariably more hectic. They described events still unfolding, and not yet fully known. They were forced to include much infor-mation that seemed portentous at the time, but in retrospect was utterly trivial. The news men, whose major editorial task was to choose what threads of news to print from a larger heap, were not particularly well qualified to make such judgements. Often this was just one of many tasks in a busy print shop. No sooner was one issue on sale than news men were gathering copy for the next. There was little mental space for reflection and explanation, even if the style adopted in the newspapers (inherited from the manuscript newslet-ters) had allowed for this, which it did not.

News pamphlets could adopt a very different approach. Most pamphlets would appear only at the conclusion of a siege or campaign, when the outcome was known (a luxury not available to a weekly publication). In a pamphlet facts could be marshalled and shaped towards this known outcome. For those wanting to make sense of troubled times this must have seemed a much more logical form of news reporting. Pamphlets also offered more opportunity for erudite and fine writing, for commitment and advocacy.

So there were good reasons, quite apart from professional competition, why many regarded the newspapers as a fad, and a retrograde step for news publication. But when Ben Jonson took aim at the new naïve readers, he need not have worried, because these were hardly the intended audience: these neophyte consumers were far more likely to buy, if anything, a pamphlet which gave them a complete view of a single subject. An individual issue of a newspaper would always be like coming into a room in the middle of a conversation; it was hard to pick up the thread, and the terse factual style offered little help. This was not how they were intended to be read, or collected: most newspaper issues passed safely into the hands of more sophisticated readers, who followed events on a regular basis.

The Scourge of Opinion

The rising tide of criticism reflected the fact that by the late seventeenth century a serial press was a fixed and unavoidable feature of the commerce of news. While the lands in northern Europe had taken most enthusiastically to the newspapers, by late in the century Italian cities also had a decent scattering of papers, and the form was even beginning to establish a foothold in Spain. Germany, with its patchwork of independent jurisdictions, achieved by far the best coverage, and it was here too that the critics of newspapers made their voices heard. In the third quarter of the seventeenth century a number of writers articulated their disquiet at the proliferation of the serial press, and the dangers to society if newspapers fell into the wrong hands. In 1676 the court official Ahasver Fritsch published a brief pamphlet on the use and abuse of newspapers.[32] Fritsch was a firm supporter of princely power, and was strongly of the view that the circulation of newspapers should be confined to public persons who had an occupational need to remain informed (that is, the traditional readers of *avvisi*). The fact that he published his tract in Latin indicates that these were very much his intended audience.

Fritsch's theme was taken up a few years later by Johann Ludwig Hartman, a Lutheran pastor and prolific author. Hartman had developed a line in sermons denouncing the sins of dancing, gambling, drinking and idleness; to these he added, in a trenchant discourse of 1679, the sin of newspaper reading.[33] Hartman was prepared to concede that merchants needed to read newspapers; but otherwise they should be forbidden to the general public. Fritsch and Hartman set the tone for a debate that focused on defining which social groups could safely be entrusted with political news. Daniel Hartnack, a skilled and imaginative publisher, also tried to draw a distinction between useful reading and mere curiosity. In normal times, Hartnack agreed, reading of newspapers

THE WORLD IS RVLED & GOVERNED by OPINION.

Viator. Who art thou Ladie that aloft art set
In state Maiestique this faire spredding
Vpon thine head a Towre-like Coronet,
The Worldes whole Compasse, resting on thy knee,

Opinio. I am OPINION who the world do swaie
Wherefore, I beare it, on my head that Towre
Is BABELS: meaning my confused waie
The Tree so shaken, my unsetled Bowre.

Viator. What meaneth that Chameleon on thy fist
That can assume all Cullors saving white.

Opinio. OPINION thus can everie waie shee list.
Transforme her self, save into TRVTH, the right

Viator. And Ladie what's the Fruite, which from thy Tree
Is shaken of with everie little wind
Like Bookes and papers this amuseth mee
Beside thou seemest (veiled) to bee blind

Opinio. Tis true I cannot as cleare IVDGMENTS see
Through self CONCEIT and haughtie PRIDE
The fruite those idle bookes and libells bee
In everie streete, on everie stall you find

Viator. Cannot OPINION remedie the same.

Opinio. Ah no then should I perish in the throng
O'th giddie Vulgar, without feare ~ shame
Who censure all thinges, bee they right or wrong

Viator. But Ladie deare, whence came at first this fruite
Or why doth WISEDOME suffer it to grow
And what's the reason its farre reaching roote
Is water'd by a sillie Foole below

Opinio. Because that FOLLIE giveth life to these
I but retaile the fruites of idle Aire
Sith now all Humors utter what they please
Toth loathing loading of each Mart and Faire.

Viator. And why those saplings from the roote that rise
In such abundance of OPINIONS tree

Opinio. Cause one Opinion many doth devise
And propagate, till infinite they bee

Viator. Adieu sweete Ladie till againe wee meete

Opinio. But when shall that againe bee, *Viator* Ladie saie

Opinio. Opinions found in everie house and streete
And going ever, never in her waie.

VIRO CLAR: Dr: FRANCISCO PRVIEANO D: MEDICO, OMNIVM BONARVM AR:
tium, et Elegantiarum, fautori et Admiratori summo. D.D.D.   *Henricus Peachamus.*

12.3 *The world ruled and governed by opinion.* Opinion is represented as a blindfolded woman, crowned with the Tower of Babel. The fruits of the tree are pamphlets.

should be restricted to the informed who could apply proper critical judgement. Only in time of war should everyone read papers.[34]

This sense of social exclusivity is a warning against overestimating the reach of the first generations of newspapers. Those in the circles of power, with access to good sources of news, were deeply sceptical as to whether much good would come of extending these privileges to untrained minds. It was only at the very end of the seventeenth century that a German author would join the debate with an unambiguous statement in favour of reading newspapers. Kaspar Stieler's *Zeitungs Lust und Nutz* (*The Pleasure and Utility of Newspapers*) was a ringing endorsement of the right to follow the news:

> We who live in this world, must know the present world; we get no help here from Alexander, Caesar or Mohammed if we wish to be wise. Whoever seeks this wisdom and wishes to partake in society must follow the papers: must read and understand them.[35]

Stieler had no patience with the attempt to limit access. All people, he believed, had the natural instinct to learn, and this extended to the latest current events. By enumerating the groups that would profit from newspaper reading, Stieler answered critics of the press directly. Teachers and professors needed to follow the news to stay up to date. Clergymen could incorporate material from the papers into their sermons (and find in them instances of God's interventions in human affairs). Merchants and itinerant workmen would be informed of the conditions on Europe's hazardous roads. Country nobles read newspapers to ward off boredom, and their ladies should read them too: better they prepared themselves to discuss serious subjects than waste time on gossip. Those who objected that newspapers were full of material unsuited to gentle eyes should remember that the Bible was also 'full of examples of murder, of adultery, of theft and many other sins'.[36]

Stieler's broadside was timely, because at the beginning of the eighteenth century the virtues of news reading were far from universally acknowledged. On the contrary, the intensification of participatory politics brought a host of new anxieties that called into question the value – and the values – of the serial press. Critics of the newspapers focused on three main issues which they felt compromised the media contribution to public debate. They complained of information overload: that there was simply too much news, much of it contradictory. They worried that the old tradition of straight reporting was being contaminated by opinion. This they believed, not without reason, was because statesmen were seeking to manipulate the news for their own purposes. All of these factors were likely to distort or obscure the truth, and leave readers confused and bamboozled.

The complaint that good sense was being drowned in a torrent of print was not entirely new at this time. Since the first decades of the sixteenth century, and the surge of pamphlets that accompanied the Reformation, contemporaries had been startled and unsettled by the pamphlet warfare stimulated by successive crises of European affairs. To apply the same criticism to the newspapers at the beginning of the eighteenth century may seem wide of the mark. In most parts of Europe a single newspaper still enjoyed a local monopoly. Only in London and a few German cities (notably Hamburg) was a larger number of regular serials in direct competition. Here rivalry could bring damaging consequences.[37] Papers were all too gleefully eager to point up each other's errors. It seems not to have occurred to them that by impugning their rivals they damaged the credibility of the genre as a whole. Daniel Defoe, who was hardly innocent of hyperbole or partisan exaggeration, at one time or another attacked the truthfulness or integrity of most of his competitors, including *The Daily Courant, The English Post, The London Gazette, The Post Boy* and *The Post Man*.[38] *The Tatler* sneered intermittently at the contradictions and exaggerations of the press, concluding, with lofty hyperbole, that 'the newspapers of this island are as pernicious to weak heads in England as ever books of chivalry to Spain'.[39]

Partly this professional warfare was the consequence of a crowded market. London papers drew very largely on the same sources of information for the bulk of their copy, made up of news from abroad. The search for an original angle naturally gave occasion for some artful embroidery. This inevitably caused readers some perplexity, particularly if they read the same report in different places. As Joseph Addison expressed it, with characteristic elegance, in his *Spectator*:

> All of them receive the same advices from abroad, and very often in the same words; but their way of cooking it is so different, that there is no citizen, who had an eye to the public good, that can leave the coffee-house with peace of mind, before he has given every one of them a reading.[40]

Addison reproved the dangers of journalistic licence; but this largely commercial pressure to embroider news was greatly compounded by anxieties that news was deliberately framed to a partisan agenda. This, the scourge of opinion, was a concern that extended far beyond the crowded London market.

Here it is important to remember the historical roots of the newspapers in the manuscript newsletters: a form of news reporting that valued unadorned

12.4 An attack on *The London Gazette*. The author may not have reflected that such an attack on the English paper of record did nothing to enhance the credibility of the medium as a whole.

fact almost to a fault. Those who subscribed to the *avvisi* and their print successors valued the total separation of news from the more discursive, analytical and frankly polemical style of news pamphlets. The fear that the serial news publications might be polluted by this parallel strand of news reporting was widespread and increasing in the early eighteenth century. The publication of what were in effect serial polemics in the English Civil War was an extreme case. But even the German newspapers could not be entirely oblivious to the loyalties of their local readership in times of war. By the early decades of the eighteenth century English newspapers were openly abusing each other for their partisan loyalties, as much as their inaccuracies. Even so, newspapers still by and large fought shy of explicit attempts to direct their readers' opinions. The first leading article or editorial in a German newspaper was published in Hamburg in 1687, but this proved to be an aberration: a product of a market where competing serials encouraged experimentation to win readers.[41] More typical was the high-minded declaration with which the editor of *The Daily Courant* addressed his readers in the first issue in 1702:

> He will quote the foreign papers from whence 'tis taken, and the public, seeing from what country a piece of news comes with the allowance of that government, may be better able to judge of the credibility and fairness of the relation. Nor will he take upon him to give any comments or conjectures of his own, but will relate only matter of fact; supposing other people to have sense enough to make reflections for themselves.[42]

This was all well and good, but how could the reader be certain of this? Even if the proprietor held to this worthy intention, how could the reader be assured that the papers would not be suborned by politicians with their own agendas?

The Heavy Hand of Power

From the first days of print Europe's rulers had recognised the need to regulate the new industry. The religious conflicts of the Reformation brought a new sensitivity to the power of the printed word, but magistrates also wished to control any debate on public policy that seemed to infringe their prerogatives. Systems of control evolved very rapidly in the course of the sixteenth century. Both Protestant and Catholic regimes practised censorship, though with a rather different emphasis. In Catholic countries it became the norm, following the example of Rome, to issue a comprehensive list or 'index' of forbidden books and authors. In Protestant jurisdictions it was more usual to require the examination of any text to be published locally before it was sent to the printer.

It was this second system that provided the model for the regulation of news publications. But whereas it could be applied with reasonable success to the production of books and pamphlets, such a system was far less suited to monitoring serials. Those nominated to undertake pre-publication examination of texts were generally busy men. Publishers complained of long delays and oppressive fees even for relatively uncontroversial books. When it came to news serials, which had to be printed on a particular day of the week, any delay was unconscionable. Pre-publication censorship seldom worked well in practice.

In general, then, most places where newspapers were established relied on a third scheme of control: the punishment, after publication, of anyone who printed anything the authorities deemed to be offensive. These interventions were all the more effective for being infrequent. Newspaper publishers knew that they put their livelihoods at risk with every issue. Where printers might risk a cheeky pamphlet, particularly if it could be sent out under the cloak of anonymity, this option was simply not available to publishers of newspapers. Their address had to feature prominently on every issue, so that subscribers could know where to send payments, and drop-in customers could find their shop.

So newspapers were very careful to avoid giving offence. As so often, self-censorship was far more effective than any system of regulation. The pressure to conform was particularly intense where any newspaper held a local monopoly; this applied to most parts of Europe where papers were published. In France the *Gazette* was an unapologetic cheerleader for royal power, but this was only the most extreme example of a general phenomenon. In Italy, newspaper proprietors in Milan and Piedmont were happy to establish their papers in the government printing house, in the case of Piedmont with a government pension for the publisher.[43] Even in the Dutch Republic, famed as a haven of toleration, the exuberant cacophony of mid-century had been quietly suppressed by 1690. Now each city had a single paper enjoying a lucrative monopoly.

It was generally understood that papers would abstain from comment on matters of political sensitivity; this explains the long-standing prejudice against the publication of domestic political news. But sometimes political pressures went beyond this, and the reporting of foreign news had to be slanted to conform to the policy priorities of the local power. Even the most enthusiastic defender of a wider readership for newspapers, Kaspar Stieler, believed that they should never publish anything that might impugn their sovereign's reputation. 'A publisher has to remember who he is and where he lives, who his lord and master is.'[44] If the authorities required it, the newspapers should be willing to circulate news they knew to be false. No wonder Stieler urged the reader to show a sharp critical sense, paying close attention to the origin of a report, and whether it came from a Protestant or Catholic locality.

None were more aware of the difficulties of a compromised, tainted source than the news men themselves. Newspaper editors returned repeatedly to the theme, promising only the best impartial news. 'In one thing,' claimed Théophraste Renaudot in the Paris *Gazette*, 'I yield not to anyone, in the search for truth.' *The London Courant* of 1688 promised to write 'with the integrity of an unbiased historian to do justice to all parties, in representing things as they shall really happen'.[45]

Nowhere were these truth claims more insistently repeated, and more tenaciously challenged, than in London, home to the most robustly contentious press of the era. But the hope that a less stringently regulated market would promote a civil discourse of truth-telling went unrequited, as it would a century later in revolutionary France.[46] The London papers may have been free of the oppressive burdens that bore down on a single paper in a monopoly market; but they were not, for all that, free of political pressure. Rather, English statesmen swiftly realised that to make their case they needed to have tame papers. Newspapers were quickly identified as Whig or Tory; leading writers accepted pensions to write in the party interest. In 1726 *The Craftsman* was set up by the Tory Lord Bolingbroke explicitly to mobilise political opinion against the Walpole administration. Robert Walpole responded sensibly enough by marshalling his own press. In his last decade as prime minister he controlled five papers, and paid out a total of £50,000 – a quite enormous sum – to compliant news men.[47]

What price a free press? Of what value the insistent claim of devotion to the unvarnished truth? As the newspaper passed the end of its first century, the serial press presented an awkward paradox. The more the newspapers extended their readership and their political influence, the less they were trusted. It was a difficult and complex legacy to carry into the age of Enlightenment.

CHAPTER 13

The Age of the Journal

THE debate about truth represented a crisis of authority for the reporting of news. With the development of a more adversarial political culture, news reporting seemed in some ways to have regressed. The search for facts came to be smothered in a fog of opinion, and the abuse and manipulation that went with factious politics. Politics had polluted the news. This, of course, is a problem that would never truly be resolved. The need for news prints also to be agents of persuasion would continue to challenge the critical faculties of readers into the modern age. But the first hints of a way forward emerged in the eighteenth century in a new form of periodical publication quite distinct from the noisy and insistent newspaper press. This would be the age of the journal.

The eighteenth century witnessed a spectacular rise in the periodical press. As the century wore on, newspapers would comprise only a small portion of this. Instead, the new century saw the establishment of a large number of other publications presented in serial form for a regular subscribing readership: literary, cultural, scientific and learned journals circulating on a weekly or monthly basis. The new periodicals proved to be enormously popular. This was an era of rising prosperity, and rising literacy. The expansion of professional elites was accompanied by a growth in confidence in scientific and professional expertise which the new periodicals were able to exploit by enrolling these professional groups as both writers and subscribers. These publications, in contrast to the newspapers, would draw on traditional founts of authority, expert writers and discursive analysis. This was also a period that witnessed the emergence of a bourgeoisie with larger amounts of disposal income.[1] These new members of an increasingly vibrant consumer society had more money for polite diversions: literature, music, the theatre. But they were also amenable to guidance as they took their first cautious steps into society: those new to refined pursuits welcomed help in matters of taste and fashion.

For publishers, the development of a market for journals was also to be welcomed. The avoidance of direct comment on contemporary events minimised the risk of official disapproval, though many more journals espoused such a policy than strictly adhered to it. They certainly regarded high society, and the fashionable doings of the great, as a subject of obsessive interest. What was in vogue became the business of the journals; and the social elite, and their enterprises, were often very much *à la mode*.

The rise of the journal was important both as a social phenomenon and for its impact on the news market. The growth of journals with their longer articles and more personal tone encouraged the development of a journalistic tradition that had so far eluded news reporting. In fact, many of the critical and stylistic features that we regard as inherent in journalism emerge first in these eighteenth-century journals. They gave the public what they had so far missed in the newspapers, with their worthy recitations of battles and court levées. Journals offered criticism, taste and judgement, but in a lighter tone than the hectoring political review papers. They spoke directly to their audience; they took time to explain and develop an argument. They were funny and diverting. Most of all they offered something entirely new to an audience that had not previously experienced anything like the sort of recreational miscellany presented in the eighteenth-century 'spectators': a distinctive voice that would return to their drawing rooms week after week, bringing both familiar characters and new fashions. It was a beguiling, intoxicating mixture.

Tools of Enlightenment

In 1665 there appeared in the highly controlled French market a wholly new periodical to set alongside the venerable *Gazette*: the *Journal des sçavans*. This was a major innovation in the European book trade: a journal devoted primarily to discoveries in the arts and sciences, with some additional notification, for legal customers, of decisions taken by the civil and ecclesiastical courts. It was set to appear weekly, on the grounds that novelties lost their lustre if held back for a monthly or annual publication. But pagination was continuous through the year's issues, indicating that they were intended to be bound up together at the end of the year. The volume was also provided with a full scholarly apparatus: tables, notes, index and cumulative bibliography. Like the *Gazette*, this was to be a privileged enterprise, enjoying a protected monopoly in this section of the market. And it was expected to be lucrative. For the French intellectual community the *Journal des sçavans* would be both an inspiration and an essential prop, a means to keep abreast of a vast literature that they could not hope to traverse alone.

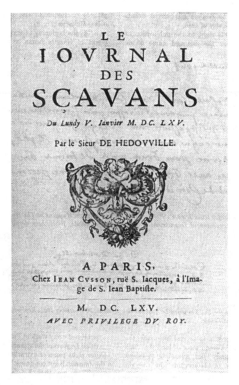

13.1 The *Journal des sçavans*.

The *Journal des sçavans* provided the prototype of a new scholarly journal that would prove enormously influential.[2] Its impact was most immediately felt across the Channel in London. Here within a few months a similar venture was established, the *Philosophical Transactions*. As its name would suggest, this was more earnestly scientific. Its editors were closely connected to the recently founded Royal Society, whose fellows provided a large proportion of its articles.[3] But the journal was not formally under the Society's control, a circumstance that led to some difficulty when the two branches of the Society, based in London and Oxford, fell out and used the pages of the *Transactions* to impugn each other's scholarly credentials. Just as the *Journal des sçavans* was published in French, the articles in the *Philosophical Transactions* were published in English. This was far from a matter of course. Educated men were expected to be Latinate, and Latin was still the language of international scientific discourse. In fact, scholars were soon complaining that the retreat from Latin made their life more difficult, as they now had to master so many languages. But the first editor of the *Transactions*, Henry Oldenburg, was adamant that it should be so: 'Because they are intended to be for the benefit of such Englishmen as are drawn to curious things, yet perhaps do not know Latin.'[4] Here the Society was making a statement of importance for the future of European culture. It proposed the vernacular as a language of erudition, notwithstanding that this went against all the established traditions of European culture, letters, and the social hierarchy represented by a good education. It was a significant symbolic step in the process of liberation from the long shadow of the humanist tradition.

The *Philosophical Transactions* was nevertheless a more elitist venture than the *Journal des sçavans*. The three hundred copies printed were more than enough for the fellows, and the Society made little attempt to spread its reach beyond the circle of experts. Both periodicals, however, were self-consciously a part of the international community of learning and discovery: the Republic of Letters celebrated in Pierre Bayle's monumental and long-running review journal, *Nouvelles de la république des lettres* (1684–1718). The first issue of the *Philosophical Transactions* contained one article contributed from France, and another from Italy; subsequent numbers frequently carried articles translated from the *Journal des sçavans*.

The scientific journals also profited from the widespread scholarly concern to organise knowledge into large encyclopaedic publications, many published in parts. The journal was now conceived in much the same way, as a tool of reference to be archived and searched. Eighteenth-century readers were increasingly prone to treat their newspapers in precisely this way.[5] A journal, or paper, would have a double value: as a topical information sheet, and as an incremental archive of knowledge. It was a knowledge bank in which science played an increasingly important role.

The *Philosophical Transactions* and *Journal des sçavans* paved the way for a growing market in serious specialist journals, which would eventually cover a large range of topics. This would be one of the most buoyant and lucrative areas of the eighteenth-century book market. It would prove particularly important in France, where the market for news and current affairs publications was so constrained by the strictly enforced monopoly of the *Gazette*.[6] Around two hundred journals made their appearance there before the end of the seventeenth century. Between 1700 and the outbreak of the French Revolution in 1789 the figure was in excess of eight hundred. This was the age of specialist journals: among the most important were the prestigious *Journal économique* (1751–72), the *Observations de la physique* (1752–1823) and the *Journal de médecine* (1754–93). The journals established in this mid-century period were particularly successful, as these long-lived ventures bear witness: of 115 periodicals established between 1750 and 1759, 63 lasted a year and

21 ten years or more. Other journals served communities of interest in medicine, agriculture, commerce, music and art.

The development of a serious scholarly press added depth and weight to the periodical press pioneered by the newspapers. The serial model proved a highly effective mechanism for spreading the risk of encyclopaedic publications, improving cash flow and allowing the market to dictate the size of an edition. Publishers were not faced, as they were in the case of conventionally published books, with the prospects of warehouses full of unsold copies. The new periodicals also progressively broadened the market for professional research in a wide variety of fields, based on serious investigation backed by empirical data. This inevitably had its impact on the reporting of current affairs, encouraging both a turn towards analysis and an increasingly sceptical approach to tales and wonders that fell outside the range of explicable phenomena. It is in precisely this period that we witness a retreat, particularly in the metropolitan press, from the reporting of bizarre or supernatural events (unless they could be used to expose the credulity of country folk).[7]

The market for science also proved remarkably broad. This was demonstrated when in 1691 John Dunton, an experienced London bookseller and publisher, embarked on one of the most innovative serial publications of this restless age. *The Athenian Mercury* was a periodical entirely devoted to readers' questions, in all fields: science, religion, manners, courtship and history.[8] Readers sent their questions by penny post to Mr Smith's coffee house adjacent to Dunton's shop in the Stocks Market. The questions were answered by the Athenian Society, in essence Dunton and his two brothers-in-law. Correspondents were never identified, which allowed them to ask their questions without worrying about exposing their ignorance. It proved to be a winning formula. The *Athenian Mercury* was sold twice weekly for a penny, and Dunton and his fellow Athenians were inundated with questions. The editor was obliged to warn readers that they would not answer the same question twice, which of course obliged enthusiasts to collect back numbers to have access to the full range of the wisdom on offer.

The *Athenian Mercury* demonstrated to the English public, probably to their great surprise, that science was one of their greatest interests.[9] Science, broadly defined, provided 20 per cent of the questions. This was very different from the science of the *Philosophical Transactions*, but on the other hand it was also a far cry from the news-books and their monstrous births. Readers wanted to know the answers to simple, practical things and phenomena that they observed in the course of their everyday lives. Why is the water in the Baths hotter than in either springs or rivers? Whence the wind has its force, and the reason for its changes; where extinguished fire goes.[10] All good questions.

Dunton closed the *Athenian Mercury* in 1697. The resumption of political journalism with the lapsing of the Licensing Act of 1695 had extended the range of serials available, and sales of his periodical were falling. But it is likely Dunton felt the venture had run its course. When a periodical depended so wholly on the personality and charisma of one individual, the pressure of weekly or bi-weekly publication was relentless; perhaps both Dunton and his readers were ready to move on. The *Athenian Mercury* nevertheless made a critical contribution to the development of the periodical genre. Beyond the inventive format of the interactive dialogue with readers, Dunton had also struck gold with his college of sages who delivered the responses. By creating this club, of which readers enjoyed a vicarious membership, Dunton had developed a conceit that found a lasting resonance both with readers and with the authors of future serials.[11] Invited for their penny subscription to join a society of erudite and witty companions, readers could be drawn into a regular web of relationships that became a virtual neighbourhood, or a substitute for their family circle. This had a particular appeal for new city dwellers often disconnected from home, and open to new associations and new experiences. Here Dunton had planted a seed that would germinate in one of the most creative phases of English letters.

Mr Spectator

In 1672 another Mercury appeared in France, a journal that over the course of years would soar far above the high-minded *Journal des sçavans*. This was the *Mercure galant* and, as its name suggests, it had in mind a rather different set of readers. The *Mercure galant* offered a vivid miscellany of topical cultural and literary news. Court gossip was mixed with a hodge-podge of verses, melodies, literary reviews, obituaries, marriage and birth announcements. Its first editor, Jean Donneau de Visé, can be regarded as the founder of the society journal.[12]

The *Mercure galant* was not above a certain high-mindedness. De Visé was a serious man, and a critic of the comedies of Molière. The *Mercure galant* was also, as was the way in France, protected by a royal monopoly, and de Visé enjoyed a handsome royal pension. So naturally the *Mercure galant* remained friendly to the court. The frequent articles flattering Louis XIV and lauding his conquests were not easily distinguishable from similar effusions in the *Gazette*. The *Mercure galant* would never be a tool of satire; its real influence

13.2 The Athenian Society. Dunton's brains' trust in fact consisted of himself and his two brothers-in-law.

was in showing the way to a new genre of periodical, the journal of society and manners. It was the signature creation of the eighteenth-century press.

It took some time before the English press found a response to the success of the *Mercure galant*. Various review papers came and went; some were too high-minded, some, like Pierre Antoine Motteux's monthly *Gentleman's Journal*, too infrequent to catch the febrile temper of the times. But the *Gentleman's Journal*, with its rich miscellany of news, culture and entertainment, pointed the way towards a form of publication that offered the man of refinement a fresh window on contemporary affairs. If this could be mixed with wit and irony the result would be the talk of the town. So it was when in 1709 Richard Steele launched *The Tatler*, a thrice-weekly miscellany printed on both sides of a single folio half sheet.[13] Steele was already an experienced news man. Since 1707 he had been the editor of the *Gazette*, a lucrative but to Steele dull assignment.[14] In contrast to the ponderous detached tone of the *Gazette*, *The Tatler* would be witty and personal. As Steele conceived it, the journal would offer a mix of news from home and abroad, comment on new books and plays, gossip and commentary on contemporary affairs. It would also include original fiction and poetry (always reliable fillers for publications facing stiff deadlines).

The Tatler took a little time to find its feet. Within a few months it had dropped its news reporting; this never fitted well with the facetious tone of the rest of the contents, and *The Tatler* was always likely, in any case, to be an additional purchase for regular readers of newspapers. The change of emphasis also reflected the influence of Joseph Addison, who joined Steele as a partner shortly after *The Tatler*'s launch. Under Addison *The Tatler* became less of a miscellany and more of an essay paper, each number offering an extended reflection on a single subject. *The Tatler* also vigorously pursued and gave a great deal of space to advertising: as many as 14 or 18 advertisements an issue, up to 150 a month. These promoted wigs, wheelchairs, birdcages, lotteries, cosmetics and medicines. As well as bringing in valuable revenue they held up a mirror to the changing taste of London society. Readers could look to them for tips on correct deportment as well as bargains.[15]

In 1711, after just two years and 271 issues, Addison and Steele closed *The Tatler*; it would live on in book form, in collected editions. Two months later they launched *The Spectator*.[16] This, it proved, was their true masterpiece. Advertised as the 'sober reflections of a detached observer', Mr Spectator was never quite that; rather a wry, sometimes caustic and always penetrating observer of the foibles and peculiarities of London life. The enterprise was driven by the sheer brilliance of the writing. Addison and Steele ostensibly eschewed coverage of the news, but the distinction was always more rhetorical

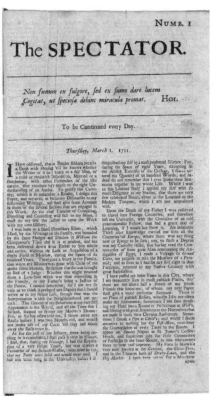

13.3 *The Tatler* and *The Spectator*.

than real. *The Tatler* included essays on the lottery and duelling, and *The Spectator* on the Bank of England, the social status of credit and the moral value of money. Was an essay on duelling addressing a social issue or writing a comedy of manners? With Steele it is hard to say. But the proclaimed bar on politics did at least give the authors licence for merciless satire of the coffee-house culture and the rage for news, never more comical than when pursued by a humourless upstart tradesman. An upholsterer, for instance:

> I found him to be the greatest newsmonger in our quarter; that he rose before day to read the *Post Man*, and that he would take two or three turns to the other end of the town before his neighbours were up, to see if there were any Dutch mails come in. He had a wife and several children, but was much more inquisitive to know what passes in Poland than in his own family. . . . He looked extremely thin in a dearth of news, and never enjoyed himself in a westerly wind. [That is, when contrary winds prevented news

bulletins crossing the English Channel.] This indefatigable kind of life was the ruin of his shop.

   This man and his affairs had been long out of my mind, till about three days ago, as I was walking in St James's Park, I heard somebody at a distance hemming after me: and who should it be but my old neighbour the uphol-sterer? I saw he was reduced to extreme poverty, by certain shabby super-fluities in his dress. . . . But pray, says he, tell me sincerely what are your thoughts of the King of Sweden? For though his wife and children were starving, I found his chief concern at present was for this great monarch.[17]

This, by Addison, was presented as the reflections of Isaac Bickerstaff, Esq., the fictional persona of *The Tatler*. It was a device that allowed the authors great licence. The views expressed were never quite those of Addison or Steele; the uncomfortable and sometimes quite cruel satire of aspirant tradesmen and empty-headed fops was placed in the mouth of a third party. Mr Spectator could advance prescriptions for the reform of taste, the theatre or the Bank of England without pausing to reflect whether they made much sense; all was in the service of wit and raillery. The tone was very different from the impas-sioned advocacy of Defoe's *Review*, but perhaps no less effective for that. And for all Mr Spectator's denial of serious political intent, this was a Whig paper, deeply rooted in the salons and coffee houses of that political interest. When Jonathan Swift was enrolled to write for *The Examiner* in 1710, this was specifically intended to provide a Tory counter-weight to the prevailing Whig tone of the leading essay periodicals.[18]

   Just as they had with *The Tatler*, Steele and Addison closed *The Spectator* after only two years. This was not because the paper had lost its way; rather, the pressures of production had become too great. Many of the most successful topical periodicals were remarkably short-lived: the ten years of Defoe's *Review* proved an exceptional run. Their fate reveals the weakness of a peri-odical dependent on a single source of inspiration. However gifted the writer, the pressure of writing regularly with passion and wit, on a sufficient variety of subjects to keep the readership entertained, would eventually tell. Periodicals folded – not because their audience fell away, but because their creators became exhausted.

   The long-term future required the development of a production model that depended less on a single creative genius. In England the way forward was indicated by Edward Cave's *Gentleman's Magazine* (1731).[19] This preserved the miscellaneous content but abandoned the highly personalised identity of the essay periodical. Begun as a digest of other topical publications, it gradu-ally evolved into an independent periodical with original content, written by

professional writers hired for the task. This was a model of collective production that the newspaper press was not yet ready to follow.

For the moment it was Mr Spectator who captured the imagination. *The
Spectator* epitomised the qualities that had made the essay paper so intoxicating: the invitation to take a walk through the city's crowded streets in the
company of a witty and urbane guide, a worldly and cultured man with access
to the smartest salons and the most advanced literary circles. *The Spectator*
found many imitators in England and abroad. The new ventures that attempted
to fill the void in the London press left by its closure mostly failed; there was
no substitute for its original authors, who had now moved on to other literary
pursuits. But abroad the 'Spectators' flourished. In the Netherlands Spectatorial
publications helped revive a periodical trade constrained by the urban magistrates' determination to limit their city to one regular paper. There was no such
restriction on the essay papers, and readers would often take several.[20] In
France one can enumerate as many as one hundred such journals established
between 1720 and 1789.[21] French readers took to their mix of literary criticism,
wit, and advice on matters of taste. The Spectators were familiar and accessible;
they offered for the first time in the French periodical press direct dialogue
with the public. They represented all that had been lacking in journalism until
this point in the highly controlled and reverential French market; the effect
was like a jolt of electricity through French literary culture and the book trade.
Naturally, such a transformation was not without its critics. The sheer frivolity
of some of the periodicals irritated the more high-minded readership, but the
publishers were unapologetic. After all, as one editor put it,

> Should one write only for savants, or for those who want to become learned?
> There is something between total ignorance and profound erudition. The
> multitude is incapable of studying and learning, so brochures and periodi-
> cals are necessary for our century.[22]

The earliest French Spectators by and large preserved the cautious tradition
of anonymity, but gradually adopted a more robust authorial identity. Between
1720 and 1739 writers like Marivaux, d'Argens, the Abbé Prévost and critics
like Desfontaines, La Varenne and La Barre de Beaumarchais all established
their own personal vehicles.[23] Some of these maintained a more serious tone,
but across the whole spectrum cultural reviews made up three-quarters of the
periodical literature, particularly in the more restrictive political environment
of the earlier half of the century. From all of this, there was money to be made;
after 1730 all major French publishers had journals on their list. The trade in
periodicals provided a substitute for the saucy fiction and 'philosophical'

works forbidden by the censors and therefore published abroad and imported back into France; this trade had reached massive proportions by the latter part of the eighteenth century.[24] It was therefore fortunate for the Parisian publishers that the trade in periodicals offered more of an outlet; though it in no way prepared them for the extraordinary surge in news publication that would follow with the revolutionary events in the century's last years.

'Riens délicieux'

In his issue of 5 May 1691, John Dunton published in the *Athenian Mercury* a daring and dramatic announcement:

> We have received this week a very ingenious letter from a lady in the country, who desires to know whether her sex might not send in questions as well as men, to which we answer yes they may, our design being to answer all manner of questions sent to us by either sex, that may be either useful to the public or to particular persons.[25]

To drive home his point Dunton followed his editorial statement with fifteen questions on marriage. This was not an unconsidered initiative. The *Athenian Mercury* had now been going for two months, and Dunton had taken the temperature of his readership. This was the most dramatic declaration possible: that women were a welcome contributing part of the reading community, and Dunton eagerly embraced his role as torchbearer. The issue of 22 May was entirely made up of questions from women, and Dunton now announced that on the first Tuesday of every month the issue would be set aside to address feminine concerns.

Although the French had been the great innovators in the seventeenth-century periodical market, it was English publishers who showed the most lively awareness of the potential of an expanding female readership. Both *The Tatler* and *The Spectator* actively courted female readers. In setting out his agenda for *The Tatler* in 1709, Richard Steele appealed explicitly to 'public-spirited' men, but not exclusively: 'I resolve also to have something which may be entertainment to the fair sex, in honour of whom I have invented the title of this paper.' It was a back-handed compliment, with its implication of inconsequential gossip, to which women were seen as particularly prone. It sets the tone of elaborate gallantry and condescension that characterised much of the engagement of essay periodicals with their female readers.[26] *The Spectator* followed with Addison's insistence that 'there are none to whom this paper will be more useful than to the female world', and the evident success of the

Spectator genre soon inspired a number of periodicals specifically directed at women readers. These proved less successful. Both *The Female Tatler* and *The Whisperer*, written in the persona of Jenny Distaff, Isaac Bickerstaff's half-sister, were blatant attempts to exploit the success of the Spectator brand, and neither succeeded.[27] It would be a further thirty years before a periodical emerged with a robust and genuine female voice: Elizabeth Haywood's *Female Spectator*.

The relationship between the earliest society periodicals and their female readers was complex. The editors were emphatic that their essays on morals and manners were particularly suitable for women, but they were also teasing and condescending. The essays were often couched as replies to a plaintive, tragicomical appeal for advice from a distressed female reader in a fix, confounded by some perplexing piece of social etiquette, or trapped by an unsuitable lover. Many of these letters give every appearance of having been written by the editors themselves. The convoluted explanations of the circumstances in which the correspondents found themselves certainly have more in common with the plots of contemporary dramatic pieces than with the lives of the allegedly inexperienced writers supposed to have penned them. These transparent devices allowed the essayists to have the best of both worlds: they could both titillate their readers and inhabit the moral ground with their responses; a device still widely practised, of course, in the serious papers' reporting of scandal or celebrity today.

The relentless definition of female consciousness – the home, manners, social etiquette and love affairs – is often grating. This preoccupation was neatly expressed in the French *Journal des dames*, launched in 1759 offering its readers a diet of 'riens délicieux', delicious nothings. But this was only ever part of the story. It is worth recalling that the *Journal des dames* soon became something more than an entertainment paper, supporting the agenda of the Enlightenment and vigorously criticising both state-privileged cultural institutions and ministerial policy. The driving force behind this transformation was a sequence of three strong women, who successively managed the journal and gave it its distinctive voice.[28] The *Journal des dames* was suppressed twice by angry ministers, in 1769 and finally in 1776.[29]

The changing shape of the *Journal des dames* is not unusual in the periodical press. New ventures sprung up and often failed to find an audience; a journal could not survive without close attention to its readers' priorities. These were partly set by women, as readers but also as engaged protagonists in the press. Women had played an active role in the print industry virtually since its beginning, almost certainly a more active role than in any other craft industry.[30] Many presses were very effectively managed by the women to whom they were entrusted, sometimes but not always after the death of their

husbands. John Dunton's sensibility to his female readers may owe something
to the fact that his business prospered mightily when his wife was at the helm,
and declined steeply after her death. Countess Alexandrine de Rye, widow of
Leonhard II von Taxis, effectively ran the Taxis postal network for eighteen
years after her husband's death, and steered the company through the notably
turbulent decades of the latter part of the Thirty Years War.[31] Among those
challenging her authority was the female Hamburg newspaper proprietor,
Ilsabe Meyer.[32] At the other end of the social spectrum the London press
would not have been able to function without the army of 'Mercury women'
who brought periodicals to their readers and sold them on the streets.[33]

The industry also found a place for an entrepreneur like Eliza Haywood,
author and proprietor of *The Female Spectator*.[34] Haywood started this periodical after a long and successful career as a novelist, and a less successful turn
as a stage actress. She gave herself no airs: the first issue confided that the
author 'never was a beauty, and am very far from being young'. But its witty
sequence of essays, on subjects that ranged from the immoderate use of tea to
the conduct of military gentlemen (likely to be bad) found a ready audience.
After it ceased publication *The Female Spectator* was several times republished
as a collected volume, and translated into both French and Dutch.[35] Haywood
was even sufficiently confident to satirise the alleged female aversion to political affairs. In reply to a dyspeptic (though almost certainly invented) correspondent, who took her to task for promising more in the way of politics than
she had delivered, Haywood defended her editorial choices:

> Armies marching – battles fought – towns destroyed – rivers crossed and the
> like: I should think it ill became me to take up my own, or reader's time with
> such accounts as are every day to be found in the public papers.[36]

This was the point; there were other places where such matters were exhaus-
tively discussed, and the journals did not have to regurgitate material freely
available in the newspapers. Plenty of male readers also found their appetite for
battles and sieges much reduced when the society papers provided an alternative diversion. But this was generally not a choice that had to be made.
Articulate female readers followed the news closely, even if social convention
forbade them from making much reference to this in their correspondence.[37]
It is significant that when Dorothy Osborne read a news publication in 1653,
she could only acknowledge this in an oblique way: 'I know not how I stumbled
upon a news book this week, and for want of something else to do read it.'[38]
This was in a letter to her suitor, Sir William Temple, and she may have
thought he would consider an interest in news unseemly in a potential bride.

Married women could take a close interest in politics that impacted on their family with less constraint.[39]

Critically the hundred years between Dorothy Osborne's letter and Eliza Haywood's *Female Spectator* saw a giant leap forward in female literacy. The number of female readers had increased three or fourfold; this was a substantial market that publishers could not afford to ignore. Women as consumers and arbiters of taste were an important economic force and therefore an important driver of the periodical market. The first daily paper in France, the *Journal de Paris* (1777), was a cultural listing, offering notes on the current theatrical performances and literary gossip. In the second half of the eighteenth century essay journals like *The Female Spectator* were gradually superseded by a new generation of monthly magazines. *The Lady's Magazine* (1759) and *The Lady's Museum* (1760) were part of a general trend away from the single editor-persona towards a substantial periodical offering a collection of features by various hands.[40] Both these journals offered a variety of instructional features, including articles on geography, history and popular science, tempered by fiction and poetry. Nor were female readers spared the harsher aspects of contemporary life. In an earlier manifestation of *The Lady's Magazine*, a fortnightly established in 1749, readers were treated to a monthly account of the trial, confession or execution of some notorious criminal. Sometimes these malefactors were female: 'an account of three unhappy women executed at Tyburn'; 'the trial of Mary Blandy for poisoning her late father'.[41] The windows of the polite parlour could never entirely shut out the life of the teeming metropolis beyond.

The Political Journal

The periodical press did not – could not – ignore politics. Whether it was the whimsical rapier thrusts of the Spectator genre, or the increasingly bold editorialising in some parts of the newspaper industry, this was the age that finally began to achieve the integration of news and commentary that we take for granted in the printed news media today. An important catalyst was the emergence of a new generation of journals of political analysis. These played a particularly important role in parts of Europe where the newspapers remained wedded to a conservative vision of news reporting that left them little scope for political commentary. This was true for both the Low Countries and Germany, where most newspapers remained local monopoly providers, and obsessively careful not to cause offence to local magistrates. An escape from this studied neutrality was provided by Gottlob Benedikt von Shirach's *Politische Journal*, one of the most successful periodical ventures of the century. Established in

1781, the *Politische Journal* became the most widely read periodical in the German-speaking world, with an audience transcending the micro-markets of the German city and princely states.[42]

By the 1780s Germany had 183 newspapers. With rare exceptions, however, such as the widely circulating Hamburg papers, most served a purely local clientele. Their format and priorities were barely distinguishable from their predecessors a century before. Foreign news predominated, and much of the remaining space was taken up by advertisements and a local court circular, a Lilliputian version of the Paris *Gazette*'s despatches from Versailles: 'all the honours and favours dispensed at the court, festivities, voyages, ceremonies, banquets, and the endless list of irrelevancies, rumours, suppositions, contradictions and private affairs', as von Shirach put it in one of the first issues of the *Politische Journal*.[43] Von Shirach also believed that the newspaper itself – its barrage of fragmentary reports – posed a barrier to understanding. Even with the best-informed paper, the urgent periodicity of a weekly production could hardly provide more than a part of the picture, with little context and no scope for sober analysis. With the *Politische Journal* von Shirach created a journal that he hoped could combine the traditional analytical function of pamphlets with the contemporaneity of the newspapers. Monthly publication should ensure that the shape of events had become clearer, and eliminate the misleading, false or trivial reports that found their way into the newspapers.

A true child of the Enlightenment, von Shirach adhered to a clear and rational plan. Each monthly issue consisted of three parts. The first presented background information necessary to understand the issues of the day: statistics and excerpts from official documents. There then followed analytical articles written by von Shirach summarising events in various parts of Europe. The final third consisted of letters from the *Journal*'s correspondents from the self-same capitals, timed to arrive in Hamburg just before he went to press.

It was an innovative formula and it found a ready public: the readership grew steadily to around 8,000 subscribers. But the *Politische Journal* also attracted criticism, much of it focused on von Shirach's own editorial style. Von Shirach never understated the potential importance of the events he described: each shift in the balance of European power portended revolution, and he often saw war looming. Von Shirach's views were strongly held, but he sometimes put himself on the wrong side of history, as with his trenchant opposition to both the American and French revolutions. An unfortunate talent for unsuccessful prognostication was revealed early in his reporting of the Franco-Spanish siege of Gibralter in 1782. Subscribers would have received his careful analysis of the strength of the investing forces, and confident predictions of their success, just as the newspapers brought news of the crushing English victory. This was the danger of a monthly publication dealing with fast-moving events. For all that, the *Politische Journal* was a carefully conceived and ground-breaking publication, not least in the degree of attention it gave to German news. The *Politische Journal* devoted at least half of its space to news and analysis of events in Germany and Austria: a radical departure from the newspaper tradition with its continuing concentration on foreign news. This, along with the *Politische Journal*'s wide circulation, played an important role in the growth of pan-German political consciousness.

In France the publication of political journals was a feature of the general loosening of political controls before the Revolution. The catalyst was a political crisis of a very traditional sort. In 1770 Louis XV, exasperated by a long conflict of attrition with the Paris Parlement, dismissed his veteran chief minister Choiseul and sought more decisive leadership from a triumvirate of determined officials, led by Chancellor Maupeou. The triumvirate in turn sought to out-manoeuvre the opposition of the Parlement by replacing sitting magistrates with a reorganised court system. This flagrant provocation initiated the largest wave of pamphleteering since the *Mazarinades* more than a century before.[44] The outpouring of publications on both sides awakened Paris's normally conservative publishing community to the tremendous public interest in current affairs. Encouraged by the weakening of censorship that always followed from a major political conflict in France, publishers began to issue pamphlets in a quasi-periodical form, with each successive issue consecutively numbered. This shift towards serial publication continued after the initial crisis had subsided, most notably with the *Mémoires secrets*, a thirty-six volume series of gossip and anecdotes. Other notable ventures included the *Observateur anglois*, and, most notorious of all, the *Annales politiques* of Simon-Nicolas-Henri Linguet.

Linguet had earned his journalistic spurs as an employee of the publisher-entrepreneur Charles-Joseph Panckoucke. Dismissed for intemperate attacks on the *philosophes*, Linguet withdrew to London, from where he crafted an immediate publishing sensation. The contemporary renown of Linguet's *Annales* lay in the quality of its writing, for Linguet, already a well-known and distinguished lawyer, revealed himself as a natural exponent of advocacy journalism. More remarkable still was his success, as an independent editor operating outside the country, in securing the printing and distribution of the *Annales* in France. Somehow Linguet's agent in his home country managed to ensure that circulation of the journal would be tolerated, but its instant celebrity brought new problems in the form of unauthorised reprints, which Linguet was powerless to prevent. Briefly interrupted when Linguet was lured to Paris and imprisoned in the Bastille, the *Annales* were resumed in 1783. Linguet's adventures provided a vivid illustration of the enduring problem that faced the French political press. Although political periodicals circulated widely, censorship was never formally abandoned. This meant that political journals could never be openly marketed or advertised; circulation required accommodations and private understandings that could always be revoked. This was one reason why the French periodicals did not achieve the same regularity and exact periodicity that characterised similar ventures in other countries. However, they made up for this with a passionate engagement and wit that entranced readers greedy for political debate after the long years of a controlled and subservient press. Linguet's *Annales*, boosted by the unofficial reprint, maintained an international circulation of as much as twenty thousand copies per issue. Despite his angry denunciations of pirate publishers, Linguet was reported to have made large sums from the *Annales*, as much as 80,000 *livres* a year.[45]

A Man of Property

The full potential of this buoyant market for political journalism would ultimately be demonstrated by Linguet's former patron, Charles-Joseph Panckoucke. Panckoucke was Europe's first media mogul.[46] He had been born into the business of books, the son of a provincial bookseller in Lille. Educated in the *philosophe* spirit, he considered a career as an academic or military engineer (he was an especially gifted mathematician) before accepting that his fate was to take over the family business.[47] In the early 1760s, working in partnership with his two sisters, Panckoucke transferred the bookshop to Paris. Immersing himself in the intellectual culture of the capital, Panckoucke continued to write; among the books he published were a number of his own works. Most important of all, Panckoucke had the gift of friendship. He was close to Voltaire from an early age, and later to Jean-Jacques Rousseau. The distinguished naturalist Georges-Louis Leclerc, Comte de Buffon, was a confidant and friend.[48]

Moving in these circles Panckoucke conceived the wish to make a substantial contribution to the Encyclopedist movement. In 1769 he approached Diderot with a plan to publish a supplement to the *Encyclopédie*. Initially rebuffed, he persisted and obtained the necessary permission. A decade later he embarked on what would be his chief monument, the *Encyclopédie méthodique*, arranged by subject matter rather than alphabetically. Secure in the esteem of France's leading thinkers, Panckoucke might have been expected to be content. But he had other plans. A shrewd reader of markets as well as men, Panckoucke had for some years been contemplating the rich potential of the periodical press. The original transaction through which Panckoucke bought the shop and stock of the Paris bookseller Michel Lambert in 1760 had also brought him Lambert's printing contracts, which included the *Année littéraire* and the

Journal des sçavans; the latter in particular was a prestigious venture, though Panckoucke claimed it was running at a loss when he bought it.[49] Profitable or not, this provided the foundation for an expanding portfolio of periodicals. In due course Panckoucke was prepared to try his hand at the political press. Gradually he built up a stable that included the *Journal politique de Bruxelles*, *Journal des dames*, *Journal des spectacles*, *Journal des affaires d'Angleterre et d'Amérique* and the *Gazette des tribunaux*. With his *Journal politique de Bruxelles* and the *Journal de Genève*, Panckoucke nodded towards the tradition that all political papers apart from the official *Gazette* should be published outside the country. In fact both periodicals, despite their name, were published in France, an arrangement that had the blessing of the ministry.

The crucial moment came in 1778 when Panckoucke purchased control of the *Mercure de France*, the venerable but ailing successor to the *Mercure galant*. The *Mercure* had been established in 1672 as a monthly stablemate to the *Gazette*, but had failed to maintain its position in the proliferating eighteenth-century market for journals. Panckoucke transformed it into a weekly, and in the process built its circulation from 2,000 to 15,000. This coup had been

13.4 Charles-Joseph Panckoucke, media mogul and Enlightenment man.

prepared by careful politics. By cultivating a relationship with the Comte de Vergennes, minister of foreign affairs from 1774, Panckoucke received the exclusive privilege to publish political news. That the foreign minister should have dealt such a critical blow to the official *Gazette* tells us much about the essential frivolity, as well as the brutality, of Ancien Régime politics. Other newspapers now had to pay Panckoucke for the privilege of reprinting his information. Secure in the confidence of both official Paris and the leading figures of the Enlightenment, Panckoucke flourished. By 1788 he had built up an extraordinary business empire, with 800 workmen and employees. His workshops and offices, it was said, were one of the sights of Paris.

In 1789 Panckoucke won what would previously have been considered one of the greatest prizes of all: he became publisher of the *Gazette*. But these were strange times for the reporting of current affairs in France. Events would soon take a turn beyond the imagining of the philosophers of the old order. These events would test to destruction the capacities of the antiquated, prosperous print world of the Ancien Régime; men like Panckoucke, who had done well in its strangely constrained politics but extraordinarily diverse intellectual culture, would face a fight for survival.

The age of the journal witnessed the emergence of a thoughtful, self-confident industry that facilitated intellectual exchange over a wide spectrum of disciplines. For publishers this offered a welcome field of innovation in new ventures positioned between the established but sometimes complaisant world of book publishing and the turbulent world of pamphlets and ephemeral print. Even for the most established and conservative publishing houses, journals were an attractive economic proposition. They offered a regular and predictable sale thanks to the subscription system. For major new enterprises the compilation of a subscription list provided both valuable advertising and a means of testing the water before printing got underway. The extended friendship and correspondence network of the Republic of Letters provided a natural conduit for such information, and both editors and publishers were happy to move in these circles. The publication of even very substantial intellectual enterprises in numbered sections ensured that there was no risk of the unsold portion of an edition rotting in the warehouse, as had been the case with many overly ambitious scholarly works issued in the first centuries of print.[50] With periodicals, customers paid in advance and each issue had a built-in sequel, whereas books were individual events, dangerous and unpredictable in their success. It is no wonder that periodicals became the fastest growing sector of eighteenth-century publishing.

CHAPTER 14

In Business

In June 1637 Hans Baert found himself in a difficult spot. Baert was a wealthy Haarlem merchant, and in recent times he had involved himself heavily in the trade in tulips.[1] For a time he had prospered. The price of the bulbs had increased steadily, and more recently at a phenomenal rate. But in February of this year the bottom had dropped out of the market; and none of those who had bought from Baert at the higher prices would pay their debt.

The tulip trade was, it must be admitted, a very unusual form of commodity trading. These most exotic of plants flowered, often only for a week or two, in spring. The bulbs were then lifted, dried and in September replanted; thus for most of the trading year they could not be seen, or physically delivered to their new owners. This was little problem to the adventurous Dutch, who through their lengthy experience of long-distance voyages were used to managing a futures market, but it was bad news for Hans Baert. The price for tulips had reached its unlikely zenith in February 1637, when his bulbs were deep underground; now, in June, they had to be lifted, which could only be done in the presence of their new owners to prevent fraudulent substitution of less valuable varieties. Since his clients would not come, Baert stood to lose his money.

The tulipmania has gone down in history as one of the first great financial bubbles: an extravagant boom, followed by a ruinous bust. In fact, much of what was assumed to be known about this episode turns out to be myth. Most of those involved in the trade were prosperous citizens who could absorb the losses. There were few bankruptcies and the wider Dutch economy was barely affected. The tulipmania did not lead simple artisans, tempted into the market by hopes of a quick fortune, into penury. The most extravagant stories of destitute carpenters and weavers emanate from the moralising pamphlets that followed the collapse of the market.[2] During the sharp, and ultimately spectacular rise in the prices of bulbs there was little adverse comment; in fact, the States of Holland were most concerned to profit from the boom by taxing the trade. What is in fact most extraordinary about this colourful episode is how little interest it evoked in the contemporary news media. That a pound of bulbs could change hands for 1,000 guilders (three years' wages for a master carpenter) caused no adverse comment. Perhaps events moved too quickly. In five weeks Switzers, one of the most sought-after bulbs, went from 125 guilders a pound to a high of 1,500: 1,200 per cent appreciation in just over a month.[3]

In this same year Amsterdam had two functioning newspapers, yet neither paid this sudden appreciation in the price of tulips much attention. Even in this sophisticated news market, the boom in tulip futures was a word-of-mouth phenomenon. Deals were struck and prices talked up in meetings between *bloemisten*, as those who got into the trade became known, in closed circles: at private dinners, in taverns, or in meetings in the gardens where the tulips were planted. The print media discovered the tulipmania only when the trade had collapsed, when pamphleteers had many things to say about greed, the credulity of traders, and the transitory nature of earthly wealth. Those who had had their fingers burned faced a deal of mockery. In 1637 the bad blood between thwarted sellers and rebellious buyers threatened to become a problem of public order. This too was unwelcome in a state where the good conduct of business and national reputation were closely aligned. In March the Burgomasters of Holland forbade 'the little song and verses which are daily sold by the booksellers about the tulip trade'. The council sent round bailiffs to confiscate the printed copies.[4] It was time to draw a veil over the business, and move on.

The Business Press

The tulipmania casts an interesting light on the psychology of business in this period, but offers few hints regarding the development of a business press. This seems all the more surprising when we remember the important role that merchants had played in the creation of the international news market: from the business correspondence of the late Middle Ages, through the creation of the first courier services and the first commercial manuscript newsletters.[5] But at the point news became a commercial product it took a decisive turn away from the reporting of business news. *Avvisi*, and their successors the printed newspapers, offered almost exclusively political, diplomatic and military news. This could be of great importance to merchants with goods on the road, but it did not mesh with their day-to-day concerns with regard to the prices they would pay, or could charge, for commodities. Merchants also needed to

14.1 A satire on the tulipmania. *Bloemisten* conclude their bargains in a fool's cap while peasants cart off the worthless bulbs.

keep a close eye on the rates of exchange between Europe's various currencies. Although bills of exchange had functioned efficiently for the discharge of debt and the transfer of money over long distances for some centuries, fortunes could still be won and lost through trading in the currency markets.

These more prosaic mercantile concerns spawned a different and highly specialised printed business literature: the publication of lists of commodity prices and exchange rates. Some of the most ephemeral of all forms of printed literature, they are far more likely to have been lost than to survive. The early history of the financial press can only be reconstructed from fragmentary evidence of flimsy scraps of print, often tucked away in bundles of commercial correspondence.[6]

So although there is evidence that printed lists of commodity prices were published in Venice and Antwerp as early as the 1540s, the earliest surviving copies date from forty years later. These printed price lists were the very simplest form of print: a single strip of paper, characteristically about 14 by 48 centimetres. This suggests a large folio sheet had been set with two or three settings of the same text across the page, which was then cut up. The format was closely modelled on the handwritten price lists compiled by brokers and agents in Europe's major trading centres in the medieval period. Examination of these early manuscript lists reveals a remarkable level of uniformity. Lists compiled in widely spread cities such as London and Damascus, and at very different dates, record much the same commodities (and often in the same order).[7] The commodities were named in Italian and this practice was largely continued into the print era, whether the price lists were issued in Venice, Frankfurt or Antwerp.[8] Amsterdam, where the commodities were listed in Dutch, was an exception; Hamburg also used Dutch in its earliest lists. All of these cities had published regular weekly lists by the end of the sixteenth century. London, Danzig and Lisbon soon followed. In the earliest surviving examples only the actual form was printed, leaving the date and the current prices to be added by hand.

In Amsterdam the fixing of prices was delegated to a committee of five brokers.[9] The data could then be passed to a scribal office for the prices to be added to a pre-printed form. By the middle of the seventeenth century Amsterdam had moved to a fully printed form, still produced under official supervision. The regulations established by the city burgomasters also stipulated the terms of sale: subscribers were to pay 4 guilders a year (one and a half stuivers per copy). So that merchants who traded in Amsterdam on an irregular basis could have access to them, individual issues could be purchased at the Exchange for 2 stuivers each. The commodities listed were grouped into convenient categories, and covered a wide range of raw materials and finished products, including spices, foodstuffs and a range of clothes and textiles. Of course those actually striking bargains would always want to check up on the latest prices, which could move quite significantly during the course of a week. This suggests that the printed sheets served primarily as a reference tool, particularly for traders who wanted to assemble a run of weekly lists and check how prices had moved over an extended period. That the Amsterdam lists were used in this way, and circulated widely both in the Netherlands and abroad, is indicated by the provision for subscribers to take two or more copies at a reduced rate: presumably to send the duplicates to out-of-town correspondents.

Lists of currency exchange rates were published in much the same way, on a weekly basis under official supervision. Here the published form consisted of a list of European cities, alongside which the prevailing rates of exchange could be added. In Venice the currencies and their rates were both printed on the sheet, though this was rather the exception.[10] Elsewhere the rates were added by hand. As with commodity prices, each city published a single official

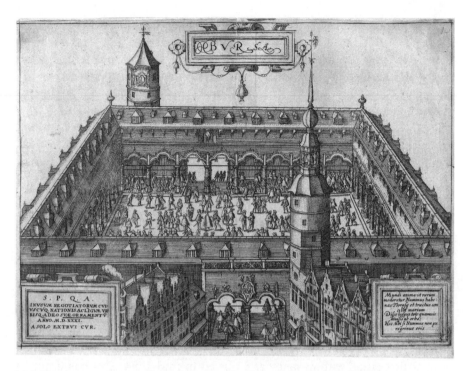

14.2 The Antwerp Bourse. Such places were hotbeds of rumour and disinformation, as well as commercial hubs.

list, consigning the task to a trusted official or, in the case of Venice, a publishing firm. In the second half of the seventeenth century the principle of this official monopoly was increasingly under strain. Twice, in 1670 and 1683, the Amsterdam authorities had to intervene to defend the privileges of the appointed exchange brokers from interlopers. The crucial change seems to have come with the introduction of a third major piece of financial data: share prices. In the second half of the seventeenth century the previously rather small number of joint stock companies expanded rapidly. Trading in their stock encouraged the development of specialist financial publications, which listed shares alongside commodity prices, exchange rates and shipping news. Nowhere was this development more pronounced than in the emerging powerhouse of northern commerce, London.

Bubble

In the publication of business data England chose a separate path, almost from the beginning. Uniquely, in England the publishing of commodity data does not seem to have been an official monopoly. Merchants and traders could instead avail themselves of a wide range of publications. The *Prices of Merchandise in London*, published from 1667 and the successor to the earliest London price lists, was joined from 1680 by Whiston's *Weekly Remembrancer* and from 1694 by Proctor's *Price Courant*.[11] A few years later John Castaing began publication of his *Course of the Exchange*. London had never had its own listing of exchange rates, and this provided Castaing's opportunity. But he improved on it by adding a list of share prices. Castaing, a member of the Protestant Huguenot community settled in London since their expulsion from France by Louis XIV, was an active stock-jobber, and saw here the chance to combine this business with financial journalism. In March 1697 he placed an advertisement for his paper: 'J. Castaing at Jonathan's Coffee House delivers the Course of Exchange, the price of Blank-Notes, Bank Stock, East India Stock and other things every Post-Day, for 10s per annum.'[12]

This advertisement appeared in Houghton's *A collection for the improvement of husbandry and trade*, another innovative financial publication. In contrast to the price lists, Houghton's *Collection* included in each weekly issue an article on a topic of economic or financial interest. This was followed by a select commodity price list and a list of shares. The number of shares quoted was at first large, with as many as 64 listed in mid-1694. This could not be sustained; the list of companies shrank quite rapidly, and in 1703 Houghton's paper ceased publication.[13] Houghton's collection had also included details of the arrivals and departures of ships, trading information that also generated its own specialist publication with the foundation in 1694 of Edward Lloyd's *Ships arrived at and departing from the several ports of England and foreign ports*. This, renamed *Lloyd's list*, continues to this day.

These technical specialist papers remained, however, rather separate from the general press. Although England experienced a rapid proliferation in the number of newspapers after the lapse of the Licensing Act in 1695, these papers offered only very limited comment on the economic life of the capital. The *Gazette* followed the progress of the subscription to the Bank of England in 1694, but once this was accomplished Bank matters were not often alluded to. In 1699 *The Post Boy* mentioned a meeting to discuss a union of the East India and English Companies; but there was no comment on the likely effect of such a union, or, in subsequent issues, on the outcome.[14] From 1697 *The Post Boy* included a brief passage with the major share prices, but business news intruded most obviously through the placing of paid advertisements. Companies took space to advertise meetings of their General Court. The launch of companies, and particularly projects, took up many inches of news print. This was a great era of projecting. Schemes of land reclamation, patent diving bells, new inventions and trading schemes made their optimistic pleas for investors' money. Between 1695 and 1699 lottery schemes often occupied nearly all the available advertising space.[15] This proliferation of lotteries, such as the Million Adventure, the Unparalleled Adventure and the Honorable Undertaking, was a sign of the emergence of a new class of potential investors with little experience in the marketplace and searching for alternative opportunities for investment. It was a potentially combustible mix.

In the two decades after the Glorious Revolution of 1688 the London economy embarked on a period of sustained growth. The more settled political climate allowed for a degree of fundamental institutional innovation: the foundation of the Bank of England, the consolidation of the national debt, the re-coinage of 1696.[16] All of these remarkable developments, and the extraordinary boom in venturing and new companies, inspired a sustained effort to understand the changes under way. Most of these disquisitions on trade appeared in traditional pamphlet form, though the periodical press also did what it could to help readers understand the new markets. Between June and July 1694 John Houghton wrote a series of seven articles in his *A collection for the improvement of husbandry*, attempting to explain the new financial markets to his subscribers. His articles gave a brief history of joint stock companies and explained how trades were made, including such relatively sophisticated instruments as options and time bargains.[17] Defoe's *Review* also discoursed frequently on economic matters, and Defoe was more inclined than most to muse on the general state of the economy. Defoe of course had personal experience of the hazards of projecting, having been a bankrupt in an unsuccessful business career. He never entirely kicked the habit; although the *Review* was drawn off into political topics, his last valedictory issue would comment rather wistfully that 'writing upon trade was the whore I really doted upon'.[18] The choice of language is significant; the tone of contemporary pamphlet comment was deeply suspicious of projecting, reflecting the perceived moral ambiguity of making money through financial dealings. The questions posed in the correspondence columns of the *Athenian Mercury* focused on the moral hazard of lotteries. Could, asked one correspondent in 1694, a godly man in good conscience partake in a lottery when the lots were disposed by Divine Providence?[19]

Despite the considerable amount of ink spilled on economic discussions, and the amount of financial data being published in the business press, it remains very questionable whether this was sufficient, or offered the right sort of information, to be of much use to those entering the markets; particularly at times of rapid price movements. London was a very unusual financial market. To a quite unique extent the capital city concentrated the political

power and financial muscle of the whole nation. It was also of course a port
with constant connections to all major European markets. Yet within this
sprawling metropolis the financial trading district was concentrated into a
very small space. The principal centres of financial power, the Royal Exchange,
the East India Company and Exchange Alley (whence stock-jobbers had
removed from the Exchange in 1698) were all within a few hundred paces of
each other. Visitors venturing into this bear-pit in trading hours found it a
cacophony of noise, where those experienced in affairs exchanged information
and made trades, all at a speed and in a jargon that outsiders found utterly
bewildering. Defoe, whose *Essay on Projects* and *The Villainy of Stock-Jobbers
detected* reflect the general scepticism of the age, used his *Review* for a wonderfully inventive denunciation of the lack of scruples in the financial market. The
following imagined dialogue caught the irrationality of trading in a market
where rumour and the herd mentality could easily trump rational analysis:

> One cries, is there a Post? Answer, no; but they have it in Exchange Alley
>   Has the Government any Express? No, but it is in everybody's mouth in
> Exchange Alley.
>   Is there any account of it at the Secretary's Offices? No, but 'tis all the news
> in Exchange Alley.
>   Why, but how does it come? Nay, nobody knows; but 'tis very hot in
> Exchange Alley.[20]

Those that flourished in this world did so because they had developed their
own networks of information and intelligence.[21] It took experience to filter
from the cacophony of rumour, reports and advice the news that would move
markets, particularly as it was widely believed that some would deliberately
circulate false reports to make a profit. Those at the very pinnacle of this
edifice of power and money could also be very secretive with commercially
sensitive information, the directors of the East India Company and the Bank
notoriously so.

The result was that when the markets moved rapidly, as was the case with
the notorious South Sea adventure, the printed word offered no real help. The
weekly price lists were too infrequent to keep up with the market, and the web
of speculation and rumour made little impact on the non-financial papers.
This mattered less than one might think, for most citizens were simply the
astonished audience for this first great bull market. Rather like tulipmania, the
vast majority of dealings occurred within the closed circles of the privileged.
The South Sea Bubble was that most satisfying thing: a fraud perpetrated by
the elite on itself.

Defoe's *Review* had ceased publication before the South Sea calamity, but it is not likely that he would have spoken out against it. Few voices were raised in criticism as the financial miracle of 1720 unfolded. The South Sea venture was never in any real respect a trading company.[22] To establish a trade with South America depended on an unlikely conjuncture of political circumstances opening a previously closed market, and this prospect had in any case disappeared by 1718. Where it did find success was in creating a counterweight to the Whig-dominated East India Company and Bank of England, and by sucking in surplus liquidity it had soon raised a huge capital. With no trade in view the directors now made an audacious attack on the Bank by proposing to take on the whole national debt. In a period of frantic negotiation a counter-bid from the Bank was seen off, and the South Sea Company emerged victorious. Such a huge liability, however, required a greatly increased share capital, and a rising share price would also greatly increase the prospects of meeting the Company's obligations. By judicious management of the market this was for a time achieved. Between January and April 1720 the price of South Sea stock had risen from 130 to 300; in the next two months stock appreciated a further 300 per cent. The South Sea stock was not an isolated beneficiary of this frantic activity. Bank and East India stock also rose sharply, and during the year to August a further 190 projects were floated, most as joint stock companies. All were seeking to catch the same hopeful tide that created money from nothing.

At the height of the Bubble newspapers had remarkably little to say about the astonishing events unfolding at the heart of the financial district. *The Daily Courant*, a single-page daily news sheet established in 1702, was the only organ in a position to chart the day on day rises, which seemed so miraculously to be enriching those blessed with stock. On 31 May, South Sea stock moved from 590 to 610; on 1 June from 610 to 760; on 2 June it touched a high of 870 before falling back to 770. Then on 24 June, after South Sea stock had traded at 750 the day before, *The Daily Courant* offered this momentous, but curiously dispassionate announcement: 'yesterday South Sea stock was 1000'.[23]

In such extraordinary times, the weekly or tri-weekly news-sheets despatched to out-of-town subscribers by post could scarcely keep up. Those in the provinces, who would not normally have been subscribers to the *Courant*, generally heard of developments through correspondence with London friends. The papers also gave notice of meetings of the court, and publicised its determinations, as during the summer the Company took steps to enhance its capital further. These heady days, before Parliament intervened to curb projecting, brought a cascade of other calls for capital.[24] The London newspapers were happy to find room for the numerous advertisements placed by these hopeful entrepreneurs. There were also an increasing number of advertisements placed by those seeking to cash in their shares and invest the profits in property or the accoutrements of wealth. At this point there was little adverse comment; this was reserved for the inevitable search for scapegoats when the Company's share price first faltered and then tumbled precipitously: 'All is floating, all falling, the directors are cursed, the top adventurers broke.'[25]

The social consequences of the Bubble should not be exaggerated. Most of those who had invested were moneyed, and few were left destitute.[26] The collapse of the Company was most deadly for its directors, who had made stock available, often on very preferential terms, to numerous Parliamentarians. Faced with personal losses, the Members of Parliament were at their most virtuous and censorious. The directors were summoned before the House of Commons and stripped of much of their personal wealth. Having performed this ritual sacrifice, the appetite for more fundamental investigation palled. The most scandalous aspect of the project had been the terms under which stock had been made available to persons of influence. They were allowed an option to buy at a stipulated rate, at no payment. It was a risk-free trade: if the stock went up, they took the profit, and if it did not the option lapsed.[27] This irregular procedure, a bribe by any other name, had been recorded in the famous green book of the Company Secretary, Robert Knight. This mysterious volume had disappeared when Knight fled the country, but its pages included many surprising names, including that of the king, George I. When Knight was taken into custody in the Austrian Netherlands, the ministry was obliged to make energetic public efforts to secure his return to face trial, while simultaneously making equally urgent representations to the Habsburg authorities to ensure that these formal requests were denied. Incredibly, this tortuous procedure was successful; still more surprisingly, it remained secret. Although long suspected, the full extent of the ministry's duplicity was only revealed by documents discovered in the imperial archives in Vienna during the past twenty years.[28] The famous green book was never seen again.

By 1720 London had a large and vibrant press: at least twenty competing papers sold many thousands of copies every week. It could hardly have been said to have covered itself in glory. Perhaps the failure to anticipate the crash should not be too heavily censured. A bubble is only identified as such when it bursts; until that point the steady upward march of share prices can easily seem the natural order of things. Those who identify a downturn too early, and miss out on the easiest profits, can end up as the biggest losers.[29] In a stampede the middle of the herd can be the safest place. In the Bubble the press did what it does best: joined the torrent of virtuous indignation unleashed on those who gave too much, too generously, to men who would not accept that their unearned windfall could vanish as easily as it had been conjured up. As the share price slid towards oblivion in the autumn of 1720, the advertisements in *The Daily Courant* for coach horses and fine houses were replaced by notices of recently published pamphlets seeking to make sense of these unprecedented events. This day is published, offered the *Courant* on 31 October, *The Battle of the Bubbles from their first sudden rise to their late speedy decay*. It was clearly popular: a second edition was on sale only a week later.[30] Once again it was specially penned pamphlets, rather than the weekly or daily press, that offered the natural place to analyse great events.[31] And there was always the catharsis of ridicule. *The Post Boy* of 22 October offered (for six pence) a newly written play, *The Broken stock-broker: or work for the bailiffs: a new farce as it was lately acted in Exchange alley*. And those with time on their hands could at least invest in a new pack of playing cards, 'wherein are represented several bubbles, with a satirical epigram on each card'. The enterprising makers clearly anticipated a large sale, since *The Post Boy* advertised a long list of places where the cards could be purchased (at a cost of three shillings).[32]

The real economy, meanwhile, adapted smoothly to the humbling of the South Sea Company. The primacy of the Bank resumed; coach-makers and smart London tailors enjoyed a difficult season; above all commerce continued to fuel the steady enrichment of the emerging bourgeoisie. By 1727 London had come close to equalling Amsterdam as the financial capital of northern Europe, an outcome that would have been unimaginable when in the previous century England was repeatedly humbled by Dutch sea power.[33]

Advertising

The early business press, it seems, offered very little in the way of advice to those seeking to take advantage of the new investment opportunities of the age; still less to those with money but no wisdom, seeking to avoid its pitfalls. The business press produced no seers of prophecy, no masters of divination. Economic journalism learned from its earliest days that it was far easier to be wise after the event. Those seeking visions into the future were as well advised to pore over the printed almanacs, with their opaque and tantalising fore-telling of the year ahead. These continued to sell in huge numbers, and also provided useful fillers as excerpts for newspapers short of material.[34]

The world of commerce made its principal impact upon the newspapers not in discussions of high policy or investment strategy, but as an adjunct to the trade in goods and services: through paid advertising. By the eighteenth

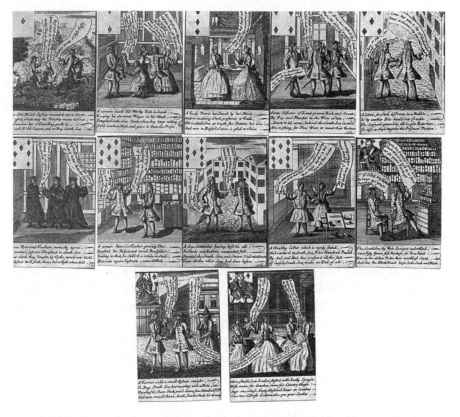

14.3 Bubble playing cards. An opportunity to beguile care and forget fortunes lost for three shillings a pack.

century advertisements were a ubiquitous part of the market in periodical news. They throw a fascinating light on the developing marketplace; they also played an increasingly important part in underpinning the economics of the news industry.

Advertisements made their first appearance in newspapers in that most commercial of societies, the Dutch Republic. Newspapers in Amsterdam carried advertisements from the 1620s. The very first, for a forthcoming book of emblems, in fact appeared simultaneously in the two competing Amsterdam papers, on 10 August 1624.[35] Neither stated the price of the book. Advertisements for books would make up a large proportion of the earliest advertisements in Dutch papers, as they would also in England, where advertisements would first appear in news periodicals in any number during the Interregnum.[36] Booksellers, who often sold newspapers from their stalls or shops, clearly saw the opportunity to tempt buyers in to view other interesting new stock.

The range of advertisements carried by Dutch papers broadened rapidly. They normally fell into one of three categories: notifications of sales or services; public service notices; and personal items. The Republic was an early centre of public auctions, of pictures and books, and these forthcoming events were often advertised in the newspapers. Tutors and schoolmasters advertised their services; the city of Utrecht even took out a series of advertisements to announce the opening of the new university in 1636. Other public notices included of market days, new postal routes, and wanted posters: the oldest, a hue and cry for a shoemaker suspected of murdering the mayor of Weesp. Amsterdam was also the centre of the European diamond trade, and dealers were happy to promise a reward to see stolen goods returned. Individual citizens would advertise for the return of lost property or fugitive servants; in one poignant case, a mother was seeking to be reunited with her young children.[37]

The Dutch were precocious in their development of the newspaper trade. By the 1650s advertisements frequently occupied half of the last column, that is, one eighth of the total space. The early German newspapers were in contrast reluctant to admit much beyond book notices in their early years, and here the market in paid advertisements developed more slowly. In England, although advertisements appear in any numbers only in the 1650s, they proliferated very rapidly. Here again, notifications of newly published books were most common, but newspapers also soon found space for lost and found goods, runaway servants and patent medicines. Medicinal remedies would become a mainstay of English advertising, partly because booksellers often stocked a few patent potions alongside their books.[38] The *Gazette*, as a paper of record, resisted advertisements for six years, until in 1671 it started to accept personal ads. These were often, it must be admitted, of a rather superior nature. In the issue of 21 September 1671 the queen appealed for the return of a missing spaniel, with furry feet and liver-coloured spots. And who could imagine a grander lost-property notice than that inserted in The *Gazette* of 4 May 1685 after the coronation of James II:

> Lost at their Majesties coronation the button [knob] of his Majesty's sceptre, set about with 24 small diamonds, three rubies and three emeralds; a pendant pearl from his Majesty's gown about 9 carets of 30 common grains, and about 16 great links of a gold chain. Whoever gives notice thereof to the officers of her Majesty's Jewel-house, shall be well rewarded.[39]

Advertising was important for the development of the news industry in two very different ways. Firstly, in newspapers still overwhelmingly dominated by foreign, military and diplomatic despatches, they introduced an important element of the local and often parochial. Sometimes the advertisements were the only local or domestic news to be found in the entire paper. Secondly, they rapidly came to play an increasingly important role in underpinning the economics of the industry. In mid-seventeenth-century England advertisers were customarily charged sixpence per notice, but when Marchamont Nedham was granted the monopoly under Cromwell he raised rates to two shillings and sixpence. This helped make him a rich man. In 1657 he was sufficiently confident of the market to attempt an advertising paper, *The Public Advertiser*.[40] This contained a variety of publicly useful information, such as shipping and stagecoach schedules, sales of real estate and horses, advertisements for serv-ants and commodities, such as chocolate and coffee. When John Houghton's commercial information sheet, *A collection for the improvement of husbandry*, failed after its first issues, Houghton was able to revive it by a carefully consid-ered strategy for advertising. Restored by an injection of cash from interested subscribers, Houghton used his next issues to test the market for different sorts of services. Thus in April 1694 he asked his customers, 'whether adver-tisements of schools, or houses and lodgings about London, may be useful, I submit to those concerned'. By June he was ready to lay out his full list of services:

> I sell chocolate, which I know to be a great helper of bad stomachs and restorative to weak people. I'll answer for their goodness.
> I also sell true German Spa-water and sago.
> If applied to, I'll strive to help masters to clerks, apprentices and other valuable servants and such to masters. Also masters of ships to chirurgians and they to masters.
> I find advertisements of schools, or houses and lodgings to be let, are useful.
> I know of valuable estates to be sold.
> I want several apprentices for valuable tradesmen.
> I can help to ready money for any library great or small.[41]

These years also saw the publication of a number of free sheets consisting entirely of advertising. Usually distributed in the vicinity of the Royal Exchange, these *City Mercuries* had a chequered history.[42] They were gener-ally single sheets, and did not observe perfect regularity, being printed and distributed when sufficient advertisements had been received to turn a profit. Even so they seem to have been viable only in times of the *Gazette* monopoly; when that was broken they were soon superseded by papers combining news and advertising.

Though these free sheets make only a modest contribution to the history of consumption, they have a distinguished ancestry, for it was no less a figure than the French thinker Montaigne who in 1591 had first proposed a bureau of commercial exchange, bringing buyers together with those who had something to sell. This proposal would be extraordinarily influential: the first attempt to set up such a bureau in England quoted directly from Montaigne in its prospectus.[43] This scheme, in 1611, fell victim to the Crown's desire to extract too high an annual fee in return for the proposed monopoly, but similar schemes recurred at intervals through the century, leading ultimately to the establishment of Marchamont Nedham's short-lived advertising paper, *The Public Advertiser*. Most successful of all was the Bureau d'Adresse established in Paris by Théophraste Renaudot, later the editor of the Paris *Gazette*. Renaudot conceived his commercial exchange service as a means of supporting his medical duties as Commissioner General for the Poor. This altruism aroused considerable suspicion, and in 1644 Renaudot was obliged to close his bureau. Henceforth he and his heirs would have to console themselves with the advertising revenue that came with their monopoly of news publications in France. The concept of an advertising paper found its purest expression in the foundation of *The Daily Advertiser* in London in 1731, but this again soon faltered. Within a month it was recognised that this was not viable: the familiar mix of advertising with news was now too well established. By undertaking to 'publish daily the latest and freshest accounts of all occurrences foreign and domestic', *The Daily Advertiser* joined the ranks of general newspapers.[44]

Despite this mis-step, it is obvious that the late seventeenth-century proliferation of newspapers in England would have been unthinkable without the healthy advertising revenue generated. In the early eighteenth century the new journals also relied heavily on advertisements. By the end of its run *The Tatler* carried as many as eighteen in each issue, and in *The Spectator* they took up half the total space.[45] They also generated the entirety of the profits. These more upmarket periodicals advertised a more exotic variety of goods reflecting the commercial vitality of London: wigs, slaves, birdcages, shoe polish, cosmetics and medicines.

Advertisements played an even more crucial role in the development of a provincial press. With far more limited pools of potential customers who were prepared to pay two pence for a weekly news-sheet, it was hard to envisage turning a profit from the cover price alone. Allowance had to be made for the profit to the seller and the cost of cartage to bring copies to a dispersed circle of readers. The grim economics were set out with brutal economy by Thomas Avis, editor of *The Birmingham Gazette*. Because of local competition, Avis was attempting to sell his paper for three halfpence. This was an uphill struggle:

> That a great deal of money may be sunk in a very little time by a publication of this nature, cannot seem strange to anyone who considers, that out of every paper one half-penny goes to the Stamp-Office, and another to the person who sells it; that the paper it is printed on costs a farthing; and that consequently no more than a farthing remains to defray the charges of composing, printing, London newspapers, and meeting as far as Daventry the post; which last article is very expensive; not to mention the expense of our London correspondent.[46]

With these considerable expenses to meet from a residual farthing a copy, this paper would have run at a loss had it not been for advertising income. Here we might consider the sounder economics of the *Western Flying Post*, which by the mid-eighteenth century might cram up to forty advertisements into its four pages. At a profit of one shilling and sixpence each (after tax) the income, £3 4s 6d, would exceed the profits from sales of over 1,500 copies (an unlikely print run for a paper serving rural Somerset and Dorset).[47] If the paper was only clearing the farthing claimed by Avis, then this advertising revenue returned more than selling 3,000 copies. Advertising was a lifeline.

To secure this revenue stream proprietors had to convince their readers that their advertisements would reach a wide circle of potential readers. County papers expended considerable effort to create markets in towns and villages round about. Most papers maintained a standing arrangement with networks of booksellers or grocers where papers could be purchased and advertisements delivered for placement in the next paper; these addresses were usually listed on the final page. One of the most ambitious of these networks was that set out in *The Gloucester Journal* of 1725, which described thirteen divisions or circuits that carried the paper into twelve English and Welsh counties spread over an area of 11,000 square miles.[48] *The Gloucester Journal* could be read in Glamorgan, in Ludlow in Shropshire, and as far away as Berkshire. In these farthest reaches *The Gloucester Journal* would be rubbing up against papers printed in other cities (most obviously Bristol and Birmingham) and the competition for advertising revenue was undoubtedly intense. Nowhere was this more the case than in London, with its numerous papers and journals. By the mid-eighteenth century the market for advertisements was itself beginning to segment, with different papers specialising in particular sub-markets: medical elixirs, theatre announcements, and so on.[49] All sought to impress potential advertisers with their wide circulation, and, increasingly, the quality of their readership.

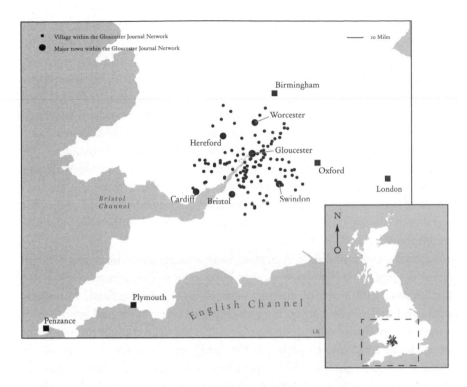

Map 3 The circulation network of the *Gloucester Journal*, 1725

It is in this context that one needs to see Addison and Steele's celebrated and much cited boast that each copy of *The Spectator* would be seen by twenty readers.[50] The claim actually originates rather earlier, in *The City Mercury* in 1694, one of the London advertising papers.[51] It is a multiplier frequently cited by scholars of the newspaper industry when calculating the impact and reach of eighteenth-century papers, but this is not what Addison intended. An, optimistic assessment, it was based on no systematic data, and was little more than a well-judged pitch for advertising business in a crowded market.[52] As a generalisation on which to build calculations of readership it has little value.

Nevertheless such claims do point up the energy with which publishers pursued advertising, which played a crucial role in the development of the news industry not just in the most obvious sense of making marginal operations viable. We may identify, in addition, three consequences of long-term significance. Firstly, the inclusion of advertisements was an important way in which printed newspapers differentiated themselves from manuscript news-books.[53]

Until this time the two traditions had been utterly intermingled, mutually furnishing intelligence and copy, and serving overlapping readerships. But manuscript news services never included advertisements; and although they continued into the eighteenth century (robustly in places like France where newspaper publication remained more restricted),[54] the two traditions now began to diverge more dramatically. In the eighteenth century, newspapers served far broader and more numerous clienteles, and finally developed as a self-consciously independent genre. The importance of advertising to this process is signalled by the developing practice of reserving the whole front page of a newspaper for advertising, rather than placing advertisements at the end. This had become the habitual practice of the London papers by the end of the eighteenth century (and in some cases would only be abandoned in relatively recent times).[55]

Secondly, by providing a robust income stream, advertisements brought closer the day when newspapers could hope to be self-financing, and furnish their editors with a decent income: perhaps ultimately the funds to employ additional staff. To this point, the publishing of newspapers had been almost always the enterprise of a single man, and this left little enough time or space for editorial creativity. In principle the rising financial returns from advertising revenue might over time encourage a tradition of genuine editorial independence. In the short term governments were too wary of the press to allow this to happen. It is surely relevant in this connection that the Stamp Act of 1712 imposed, in addition to the obligation of stamped paper, a swingeing fee for each advertisement. The precipitate fall in advertising revenue that inevitably followed was probably a greater cause of newspapers failing than the stamp itself.[56]

Finally, advertisements played an important role in humanising the press. The first papers were, as we have seen, rather clinical and distant. They offered a sequence of reports of overwhelmingly foreign news. The reader might be flattered to be incorporated into these previously closed circles of knowledge, but it was hard going. Advertisements brought the everyday lives of the local public directly into the reading experience of their fellow customers. They could marvel at the rich furnishings and clothing that citizens had somehow mislaid; empathise with the experience of unreliable servants; enjoy the wicked, guilty pleasure at the humiliated and exasperated husband forced to make a public declaration that he would no longer be responsible for his wife's debts.[57]

Readers could revel in these vignettes of chaotic and disturbed lives; they could feel the pain of those who had lost all their worldly goods by fire; they could wrestle with the conflicting emotions of incredulity and hope raised by advertisements for patent medicines. They could marvel at the villainy of fugitive criminals, whose crimes and physical characteristics were often described at some length, and they could share with anxious neighbours their fears that such villains could be lurking in the vicinity. It has been suggested that these crime reports, placed by the local authorities as advertisements, made a significant contribution to law enforcement at a time when policing was rudimentary and citizens were necessarily required to contribute to upholding public order.[58] Certainly, in an age before the editorial, and where a large portion of the news continued in the hallowed tradition of the foreign despatches, these advertisements allowed papers to offer some echo of the vivacity and merriment purveyed by pamphlets and broadsheets. It is no accident that in the early eighteenth century, when the metropolitan news market was first embracing the culture of advertising, the circulation of *The London Gazette*, necessarily committed to a more conservative style of dry official announcements, fell precipitously.[59] These scenes of everyday life and titillating visits to the darker reaches of society brought energy, variety and a hint of danger to the news. From this point on advertisements were a staple of the industry.

CHAPTER 15

From Our Own Correspondent

THERE can be no doubt that by the eighteenth century the reading public's appetite for news had generated a considerable industry. In Germany, the Low Countries and particularly England newspapers had captured the public imagination. In London a multiplicity of competing papers fuelled the poisonous politics of the age, and posed those in power unfamiliar problems of news management. But who exactly lay behind this vast increase in the weekly and sometimes daily output of news? Who provided the necessary continuous stream of copy?

It will not have escaped the attention of readers that so far we have met remarkably few of those involved in the actual writing of news. Most of the news men who have featured in these pages have been either the proprietors of manuscript news services, or authors who made their name through the publication of what were essentially advocacy pamphlets in serial form – men like Marchamont Nedham or Daniel Defoe. Most of the great journalists of the eighteenth century were either pamphleteers (Defoe and Swift) or wits (Addison and Steele). So although this was the age when the word 'journalist' was first coined, it did not yet describe an independent craft.

The word 'journalist' first made its way into the English language at the end of the seventeenth century: the first reported usage is 1693.[1] But like the use of the German *Zeitung* two hundred years before, it did not yet have its modern meaning. A journalist was one who made his living from writing, but not necessarily for the newspapers. The implication was generally disparaging. When the essayist John Toland described the now scarcely known Lesley as a 'journalist' in 1710, he was referring scornfully to an emerging class of hired hack who wrote to order, sometimes copy for the newspapers, more often in partisan pamphlets. 'They [the Tories] have one Lesley as their journalist in London, who for seven or eight years past did, three times a week, publish rebellion.' The term was opprobrious and unstable. When Addison in *The Spectator* of 1712 referred to a female correspondent as a journalist, he meant someone who kept a journal or diary 'filled with a fashionable kind of gaiety and laziness'. The coinage remained occasional. Jonathan Swift tried another variation, 'journalier', for newspaper writer, but this did not really catch on. At best the term, derived from the French *journal* ('newspaper'), and ulti-mately *jour* ('day'), represented a new emphasis on timeliness in the reporting of current affairs; a circumstance that in the politically charged atmosphere of turn-of-the-century London brought a promise of abundant opportunity for the aspiring writer not overburdened with scruples.

Grub Street

The first true news professionals were the purveyors of manuscript news services. They generally managed the whole business, building their reputa-tion through collecting and redacting the news, and personally writing the master copy. The same was by and large true of the first generation of news-paper proprietors, who usually managed the whole editorial process single-handed. The most significant exception to this, right through to the end of the eighteenth century, was the busy London market. Here the weekly or bi weekly news-sheets could sometimes afford to retain one or two staff reporters. This was a tenuous existence, and the jobbing news man would often make ends meet by working for more than one paper. This was not well-paid work. Even in regular employment it was scarcely possible to make more than a pound a week, the sort of money a printer paid to a trained compositor. A compositor was a vital part of the production process; at this point a reporter was not.

It is seldom possible to put a name or a face to these drones of the news industry. We normally meet them only through the hostile caricature of a sneering competitor. Thus *Read's Journal* wrote of the men who gathered news for *Mist's*:

> [One] has a commission for scraping the jails in Middlesex and Surrey of their commitments; another has a warrant for scouring the ale-houses and gin-shops for such as die of excessive drinking. A person is posted at the Savoy to take up deserters; and another in the park to watch the motions of the guards and their military punishments.[2]

A pamphlet published on behalf of the coffee houses attacked news gatherers who would 'hang and loiter about the public offices, like house-breakers, waiting for an interview with some little clerk'.[3] This at least is plausible; less so the wild and gleeful suggestion of *The Flying Post* that to improve its coverage of domestic news *The Universal Spectator* had 'settled fixed salaries of two pence per diem on a considerable number of antiquated herb women'.[4] This is the savage sarcasm of an industry competitor, but it does point obliquely to an underlying truth: that women were becoming an essential element of the eighteenth-century news industry, if not as news writers then certainly in the distribution process.

In truth the professional infrastructure of news in the eighteenth century – those regularly involved on a paid basis in the industry – was much more concerned with distribution than the generation of copy. From the point that the manuscript text of an issue left the proprietor's hand a substantial company of business associates and casual employees was required to deliver

15.1 *The Three Champions*. The writers Richard Steele, Daniel Defoe and George Ridpath, here denounced for their partisanship and political connections.

the newspaper to the reader's hands. The copy went first to the print shop to be set up in type, and from there to booksellers or wholesalers, for distribution through a whole network of street-sellers. This sales force ensured the papers were delivered to subscribers, or sold copies on the streets. In London, during the early years of the eighteenth century, the wholesale trade had fallen almost entirely into the hands of female publishers known as 'Mercury women'. Elizabeth Nutt and her daughters owned several bookshops in the heart of London in the 1720s; they were responsible for distributing, through their network of hawkers, *The Daily Post, The London Journal* and *The London Evening Post*.[5] Mercury women were often the wives or widows of established printers, so they could rely on a wide network of contacts. Many of their hawkers were also female. These humble and often near indigent day labourers were a constant source of concern for government authorities, particularly when they were thought to be distributing seditious material or opposition newspapers.[6] When in 1728 the government attempted to stifle *Mist's Weekly Journal*, twenty-four people were arrested, including two Mercury women and the hawker Judith Salmon. A similar attempt to silence the radical politician John Wilkes thirty-five years later led to forty-nine arrests.[7] The numbers who were making a living from the press in this way were very considerable. And these, we must remember, were enterprises where the journalistic content was essentially the responsibility of one individual. If there was, in this age, the beginnings of a newspaper industry, it relied far more on the artisans of the trade than on a new profession of career news writers.

Booksellers had a slightly schizophrenic relationship with hawkers, denouncing them as competitors who did not bear any of the usual fixed costs of running a bookshop, but then making use of them to distribute their own stock. By the last decades of the eighteenth century it required fifty hawkers to carry the copies of a single issue of the *Amsterdamsche courant* around town: however lowly, they were an indispensable part of the industry.[8] But hawkers could also play a role, seldom appreciated, in the evolution of a newspaper's style and market position. They knew better than most what sort of news encouraged casual sales, particularly at the lower end of the market, since for them a good pitch was the difference between a full belly and going hungry. By reporting back what stories went down well they could help a canny publisher shape his publishing strategy. It may have been this sort of relationship which *The Flying Post* had in mind in its reference to *The Universal Spectator*'s herb women.

These ill-natured jibes come from the first exuberant growth of competing papers in the early part of the eighteenth century; as the business model became more secure, and the proportion of space devoted to domestic news mounted, papers could invest rather more in news gathering. In the 1770s the editor of *The Gazetteer* listed fourteen correspondents who were paid for contributions, including information from the City, the Law Courts, and the shipping news.[9] These were not yet members of staff, and as casual workers they were free to work for more than one paper; but this was definitely a change from a century before, when the correspondents of Williamson's news service had been customs officials and postmasters, supplying news as an (unpaid) adjunct to their normal duties.[10] Note, too, that these informants were by and large local stringers operating in the metropolis. Few if any papers would maintain a correspondent abroad, relying instead on the traditional and highly effective services of the manuscript newsletters and foreign newspapers for their foreign news. Paying the subscriptions for these services could of course add up to a considerable financial outlay.

Considered in the round, an eighteenth-century newspaper business dispensed a remarkably small proportion of its outlay on writers. Few newspapers felt the need to secure the exclusive services of the men who wrote for them. The special skills of old lags who snuffled about the court house to root out a story were no doubt appreciated, but such low characters could never expect their efforts to be openly acknowledged. The concept of a journalist as an informed observer with specialist expertise had yet to be invented. No papers carried reports from named journalists writing under their own byline. The tradition of anonymity inherited from the manuscript newsletter cast a long shadow, to the frustration of anyone ambitious to make their name through the burgeoning press. In 1758 Ralph Griffith, founder of the *Monthly Review*, painted a bitter portrait of the life of the man who wrote for hire. 'There is no difference between the writer in his garret and the slave in the mines. Both have their tasks assigned them alike: both must drudge and starve; and neither can hope for deliverance.'[11] Griffith thought that if all the writers were to withdraw their labour the sudden disappearance of the papers and journals would bring the reading public to some appreciation of their skills; needless to say, the call fell on deaf ears. Revealingly, although 'journalist' had made its hesitant debut in the English language by the end of the seventeenth century, 'journalism', describing the trade of writing, is not known until 1833, 140 years later.[12]

Not Quite a Gentleman

Even in this grudging employment of piecework news gatherers, the London papers were very much the exception. Elsewhere in Europe (and elsewhere in England) a large proportion of newspapers were essentially produced single-handed until the end of the eighteenth century. The publisher or editor would gather the copy from manuscript news-sheets and other newspapers, and deliver it to the printer. He would supervise the network of hawkers or carters that brought the papers to their readers. He would maintain and chase up subscriptions and solicit advertising. Sometimes, notwithstanding this over-whelming miscellany of tasks, the newspaper was not his exclusive occupa-tion. In some English towns the newspaper was published by the local printer, elsewhere often by a man who simultaneously ran a bookshop. In Germany, and later in colonial America, it was common for the local postmaster to be proprietor of the local newspaper, exploiting his privileged first access to the foreign despatches, and relying on the fact that potential customers would routinely drop by his premises.

This extraordinarily busy life left little time for activities we associate with journalism: the searching out or development of stories, research and crafting of articles. Composition of the weekly issue would continue up to the last minute, but to set a whole issue of a thousand copies printed on a single press demanded that the composition of the text began almost as soon as the last issue was complete. Advertisements or letters held over from the previous week could be set up first, but publishers were aware that it was for news that subscribers bought their paper, and they would only tolerate so many thin issues before cancelling an order. 'I desire you to erase out my name from among the number of your subscribers,' wrote a reader of *The British Spy* in December 1728, 'unless in your next you give me a just reason for the barren-ness of your intelligence.'[13] So while it was tempting for proprietors to increase revenue with several columns of advertisements, they could only go so far. Letters and other contributed pieces could not be allowed to crowd out news. As Samuel Johnson correctly remarked, writing for the first issue of *The London Chronicle* (January 1757), 'The first demand made by the reader of a journal is that he should find an accurate account of foreign transactions and domestic incidents.'[14]

For foreign news, which continued to claim first place in every newspaper, publishers were entirely dependent on traditional sources. Few could afford to maintain paid correspondents in any foreign city. Working with limited resources and under severe time constraints, their regular weekly issue was in its way a marvel of creation; a tribute to ingenuity and the dense network of communication that brought news from Lyon to Berlin, and Vienna to Birmingham. But the urgency of deadlines left little time for reflection. Eighteenth-century newspapers are striking for an absence of design innova-tion. Such advances as we see in the creative use of white space and ruling to separate different items are slow and incremental. Virtually no use is made of headlines, or of illustration, beyond small woodcuts of ships to identify the shipping news. The order of news was determined largely by external factors: that is, the order in which reports were received in the shop. There was no guarantee that the most important items would appear first, or even on the first page.

Newspapers continued, by and large, to steer clear of editorial comment. This was particularly true of papers published in towns where theirs was the only newspaper. Since this was the case in the vast majority of places that boasted a newspaper in eighteenth-century Europe, the contentious press of London was very much the exception. But occasionally a newspaper man rose above the anonymity of the everyday to espouse a cause. Such a man was Andrew Brice of Exeter, editor of *Brice's Weekly Journal*. In 1726 he was moved to protest against the dire conditions endured by inmates of the West Country prisons. Having fired his opening salvo in a pamphlet *Appeal for Justice*, Brice was contacted by several prisoners held in Exeter prison, and he used the columns of his paper to publicise their plight. Matters came to a head when a confined merchant made specific accusations against the Keeper of the Exeter prison, George Glanvill. Glanvill sued Brice, and although Brice pleaded his cause in the *Weekly Journal*, the case went against him. Unable to pay a fine of £103, the editor absconded. The story ends badly, and there is little doubt that the stalwart citizens of Devon would have stood stoutly behind the officers of the law rather than the quixotic defender of the rights of felons. A man ahead of his time, Brice was a rare example of a type that later generations would come to honour: the campaigning journalist.[15]

The courageous Brice found few imitators in the eighteenth-century press. Most newspaper publishers maintained strict neutrality in local political issues. The exception was, once again, London. Here the rise of political journalism in the late eighteenth century introduced significant change, but not necessarily advantageous to newspaper writers. In England most of the professional writers whose names have come down to us were paid agents of government. They were not employed on the staff of any particular title, but simply supplied copy to papers friendly to the ministry as required, putting the best face on foreign news or casting aspersions on the motives and blackening the names of opposition politicians. They also wrote pamphlets: just like Defoe a half century before, whether a piece of persuasive writing appeared in a serial publication or a free-standing pamphlet was largely immaterial. We know of their work not because they were especially gifted, but because their names appear in Treasury accounts of their payments. For the most part their careers were mean and inglorious, though government newspapers were willing to pay substantial sums to attract the best talent. Even the sententious Samuel Johnson was prepared to accept a pension from the Earl of Bute, favourite and minister of George III. John Wilkes, who served the contrary cause, gleefully referred to him as 'Pensioner Johnson'. A few years earlier in the *Dictionary* that made his name (1755) Johnson reflected the cynicism of the time, defining 'Gazetteer' as a term 'lately of the utmost infamy, being usually applied to wretches who were hired to vindicate the court'.[16] Clearly, he was not yet conscious of his own lucrative future as a hired pen.

The assumption that a newspaper writer was little more than a paid agent of politicians ensured that 'journalist' would be a term of opprobrium well into the nineteenth century. Writing for the newspapers was not considered a respectable occupation. Probably greatly to their advantage, it was thought mildly degrading to fight a duel against a newspaper man. To have taken paid employment for a newspaper also ensured a man would be barred from the legal profession in England, according to a regulation of 1807. As late as 1860 it apparently merited serious discussion whether a man who had been a staff writer on *The Times* was thereby disqualified from potential nomination as a magistrate.[17]

Politicians had a complex view of the men of the press. Although absolutely convinced of the need to manage the press, they continued to hold in contempt those who made their living in this way. Even a professional writer like Sir Walter Scott affected to regard journalism as a disreputable calling. 'Nothing but a thorough-going blackguard ought to attempt the daily press unless it is some quiet, country diurnal' was a typically forthright view. When attempts were made to entice his friend John Gibson Lockhart to edit a new London paper, Scott advised against it. 'I should think it rash for any young man, of whatever talent, to sacrifice nominally at least, a considerable portion of his respectability in society in hopes of being an exception to a rule which is at present pretty general.' Another friend agreed: 'I should not receive an offer of the editorship of a newspaper as a compliment to my feelings as a barrister and a gentleman, however complimentary it might be as to my talents.' Even after the passage of the Great Reform Bill (1832), a drama in which the newspapers played so material a part, the same stigma applied. In 1835 *The London Review* was firm on the point: 'Those who are regularly connected with the newspaper press are for the most part excluded from what is, in the widest extension of the term, called good society.'

Interestingly, such strictures applied specifically to newspapers; the same consideration did not apply to the new political journals. Here a gentleman could offer his talents and, indeed, make a reputation, the point being that contributors to journals wrote under their own name, whereas newspaper men sheltered behind the cloak of anonymity. It was this, along with their tendency to switch sides with the seasons, that drew down on them such opprobrium:

> How can men help shunning contact with men who have the power of inflicting secret injury, and who are known to be in the habit of using that power against the members of society. . . . How can society respect men who show so little respect for themselves and each other; who, when their gains are threatened, can talk, it is true, in a lofty tone about the high character of the Press of their country for talent and integrity, but who, in general, are occupied in bandying with each other the lowest slang of the pothouses, or imputations of gross dishonesty and dense ignorance?[18]

It is a singular fact that in contrast to the newspapers, not only the political journals but also pamphlets were held in high esteem. At the end of the eighteenth century, pamphlets were considered an entirely reputable medium for political discussion; a remarkable enhancement of their status since the early days of print. It is a reminder, if one were needed, that too simple a view of news gathering as a series of evolutionary steps, from manuscript to print, and from pamphlets to newspapers, risks distorting reality. Well into the nineteenth century, great reformers and political philosophers addressed a wide public in pamphlets.

Newspaper men did not help their cause by accepting fees to suppress stories about the private lives of the great (this was known as selling 'paragraphs'). Some low-rent ventures were effectively established for this specific purpose.[19] In the view of the great campaigner William Cobbett, the failure of his short-lived newspaper was explained by his refusal to stoop to such practices:

> It was not, I found, an affair of talent but of trick. I could not sell paragraphs. I could not throw out hints against a man's or woman's reputation in order to bring the party to pay me for silence. I could do none of those mean and infamous things by which the daily press, for the far greater part, was supported, and which enabled the proprietors to ride in chariots, while their underlings were actually vending lies by the line and inch.[20]

Letters Lately Arrived

Here we are confronted with one of the great paradoxes of the eighteenth-century news world: that the increased involvement of professional news men in news production was seen as diminishing, rather than enhancing, the credibility of news. This is why so many newspapers published official communications verbatim: the lack of editorial intervention was seen as a guarantee of their integrity. Equally in demand were reports from participants: a despatch penned by a general at the front, or an eyewitness account of some great event or disaster.[21]

This use of private or semi-public letters as a cornerstone of news reporting drew on a long-standing tradition where the authority of a report was closely connected to the standing of the news bearer. We have seen this in the instructions despatched with trusted couriers along the post roads of the Roman Empire, and in the exchange of correspondence in medieval Europe. The tradition persisted in the assumption that news exchanged in private correspondence between persons of rank could be believed because the credit – the honour – of the writer lay behind the intelligence conveyed. This assumption of reliability was obviously compromised when news was published, in pamphlet form for profit, by men of lower rank.[22]

Publishers attempted to counter this insinuation by appropriating for the commercial news market the forms and conventions of the private letter. Thousands of news pamphlets in the sixteenth century describe themselves as 'a letter' (French *lettre*, German *Brief*, Italian *lettera*), a 'true despatch' and so on. Sometimes they do indeed give the text of such a despatch, often verbatim and in full, complete with the opening salutation and closing greeting.

This epistolary form could also be abused. In the inflamed international confessional conflicts of the later sixteenth century nothing was more telling than the publication of intercepted letters revealing the perfidious plans of one's devious opponents. The inevitable response of the embarrassed writer was to complain that the published letters were a forgery or invention. Sometimes they were, though the authenticity of tone of such correspondence was often damning. In the seventeenth century the letter form was also a predictable vehicle for political satire, never more so than during the French Fronde. In this period of wild protest against the rule of Cardinal Mazarin, almost five hundred pamphlets described themselves as 'letters': the fact that some were entirely in verse rather undermined the claim.[23] But the publication of genuine intercepted correspondence continued to be practised right through to the end of the eighteenth century, and often with telling effect. In the American War of Independence the British army routinely published such of General Washington's despatches as fell into their hands, and carefully monitored the effect this had on enemy morale.[24]

The letter enjoyed an uncommon status because it was, until the end of the sixteenth century, the attribute of men of power and rank. To be able to write a letter, observing the correct forms, marked one out as a person of education. Ensuring that it reached its destination was only possible if the writer had access to the postal network, or could employ a courier. All of these aspects of correspondence were expensive, and therefore likely to be the prerogative of members of the social elite. These were, aside from scholars, generally individuals who by virtue of their social status were politically active and informed. Private correspondence among these higher ranks of society was a natural extension of their public life. Alongside family news they could be expected to discuss business dealings and political events likely to impact on their prospects and standing. A good example is the correspondence of Viscount Scudamore, a Justice of the Peace and Member of Parliament who also served several years as Charles I's ambassador to Paris.[25] Scudamore lived through turbulent times, and while resident at his family seat in Herefordshire felt the need to keep in touch with events. He also had the means to do so. Four of his regular correspondents were professional news men, who charged up to £20 per annum for their weekly newsletters (a reasonable living wage for a country vicar). Scudamore also heard regularly from several government officials, the Tuscan ambassador in London and a lifelong friend, Sir Henry Herbert. Scudamore's brothers provided military news, and other relatives sent printed pamphlets. Many of these letters were personal but not wholly private. They were expected to be shared with further family members, neighbours and other leaders of local society. In this way local hierarchies built a network of news-sharing equivalent to that operated for some centuries by international merchants.

Such news networks however, remained, for some centuries the exclusive preserve of the social elite. It was only in the eighteenth century that the capacity for correspondence was extended to a wider range of citizens. The potential implications for Europe's news networks were very significant.

The Age of Correspondence

George Washington was admirably sanguine about the occasional publication of his captured letters. He wrote so many – around twelve thousand are still extant – that some were bound to go astray. By this point the exchange of letters, with friends, family and business partners, had become routine, and not just for the established leaders of society who, like Washington, had access to privileged circuits of communication. In the eighteenth century the practice of letter-writing moved beyond the elites; it became a familiar social practice for many millions of people in Europe and North America.

The eighteenth century was the age of correspondence. Advances in education, postal networks and the falling costs of writing materials fuelled the boom in letter-writing. And this was, for the first time, a communications revolution that affected men and women in almost equal measure. The eighteenth century went a long way to closing the yawning educational gap between the sexes. In Amsterdam by 1780 betrothal agreements were personally signed by 85 per cent of men and 64 per cent of women, compared to 57 per cent of men in 1630 and 30 per cent of women. In France only 29 per cent of men and 14 per cent of women signed in 1690; one hundred years later the percentages were 48 and 27 per cent. These figures were depressed by the leavening effect of France's large rural hinterland (literacy was much higher in the cities and especially so in Paris), but even in rural areas the advance was striking. In the rural territory governed by the city of Turin in northern Italy the percentage of male readers rose from 21 to 65 per cent in eighty years, and female readers from 6 to 30 per cent. In the city itself 83 per cent of husbands and 63 per cent of wives could sign their marriage contracts in 1790.[26]

Women were also well represented among the social classes propelled by the expanding world economy into the unfamiliar possession of a modicum of surplus income. Younger, unmarried women, unencumbered by family responsibilities, embraced with particular eagerness the opportunities to engage in regular communication with family friends and potential suitors.

The new craze for letter-writing was supported by a powerful infrastructure. The expansion of school education (and particularly schooling for girls)

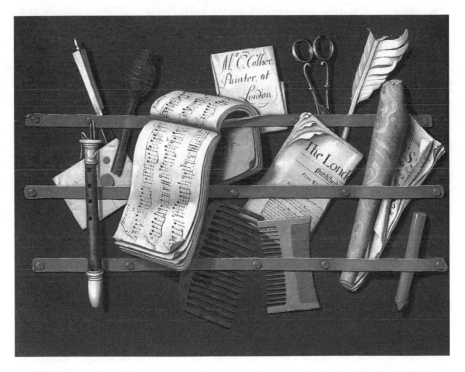

15.2 Edward Collier, *The Letter Rack*. The writing and communication media of the late seventeenth century presented as a still-life tableau.

was particularly important. Thereafter induction in the particular craft and conventions of correspondence was encouraged by a host of epistolary hand-books. This was a venerable genre, and popular in polite society from the time Erasmus had placed correspondence at the heart of humanist self-fashioning. His two primers of letter-writing were instant best-sellers.[27] Erasmus provided one model and Cicero another; but as letter-writing moved beyond the elite, so the letter-writing manuals adapted their style and contents to less confident purchasers. This was a gradual process; the medieval *dictamen* convention, so stifling to individuality in the letter-writing culture of the Middle Ages, proved very powerful. George Snell's *Right Teaching* of 1649 advocated a letter-writing structure clearly modelled on these medieval prescriptions, as did several of the French *Secrétaires*.[28] In January and February 1789, on the very eve of the French Revolution, an inventory was compiled of the goods of Estienne Garnier, a deceased printer and bookseller from the northern French city of Troyes. Among his very considerable stock were three letter-writing manuals: the *Secrétaire à la mode*, the *Nouveau Secrétaire Français* and *Secrétaire des dames*.[29] They contained a selection of model letters for a variety of social situations. The *Secrétaire à la mode* was conveniently divided into two categories, business letters (letters of notification, complaint or making excuses) and complimentary letters (congratulations, thanks, consolation or letters announcing a visit).

Although Garnier catered mostly for customers with low disposable income – he was a specialist in the coarse and cheaply produced books known collec-tively as the *Bibliothèque bleue* – these manuals were extremely popular.[30] Together he held in stock some 5,832 copies of these three titles. For his normal customer base they would have been a curious purchase: model letters exchanged between persons of civility and social stature could scarcely have been of practical use to the artisans and tradesmen who patronised the *Bibliothèque bleue*. A number of these volumes had been continuously in print for over a century. Yet as time went on enterprising publishers also began to compile collections of letters more carefully adapted to the real practical needs of the new corresponding classes. One such was the *Letters written to and for particular friends*, a collection of 272 model letters assembled and published by the London publisher Samuel Richardson. The book was successful enough, but entirely overshadowed by another of Richardson's ventures in this same year: *Pamela, or virtue rewarded*, a novel in which the narrative proceeded entirely through a series of personal letters. Encapsulating the new vogue for correspondence, the epistolary novel became an eighteenth-century sensation, offering a breathless window on the intimate lives of their protagonists while exploiting the established reputation of the letter as a truth-bearing medium.

The eighteenth-century rage for correspondence opened up an important new flank of the communication network, and it would be reasonable to hope that these letters, which survive in private and public archives in hundreds of thousands, would be a rich source of news reporting. In fact this does not prove to be the case. Those neophyte writers who entered the world of correspondence in this period did not on the whole use their letters for discussions of public affairs; one can work one's way through many hundreds of these letters and find only a meagre harvest of comment on the news, beyond the intimate, purely familial and business transactions.[31] There are good practical reasons why this should have been so. In the first place the use of the postal system, though now far simpler and far more reliable, was still expensive. The cost of letters was carefully gradated to the weight of the package and the distance they would be carried. Only a small proportion was delivered post-paid. For many correspondents the joy of receiving a letter was tempered by the need to find ready cash to pay for it; and this could be a considerable sum. Although letters moved smoothly enough along the postal routes, arrangements for delivery from the depot on their arrival were often rudimentary. Only habitual correspondents (mostly business users) would make regular visits to the post office to pick up mail.

Use of the postal system would therefore remain through this period a carefully weighed expenditure for most letter writers. In colonial Philadelphia Benjamin Franklin thought it perfectly reasonable that his wife should forebear writing a letter of consolation to her recently widowed sister on grounds of cost.[32] While many more people were using the post, a very large proportion were tradesmen and business users. A survey of 608 letters despatched from Paris between 1830 and 1865 (and kept in the Musée de la poste as evidence of franking practice) reveals that only 15 per cent of the corpus were of a personal nature. The rest concerned commercial or banking transactions (47 per cent) or were letters from notaries and advocates concerning legal business (38 per cent).[33] These, of course, were the intended users of the post: most of the government-led improvements in postal services of the eighteenth century were justified on commercial grounds.[34] These business users tended to follow the conventions and models laid down in the letter-writing manuals with particular care, betraying the fragile social self-confidence of neophyte correspondents. There was little space for digression, opinion or gossip.

The eighteenth century did witness significant changes in epistolary style. Whereas in the sixteenth century the emphasis had been on the display of formal rhetorical training, the eighteenth century strayed more easily into the familiar and familial. Letters, it was now thought, should give 'a true picture of the heart'.[35] This was all the more the case as letter-writing became increasingly feminised, encouraged not only by writing manuals directed specifically at female readers, but by the female protagonists in the epistolary novels. But this newly emboldened class of literate and educated female writers seldom strayed into the political domain. These were, in any case, the members of literate society most likely to be outside news circles; and they were not encouraged by social convention to share their opinions. Many such letters kept to the safe ground of family matters, small domestic dramas, servants and local diversions, the weather – or the receipt of other letters.

In terms of their contribution to the news networks, the new letter writers of the eighteenth century were probably most important in their enthusiastic interaction with new forms of news periodicals: journals, magazines and newspapers. All newspapers carried copy derived from letters, whether official despatches reprinted in their entirety or letters from their own subscribers. Readers bombarded the editorial office with their comments, complaints and suggestions; this was a form of letter that could often be hand-delivered, and therefore involved minimum expense on the part of the correspondent. The burden of this incoming mail – *The London Gazette* claimed to have received 861 letters in four months in 1761[36] – must have been very considerable, particularly when set alongside numerous other claims on an editor's time. But the readers could not be ignored. Sometimes they offered snippets of news for inclusion. Particularly in towns off the main news networks these could be extremely useful; but relying on volunteer enthusiasts had its dangers, as publishers were all too aware. 'We are assured from Shrewsbury,' wrote the editor of the *Birmingham Gazette* in May 1749, 'that the account sent from thence, and inserted in this paper, in relation to the fireworks there, was an entire falsehood.'[37] The safest course, in reporting an apparent sensation, was to name the informant, and thus distance the paper from any accusation of unprofessional credulity. Thus in *The British Spy, or Derby Postman* of 1727:

One Thomas Bostock of Buzlum near Newcastle under Lime, gives us the following narrative, viz. he says that a noted farmer living at Wiln-House . . . having a daughter about five or six years old, the girl has for as many weeks past seen, and still continues to see some daemon, spectre or airy composure assuming human shape, but of little magnitude, and imperceptible to all but his child.[38]

Keeping their subscribers satisfied was not an easy task, and some editors occasionally allowed their impatience to show. Readers were particularly insistent in proposing their own literary effusions, for which they hoped the paper would find room. Although newspapers usually only turned to them in desperation, when they had insufficient news to fill their pages, these seem to have been genuinely popular features. In this way it was readers who moved papers away from exclusive concentration on news to a more varied diet of features and soft items increasingly familiar to them from magazines. These would, in the future, be an important part of the more rounded mix of news and entertainment that became an essential element of the newspapers' appeal in the centuries to come.

The Theatre of Current Events

On the whole, then, private correspondence is a frustrating and disappointing resource for writing a history of news; or, indeed, for trying to establish how these newly empowered eighteenth-century citizens reacted to the ebb and flow of current events. We can expect attention to politics only in the circles of upper-class correspondents: much the same people who would have used their letters to share news of recent events from the sixteenth century onwards. Sometimes the mix of news, gossip and personal information we are offered from these correspondents can be a little disconcerting. Remarks on riots, famine or the execution of notorious criminals are interspersed with society scandal or complaints about pinching shoes. Crime and punishment attracted especial interest, particularly in Paris where the fashion for attending public executions had been eagerly embraced by upper-class society. This led to considerable competition for windows that overlooked the prisoner's route or, still better, the actual place of suffering.[39] This was particularly the case when the condemned was also high-born. In 1699 the wife of a counsellor of the Parlement of Paris, Madame Ticquet, was accused of hiring men to murder her husband, a crime to which she ultimately confessed. On the day of her execution at the notorious Place de Grève, Paris high society turned out in force to see her die. According to Anne Marguerite du Noyer, who knew the prisoner, 'the entire court and the city ran to see this spectacle'. Some houses with a good view 'brought more money to their owners than they had ever cost them'.

Du Noyer reported events rather like a visit to the theatre where she had secured a prime seat; and happily the principal actor was prepared to put on a good show:

I was in the windows of the Hôtel de Ville, and I saw poor Mme Ticquet arrive around five o'clock in the evening, dressed in white. . . . One would have said that she had studied her role, because she kissed the chopping block and attended to all the other particulars as if it were simply a matter of performing in a play. In the end, one had never seen such self-possession, and the curé of Saint-Sulpice said that she died a true Christian heroine. The hangman was so moved that he missed [her head] and had to repeat his job five times before he managed to behead her. . . . Thus ended the beautiful Mme Ticquet, who was the ornament of all Paris.[40]

Twenty years later Paris prepared to witness the execution of the notorious Cartouche, convicted of running a massive criminal enterprise in the city. The scale and sensational nature of his crimes, along with the insouciance with which he faced the horror of being broken on the wheel ('a bad quarter of an hour passes quickly'), combined to create a media circus. Even before he came to trial the actors of the Comédie française considered staging a play based on his life and crimes. Some thought this in bad taste, but the play went ahead. The *Mercure*, which had previously condemned the enterprise, thought it 'very funny'. After conviction and sentencing, Cartouche was remitted to questioning, in the hope that he would name his accomplices; nevertheless spectators flocked to the Place de Grève for fear of missing the dramatic denouement. Even after his execution, Cartouche fever took time to subside. 'For several days,' reported a breathless Caumartin de Boissy to his sister, 'no one has spoken of anything but Cartouche.' The Regent's own mother, the Duchess of Orléans, recorded: 'I ran into the comte d'Hoïm and the chevalier de Schaub. They told me about Cartouche having been executed yesterday; this detained me for quite a while.'[41]

These events, and their reporting, serve as a vivid reminder that even in the eighteenth century the dissemination of news still relied on a vivid collage of eyewitness accounts, correspondence and word of mouth alongside the new printed media. They also offer a sobering view of the emotional temper of Enlightenment Europe. Of course, this sense of an execution as public entertainment was not exclusive to France, though the more routine executions at London's Tyburn tended to attract a more rowdy, less socially exclusive clientele.[42] But it fell well short of the original intention, which was for a community to come together to witness and affirm the justice of an offender's punishment: a form of ritual expulsion intended to heal a community.[43] In the eighteenth century, an age that prided itself on rational sensibility, this dry-eyed enjoyment of human suffering seemed especially jarring. Louis XIV reproved several of the ladies of the court for their presence at the execution of Madame Ticquet; if human beings were compassionate, women were meant to be the epitome of this emotion. A significant turning point seems to have arrived with the execution of Robert-François Damiens, convicted of attempting to kill Louis XV. He was subjected to the traditional punishment for regicides. His flesh was torn with hot pincers and the wounds filled with molten lead and oil, after which he was torn apart by four teams of horses.[44]

Crowds gathered in the square from the previous evening to watch this spectacle. Those who could find no place lined the streets from Notre Dame, where Damiens had made his last confession. The torture lasted for several hours: the horses strained for an hour and a half before they could detach a limb. This obscene performance seems finally to have mobilised philosophers and penal reformers against such festivals of retribution. The search began for a more rational and clinical means of executing justice: still in public, but without the baroque ceremonies and careful gradations of crime and rank that had previously attended executions.

The result, after thirty-five years of debate, was the adoption, in 1792, of a new decapitation machine: a killing device for the age of reason. This, to be applied equally to all condemned without distinction of status, would sweep away all of the macabre ritual that had previously attended the executioner's craft, and consign justice to a simple, easily replicated device, soon dubbed the guillotine after the distinguished doctor who had first designed a prototype. The first execution drew a large crowd but proved rather a disappointment. There was little to see and events proceeded so quickly that the crowd began chanting, 'bring me back my wooden gallows, bring me back my gallows'.[45]

What the disappointed viewers did not realise was that they had witnessed the debut of one of the principal actors in the concluding news event of this era, the French Revolution; an event that would both create the first generation of celebrity journalist/politicians and move the reporting of news, and the development of a news market, into quite uncharted waters.

Cry Freedom

THE mid-eighteenth century had been a period of consolidation for the European press. The development of the weekly journal and monthly magazines extended the range of comment and reflection on political topics. The number of newspapers expanded gradually, as new titles were established and existing papers failed; markets were sustained by a steadily rising tide of new readers. Publishers could earn a good living from providing subscribers with a weekly or thrice-weekly diet of news. But this was not a period of enormous innovation in the news market. In Britain, Parliamentary politics (now settled into an established pattern of annual sessions) ensured that intermittent crises of faction or policy could bring sudden spasms of press fury. A newspaper campaign undoubtedly helped force a humiliating retreat for the ministry in the excise crisis of 1737, and generated a passionate intensity in the opposition to Walpole; but after his fall in 1742 the fizz went out of the bottle. In France the *Gazette* sailed serenely on, protected from competition. The most rapid growth in press activity was away from the major centres of population: in English and French provincial towns (in the latter, it must be said, largely apolitical advertising journals) and in the American colonies.[1] More and more middle-sized communities were served by a single newspaper, usually faithfully modelled on the papers of the metropolitan hubs. By adopting the style of the cosmopolitan centre, on which they largely relied for copy, these papers succeeded by a conscious lack of innovation. An authentic local voice had yet to be developed.

In the last decades of the eighteenth century, and with remarkable rapidity, this busy, prosperous but rather undemanding news world was completely reshaped. In France, England and the American colonies new political controversies brought both a changed role for the press and a vast increase in the number and circulation of newspapers. For the first time, newspapers played a vital role not only in recording but in shaping political events. It was a critical milestone on the road to a recognisably modern newspaper industry.

Wilkes and Liberty

For the Enlightenment philosopher, John Wilkes made a rather unlikely champion.[2] Unscrupulous, devious and nakedly ambitious, Wilkes combined a rackety private life with a cavalier attitude to public affairs. Continuously in debt and careless of friends and obligations, in the middle years of a hitherto undistinguished career Wilkes discovered both a cause and a flair for publicity. That cause would be the freedom of the press. By the time he had concluded his long struggle the acceptable boundaries of public debate, and the part of the newspapers in the political process, had been radically redrawn.

Wilkes was lucky to be feeling his way towards a public career at a moment when the accession of a new king, George III, had brought a revival of party politics. The change of monarch caused an inevitable turbulence in the governing elite, as the king sought to impose his own stamp on affairs; determined to play an active part in government, George III chose to be advised by Lord Bute, a brittle and sensitive Scot not afraid to use the patronage powers of government to reward his friends and punish his enemies. The discontents of the dispossessed Whigs found a political cause in the negotiations for the unpopular peace that would in 1763 end the Seven Years War. Wilkes was happy to be their most pungent instrument.

Wilkes's famous political paper, *The North Briton*, was a direct response to Bute's attempt to cultivate opinion through his own recently established organ, *The Briton*.[3] Wilkes opened the first issue with a high-minded defence of the principle of a free press, 'the firmest bulwark of the liberties of this country. . . the terror of bad ministers'. But if this seemed to promise elevated political philosophy, Wilkes's journalistic principles were better encapsulated by a typically frank avowal to his financial backer, Lord Temple: 'no political paper would be relished by the public unless well-seasoned with personal satire'.[4] *The North Briton* was relentlessly rude, personal and daringly outspoken. Fed a constant stream of damaging information by his Whig allies, a well-sourced exposé of embezzlement in the army concluded with a frantic denunciation of the Secretary of State: 'the most treacherous, base, selfish, mean, abject, low-lived and dirty fellow that ever wriggled himself into a secretaryship'.

Wilkes did not take this too seriously. Challenged by James Boswell for his abuse of Samuel Johnson when they met on neutral ground in Italy, Wilkes was happy to admit that he held a high opinion of Johnson in private: but

'I make it a rule to abuse him who is against me or any of my friends.'[5] Here was journalism concerned not with the transmission of news, but as a vehicle of partisan invective. *The North Briton* existed 'to plant daggers in certain breasts'. Not all his victims would show the same insouciance, but Wilkes did not lack personal courage, and a well-publicised duel with one outraged aristocratic victim, Earl Talbot, only served to enhance his fame. When the ministry attempted to silence him with the promise of office, Wilkes ensured that this too became known.

Much of this would have been familiar from the ferocious press campaign against Walpole. Where Wilkes truly broke new ground was in associating these criticisms with the king personally. In the infamous number 45 of *The North Briton*, Wilkes denounced the king's speech, delivered on behalf of the monarch at the opening of Parliament, with unprecedented freedom:

> Every friend of this country must lament that a prince of so many great and amiable qualities, whom England truly reveres, can be brought to give the sanction of his sacred name to the most odious measures. . . . I wish as much as any man in the kingdom to see the honour of the crown maintained in a manner truly becoming royalty. I lament to see it sunk even to prostitution.[6]

This could not be allowed to go unanswered. The ministry now issued a general warrant for the arrest of anyone connected with the publication. This raised the stakes. Until this point *The North Briton* had been the tool of what was, in essence, a dispute within the political elite. Now with the arrest of his publisher, printer, journeymen and hawkers (forty-nine in all), Wilkes had the opportunity he craved to test an issue of real importance: the limits of press freedom.

The legal actions revolved around two issues: whether Wilkes as a Member of Parliament enjoyed immunity from arrest for a libel (albeit a heinous one); and the validity of a general warrant, which named the crime rather than listing the alleged perpetrators by name. On both points *The North Briton* was triumphantly vindicated. Its printers were freed and awarded substantial damages for wrongful arrest. Wilkes became a celebrity. Before his trial Wilkes had fretted that his face was hardly known to the general public. Now the deficiency was repaired, first by a hostile but widely circulated print by William Hogarth (a Tory, and an enemy). Soon his features seemed to be everywhere: on broadside ballads celebrating his release, stamped on porcelain dishes, teapots and tobacco papers.[7] Such were the fruits of fame in eighteenth-century London. Despite muddying the waters with a conviction for obscenity and flight abroad, Wilkes continued to attract considerable loyalty. His fight to be allowed to take his seat as an MP for Middlesex in 1768 and 1769 made his a national cause.

The emboldened press now pushed forward on other fronts. *The London Daily Post and General Advertiser* was largely an advertising paper until new editors, Henry Woodfall and his son Henry Sampson Woodfall, gave it a new lease of life. Rebranded as *The Public Advertiser*, their key innovation, to accompany the paper's enhanced coverage of domestic politics, was a series of trenchant political essays, published anonymously as the *Letters of Junius*. Strongly anti-ministerial in tone, in 1769 a letter addressed to the king resulted in the arrest of the younger Woodfall and several other editors whose papers had reprinted what was, in truth, an astonishingly direct and personal attack. 'It is the misfortune of your life,' Junius informed the king, 'that you should never have been acquainted with the language of truth, until you have heard it in the complaints of your people.'[8]

Three editors were committed to trial. Lord Chief Justice Mansfield directed the jury to convict, on the grounds that the judge alone could determine whether a seditious libel had occurred. The jury had solely to establish whether the accused were responsible for its publication. The jury's stubborn

16.1 The fruits of celebrity. John Wilkes immortalised in enamel.

refusal to follow this direction drastically rewrote the law of libel and much diminished its usefulness as a tool of press control. Though convictions for seditious libel still hung over the press, English regimes now had to be assured of a sympathetic jury, and not just a compliant judge; a much more demanding test.

Thus far the papers had directed their attacks at the conduct of government, a cause in which they could usually rely on the support of disaffected factions in the political elite. Now attention shifted to the prerogatives of Parliament itself. The right to publish Parliamentary proceedings had been a contested issue for over a century, ever since reporting had been encouraged by the Parliamentary opposition to Charles I in 1640. This freedom had been withdrawn by Charles II on the Restoration, and periodically reaffirmed and removed thereafter. This was generally an opposition cause, and one easily abandoned if the opposition found itself in power. The papers chipped away, publishing 'extracts' of speeches which frequently owed more to the imagination of the writer than any real knowledge of what had been said. Samuel Johnson, who built a considerable reputation as a Parliamentary reporter, confessed to friends that a much admired speech of the Elder Pitt was entirely Johnson's work: 'that speech I wrote in a garret in Exeter Street'.[9]

The matter came to a head in 1771, when the printer of the admirably named *Middlesex Journal or Chronicle of Liberty* was summoned with others to answer the charge of having printed the debates of the House of Commons in contravention of regulations. Wilkes, now a London magistrate, was able through shameless manipulation of the legal process to ensure that the case was struck down, on the ground that the alleged offence contravened no statute, but only a proclamation that violated inalienable rights. Rather than risk outright confrontation with London opinion, Parliament backed down. No further attempt was made to impede the reporting of Parliamentary debates; though, since notetaking remained forbidden, journalists were still forced to rely on imperfect memory and lively imagination.[10]

These three great set-piece confrontations together constituted a remarkable breakthrough for the principle of a free press, and the rights it should enjoy both to report the news and offer opinion (and, indeed, pungent criticism). At the beginning of the eighteenth century Chief Justice Holt could argue that criticism of the government was criminal, because 'it is very necessary for all governments that the people should have a good opinion of it'.[11] Sixty years later such a view was redundant; it had become axiomatic that 'statesmen may be corrected in their blunders, or chastened for their villainy' by the press.[12] A man like John Wilkes could only have survived – indeed, thrived – because of this sea change in attitudes. It protected him from the consequences of a wild impudence that a generation before would surely have brought about his downfall.

How the press would use these new freedoms would remain to be seen. For some it seemed that the papers had merely won the right to be incredibly rude. When in 1772 *The Middlesex Journal* offered this comment on a proposed royal progress, it would have seemed to many that established boundaries of respect and propriety had been dissolved:

> His majesty, we are told, intends to make the tour of England. Weak as he is, he has got more wisdom. He knows too well the contempt or detestation in which he is held in all parts of the Kingdom, to expose himself to the neglect or insults he would everywhere meet with. Instead of travelling through England, he will bury himself at Kew.[13]

The best hope for politicians was that this rampant press might be drawn off the scent by other more alluring quarry. In the summer of 1776, for instance, one might have thought that the papers would have been consumed by anxious introspection at the portentous events unfolding in the American colonies. In fact, for several months London was preoccupied with two extraordinary (and interlinked) trials: the prosecution of the Duchess of Kingston for bigamy, and the subsequent trial of the comic dramatist Samuel Foote, her principal perse-cutor, for sodomy. In the case of the duchess no great legal issues were at stake. Depending on the outcome she would either be duchess or, if her first marriage was proved, Countess of Bristol. But for the trial of a peeress by the entire House of Lords, Westminster Hall was crammed and sittings of the House of Commons were suspended. Foote, who had made a fortune, and many enemies, by his impersonations of society figures, commanded less attention, but at least he was acquitted (after an extraordinary personal intervention by the king).[14] In London, as in contemporary Paris, theatre played a crucial role in the development of a celebrity culture, as well as providing an increasing amount of copy for the voracious newspapers.

There is no doubt that a reinvigorated and saucy press was more attractive to readers. In the last decades of the eighteenth century politics became a national sport. Just as in the 1760s and 1770s the prolonged controversy over Wilkes's membership of the House of Commons achieved considerable coverage in the provincial papers, from the 1780s onwards a robust campaign for Parliamentary reform won advocates in the press throughout the nation.[15] The provincial papers generally stuck to their routine of weekly publication. The London press, in contrast, was increasingly dominated by daily news. These papers were now a successful part of the political scene; they were also

16.2 The notorious Samuel Foote. His form of political satire eventually made him too many influential enemies.

increasingly professional in their deft integration of political comment with advertising, society gossip and foreign news. The outlines of the mature newspaper were gradually emerging from the turmoil of metropolitan politics and commercial life.

A Family Divided

This transformation in the English press owed a great deal to the reinvigorated interest in politics: not least, through the prolonged crisis with the American colonies. But it was surely significant – and a real milestone – that even this first traumatic challenge to the integrity of British imperial power did not bring about a retreat into dull loyalism. The crisis of American identity stimulated a real debate in England, where the colonists' insistence on their own rights and prerogatives found many English defenders.

Approaching the American Revolution through the history of the press brings home that this was always a family feud, and all the more painful for that. The sense of kinship ran very deep, a connection that made the disputes that festered through the 1760s so bitter and bewildering. The umbilical cord to London wholly shaped the early history of American newspapers: London was the source of news, and its papers the model to be emulated.

Newspapers developed only very haltingly in the American colonies.[16] Although Boston had a printer as early as 1634, it was not until 1690 that an attempt was made to establish a news periodical, and this, Benjamin Harris's *Publick Occurrences Both Forreign and Domestick*, was suppressed after just one issue. It was only in 1704 that, with the support of the authorities, the local postmaster John Campbell was allowed to begin distributing his *Boston News-Letter*. Like the earliest European newspaper, Campbell was here mechanising an existing service, since the postmaster had already learned to exploit his privileged position as distributor of incoming despatches by sending a regular manuscript newsletter to favoured clients. His printed weekly newspaper scarcely deviated from this model. *The Boston News-Letter* was throughout his custodianship essentially a digest of European and primarily London news.

Campbell was not an ideal news man. Cantankerous and given to self-pity, if he believed his readers did not appreciate his efforts he would write long self-justifying notices to say so. But his vision of what a newspaper should be proved deeply influential. Benjamin Harris, the battle-scarred London controversialist whose newspaper had been so quickly suppressed in 1690, had attempted to engage the local community in debate about Boston affairs. Campbell, in contrast, published very little local news. *The Boston News-Letter* was a scrupulous and often scrupulously dull litany of despatches extracted from London papers. So determined was he not to deviate from this programme that his reports of European news fell steadily behind. By 1719 he was meticulously reporting European events over a year old.

This was taking the principle of the journal of record to bizarre extremes, and thankfully other colonial news men did not feel the same compulsion. From 1719 Campbell had a Boston competitor, and papers were established shortly thereafter in Philadelphia, New York, Newport and Charleston. But none broke free from the preoccupation with European affairs. Analysis of the contents of *The Pennsylvania Gazette* between 1723 and 1765 reveals that over this extended period 70 per cent of news items were devoted to continental Europe and the British Isles.[17]

For all that, geography and logistics ultimately mandated that American newspapers would evolve in different ways to their European progenitors. The sheer distance between communities, strung out along a rocky coastline in colonies of different settlement patterns, created a series of largely self-contained markets. And notwithstanding the preoccupation with European affairs, the long winter season during which the transatlantic passage was interrupted meant that the stream of London papers was for several months abruptly terminated. The papers were obliged to seek more imaginative solutions to fill their pages: advertisements, correspondence, witty and diverting articles. The 1730s saw a wave of what might be termed literary papers. There was also increasing comment on local political controversies, such as the great immunisation debate that convulsed Boston in the 1720s.[18]

The period before 1740 also witnessed a slow but perceptible rise in the amount of news from other colonies. In this way the newspapers played an important part in the growth of an American inter-colonial community consciousness. But the community of shared values was essentially transatlantic. The social assumptions of the early American readership – a strong belief in Protestantism, property, retributive justice, the virtues of family, hard work and the superiority of the English over all other nations – these were virtually indistinguishable from those of the Englishmen who would have been reading, a few months earlier, largely the same news.

This made the quarrel, when it came, all the more destructive. The proximate cause was a European conflict fought largely on the American continent, the Seven Years War of 1756–63. Because the fighting was so much closer to home, this greatly increased coverage in colonial papers of events in the western hemisphere. This crisis also inspired one of the most memorable images of the colonial era, Benjamin Franklin's representation of the colonies as a severed snake, with the caption 'Join, or Die.' Ironically in its first manifestation, this cartoon (plausibly the first on the American continent) was pro-British: an admonition to the colonies to combine in their own defence or face destruction at the hands of the French. Its debut was modest enough, tucked away with little fanfare on the second page of Franklin's *Pennsylvania Gazette*.[19] But it was soon taken up and reprinted in papers in New York and Boston.[20] Rediscovered at the time of the Stamp Act Crisis, it would pass into history as one of the most potent patriot rallying cries.

The Seven Years War left the British victorious, but with an empty treasury. The territorial gains in the Americas had to be defended by a permanent military presence. It was to pay for this that the British Parliament determined to raise new revenues, laid partly on the colonies. One way of doing this was to tax colonial newspapers in the same way that English papers were taxed: by requiring them to use stamped, that is specially authorised and certified, paper.

If the Stamp Act crisis of 1765 proved one thing, it was that the press is never more eloquent, self-righteous and clamorous in the defence of liberty

16.3 Join, or Die. Benjamin Franklin's inspired piece of pro-British propaganda.

than when its own economic interests are concerned. Perhaps the English administration had been lulled by the experience of the imposition of the English stamp duty in 1712. Despite prognostications of the direst consequences the English press had absorbed the tax obligation with relatively little turbulence.[21] But the American press did not have the same deep roots, and securing supplies of the stamped paper from London posed extra logistical difficulties. The duty was repealed within a year, but American opinion, deftly marshalled by the press, had experienced its first taste of success.[22]

The Stamp Act crisis was also decisive in one other way. The short but furious agitation had engaged the loyalties of most of the established papers, though often initially with some reluctance. The partisan tone of the agitation, which would continue through the next decade of revolutionary controversies, ran wholly contrary to the established traditions of the colonial press. As colonial newspapers were, most usually, the only papers serving a community, their proprietors had striven, above all, to avoid giving offence.[23] A studied neutrality in local political controversy, made possible by the relatively limited coverage of local political news, had served them well. This could be presented as a point of principle, enunciated most famously by Benjamin Franklin in his *Apology for printers* (1731). 'Printers are educated in the belief,' he wrote, 'that when men differ in opinion, both sides ought equally to have the advantage of being heard by the public.'[24] The new temper of the times left no room for such Olympian sentiments. Printers exhibiting an insufficient zeal for the cause of liberty found subscriptions cancelled, and a chilly reception from former friends. Charleston's Peter Timothy found himself transformed from 'the most popular' to 'the most unpopular man in the province'.[25] In Charleston as elsewhere local patriots supported the establishment of a rival paper, warmer in the cause of liberty. Many printers were reluctant patriots. But the passions of public debate were too strong for the old ways.

In this sense the overwhelmingly patriot tone of the press during the Revolution was not always the result of free choice. Whereas the freedom of the press was vehemently proclaimed as a fundamental principle of the revolutionary movement, it was widely understood that this should not extend to the publication of sentiments injurious to the public good.[26] The careful distinctions enunciated by patriot authors were more rudely enforced by the populace, who installed their own form of popular censorship, harrying printers insufficiently enthusiastic for revolutionary politics and, if necessary smashing their shops and ruining the type.

The beguilingly easy triumph of the Stamp Act revolt would in one respect prove misleading. Never again would colonial opinion speak with such apparent unity. The long, slow descent to confrontation left the colonies badly divided. Harassed news men found it difficult to satisfy readers often fundamentally at odds on the issues of the day. Happily newspapers were not left to bear alone the burden of shaping the political agenda during these years. The most significant and influential political statements were all published as pamphlets. The most successful, such as Thomas Paine's Common Sense, sold in huge numbers (a reputed 120,000 copies). A brilliant exposition of the case for independence, which cut through the legalistic prose in which the debate had to this point been largely conducted, Common Sense was printed in twenty-five editions in thirteen American cities.[27] This was only the most notable example of a surge of pamphlet publication that reached a first climax with the Stamp Act, and a second with the commencement of hostilities in 1775–6.[28] Thereafter, both news men and pamphleteers found this intensity hard to sustain. Fighting disrupted distribution networks and forced many printers to shift location. Resources had to be redeployed to military purposes; sensitive information on troop movements could obviously not be widely reported.

This was a very slow-moving revolution. Between the battle of Concord and the Treaty of Paris the war lasted eight years (1755–83). A full twenty-four years elapsed between the Stamp Act and the inauguration of the first president, George Washington. The ardent young men of the 1760s had grown old before the United States emerged as an independent nation. The dramatic moments of crisis were interspersed with long periods of relative inactivity. The shift to outright rebellion was characterised by repeated hesitancy, as proposals, loyal addresses and pained remonstrances passed back and forth across the great expanse of the Atlantic. Even after the fighting was concluded, the various legislative and constitutive bodies moved with agonising slowness.

The rebellious provinces presented a very particular context for the distribution of news, as settlements with quite separate heritages attempted to forge a common cause across great expanses of coast and barely tamed interior. Reading the successive issues of the newspapers can present an unexpected impression of tranquillity, of societies going about their business into which great events only intermittently intrude. *The Virginia Gazette* of 1775 was a weekly four-page folio in three columns, with supplements issued as necessary. The issue of 28 April opened with news from Constantinople.[29] The Parliamentary debate from London of 2 February featured a long speech from Lord Chatham in the House of Lords. The advertisements, starting in the middle column of the second page and consuming the rest of the paper, feature horses for stud and appeals for the return of runaway slaves. The first news of the battles of Lexington and Concord is included with an extra half sheet, dated from Philadelphia on 24 April (five days after the engagement). Often it is the advertisements that give a hint of the growing turbulence in a community, as in the announcement of sales of goods of those leaving the colony. But life goes on. *The Virginia Gazette*, 'Always for Liberty and the Public Good', continued to run its advertisement for the recovery of fugitive servants and slaves, and its occasional tantalising hint of domestic discord:

> Whereas my wife Frances has behaved in a very uncommon manner to me of late, this is to forewarn all persons from having any dealings with her on my account, as I will not be answerable for any debts of her contracting after this date.[30]

It can indeed plausibly be argued that the Revolution encouraged newspapers to take themselves too seriously. In the densely settled port towns – precisely the place of publication of most newspapers – residents had access, through overlapping networks of family, workplace and commercial connections, to a great deal of news far fresher and more pertinent than much of what they read in their newspapers.[31] Most newspapers still only published once, or at most twice a week. Months-old news from distant parts might be of limited interest, and commercial notices placed in the advertisement columns were of little use to rural subscribers. During the war years in particular word of mouth, communications from travellers, ships' captains and returning soldiers, played a vital part in keeping people abreast of uncertain events.

Irrespective of what the press did for the Revolution, the Revolution certainly had a profound impact on the press. The number of papers published doubled between 1763 and 1775, and again by 1790. In that year the American states supported ninety-nine newspapers in some sixty-two separate locations. Newspaper publication was now one of the most significant props of the American publishing industry.[32] In an era when substantial volumes of literature, history and scholarship were still by and large imported, it was almost necessary for a printer to have a newspaper to stay in business.

In this way it was not just patriotism but economic interest that tied the press to the cause of the emerging nation. The same tone of patriotic commitment enunciated during the revolutionary agitation continued after the British defeat and through the subsequent constitutional debates. The press was overwhelmingly Federalist; a commitment all the more notable given that one of the first acts of the Federal Convention was to resolve to keep its debates secret. The intention was to insulate delegates from public pressure, but it also deprived the newspapers of a constant supply of good copy during its protracted deliberations. A few years later the French revolutionaries would adopt a conspicuously contrary view, encouraging journalists to attend and report the debates of the successive legislative bodies. The press came into its own during the campaign for ratification, which was far from a foregone conclusion. Only when Virginia came reluctantly into line, and the presumed Anti-Federalist majority in New York was narrowly defeated, could the new constitution be put into effect.

The zealous commitment of the press to the establishment of the new nation did not go unrewarded. When James Madison was entrusted with preparing the Bill of Rights in 1790, the first amendment to the constitution guaranteed that Congress would 'make no law. . . abridging the freedom of speech, or of the press'. But these freedoms would still be forced to run the test of prevailing morality, social convention and partisan politics. Contemporary opinion saw no contradiction between the assertion in Virginia's Bill of Rights 'that the freedom of the press is one of the great bulwarks of liberty, and can never be restrained but by despotic governments' and the state's 1792 'Act against divulgers of false news'.[33] The unacknowledged tensions set the scene for an exuberant, rancorous and highly partisan culture of public debate that was both the adornment and curse of politics in the new nation.

The Empty Prison

On 14 July 1789 a crowd of around nine hundred local people gathered outside the Bastille, the old prison building of Paris that now served mostly as an armoury. Very little remained of the old autocratic system of *lettres de cachet* that had incarcerated prisoners without trial; nevertheless, the building still constituted a potent symbol and the crowd were determined to liberate, if not its few remaining prisoners, then at least its stock of gunpowder. The morning was consumed in nervous negotiations between the insurgents and the marquis de Launay, commander of the small garrison. These achieved little, and by afternoon, in an increasingly chaotic melee, shots were exchanged. The arrival of more revolutionary forces, including trained soldiers, compelled the garrison's surrender. Launay and some of his soldiers were hauled out and butchered; the rest were escorted away as the crowd took possession of the artillery.[34]

In such a turbulent and politically momentous season, there was little in these events to suggest why this should become such an iconic day in French history: since 1880, indeed, the nation's primary day of national celebration. The haul of liberated prisoners, seven, was meagre. This included four convicted forgers and two who had to be reincarcerated in mental institutions; hardly the political detainees of the Bastille's fearsome legend. The immediate response of the established periodical press, both at home and abroad, was restrained. The *Gazette de France*, naturally, ignored the disturbance altogether. The foreign press reported it as an incident of riotous disorder, rather than suggesting any wider significance. In real political terms it scarcely merited being privileged ahead of the calling of the Estates General, the Tennis Court Oath, or the subsequent forced return of the king from Versailles. As a revolutionary event, the 1788 insurrection in Grenoble was a far more potent challenge to the *ancien régime*, though it scarcely now registers in the revolutionary canon.

It was the newly emboldened pressmen of Paris who ensured that the storming of the Bastille did not suffer the same fate. A rush of celebratory pamphlets and illustrated broadsheets proclaimed the fall of the empty prison as the symbolic awakening of an oppressed people.[35] The same themes were rapidly taken up in the developing newspaper press. Yesterday, wrote Antoine-Louis Gordas in his *Courier de Versailles à Paris*, 'will be forever remembered in the records of our history: it opens the way for the greatest and perhaps the most fortunate of revolutions.'[36]

The extraordinary events that unfolded in France between 1789 and 1794 were accompanied by a torrent of newsprint in every media: pamphlets, journals, broadsheet images and political song.[37] The pre-revolutionary political crisis and the calling of the Estates General had stimulated a steadily rising drum roll of political pamphlets: around 1,500 different titles in 1788 and at least 2,600 during the elections to the Estates in the first four months of 1789: a stratospheric rise compared to the four hundred or so published in the twelve years before 1787.[38] The carefully constructed edifice of press control established during the *ancien régime*, and sustained for over 150 years, now simply evaporated. While the National Assembly engaged in long and earnest debates over press freedom, events and the book trade moved on.

In the years after 1789 the pampered and privileged members of the Paris Book Guild saw their world turned upside down.[39] For the previous two centuries it had been the conscious policy of the French monarchy to concentrate the printing industry in the capital, and to favour a small number of large firms. An effective monopoly on book production for a large and prosperous population was a predictable disincentive to innovation. Faced with the Parisian presses' outdated stock of worthy reproductions of the seventeenth-century canon, readers looked elsewhere, cultivating a lively market in semi-tolerated illicit imports from abroad.[40] Now, under the pressure of unprecedented events, the market of the established printing magnates simply melted away. Despite Crown efforts to support allies in the press with substantial covert subsidies, between 1789 and 1793 many of the giants of Parisian printing filed for bankruptcy. Their place was taken by an entirely new generation, many of them booksellers, who had detected the hunger for contemporary political works. To feed this demand they now set up their own presses.

From 1789 these news publishers/booksellers also began to convert their pamphlet output into periodical series. This was neither immediately nor universally successful. Only one of the pamphlets celebrating the fall of the Bastille was announced as part of a serial. Many of the newly established titles disappeared equally rapidly. But during the course of 1789 and 1790 the journal – a daily, tri-weekly or weekly newspaper – would establish itself as the characteristic organ of revolutionary debate.

For a country deliberately starved of choice in the periodical press during the *ancien régime*, this was a momentous change. The pamphlet surge of the revolutionary period was in some respects quite traditional: the previous collapse of royal authority during the Fronde in the mid-seventeenth century had been accompanied by a similar deluge of pamphlet literature.[41] But the explosion of journal publication in Paris during these years was on a scale not witnessed anywhere in Europe. From four journals published in the capital in 1788, the number skyrocketed to 184 in 1789 and 335 in 1790. During the height of the revolutionary agitation, as many as 300,000 copies a day of these various publications would have been available on the streets.[42] Paris was suddenly awash with a flood of exuberant, passionate, committed news-sheets. Soon they had come to dominate the political agenda.

Most of these new serials were, it must be admitted, rather unprepossessing little booklets, scarcely distinguishable from the grubby cheap pamphlets with which their printers and readers were already familiar. Without the fifty years of steady growth and evolution that had characterised the development of the newspapers in England, the printers of this sudden rush of new titles had little time or resources for questions of design. Most of the first news serials kept close to the familiar pamphlet format: published in the customary small octavo of the established genre, they generally consisted of eight closely written pages of political advocacy. The experienced Charles-Joseph Panckoucke, skilfully surfing the wave of political change, could envisage his *Moniteur* imitating the three-column folio format of the London press.[43] But this was very much the exception. Most of the revolutionary papers were the product of less well-established printing houses. The urgency of the moment called for quick work rather than sophistication.

These papers, then, had none of the elegance and balance of the established press in other parts of Europe; nor the variety of content and subject matter. The Paris papers of the Revolution were devoted wholly and passionately to politics. Here they had the advantage of an almost inexhaustible supply of subject matter. With the National Assembly and its successor bodies in almost continuous session, the debates and speeches became the staple diet of many papers, sometimes excessively so. Those high-minded papers that attempted to provide verbatim reports of debates, down to the last cough and heckled interjection, found within a few months that this was a most unsatisfactory form of journalism, likely to leave their readers baffled rather than enlightened. But the commitment to accurate reporting was impressive. All the major events of the revolutionary years, even such brutal spasms as the prison massacres of September 1792, were fully and relatively accurately reported and interpreted.

Experiments in exhaustive factual reporting aside, it was with advocacy journalism that the French revolutionary newspapers found their characteristic voice. All the major figures of the revolutionary era, including Marat, Danton and Robespierre, were at some point journalists.[44] Many, including Marat, Camille Desmoulins and George Hébert, established their political profile almost entirely through their writing. Marat was here the pivotal figure: his intemperate prose and open advocacy of violence created a darker palette for revolutionary rhetoric, foreshadowing the horrific violence of the Terror, when the Revolution consumed its own. Hébert, speaking as the witty and scabrous representative of the *sans-culottes*, the Père Duchêne, was also not for the weaker constitution, with his eager embrace of the cruelty of revolutionary justice. But most of all, revolutionary journalists needed to be able to turn out copy at speed, and to a deadline. 'The necessity of writing every day,' according to Benjamin Constant, 'is the tomb of talent.'[45] Many journalists would agree; the most successful and best-known newspapers of the

Revolution were generally weekly or thrice-weekly publications. For all that the most successful journalists of the Revolution maintained, sometimes over a sustained period, a remarkable output. Madame Roland acknowledged that the great success of her friend Jacques-Pierre Brissot was that he 'worked very easily, and he composed a treatise the way someone else would copy a song'.[46] This left little space for profound reflection, but that was hardly necessary: the potency of revolutionary journalism lay in the constant regurgitation of political advocacy. 'How does it happen that this petty individual does so much harm to the public welfare,' asked one of Brissot's Jacobin enemies in 1792. 'It is because he has a newspaper. . . . It is because Brissot and his friends have all the trumpets of renown at their disposal.'[47]

The trumpets of renown could also be very lucrative. Demand for the news was enormous, and there was plenty of room for competing ventures. The most successful papers swiftly built a substantial readership. The *Journal du soir* employed five presses and sixty workmen, and needed two hundred street vendors to distribute its 10,000 daily copies.[48] But it did not require an operation on this industrial scale to make money. A single press could crank out around 3,000 copies of a simple news pamphlet in a day, more than enough to make money: the break-even point for such publications was probably as low as four hundred copies per issue. The printers protected their investment by operating an informal price cartel. Although they would furiously denounce their competitors' opinions, publishers never attempted to undercut rivals by lowering their price. Almost all set their subscription rates close to the customary rate for the pre-revolutionary imported newspapers, around 36 *livres* a year. Given the extraordinary political events they record, this industry conservatism seems rather quaint; but it served the printers well, allowing them to ride out the political turbulence and compensating them for the undoubted risk of this form of publication. The only significant technical innovation introduced by the revolutionary papers was the provision, in the opinion papers, of short summaries of the contents or argument at the top of the first sheet, under the title. This was intended to assist the hawkers, crying out the papers on the streets.[49]

For the leading journalists of the Revolution, as well as their printers, the market for news also brought considerable financial rewards. Brissot was paid 6,000 *livres* a year to edit his newspaper (the same salary as a minister in the government) and his was not a unique case.[50] In truth, for the principal actors this was undoubtedly a subsidiary concern: journalism, for them, was a weapon of revolution, a means to shape fast-moving events. With influence came hazard. This was, to a quite unprecedented extent, a deadly trade. The Terror would claim the lives of at least one-sixth of the journalists writing in the first full years of the Revolution (1790–1), including most of the major journalist-politicians. Marat was assassinated in his bath; Brissot fell with the Girondins and died with Danton. Hébert, whose Père Duchêne had gleefully recorded the last moments of so many victims of the guillotine, attracted a large crowd when he, in turn, went to his death. Camille Desmoulins was one of the last victims of Robespierre, the godfather of his young son.

It was in these most vicious months that the Revolution finally abandoned the vision of press freedom that had animated many of the early debates in the National Assembly.[51] Robespierre, a consistent advocate of the principle from 1789 to 1793, now recognised the error of his ways. On 16 June he invited the Committee of Public Safety to punish 'treacherous journalists who are the most dangerous enemies of liberty'.[52] Shortly before concluding his ascent to power, Robespierre had sketched an extraordinary political catechism. This demonstrates the extent to which he now saw unlicensed freedom as the heart of the discord that had engulfed the revolutionary movement:

What is our aim? It is the use of the Constitution for the benefit of the people.

Who is likely to oppose us? The rich and the corrupt.

What methods will they employ? Slander and hypocrisy.

What factors will encourage the use of such means? The ignorance of the sans-culottes.

The people must therefore be instructed.

What are the obstacles to their enlightenment? The paid journalists who mislead the people every day by shameless distortions.

What conclusion follows? That we ought to proscribe these writers as the most dangerous enemies of the country, and to circulate an abundance of good literature.[53]

In the early, hopeful days of revolution, Mirabeau and Brissot had believed that the press would unify public opinion. In this at least they were to be disappointed. The coup that toppled Robespierre was accompanied by stringent measures to rein in the press. Both the Directory and the subsequent Napoleonic regime recognised the corrosive danger of unbridled political criticism. Of the eighty Parisian printing houses chosen to be retained under the Napoleonic system of press control, only nineteen specialised in journals and periodicals.[54]

At the height of the revolutionary agitation the interested reader could choose between as many as one hundred serial publications. The scale of the transformation from the staid, controlled world of the *ancien régime* is obvious, though this is not to say that the newspapers exercised all the influence attributed to them by the revolutionary leadership. Serial publication vied for influence with other traditional forms of persuasive literature, not least non-serial political pamphlets which were also published in huge numbers.[55] While Paris was a highly literate society (with high levels of male and female literacy), the combined readership of newspapers probably never exceeded 3 million, out of a total national population of 28 million. Although provincial cities like Lyon and Toulouse also experienced a rapid expansion of a newly established provincial press, the disjunction between the political melting pot of the capital and provincial society was still stark.[56] In Paris itself, much political activism was face to face and word of mouth, in the Jacobin clubs and, among delegates to the successive national assemblies, in private drawing rooms or on the floor of the debating chamber itself. Among the wider population most citizens, called to action regardless of social station, would have been roused to arms by speeches or conversation in impromptu street gatherings and taverns. The French Revolution was an extraordinarily fertile period for the composition of political song, of which the Marseillaise was only the most famous and enduring example.[57]

Periodicals, for all their eloquent advocacy of universal enfranchisement, still spoke in the voice of the educated elite. Marat's tirades of denunciation could be couched in a severely classical vocabulary. He made no attempt whatsoever to address the common people in their own patterns of speech; rather there was a conscious sense of distance. Several times a week his *Ami du peuple* would conclude with an 'Address to the Citizenry', where in the exasperated tones of an Old Testament prophet he offered a foreboding vision of the future that would unfold should his readers ignore his injunctions.

At least in these revolutionary papers the Paris readership would have a clear sense of the context of events discussed: there was far less of the baffling recitation of foreign diplomatic and military events that had made up the stock in trade of European newspapers for the past two centuries. And in the newspapers published under the title of the *Père Duchêne* we witness a radical and imaginative attempt to adopt the personality, and patterns of speech, of the less well-educated foot-soldiers of the revolutionary era. Père Duchêne was a lusty old salt; vulgar, forthright and not afraid to stand up to his social betters. Although Hébert was the best known and most successful, a dozen or more different writers at some point adopted this persona – an eloquent testimony to the difficulties faced by political activists who recognised the need to mobilise a mass movement but realised these citizens did not yet have the political vocabulary to articulate shared political goals. It is also a reminder that the market for revolutionary newspapers, though very large, was also highly competitive. New ventures shamelessly poached the titles of successful rivals, or shifted their own clothes as the political wind turned. Many vanished as easily as they had appeared. At a time when many other European nations had established papers of many years standing (and some with centuries of continuous publication ahead of them), most revolutionary papers lasted three or four years at most.

With the perspective of hindsight, the revolutionary papers can be seen as a relatively brief interlude in France between two stable eras of controlled, cautious news-making. For all that they nevertheless represent a true milestone in the history of European journalism. The French Revolution was arguably the first European event to which a periodical press was truly indispensable. For the first time newspapers became, albeit fleetingly, the dominant medium of printed text, displacing their more aristocratic progenitor, the book, and even the characteristic carrier of political discussion, the pamphlet. France was in this respect ahead of its time. In other parts of Europe, for instance Ireland, the political pamphlet was still the dominant medium for political agitation – as it was indeed during the American Revolution.[58] In France, and to a lesser extent in the other cases studied in this chapter, we see the first instances of a fundamental realignment in the European culture of news. From henceforth the periodical rhythms of regular news publication would come to characterise the public perceptions of the shape of current events. Domestic news was suddenly the most urgent order of business. The great age of the daily newspaper was at hand.

How Samuel Sewall Read his Paper

O N 24 April 1704 Samuel Sewall, citizen of Boston, travelled across the Charles River to Cambridge, carrying with him the first issue of John Campbell's weekly news-sheet, *The Boston News-Letter*. Sewall was on his way to present a copy to his friend Reverend Samuel Willard, Vice-President of Harvard College; Willard was delighted to receive it, and promptly shared it with the other Fellows. Samuel Sewall was at this point one of the leading citizens of the largest city in the American colonies. For the best part of fifty years he was at the heart of its commerce and government, named to the Governor's Council in 1691 and re-elected annually until his retirement in 1725. As a magistrate, father and neighbour, Sewall was a model citizen of this potent emerging society.

Sewall also kept a diary. That, for our purposes, puts him in a special category beyond all his other accomplishments. For Sewall recorded, on a regular basis, his daily round: his work, his conversations, the sermons he attended, and how he heard the news.[1]

This evidence is, for a student of news, very precious. Over the course of this narrative we have witnessed a real transformation in the supply and availability of news. By the eighteenth century the number of those who had access to news on a regular basis was vastly increased. Newspapers were an established part of life; in some places a daily newspaper was becoming if not the norm, then increasingly available. But whereas we can chart easily enough the history of news from the production side, it is far more difficult to experience at first hand what readers made of this. The articulate reader, who went on to record how he experienced day-to-day news culture, is comparatively rare.

Sometimes, indeed, the available sources tell us more about the relatively inarticulate consumer of news. This is certainly true of one precious source of which we have made intermittent use in this book, court records and judicial proceedings. These provide a detailed record of occasions when the discussion of public affairs was deemed by Europe's rulers to be injurious to the public good. What is particularly striking is the extent to which this regulation of opinion concentrated not on print, but on the spoken word: what the city council of Augsburg described as 'dangerous and idle talk'.[2] For news respected no boundaries. What was printed in one city could be sold and read in another; once news was in the public domain it was extremely difficult to arrest its flow. News moved easily from manuscript to print and from print to speech.

This subtle understanding of the interconnectedness of different media is exhibited in a very revealing edict published by the time of the Catalan revolt in 1640:

> Let nobody own, read or hear any book or paper, be it printed or hand-written, which justifies, warns, counsels and encourages the uprising in this principality and the continuance of the war; and be it forbidden that *anyone who knows by heart* any part of those books or papers should relate them or that anyone should hear them.[3]

Scholars tend to privilege the printed word because it has provided the vast bulk of surviving evidence of past events. But hard-pressed magistrates never underestimated the potency of speech (or, as this Spanish example makes clear, of memory). Reading their Bible they knew that 'death and life are in the power of the tongue'. They also knew that 'the wicked is snared by the transgression of his lips'; indeed, they counted upon it.[4] In Europe's teeming cities, where living conditions were cramped, privacy virtually unknown, and strong drink ubiquitous, rumours spread like wildfire. When the city authorities cornered someone who had uttered seditious words, they always took the greatest pains to reconstruct how these miscreants had first heard the rumour, and who they had spoken to afterwards.

The new world was emerging, but the old world was not banished. The multi-media world of news exchange, the subtle chain of interactions between those who brought the news and those who heard it, did not dissolve in the face of the on-rushing periodical press. Court transcripts provide some of the best evidence of how news spread in the pre-modern era: they reveal a turbulent, combustible world of shouting, insult, rumour and song. Song, in particular, was a particularly potent vector of criticism throughout the period under study: the Parisian police authorities were still greatly concerned at the circulation of satirical verses on the eve of the French Revolution, and with good reason.[5] In this rich and diverse world of information exchange, it is clear that despite the proliferation of commercial news-sheets in various shapes and varieties, many citizens would still have got all the news they wanted for free.

Those who bought the news are already in some senses in a special category; those who record their reflections on current events are even more rare. So it will be helpful to spend a little time with three men who did keep track of their thoughts in their own way. They are a varied bunch: an English workman, a Dutch clerk and the North American magistrate Samuel Sewall. All were in some respects unusual, and not just in their meticulous diary keeping. But time in their company does tell us a great deal about the multi-media world we have traversed in this book. Despite the increased sophistication of the available news media, much had remained surprisingly unchanged.

Turning the Tables

Nehemiah Wallington was a modest and self-effacing man. The son of a London wood-turner, he spent his whole life practising his father's trade, living in a house close to the place where he was born, a few yards north of London Bridge. Wallington did not aspire to a life in public affairs; but he lived in troubled times, and it is as a chronicler of these times that he has latterly found fame.[6] For Wallington was a quite exceptional man. In 1618, shortly before he was admitted to the Turners' Company as an independent master, Wallington began to write in the first of many notebooks, which he would fill with his religious reflections, notes on current events, letters and transcribed portions of printed news-books.[7] By the time he decided to desist in 1654 he had compiled fifty volumes containing at least twenty thousand closely written pages, and earned his place as one of the premier artisan chroniclers of his day.

Wallington, an intensely introspective character, sometimes wondered whether this obsessive concern to record the everyday experiences of his spiritual journey was rather unhealthy. Despite the intermittent money worries that afflicted all tradesmen, Wallington spent heavily on books. During the dramatic early years of the Civil Wars he bought hundreds of news pamphlets. Ruefully contemplating the piles heaped up around his house, he recognised in 1642 that these had been an extravagance: 'these little pamphlets of weekly news . . . were so many thieves that had stolen away my money before I was aware of them'.[8]

Wallington is an especially valuable witness because he wrote in a period when the news environment was changing very rapidly. In the 1620s and 1630s, when Wallington was first compiling his journals, the publication of news serials in England was intermittently banned, and always closely controlled. But as a citizen of London, and as an ardent puritan, Wallington was an impassioned observer, and occasional actor, in the turbulent political events played out in the capital. In 1638 Nehemiah was questioned by the Star Chamber about the distribution of seditious books. Given the savage punishment meted out to their author, William Prynne, he was understandably alarmed.[9] Three years later he was among the reputed fifteen thousand Londoners who descended on Westminster to persuade the House of Lords to condemn the hated Earl of Strafford. 'I never did see so many together in all my life,' Wallington reflected, 'and when they did see any Lord coming, they all cried with one voice, Justice! Justice!'[10]

Wallington was very conscious of living at the hub of events, all of which he interpreted through the prism of his deeply held religious beliefs. Almost all of the news events he records were seen as evidence of divine purpose: to punish the sinful, or test the faith of the Lord's children. One whole volume of his chronicles is devoted to the evil consequences that befell those who

17.1 Nehemiah Wallington's writing books.

profaned the Sabbath, instances all too frequent in the teeming metropolis. In 1632 he recorded the salutary tale of two young men larking in the rigging of a ship at Whitechapel on a Sunday, when one fell to his death.[11] Wallington had this from the chastened survivor, and many of these stories – of a child who fell into the fire while their mother was doing the monthly wash, or a house burned down when the family was gadding forth on the Sabbath – came to him in this way, by word of mouth. Once the Civil War fighting was underway Wallington was equally meticulous in collecting instances of sudden calamity that had fallen upon the king's troops when they spoke contemptuously of the Godly as Roundheads. Wallington's God was not slow to indicate through such signs his partiality towards those who held to the straight and narrow path. A fine example is his wonderfully idiosyncratic account of the battle of Edgehill: 'The wonderful work of God in the guidance of bullets.'[12]

In searching out evidence of the workings of God's Providence, Wallington noted without scepticism many strange and threatening portents: a fearful storm in 1626, the sighting of a meteor in Berkshire in 1628. Seventy years later to the sophisticated London newsmen such reports would be an implicit comment on the credulity of country folk, but Wallington's generation had no such doubts.[13] A terrible tempest near Norwich in 1643, resulting in the death of 111 rooks and jackdaws, inspired an ingenious explanation: 'we may conjecture that it may mean God's judgement upon the plundering and pillaging cavalier rebels, who, like rooks and daws, live now raucously by the sweat of honest men's brows'.[14]

Wallington's meticulous record-keeping provides eloquent witness to the emerging power of the urban population to influence great events. Some years before Nehemiah was born Sir Thomas Smith had laid down with lofty precision the division of the English Commonwealth between those 'that bear office, the other of them that bear none'. Artisans and tradesmen belong to the latter sort, and 'have no voice nor authority in our commonwealth'.[15] Wallington was of the generation that subverted these comfortable assumptions. Although he spent freely on news publications when these became available, most of his news came to him through friends, casual acquaintance, and the closely knit network of his fellow believers. Some great events, like the burning of London Bridge, he could record as an eyewitness. Others, like his account of the comet that had so alarmed King James in 1618, he copied from a pamphlet.[16]

In what ways did the news serials of the 1640s, which he bought so recklessly, impact on this developed news consciousness? Wallington certainly did acquire a sophisticated sense of the wider strategic issues that would determine the outcome of the conflict. He saw that Ireland, where he had family, would play a key role, and lamented the cleavage that emerged between the Godly congregations of England and Scotland in the latter stages of the conflict. An insightful letter to his friend James Cole in New England analyses the various phases of the wars, which he defines as the 'prelatical war' of 1639–40, the 'profane war' of 1642, and the 'hypocritical war' of 1648. Historians have varied the judgemental titles, but hardly improved on the chronology.[17] Nor was Wallington's interest confined to the British wars. In 1638 a book came into his hands that laid bare the miserable estate of the Christian peoples in Germany, and he mourned the fate of the Huguenot congregation in La Rochelle in 1628.[18]

Wallington's pamphlets were assembled for a particular purpose, the creation of a historical narrative to enable 'the generation to come [to] see what God hath done'. The journal would teach posterity the trials undergone by the children of God. And Wallington felt these trials very acutely, as the fighting took its toll: the death of an apprentice, the loss of a close friend. Where the personal meets the political, the news networks did not always function smoothly. Only in 1643, in a section devoted to Catholic atrocities in Ireland, could Wallington record the death of a brother-in-law, murdered two years previously. Presumably only now was he receiving this grim news.

Wallington was a sophisticated reader. Sometimes he would transcribe from news-books accounts of events he had attended in person: here he used his notebooks to marshal and order his recollections. His detailed narrative of the war years provides a gripping contemporary history, compiled largely from his collection of pamphlets and his own experiences. Few were as committed as our master turner to bringing order to current events; in a world view shaped by piety his notebooks served as a means to record and divine God's ineffable purposes for humanity.

First among Equals

Like Nehemiah Wallington, Samuel Sewall was a committed churchman. Before his marriage he had trained at Harvard and originally intended ordination, and the imprint of his theological training remained with him for life. He was a regular and judicious attender of sermons, often twice on Sunday, and a rigorous defender of the Sabbath. Boston's leading ministers were among his closest friends. As commissioner of the local court of judiciary one of Sewall's first duties was to participate in the condemnation of the accused in the famous Salem witch trials. He quickly came to regret his part in this dark business, and he was the only judge to publicly repudiate his role, standing bare-headed before his congregation while his minister read out a formal act of contrition.[19]

Sewall began his diary at the age of twenty-one, and continued it until the last year of his life: a span of over fifty years. During this time Boston was transformed from an insular provincial place to a bustling Georgian city. Sewall remained faithful to the values of the old school, but his patent integrity and lack of personal vanity ensured that he retained the respect of the whole community.

As a member of Boston's commercial and political elite, Sewall had access to the best sources of information. He was an avid reader of the incoming mails, and, as we have seen, he eagerly welcomed the publication of Boston's first weekly newspaper. He subscribed to the paper throughout his lifetime, and bound successive issues into neat volumes for inclusion in his library. But for all his delight in this refined specimen of European sophistication, what he read in *The Boston News-Letter* seemed to have had only a marginal impact on his news world. As we can see from his diary, even before the coming of the newspaper Sewall had been at the centre of a series of inter-locking news networks: family, commercial, the judicial circuit and colonial government.

When Sewall moved into his father-in-law's house after his marriage he immediately joined a substantial news hub. Visitors and messengers brought information from family members settled in farms and settlements around Massachusetts Bay. At times of crisis Sewall would have been one of the first to know of threats to what was still a frontier society. When a messenger in 1690 brought news of an Indian assault, Sewall wrote immediately to his father and brother. Even the wedding party of Sewall's son, who was marrying the Governor's daughter, was briefly interrupted so the Governor could read aloud a letter from his own son (the colony's Attorney General) describing the business that had kept him away: the capture of a pirate.[20]

Pirates and their fate feature regularly in Sewall's diary. As a judge he was often concerned with their trials, and as a merchant trading in export goods he was acutely conscious of the threat they posed to the colony's economy. Despite this he was, more often than not, on the side of mercy. Possessed of an enviably robust constitution, Sewall travelled incessantly, riding out of Boston on commercial business or as a judge on circuit. A single entry from relatively early in the diary gives a sense of the rich intermingling of his circles of acquaintance, and their role as conduits of news:

Joshua Moodey and self set out for Ipswich. I lodge at Sparkes's. Next day, Feb 12, go to lecture which Mr Moodey preaches, then I dine with Mr

17.2 *The Boston News-Letter*. A slavish imitation of *The London Gazette*, down to the sub-heading and style of date.

Cobbet, and so ride to Newbury; visit Mr Richardson sick of the dry belly ache. Monday, Feb 16, get Mr Philips and Payson to town and so keep a fast day. Mr Moodey preaching forenoon, Mr Phillips afternoon, Mr Woodbridge and Payson assisting in prayer; was a pretty full Assembly, Mr Moodey having given notice the Sabbath day, on which he preached all day. At Wenham and Ipswich, as we went, we were told of the earthquake in those parts and at Salem (Feb 8) the Sabbath before about the time of ending afternoon exercise. That which most was sensible of was a startling doleful sound; but many felt the shaking also.[21]

Sewall, like Wallington, was an unsceptical recorder of natural phenomena and heavenly apparitions. There is good reason why devout Protestants feature so prominently among the early keepers of diaries, often unsparingly frank: under the eye of an all-seeing God it was useless to dissemble. When

Sewall lost his wife in 1717, his humbling search for a suitable widow with whom to spend his declining years is fully and painfully recorded. It was in these last years of his life that the public printed media came to play a more important role in Sewall's access to news. This was not because the newspaper itself had improved; as we have seen, John Campbell took a remorselessly old-fashioned approach to the newsman's craft. Rather as Sewall cut back on his public responsibilities he was increasingly dependent on second-hand information. In his declining years he even relied on younger female relatives for news, as when 'cousin Mrs Jane Green told me of Governor Burnet's commission being come, which I heard not of before; though 'twas known of in the town the evening before'.[22]

What Sewall's diary reveals most vividly, in the first decades of the eighteenth century, is the survival of an essentially hierarchical structure of news gathering and dissemination. The public prints were part of the culture of society, and local debates could be stoked by pamphlets published in the Boston print shop. But the most important news inevitably came first to the colony's leading citizens, who passed on to kin, workmates and other citizens such as they thought fit. News sufficiently momentous was announced publicly from the pulpits of Boston's eleven churches. But there was much with which Sewall and his colleagues thought it unnecessary to trouble their social inferiors. The best news still, in Georgian Boston, passed around the circles of trust. Even a society built on principles of the spiritual democracy of equality before God had imposed its own social filters on that most precious of commodities, information.

Boston was not a typical place. It was only towards the end of Sewall's life (and not with his approval) that the city relaxed its very strict control of licensed premises. Business that in other places might have been conducted at home or in the tavern was often transacted in communal gatherings: the meeting house, around the courtroom, even at funerals. Boston, of course, was as prone as other places to the circulation of uncontrolled rumour, either of dramatic events in the interior or momentous happenings from Europe. On 22 September 1685 Sewall picked up a rather garbled story from 'neighbour Fyfield', a less eminent citizen who did not move in Sewall's normal circles, of the execution of the Duke of Monmouth (this had taken place in London on 15 July). Fyfield had it from the 'crier of fish', who had apparently picked up the news from a sea captain.[23] Further diary entries in the following week record a corrected narrative from more reliable sources. Here, as often, rumour had moved more rapidly, though less accurately, than the normal channels of elite diffusion.

Boston was a unique laboratory: a place where news was funnelled through more restricted filters than in more densely settled European lands. Here the newspaper played a secondary role as the first source of news. Sewall was committed to print – he had supervised the Boston press for three years as a young man and he was a published author – and he collected the newspaper assiduously. But mostly he used his carefully bound copies as a source of reference: for names and dates or for the political texts, the speeches and proclamations that they reprinted in full.[24] The Boston paper also provided some useful commercial reference material such as the dates of landing of incoming vessels; though the attempt to include commodity prices, an innovation of the second Boston paper the *Gazette*, was dropped at the behest of Boston merchants who did not want to lose their commercial edge over competitors in Connecticut and Rhode Island.[25]

In some years Sewall prepared for his bound volumes an index of the principal events, and he also added marginal notes as appropriate. For all this, the local paper played a small part in Sewall's network of information: smaller, indeed, than the imported papers brought by incoming vessels from London and Amsterdam. Perhaps for those less well connected than Sewall it was different: Campbell's paper had a more important role bringing the news to subscribers in the smaller outlying settlements around Boston. The arrival of competing papers brought different perspectives, and a certain loosening of elite domination of news. But in places like Boston, word of mouth communication, closely bound to the credit and reputation of the teller, remained at the heart of news communication throughout the colonial period.

The Amateur Newshound

By the mid-eighteenth century the Dutch Republic had lost something of its early lustre. It no longer inspired fear for the ruthlessness of its command of international trade, or awe at its sudden rise to the first rank of European powers. But it was still a marvellously sophisticated and ingenious society; and it still possessed one of Europe's most highly developed news markets. Each of its largest cities was served by a regular paper, some now long established. The *Oprechte Haerlemsche Courant* was the direct descendant of the paper established in the mid seventeenth century. Between 1650 and 1750 its circulation had expanded tenfold, to about 4,300 subscriptions for its thrice-weekly issues; the *Amsterdamsche Courant* sold about 6,000.[26] These were impressive figures for the publisher, though perhaps less so when one considers the size of the population and the lack of local competition. Each of the ten Dutch papers published in the mid-eighteenth century enjoyed a local monopoly, protected and regulated by the local authorities. Such competition as there was came from overlapping markets: half of the *Haerlemsche Courant*'s print run was sold through its Amsterdam distributor.

The vibrancy of Dutch news culture emerged from a long and distinguished tradition of pamphlet production, significantly more uninhibited in its approach to public affairs in one of the most urbanised, literate and bourgeois of European societies. There was no better place to be a lover, an amateur, of news; and there was none more ardent than Jan de Boer.

Jan de Boer was a clerk.[27] He spent three days a week working in the office of a vintner, an occupation that left him plenty of time for other activities. He was clearly in relatively leisured circumstances. He paid decent levels of tax, and possessed a small house in Haarlem that he was able to let rent free to 'destitute persons'. De Boer was also a Catholic, a member of a minority Church that attracted some disapproval but whose members were generally left to practise their religion in peace. But de Boer was very aware that they owed this protection to the local magistrate, and a section of the population wished them no good.

De Boer's news diary is very unusual. Unlike the documents left by Wallington or Sewall it contained very little autobiographical material. De Boer seldom wrote about everyday activities: he devoted his energies entirely to chronicling the news. He began his diary at a moment of political crisis: the appointment of William IV as Stadtholder, and the tax riots of 1748 that allowed William to entrench his power. De Boer continued it for twelve years before laying aside his beautifully presented volume, for which he had prepared a highly decorated title-page. Although he applied all his professional skills to crafting his book it was not intended for wider circulation. As soon as it was concluded de Boer put it away in a locked cupboard with his other manuscripts. He got his wish: the news chronicle remains an unpublished manuscript to this day.[28]

De Boer wrote up his chronicle most days. Apart from the news that came to him by word of mouth, he also included reports from written sources, many of which he pasted into the volume at the appropriate places. De Boer was a gifted news-gatherer; he had the instincts of a true reporter. On a day when two ring-leaders of the thwarted tax riot were to be executed, de Boer made sure he arrived early at Dam Square, so he could study the exact disposition. He was convinced that the arrangements made to marshal the crowd, with narrow entry and exit points, would lead to trouble, and so it proved. The huge crowd proved unmanageable, shots were fired and in the rush to escape many were crushed to death. Even in this tragedy de Boer could congratulate himself on the quality of his reporting: 'I know that there was no-one else who had observed the events as closely and deliberately as I and who had immediately made notes on it all.'[29]

De Boer was also an avid reader of newspapers. He was a regular reader of the *Amsterdamsche Courant*, but the *'s Gravenhaegse Courant* was cited in his diary almost as frequently. Because the two papers were published on alternate days (Tuesday, Thursday and Saturday locally, Monday, Wednesday and Friday in The Hague), readers with subscriptions to both could in effect purchase a daily paper. During times of particular excitement de Boer could also get hold of other papers: the *Leidse Courant*, and papers from Haarlem, Rotterdam and Groningen. Most could be purchased in one or other of the Amsterdam bookshops. De Boer also read and collected pamphlets. The Doelist riots led to a search for scapegoats for current economic ills, and a number of pamphlets openly questioned whether Catholics could be loyal Dutch citizens. De Boer was both a contributor to and an observer of this debate: his poem *De Patria* went through several editions, as he noted with considerable pride. Pamphlets were often purchased from street vendors, and sometimes offered to de Boer by friends who had obtained something known to be disapproved of by the magistrates. The generally law-abiding de Boer enjoyed the frisson that attended the trade in semi-clandestine, if not particularly dangerous, books.

Because de Boer notes so carefully where he obtained his news, we are able to anatomise with some accuracy the news networks to which an engaged but not privileged citizen had access in eighteenth-century Amsterdam. The results are very revealing. In 1748, for instance, de Boer noted the source of 179 news stories that he wrote up in his chronicle. Of these, one-fifth were events he witnessed himself, and a further 40 per cent were stories that he had heard from third parties. Less than 40 per cent of his news came from the reading of printed matter. This was a particularly turbulent year in Amsterdam politics, but even in a year when most of the notable events occurred else-where, like the Lisbon earthquake in 1755, fewer than half of his reports emanated from printed sources.[30] Even among the printed matter, newspapers were far from the predominant source of news. If we examine the pieces that de Boer inserted into his news chronicle, most came from other types of printed media: pamphlets, government publications, and a few engraved pictures. Despite its heritage as one of the first centres of the newspaper trade in the seventeenth century (at one point, remember, the city had nine competing papers), newspapers played a relatively modest role in the news world of eighteenth-century Amsterdam.

Disgusted of Sneek

Why, for even so devoted a follower of news as Jan de Boer, were newspapers still such an unsatisfactory source of news in the mid-eighteenth century? In the Dutch Republic the exuberant, innovative newspaper world inherited from the seventeenth century had actually become more restrictive. Each city allowed only one paper. In return for its monopoly the paper paid a considerable fee, and the editors were careful not to compromise their investment by publishing anything of which the magistrates might disapprove. The self-imposed restraints that governed the contents of newspapers were not blown away by the great late century revolutions. In both France and the Low Countries the nineteenth century witnessed a retreat to a familiar, more conservative pattern of reporting. In this respect the contentious political cultures of Britain and America were very much the exception. More typical is this editorial notice in the *Leidsche Courant*, the paper of the leading intellectual centre of the Dutch Republic, published in 1785:

> Since a newspaper is meant to publish news events, and print official documents, and is not designed to be a collection of contesting articles, we kindly request our contributors not to bother us with this kind of copy.[31]

Dutch readers did wish to take part in political debate. But this was largely confined to pamphlets and a new class of political journals. The newspapers, privileged, cautious and profitable, remained inviolate. In the nineteenth century coverage of domestic news would expand, to become the core business of newspapers. But in the eighteenth century this had not been achieved.

Dutch newspapers were resolute in their refusal to publicise local political controversies. A letter of the Frisian patriots in 1786 was published in every Dutch newspaper except Friesland's own newspaper, the *Leeuwarder Courant*. The paper, conscious of its vulnerability to local government disapproval and the removal of its lucrative privileges, contented itself instead with reprinting provincial ordinances: such as a ban on fruit baskets from the town of Sneek (apparently they were smaller than those used in the rest of Friesland, and customers could be given short measure).[32]

This seems an absurd banality, though the tradition of the mundane and parochial still lives on in many a local newspaper. But it does draw attention to the extent to which governments were still the direct source of a large part of the newspapers' copy. Even at the end of the eighteenth century official publications remained a crucial conduit of news and information. This was last discussed in this book as an element of the expanding sixteenth-century news market, when governments across Europe began to pump out printed proclamations and ordinances, both as broadsheets and in pamphlet form.[33] But this did not end with the arrival of new commercial forms of news publication. From the seventeenth century excerpts and entire texts of official publications were simply absorbed into serial news publications. And governments continued to issue their ordinances in traditional ways, posted up in public places and cried out on the market square. In an age before universal literacy such verbal publication continued to play an important role in the dissemination of news.

For the new classes of readers newspapers were unsatisfactory in other ways. Right up until the end of the eighteenth century, newspapers were wholly unillustrated. Those who wanted to obtain a visual representation of great events had, like Jan de Boer, to buy engravings or woodcuts as separate sheets. This intermittently vibrant market helped those who followed the news to create a picture of great events.[34] But the illustrated sheets had then to be combined with the narrative account in the newspaper or pamphlet by the purchasers themselves. The striking, dramatic juxtaposition of words and pictures artfully deployed in the painting of news stories still lay in the future.

Customers also worried about the accuracy of the newspapers. In 1757 de Boer was trying to keep up with reports of the war between Prussia and Austria. Although he followed the news closely, he was bewildered by contradictory reports: 'How one is to reconcile all these different reports is quite beyond me, and I shall leave it to those wiser than myself.'[35] The real problem was that news from faraway places, which still dominated the newspapers' pages, was so slow to arrive. In this respect there was no great improvement in the provision of the news from the seventeenth to the nineteenth centuries. Groningen papers were actually more up-to-date in their coverage of news stories in 1750 than they would be in 1800.[36] The truth was that once the European postal network had been completed in the mid-seventeenth century, nothing much further could be done to speed the news. It would require the major technological innovations of the nineteenth century, the telegraph and the railways, to bring significant change. At that point the results were spectacular. In 1823 foreign news took an average of eighteen days to reach the *Leeuwarder Courant*. Fifty years later this was reduced to four.[37]

Did this matter? In one sense news is fresh to anyone who hears or reads it for the first time. Its value as a recreational or didactic text is not reduced by the time it takes in transit; if it is an older tale refreshed it does not need to be new at all to make its point. This is true for many of the new consumers of news in this book, but certainly not for opinion formers for whom speed of transmission had always been critical. For them, just as four hundred years previously, access to reliable sources of news was a central attribute of power, and they continued to look beyond the newspapers to procure it.

The Itch Grown a Disease

Between the fourteenth and the eighteenth centuries the number of those who had regular access to news had expanded enormously. The news media were slow to adapt to this changing public, particularly in their tone and style. It is important to remember that professional news services made their debut in an age when the word 'client' described the producer, not the potential purchaser. A news man offered himself to a great nobleman or prince in much the same way that a poet would present his sonnets, or an artist a portrait, in the hope of reward. Even when this service was monetised, the tone in which news writers tendered for custom was very much that of a tradesman plying his wares.[38] This tradition of clientage was maintained through to the eighteenth century when paid hands like Daniel Defoe or Samuel Johnson wrote in return for pensions or salaries; or indeed in the long, languid and pampered career of the Paris Gazetteer, his respectful and undemanding hymns to royal prerogatives protected from competition by royal monopoly.

In a similar way the style of newswriting adhered stubbornly to that developed to inform and brief Europe's ruling classes. News evolved from confidential briefings, to commercial newsletters, and then became embedded in the first newspapers, without substantial change in style or organisation. One could argue that the new generations of readers who bought these papers would be flattered to be treated to information that had previously passed only among the secret counsels of the governing classes. Perhaps they were; but they would have been hard put to understand it. Newspaper men recognised no duty to explain. If readers chose to have these reports of foreign politics explained to them, or indeed if they wanted to find out what was going on in areas more relevant to their own lives, they were forced to rely on traditional mechanisms of news distribution, primarily conversation.

So much news and most interpretation and analysis were conveyed by word of mouth. This indifference to the real-life experience of the reader, or construction of an imagined reader, continued into the lofty classical allusions of Jean-Paul Marat in the French Revolution. To the end of our period news men give a distinct impression that they are more concerned to earn the approbation of their social superiors, or their fellow writers, than of their hard-pressed readers. News was writer, rather than public, centred. The reader is obliged to take it or leave it; they must buck up and keep up.

The remarkable thing is that so many of Europe's citizens did choose to enter this esoteric world of printed news. 'You cannot imagine,' wrote John Cooper in 1667, 'to what a disease the itch of news is grown.' The medical analogy is telling; for many news had become one of the necessities of life.[39] That in times of great events they should purchase pamphlets is less surprising. The need for explanations, exhortations or tokens of fidelity provides sufficient explanation of the huge pamphlet surges that accompany all great events in this period. More surprising is the desire to take a regular diet of news even in times, as the newspapers would sometimes disarmingly confess, when there really was none.

The answer seems to be that newspapers were valued only partly for what they contained, and at least as much for what they represented. They offered readers a glimpse into a world far beyond the experience of the everyday. A glimpse, indeed, into many worlds: of countries they would never visit; battles they would thankfully never fight; of potentates and princes they would never meet, and who would barely spare them a glance if they did. Such worlds they could sample in works of history or travel narratives, but in the newspapers they were brought to them in an unpredictable miscellany, without narrative, and all for the price of a steak pie or a quart of ale. It was possible to be without the newspaper, but once it was there it quickly became an accoutrement of a polite life; a sign that a citizen had reached a certain place in society from which retreat would be painful. Newspapers had entered the lifeblood of European society. There would be no going back.

Conclusion

IT is easy to see why, for those engulfed by the tumultuous events at the end of the eighteenth century, it seemed that a decisive moment had been reached in the history of communication. The newspaper had come of age. A French revolutionary journalist, Pierre-Louis Roederer, set out the case with admirable clarity in an essay 'on the different means of communication of ideas among men in society'. Newspapers, he argued,

> contained only the latest and most pressing news; they had more readers than books or other forms of printed matter that customers had to seek out in bookstores, because, thanks to hawkers and postmen, newspapers sought out their audiences. Journals had a greater social impact than other media because they were read by all classes and because they reached their audience every day, at the same time . . . in all public places, and because they were the almost obligatory diet of daily conversation.[1]

News men had endured much in the three centuries since, at the beginning of the sixteenth century, news had first become a commodity. Now they saw the means to achieve not only influence, but dignity. No longer would they be, in their own eyes at least, despised and put-upon tradesmen, but 'the tribunes of the people'. Here is Camille Desmoulins, writing in *Révolutions de France et de Brabant*:

> Here I am a journalist, and it is a rather fine role. No longer is it a wretched and mercenary profession, enslaved by the government. Today in France, it is the journalist who holds the tablets, the album of the censor, and who inspects the senate, the consuls and the dictator himself.[2]

The sense of unlimited possibilities is palpable, and it captures very well a strand of commentary that continued through the nineteenth century. This would be a great age of newspaper triumphalism. By 1835 an American commentator (naturally a journalist) could ask: 'What is to prevent a daily newspaper from being made the greatest organ of social life?' 'Books have had their day – theatres have had their day – religion has had its day. . . . A newspaper can be made to take the lead in all these great moments of human thought.'[3]

This was heady stuff. One can see why the French Revolution, which witnessed the sudden, tumultuous emergence of a voracious press, should have made such an impact on contemporaries. In France the contrast between the controlled press of the Ancien Régime and the freedom of the revolutionary years was particularly stark. But even in their own terms the claims made for the press were somewhat overblown. Was the press really more important than the agitation on the streets, the debates in the National Assembly, or the heated discussions in the Jacobin Club that, for instance, sealed Danton's fate? The Terror was underpinned by Robespierre's control of the Committee of Public Safety, a body of no more than a dozen people.

In this triumphant praise of the periodical press we see strong echoes of the salutations that accompanied the birth of printing in the mid-fifteenth century, and intermittently ever since. Print was widely celebrated by scholars and printers, themselves heavily involved in the new industry, for its transformative role in society. Looking back we can see in those wide-eyed encomia to progress a great deal of false prophecy and rationalised self-interest. It reminds us that of all the technological innovations of that busy era, print was unique in its capacity for self-advertisement. Guns, sailing ships and improvements in navigation were all critical to the European domination of the non-European world, but none could hymn their own achievements in quite the same way.

All of this helps explain why, since the history of news first came to be written, the development of the newspaper has traditionally taken centre stage. The first systematic histories of news were all written during a period when the newspaper was not only the dominant form of news delivery, but appeared likely to remain so. The history of news was to a very large extent, at least before the advent of television, the history of newspapers. The period before the invention of the newspaper is reduced to the status of pre-history.

Now, as we re-enter a multi-media environment in which the future of newspapers looks decidedly uncertain, we can take a rather different perspective. As the first chapters of this book have demonstrated, there was plenty of scope for the circulation of news before newspapers, indeed, before the invention of printing. When newspapers made their appearance their progress was halting and uncertain. From the first (and at the time widely celebrated) experiments with a periodical press at the beginning of the seventeenth century, to the decisive breakthrough at the end of the eighteenth, would be a full two hundred years. Even during this time, a period of rapid expansion for the European economy in every way conducive to the development of an ever more sophisticated news market, the coverage of the periodical press was decidedly patchy. Spain lagged a long way behind developments in other countries, and this was also true of Italy, which had been until the end of the sixteenth century the very heart of the world's news market. Rome had no newspaper before the eighteenth century; here, the manuscript newsletters remained at the heart of the city's vibrant marketplace of news.[4] In Spain, even the traditional leaders of society pursued their power struggles by paying for the publication of broadsheet libels that could then be distributed on the streets.[5] It would not be until the mid-nineteenth century that newspapers established a relatively full coverage in all parts of western Europe.

Why was the advance of the newspaper not more rapid? One reason, it is clear, is that the periodical press was attempting to make its way in a complex communications environment, where news was already disseminated relatively effectively in a large variety of ways, by word of mouth, letter, non-serial print, proclamations, pamphlets and so on. To many consumers newspapers did not seem much of an advance on these well-established conduits of news: indeed, in some respects they represented a retrograde step. To drive this point home we only need to look at what have traditionally been regarded as the defining characteristics of periodical news: periodicity and regularity; contemporaneity; miscellany (presenting many different strands of news) and affordability. We can see that what scholars have described as important advances all had drawbacks when seen through the eyes of contemporary consumers.

First, periodicity. We have seen that the idea of a newspaper, a gather-up of the week's news from many parts of Europe that could be delivered economically to subscribers, initially appeared very attractive. It offered a window onto a sophisticated world of politics and high society previously closed to all but the few. At first it was rather gratifying to be initiated into the complex, exotic world of court life and international diplomacy; but with time it became rather wearing. The constant enumeration of diplomatic manoeuvres, arrivals and departures at court and military campaigns could be repetitive and increasingly mundane: particularly as the significance of these events, if not immediately apparent, was never explained. The apparent virtue of a newspaper, its regularity, became something of a burden.

18.1 An early issue of a Spanish paper. Despite almost a century since the first newspaper in Germany, the style is still very rudimentary.

This was not just a new way of reading the news. To many it involved a total redefinition of the concept of news. Most of those who had followed the news to this point would have done so irregularly. When news piqued their interest they could purchase a pamphlet; they were most likely to do so when, for one reason or other, they felt personally touched by events. Now with the newspapers they were offered an undigested and unexplained miscellany of things that scarcely seemed to concern them at all. Much of it must have been completely baffling.

The extent of this transformation appears more starkly if we look a little more closely at the pamphlets that bore the main burden of reporting contemporary events in the first age of print. Reading these works we get a vivid sense of our ancestors' fascination with the extraordinary. News pamphlets are filled with disasters, weather catastrophes, heavenly apparitions, strange beasts, battles won, shocking crimes discovered and punished. In contrast, much of what was reported in the newspapers was necessarily routine and unresolved: ships arrive in port, dignitaries arrive at court, share prices rise and fall, generals are appointed and relieved of command. This might have been critical information for those in the circles of power and commerce, but for occasional news readers there was nothing to compare with the sighting of a dragon in Sussex.[6]

Pamphlets and news broadsheets allowed the discerning reader to dip in and out of the news as they chose. They also reflected accurately one great truth inimical to the periodical press: that news was actually more urgent at some times than others. Two centuries of regular daily papers and news bulletins have trained us out of an appreciation of this. Yet when we turn on a news bulletin and hear, as the first item, that a committee of legislators has reported that some government activity could be accomplished a little bit better, then perhaps we may conclude that our ancestors had a point.

So it is with the other great 'advances' introduced with the newspapers. The contemporaneity of newspapers, a recital of the latest despatches from nine or ten of Europe's capitals, represented an abandonment of the customary narrative structure of news. A pamphlet would most usually describe a single event from beginning to end. It would be conditioned by knowledge of how matters had concluded – who had won a battle or how many had died in an earthquake. It could offer proximate causes, explanations and draw lessons. The newspapers in contrast offered what must have seemed like random pieces from a jigsaw, and an incomplete jigsaw at that. Even for regular subscribers there was no guarantee that the outcome of events described would be reported in the following issues. There was no way that editors could know which of the strands of the information reported from Cologne or Vienna would turn out to be important. And they had no way to pursue stories independent of the manuscript newsletters and foreign newspapers from which they constructed their copy: they could not contact their own correspondent in those places, because they did not yet have one.

Confronted with this miscellany of brief reports from Europe's news centres, newspaper readers were offered little help in finding their way to the news of most critical importance. Newspapers had not yet developed the design sophistication, or editorial capacity, to point up the most important stories, or lead their readers into understanding. Because verbatim reports and despatches were regarded as inherently more truthful, newspapers tended to avoid interpolations that would actually have assisted their readers in following the news. This form of editorial guidance was far more likely to be found in pamphlets. As for affordability, in the case of periodicals this was often more apparent than real. Although an individual copy of a newspaper might only cost a couple of pence, a regular subscription represented a more substantial investment. It also required the development of a considerable infrastructure on the part of the publisher so that copies could be delivered to their readers.

All of this helps explain how, despite the undoubted interest in the concept of a newspaper, so many news serials failed; or only succeeded with official subsidy. It is also no surprise that the periodical press flourished most in periods of high political excitement (when of course pamphlet production also rose substantially).

All of this prompts the question why, if newspapers were so testing to new readers, they did finally become an established (and then ultimately a dominant) part of the news infrastructure. Given how indigestible were their contents, we may conclude that the newspapers succeeded partly because of what they represented, rather than what they contained. For the first time the reading public was offered news of a type, and in a form, that had previously only been available to those in the circles of power. If their newspaper was a peepshow, it was a peepshow of the most flattering sort. Even if a country squire in Somerset or a physician in Montpellier had no particular interest in a dynastic crisis in Muscovy, merely to have access to such intelligence conveyed status. Newspapers were a non-essential purchase for those with a degree of disposable income, and it helped that the number of people in this position increased very rapidly in this era. A consumer society is driven as much by fashion as by utility, and in the eighteenth century a newspaper became an important accoutrement of polite society.

Towards the end of this period the newspaper also gained traction by throwing off many of the chaste virtues that had characterised its first century. Here the gradual expansion into the reporting of domestic news was absolutely decisive. This occurred at very different times in different parts of Europe. The competitive and vibrant London news market was unusually precocious in plunging so boldly into the contentious partisan politics of the early eighteenth century. Elsewhere, the development of domestic news reporting was essentially a feature only of the last years of the eighteenth century, and in some places even later.

This undoubtedly made newspapers interesting to an expanding public, who were encouraged to believe that they too could play an informed and active role in political discussion. The arrival, with the great crises of the late eighteenth century, of advocacy journalism also finally dissolved the distinction between news and opinion, and between the newspaper and other forms of writing on current affairs: pamphlets of course, but also the new, and highly respected, political journals. This transformation was not universal; the tradition of political neutrality lived on in many places where a single paper served

18.2 *An Englishman's delight or news of all sorts*. The list of titles on his topmost sheet comprises ten different papers.

a local market, and had no wish to alienate a portion of its readers. But the effect was, nonetheless, profound and enduring.

This transformation came at a cost. If newspapers were to play a direct role in shaping opinion, then statesmen would wish to control them; and journalists, eager above all to secure a competent living, were not always unhappy to be controlled. By 1792 in England the government had bought up half the press.[7] The *Diary or Woodfall's Register* was subsidised by the Treasury throughout its existence for £400 a year. The editor of the more established *Morning Herald* was confronted in 1790 with the choice of prison or leasing his title to the government, for £600 a year. He chose the latter. Six hundred pounds seems to have been very much the going rate, and enough in 1795 to secure the support of *The Times*. Other papers, whose political influence was not thought worthy of Treasury subsidies, turned instead to extortion, accepting cash from public figures in return for suppressing disobliging gossip. The London press was an extreme example, but not unique. The press in America, widely praised as a bastion of liberty in revolutionary times, soon earned a bleaker reputation.[8] 'There has been more error propagated from the press in the last ten years than in a hundred years before,' was the jaundiced judgement of John Adams, second president of the United States, and a frequent victim of press vituperation and ridicule.[9]

Thomas Jefferson, his one-time friend and ultimate nemesis, of course disagreed. Jefferson's famous declaration on the question, 'were it left to me to decide whether we should have a government without newspapers or newspapers without a government I should not hesitate for a moment to prefer the latter', was more of a rhetorical device than a proposal for action. But its spirit strongly animated the work of the Founding Fathers and saw its monument in the first amendment to the American constitution, guaranteeing freedom of the press.

There is little doubt that in this period the news media, and the news market, were both entering a new phase of their development. What, finally, was the contribution of the preceding four centuries to preparing this new world? Even before the vast acceleration of change in the last part of the eighteenth century, the news world of 1750 was palpably different from that of 1400 or 1500. This change was underpinned by three critical developments in European society. First was the movement, in contemporary thinking, from an emphasis on divine to human agency in the explanation of events. This was by no means complete. Western society was still overwhelmingly populated by believers, who continued to seek God's Providence in events. 'It is God that has done it, therefore what can I say,' was the response of one soldier in the Continental Army to the British victory at New York in 1776.[10] But there is a palpable shift from the pamphlet literature of the sixteenth century, where virtually every event could be framed as a parable of God's Providence, to the more dispassionate reporting in the routine despatches of eighteenth-century newspapers.

Second, and not unconnected with this, was the increasing emphasis on timeliness in the reporting and reception of news. Previously, when people looked to the news for the key to eternal verities, contemporaneity had been a much less urgent concern. An account of a flood, murder, or diabolical possession could be as pungent whether it occurred last week or some time ago, whether locally or in some distant region. Its moral force was in this respect timeless. But when news was regarded less as a key to God's purpose and more as a catalyst for action, then timeliness became critical. In the eighteenth-century clash of empires that provided so much of the copy for newspapers, this sense of urgency became far more evident, and also helped spur the progressive improvements of the infrastructure that underpinned the increasing density of news communication. Throughout the period under study the postal network made a series of giant leaps forward: first with the completion of the transcontinental European post; then with the addition of new branch lines. The rise of the north European trading empires in turn stimulated a concerted effort to repair the chronic deficiencies of the English and French postal networks, and ultimately to extend these improvements across the Atlantic.[11]

Governments had always been aware that knowledge was power. One of the first acts of the Massachusetts Assembly after the outbreak of the revolutionary conflicts was to set up a whole network of new post offices up-state. Control of the communications network was one aspect of the war in which the insurgents enjoyed total supremacy; in a long defensive war it was potentially decisive.[12]

Finally we should not underestimate the importance of the sheer volume of news in circulation. This was experienced in Europe as a series of surges: the first pamphlet fury of the Reformation; the later political convulsions of the Paris League, the British Civil Wars and the Fronde; the baptism of fire for news print in the Thirty Years War; the birth of party politics in England; the American and French Revolutions. This allowed European society to experience not only the expansion of access to new markets, but also the persuasive power of volume and repetition. Benjamin Franklin, one of the most perceptive and analytical minds to observe the power of contemporary reporting (his first career was as a printer), reflected openly on the potency of an orchestrated press campaign:

> The facility with which the same truths may be repeatedly enforced by placing them daily in different lights in newspapers which are everywhere read, gives a great chance of establishing them. . . . It is not only right to strike when the iron is hot, it may be very practicable to heat it by continually striking.[13]

With these three developments the building blocks were in place for the dramatic developments in the nineteenth-century news market. It was then, and only then, that the daily newspaper became the predominant instrument of news distribution. In North America the number of newspapers increased between 1790 and 1800 from 99 to 230. This represented not only the emergence of a reading public, but a deliberate act on the part of the Founding Fathers to create an informed citizenry. In this case the federal government provided a powerful financial inducement by offering the newspapers highly privileged access to the postal network to ensure economical and timely distribution.[14] In continental Europe the development of the press was more uneven; but by the middle of the new century the daily newspaper had largely superseded the weekly or bi-weekly paper as the predominant form.

These nineteenth-century developments were made possible by two further critical technological innovations: the invention of the steam-press and the substitution of wood pulp for rag-based paper. 'Steam-powered knowledge' propelled the capacities of the daily edition, which had reached an effective ceiling of 3,000 copies in the hand-press era, to many multiples of this figure.[15] Paper based on wood pulp permitted the exploitation of a new and abundant resource. The impact of these technological developments was compounded by the approach to something closer to universal literacy, at least among the urban populations that were the most important consumers of news. This in turn encouraged a heightened political activism among the previously unenfranchised, a great driver of demand for newspapers. It also encouraged the profound diversification of papers in terms of subject matter and content, as newspapers began to feed the appetite for information and diversion across a whole range of cultural and recreational activities. In this way newspapers became both longer and qualitatively different from anything that had come before.

This, the great age of the newspaper, would last for a century and a half, a period when the contest for power within Europe's nations gave impetus to the long struggle for democracy, and the contests between rival powers sowed the seeds of the catastrophic warfare of the twentieth century. In these conflicts, too, newspapers would play their part, but no longer as monopoly providers. As European ingenuity designed ever more destructive weaponry and ideologies, so too the march of science created new competitors for news print: first radio, then television. As these new media became embedded in society they swiftly demonstrated their potential for the distribution of news. They too had to be shaped and manipulated by those to whom the control of information was a crucial attribute of power. But it was only with the arrival of digital media that the role of printed news in this evolving ecology would seriously be questioned.

The dominant role of print in the delivery of prompt, regular digests of news can no longer be taken for granted. Put in this context, the age of the newspaper seems comparatively fleeting, rather than, as it was when the first histories of news were written, the natural order of things. Still less does the newspaper appear, as its admirers would once have seen it, as an instrument of empowerment and emancipation that represented the natural culmination of the civilising process.[16]

Living as we now do through the uncertainties of the evolving and unstable multi-media world that characterises the early twenty-first century, it is perhaps easier to see why a similar variety of news delivery would have seemed utterly appropriate to the four centuries that have been the central concern of this book. The arrival of print in the mid-fifteenth century offered many new opportunities; but it had to make its way in a world where networks for the distribution of news had already been developed: networks with standards, conventions and social freight with which those in circles of power were fully conversant. In the centuries that followed print disrupted and then reshaped this infrastructure, bringing new customers into the circle of news but without fully superseding the established norms. The news media of this era presented every bit as much a multi-media phenomenon as our own. It is that which gives this period its particular fascination.

Notes

Introduction: All the News that's Fit to Tell

1. *Weekly Review of the Affairs of France* (17 February 1704). A magnificent new edition, edited by John McVeagh, is *Defoe's Review* (London: Pickering & Chatto, 2003-11). An atmospheric selection is available in William L. Payne, *The Best of Defoe's Review: An Anthology* (New York: Columbia University Press, 1951).
2. *Review* (fasc. edn, New York, 1938), viii, 708, book 21. Quoted Harold Love, *The Culture and Commerce of Texts* (Amherst, MA: University of Massachusetts Press, 1998), p. 3. See now also Dror Wahrman, *Mr. Collier's Letter Rack: A Tale of Art and Illusion at the Threshold of the Modern Information Age* (Oxford: Oxford University Press, 2012), pp. 19-29.
3. Instances can be found, for example, in at least ten of Shakespeare's plays: *King Henry VI, Part 2*, Act IV, scene 4; *King Henry VI, Part 3*, Act II, scene 1; *King Richard III*, Act IV, scenes 2 and 4; *The Taming of the Shrew*, Act V, scene 2; *The Merchant of Venice*, Act 1, scene 2; *Twelfth Night*, Act 1, scene 1; *Hamlet*, Act IV, scene 7; *Timon of Athens*, Act 1, scene 2; *King Lear*, Act 1, scene 2; *Macbeth*, Act 1, scene 7. Instances supplied by Paul Arblaster.
4. Claude Holyband, *The French Littelton* (London: Richard Field, 1593). Below, Chapter 6.
5. This regular exchange, between Aberconwy and Strat Florida, is reported in *The historie of Cambria, now called Wales* (1584), sig. vr. I am grateful to my colleague Alex Woolf for this reference.
6. Jürg Zulliger, '"Ohne Kommunikation würde Chaos herrschen". Zur Bedeutung von Informationsaustauch, Briefverkehr und Boten bei Bernhard von Clairvaux', *Archiv für Kulturgeschichte*, 78 (1996), pp. 251-76. Below, Chapter 1.
7. Below, Chapter 2.
8. Below, Chapter 7.
9. Nate Silver, *The Signal and the Noise: Why So Many Predictions Fail but Some Don't* (New York: Penguin, 2012).
10. Ulinka Rublack, *The Crimes of Women in Early Modern Germany* (Oxford: Oxford University Press, 1999), pp. 16-19.
11. Matthew Lundin, *Paper Memory: A Sixteenth-Century Townsman Writes his World* (Cambridge, MA: Harvard University Press, 2012).
12. Ibid., p. 243.
13. Below, Chapter 5.
14. Andrew Pettegree, *The Book in the Renaissance* (New Haven, CT, and London: Yale University Press, 2010).
15. Below, Chapter 4.
16. Below, Chapter 7.
17. Allyson Creasman, *Censorship and Civic Order in Reformation Germany, 1517-1648* (Aldershot: Ashgate, 2012).

18. Jan Bloemendal, Peter G. F. Eversmann and Else Strietman (eds), *Drama, Performance and Debate: Theatre and Public Opinion in the Early Modern Period* (Leiden: Brill, 2013); and see the remarks about competition between the London theatre and newspapers below, Chapter 12.
19. As in the French *publier*. See Kate van Orden, 'Cheap Print and Street Song Following the Saint Bartholomew's Massacres of 1572', in van Orden (ed.), *Music and the Cultures of Print* (New York: Garland Publishing, 2000), pp. 271–323.
20. Maximilian Novak, *Daniel Defoe, Master of Fictions: His Life and Ideas* (Oxford: Oxford University Press, 2001).
21. Below, Chapter 15.

Chapter 1 Power and Imagination

1. Larry Silver, *Marketing Maximilian: The Visual Ideology of a Holy Roman Emperor* (Princeton, NJ: Princeton University Press, 2008).
2. Wolfgang Behringer, *Thurn und Taxis: Die Geschichte ihrer Post und ihrer Unternehmen* (Munich: Piper, 1990); idem, *Im Zeichen des Merkur: Reichspost und Kommunikationsrevolution in der Frühen Neuzeit* (Göttingen: Vandenhoeck & Ruprecht, 2003).
3. A. M. Ramsay, 'A Roman Postal Service under the Republic', *Journal of Roman Studies*, 10 (1920), pp. 79–86.
4. Alan K. Bowman, *Life and Letters on the Roman Frontier: Vindolanda and its People*, 2nd edn (London: British Museum, 2003); Anthony Birley, *Garrison Life at Vindolanda* (Stroud: History Press, 2007).
5. Alan K. Bowman and Greg Woolf, *Literacy and Power in the Ancient World* (Cambridge: Cambridge University Press, 1994); Greg Woolf, 'Monumental Writing and the Expansion of Roman Society in the Early Empire', *Journal of Roman Studies*, 86 (1996), pp. 22–39.
6. M. T. Clanchy, *From Memory to Written Record: England 1066–1307* (Oxford: Blackwell, 1979).
7. Ibid., p. 261.
8. Jürg Zulliger, '"Ohne Kommunikation würde Chaos herrschen": Zur Bedeutung von Informationsaustauch, Briefverkehr und Boten bei Bernhard von Clairvaux', *Archiv für Kulturgeschichte*, 78 (1996), pp. 251–76.
9. Chris Given-Wilson, *Chronicles: The Writing of History in Medieval England* (London: Hambledon, 2004), p. 21.
10. Ibid., p. 13.
11. J. K. Hyde, 'Italian Pilgrim Literature in the Late Middle Ages', in his *Literacy and its Uses: Studies on Late Medieval Italy* (Manchester: Manchester University Press, 1993), pp. 136–61.
12. Sophia Menache, *The Vox Dei: Communication in the Middle Ages* (New York: Oxford University Press, 1990), p. 116.
13. Lorraine Daston and Katharine Park, *Wonders and the Order of Nature, 1150–1750* (New York: Zone, 2001).
14. Hyde, 'Ethnographers in Search of an Audience', in his *Literacy and its Uses*, pp. 162–216.
15. Jonathan Sumption, *Pilgrimage: An Image of Medieval Religion* (London: Faber, 1975), p. 257; Debra Birch, 'Jacques de Vitry and the Ideology of Pilgrimage', in J. Stopford (ed.), *Pilgrimage Explored* (Woodbridge: York Medieval Press, 1999).
16. Dianna Webb, *Pilgrims and Pilgrimage in the Medieval West* (London: I. B. Tauris, 2001); Sumption, *Pilgrimage*.
17. Albert Kapr, *Johann Gutenberg: The Man and his Invention* (London: Scolar Press, 1996), pp. 71–5.
18. Debra Birch, *Pilgrimage to Rome in the Middle Ages* (Woodbridge: Boydell, 1998).
19. It is illustrated in Peter Spufford, *Power and Profit: The Merchant in Medieval Europe* (London: Thames and Hudson, 2002), p. 23.
20. Ambassadorial correspondence is discussed below, Chapter 5.
21. Yves Renouard, 'Comment les papes d'Avignon expédiaient leur courrier', *Revue historique*, 180 (1937), pp. 1–29; idem, *The Avignon Papacy, 1305–1403* (London: Faber, 1970); Anne-Marie Hayez, 'Les courriers des papes d'Avignon sous Innocent VI et Urbain V (1352–1370)', in *La circulation des nouvelles au moyen âge* (Paris: Sorbonne, 1994), pp. 37–46.
22. Renouard, 'Les papes d'Avignon', pp. 20–3.

23. A letter destined for Rome written on 3 March 1321 did not depart Avignon until 18 April. A letter for Venice written on 6 October 1321 departed on 31 October. A letter for Poitiers in 1360 was delayed for two months before despatch. Renouard, 'Les papes d'Avignon', p. 28.
24. Suzanne Budelot, *Messageries universitaires et messageries royales* (Paris: Domat, 1934).
25. The four 'nations' in Paris, rather loosely defined, were France, Picardy, Normandy and England. The English 'nation' included the students from central and northern Europe. Hilde de Rodder-Symoens (ed.), *A History of the University in Europe. Volume I: Universities in the Middle Ages* (Cambridge: Cambridge University Press, 1992), p. 114.
26. C. H. Haskins, 'The Lives of Mediaeval Students as Illustrated in their Letters', in his *Studies in Mediaeval Culture* (Oxford: Oxford University Press, 1929), pp. 1–35.
27. Alain Boureau, 'The Letter-Writing Norm, a Mediaeval Invention', in Roger Chartier (ed.), *Correspondence: Models of Letter-Writing from the Middle Ages to the Nineteenth Century* (Cambridge: Polity, 1997), pp. 24–58.
28. Haskins, 'Lives of Medieval Students', p. 10.
29. Ibid., pp. 15–16.
30. Below, Chapter 15.
31. Philip O. Beale, *A History of the Post in England from the Romans to the Stuarts* (Aldershot: Ashgate, 1998), p. 22.
32. Ibid., pp. 24–7.
33. J. K. Hyde, 'The Role of Diplomatic Correspondence and Reporting', in his *Literacy and its Uses*, pp. 217–59, here pp. 224–6.
34. Ibid., p. 244.
35. Below, Chapter 5.
36. Beale, *History of the Post*, pp. 30–39.
37. Given-Wilson, *Chronicles*, p. 109.
38. Beale, *History of the Post*, pp. 84–6.
39. *La circulation des nouvelles*.
40. C. A. J. Armstrong, 'Some Examples of the Distribution and Speed of News in England at the Time of the Wars of the Roses', in his *England, France and Burgundy in the Fifteenth Century* (London: Hambledon, 1983), pp. 97–122.
41. See Armstrong, 'Some Examples', p. 100; James Gairdner (ed.), *Three Fifteenth Century Chronicles* (London: Camden Society, 1880), pp. 156 ff.
42. Below, Chapter 4.
43. B. Guenée, 'Les campagnes de lettres qui ont suivi le meurtre de Jean sans Peur, duc de Bourgogne (septembre 1419–février 1420)', *Annuaire-Bulletin de la Société de l'Histoire de France* (1993), pp. 45–65.
44. Craig Taylor, 'War, Propaganda and Diplomacy in Fifteenth-Century France and England', in Christopher Allmand (ed.), *War, Government and Power in Late Medieval France* (Liverpool: Liverpool University Press, 2000), pp. 70–91.
45. Armstrong, 'Some Examples', p. 99.
46. Budelot, *Messageries universitaires et messageries royales*; E. John B. Allen, 'The Royal Posts of France in the Fifteenth and Sixteenth Centuries', *Postal History Journal*, 15 (January 1971).
47. Armstrong, 'Some Examples', p. 107.
48. Menache, *Vox Dei*.
49. Armstrong, 'Some Examples', p. 101.

Chapter 2 The Wheels of Commerce

1. Iris Origo, *The Merchant of Prato: Francesco di Marco Datini* (London: Jonathan Cape, 1957), p. 90.
2. In addition there are ten thousand letters exchanged between Datini and his wife, who was left to manage the household in Prato when Datini moved to Florence. These are the main focus of Origo's study.
3. David Nicholas, *Medieval Flanders* (London: Longman, 1992). James M. Murray, *Bruges, Cradle of Capitalism, 1280–1390* (Cambridge: Cambridge University Press, 2005).

4. Edwin S. Hunt, *The Medieval Super-Companies: A Study of the Peruzzi Company of Florence* (Cambridge: Cambridge University Press, 1994).
5. Raymond de Roover, *Money, Banking and Credit in Medieval Bruges* (Cambridge, MA: 1948).
6. See here the fourteenth-century 'Itinéraire de Bruges', ed. E.-T. Hamy, in Gilles le Bouvier, *Le livre de la description des pays* (Paris: Leroux, 1908), pp. 157–216.
7. Peter Spufford, *Power and Profit: The Merchant in Medieval Europe* (London: Thames and Hudson, 2002), pp. 143–52.
8. Frederic C. Lane, *Andrea Barbarigo, Merchant of Venice, 1418–1449* (Baltimore, MD: Johns Hopkins University Press, 1944), p. 20.
9. Spufford, *Power and Profit*, pp. 25–8.
10. Lane, *Andrea Barbarigo*, pp. 199–200. Barbarigo's letters from Valencia seldom arrived in under thirty days, and the norm was nearer forty.
11. Federigo Melis, 'Intensità e regolarità nella diffusione dell'informazione economica generale nel Mediterraneo e in Occidente alla fine del Medioevo', in *Mélanges en l'honneur de Fernand Braudel*, 2 vols (Toulouse: Privat, 1973), I, 389–424. Spufford, *Power and Profit*, p. 27.
12. Philip O. Beale, *A History of the Post in England from the Romans to the Stuarts* (Aldershot: Ashgate, 1998), p. 33.
13. C. A. J. Armstrong, 'Some Examples of the Distribution and Speed of News in England at the Time of the Wars of the Roses', in his *England, France and Burgundy in the Fifteenth Century* (London: Hambledon, 1983), pp. 97–122, here p. 109.
14. A. Grunzweig, *Correspondance de la filiale de Bruges de Medici* (Brussels: Lamertin, 1931), I, 130–45.
15. Below, Chapter 5.
16. Hunt, *Medieval Super-Companies*, p. 73.
17. A point appreciated by the Milanese ambassador when he recommended the use of the merchant post: 'the Genoa letter bag will be of good use, but get more such Florentine merchants as are in your confidence, as their correspondence passes through France without impediment and is but little searched'. Quoted in Beale, *A History of the Post in England*, p. 160.
18. E. John B. Allen, *Post and Courier Service in the Diplomacy of Early Modern Europe*, vol. 3 (The Hague: Nijhoff, International Archive of the History of Ideas, 1972).
19. Richard Goldthwaite, *The Economy of Renaissance Florence*, (Baltimore, MD: Johns Hopkins University Press), p. 94.
20. Origo, *Datini*, pp. 85–6.
21. Ibid., p. 86.
22. Robert S. Lopez and Irving W. Raymond, *Medieval Trade in the Mediterranean World: Illustrative Documents* (Oxford: Oxford University Press, 1955), no. 193; Gunnar Dahl, *Trade, Trust and Networks: Commercial Cultures in Late Medieval Italy* (Lund: Nordic Academic Press, 1998), p. 82.
23. Lopez and Raymond, *Medieval Trade*, no. 194; Dahl, *Trade*, p. 82.
24. Dahl, *Trade*, p. 83.
25. Gertrude R. B. Richards (ed.), *Florentine Merchants in the Age of the Medici: Letters and Documents from the Selfridge Collection of Medici Manuscripts* (Cambridge, MA: Harvard University Press, 1932), p. 109; Dahl, *Trade*, p. 83.
26. Paolo da Certaldo, *Libro di buoni costumi*, ed. Alfredo Schiaffini (Florence, 1946), pp. 149–50.
27. Goldthwaite, *Economy of Renaissance Florence*, p. 95.
28. Theodor Gustav Werner, 'Das kaufmännische Nachrichtenwesen im späten Mittelalter und in der frühen Neuzeit und sein Einfluss auf die Entstehung der handschriftlichen Zeitung', *Scripta Mercaturae* (1975), pp. 3–51.
29. Goldthwaite, *Economy of Renaissance Florence*, p. 94.
30. George Christ, 'A Newsletter in 1419? Antonio Morosini's Chronicle in the Light of Commercial Correspondence between Venice and Alexandria', *Mediterranean Historical Review*, 20 (2005), pp. 35–66, here pp. 41–2.
31. Richards, *Florentine Merchants*, 263; Dahl, *Trade*, p. 116.

32. Dahl, *Trade*, p. 104. They were, however, permitted to play chess, to while away the long evenings.
33. Dahl, *Trade*, p. 119.
34. Lane, *Andrea Barbarigo*, pp. 127–8.
35. Marin Sanudo, *I diarii*, 58 vols (Venice: Visentini, 1879–1903); Pierre Sardella, *Nouvelles et spéculations à Venise au début du XVIe siècle* (Paris: Colin, 1949). An elegant English translation of selections from Sanudo can be found in Patricia H. Labalme and Laura Sanguieti White (eds), *Città Excelentissima: Selections from the Renaissance Diaries of Marin Sanudo* (Baltimore, MD: Johns Hopkins University Press, 2008).
36. Sardella, *Nouvelles*, p. 21.
37. Ibid., p. 32.
38. G. Priuli, *I diarii*, 4 vols (Bologna: Zanichelli, 1912–39), I, 153, cited by Mario Infelise, 'From Merchants' Letters to Handwritten Political *Avvisi*: Notes on the Origins of Public Information', in Francisco Bethercourt and Florike Egmond (eds), *Correspondence and Cultural Exchange in Europe, 1400–1700* (Cambridge: Cambridge University Press, 2007), pp. 33–52.
39. Sardella, *Nouvelles*, p. 42.
40. Ibid., p. 50.
41. The scale of charges comes from an example of 1538; Sardella, *Nouvelles*, p. 50.
42. Wolfgang Behringer, *Im Zeichen des Merkur: Reichspost und Kommunikationsrevolution in der Frühen Neuzeit* (Göttingen: Vandenhoeck & Ruprecht, 2003), p. 51.
43. Sardella, *Nouvelles*, pp. 56–71.
44. Philippe Dollinger, *The German Hansa* (London: Macmillan, 1970); Tom Scott, *The City State in Europe, 1000–1600* (Oxford: Oxford University Press, 2012).
45. Lore Sporhan-Krempel, *Nürnberg als Nachrichtenzentrum zwischen 1400 und 1700* (Nuremberg: Vereins für Geschichte der Stadt Nürnberg, 1968), p. 19.
46. Steven Ozment, *Three Behaim Boys: Growing up in Early Modern Germany* (New Haven, CT: Yale University Press, 1990).
47. Sporhan-Krempel, *Nürnberg als Nachrichtenzentrum*, p. 21; below, Chapter 3.
48. Werner, 'Das kaufmännische Nachrichtenwesen', p. 11.
49. Sporhan-Krempel, *Nürnberg als Nachrichtenzentrum*, p. 23.
50. Werner, 'Das kaufmännische Nachrichtenwesen', p. 7; Sporhan-Krempel, *Nürnberg als Nachrichtenzentrum*, p. 21.
51. Sporhan-Krempel, *Nürnberg als Nachrichtenzentrum*, p. 23.

Chapter 3 The First News Prints

1. Phyllis Goodhart Gordan, *Two Renaissance Book Hunters: The Letters of Poggius Bracciolini to Nicolaus de Niccolis* (New York: Columbia University Press, 1974).
2. Albert Kapr, *Johann Gutenberg: The Man and his Invention* (Aldershot: Scolar Press, 1996).
3. For more on these events see Andrew Pettegree, *The Book in the Renaissance* (New Haven, CT, and London: Yale University Press, 2010).
4. Margaret Meserve, 'News from Negroponte: Politics, Popular Opinion and Information Exchange in the First Decade of the Italian Press', *Renaissance Quarterly*, 59 (2006), pp. 440–80. For Rhodes see the Universal Short Title Catalogue (USTC) (search 'Rhodes – 1480').
5. Victor Scholderer, 'The Petition of Sweynheim and Pannartz to Sixtus IV', *The Library*, 3rd ser., 6 (1915), pp. 186–90, reprinted in his *Fifty Essays in Fifteenth- and Sixteenth-Century Bibliography* (Amsterdam: Hertzberger, 1966), pp. 72–3.
6. Chapter 4, below.
7. See here especially Falk Eisermann, *Verzeichnis der typographischen Einblattdrucke des 15. Jahrhunderts im Heiligen Römischen Reich Deutscher Nation: VE 15* (Wiesbaden: Reichert, 2004).
8. R. N. Swanson, *Indulgences in Late Mediaeval England: Passport to Paradise?* (Cambridge: Cambridge University Press, 2007).
9. Pettegree, *Book in the Renaissance*, pp. 93–4; Paul Needham, *The Printer and the Pardoner* (Washington, DC: Library of Congress, 1986), p. 31.
10. See, for instance, USTC 743954, the indulgence of 1454 for contributions to the war against the Turks.

11. *Eyn Manung der Christenheit Widder die Durken* (1454). ISTC it00503500. GW M19909; Kapr, *Gutenberg*, pp. 212–14.
12. Calixtus III, *Bulla Turcorum* (1456). ISTC ic00060000. GW 0591610N. *Die Bulla widder die Turcken*. ISTC ic00060100. GW 05916.
13. Robert Schwoebel, *The Shadow of the Crescent: The Renaissance Image of the Turk (1453–1517)* (Nieuwkoop: De Graaf, 1967).
14. Ibid., pp. 157–60, 166–71.
15. Janus Møller Jensen, *Denmark and the Crusades, 1400–1650* (Leiden: Brill, 2007), pp. 131–2; Schwoebel, *Shadow of the Crescent*, pp. 157–60, 166–71.
16. The ISTC identifies 179 items published in Germany either by or for Peraudi. Of these the vast proportion (170) are broadsheets. See also Nikolaus Paulus, 'Raimund Peraudi als Ablasskommissar', *Historisches Jahrbuch*, 21 (1900), pp. 645–82.
17. Falk Eisermann, 'The Indulgence as a Media Event', in R. N. Swanson (ed.), *Promissory Notes on the Treasury of Merits: Indulgences in Late Mediaeval Europe* (Leiden: Brill, 2006), pp. 309–30, here pp. 315–16.
18. Jensen, *Denmark and the Crusades*, p. 138.
19. Ingrid D. Rowland, 'A Contemporary Account of the Ensisheim Meteorite, 1492', *Meteoritics*, 25 (1990), pp. 19–22.
20. Martin Davies, *Columbus in Italy* (London: British Library, 1991).
21. Renate Pieper, *Die Vermittlung einer Neuen Welt: Amerika im Nachrichtennetz des Habsburgischen Imperiums, 1493–1598* (Mainz: Von Zabern, 2000), pp. 86, 287.
22. Above, Chapter 2.
23. The USTC lists editions of his *Mundus novus* in Latin, Italian, French and German, published in fourteen different locations.
24. Pieper, *Die Vermittlung einer Neuen Welt*.
25. Meserve, 'News from Negroponte'.
26. The three known printed editions are listed in Josef Benzing, *Lutherbibliographie. Verzeichnis der gedruckten Schriften Martin Luthers bis zu dessen Tod*, 2nd edn (Baden-Baden: Heitz, 1989), nos 87–9. The two broadsheet editions are not included in VD16, since broadsheets were excluded from the terms of reference of this bibliography.
27. Theodor Gustav, Werner, 'Das kaufmännische Nachrichtenwesen im späten Mittelalter und in der frühen Neuzeit und sein Einfluss auf die Entstehung der handschriftlichen Zeitung', *Scripta Mercaturae* (1975), p. 32.
28. Léon-E. Halkin, *Erasmus: A Critical Biography* (Oxford: Blackwell, 1993), pp. 146–59.
29. *Ein Sermon von Ablass und gnade*; Benzing, *Lutherbibliographie*, nos 90–112.
30. Mark U. Edwards, *Printing, Propaganda and Martin Luther* (Berkeley, CA: University of California Press, 1994), p. 21, adjusted to take account of work subsequently undertaken for the USTC, http://www.ustc.ac.uk/.
31. The USTC lists 9,469 titles printed in Wittenberg before 1601, of which only 123 were published before 1517.
32. On Cranach see, most recently, Steven Ozment, *The Serpent and the Lamb* (New Haven, CT, and London: Yale University Press, 2011).
33. Max J. Friedländer and Jakob Rosenberg, *The Paintings of Lucas Cranach* (New York: Tabard Press, 1978); Werner Hofmann, *Köpfe der Lutherzeit* (Munich: Prestel, 1983).
34. *Cranach im Detail. Buchschmuck Lucas Cranachs des Älteren und seiner Werkstatt* (exhibition, Lutherhalle Wittenberg, 1994). On the development of the title page, see also Margaret Smith, *The Title Page: Its Early Development, 1460–1510* (London: British Library, 2000).
35. Paul Roth, *Die Neuen Zeitungen in Deutschland im 15. und 16. Jahrhundert* (Leipzig: B. G. Teubner, 1914).
36. An example being the long after-history of the defeat of Louis Jagiello at Mohács in 1526; Carl Göllner, *Turcica. Die europäischen Türkendrucke des 16. Jahrhundert*, 3 vols (Bucharest: Academiei, 1961–78).
37. William Layher, 'Horrors of the East: Printing *Dracole Wayda* in 15th-Century Germany', *Daphnis*, 37 (2008), pp. 11–32.
38. Below, Chapter 5.
39. The first use of the term 'Neue Zeitung' is found in a double-sided broadsheet of 1502, the *Newe zeytung von orient und auff gange*, but here as a subheading to a subsidiary news item.

There is a facsimile edition, Hans H. Bockwitz, *Newe zeytung von orient und auff gange. Facsimileabdruck eines zeitungsgeschichtlichen Dokuments vom Jahre 1502 mit Begleitwort* (Leipzig: Deutsches Museum für Buch und Schrift, 1920).

40. This calculation rests on an analysis of the data in the USTC.
41. *Newe Tzeittug von Padua und von vil anderen Stetten in welschen landen gelegen kurtzlich ergangen* (Nuremberg, s.n., 1509); USTC 677285. *Neutzeytug ausz welschen landen eyns handels fryde czu machen czwischen Bebstlicher Heyligkeit unnd dem Koenige von Franckreich durch mittel der oratores Kayserlichen Majestat der Koenige von Hyspanien und Engelant* (Nuremberg: Johann Weißenburger, 1510); USTC 677019.
42. Göllner, *Turcica*, provides a useful, though now somewhat outdated survey.
43. Below, Chapters 4 (broadsheets) and 6 (ballads).
44. USTC 705457: 'Von Rom geschriben an einen guten freund in Deudtschlandt'; USTC 705584: 'Von einer glaubwirdigen person auß Bibrach einem guten freunde zugeschrieben'; USTC 705464: 'Auß der statt Achen an einen guten freundt geschriben'; USTC 705068: 'Von einer glaubwirdigen person entpfangen: an seinen guten freund einen geschrieben und erklehret'.
45. USTC 659718: 'Aus gewissen Zeitungen so ausser dem feldlager uberschickt worden'.
46. Lisa Ferraro Parmelee, *Good Newes from Fraunce: French Anti-League Propaganda in Late Elizabethan England* (Rochester, NY: University of Rochester Press, 1996).

Chapter 4 State and Nation

1. Augsburg, Magdeburg, Mainz, Passau, Strasbourg, Stuttgart and Ulm. There was also an edition in Antwerp. USTC (search Maximilian – 1486).
2. *Gefangenschaft des Römischen Königs Maximilian in Brügge* (Augsburg: Erhard Ratdolt, 1488). USTC 747013. A further Augsburg edition (Augsburg: Peter Berger, 1488), USTC 747014. A Nuremberg edition (Nuremberg: Marx Ayrer, 1488), USTC 747015.
3. Chapter 1, above.
4. Jean-Pierre Seguin, 'L'information à la fin du XVe siècle en France. Pièces d'actualité sous le règne de Charles VIII', *Arts et traditions populaires*, 4 (1956), pp. 309–30, 1–2; (1957), pp. 46–74; David Potter, *Renaissance France at War: Armies, Culture and Society, c. 1480–1560* (Woodbridge: Boydell, 2008), pp. 255–84.
5. Three editions: ISTC it00421850; ISTC it00421880; ISTC it00421860.
6. David Potter, 'War, Propaganda, Literature and National Identity in Renaissance France, c. 1490–1560', in Robert Stein and Judith Pollmann (eds), *Networks, Regions and Nations: Shaping Identity in the Low Countries, 1300–1650* (Leiden: Brill, 2010), pp. 173–93, here p. 188.
7. Jean-Pierre Seguin, *L'information en France de Louis XII à Henri II* (Geneva: Droz, 1961).
8. Frederic J. Baumgartner, *Louis XII* (London: Macmillan, 1996), p. 216; Michael Sherman, 'Political Propaganda and Renaissance Culture: French Reactions to the League of Cambrai, 1509–1510', *Sixteenth Century Journal*, 8 (1977), pp. 97–128.
9. Seguin, *L'information en France*, now enhanced by the USTC.
10. Lauro Martines, *Strong Words: Writing and Social Strain in the Italian Renaissance* (Baltimore, MD: Johns Hopkins University Press, 2001), Chapter 11, 'Crisis in the Generation of 1494'.
11. USTC; Stefano Dall'Aglio, *Savonarola and Savonarolism* (Toronto: Center for Reformation and Renaissance Studies, 2010).
12. USTC (search 'Antwerp + news'). Steven Gunn, David Grummitt and Hans Cool, *War, State and Society in England and the Netherlands, 1477–1559* (Oxford: Oxford University Press, 2007).
13. Seguin, *L'information en France*, nos 167–70.
14. Andrew Pettegree, 'A Provincial News Community in Sixteenth-Century France', in his *The French Book and the European Book World* (Leiden: Brill, 2007), pp. 19–42.
15. Potter, *Renaissance France at War*, p. 267.
16. Ibid., p. 277.
17. Gunn, Grummitt and Cool, *War, State and Society*, p. 263.
18. Steven Gunn, 'War and Identity in the Habsburg Netherlands', in Stein and Pollman (eds), *Networks, Regions and Nations*, p. 160.

19. Alastair Duke, 'From King and Country to King or Country? Loyalty and Treason in the Revolt of the Netherlands', in his *Reformation and Revolt in the Low Countries* (London: Hambledon, 1990), pp. 175–97.
20. Potter, *Renaissance France at War*, pp. 267–8.
21. Lauren Jee-Su Kim, 'French Royal Acts Printed before 1601: A Bibliographical Study' (University of St Andrews PhD dissertation, 2007); Potter, *Renaissance France at War*, p. 262.
22. Paul L. Hughes and James F. Larkin, *Tudor Royal Proclamations*, 3 vols (New Haven, CT: Yale University Press, 1969), no. 390.
23. Adam Fox, *Oral and Literate Culture in England, 1500–1700* (Oxford: Oxford University Press, 2000), p. 367.
24. Wallace T. MacCaffrey, 'The Newhaven Expedition, 1562–1563', *Historical Journal*, 40 (1997), pp. 1–21.
25. Hughes and Larkin, *Tudor Royal Proclamations*, no. 510.
26. G. R. Elton, *Policy and Police: The Enforcement of the Reformation in the Age of Thomas Cromwell* (Cambridge: Cambridge University Press, 1972), p. 134.
27. They are listed in Léon Voet, *The Plantin Press (1555–1589): A Bibliography of the Works Printed and Published by Christopher Plantin at Antwerp and Leiden*, 6 vols (Amsterdam: Van Hoeve, 1980–3).
28. Ordinances regulating the poultry trade can be found in Voet, *The Plantin Press*, nos 144, 169, 438, 528.
29. Pieter Spierenburg, *The Spectacle of Suffering* (Cambridge: Cambridge University Press, 1984).
30. Matthias Senn, *Die Wickiana. Johann Jakob Wicks Nachrichtensammlung aus dem 16 Jahrhundert* (Zurich: Raggi, 1975); Franz Mauelshagen, *Wunderkammer auf Papier. Die "Wickiana" zwischen Reformation und Volksglaube* (Zurich: Bibliotheca academica, 2011).
31. Zurich ZB, Pas II 12:76, reproduced in Walter L. Strauss, *The German Single-Leaf Woodcut, 1550–1600*, 3 vols (New York: Abaris, 1975), p. 842. Wick possessed no fewer than four separate broadsheet descriptions of this clearly notorious crime.
32. Strauss, *German Single-Leaf Woodcut*, pp. 246, 700, 701, 831.
33. Ibid., p. 1,086 (separate panels), Zurich ZB Pas II 27:7; ibid., 848 (narrative), Zurich ZB, Pas II 22:10.
34. *A most straunge, rare, and horrible murther committed by a Frenchman of the age of too or three and twentie yeares who hath slaine and most cruelly murthered three severall persons* (London: Purfoot, 1586); STC 11377.
35. Joseph H. Marshburn, *Murder and Witchcraft in England, 1550–1640, as Recounted in Pamphlets, Ballads, Broadsides, and Plays* (Norman, OK: University of Oklahoma Press, 1971); Peter Lake and Michael Questier, *The Antichrist's Lewd Hat: Protestants, Papists and Players in Post-Reformation England* (New Haven, CT: Yale University Press, 2002), pp. 3–53.
36. J. A. Sharpe, 'Last Dying Speeches: Religion, Ideology and Public Execution in Seventeenth-Century England', *Past and Present*, 107 (1985), pp. 144–67.
37. Senn, *Wickiana*, p. 149.
38. Strauss, *German Single-Leaf Woodcut*, p. 488.
39. Jennifer Spinks, *Monstrous Births and Visual Culture in Sixteenth-Century Germany* (London: Chatto & Pickering, 2009); Aaron W. Kitch, 'Printing Bastards: Monstrous Birth Broadsides in Early Modern England', in Douglas A. Brooks (ed.), *Printing and Parenting in Early Modern England* (Aldershot: Ashgate, 2005), pp. 221–36.
40. Zurich ZB, PAS II 15:17, Strauss, *German Single-Leaf Woodcut*, p. 481.
41. Senn, *Wickiana*, pp. 216–17.
42. Ulinka Rublack, *The Crimes of Women in Early Modern Germany* (Oxford: Oxford University Press, 1999).
43. Strauss, *German Single-Leaf Woodcut*, p. 936.
44. Ibid., p. 395, Zurich ZB PAS II 2:23; Zurich ZB PAS II 12:78. For the same event as a pamphlet, USTC 699843; 'Shower of Wheat that Fell in Wiltshire', in J. Paul Hunter, *Before Novels: The Cultural Contexts of Eighteenth-Century English Fiction* (New York: Norton, 1990), p. 186.
45. Burkard Waldis, *Eyne warhafftige und gantz erschreckliche historien* (Marburg, 1551). Quoted in Joy Wiltenburg, 'Crime and Christianity in Early Sensationalism', in Marjorie

Plummer and Robin Barnes (eds), *Ideas and Cultural Margins in Early Modern Germany* (Aldershot: Ashgate, 2009), pp. 131–45, here p. 135.

46. Wiltenburg, 'Crime and Christianity', p. 140.
47. Joy Wiltenburg, 'True Crime: The Origins of Modern Sensationalism', *American Historical Review*, 109 (2004), pp. 1,377–1,404.
48. As eloquently argued by Wolfgang Behringer, 'Witchcraft and the Media', in Marjorie Plummer and Robin Barnes (eds), *Ideas and Cultural Margins in Early Modern Germany* (Aldershot: Ashgate, 2009), pp. 217–36.
49. We record twenty-six editions published before 1600 in the USTC.
50. *De lamiis et phitonicis mulieribus*, twenty-five editions in Latin and German translation.
51. Max Geisberg, *The German Single-Leaf Woodcut, 1500–1550* (New York: Hacker, 1974), vol. 1,206.
52. Behringer, 'Witchcraft and the Media', pp. 221–2.
53. Though the French scholar Jean Bodin was an important counterweight, and a firm believer in malevolent witchcraft. Johannes Weyer, *Cinq livres de l'imposture et tromperie des diables, des enchantements et sorcelleries* (Paris: Jacques du Puys, 1567); USTC 1465; Jean Bodin, *De la demonomanie des sorciers* (Paris: Jacques du Puys, 1580); USTC 1660.
54. *Zwo Newe Zeittung, was man für Hexen und Unholden verbrendt hat* (Basel, 1580); USTC 707209; Behringer, 'Witchcraft and the Media', p. 227.

Chapter 5 Confidential Correspondents

1. A point made by David Randall, *Credibility in Elizabethan and Early Stuart Military News* (London: Pickering & Chatto, 2008).
2. M. S. Anderson, *The Rise of Modern Diplomacy, 1450–1919* (London: Longman, 1993), p. 9. The seminal texts are Garrett Mattingly, *Renaissance Diplomacy* (London: Jonathan Cape, 1955), and Donald E. Queller, *The Office of Ambassador in the Middle Ages* (Princeton, NJ: Princeton University Press, 1967).
3. Quoted Mattingly, *Renaissance Diplomacy*, p. 45.
4. J. K. Hyde, 'The Role of Diplomatic Correspondence and Reporting: News and Chronicles', in his *Literacy and its Uses: Studies on Late Medieval Italy* (Manchester: Manchester University Press, 1993), pp. 217–59.
5. Donald E. Queller, *Early Venetian Legislation on Ambassadors* (Geneva: Droz, 1967), p. 82 (no. 43).
6. Donald E. Queller, 'The Development of Ambassadorial Relazioni', in J. R. Hale (ed.), *Renaissance Venice* (London: Faber & Faber, 1973), pp. 174–96.
7. Queller, 'Development', pp. 177–8.
8. *Traité du gouvernement de la cité et seigneurie de Venise*, in P.-M. Perret, *Relations de la France avec Venise*, 2 vols (Paris, 1896), II, 292.
9. Mattingly, *Renaissance Diplomacy*, pp. 135–6.
10. There has been no full study dedicated to Chapuys since Garrett Mattingly's unpublished doctoral dissertation of 1935. See Mattingly, *Renaissance Diplomacy*, pp. 232–5; Richard Lundell, 'Renaissance Diplomacy and the Limits of Empire: Eustace Chapuys, Habsburg Imperialisms, and Dissimulation as Method', in Tonio Andrade and William Reger (eds), *The Limits of Empire: European Imperial Formations in Early Modern World History: Essays in Honour of Geoffrey Parker* (Farnham: Ashgate, 2012), pp. 205–22.
11. Michael J. Levin, *Agents of Empire: Spanish Ambassadors in Sixteenth-Century Italy* (Ithaca, NY: Cornell University Press, 2005), p. 44.
12. Mai to Charles V, 31 July 1530; quoted Levin, *Agents of Empire*, p. 52.
13. Catherine Fletcher, *Our Man in Rome: Henry VIII and his Italian Ambassador* (London: Bodley Head, 2012); idem, 'War, Diplomacy and Social Mobility: The Casali Family in the Service of Henry VIII', *Journal of Early Modern History*, 14 (2010), pp. 559–78.
14. Levin, *Agents of Empire*, pp. 18–23.
15. Ibid., p. 167.
16. Frederic J. Baumgartner, 'Henry II and the Papal Conclave of 1549', *Sixteenth Century Journal*, 16 (1985), pp. 301–14.
17. Levin, *Agents of Empire*, p. 65.

18. Ermolao Barbaro, *Epistolae, Orationes et Carmina*, ed. V. Branca, 2 vols (Florence: Bibliopolis, 1943).
19. Quoted Mattingly, *Renaissance Diplomacy*, p. 188.
20. Geoffrey Parker, *The Grand Strategy of Philip II* (New Haven, CT, and London: Yale University Press, 1998), p. 214; Katy Gibbons, *English Catholic Exiles in Late Sixteenth-Century Paris* (Woodbridge: Boydell & Brewer, 2011).
21. Parker, *Grand Strategy*, pp. 209–23; M. Leimon and Geoffrey Parker, 'Treason and Plot in Elizabethan England: The Fame of Sir Edward Stafford Reconsidered', *English Historical Review*, 106 (1996), pp. 1,134–58.
22. A helpful introduction to Spanish diplomatic ciphers, with some examples, can be found in an appendix to De Lamar Jensen, *Diplomacy and Dogmatism: Bernardino de Mendoza and the French Catholic League* (Cambridge, MA: Harvard University Press, 1964), pp. 231–8.
23. John Bossy, *Under the Molehill: An Elizabethan Spy Story* (New Haven, CT: Yale University Press, 2001).
24. René Ancel, 'Étude critique sur quelques recueils d'avvisi', *Mélanges d'archéologie et d'histoire*, 28 (1908), pp. 115–39, here p. 130.
25. Philip Beale, *A History of the Post in England from the Romans to the Stuarts* (Aldershot: Ashgate, 1988), p. 148. This was presumably Sir Francis Englefield, one of the most notorious of the English Catholic exiles.
26. Jensen, *Diplomacy and Dogmatism*, pp. 171–89.
27. Wolfgang Behringer, *Im Zeichen des Merkur: Reichspost und Kommunikationsrevolution in der Frühen Neuzeit* (Göttingen: Vandenhoeck & Ruprecht, 2003), p. 340.
28. The fundamental literature is the work of Mario Infelise, *Prima dei giornali: alle origini della pubblica informazione (secoli XVI–XVII)* (Rome: Laterza, 2002). See also his 'From Merchants' Letters to Handwritten Political Avvisi: Notes on the Origins of Public Information', in Francisco Bethercourt and Florike Egmond (eds), *Correspondence and Cultural Exchange in Europe, 1400–1700* (Cambridge: Cambridge University Press, 2007), pp. 33–52, and 'Roman Avvisi: Information and Politics in the Seventeenth Century', in Gianvittorio Signorotto and Maria Antonietta Visceglia (eds), *Court and Politics in Papal Rome, 1400–1800* (Cambridge: Cambridge University Press, 2002).
29. George Holmes, 'A Letter from Lucca to London in 1303', in Peter Denley and Caroline Elam (eds), *Florence and Italy: Renaissance Studies in Honour of Nicolai Rubinstein* (London: University of London, 1988), pp. 227–33.
30. Chapter 2, above.
31. Carolyn James (ed.), *The Letters of Giovanni Sabadino degli Arienti (1481–1510)* (Florence: Olschki, 2001); Bernard Chandler, 'A Renaissance News Correspondent', *Italica*, 29 (1952), pp. 158–63.
32. C. Marzi, 'Degli antecessori dei giornali', *Rivista delle biblioteche e degli archivi*, 24 (1913), 181–5. The translated excerpts are from Infelise, 'Merchants' Letters', p. 39.
33. James, *Letters of Giovanni Sabadino degli Arienti*, pp. 48–50.
34. Infelise, 'Merchants' Letters', pp. 39–40.
35. Jean Delumeau, *Vie économique et sociale de Rome dans la seconde moitié du XVIe siècle* (Paris: Boccard, 1957–9), pp. 26–79, here p. 28.
36. *The Merchant of Venice*, Act 3, scene 1, echoing Shylock to Bassano, Act 1, scene 3.
37. Delumeau, *Vie économique et sociale de Rome*, pp. 877–8.
38. Infelise, 'Roman Avvisi', p. 216.
39. Brian Richardson, *Manuscript Culture in Renaissance Italy* (Cambridge: Cambridge University Press, 2009), p. 159.
40. Ibid., pp. 117–21.
41. See Chapter 7 below.
42. Delumeau, *Vie économique et sociale de Rome*, p. 31.
43. Richardson, *Manuscript Culture*, p. 159.
44. Delumeau, *Vie économique et sociale de Rome*, p. 64.
45. See Chapter 8 below.
46. Mark Häberlein, *The Fuggers of Augsburg: Pursuing Wealth and Honor in Renaissance Germany* (Charlottesville, VA: University of Virginia Press, 2012); Jacob Strieder, *Jakob Fugger the Rich: Merchant and Banker of Augsburg, 1459–1525* (Westport, CT: Greenwood Press,

1984); Götz von Pölnitz, *Die Fugger* (Frankfurt: Scheffler, 1960); Richard Ehrenberg, *Das Zeitalter der Fugger: Geldkapital und Creditverkehr im 16. Jahrhundert* (Jena: Fischer, 1922).

47. Vienna, ONB, Cod. 8949–8975; Mathilde A. H. Fitzler, *Die Entstehung der sogenannten Fuggerzeitungen in der Wiener Nationalbibliothek* (Baden bei Wien: Rohrer, 1937); Oswald Bauer, *Zeitungen vor der Zeitung. Die Fuggerzeitungen (1568–1605) und das frühmoderne Nachrichtensystem* (Berlin: Akademie Verlag, 2011).

48. Ancel, 'Étude critique', pp. 115–39.

49. Behringer, *Im Zeichen des Merkur*, p. 327.

50. Fitzler, *Entstehung*, p. 22.

51. Behringer, *Im Zeichen des Merkur*, p. 328.

52. Fitzler, *Entstehung*, p. 78. It was published as *Warhafftige Abconterfectur und eigentlicher bericht der gewaltigen Schiffbrucken, Blochheusser und unerhörter wundergebew die der Printz von Barma vor der Statt Antorff auf dem Wasser hat bawen lassen*. A copy is in the Munich State Library, Cod. Germ. 5864/2 f. 38.

53. Albert Ganado and Maurice Agius Valadà, *A Study in Depth of 143 Maps Representing the Great Siege of Malta of 1565* (Valetta: Bank of Valetta, 1994).

54. Behringer, *Im Zeichen des Merkur*, pp. 330–1.

55. William S. Powell, *John Pory, 1572–1636: The Life and Letters of a Man of Many Parts* (Chapel Hill, NC: University of North Carolina Press, 1976).

Chapter 6 Marketplace and Tavern

1. G. R. Elton, *Policy and Police: The Enforcement of the Reformation in the Age of Thomas Cromwell* (Cambridge: Cambridge University Press, 1972).

2. Adam Fox, *Oral and Literate Culture in England, 1500–1700* (Oxford: Oxford University Press, 2000), pp. 346, 349.

3. Peter Clark (ed.), *Small Towns in Early Modern Europe* (Cambridge: Cambridge University Press, 1995).

4. Adam Fox, 'Rumour, News and Popular Political Opinion in Elizabethan and Early Stuart England', *Historical Journal*, 40 (1997), p. 604.

5. Ibid., p. 605.

6. Ibid., p. 609.

7. Pieter Spierenburg, *The Spectacle of Suffering* (Cambridge: Cambridge University Press, 1984); Paul Friedland, *Seeing Justice Done: The Age of Spectacular Capital Punishment in France* (Oxford: Oxford University Press, 2012); David Nicholls, 'The Theatre of Martyrdom in the French Reformation', *Past and Present*, 121 (188), pp. 49–73; J. A. Sharpe, 'Last Dying Speeches: Religion, Ideology and Public Execution in Seventeenth-Century England', *Past and Present*, 107 (1985), pp. 144–67.

8. See Chapter 4.

9. For a more realistic timetable, see the case of the notorious axe murderer Enoch ap Evan, executed at Shrewsbury on 20 August 1633. Two short pamphlet accounts were published by the end of the year, the first registered by the Stationers' Company on 20 September. Peter Lake and Michael Questier, *The Antichrist's Lewd Hat: Protestants, Papists and Players in Post-Reformation England* (New Haven, CT: Yale University Press, 2002), pp. 6–7.

10. Laurence Fontaine, *History of Pedlars in Europe* (Durham, NC: Duke University Press, 1996).

11. Clive Griffin, 'Itinerant Booksellers, Printers and Pedlars in Sixteenth-Century Spain and Portugal', in Robin Myers, Michael Harris and Giles Mandelbrote, *Fairs, Markets and the Itinerant Book Trade* (London: British Library, 2007), pp. 43–59.

12. E. M. Wilson, 'Samuel Pepys's Spanish Chapbooks', *Transactions of the Cambridge Bibliographical Society*, 2 (1955–7), pp. 127–54, 229–68, 305–22.

13. Clive Griffin, *Journeymen Printers, Heresy and the Inquisition in Sixteenth-Century Spain* (Oxford: Oxford University Press, 2005).

14. Alastair Duke, 'Posters, Pamphlets and Prints', in his *Dissident Identities in the Early Modern Low Countries* (Aldershot: Ashgate, 2009), pp. 157–77.

15. F. Madan, 'The Daily Ledger of John Dorne, 1520', in C. R. L. Fletcher (ed.), *Collectanea* (Oxford: Oxford Historical Society, 1885), pp. 71–177. He also sold Christmas carols, again in single sheets, for the same price.

16. Rosa Salzberg and Massimo Rospocher, 'Street Singers in Italian Renaissance Urban Culture and Communication', *Cultural and Social History*, 9 (2012), pp. 9–26.
17. Giancarlo Petrella, 'Ippolito Ferrarese, a Travelling "Cerratano" and Publisher in Sixteenth-Century Italy', in Benito Rial Costas (ed.), *Print Culture and Peripheries in Early Modern Europe* (Leiden: Brill, 2013), pp. 201–26.
18. Salzberg and Rospocher, 'Street Singers'.
19. Massimo Rospocher, 'Print and Political Propaganda under Pope Julius II (1503–1513)', in Pollie Bromilow (ed.), *Authority in European Book Culture* (New York: Ashgate, 2013).
20. Salzberg and Rospocher, 'Street Singers'.
21. *Cantique de victoire pour l'Eglise de Lyon. A Lyon, Le jour de la victoire, dernier du mois d'Avril. 1562* (Lyon: Jean Saugrain, 1562). USTC 37138.
22. The conclusion, and telling phrase of Rosa Salzberg. Salzberg and Rospocher, 'Street Singers'.
23. Above, Chapter 5.
24. Tommaso Garzoni, *La piazza universale di tutte le professionini del mondo* (1585).
25. Andrew Pettegree, *Reformation and the Culture of Persuasion* (Cambridge: Cambridge University Press, 2005), Chapter 3.
26. Nathan Rein, *The Chancery of God: Protestant Print, Polemic and Propaganda against the Emperor, Magdeburg 1546–1551* (Aldershot: Ashgate, 2008).
27. Listed in an appendix to Thomas Kaufmann, *Das Ende der Reformation: Magdeburgs "Herrgotts Kanzlei" (1548–1551/2)* (Tübingen: Mohr Siebeck, 2003).
28. Rebecca Wagner Oettinger, *Music as Propaganda in the German Reformation* (Aldershot: Ashgate, 2001), p. 137, and the chapter, 'Popular Song as Resistance.'
29. Wagner Oettinger, *Music as Propaganda*, pp. 118–19. Oettinger's table 4.2 (p. 113) provides a list of *contrafacta* of the 'Judaslied'.
30. Jane Finucane, 'Rebuking the Princes: Erasmus Alber in Magdeburg, 1548–1552', in Bromilow (ed.), *Authority in European Book Culture*. For Alber's works, Kaufmann, *Ende der Reformation*, appendix I and pp. 371–97.
31. Allyson Creasman, *Censorship and Civic Order in Reformation Germany, 1517–1648* (Aldershot: Ashgate, 2012), pp. 27–30, 73.
32. Ibid., p. 106.
33. Ibid., pp. 147–84. See also on the Calendar controversies C. Scott Dixon, 'Urban Order and Religious Coexistence in the German Imperial City: Augsburg and Donauwörth, 1548–1608', *Central European History* (2007), 40, pp. 1–33.
34. Alexander J. Fisher, 'Song, Confession and Criminality: Trial Records as Sources for Popular Music Culture in Early Modern Europe', *Journal of Musicology*, 18 (2001), pp. 616–57.
35. Creasman, *Censorship and Civic Order*.
36. Allyson F. Creasman, 'Lies as Truth: Policing Print and Oral Culture in the Early Modern City', in Marjorie Plummer and Robin Barnes (eds), *Ideas and Cultural Margins in Early Modern Germany* (Aldershot: Ashgate, 2009), pp. 255–70.
37. Tessa Watt, *Cheap Print and Popular Piety, 1550–1640* (Cambridge: Cambridge University Press, 1991); Natasha Würzbach, *The Rise of the English Street Ballad, 1550–1650* (Cambridge: Cambridge University Press, 1990); Christopher Marsh, *Music and Society in Early Modern England* (Cambridge: Cambridge University Press, 2010).
38. Marsh, *Music and Society*, p. 255.
39. Ibid., p. 251.
40. Nancy Lyman Roelker, *The Paris of Henry of Navarre as Seen by Pierre de L'Estoile* (Cambridge, MA: Harvard University Press, 1958).
41. Patricia Fumerton and Anit Guerrini, 'Introduction: Straws in the Wind', in their *Ballads and Broadsides in Britain, 1500–1800* (Aldershot: Ashgate, 2010), p. 1.
42. Marsh, *Music and Society*, pp. 245–6.
43. Ibid., p. 246.
44. Alan Everitt, 'The English Urban Inn, 1560–1760', in idem, *Perspectives in English Urban History* (London: Macmillan, 1973), pp. 91–137, here p. 93; see also Peter Clark, *The English Alehouse: A Social History, 1200–1830* (London: Longman, 1983).
45. Peter Spufford, *Power and Profit: The Merchant in Medieval Europe* (London: Thames and Hudson, 2002), pp. 205–6.
46. Everitt, 'English Urban Inn', pp. 104–5.

47. Beat Kümin, *Drinking Matters: Public Houses and Social Exchange in Early Modern Central Europe* (London: Palgrave Macmillan, 2007), p. 121.

48. Ibid.

49. Ibid., pp. 134–5.

50. Famously, the White Horse Tavern in Cambridge. Elisabeth Leedham-Green, *A Concise History of the University of Cambridge* (Cambridge: Cambridge University Press, 1996), p.44.

51. M. Kobelt-Groch, 'Unter Zechern, Spielern und Häschern. Täufer im Wirtshaus', in N. Fischer and M. Kobelt-Groch (eds), *Aussenseiter zwischen Mittelalter und Neuzeit* (Leiden: Brill, 1997), pp. 111–26.

52. See here particularly Tom Scott, *Freiburg and the Breisgau: Town–Country Relations in the Age of Reformation and Peasants' War* (Oxford: Oxford University Press, 1986).

53. Hans-Christoph Rublack (ed.), 'The Song of Contz Anahans: Communication and Revolt in Nördlingen, 1525', in R. Po-Chia Hsia (ed.), *The German People and the Reformation* (Ithaca, NY: Cornell University Press, 1988), pp. 108–9.

54. For the sheer dogged persistence of Inquisition interrogations, see especially Clive Griffin, *Journeymen-Printers, Heresy and the Inquisition in Sixteenth-Century Spain* (Oxford: Oxford University Press, 2005).

55. Guarinonius quoted by Kümin, *Drinking Matters*, p. 129.

56. Michael Frank, 'Satan's Servants or Authorities' Agent? Publicans in Eighteenth-Century Germany', in Beat Kümin and B. Ann Tlusty (eds), *The World of the Tavern: Public Houses in Early Modern Europe* (Aldershot: Ashgate, 2002), p. 32. See also B. Ann Tlusty, *Bacchus and Civic Order: The Culture of Drink in Early Modern Germany* (Charlottesville, VA: University of Virginia Press, 2001).

57. Fox, *Oral and Literate Culture*, p. 364.

58. Ibid., p. 369.

59. Adam Fox, 'Rumour, News and Popular Political Opinion in Elizabethan and Early Stuart England', *Historical Journal*, 40 (1997), pp. 597–620; Rebecca Lemon, *Treason by Words: Literature, Law, and Rebellion in Shakespeare's England* (Ithaca, NY: Cornell University Press, 2006).

60. Fox, 'Rumour', p. 599.

61. Fox, *Oral and Literate Culture*, p. 341.

62. Claude Holyband, *The French Littelton* (London: Richard Field, 1593), pp. 46 7. STC 6742. USTC 75635.

63. Fox, 'Rumour', p. 601.

64. Carolyn Muessig (ed.), *Preacher, Sermon and Audience in the Middle Ages* (Leiden: Brill, 2002).

65. Above, Chapter 3.

66. See especially Larissa Taylor (ed.), *Preachers and People in the Reformations and Early Modern Period* (Leiden: Brill, 2001); Pettegree, *Reformation and the Culture of Persuasion*, Chapter 2.

67. Pettegree, *Reformation and the Culture of Persuasion*, p. 18.

68. Ibid., pp. 24–5. For an account of the surprising consequences that sometimes followed from this sermon tourism see the account of Florimond de Raemond in Alastair Duke, Gillian Lewis and Andrew Pettegree (eds), *Calvinism in Europe: A Collection of Documents* (Manchester: Manchester University Press, 1992), pp. 37–8.

69. A good example from his sermons on Micah is transcribed in Duke, Lewis and Pettegree (eds), *Calvinism in Europe*, pp. 30–34.

70. William G. Naphy, *Calvin and the Consolidation of the Genevan Reformation* (Manchester: Manchester University Press, 1994), pp. 159, 161.

71. Heiko Oberman, *Luther: Man between God and the Devil* (New Haven, CT: Yale University Press, 1992), pp. 3–12.

72. Arnold Hunt, *The Art of Hearing: English Preachers and their Audiences, 1590–1640* (Cambridge: Cambridge University Press, 2010), p. 106. For the expedition as a news events see Chapter 9.

73. A point demonstrated convincingly by Hunt, *The Art of Hearing*, pp. 150–4. For the highly politicised sermons of seventeenth-century England see Tony Clayton, 'The Sermon, the "Public Sphere" and the Political Culture of Late Seventeenth-Century England', in L. A.

Ferrell and P. McCullough (eds), *The English Sermon Revised: Religious Literature and History, 1600–1750* (Manchester: Manchester University Press, 2001), pp. 208–34.

74. Millar MacLure, *The Paul's Cross Sermons, 1534–1642* (Toronto: University of Toronto Press, 1958); idem, *Register of Sermons Preached at Paul's Cross, 1534–1642* (Ottawa: Dovehouse editions, 1989).

75. Hunt, *The Art of Hearing*, p. 212. On the highly political and topical character of Paul's Cross sermons, see Lake and Questier, *Antichrist's Lewd Hat*, pp. 335–76.

76. Emily Michelson, 'An Italian Explains the English Reformation', in Michelson et al. (eds), *A Linking of Heaven and Earth* (Aldershot: Ashgate, 2012), pp. 33–48.

77. Hunt, *The Art of Hearing*, Chapter 1.

78. Ibid., p. 64.

79. Margo Todd, *The Culture of Protestantism in Early Modern Scotland* (London: Yale University Press, 2002), pp. 28–48.

Chapter 7 Triumph and Tragedy

1. Iain Fenlon, *The Ceremonial City: History, Memory and Myth in Renaissance Venice* (New Haven, CT, and London: Yale University Press, 2007).

2. Margaret Meserve, 'News from Negroponte: Politics, Popular Opinion and Information Exchange in the First Decade of the Italian Press', *Renaissance Quarterly*, 59 (2006), pp. 440–80; Robert Schwoebel, *The Shadow of the Crescent: The Renaissance Image of the Turk (1453–1517)* (Nieuwkoop: De Graaf, 1967); Carl Göllner, *Turcica. Die europäischen Türkendrucke des XVI Jahrhunderts*, 3 vols (Bucharest: Academiei, 1961–78).

3. Above, Chapter 3.

4. Margaret Meserve, *Empires of Islam in Renaissance Historical Thought* (Cambridge, MA: Harvard University Press, 2008).

5. Albert Ganado and Maurice Agius-Vadalà, *A Study in Depth of 143 Maps Representing the Great Siege of Malta of 1565* (Valetta: Bank of Valetta, 1994).

6. Henry Kamen, *Philip of Spain* (New Haven, CT, and London: Yale University Press, 1997), p. 139.

7. Geoffrey Parker, *The Grand Strategy of Philip II* (New Haven, CT, and London: Yale University Press, 1998), p. 19, and see below for Philip's pattern of work.

8. Fenlon, *Ceremonial City*.

9. Barbarics Zsuzsa and Renate Pieper, 'Handwritten Newsletters as a Means of Communication in Early Modern Europe', in Francisco Bethercourt and Florike Egmond, *Correspondence and Cultural Exchange in Europe, 1400–1700* (Cambridge: Cambridge University Press, 2007), pp. 75–6.

10. Göllner, *Turcica*, vol. 2, no. 1,396.

11. Listed ibid., vol. 2.

12. Ibid., nos 1,435–1,439.

13. Interestingly, both those listed by Göllner are based on lost originals.

14. Basel, Ulm, Nuremberg, Leipzig and Breslau. Göllner, *Turcica*, nos 1398–1404, 1448, 1477–1496.

15. Zurich ZB: PAS II 24/17.

16. Barbara Diefendorf, *Beneath the Cross: Catholics and Huguenots in Sixteenth-Century Paris* (New York: Oxford University Press, 1991). For the provincial massacres and recantations, Philip Benedict, *Rouen during the Wars of Religion* (Cambridge: Cambridge University Press, 1981).

17. Robert M. Kingdon, *Myths about the St Bartholomew's Day Massacre* (Cambridge, MA: Harvard University Press, 1988).

18. *Correspondance de Théodore de Bèze, 13 (1572)*, ed. Hippolyte Aubert (Geneva: Droz, 1988), no. 938, p. 179; Scott M. Manetsch, *Theodore Beza and the Quest for Peace in France, 1572–1598* (Leiden: Brill, 2000), p. 34.

19. Manetsch, *Theodore Beza and the Quest for Peace*, p. 34.

20. *Correspondance de Théodore de Bèze*, no. 939.

21. Donald Kelley, *François Hotman: A Revolutionary's Ordeal* (Princeton, NJ: Princeton University Press, 1973), p. 219.

22. John Cooper, *The Queen's Agent: Francis Walsingham at the Court of Elizabeth I* (London: Faber & Faber, 2011); Conyers Read, *Mr. Secretary Walsingham and the Policy of Queen Elizabeth*, 3 vols (Oxford: Clarendon Press, 1925).

23. Bertrand de Salignac de La Mothe Fénélon, *Correspondance diplomatique*, ed. T. H. A. Teulet, 7 vols (Paris, 1838–40), V, 21; Conyers Read, *Lord Burghley and Queen Elizabeth* (London: Jonathan Cape, 1960), p. 87.

24. Read, *Lord Burghley and Queen Elizabeth*, p. 91.

25. Pierre Hurtubise, 'Comment Rome apprit la nouvelle du massacre de la Saint-Barthélemy', *Archivum Historiae Pontificiae*, 10 (1972), pp. 187–209.

26. Ibid., pp. 198–9.

27. Kamen, *Philip of Spain*, p. 141.

28. Parker, *Grand Strategy*, p. 101.

29. Paula Sutter Fichtner, *Emperor Maximilian II* (New Haven, CT: Yale University Press, 2001), pp. 183–4.

30. *Declaration de la cause et occasion de la mort de l'admiral* (Paris: Jean Dallier, 1572); FB 12209–12217, 12230–12231.

31. Hurtubise, 'Comment Rome apprit la nouvelle', p. 202.

32. *Le stratagem ou la ruse de Charles IX* (Geneva: Jacob Stoer, 1574); FB 8814. The original Italian edition (Rome, 1572) is USTC 818499.

33. Kingdon, *Myths about the St Bartholomew's Day Massacre*. The classic treatment of this literature is Quentin Skinner, *The Foundations of Modern Political Thought* (Cambridge: Cambridge University Press, 1978).

34. Kingdon, *Myths about the St Bartholomew's Day Massacre*, pp. 28–50. Many of the most important contemporary published documents are collected in Simon Goulart, *Mémoires de l'estat de France sous Charles neufiesme* (Geneva: Vignon, 1576).

35. The best account is Colin Martin and Geoffrey Parker, *The Spanish Armada*, 2nd edn (Manchester: Manchester University Press, 1999). For the ground-breaking archaeological investigations that underpin this study, Colin Martin, *Full Fathom Five: The Wrecks of the Spanish Armada* (London: Chatto & Windus, 1975).

36. Jean Delumeau, *Vie économique et sociale de Rome dans la seconde moitié du XVIe siècle* (Paris: Boccard, 1957–9), p. 60.

37. Ibid., p. 35.

38. De Lamar Jensen, *Diplomacy and Dogmatism: Bernardino de Mendoza and the French Catholic League* (Cambridge, MA: Harvard University Press, 1964), pp. 156–7.

39. *Copie d'une lettre envoyée de Dieppe, sur la rencontre des armées d'Espaigne & d'Angleterre* (Paris: Guillaume Chaudiere, 1588); USTC 8949. There were four 1588 editions in all, including reprints in Lyon and Toulouse. USTC 12721, USTC 53285.

40. *Discours veritable de ce qui s'est passé entre les deux armées de Mer d'Angleterre & d'Espaigne* (s.l, s.n. 1588). It was, though, republished in stoutly Protestant La Rochelle, and anonymously elsewhere. USTC 19491 for the La Rochelle edition.

41. Bertrand T. Whitehead, *Brags and Boasts: Propaganda in the Year of the Armada* (Stroud: Alan Sutton, 1994), p. 109.

42. Parker, *Grand Strategy*, pp. 223–4. For the Elizabethan efforts at intelligence gathering, Alan Haynes, *Invisible Power: The Elizabethan Secret Service, 1570–1603* (Stroud: Sutton, 1992); Stephen Alford, *The Watchers: A Secret History of the Reign of Elizabeth I* (London: Allen Lane, 2012).

43. Parker, *Grand Strategy*, p. 270.

44. Stuart Carroll, *Martyrs and Murderers: The Guise Family and the Making of Europe* (Oxford: Oxford University Press, 2009), pp. 281–92.

45. Delumeau, *Vie économique et sociale de Rome*, p. 54.

46. Ibid., p. 59.

47. Ibid., p. 61.

48. See, for the context of these negotiations, Michael Wolfe, *The Conversion of Henry IV* (Cambridge, MA: Harvard University Press, 1993).

49. Delumeau, *Vie économique et sociale de Rome*, p. 58.

50. *Corte verhael vande groote victorie die Godt almachtich de conincklijcke mayesteyt van Enghelant verleent heft, over de Spaensche armada* (Amsterdam: Barent Adriaesnz, 1588); USTC 422639.

51. *Le discourse de la deffette des Anglois par l'armée espagnolle conduicte par le marquis de Saincte Croix espagnol, aux Illes Orcades* (Paris: François Le Fèvre, 1588); USTC 9650.

52. As reported in a newsletter of 3 September. Brendan Dooley, 'Sources and Methods in Information History: The Case of Medici Florence, the Armada and the Siege of Ostende', in Joop W. Koopmans (ed.), *News and Politics in Early Modern Europe (1500–1800)* (Louvain: Peeters, 2005), p. 39.

53. The ballads entered for publication in the Stationers' registers are listed in Whitehead, *Brags and Boasts*, pp. 209–11. John J. McAleer, 'Ballads on the Spanish Armada', *Texas Studies in Literature and Language*, 4 (1963), pp. 602–12.

54. STC 6558. Illustrated Whitehead, *Brags and Boasts*, p. 126.

55. *A true discourse of the Armie which the kinge of Spaine caused to be assembled in the haven of Lisbon* (London: John Wolfe, 1588); STC 22999, USTC 510911.

56. *Le vray discours de l'armee, que le roy catholique a faict assembler ay port de la ville de Lisbone* (Paris: Chaudière, 1588); USTC 19534. There is also an abbreviated Dutch version: *De wonderlijcke groote Armade die den Coninck van Spaengien heft toegherust op Enghelandt* (Gent: Jan van Salenson, 1588); USTC 413911.

57. *A pack of Spanish lyes sent abroad in the world* (London: Christopher Barker, 1588); STC 23011, USTC 510912; Whitehead, *Brags and Boasts*, pp. 197–8. The irony, of course, is that England was one of the last print cultures to abandon the old-fashioned Gothic in favour of Roman type. Spain was well ahead in this respect.

58. Christina Borreguero Beltrán, 'Philip of Spain: The Spider's Web of News and Information', in Brendan Dooley (ed.), *The Dissemination of News and the Emergence of Contemporaneity in Early Modern Europe* (Aldershot: Ashgate, 2010), pp. 23–49, here p. 31.

59. Beltrán, 'Philip of Spain', p. 33.

60. Below, Chapter 8.

61. Parker, *Grand Strategy*, p. 244.

62. No fewer than ten Italian states kept resident ambassadors in Spain, quite apart from those from the western nation states. Parker, *Grand Strategy*, p. 218.

63. Ibid., p. 20.

64. Ibid.

65. Ibid., p. 65.

66. Geoffrey Parker, *The Dutch Revolt* (London: Allan Lane, 1977).

Chapter 8 Speeding the Posts

1. Johannes Weber, 'Strassburg 1605: The Origins of the Newspaper in Europe', *German History*, 24 (2006), pp. 387–412.

2. See below; and above, Chapter 2.

3. Wolfgang Behringer, *Thurn und Taxis. Die Geschichte ihrer Post und ihrer Unternehmen* (Munich: Piper, 1990); idem, *Im Zeichen des Merkur. Reichspost und Kommunications-revolution in der Frühen Neuzeit* (Göttingen:Vandenhoeck & Ruprecht, 2003). A summary of the argument is presented in Wolfgang Behringer, 'Communications Revolutions', in *German History*, 24 (2006), pp. 333–74.

4. Behringer, *Thurn und Taxis*, p. 18.

5. Ibid., pp. 41–6; idem, *Im Zeichen des Merkur*, p. 63.

6. Behringer, *Im Zeichen des Merkur*, pp. 80–82.

7. Behringer, *Thurn und Taxis*, pp. 52–4, 79–83.

8. E. John B. Allen, 'The Royal Posts of France in the Fifteenth and Sixteenth Centuries', *Postal History Journal*, 15 (1971), pp. 13–17.

9. Philip Beale, *A History of the Post in England from the Romans to the Stuarts* (Aldershot: Ashgate, 1988).

10. Ibid., p. 119.

11. Ibid., p. 122.

12. Ibid., p. 142.

13. Philip Beale, Adrian Almond and Mike Scott Archer, *The Corsini Letters* (Stroud: Amberley, 2011).

14. Behringer, *Thurn und Taxis*, pp. 49–50.

15. Wolfgang Behringer, 'Fugger und Taxis. Der Anteil Augsburger Kaufleute an der Entstehung des europäischen Kommunikationssystems', in Johannes Burkhardt (ed.), *Augsburger Handelshäuser im Wandel des historischen Urteils* (Berlin: Akademie Verlag, 1996), pp. 24–48.

16. Hans and Marx Fugger stood godfather to Octavia von Taxis in 1572, and Hans Fugger acted as executor for the Augsburg postmaster Seraphin in 1582. Behringer, 'Fugger und Taxis', in Burkhardt (ed.), *Augsburger Handelshäuser*, pp. 241–8.

17. Von Sautter, 'Auffindung einer grossen Anzahl verschlossener Briefe aus dem Jahre 1585', *Archiv für Post und Telegraphie*, 4 (1909), pp. 97–115.

18. Von Sautter, 'Briefe aus dem Jahre 1585', pp. 107–9.

19. A. L. E. Verheyden, 'Une correspondance ineditée addressée par des familles protestantes des Pays-Bas à leurs coreligionnaires d'Angleterre (11 novembre 1569–25 février 1570)', *Bulletin de la Commission Royale d'Histoire*, 120 (1955), pp. 95–257.

20. The letters are discussed in Andrew Pettegree, *Foreign Protestant Communities in Sixteenth-Century London* (Oxford: Oxford University Press, 1986), pp. 221–5.

21. See Chapter 7 above.

22. M. A. H. Fitzler, *Die Entstehung der sogenannten Fuggerzeitungen in der Wiener Nationalbibliothek* (Vienna: Rohrer, 1937), p. 61.

23. Behringer, *Thurn und Taxis*, p. 52.

24. Ibid., p. 56.

25. Behringer, *Im Zeichen des Merkur*, pp. 132–6.

26. Erich Kuhlmann, 'Aus Hamburgs älterer Postgeschichte', *Archiv für deutsche Postgeschichte*, *Sonderheft* (1984), pp. 36–68.

27. Behringer, *Thurn und Taxis*, p. 58.

28. Reproduced in ibid., pp. 70–1.

29. Behringer, *Im Zeichen des Merkur*, pp. 177–88.

30. Ibid., p. 178.

31. Ibid., pp. 205–11.

32. Swedish involvement in the international diplomacy of these years was graphically demonstrated by the discovery in 1936 of the largest known surviving collection of seventeenth-century newspapers in the stacks of the Royal Library in Stockholm. See Folke Dahl, *The Birth of the European Press as Reflected in the Newspaper Collection of the Royal Library* (Stockholm: Rundqvists Boktryckeri, 1960).

33. See below, Chapter 10.

34. Klaus Beyrer, *Die Postkutschenreise* (Tübingen: Ludwig-Uhland-Instituts, 1985); idem, 'The Mail-Coach Revolution: Landmarks in Travel in Germany between the Seventeenth and Nineteenth Centuries', *German History*, 24 (2006), pp. 375–86.

Chapter 9 The First Newspapers

1. Johannes Weber, 'Strassburg 1605: The Origins of the Newspaper in Europe', *German History*, 24 (2006), pp. 387–412.

2. Elizabeth Armstrong, *Before Copyright: The French Book-Privilege System, 1498–1526* (Cambridge: Cambridge University Press, 1990).

3. The University of Heidelberg has an almost complete run for this year, which has now been digitised: http://digi.ub.uni-heidelberg.de/diglit/relation1609.

4. Johannes Weber, '"Untherthenige Supplication Johann Caroli, Buchtruckers." Der Beginn gedruckter politischer Wochenzeitungen im Jahre 1605', *Archiv für Geschichte des Buchwesens*, 38 (1992), pp. 257–65.

5. The standard directory of early German newspapers is Else Bogel and Elgar Blühm, *Die deutschen Zeitungen des 17. Jahrhunderts. Ein Bestandverzeichnis*, 2 vols (Bremen: Schünemann, 1971); *Nachtrag* (Munich: Saur, 1985). See also Holger Böning, *Deutsche Presse. Biobibliographische Handbücher zur Geschichte der deutschsprachigen periodischen Presse von den Anfängen bis 1815*, 6 vols (Stuttgart-Bad Cannstatt: Frommann-Holzboog, 1996–2003).

6. Paul Ries, 'The Anatomy of a Seventeenth-Century Newspaper', *Daphnis*, 6 (1977), pp. 171–232; idem, 'Der Inhalt der Wochenzeitungen von 1609 im Computer', *Deutsche Presseforschung*, 26 (1987), pp. 113–25.

7. Weber, 'Strassburg 1605', p. 398.

8. Karl Heinz Kremer, *Johann von den Birghden, 1582–1645. Kaiserlicher und koniglich-schwedischer Postmeister zu Frankfurt am Main* (Bremen: Lumière, 2005); idem, 'Johann von den Birghden, 1582–1645', *Archiv für deutsche Postgeschichte* (1984), pp. 7–43.
9. Listed in Bogel and Blühm, *Deutschen Zeitungen*, no. 5.
10. Ibid., no. 15.
11. Ibid., no. 16.
12. In this respect Meyer's decision to call his second weekly issue, started in 1630, also *Postzeitung*, was a definite and unnecessary provocation.
13. Thus, in the case of Meyer's *Wöchentliche Zeitung auss mehrerley örther*, the Tuesday edition was given the title *Prima*, and the Thursday edition, *Wöchentliche Zeitung*. See Bogel and Blühm, *Deutschen Zeitungen*, no. 15.
14. Folke Dahl, *Dutch Corantos, 1618–1650: A Bibliography* (The Hague: Koninklijke Bibliotheek, 1946); Folke Dahl, *The Birth of the European Press as Reflected in the Newspaper Collection of the Royal Library* (Stockholm: Rundqvists Boktryckeri, 1960).
15. Folke Dahl, 'Amsterdam, Earliest Newspaper Centre of Western Europe: New Contributions to the History of the first Dutch and French Corantos', *Het Boek*, XXV (1939), III, pp. 161–97, with a reproduction of this issue from the copy in Stockholm Royal Library. See also D. H. Couvée, 'The First Couranteers – The Flow of the News in the 1620s', *Gazette*, 8 (1962), pp. 22–36.
16. This means that in cases where copies of both printings survive, they are likely to exhibit small typographical differences. Dahl, *Dutch Corantos*, pp. 20–23, with reproductions of the copies in the Royal Library in Stockholm and the Mazarine Library in Paris.
17. Dahl, *Dutch Corantos*, pp. 23–6.
18. Dahl, 'Amsterdam, Earliest Newspaper Centre', pp. 190–91.
19. Ibid., pp. 185–6.
20. On advertising see ibid., pp. 161–98, and Chapter 14 below.
21. Michiel van Groesen, 'A Week to Remember: Dutch Publishers and the Competition for News from Brazil, 26 August–2 September 1624', *Quaerendo*, 40 (2010), pp. 26–49.
22. Paul Arblaster, 'Current Affairs Publishing in the Habsburg Netherlands, 1620–1660' (Oxford University DPhil dissertation, 1999); Leon Voet, 'Abraham Verhoeven en de Antwerpse pers', *De Gulden Passer*, 31 (1953), pp. 1–37. See also, most recently, Stéphane Brabant, *L'imprimeur Abraham Verhoeven (1575–1652) et les débuts de la presse 'belge'* (Paris: A.E.E.F, 2009).
23. See Christiaan Schuckman, *Hollstein's Dutch and Flemish Etchings, Engravings and Woodcuts, ca. 1450–1700*, vol. XXXV (Roosendaal: van Poll, 1990), pp. 217–26, nos 2–5.
24. The text of the privilege is given in Brabant, *Verhoeven*, p. 281.
25. Illustrated in Dahl, *The Birth of the European Press*, p. 18.
26. Augustus, 1621, 112. *Tijdinghe wt Weenen, ende hoe dat het doodt lichaem . . . van Bucquoy, binnen . . . Weenen op chrijschmaniere . . . is ghebrocht, ende in baren ghestelt, inde kercke vande minimen.* Copies in Antwerp, Heritage Library: B 17885: II, 112, and London, British Library: PP.3444 af (269).
27. Paul Arblaster, *Antwerp and the World: Richard Verstegen and the International Culture of Catholic Reformation* (Louvain: Louvain University Press, 2004).
28. As demonstrated in Andrew Pettegree, 'Tabloid Values: On the Trail of Europe's First News Hound', in Richard Kirwan and Sophie Mullins (eds), *Specialist Markets in the Early Modern Book World* (Leiden: Brill, 2014).
29. Quoted Paul Arblaster, 'Policy and Publishing in the Habsburg Netherlands, 1585–1690', in Brendan Dooley and Sabrina Baron (eds), *The Politics of Information in Early Modern Europe* (London: Routledge, 2001), p. 185.
30. Lisa Ferraro Parmelee, *Good Newes from Fraunce: French Anti-League Propaganda in Late Elizabethan England* (Rochester, NY: University of Rochester Press, 1996).
31. I. Atherton, 'The Itch Grown a Disease: Manuscript Transmission of News in the Seventeenth Century', in Joad Raymond, *News, Newspapers, and Society in Early Modern Britain* (London: Cass, 1999). For the career of one particular newsletter agent, see William S. Powell, *John Pory, 1572–1636: The Life and Letters of a Man of Many Parts* (Chapel Hill, NC: University of North Carolina Press, 1976).

32. Folke Dahl, A *Bibliography of English Corantos and Periodical Newsbooks, 1620–1642* (London: Bibliographical Society, 1952), nos 1–16 (with illustrations). The printer was Joris Veseler, the same man who had printed the Dutch edition for van Hilten. Dahl, *Birth of the European Press*, p. 29. See STC 18507.1–17.
33. Dahl, *Birth of the European Press*; STC 18507.18–25 (Amsterdam: Jansz.; or London for Thomas Archer). STC 18507.29–35 (London: N. Butter).
34. STC 18507.35–81.
35. Dahl, *Bibliography*, nos 80 ff.
36. Illustrated Dahl, *Birth of the European Press*, p. 30.
37. Nicholas Brownlees, *Corantos and Newsbooks: Language and* Discourse *in the First English Newspapers* (1620–1641) (Pisa: Ets, 1999); Nicholas Brownlees, *The Language of Periodical News in Seventeenth-Century England* (Newcastle: Cambridge Scholars, 2011).
38. C. John Sommerville, *The News Revolution in England: Cultural Dynamics of Daily Information* (Oxford: Oxford University Press, 1996), p. 26.
39. Ibid.
40. An example in Jason Peacey and Chris R. Kyle, *Breaking News: Renaissance Journalism and the Birth of the Newspaper* (Baltimore, MD: Johns Hopkins University Press, 2009), p. 55: 'I send you here enclosed the Currantos that are come out since my last letter, which is in effect all our present foreign news.'
41. Michael Frearson, 'The Distribution and Readership of London Corantos in the 1620s', in Robin Myers and Michael Harris (eds), *Serials and their Readers, 1620–1914* (Winchester: St Paul's Bibliographies, 1993), p. 17.
42. Thomas Cogswell, '"Published by Authoritie": Newsbooks and the Duke of Buckingham's Expedition to the Ile de Ré', *Huntington Library Quarterly*, 67 (2004), pp. 1–26, here p. 4.
43. In the original: '1. To settle a way when there shall be any revolt or back sliding in matters of religion or obedience (which commonly grows with rumours among the vulgar) to draw them in by the same lines that drew them out, by spreading among them such reports as may best make for that matter to which we would have they drawn. 2. To establish a speedy and ready way whereby to disperse in the veins of the whole body of a state such matter as may best temper it, and be most agreeable to the disposition of the head and principal members. 3. To devise means to raise the spirits of the people and to quicken their concepts. . . . It extends the sense by degrees to the concept of the right rules of reason, whereby they are wrought easily to obey those which by those rules shall command them.' Powell, *Pory* (1976), p. 52.
44. See here the brilliant article by Thomas Cogswell, '"Published by Authoritie"'.
45. Ibid., p. 14.
46. Frearson, 'London Corantos', p. 3.
47. Jayne E. E. Boys, *London's News Press and the Thirty Years War* (Woodbridge: Boydell, 2011).
48. Jeffrey K. Sawyer, *Printed Poison: Pamphlet Propaganda, Faction Politics, and the Public Sphere in Early Seventeenth-Century France* (Berkeley, CA: University of California Press, 1990).
49. Christian Jouhaud, 'Printing the Event: From La Rochelle to Paris', in Roger Chartier (ed.), *The Culture of Print: Power and Uses of Print in Early Modern Europe* (Princeton, NJ: Princeton University Press, 1989), pp. 290–333.
50. Dahl, *Birth of the European Press*, pp. 23–4.
51. See the article by Gilles Feyel in Jean Sgard, *Dictionnaire des Journaux 1600–1789* (Paris: Universitas, and Oxford: Voltaire Foundation, 1991), pp. 967–70.
52. Howard M. Solomon, *Public Welfare, Science, and Propaganda in Seventeenth-Century France: The Innovations of Théophraste Renaudot* (Princeton, NJ: Princeton University Press, 1972); Christian Bailly, *Théophraste Renaudot: un homme d'influence au temps de Louis XIII et de la Fronde* (Paris: Le Pré aux Clercs, 1987).
53. Gilles Feyel, *L'annonce et la nouvelle. La presse d'information en France sous l'ancien régime (1630–1788)* (Oxford: Voltaire Foundation, 2000), pp. 131–90.
54. Solomon, *Public Welfare*, p. 126.
55. Ibid., p. 129; see also idem, 'The *Gazette* and Antistatist Propaganda: The Medium of Print in the First Half of the Seventeenth Century', *Canadian Journal of History*, 9 (1974), pp. 1–17.

56. Feyel, *L'annonce et la nouvelle*, pp. 476–503.
57. The standard work is C. Moreau, *Bibliographie des Mazarinades* (Paris: Société de l'histoire de France, 1850–51), though this makes only the most rudimentary attempt to distinguish between different editions of the same title.
58. *Remerciment des imprimeurs a monseigneur le Cardinal Mazarin* (N. Boisset, 1649), p. 4; Moreau, *Mazarinades*, no. 3,280.
59. *Avis burlesque du cheval de Mazarin à son maître* (Paris: veuve Musnier, 1649); Moreau, *Mazarinades*, no. 494.
60. Moreau, *Mazarinades*, nos 811–835 (*Courier*), 1,466–1,472 (*Gazette*), 1,740–1,764 (*Journal*), 2,451–2,457 (*Mercury*).
61. *Le gazettier des-interressé* (Paris: Jean Brunet, 1649), sig. B2r; Moreau, *Mazarinades*, no. 1,466.
62. Moreau, *Mazarinades*, no. 830.
63. Ibid., I, pp. 249–50, for the identification of Eusèbe and Isaac Renaudot as publishers of the *Courier*. See now H. Carrier, *La Presse de la Fronde (1648–1653): les Mazarinades* (Paris: Droz, 1989), I, 188–189 and note 605.
64. Moreau, *Mazarinades*, no. 718.
65. Below, Chapter 11; Stéphane Haffemayer, *L'information dans la France du XVIIe siècle: La Gazette de Renaudot de 1647 à 1663* (Paris: Champion, 2002).
66. Filippo de Vivo, *Information and Communication in Venice: Rethinking Early Modern Politics* (Oxford: Oxford University Press, 2007).
67. Quoted Brendan Dooley, *The Social History of Skepticism: Experience and Doubt in Early Modern Culture* (Baltimore, MD: Johns Hopkins University Press, 1999), p. 34.
68. Ibid., Filippo de Vivo, 'Paolo Sarpi and the Uses of Information in Seventeenth-Century Venice', *Media History*, 11 (2005), pp. 37–51.
69. Dooley, *Skepticism*, p. 54.
70. Examples of profits from ibid., p. 42.
71. Ibid., p. 46.

Chapter 10 War and Rebellion

1. Johannes Weber, 'Der grosse Krieg und die frühe Zeitung. Gestalt und Entwicklung der deutschen Nachrichtenpresse in der ersten Hälfte des 17. Jahrhunderts', *Jahrbuch für Kommunikationsgeschichte*, 1 (1999), pp. 23–61, here p. 25.
2. Karl Heinz Kremer, *Johann von den Birghden, 1582–1645. Kaiserlicher und koniglich-schwedischer Postmeister zu Frankfurt am Main* (Bremen: Lumière, 2005); idem, 'Johann von den Birghden, 1582–1645', *Archiv für deutsche Postgeschichte* (1984), pp. 7–43.
3. Esther-Beate Körber, 'Deutschsprachige Flugschriften des Dreissigjährigen Krieges 1618 bis 1629', *Jahrbuch für Kommunikationsgeschichte*, 3 (2001), pp. 1–37.
4. Weber, 'Der grosse Krieg und die frühe Zeitung', p. 25: the victims were described as Herr Slawata, Herr Schmozonsky, and Herr Philip P, Secretarius.
5. Ibid., p. 29.
6. Else Bogel and Elgar Blühm, *Die deutschen Zeitungen des 17. Jahrhunderts. Ein Bestandverzeichnis*, 2 vols (Bremen: Schünemann, 1971); Else Bogel and Elgar Bluhm, *Nachtrag* (Munich: Saur, 1985), vol. I, pp. 48–51; II, pp. 50–51.
7. Johannes Weber, 'Kontrollmechanismen im deutschen Zeitungswesen des 17. Jahrhunderts', *Jahrbuch für Kommunikationsgeschichte*, 6 (2004), pp. 56–73.
8. See for the following especially John Roger Paas, *The German Political Broadsheet, 1600–1700*, 11 vols (Wiesbaden: Harrassowitz, 1985–2012); Elmer A. Beller, *Propaganda during the Thirty Years War* (Princeton, NJ: Princeton University Press, 1940), offers a small selection of the broadsheets, but usefully also has an English translation of the accompanying texts.
9. Above, Chapter 4.
10. The classic study is Robert W. Scribner, *For the Sake of Simple Folk: Popular Propaganda for the German Reformation* (Cambridge: Cambridge University Press, 1981). For criticism of the implicit argument that the customers were generally from lower social classes than the buyers of pamphlets, see my *Reformation: The Culture of Persuasion* (Cambridge: Cambridge

University Press, 2005), Chapter 5. For examples of effective Catholic use of polemical images in the second half of the sixteenth century, see Andrew Pettegree, 'Catholic Pamphleteering', in Alexandra Bamji et al. (eds), *The Ashgate Research Companion to the Counter-Reformation* (Aldershot: Ashgate, 2013), pp. 109–26.

11. Paas, *German Political Broadsheet*, vol. 2, P272–337.
12. William A. Coupe, *The German Illustrated Broadsheet in the Seventeenth Century: Historical and Iconographical Studies*, 2 vols (Baden Baden: Heintz, 1966).
13. Beller, *Propaganda*, plate II, pp. 18–20.
14. Paas, *German Political Broadsheet*, vol. 2, P452–6.
15. Ibid., vol. 3, P652–9, for this and other representations of the search for Frederick. There were even French and Dutch versions: vol. 3, PA133–9.
16. Ibid., P784–90.
17. Ibid., P708–13.
18. Ibid., P675–6.
19. Ibid., vol. 1, P23.
20. W. Lahne, *Magdeburgs Zerstöring in der zeitgenössischen Publizistik* (Magdeburg: Verlag des Magdeburger Geschichtsvereins, 1931). For a shorter treatment in English, see Andrew Cunningham and Ole Peter Grell, *The Four Horsemen of the Apocalypse: Religion, War, Famine and Death in Reformation Europe* (Cambridge: Cambridge University Press, 2000), pp. 170–99.
21. Weber, 'Der grosse Krieg und die frühe Zeitung', pp. 36–7.
22. Ibid., pp. 38–9.
23. Paas, *German Political Broadsheet*, vol. 5, P1,336–47.
24. Lahne, *Magdeburgs Zerstörung*, pp. 147–55; Cunningham and Grell, *Four Horsemen*, p. 182.
25. For Swedish propaganda, see particularly G. Rystad, *Kriegsnachrichten und Propaganda während des Dreissigjährigen Krieges* (Lund: Gleerup, 1960).
26. Paas, *German Political Broadsheet*, vol. 5, P1,430–52; Beller, *Propaganda*, plate XI, pp. 30–1, for a reproduction with translation of one of the texts.
27. Paas, *German Political Broadsheet*, vol. 6, P1,585, 1,587.
28. Kremer, 'Johann von den Birghden', pp. 31–4.
29. Ibid., pp. 34–9.
30. Paas, *German Political Broadsheet*, vol. 6, P1,770–8.
31. Ibid., P1,554–5, 1,614–15.
32. Ibid., P1,635–6, 1,812.
33. As for instance in the case of British Library 1750.b.29, a folio of over one hundred items.
34. Weber, 'Der grosse Krieg und die frühe Zeitung', pp. 39–40.
35. Paas, *German Political Broadsheet*, vol. 7, P2,174–5.
36. Nadine Akkerman, 'The Postmistress, the Diplomat and a Black Chamber?': Alexandrine of Taxis, Sir Balthazar Gerbier and the Power of Postal Control', in Robyn Adams and Rosanna Cox (eds), *Diplomacy and Early Modern Culture* (Basingstoke: Palgrave, 2011), pp. 172–88.
37. Above, Chapter 9.
38. On this period, which has attracted considerable scholarly attention, see particularly Joad Raymond, *Pamphlets and Pamphleteering in Early Modern Britain* (Cambridge: Cambridge University Press, 2003); Jason Peacey, *Politicians and Pamphleteers: Propaganda during the English Civil Wars and Interregnum* (Aldershot: Ashgate, 2004). Still useful is the older study by Joseph Frank, *The Beginnings of the English Newspaper, 1620–1660* (Cambridge, MA: Harvard University Press, 1961).
39. Caroline Nelson and Matthew Seccombe, *British Newspapers and Periodicals, 1641–1700: A Short-Title Catalogue* (New York: Modern Language Association of America, 1987).
40. The figures are in John Barnard and Maureen Bell, 'Statistical Tables', in Barnard and D. F. McKenzie (eds), *The Cambridge History of the Book in Britain. Volume IV, 1557–1695* (Cambridge: Cambridge University Press, 2002), pp. 779–84; Raymond, *Pamphlets and Pamphleteering*, pp. 202–75.
41. Jason McElligott, '1641', in Joad Raymond (ed.), *The Oxford History of Popular Print Culture. I: Cheap Print in Britain and Ireland to 1660* (Oxford: Oxford University Press), pp. 599–608.

42. Ethan Shagan, 'Constructing Discord: Ideology, Propaganda and the English Responses to the Irish Rebellion of 1641', *Journal of British Studies*, 36 (1997), pp. 4–34.
43. For excerpts from the diurnals, see Joad Raymond, *Making the News: An Anthology of the Newsbooks of Revolutionary England 1641–1660* (Moreton-in-Marsh: Windrush Press, 1993), pp. 35–52.
44. Sometimes in very large editions. For broadsheet proclamations to be distributed to all the parishes of England in 1649, between nine and twelve thousand copies were ordered from the printers. Angela McShane, 'Ballads and Broadsides', in Raymond (ed), *Popular Print Culture*, p. 348.
45. C. John Sommerville, *The News Revolution in England: Cultural Dynamics of Daily Information* (Oxford: Oxford University Press, 1996).
46. Ibid., p. 35.
47. Raymond, *Making the News*, pp. 92–9. For its principal editor see P. W. Thomas, *Sir John Berkenhead, 1617–1679: A Royalist Career in Politics and Polemics* (Oxford: Oxford University Press, 1969).
48. Sommerville, *News Revolution*, p. 51.
49. Jason Peacey, 'The Struggle for Mercurius Britanicus: Factional Politics and the Parliamentarian Press, 1643–6', *Huntington Library Quarterly*, 68 (2005), pp. 517–43.
50. Joseph Frank, *Cromwell's Press Agent: A Critical Biography of Marchamont Nedham, 1620–1678* (Lanham, MD: University Press of America, 1980). For excerpts from the *Mercurius Britanicus*, see Raymond, *Making the News*, pp. 332–50.
51. Sommerville, *News Revolution*, p. 40.
52. Raymond, *Making the News*, pp. 350–74.
53. Helmer J. Helmers, 'The Royalist Republic: Literature, Politics and Religion in the Anglo-Dutch Public Sphere (1639–1660)' (Doctoral Dissertation, Leiden, 2011).
54. Paas, *German Political Broadsheet*, vol. 8, P2,225–36.
55. Peacey, *Politicians and Pamphleteers*, pp. 132–54.
56. Francis F. Madan, *A New Bibliography of the Eikon Basilike* (Oxford: Oxford Bibliographical Society Publications, III, 1949).
57. Blair Worden, *Literature and Politics in Cromwellian England: John Milton, Andrew Marvell, Marchamont Nedham* (Oxford: Oxford University Press, 2007); idem, 'Marchamont Nedham and the Beginnings of English Republicanism, 1649–1656', in David Wootton (ed.), *Republicanism, Liberty and Commercial Society, 1649–1776* (Stanford, CA: Stanford University Press, 1994), pp. 45–81.
58. Jason Peacey, 'Cromwellian England: A Propaganda State?', *History*, 91 (2006), pp. 176–99; Raymond, *Making the News*, pp. 364–79.
59. The best modern study is Jonathan Israel, *The Dutch Republic: Its Rise, Greatness and Fall, 1477–1806* (Oxford: Oxford University Press, 1995).
60. Folke Dahl, 'Amsterdam, Earliest Newspaper Centre of Western Europe: New Contributions to the History of the First Dutch and French Corantos', *Het Boek*, XXV (1939), 3, pp. 185–6.
61. Helmers, 'Royalist Republic'.
62. See below, Chapter 14.
63. Meredith Hale, 'Political Martyrs and Popular Prints in the Netherlands in 1672', in Martin Gosman (ed.), *Selling and Rejecting Politics in Early Modern Europe* (Louvain: Peeters, 2007), pp. 119–34.
64. Michel Reinders, *Printed Pandemonium: Popular Print and Politics in the Netherlands 1650–72* (Leiden: Brill, 2013).
65. Above, Chapter 9. Hubert Carrier, *La presse et la Fronde, 1648–1653: Les Mazarinades. I. La conquête de l'opinion. II. Les hommes du livre*, 2 vols (Geneva: Droz, 1989–91).

Chapter 11 Storm in a Coffee Cup

1. Maximillian E. Novak, *Daniel Defoe, Master of Fictions* (Oxford: Oxford University Press, 2001), pp. 289–328.
2. Craig Calhoun (ed.), *Habermas and the Public Sphere* (Cambridge, MA: Harvard University Press, 1992); Nick Crossley and John Michael Roberts, *After Habermas: New Perspectives on the Public Sphere* (Oxford: Blackwell, 2004).

3. Aytoun Ellis, *The Penny Universities: A History of the Coffee-House* (London: Secker & Warburg, 1956); Heinrich Jacob, *Coffee: The Epic of a Commodity* (London, 1935; reprinted Short Hills, NJ: Burford Books, 1998); Brian Cowan, *The Social Life of Coffee: The Emergence of the British Coffeehouse* (New Haven, CT: Yale University Press, 2005); Steve Pincus, 'Coffee Politicians Does Create: Coffeehouses and Restoration Political Culture', *Journal of Modern History*, 67 (1995), pp. 807–34; Mark Knights, *Representation and Misrepresentation in Later Stuart Britain: Partisanship and Political Culture* (Oxford: Oxford University Press, 2005).
4. Gilles Feyel, *L'annonce et la nouvelle. La presse d'information en France sous l'ancien régime (1630–1788)* (Oxford: Voltaire Foundation, 2000).
5. Peter Burke, *The Fabrication of Louis XIV* (New Haven, CT: Yale University Press, 1992).
6. Roger Mettam, 'Power, Status and Precedence: Rivalries among the Provincial Elites of Louis XIV's France', *Transactions of the Royal Historical Society* (5th series), 38 (1988), pp. 43–62.
7. Feyel, *L'annonce et la nouvelle*, pp. 476–92.
8. This schedule is reconstructed ibid., pp. 486–92.
9. Burke, *Fabrication*, p. 76.
10. *Gazette extraordinaire*, 77, July 1673. Quoted Feyel, *L'annonce et la nouvelle*, p. 435.
11. Feyel, *L'annonce et la nouvelle*, p. 501.
12. Ibid., p. 466.
13. François Moureau, *Répertoire des Nouvelles à la Main. Dictionnaire de la presse manuscrite clandestine XVIe–XVIIIe siècle* (Oxford: Voltaire Foundation, 1999); Moreau (ed.), *De bonne main. La communication manuscrite au XVIII siècle* (Paris: Universitas, and Oxford: Voltaire Foundation, 1993).
14. Joseph Klaits, *Printed Propaganda under Louis XIV: Absolute Monarchy and Public Opinion* (Princeton, NJ: Princeton University Press, 1976), pp. 50–6.
15. Jane McLeod, *Licensing Loyalty: Printers, Patrons and the State in Early Modern France* (University Park, PA: Pennsylvania State University Press, 2011).
16. It was generally published under the more unwieldy title of *Nouvelles extraordinaires de divers endroits*.
17. Jeremy D. Popkin, *News and Politics in the Age of Revolution: Jean Luzac's Gazette de Leyde* (Ithaca, NY: Cornell University Press, 1989).
18. Klaits, *Propaganda*, p. 91.
19. Quoted ibid., p. 169.
20. Quoted ibid., p. 248.
21. James Sutherland, *The Restoration Newspaper and its Development* (Cambridge: Cambridge University Press, 1986); Harold Weber, *Paper Bullets: Print and Kingship under Charles II* (Lexington, KY: University Press of Kentucky, 1996); Knights, *Representation and Misrepresentation*.
22. J. G. Muddiman, *The King's Journalist* (London: Bodley Head, 1923).
23. Anne Dunan-Page and Beth Lynch (eds), *Roger L'Estrange and the Making of Restoration Culture* (Aldershot: Ashgate, 2008).
24. *The Intelligencer*, 31 August 1663.
25. P. M. Handover, *A History of the London Gazette, 1665–1965* (London: HMSO, 1965).
26. Ibid.; Peter Fraser, *The Intelligence of the Secretaries of State & their Monopoly of Licensed News, 1660–1688* (Cambridge: Cambridge University Press, 1956), pp. 43–56; Alan Marshall, *Intelligence and Espionage in the Reign of Charles II* (Cambridge: Cambridge University Press, 1994).
27. Fraser, *Intelligence*, pp. 30–32.
28. Alan Marshall, *The Strange Death of Edmund Godfrey: Plots and Politics in Restoration London* (Stroud: Sutton, 1999); Peter Hinds, *The Horrid Popish Plot: Roger L'Estrange and the Circulation of Political Discourse in Late Seventeenth-Century London* (Oxford: Oxford University Press, 2010). The classic treatment is John Kenyon, *The Popish Plot* (London: Heinemann, 1972).
29. Sutherland, *Restoration Newspaper*, p. 15.
30. The classic survey is Bryant Lillywhite, *London Coffee Houses: A Reference Book of the Coffee Houses of the Seventeenth, Eighteenth and Nineteenth Centuries* (London: George Allen & Unwin, 1963).

31. Quoted Fraser, *Intelligence*, p. 119.
32. Cowan, *The Social Life of Coffee*, pp. 196–8.
33. Frank Staff, *The Penny Post, 1680–1918* (London: Lutterworth, 1964), pp. 34–51; Thomas Todd, *William Dockwra and the Rest of the Undertakers: The Story of the London Penny Post, 1680–2* (Edinburgh: Cousland, 1952); Duncan Campbell-Smith, *Masters of the Post: The Authorised History of the Royal Mail* (London: Allen Lane, 2011), pp. 59–61.
34. Fraser, *Intelligence*; Marshall, *Intelligence and Espionage*, pp. 78–95.
35. Sutherland, *Restoration Newspaper*, p. 18.
36. Mark Goldie, 'Roger L'Estrange's *Observator* and the Exorcism of the Plot', in Dunan-Page and Lynch (eds), *Roger L'Estrange*, pp. 67–88.
37. Mark Knights, *Politics and Opinion in the Exclusion Crisis, 1678–1681* (Cambridge: Cambridge University Press, 1994), p. 168. The overall levels of printing activity are charted in John Barnard and Maureen Bell, 'Statistical Tables', in Barnard and D. F. McKenzie (eds), *The Cambridge History of the Book in Britain. Volume IV, 1557–1695* (Cambridge: Cambridge University Press, 2002), pp. 779–84.
38. Knights, *Politics and Opinion*, p. 169.
39. Sutherland, *Restoration Newspaper*, p. 23.
40. William B. Ewald, *The Newsmen of Queen Anne* (Oxford: Basil Blackwell, 1956), p. 7; Julian Hoppit, *A Land of Liberty? England 1689–1727* (Oxford: Oxford University Press, 2000), p. 178.
41. G. A. Cranfield, *The Development of the Provincial Newspaper, 1700–1760* (Oxford: Oxford University Press, 1962); R. M. Wiles, *Freshest Advices: Early Provincial Newspapers in England* (Columbus, OH: Ohio State University Press, 1965).
42. Wiles, *Freshest Advices*, p. 192.
43. Ibid.
44. *Daily Courant*, 15 August 1704; *Flying Post*, 2 September 1704; Ewald, *Newsmen of Queen Anne*, pp. 34–5, 38–40.
45. Sutherland, *Restoration Newspaper*, pp. 91–122.
46. *Daily Courant*, 11 March 1702, quoted Wiles, *Freshest Advices*, p. 269.
47. Hoppit, *Land of Liberty?*, p. 181; Geoffrey Holmes, *The Trial of Doctor Sacheverell* (London: Eyre Methuen, 1973); Mark Knights (ed.), *Faction Displayed: Reconsidering the Trial of Dr Henry Sacheverell* (London: Parliamentary Yearbook Trust, 2012).
48. Wiles, *Freshest Advices*, pp. 46 ff.

Chapter 12 The Search for Truth

1. *The true report of the burning of the steeple and church of Paul's in London* (London: William Seres, 1561). Modern reprint in A. F. Pollard, *Tudor Tracts, 1532–1588* (Westminster: Constable 1903), here p. 405. STC 19930. USTC 505897. There was also a French translation: *Récit veritable du grand temple et clocher de la cité de Londres, en Angleterre, nommé saint Paul, ruïné et destruit par la foudre du tonnerre* (Lyon: Jean Saugrain, 1561). USTC 37109.
2. Pollard, *Tudor Tracts*, p. 406.
3. Ibid., p. 407. The fire at St Paul's is also discussed in Alexandra Walsham, *Providence in Early Modern England* (Oxford: Oxford University Press, 1999), pp. 232–4.
4. M. A. Overall, 'The Exploitation of Francesco Spiera', *Sixteenth Century Journal*, 26 (1995), pp. 619–37. Even in the 1690s, a completely different deathbed confession of a repentant atheist could draw on the enduring fame of Spiera. This so-called *Second Spira* sold 30,000 copies before it was exposed as a fake. J. Paul Hunter, *Before Novels: The Cultural Contexts of Eighteenth-Century English Fiction* (New York: Norton, 1990), pp. 182–4.
5. Nehemiah Wallington possessed a manuscript copy of the account of Spiera published by Nathaniel Bacon in 1638. David Booy, *The Notebooks of Nehemiah Wallington, 1618–1654* (Aldershot: Ashgate, 2007), pp. 154, 274–5. For Wallington, see also below, Chapter 16.
6. Michel Chomarat and Jean-Paul Laroche, *Bibliographie Nostradamus* (Baden Baden: Koerner, 1989).
7. Norman Jones, *The Birth of the Elizabethan Age: England in the 1560s* (Oxford: Blackwell, 1993), p. 40.

8. B. S. Capp, *Astrology and the Popular Press: English Almanacs, 1500–1800* (London: Faber and Faber, 1979).
9. For Brant, see Chapter 3 above. Of the four hundred illustrated German broadsheets logged in the USTC database, over 130 deal with these heavenly apparitions. For other forms of illustrated news broadsheets see above, Chapter 4.
10. Walter L. Strauss, *The German Single-Leaf Woodcut, 1550–1600*, 3 vols (New York: Abaris, 1975), pp. 163, 480, 648, 939 (comet of 1577), 399, 656 (multiple suns).
11. Ibid., pp. 481, 949.
12. Ibid., pp. 350, 396, 860.
13. Andrew Cunningham and Ole Peter Grell, *The Four Horsemen of the Apocalypse: Religion, War, Famine and Death in Reformation Europe* (Cambridge: Cambridge University Press, 2000), p. 174.
14. Nehemiah Wallington, *Historical notices of events occurring chiefly in the reign of Charles I*, ed. R. Webb (London: Bentley, 1869), pp. 150–1.
15. Jennifer Spinks, *Monstrous Births and Visual Culture in Sixteenth-Century Germany* (London: Chatto & Pickering, 2009); Julie Crawford, *Marvelous Protestantism: Monstrous Births in Post-Reformation England* (Baltimore, MD: Johns Hopkins University Press, 2005).
16. Spinks, *Monstrous Births*, pp. 59–79.
17. *The true description of two monstrous children born at Herne in Kent* (London, 1565). STC 6774. Other broadsheets of the same period and genre are illustrated in Crawford, *Marvelous Protestantism*.
18. David Cressy, *Agnes Bowker's Cat: Travesties and Transgressions in Tudor and Stuart England* (Oxford: Oxford University Press, 2000); Jones, *Birth of the Elizabethan Age*, pp. 45–7.
19. Andrew Hadfield, 'News of the Sussex Dragon', *Reformation*, 17 (2012), pp. 99–113.
20. Above, Chapter 10.
21. Leo Noordegraaf and Gerrit Valk, *De Gave Gods: De pest in Holland vanaf de late Middeleeuwen*, 2nd edn (Amsterdam: Bakker, 1996); Cunningham and Grell, *Four Horsemen*, Chapter 5.
22. Claire Tomalin, *Samuel Pepys* (London: Viking, 2002), pp. 227–35.
23. Steven Shapin, *A Social History of Truth: Civility and Science in Seventeenth-Century England* (Chicago, IL: University of Chicago Press, 1994).
24. Above, Chapter 1. The concept of honour in news is developed particularly in David Randall, *Credibility in Elizabethan and Early Stuart Military News* (London: Pickering & Chatto, 2008). C.f. Shapin, *Social History of Truth*, pp. 65–125.
25. James Shirley, *Love Tricks or the School of Complement*, quoted Jayne E. E. Boys, *London's News Press and the Thirty Years War* (Woodbridge: Boydell, 2011), p. 170.
26. Quoted Stephen J. A. Ward, *The Invention of Journalism Ethics* (Montreal: McGill University Press, 2004), p. 119.
27. 20 October 1631, STC 18507.227; quoted Boys, *London News Press*, p. 175.
28. Quoted Boys, *London News Press*, p. 171.
29. Ibid., p. 170.
30. Ben Jonson, *A Staple of News*, Act I, scene 4, lines 10–11. A groat was worth four pence.
31. See here the elegant and insightful remarks of Massimo Petta, 'Wild Nature and Religious Readings of Events: Natural Disaster in Milanese Printed Reports (16th–17th Century)', in Bo-Jan Borstner et al. (eds), *Historicizing Religion: Critical Approaches to Contemporary Concerns* (Pisa: PLUS-Pisa University Press, 2010), pp. 199–231.
32. Ahasver Fritsch, *Discursus de Novellarum, quas vocant Neue Zeitungen, hodierno usu et abusu* (1676); Otto Groth, *Die Geschichte der Deutschen Zeitungswissenschaft* (Munich: Weinmayer, 1948), p. 15. Extracts from the various participants in the German newspaper debate are collected in Elger Blühm and Rolf Engelsing (eds), *Die Zeitung. Deutsche Urteile und Dokumente von den Anfängen bis zur Gegenwart* (Bremen: Schünemann, 1967).
33. Johann Ludwig Hartman, *Unzeitige Neue Zeitungs-sucht* (Rotenburg: Lipß, 1679).
34. Daniel Hartnack, *Erachten von Einrichtung der Alten Teutsch und Neuen Europäischen Historien* (Hamburg: Zelle, 1688).
35. Kaspar Stieler, *Zeitungs Lust und Nutz* (Hamburg: Schiller, 1695), quoted Groth, *Geschichte*, p. 19.

36. This follows the excellent discussion of Stieler in Jeremy Popkin, 'New Perspectives on the Early Modern European Press', in Joop W. Koopmans, *News and Politics in Early Modern Europe (1500–1800)* (Louvain: Peeters, 2005), pp. 127, here p. 10.
37. The consequences of an active political culture (and a vigorous press) are explored with great insight in Mark Knights, *Representation and Misrepresentation in Later Stuart Britain: Partisanship and Political Culture* (Oxford: Oxford University Press, 2005).
38. William B. Ewald, *The Newsmen of Queen Anne* (Oxford: Basil Blackwell, 1956), pp. 14–15.
39. *Tatler*, no. 178, quoted Ewald, *Newsmen*, p. 15.
40. *The Spectator*, no. 452, quoted Ewald, *Newsmen*, p. 15.
41. Johannes Weber, 'Strassburg 1605: The Origins of the Newspaper in Europe', *German History*, 24 (2006), p. 393.
42. *Daily Courant*, 11 March 1702, quoted Ewald, *Newsmen*, p. 14.
43. Brendan Dooley, *The Social History of Skepticism: Experience and Doubt in Early Modern Culture* (Baltimore, MD: Johns Hopkins University Press, 1999), p. 129.
44. Stieler, *Zeitungs Lust und Nutz*, quoted Popkin, 'New Perspectives', p. 11.
45. Ward, *The Invention of Journalism Ethics*, p. 124.
46. Below, Chapter 16.
47. C. John Sommerville, *The News Revolution in England: Cultural Dynamics of Daily Information* (Oxford: Oxford University Press, 1996), pp. 132–3.

Chapter 13 The Age of the Journal

1. John Brewer and Roy Porter, *Consumption and the World of Goods* (London: Routledge, 1993).
2. David A. Kronick, *A History of Scientific and Technical Periodicals* (Methuen, NJ: Scarecrow, 1976).
3. Margery Purver, *The Royal Society: Concept and Creation* (Cambridge, MA: MIT University Press, 1967); Steven Shapin, *A Social History of Truth: Civility and Science in Seventeenth-Century England* (Chicago, IL: University of Chicago Press, 1994).
4. David A. Kronick, 'Notes on the Printing History of the Early *Philosophical Transactions*', in his *'Devant le deluge' and Other Essays on Early Modern Scientific Communication* (Oxford: Scarecrow, 2004), pp. 153–79, here p. 164.
5. Below, Chapter 18.
6. Jack R. Censer, *The French Press in the Age of Enlightenment* (London: Routledge, 1994).
7. James Sutherland, *The Restoration Newspaper and its Development* (Cambridge: Cambridge University Press, 1986), Chapter 3: 'Country News'.
8. Gilbert D. McEwen, *The Oracle of the Coffee House: John Dunton's Athenian Mercury* (San Marino, CA: Huntington Library, 1972); Helen Berry, *Gender, Society and Print Culture in Late Stuart England: The Cultural World of the 'Athenian Mercury'* (Aldershot: Ashgate, 2003); C. John Sommerville, *The News Revolution in England: Cultural Dynamics of Daily Information* (Oxford: Oxford University Press, 1996), pp. 103–9.
9. McEwen, *Oracle*, pp. 113–40.
10. From the *Athenian Mercury* of respectively 9 June, 18 April and 14 April 1691; Sommerville, *News Revolution*, pp. 106–7.
11. Robert J. Allen, *The Clubs of Augustan London* (Hamden, CT: Archon, 1967), pp. 189–229.
12. Monique Vincent, *Mercure galant. Extraordinaire affaires du temps. Table analytique* (Paris: Champion, 1998); Jean Sgard, 'La multiplication des périodiques', in *Histoire de l'édition française. II: Le livre triomphant, 1660–1830* (Paris: Promodis, 1984), pp. 198–205.
13. Richmond P. Bond, *Tatler: The Making of a Literary Journal* (Cambridge, MA: Harvard University Press, 1972). For this and what follows, Alvin Sullivan (ed.), *British Literary Magazines: The Augustan Age and the Age of Johnson, 1698–1788* (Westport, CT: Greenwood Press, 1983), provides excellent profiles and bibliography.
14. Charles A. Knight, *A Political Biography of Richard Steele* (London: Pickering & Chatto, 2009).
15. On advertising see also below, Chapter 14.
16. Erin Mackie (ed.), *The Commerce of Everyday Life: Selections from the Tatler and the Spectator* (Boston, MA: Bedford/St. Martin's, 1998).

17. *Tatler*, 6 April 1710; Mackie, *Commerce of Everyday Life*, pp. 58–9.
18. Sullivan, *British Literary Magazines*, pp. 113–19; J. A. Downie, *Jonathan Swift, Political Writer* (London: Routledge, 1985).
19. C. Lennart Carlson, *The First Magazine: A History of the Gentleman's Magazine* (Providence, RI: Brown, 1938); Sullivan, *British Literary Magazines*, pp. 136–40.
20. P. J. Buijnsters, *Spectoriale geschriften* (Utrecht: HES, 1991); idem, 'Bibliographie des périodiques rédigés selon le modèle des Spectateurs', in Marianne Couperus (ed.), *L'étude des périodiques anciens. Colloque d'Utrecht* (Paris: Nizet, 1972), pp. 111–20; Dorothée Sturkenboom, *Spectators van de hartstocht: sekte en emotionele cultuur in de achttiende eeuw* (Hilversum: Verloren, 1998).
21. Sgard, 'Multiplication des périodiques', p. 204.
22. Quoted Jeremy D. Popkin, 'The Business of Political Enlightenment in France, 1770–1800', in John Brewer and Roy Porter (eds), *Consumption and the World of Goods* (London: Routledge, 1993), p. 413.
23. Sgard, 'Multiplication des périodiques', p. 200.
24. Robert Darnton, *The Forbidden Bestsellers of Pre-Revolutionary France* (New York: Norton, 1995).
25. Berry, *Gender, Society and Print Culture*; Bertha-Monica Stearns, 'The First English Periodical for Women', *Modern Philology*, 28 (1930–1), pp. 45–59; Sommerville, *News Revolution*, p. 105.
26. Kathryn Shevelow, *Women and Print Culture: The Construction of Femininity in the Early Periodical* (London: Routledge, 1989).
27. Ibid., p. 149.
28. Olwen Hufton, *The Prospect before Her: A History of Women in Western Europe, 1500–1800* (London: HarperCollins, 1995), p. 455.
29. Censer, *French Press in the Age of Enlightenment*, pp. 88, 99.
30. Susan Broomhall, *Women and the Print Trade in Sixteenth-Century France* (Aldershot: Ashgate, 2002); Jef Tombeur, *Femmes & metiers du livre* (Soignies: Talus d'approche, 2004); Maureen Bell, 'Women in the English Book Trade, 1557–1700', *Leipziger Jahrbuch*, 6 (1996); Helen Smith, *'Grossly Material Things': Women and Book Production in Early Modern England* (Oxford: Oxford University Press, 2012).
31. Wolfgang Behringer, *Thurn und Taxis. Die Geschichte ihrer Post und ihrer Unternehmen* (Munich: Piper, 1990), pp. 87–90; Nadine Akkerman, 'The Postmistress, the Diplomat and a Black Chamber?: Alexandrine of Taxis, Sir Balthazar Gerbier and the Power of Postal Control', in Robyn Adams and Rosanna Cox (eds), *Diplomacy and Early Modern Culture* (Basingstoke: Palgrave, 2011), pp. 172–88.
32. For Meyer, see above, Chapter 9.
33. Below, Chapter 15.
34. Eliza Haywood, *The Female Spectator*, ed. Gabrielle M. Firmager (Melksham: Bristol Classical Press, 1993); Sullivan, *British Literary Magazines*, pp. 120–3; see also Alison Adburgham, *Women in Print: Writing Women and Women's Magazines from the Restoration to the Accession of Victoria* (London: George Allen & Unwin, 1972); J. Hodges, 'The Female Spectator', in Richmond P. Bond (ed.), *Studies in the Early English Periodical* (Westwood, CT: Greenwood Press, 1957), pp. 151–82.
35. Firmager, *Female Spectator*, p. 10, for the French edition. Finny Bottinga, 'Eliza Haywood's Female Spectator and its Dutch Translation *De Engelsche Spectatrice*', in Suzan van Dijk et al. (eds), *'I have heard of you': Foreign Women's Writing Crossing the Dutch Border* (Hilversum: Verloren, 2004), pp. 217–24.
36. *Female Spectator*, November 1744; Firmager, *Female Spectator*, p. 98.
37. Ian Atherton, 'The Itch Grown a Disease: Manuscript Transmission of News in the Seventeenth Century', *Prose Studies*, 21 (1998), pp. 39–65, here p. 49.
38. D. Osborne, *Letters to Sir William Temple*, ed. K. Parker (Harmondsworth: Penguin, 1987), p. 116.
39. Jacqueline Eales, *Puritans and Roundheads: The Harleys of Brampton Bryan and the Outbreak of the English Civil War* (Cambridge: Cambridge University Press, 1990), pp. 92–5.
40. Bertha-Monica Stearns, 'Early English Periodicals for Ladies (1700–1760)', *Proceedings of the Modern Languages Association*, 48 (1933), pp. 38–60.

41. Ibid., p. 57.
42. Jeremy D. Popkin, 'Political Communication in the German Enlightenment: Gottlob Benedikt von Shirach's *Politische Journal*', *Eighteenth-Century Life*, 20, no. 1 (February 1996), pp. 24–41.
43. Ibid., p. 28.
44. Popkin, 'The Business of Political Enlightenment', pp. 414 ff.
45. Ibid., p. 420.
46. Suzanne Tucoo-Chala, *Charles-Joseph Panckoucke et la libraire française* (Paris: Éditions Marrimpouey jeune, 1977).
47. David I. Kulstine, 'The Ideas of Charles-Joseph Panckoucke', *French Historical Studies*, 4 (1966), pp. 304–19.
48. George B. Watts, 'The Comte de Buffon and his Friend and Publisher Charles-Joseph Panckoucke', *Modern Language Quarterly*, 18 (1957), pp. 313–22.
49. Ibid., p. 314.
50. See here the interesting analysis of the stock of a major scholarly publisher by Ian Maclean, 'Murder, Debt and Retribution in the Italico-Franco-Spanish Book Trade', in his *Learning and the Market Place* (Leiden: Brill, 2009), pp. 227–72.

Chapter 14 In Business

1. His story is told in Anne Goldger, *Tulipmania: Money, Honor and Knowledge in the Dutch Golden Age* (Chicago, IL: University of Chicago Press, 2007), p. 168.
2. Simon Schama, *The Embarrassment of Riches* (London: Collins, 1997), pp. 350–70. The popular perception of tulipmania also owes a great deal to the extraordinary success and longevity of Charles Mackay, *Extraordinary Popular Delusions and the Madness of Crowds*, first published in London in 1841 but still extremely influential.
3. Goldger, *Tulipmania*, pp. 202, 235.
4. Ibid., p. 238.
5. Above, Chapters 2 and 5.
6. John J. McCusker and Cora Gravesteijn, *The Beginnings of Commercial and Financial Journalism: The Commodity Price Currents, Exchange Rate Currents, and Money Currents of Early Modern Europe* (Amsterdam: NEHA, 1991).
7. Ibid., pp. 22–3.
8. John J. McCusker, 'The Role of Antwerp in the Emergence of Commercial and Financial Newspapers in Early Modern Europe', in *La ville et la transmission des valeurs culturelles au bas moyen âge et aux temps modernes* (Brussels: Crédit communal, Collection histoire, 96, 1996), pp. 303–32.
9. McCusker and Gravesteijn, *Beginnings*, pp. 44–5.
10. Ibid., pp. 399–404.
11. Ibid., pp. 291–300; Anne Murphy, *The Origins of English Financial Markets: Investment and Speculation before the South Sea Bubble* (Cambridge: Cambridge University Press, 2009).
12. McCusker and Gravesteijn, *Beginnings*, p. 313. By publishing on post-days, Castaing clearly had in mind a client base outside London, or abroad, as well as in the city.
13. Murphy, *Origins of English Financial Markets*, p. 99; Blanche B. Elliott, *A History of English Advertising* (London: Batsford, 1962), pp. 313–44.
14. Ibid., p. 91.
15. Ibid., pp. 94–5.
16. Julian Hoppit, *A Land of Liberty? England 1689–1727* (Oxford: Oxford University Press, 2000), pp. 313–44.
17. Murphy, *Origins of English Financial Markets*, p. 109.
18. Grant Hannis, 'Daniel Defoe's Pioneering Consumer Journalism in the *Review*', *British Journal for Eighteenth-Century Studies*, 30 (2007), pp. 13–26, here p. 16.
19. Murphy, *Origins of English Financial Markets*, pp. 107–8.
20. Hannis, 'Defoe's Pioneering Consumer Journalism', p. 22.
21. Murphy, *Origins of English Financial Markets*, pp. 114–36.
22. Still the best study is John Carswell, *The South Sea Bubble*, 2nd edn (Stroud: Alan Sutton, 1993).

23. *Daily Courant* for 1, 2, 3 and 24 June 1720, accessed in the Guildhall Library, London.

24. See the *Daily Courant*, 8 June 1720.

25. Quoted Hoppit, *A Land of Liberty?*, p. 335.

26. Julian Hoppit, 'The Myths of the South Sea Bubble', *Transactions of the Royal Historical Society*, 6th ser., 12 (2002), pp. 141–65.

27. Carswell, *South Sea Bubble*, pp. 95–6

28. See ibid., Chapters 13 and 14 (added as fresh material to the second edition).

29. A point made about the earliest prophets of doom in the dot-com book of the 1990s. John Cassidy, *dot.con* (New York: HarperCollins, 2002).

30. *Daily Courant* for 31 October and 7 November 1720 (2nd edn).

31. Other pamphlets advertised included *The South-Sea scheme examined* (*Daily Courant* for 18 October), *The case of contracts for South Sea Stock* (9 November), and a sober pamphlet by the bishop of Carlisle: *The honest and dishonest ways of getting wealth* (12 December).

32. *Post Boy*, issues of 18–20 October and 8–10 November 1720, accessed in the Guildhall Library, London. The whole pack is illustrated on the website of the Harvard Business School, from the pack in the Kress Collection of the Baker Library: http://www.library.hbs.edu/hc/ssb/recreationandarts/cards.html.

33. Hoppit, *A Land of Liberty?*, p. 344.

34. William B. Ewald, *The Newsmen of Queen Anne* (Oxford: Basil Blackwell, 1956), pp. 30–1.

35. Folke Dahl, 'Amsterdam, Earliest Newspaper Centre of Western Europe: New Contributions to the History of the First Dutch and French Corantos', *Het Boek*, XXV (1939), III, pp. 161–98, here p. 179.

36. Elliott, *A History of English Advertising*, pp. 22–9, discusses the very earliest examples, which date from the 1620s.

37. Dahl, 'Amsterdam, Earliest Newspaper Centre', pp. 179–82.

38. Maura Ratia and Carla Suhr, 'Medical Pamphlets: Controversy and Advertising', in Irma Taavitsainen and Paivi Pahta (eds), *Medical Writings in Early Modern English* (Cambridge: Cambridge University Press, 2011), p. 183.

39. C. John Sommerville, *The News Revolution in England: Cultural Dynamics of Daily Information* (Oxford: Oxford University Press, 1996), p. 70.

40. Elliott, *History of English Advertising*, pp. 37–45.

41. Michael Harris, 'Timely Notices: The Uses of Advertising and its Relationship to News during the Late Seventeenth Century', *Prose Studies*, 21 (1998), p. 152.

42. R. B. Walker, 'Advertising in London Newspapers, 1650–1750', *Business History*, 15 (1973), pp. 114–15; Elliott, *History of English Advertising*, pp. 57–73.

43. Elliott, *History of English Advertising*, pp. 30–6.

44. Ibid., pp. 94–5.

45. Sommerville, *News Revolution*, pp. 147–8; Lawrence Lewis, *The Advertisements of the Spectator* (London: Houghton Mifflin, 1909).

46. R. M. Wiles, *Freshest Advices: Early Provincial Newspapers in England* (Columbus, OH: Ohio State University Press, 1965), p. 101.

47. Ibid., p. 142.

48. Ibid., pp. 367–72.

49. Walker, 'Advertising', pp. 112–30.

50. *The Spectator*, no. 10, Monday 12 March 1711.

51. Sommerville, *News Revolution*, p. 43.

52. Where political influence was concerned, proprietors were prepared to make even more extravagant claims, as with an author warning against the *Craftsman*, a weekly journal critical of Walpole in 1732, that it was read by 'no less than four hundred thousand . . . allowing no more than 40 readers to a paper'. Quoted Michael Harris, *London Newspapers in the Age of Walpole: A Study of the Origins of the Modern English Press* (London: Associated University Presses, 1987), p. 48.

53. Harris, 'Timely Notices', p. 144.

54. François Moureau (ed.), *De bonne main. La communication manuscrite au XVIII siècle* (Paris, Universitas, and Oxford: Voltaire Foundation, 1993).

55. Lucyle Werkmeister, *A Newspaper History of England, 1792–1793* (Lincoln, NB: University of Nebraska Press, 1967), p. 19. *The Times* began printing news on its front page only in 1966.
56. See Walker, 'Advertising', p. 119.
57. For an example from colonial Virginia see below, Chapter 16.
58. John Styles, 'Print and Policing: Crime Advertising in Eighteenth-Century Provincial England', in Douglas Hay and Francis Snyder (eds), *Policing and Prosecution in Britain, 1750–1850* (Oxford: Oxford University Press, 1989), pp. 55–111.
59. From 11,000 in 1705 to under 2,500 in 1717. Walker, 'Advertising', pp. 116–17.

Chapter 15 From Our Own Correspondent

1. http://www.oed.com/view/Entry/101740. J. Paul Hunter, *Before Novels: The Cultural Contexts of Eighteenth-Century English Fiction* (New York: Norton, 1990), pp. 167–72.
2. *Weekly Journal or British Gazeteer*, 12 September 1724. Quoted Michael Harris, 'Journalism as a Profession or Trade in the Eighteenth Century', in Robin Myers and Michael Harris (eds), *Author/Publisher Relations during the Eighteenth and Nineteenth Centuries* (Oxford: Oxford Polytechnic Press, 1983), p. 42.
3. *The case of the coffee-men of London and Westminster* (London, 1729), p. 5.
4. *Flying Post or Weekly Medley*, 21 December 1728; Harris, 'Journalism', p. 41.
5. Paula McDowell, *The Women of Grubstreet: Press, Politics and Gender in the London Literary Marketplace, 1678–1730* (Oxford: Oxford University Press, 1998), pp. 55–7, 101–2.
6. Jeroen Salman, *Pedlars and the Popular Press: Itinerant Distribution Networks in England and the Netherlands, 1600–1850* (Leiden: Brill, 2014).
7. Below, Chapter 16.
8. Salman, *Pedlars and the Popular Press*, Chapter 4.
9. Hannah Barker, *Newspapers, Politics and Public Opinion in Late Eighteenth-Century England* (Oxford: Oxford University Press, 1998), p. 101; Robert L. Haig, *The Gazetteer, 1735–1797: A Study in the Eighteenth-Century Newspaper* (Carbondale, IL: Southern Illinois University Press, 1960), pp. 178–80.
10. Peter Fraser, *The Intelligence of the Secretaries of State and their Monopoly of Licensed News, 1660–1688* (Cambridge: Cambridge University Press, 1956), pp. 30–2.
11. James Ralph, *The case of authors by profession or trade stated* (London, 1758), pp. 22, 61–7; Harris, 'Journalism', pp. 37–8.
12. http://www.oed.com/view/Entry/101739.
13. R. M. Wiles, *Freshest Advices: Early Provincial Newspapers in England* (Columbus, OH: Ohio State University Press, 1965), p. 192.
14. Ibid.
15. Ibid., pp. 290–1.
16. P. M. Handover, *A History of the London Gazette, 1665–1965* (London: HMSO, 1965), p. 53.
17. This and the following paragraph draw heavily on A. Aspinall, 'The Social Status of Journalists at the Beginning of the Nineteenth Century', *Review of English Studies*, 21 (1945), pp. 216–32.
18. J. A. Robuck in his pamphlet *The London Review and the Periodical Press* (London, 1835), quoted Aspinall, 'Social Status of Journalists', pp. 222–3.
19. Lucyle Werkmeister, *A Newspaper History of England, 1792–1793* (Lincoln, NB: University of Nebraska Press, 1967), pp. 21, 35.
20. Cobbett, *The Political Register*, 4 January 1817, referring to his *Porcupine*, which closed in 1801; Aspinall, 'Social Status of Journalists', p. 225.
21. For examples taken from the reign of Queen Anne, see above, Chapter 11.
22. Steven Shapin, *A Social History of Truth: Civility and Science in Seventeenth-Century England* (Chicago, IL: University of Chicago Press, 1994), pp. 65–125, offers interesting reflections on the relationship between gentility and integrity.
23. C. Moreau, *Bibliographie des Mazarinades*, 3 vols (Paris: Renouard, 1850–1), nos 1,809–2,294.

24. Konstantin Dierks, *In My Power: Letter Writing and Communications in Early America* (Philadelphia, PA: University of Pennsylvania, 2009), pp. 206–14.

25. I. Atherton, 'The Itch Grown a Disease: Manuscript Transmission of News in the Seventeenth Century', *Prose Studies*, 21 (1998), pp. 39–65. Also available in Joad Raymond (ed.), *News, Newspapers, and Society in Early Modern Britain* (London: Frank Cass, 1999).

26. Data collected in Roger Chartier, 'The Practical Impact of Writing', in *A History of Private Life. III. Passions of the Renaissance*, ed. R. Chartier (Cambridge, MA: Harvard University Press, 1989), pp. 112–15.

27. Judith Rice Henderson, 'Erasmian Ciceronians: Reformation Teachers of Letter-Writing', *Rhetorica*, 10 (1992), pp. 273–302; eadem, 'Humanism and the Humanities', in *Letter-Writing Manuals*, pp. 141–9; *De conscribendis epistolis*, ed. Charles Fantazzi, *Collected Works of Erasmus*, vol. 25 (Toronto: University of Toronto Press, 1985).

28. Linda C. Mitchell, 'Letter-Writing Instruction Manuals in Seventeenth- and Eighteenth-Century England', in Carol Poster and Linda C. Mitchell, *Letter-Writing Manuals* (Columbia, SC: University of South Carolina Press, 2007), pp. 179–80.

29. Roger Chartier, 'Secrétaires for the People', in Roger Chartier, Alain Boureau and Céline Dauphin, *Correspondence: Models of Letter-Writing from the Middle Ages to the Nineteenth Century* (London: Polity Press, 1997), pp. 59–111.

30. Alfred Morin, *Catalogue descriptive de la bibliothèque bleue de Troyes* (Geneva: Droz, 1974).

31. Clare Brant, *Eighteenth-Century Letters and British Culture* (Basingstoke: Palgrave Macmillan, 2008).

32. *The Letters of Benjamin Franklin and Jane Mecom*, ed. Carl van Doren (Princeton, NJ: Princeton University Press, 1950), p. 81; David M. Henkin, *The Postal Age: The Emergence of Modern Communications in Nineteenth-Century America* (Chicago, IL: University of Chicago Press, 2006), p. 180, n. 10.

33. Roger Chartier, 'An Ordinary Kind of Writing', in *Correspondence*, p. 17.

34. Dierks, *In My Power*, pp. 25–32.

35. Ibid.; Brant, *Eighteenth-Century Letters*, Chapter 4: 'Writing as a Lover'.

36. Brant, *Eighteenth-Century Letters*, p. 172.

37. Wiles, *Freshest Advices*, p. 194.

38. Ibid., pp. 194–5.

39. This section draws heavily upon Paul Friedland, *Seeing Justice Done: The Age of Spectacular Capital Punishment in France* (Oxford: Oxford University Press, 2012).

40. Ibid., p. 156.

41. Ibid., pp. 168–72, 231.

42. V. A. C. Gatrell, *The Hanging Tree: Execution and the English People, 1770–1868* (Oxford: Oxford University Press, 1994).

43. Above, Chapter 6.

44. Michel Foucault, *Discipline and Punish: The Birth of the Prison* (London: Allen Lane, 1977).

45. Friedland, *Seeing Justice Done*, pp. 247–8.

Chapter 16 Cry Freedom

1. G. A. Cranfield, *The Development of the Provincial Newspaper, 1700–1760* (Oxford: Oxford University Press, 1962); Charles C. Clark, *The Public Prints: The Newspaper in Anglo-American Culture, 1665–1740* (New York: Oxford University Press, 1994). For the French *affiches* (advertising journals) see Gilles Feyel, *L'annonce et la nouvelle. La presse d'information en France sous l'ancien régime (1630–1788)* (Oxford: Voltaire Foundation, 2000), pp. 929–1,274.

2. Arthur H. Cash, *John Wilkes: The Scandalous Father of Civil Liberties* (New Haven, CT: Yale University Press, 2006); Peter D. G. Thomas, *John Wilkes: A Friend to Liberty* (Oxford: Oxford University Press, 1996).

3. *The Briton*, published in thirty-eight issues between 29 May 1762 and 12 February 1763, was edited for Bute by the distinguished Scottish novelist Tobias Smollett. http://www.oxforddnb.com/view/article/25947.

4. Quoted Cash, *Wilkes*, p. 79.

5. Ibid., p. 85.

6. *The North Briton*, 45, 23 April 1763. Quoted Bob Clarke, *From Grub Street to Fleet Street: An Illustrated History of English Newspapers to 1899* (Aldershot: Ashgate, 2004), p. 88.

7. Cash, *Wilkes*, p. 119.

8. *Public Advertiser*, 17 December 1769. Quoted Clarke, *Grub Street*, p. 90.

9. Clarke, *Grub Street*, p. 92.

10. Only in 1972 would Parliament formally abandon the prohibition of the reporting of its debates.

11. Robert R. Rea, *The English Press in Politics, 1760–1774* (Lincoln, NB: University of Nebraska Press, 1963), p. 5; Stephen J. A. Ward, *The Invention of Journalism Ethics* (Montreal: McGill University Press, 2004), p. 155.

12. *The political beacon: or the life of Oliver Cromwell, impartially illustrated* (London, 1770), p. 3, quoted Clare Brant, *Eighteenth-Century Letters and British Culture* (Basingstoke: Palgrave Macmillan, 2006), p. 176.

13. Clarke, *Grub Street*, p. 95.

14. This story is beautifully told by Ian Kelly, *Mr Foote's Other Leg: Comedy, Tragedy and Murder in Georgian London* (Basingstoke: Picador, 2012).

15. Hannah Barker, *Newspapers, Politics and Public Opinion in Late Eighteenth-Century England* (Oxford: Oxford University Press, 1998).

16. A thoughtful survey is Clark, *Public Prints*.

17. Ibid., p. 216.

18. John B. Blake, 'The Inoculation Controversy in Boston: 1721–1722', *New England Quarterly*, 25 (1952), pp. 489–506.

19. *Pennsylvania Gazette*, no. 1,324, 9 May 1754. Consulted in the library of the Library Company of Philadelphia.

20. The *New York Gazette*, the *New York Mercury*, the *Boston Gazette* and the *Boston Newsletter*.

21. Above, Chapter 11.

22. Arthur M. Schlesinger, *Prelude to Independence: The Newspaper War on Britain, 1764–1776* (New York: Knopf, 1958).

23. Clarence S. Brigham, *History and Bibliography of American Newspapers, 1690–1820*, 2 vols (London: Archon Books, 1962).

24. Stephen Botein, 'Printers and the American Revolution', in Bernard Bailyn and John B. Hench (eds), *The Press and the American Revolution* (Worcester, MA: American Antiquarian Society, 1980), p. 20.

25. Botein, 'Printers', p. 26.

26. Richard D. Brown, 'Shifting Freedoms of the Press', in High Amory and David D. Hall, *A History of the Book in America. Volume 1: The Colonial Book in the Atlantic World* (Cambridge: Cambridge University Press, 2000), pp. 366–76.

27. Philip Davidson, *Propaganda and the American Revolution, 1763–1783* (Chapel Hill, NC: 1941).

28. G. Thomas Tanselle, 'Some Statistics on American Printing, 1764–1783', in Amory and Hall, *Book in America*, pp. 349–57.

29. Consulted in the Special Collections of the College of William and Mary, Williamsburg, Virginia.

30. *Virginia Gazette*, 9 June 1775.

31. A point made by Richard D. Brown, *Knowledge is Power: The Diffusion of Information in Early America, 1700–1865* (New York: Oxford University Press, 1989), p. 128.

32. Clarke, 'Early American Journalism', in Amory and Hall, *Book in America*, p. 361.

33. Brown, 'Shifting Freedoms', p. 375.

34. The authoritative account is now Hans-Jürgen Lüsebrink and Rolf Reichardt, *The Bastille: A History of a Symbol of Despotism and Freedom* (Durham, NC: Duke University Press, 1997).

35. Ibid.; for the broadsheets, Rolf Reichardt, 'Prints: Images of the Bastille', in Robert Darnton and Daniel Roche (eds), *Revolution in Print: The Press in France, 1775–1800* (Berkeley, CA: University of California Press, 1989), pp. 235–51.

36. *Courier de Versailles à Paris*, 15 July 1789. Cited Jeremy D. Popkin, *Revolutionary News: The Press in France, 1789–1799* (Durham, NC: Duke University Press, 1990), pp. 127–8.

37. For song see Laura Mason, *Singing the French Revolution: Popular Culture and Politics, 1787–1799* (Ithaca, NY: Cornell University Press, 1996); idem, 'Songs: Mixing Media', in Darnton and Roche, *Revolution in Print*, pp. 252–69.
38. Popkin, *Revolutionary News*, pp. 25–6; Antoine de Baecque, 'Pamphlets: Libels and Political Mythology', in Darnton and Roche, *Revolution in Print*, pp. 165–76.
39. Carla Hesse, 'Economic Upheavals in Publishing', in Darnton and Roche, *Revolution in Print*, pp. 69–97.
40. Robert Darnton, *The Forbidden Bestsellers of Pre-Revolutionary France* (New York: Norton, 1995).
41. Around 5,000 editions, compared to at least 10,000 in the five-year period at the beginning of the revolutionary events. Christian Jouhaud, *Mazarinades: la Fronde des mots* (Paris: Aubier, 1985).
42. Pierre Rétat, *Les Journaux de 1789. Bibliographie critique* (Paris: CNRS, 1988); Hesse, 'Economic Upheavals', p. 92; Popkin, *Revolutionary News*, p. 84.
43. Despite his association with the pre-revolutionary print world, in 1793–4 Panckoucke still ran twenty-seven presses and employed one hundred workmen. Robert Darnton, 'L'imprimerie de Panckoucke en l'an II', *Revue française d'histoire du livre*, 23 (1979), pp. 359–69.
44. Jack R. Censer, 'Robespierre the Journalist', in Harvey Chisick (ed.), *The Press in the French Revolution* (Oxford: Voltaire Foundation, 1991), pp. 189–96.
45. Popkin, *Revolutionary News*, p. 57.
46. Ibid.
47. Ibid., p. 55.
48. Jeremy D. Popkin, 'Journals: The New Face of the News', in Darnton and Roche, *Revolution in Print*, pp. 145–7.
49. Popkin, *Revolutionary News*, p. 8.
50. W. J. Murray, 'Journalism as a Career Choice in 1789', in Chisick (ed.), *Press in the French Revolution*, pp. 161–88, here p. 180.
51. See here now especially Charles Walton, *Policing Public Opinion in the French Revolution: The Culture of Calumny and the Problem of Free Speech* (Oxford: Oxford University Press, 2011).
52. Hugh Gough, *The Newspaper Press in the French Revolution* (London: Routledge, 1988), p. 98.
53. Quoted Ruth Scurr, *Fatal Purity: Robespierre and the French Revolution* (London: Chatto & Windus, 2006), p. 255.
54. Hesse, 'Economic Upheavals', p. 93.
55. The collection of the Bibliothèque nationale de France alone numbers some 10,000 editions published in the years 1789–93, equivalent to a minimum of 10 million copies.
56. Gilles Feyel, 'La presse provincial au XVIIIe siècle', *Revue historique*, 272 (1984), pp. 353–74. For Lyon see Gough, *Newspaper Press*, p. 65.
57. Mason, *Singing the French Revolution*.
58. R. E. Foster, *Modern Ireland, 1600–1972* (London: Allen Lane, 1988), p. 282; Bernard Bailyn, *The Ideological Origins of the American Revolution* (Cambridge, MA: Belknap Press, 1967).

Chapter 17 How Samuel Sewall Read his Paper

1. M. Halsey Thomas (ed.), *The Diary of Samuel Sewall*, 2 vols (New York: Farrar, Straus & Giroux, 1973). The visit to Harvard is vol. I, pp. 501–2. Sewell's news world is described in Richard D. Brown, *Knowledge is Power: The Diffusion of Information in Early America, 1700–1865* (New York: Oxford University Press 1989), pp. 16–41.
2. Adam Fox, *Oral and Literate Culture in England, 1500–1700* (Oxford: Oxford University Press, 2000); Allyson Creasman, *Censorship and Civic Order in Reformation Germany, 1517–1648* (Aldershot: Ashgate, 2012); Chapter 6, above.
3. Emphasis added. Antonio Castillo Gómez, '"There are lots of papers going around and it'd be better if there weren't". Broadsides and Public Opinion in the Spanish Monarchy in the Seventeenth Century', in Massimo Rospocher (ed.), *Beyond the Public Sphere: Opinions, Publics, Spaces in Early Modern Europe* (Bologna: Mulino, 2012), p. 244.

4. Proverbs 18:21; 12:13.
5. R. Reichardt and H. Schneider, 'Chanson et musique populaires devant l'histoire à la fin de l'Ancien Regime', *Dix-huitième siècle*, 18 (1986), pp. 117–36; Robert Darnton, *Poetry and the Police: Communications Networks in Eighteenth-Century France* (Cambridge, MA: Belknap Press, 2010).
6. Mostly through the ground-breaking study of Paul Seaver, *Wallington's World: A Puritan Artisan in Seventeenth-Century London* (Stanford, CA: Stanford University Press, 1985); David Booy, *The Notebooks of Nehemiah Wallington, 1618–1654* (Aldershot: Ashgate, 2007), is an excellent selection from his unpublished journals.
7. The news-books, in particular, form the substantial part of R. Webb's edition of Wallington's *Historical notices of events occurring chiefly in the reign of Charles I* (London: Bentley, 1869).
8. Booy, *Notebooks*, p. 156.
9. His examination is retold in his *Historical notices*, pp. xxxviii–xlv.
10. Ibid., p. 242.
11. Ibid., pp. 52–3.
12. Ibid., pp. 152–3.
13. James Sutherland, *The Restoration Newspaper and its Development* (Cambridge: Cambridge University Press, 1986), pp. 98–9.
14. Booy, *Notebooks*, p. 101; *Historical notices*, pp. 148–9.
15. Sir Thomas Smith, *De Republicana Anglorum*, cited Seaver, *Wallington's World*, pp. 145–6.
16. *Historical notices*, pp. 11–12.
17. Ibid., pp. l–li.
18. Seaver, *Wallington's World*, pp. 104, 156.
19. Brown, *Knowledge*, p. 20.
20. *Diary of Samuel Sewall*, I, 256 (15 April 1690); 474–5 (15 September 1702).
21. Ibid., 58 (11 February 1685).
22. Ibid., 1,061–2 (23 June 1728).
23. Ibid., I, 78.
24. Sewall's set of early numbers of *The Boston News-Letter* is now in the library of the New York Historical Society.
25. Brown, *Knowledge*, p. 38.
26. Joop K. Koopmans, 'Supply and Speed of Foreign News in the Netherlands', in his *News and Politics in Early Modern Europe (1500–1800)* (Louvain: Peeters, 2005), pp. 185–201.
27. His news chronicle is examined in Jeroen Blaak, *Literacy in Everyday Life: Reading and Writing in early Modern Dutch Diaries* (Leiden: Brill, 2009), pp. 189–264.
28. In The Hague, Koninklijke Bibliotheek, Mss 71 A 8–12.
29. Blaak, *Literacy*, p. 211.
30. Ibid., p. 351 (tables 5 and 6).
31. Quoted Marcel Broersman, 'Constructing Public Opinion: Dutch Newspapers on the Eve of a Revolution (1780–1795)', in Joop W. Koopmans, *News and Politics in Early Modern Europe (1500–1800)* (Louvain: Peeters, 2005), p. 227.
32. Broersman, 'Constructing Public Opinion', pp. 229–30.
33. Above, Chapter 4.
34. See Roger Paas, *The German Political Broadsheet, 1600–1700*, 11 vols (Wiesbaden: O. Harrassowitz, 1985–2012).
35. Blaak, *Literacy*, p. 231.
36. Koopmans, 'Supply and Speed of Foreign News', pp. 200–1.
37. Ibid., p. 193.
38. See above, Chapter 5.
39. I. Atherton, 'The Itch Grown a Disease: Manuscript Transmission of News in the Seventeenth Century', *Prose Studies*, 21 (1998), p. 39; reprinted in Joad Raymond, *News, Newspapers, and Society in Early Modern Britain* (London: Frank Cass, 1999), pp. 39–65.

Conclusion

1. Quoted in Elizabeth L. Eisenstein, *Divine Art, Infernal Machine: The Reception of Printing in the West from First Impressions to the Sense of an Ending* (Philadelphia, PA: University of Pennsylvania Press, 2011), p. 199.
2. Ibid., p. 204.
3. From the *New York Herald*, 31 August 1835; Eisenstein, *Divine Art*, p. 208.
4. Stéphane Haffemayer, *L'information dans la France du XVIIe siècle: La Gazette de Renaudot de 1647 à 1663* (Paris: Champion, 2002), pp. 68–124, for the source of the Italian content in the Paris *Gazette*.
5. Antonio Castillo Gómez, ' "There are lots of papers going around and it'd be better if there weren't": Broadsides and Public Opinion in the Spanish Monarchy in the Seventeenth Century', in Massimo Rospocher (ed.), *Beyond the Public Sphere: Opinions, Publics, Spaces in Early Modern Europe (XVI–XVIII)* (Bologna: Mulino, 2012), pp. 230–4.
6. Andrew Hadfield, 'News of the Sussex Dragon', *Reformation*, 17 (2012), pp. 99–113.
7. Lucyle Werkmeister, *A Newspaper History of England, 1792–1793* (Lincoln, NB: University of Nebraska Press, 1967).
8. Marcus Daniel, *Scandal and Civility: Journalism and the Birth of American Democracy* (Oxford: Oxford University Press, 2009).
9. Eisenstein, *Divine Art*, p. 151.
10. Konstantin Dierks, *In My Power: Letter Writing and Communications in Early America* (Philadelphia, PA: University of Pennsylvania Press, 2009), p. 225.
11. Ibid.; Ian K. Steele, *The English Atlantic, 1675–1740: An Exploration of Communication and Community* (New York: Oxford University Press, 1986), pp. 113–31, 168–88.
12. Dierks, *In My Power*, pp. 189–234.
13. Eisenstein, *Divine Art*, p. 140.
14. Richard R. John, *Spreading the News: The American Postal System from Franklin to Morse* (Cambridge, MA: Harvard University Press, 1995).
15. Aileen Fyfe, *Steam-Powered Knowledge: William Chambers and the Business of Publishing, 1820–1860* (Chicago, IL: University of Chicago Press, 2012).
16. Eisenstein, *Divine Art*, Chapter 4.

Bibliography

Adema, Kees, *Netherlands Mail in Times of Turmoil. Vol. I: 1568–1795* (London: Stuart Rossiter Trust, 2010)

Akkerman, Nadine, 'The Postmistress, the Diplomat and a Black Chamber?: Alexandrine of Taxis, Sir Balthazar Gerbier and the Power of Postal Control', in Robyn Adams and Rosanna Cox (eds), *Diplomacy and Early Modern Culture* (Basingstoke: Palgrave, 2011), pp. 172–88

Albrecht, Peter and Holger Böning, *Historische Presse und ihre Leser: Studien zu Zeitungen und Zeitschriften, Intelligenzblättern und Kalendern in Nordwestdeutschland* (Bremen: Lumière, 2005)

Alford, Stephen, *The Watchers: A Secret History of the Reign of Elizabeth I* (London: Allen Lane, 2012)

Allen, E. John B., *Post and Courier Service in the Diplomacy of Early Modern Europe*, vol. 3 (The Hague: Nijhoff, International Archive of the History of Ideas, 1972)

Allen, Robert J., *The Clubs of Augustan London* (Hamden, CT: Archon, 1967)

Ancel, René, 'Étude critique sur quelques recueils d'avvisi', *Mélanges d'archéologie et d'histoire*, 28 (1908), pp. 115–39

Arblaster, Paul, *Antwerp and the World: Richard Verstegen and the International Culture of Catholic Reformation* (Louvain: Louvain University Press, 2004)

Arblaster, Paul, 'Posts, Newsletters, Newspapers: England in a European System of Communications', *Media History*, 11 (2005), pp. 21–36

Arblaster, Paul, 'Dat de boecken vrij sullen wesen: Private Profit, Public Utility and Secrets of State in the Seventeenth-Century Habsburg Netherlands', in Joop W. Koopmans (ed.), *News and Politics in Early Modern Europe (1500–1800)* (Louvain: Peeters, 2005)

Armstrong, C. A. J., 'Some Examples of the Distribution and Speed of News in England at the Time of the Wars of the Roses', in R. W. Hunt et al. (eds), *Studies in Medieval History Presented to Frederick Maurice Powicke* (Oxford: Oxford University Press, 1948), pp. 429–54, and his *England, France and Burgundy in the Fifteenth Century* (London: Hambledon, 1983), pp. 97–122

Aspinall, A., 'The Social Status of Journalists at the Beginning of the Nineteenth Century', *Review of English Studies*, 21 (1945), pp. 216–32

Aspinall, A., 'Statistical Accounts of the London Newspapers in the Eighteenth Century', *English Historical Review*, 62 (1948), pp. 201–32

Atherton, I., 'The Itch Grown a Disease: Manuscript Transmission of News in the Seventeenth Century', in Joad Raymond (ed.), *News, Newspapers, and Society in Early Modern Britain* (London: Frank Cass, 1999)

Bailly, Christian, *Théophraste Renaudot: un homme d'influence au temps de Louis XIII et de la Fronde* (Paris: Le Pré aux Clercs, 1987)

Bailyn, Bernard (ed.), *Pamphlets of the American Revolution, 1750–1776. Vol. 1: 1750–1765* (Cambridge, MA: Harvard University Press, 1965)

Bailyn, Bernard and John B. Hench (eds), *The Press and the American Revolution* (Worcester, MA: American Antiquarian Society, 1980)

Baker, K. M., *The French Revolution and the Creation of Modern Political Culture* (Oxford: Pergamon, 1984)

Baker, K. M., *Inventing the French Revolution* (Cambridge: Cambridge University Press, 1990)

Balsamo, Jean, 'Les origines parisiennes du Tesoro politico, 1589', *Bibliothèque d'Humanisme et Renaissance*, 57 (1995), pp. 7–23

Barbarics, Zsuzsa and Renate Pieper, 'Handwritten Newsletters as a Means of Communication in Early Modern Europe', in Francisco Bethercourt and Florike Egmond (eds), *Correspondence and Cultural Exchange in Europe, 1400–1700* (Cambridge: Cambridge University Press, 2007), pp. 53–79

Barker, Hannah, *Newspapers, Politics and Public Opinion in Late Eighteenth-Century England* (Oxford: Oxford University Press, 1998)

Barker, Hannah and Simon Burrows, *Press, Politics and the Public Sphere in Europe and North America, 1760–1820* (Cambridge: Cambridge University Press, 2002).

Bauer, Martin, 'Die 'gemain sag' in späteren Mittelalter. Studien zu eine Faktor mittelalterlicher Öffentlichkeit und seinem historischen Auskunftwert' (Diss., Erlangen-Nuremberg, 1981)

Bauer, Oswald, *Zeitungen vor der Zeitung. Die Fuggerzeitungen (1568–1605) und das frühmoderne Nachrichtensystem* (Berlin: Akademie Verlag, 2011)

Baumgartner, Frederic J., 'Henry II and the Papal Conclave of 1549', *Sixteenth Century Journal*, 16 (1985), pp. 301–14

Beale, Philip, *A History of the Post in England from the Romans to the Stuarts* (Aldershot: Ashgate, 1998)

Beale, Philip, Adrian Almond and Mike Scott Archer, *The Corsini Letters* (Stroud: Amberley, 2011)

Bec, Christian, *Les marchands écrivains. Affaires et humanisme à Florence, 1375–1434* (Paris: Mouton, 1967)

Becker, Marvin B., *The Emergence of Civil Society in the Eighteenth Century* (Bloomington, IN: Indiana University Press, 1994)

Behringer, Wolfgang, *Thurn und Taxis: Die Geschichte ihrer Post und ihrer Unternehmen* (Munich: Piper, 1990)

Behringer, Wolfgang, 'Brussel, Centrum van het internationale postnet', in *De Post van Thurn und Taxis. La poste des Tour et Tassis, 1489–1794* (Brussels: Archives Générales, 1992), pp. 21–42.

Behringer, Wolfgang, *Im Zeichen des Merkur: Reichspost und Kommunikationsrevolution in der Frühen Neuzeit* (Göttingen: Vandenhoeck & Ruprecht, 2003)

Behringer, Wolfgang, 'Communications Revolutions', *German History*, 24 (2006), pp. 333–74

Behringer, Wolfgang, 'Witchcraft and the Media', in Marjorie Plummer and Robin Barnes (eds), *Ideas and Cultural Margins in Early Modern Germany* (Aldershot: Ashgate, 2009), pp. 217–36

Beik, William, *Urban Protest in Seventeenth-Century France* (Cambridge: Cambridge University Press, 1997)

Beller, Elmer A., *Propaganda during the Thirty Years War* (Princeton, NJ: Princeton University Press, 1940)

Bennett, H. S., *The Pastons and their England: Studies in an Age of Transition* (Cambridge: Cambridge University Press, 1951)

Berry, Helen, *Gender, Society and Print Culture in Late Stuart England: The Cultural World of the 'Athenian Mercury'* (Aldershot: Ashgate, 2003)

Bertaud, Jean-Paul, 'An Open File: The Press under the Terror', in K. M. Baker (ed.), *The French Revolution and the Creation of Modern Political Culture. Vol. IV: The Terror* (Oxford: Pergamon, 1994), pp. 297–308

Bertaud, Jean-Paul, *La presse et le pouvoir de Louis XIII à Napoléon Ier* (Paris: Perrin, 2000)

Beyrer, Klaus and Martin Dallmeier, *Als die Post noch Zeitung machte. Eine Pressegeschichte* (Frankfurt am Main: Deutsches Postmuseums)

Bibliography of Studies of Eighteenth-Century Journalism and the Periodical Press, 1986–2009: *http://www.bibsocamer.org/BibSite/May/May-C18-jour.pdf*

Blaak, Jeroen, *Literacy in Everyday Life: Reading and Writing in Early Modern Dutch Diaries* (Leiden: Brill, 2009)

Black, Jeremy, *The English Press in the Eighteenth Century* (London: Croom Helm, 1987)

Bloemendal, Jan Peter, G. F. Eversmann and Else Strietman (eds), *Drama, Performance and Debate: Theatre and Public Opinion in the Early Modern Period* (Leiden: Brill, 2013)

Blühm, Elger, 'Deutscher Fürstenstaat und Presse im 17. Jahrhundert', *Hof, Staat und Gesellschaft in der Literatur des 17. Jahrhundert*, in *Daphnis*, 11 (1982), pp. 287–313

Blühm, Elger and Rolf Engelsing (eds), *Die Zeitung. Deutsche Urteile und Dokumente von den Anfängen bis zur Gegenwart* (Bremen: Schünemann, 1967)

Blum, A., *L'estampe satirique en France pendant les guerres de religion* (Paris: M. Giard and E. Briere, 1916)

Bödeker, Hans Erich, 'Journals and Public Opinion: The Politicization of the German Enlightenment in the Second Half of the Eighteenth Century', in Eckhart Hellmuth (ed.), *The Transformation of Political Culture: England and Germany in the Late Eighteenth Century* (Oxford: Oxford University Press, 1990), pp. 423–46

Bogel, Else, *Schweizer Zeitungen des 17. Jahrhunderts. Beiträge zur frühen Pressegeschichte von Zürich, Basel, Bern, Schaffhausen, St. Gallen und Solothurn* (Bremen: Schünemann, 1973)

Bogel, Else and Elgar Blühm, *Die deutschen Zeitungen des 17. Jahrhunderts. Ein Bestandverzeichnis*, 2 vols (Bremen: Schünemann, 1971); *Nachtrag* (Munich: Saur, 1985)

Bond, Richmond P. (ed,), *Studies in the Early English Periodical* (Westport, CT: Greenwood Press, 1957)

Bond, Richmond P., *Tatler: The Making of a Literary Journal* (Cambridge, MA: Harvard University Press, 1972)

Böning, Holger, *Deutsche Presse. Biobibliographische Handbücher zur Geschichte der deutschsprachigen periodischen Presse von den Anfängen bis 1815*, 6 vols (Stuttgart-Bad Cannstatt: Frommann-Holzboog, 1996–2003)

Booy, David, *The Notebooks of Nehemiah Wallington, 1618–1654* (Aldershot: Ashgate, 2007)

Borreguero Beltrán, Christina, 'Philip of Spain: The Spider's Web of News and Information', in Brendan Dooley (ed.), *The Dissemination of News and the Emergence of Contemporaneity in Early Modern Europe* (Aldershot: Ashgate, 2010), pp. 23–49

Botein, Stephen, Jack R. Censer and Harriet Ritvo, 'The Periodical Press in Eighteenth-Century English and French Society: A Cross-Cultural Approach', *Comparative Studies in Society and History*, 23 (1981), pp. 464–90

Boys, Jayne E. E., *London's News Press and the Thirty Years War* (Woodbridge: Boydell, 2011)

Brant, Clare, *Eighteenth-Century Letters and British Culture* (Basingstoke: Palgrave Macmillan, 2006)

Brayshay, Mark, 'Royal Post-Horse Routes in England and Wales: The Evolution of the Network in the Later Sixteenth and Early Seventeenth Century', *Journal of Historical Geography*, 17, 4 (1991), pp. 373–89

Brennan, Thomas, *Public Drinking and Popular Culture in Eighteenth-Century Paris* (Princeton, NJ: Princeton University Press, 1988)

Brewer, John, 'The Commercialization of Politics', in Neil McKendrick and John Brewer (eds), *The Birth of a Consumer Society* (London: Hutchinson, 1982)

Brewer, John, *The Pleasures of the Imagination: English Culture in the Eighteenth Century* (London: HarperCollins, 1997)

Brigham, Clarence S., *History and Bibliography of American Newspapers, 1690–1820*, 2 vols (London: Archon Books, 1962)

Broersman, Marcel, 'Constructing Public Opinion: Dutch Newspapers on the Eve of a Revolution (1780–1795)', in Joop W. Koopmans, *News and Politics in Early Modern Europe (1500–1800)* (Louvain: Peeters, 2005)

Brown, James R., 'Drinking houses and the politics of surveillance in pre-industrial Southampton', in Beat Kümin (ed.), *Political Space in Pre-Industrial Europe* (Aldershot: Ashgate, 2009)

Brown, Richard D., *Knowledge is Power: The Diffusion of Information in Early America, 1700–1865* (New York: Oxford University Press, 1989)

Brownlees, Nicholas, *Corantos and Newsbooks: Language and Discourse in the First English Newspapers (1620–1641)* (Pisa: Ets, 1999)

Brownlees, Nicholas, *The Language of Periodical News in Seventeenth-Century England* (Newcastle: Cambridge Scholars, 2011)

Brun, Robert A., 'A Fourteenth-Century Merchant of Italy: Francesco Datini of Prato', *Journal of Economic and Business History*, 2 (1930), pp. 451–66

Budelot, Suzanne, *Messageries universitaires et messageries royales* (Paris: Domat 1934)

Burke, Peter, *The Fabrication of Louis XIV* (New Haven, CT: Yale University Press, 1992)

Burke, Peter, 'Early Modern Venice as a Centre of Information and Communication', in John Martin and Dennis Romano (eds), *Venice Reconsidered: The History and Civilization of an Italian City-State, 1297–1797* (Baltimore, MD: Johns Hopkins University Press, 2000), pp. 389–419

Burn, Jacob Henry, *A Descriptive Catalogue of the London Traders, Tavern, and Coffee-House Tokens, Current in the Seventeenth Century* (London: Arthur Taylor, 1855)

Burrows, Simon, 'Police and Political Pamphleteering in Pre-Revolutionary France', in David Adams and Adrian Armstrong (eds), *Print and Power in France and England, 1500–1800* (Aldershot: Ashgate, 2006), pp. 99–112

Calhoun, Craig (ed.), *Habermas and the Public Sphere* (Cambridge, MA: Harvard University Press, 1992)

Campbell, Peter R., *Power and Politics in Old Regime France, 1720–1745* (London: Routledge, 1996)

Campbell-Smith, Duncan, *Masters of the Post: The Authorised History of the Royal Mail* (London: Allen Lane, 2011)

Capp, B. S., *Astrology and the Popular Press: English Almanacs, 1500–1800* (London: Faber and Faber, 1979)

Carey, James, *Communication as Culture: Essays on Media and Society* (Cambridge, MA: Harvard University Press, 1988)

Carlson, C. Lennart, *The First Magazine: A History of the Gentleman's Magazine* (Providence, RI: Brown, 1938)

Carrier, Hubert, *La presse et la Fronde, 1648–1653: Les Mazarinades. I. La conquête de l'opinion* (Geneva: Droz, 1989)

Carrier, Hubert, *La presse et la Fronde: Les Mazarinades, II. Les hommes du livre* (Geneva: Droz, 1991)

Carswell, John, *The South Sea Bubble*, 2nd edn (Stroud: Alan Sutton, 1993)

Cash, Arthur H., *John Wilkes: The Scandalous Father of Civil Liberties* (New Haven, CT: Yale University Press, 2006)

Censer, Jack R., 'Recent Approaches to the Eighteenth-Century Press', *Comparative Studies in Society and History*, 31 (1989), pp. 775–83

Censer, Jack R., *The French Press in the Age of Enlightenment* (London: Routledge, 1994)

Chandler, Bernard, 'A Renaissance News Correspondent', *Italica*, 29 (1952), pp. 158–63

Chisick, Harvey, 'The Pamphlet Literature of the French Revolution: An Overview', in *History of European Ideas*, 17 (1993), pp. 149–66

Chisick, Harvey (ed.), *The Press in the French Revolution* (Oxford: Voltaire Foundation, 1991)

Christ, George, 'A Newsletter in 1419? Antonio Morosini's Chronicle in the Light of Commercial Correspondence between Venice and Alexandria', *Mediterranean Historical Review*, 20 (2005), pp. 35–66

La Circulation des nouvelles au moyen âge (Paris: Sorbonne, 1994)

Clark, Charles C., *The Public Prints: The Newspaper in Anglo-American Culture, 1665–1740* (New York: Oxford University Press, 1994)

Clark, Charles E. and Charles Wetherall, 'The Measure of Maturity: The *Pennsylvania Gazette*, 1728–1765', *William & Mary Quarterly*, 3rd ser., 61 (1989), pp. 279–303

Clark, Charles E. and Richard D. Brown, 'Periodicals and Politics', in Hugh Amory and David A. Hall (eds), *A History of the Book in America. Vol. 1: The Colonial Book in the Atlantic World* (Cambridge: Cambridge University Press, 2000), pp. 347–76

Clark, Peter, *The English Alehouse: A Social History, 1200–1830* (London: Longman, 1983)

Clark, Peter (ed.), *Small Towns in Early Modern Europe* (Cambridge: Cambridge University Press, 1995)

Clarke, Bob, *From Grub Street to Fleet Street: An Illustrated History of English Newspapers to 1899* (Aldershot: Ashgate, 2004)

Clayton, Tony, 'The Sermon, the "Public Sphere" and the Political Culture of Late Seventeenth-Century England', in L. A. Ferrell and P. McCullough (eds), *The English Sermon Revised: Religious Literature and History, 1600–1750* (Manchester: Manchester University Press, 2001), pp. 208–34

Clegg, Cyndia, *Press Censorship in Elizabethan England* (Cambridge: Cambridge University Press, 1997)

Clegg, Cyndia, *Press Censorship in Jacobean England* (Cambridge: Cambridge University Press, 2001)

Clegg, Cyndia, *Press Censorship in Caroline England* (Cambridge: Cambridge University Press, 2008)

Cogswell, Thomas, '"Published by Authoritie": Newsbooks and the Duke of Buckingham's Expedition to the Île de Ré', *Huntington Library Quarterly*, 67 (2004), pp. 1–26

Corvisier, André, *Louvois* (Paris: Fayard, 1983), pp. 222–40

Couvée, D. H., 'The Administration of the *Oprechte Haarlemse Courant*, 1738–42', *Gazette*, 4 (1958), pp. 91–110

Couvée, D. H., 'The First Couranteers – The Flow of the News in the 1620s', *Gazette*, 8 (1962), pp. 22–36

Cowan, Brian, *The Social Life of Coffee: The Emergence of the British Coffeehouse* (New Haven, CT, and London: Yale University Press, 2005)

Cranfield, G. A., *The Development of the Provincial Newspaper, 1700–1760* (Oxford: Oxford University Press, 1962)

Cranfield, G. A., 'The *London Evening Post*, 1727–1744: A Study in the Development of the Political Press', *Historical Journal*, 6 (1963), pp. 20–37

Crawford, Julie, *Marvelous Protestantism: Monstrous Births in Post-Reformation England* (Baltimore, MD: Johns Hopkins University Press, 2005)

Creasman, Allyson F., 'Lies as Truth: Policing Print and Oral Culture in the Early Modern City', in Marjorie Plummer and Robin Barnes (eds), *Ideas and Cultural Margins in Early Modern Germany* (Aldershot: Ashgate, 2009), pp. 255–70

Creasman, Allyson, *Censorship and Civic Order in Reformation Germany, 1517–1648* (Aldershot: Ashgate, 2012)

Cressy, David, *Agnes Bowker's Cat: Travesties and Transgressions in Tudor and Stuart England* (Oxford: Oxford University Press, 2000)

Crossley, Nick and John Michael Roberts, *After Habermas: New Perspectives on the Public Sphere* (Oxford: Blackwell, 2004)

Cunningham, Andrew and Ole Peter Grell, *The Four Horsemen of the Apocalypse: Religion, War, Famine and Death in Reformation Europe* (Cambridge: Cambridge University Press, 2000), pp. 170–99

Curth, Louise, *English Almanacs, Astrology and Popular Medicine, 1550–1700* (Manchester: Manchester University Press, 2007)

Cust, R., 'News and Politics in Early Seventeenth-Century England', *Past and Present*, 112 (1986), pp. 60–90

Damme, K. van and J. Deploige, '"Slecht nieuws geen nieuws." Abraham Verhoeven (1575–1652) en de *Nieuwe Tijdinghen*: periodieke pers en propaganda in de Zuidelijke Nederlanden tijdens de vroege zeventiende eeuw', *Bijdragen en mededelinghen betreffende de geschiedenis der Nederlanden*, 113 (1998), pp. 1–22

Dahl, Folke, 'Amsterdam, Earliest Newspaper Centre of Western Europe: New Contributions to the History of the First Dutch and French Corantos', *Het Boek*, XXV (1939), III, pp. 161–97

Dahl, Folke, *Dutch Corantos, 1618–1650: A Bibliography Illustrated with 334 Facsimile Reproductions of Corantos Printed 1618–1625, and an Introductory Essay on 17th-Century Stop Press News* (The Hague: Koninklijke Bibliotheek, 1946)

Dahl, Folke, *A Bibliography of English Corantos and Periodical Newsbooks, 1620–1642* (London: Bibliographical Society, 1952)

Dahl, Folke, *The Birth of the European Press as Reflected in the Newspaper Collection of the Royal Library* (Stockholm: Rundqvists Boktryckeri, 1960)

Dahl, Folke, Fanny Petibon and Marguerite Boulet, *Les débuts de la presse française. Nouveaux aperçus* (*Acta Bibliothecae Gotoburgensis*, 4; Paris: Raymann, 1951)

Dahl, Gunnar, *Trade, Trust and Networks: Commercial Cultures in Late Medieval Italy* (Lund: Nordic Academic Press, 1998)

Dallmeier, Martin, 'Die Funktion der Reichspost für den Hof und die Öffentlichkeit', *Daphnis*, 11 (1982), pp. 399–431

Daniel, Marcus, *Scandal and Civility: Journalism and the Birth of American Democracy* (Oxford: Oxford University Press, 2009)

Darnton, Robert, 'L'imprimerie de Panckoucke en l'an II', *Revue française d'histoire du livre*, 23 (1979), pp. 359–69

Darnton, Robert, 'The High Enlightenment and the Low Life of Literature', in *The Literary Underground of the Old Regime* (Cambridge, MA: Harvard University Press, 1982), pp. 1–40

Darnton, Robert, 'The Facts of Literary Life in Eighteenth-Century France', in Keith Michael Baker (ed.), *The French Revolution and the Creation of Modern Political Culture. Vol. I: The Political Culture of the Old Regime* (Oxford: Oxford University Press, 1987), pp. 261–92

Darnton, Robert, *Poetry and the Police: Communications Networks in Eighteenth-Century France* (Cambridge, MA: Belknap Press, 2010)

Darnton, Robert and Daniel Roche (eds), *Revolution in Print: The Press in France, 1775–1800* (Berkeley, CA: University of California Press, 1989)

Daston, Lorraine and Katharine Park, *Wonders and the Order of Nature, 1150–1750* (New York: Zone, 2001)

Dauser, Regina, *Informationskultur und Beziehungswissen: Das Korrespondenznetz Hans Fuggers (1531–1598)* (Tübingen: Max Niemeyer Verlag, 2008)

Davidson, Philip, *Propaganda and the American Revolution, 1763–1783* (Chapel Hill, NC: University of North Carolina Press, 1941)

Davies, Norman, *Paston Letters* (Oxford: Oxford University Press, 1958)

Deazley, Ronan, Martin Kretschmer and Lionel Bently, *Privilege and Property: Essays on the History of Copyright* (Cambridge: Openbooks, 2010)

Deen, Femke, David Onnekink and Michel Reinders (eds), *Pamphlets and Politics in the Dutch Republic* (Leiden: Brill, 2011)

Delumeau, Jean, *Vie économique et sociale de Rome dans la seconde moitié du XVIe siècle* (Paris: Boccard, 1957–9), pp. 37–53

Dickinson, H. T., *Caricatures and the Constitution, 1760–1832* (Cambridge: Chadwyck-Healey, 1986)

Dierks, Konstantin, *In My Power: Letter Writing and Communications in Early America* (Philadelphia, PA: University of Pennsylvania Press, 2009)

Doherty, Francis, *A Study in Eighteenth-Century Advertising Methods* (Leviston: Mellen, 1992)

Doig, J. A., 'Political Propaganda and Royal Proclamations in Late Medieval England', *Historical Research*, 71 (1998), pp. 253–80

Dooley, Brendan, *The Social History of Skepticism: Experience and Doubt in Early Modern Culture* (Baltimore, MD: Johns Hopkins University Press, 1999)

Dooley, Brendan, 'The Public Sphere and the Organisation of Knowledge', in John A. Marino, *Early Modern Italy, 1550–1796* (Oxford: Oxford University Press, 2002), pp. 209–28

Dooley, Brendan (ed.), *The Dissemination of News and the Emergence of Contemporaneity in Early Modern Europe* (Aldershot: Ashgate, 2010)

Dooley, Brendan and Sabrina Baron (eds), *The Politics of Information in Early Modern Europe* (London: Routledge, 2001)

Dover, Paul M., 'Philip II, Information Overload and the Early Modern Moment', in Tonio Andrade and William Reger (eds), *The Limits of Empire: European Imperial Formations in Early Modern World History: Essays in Honour of Geoffrey Parker* (Farnham: Ashgate, 2012), pp. 99–120

Downie, J. A., *Robert Harley and the Press: Propaganda and Public Opinion in the Age of Swift and Defoe* (Cambridge: Cambridge University Press, 1979)

Downie, J. A., *Jonathan Swift, Political Writer* (London: Routledge, 1985)

Downie, J. A., 'Periodicals and Politics in the Reign of Queen Anne', in Robin Myers and Michael Harris (eds), *Serials and their Readers, 1620–1914* (Winchester: St Paul's Bibliographies, 1993), pp. 63–81

Downie, J. A. and T. N. Corns (eds), *Telling People What to Think: Early Eighteenth-Century Periodicals from the Review to the Rambler* (London: Frank Cass, 1993)

Dresler, Adolf, 'Die Neue Zeitung des Postmeisters Pelegrin de Tassis aus Rom von 1527', *Archiv für Postgeschichte in Bayern*, nf 1 (1954), p. 29

Droste, Heiko, 'Degrees of Publicity: Handwritten Newspapers in the Seventeenth and Eighteenth Centuries', *LIR Journal* (2012), pp. 68–83

Droste, Heiko (ed.), *Connecting the Baltic Area: The Swedish Postal System in the Seventeenth Century* (Huddinge: Södertörns högskola, 2011)

Duccini, Hélène, *Faire voir, faire croire: l'opinion publique sous Louis XIII* (Seyssel: Champ Vallon, 2003)

Duke, A. C. and C. A. Tamse, *Too Mighty to Be Free: Censorship and the Press in Britain and the Netherlands* (Zutphen: Walburg Pers, 1987)

Earle, Peter, *The World of Defoe* (London: Weidenfeld & Nicolson, 1976)

Eeghen, I. H. van, 'De Amsterdamse Courant in de achttiende eeuw', *Jaarboek Amstelodamum*, 44 (1950), pp. 31–58

Eisenstein, Elizabeth L., *Grub Street Abroad: Aspects of the French Cosmopolitan Press from the Age of Louis XIV to the French Revolution* (Oxford: Clarendon Press, 1992)

Eisenstein, Elizabeth L., *Divine Art, Infernal Machine: The Reception of Printing in the West from First Impressions to the Sense of an Ending* (Philadelphia, PA: University of Pennsylvania Press, 2011)

Elliott, Blanche B., *A History of English Advertising* (London: Batsford, 1962)

Ellis, Aytoun, *The Penny Universities: A History of the Coffee-House* (London: Secker & Warburg, 1956)

Elton, G. R., *Policy and Police: The Enforcement of the Reformation in the Age of Thomas Cromwell* (Cambridge: Cambridge University Press, 1972)

Emery, Edwin, *The Press and America: An Interpretative History of the Mass Media* (Englewood Cliffs, NJ: Prentice-Hall, 1972)

Ettinghausen, Henry, 'The Illustrated Spanish News: Text and Image in the Seventeenth-Century Press', in Charles Davis and Paul Julian Smith (eds), *Art and Literature in Spain, 1600–1800: Studies in Honour of Nigel Glendinning* (London: Tamesis, 1993), pp. 117–33

Everitt, Alan, 'The English Urban Inn, 1560–1760', in idem, *Perspectives in English Urban History* (London: Macmillan, 1973), pp. 91–137

Ewald, William B., *The Newsmen of Queen Anne* (Oxford: Basil Blackwell, 1956)

Farge, Arlette, *Subversive Words: Public Opinion in Eighteenth-Century France* (London: Polity Press, 1994)

Faulstich, Werner, *Medien und Öffentlichkeiten im Mittelalter* (Göttingen: Vandenhoek & Ruprecht, 1996)

Feather, John, *The Provincial Book Trade in Eighteenth-Century England* (Cambridge: Cambridge University Press, 1985)

Feather, John P., 'From Censorship to Copyright: Aspects of the Government's Role in the English Book Trade, 1695–1775', in Kenneth E. Carpenter (ed.), *Books and Society in History* (New York: Bowker, 1983)

Fenlon, Iain, *The Ceremonial City: History, Memory and Myth in Renaissance Venice* (New Haven, CT, and London: Yale University Press, 2007)

Ferdinand, Christine, *Benjamin Collins and the Provincial Newspaper Trade in the Eighteenth Century* (Oxford: Oxford University Press, 1997)

Fett, Denice, 'Information, Gossip and Rumor: The Limits of Intelligence at the Early Modern Court', in Tonio Andrade and William Reger (eds), *The Limits of Empire: European Imperial Formations in Early Modern World History: Essays in Honour of Geoffrey Parker* (Farnham: Ashgate, 2012), pp. 79–98

Feyel, Gilles, *L'annonce et la nouvelle. La presse d'information en France sous l'ancien régime (1630–1788)* (Oxford: Voltaire Foundation, 2000)

Fischer, Ernst, Wilhelm Haefs and York-Gthart Mix (eds), *Von Almanach bis Zeitung. Ein Handbuch der Medien in Deutschland 1700–1800* (Munich: Beck, 1999)

Fischer, Heinz Dietrich, *Deutsche Zeitungen des 17. bis 20. Jahrhunderts* (Pullach bei München: Verlag Dokumentation, 1972)

Fisher, Alexander J., 'Song, Confession and Criminality: Trial Records as Sources for Popular Music Culture in Early Modern Europe', *Journal of Musicology*, 18 (2001), pp. 616–57

Fitzler, Mathilde A. H., *Die Entstehung der sogennanten Fuggerzeitungen in der Wiener Nationalbibliothek* (Baden bei Wien: Rohrer, 1937)

Fletcher, Catherine, 'War, Diplomacy and Social Mobility: The Casali Family in the Service of Henry VIII', *Journal of Early Modern History*, 14 (2010), pp. 559–78

Fowler, K. A., 'News from the Front: Letters and Despatches of the Fourteenth Century', in Pierre Contamine (ed.), *Guerre et société en France, en Angleterre et en Bourgogne* (Lille: Villeneuve d'Ascq: Université Charles de Gaulle Lille III, 1991), pp. 63–92

Fox, Adam, 'Rumour, News and Popular Political Opinion in Elizabethan and Early Stuart England', *Historical Journal*, 40 (1997), pp. 597–620

Fox, Adam, *Oral and Literate Culture in England, 1500–1700* (Oxford: Oxford University Press, 2000)

Fragnito, Gigliola, *Church, Censorship and Culture in Early Modern Italy* (Cambridge: Cambridge University Press, 2001)

Frank, Joseph, *The Beginnings of the English Newspaper, 1620–1660* (Cambridge, MA: Harvard University Press, 1961)

Fraser, Peter, *The Intelligence of the Secretaries of State and their Monopoly of Licensed News, 1660–1688* (Cambridge: Cambridge University Press, 1956)

Frearson, Michael, 'The Distribution and Readership of London Corantos in the 1620s', in Robin Myers and Michael Harris (eds), *Serials and their Readers, 1620–1914* (Winchester: St Paul's Bibliographies, 1993), pp. 1–25

Freist, Dagmar, *Governed by Opinion: Politics, Religion, and the Dynamics of Communication in Stuart London, 1637–1645* (London: I.B. Tauris, 1997)

Friedland, Paul, *Seeing Justice Done: The Age of Spectacular Capital Punishment in France* (Oxford: Oxford University Press, 2012)

Geisberg, Max, *The German Single-Leaf Woodcut, 1500–1550*, 4 vols (New York: Hacker, 1974)

Given-Wilson, Chris, *Chronicles: The Writing of History in Medieval England* (London: Hambledon, 2004)

Goldgar, Anne, 'The Absolutism of Taste: Journalists as Censors in 18th-Century Paris', in Robin Myers and Michael Harris (eds), *Censorship and the Control of Print in England and France, 1600–1910* (Winchester: St Paul's, 1992)

Goldie, Mark, 'Roger L'Estrange's *Observator* and the Exorcism of the Plot', in Anne Dunan-Page and Beth Lynch (eds), *Roger L'Estrange and the Making of Restoration Culture* (Aldershot: Ashgate, 2008), pp. 67–88

Göllner, Carl, *Turcica. Die europäischen Türkendrucke des XVI Jahrhunderts*, 3 vols (Bucharest: Academiei, 1961–78)

Gómez, Antonio Castillo, '"There are lots of papers going around and it'd be better if there weren't": Broadsides and Public Opinion in the Spanish Monarchy in the Seventeenth Century', in Massimo Rospocher (ed.), *Beyond the Public Sphere: Opinions, Publics, Spaces in Early Modern Europe (XVI–XVIII)* (Bologna: Mulino, 2012), pp. 227–48

Gough, Hugh, *The Newspaper Press in the French Revolution* (London: Routledge, 1988)

Gough, Hugh, 'The French Revolutionary Press', in Hannah Barker and Simon Burrows (eds), *Press, Politics and the Public Sphere in Europe and North America, 1760–1820* (Cambridge: Cambridge University Press, 2002), pp. 182–200

Greenlaw, Ralph M., 'Pamphlet Literature in France during the Period of the Aristocratic Revolt (1787–1788)', *Journal of Modern History*, 29 (1957), pp. 349–54

Greenspan, Nicole, *Selling Cromwell's Wars: Media, Empire and Godly Warfare, 1650–1658* (London: Pickering & Chatto, 2012)

Grendler, Paul, *The Roman Inquisition and the Venetian Press, 1540–1605* (Princeton, NJ: Princeton University Press, 1977)

Grendler, Paul, *Culture and Censorship in Late Renaissance Italy and France* (London: Variorum, 1981)

Griffin, Clive, *Journeymen Printers, Heresy and the Inquisition in Sixteenth-Century Spain* (Oxford: Oxford University Press, 2005)

Griffiths, Denis, *Fleet Street: Five Hundred Years of the Press* (London: British Library, 2006)

Groesen, Michiel van, 'A Week to Remember: Dutch Publishers and the Competition for News from Brazil, 26 August–2 September 1624', *Quaerendo*, 40 (2010), pp. 26–49

Grunzweig, A., *Correspondance de la filiale de Bruges de Medici* (Brussels: Lamertin, 1931)

Gunn, J. A. W., *Queen of the World: Opinion in the Public Life of France from the Renaissance to the Revolution* (Oxford: Studies on Voltaire and the Eighteenth Century, 328, 1995)

Gunn, Steven J., David Grummitt and Hans Cool, *War, State, and Society in England and the Netherlands 1477–1559* (Oxford: Oxford University Press, 2007)

Habel, Thomas, *Gelehrte Journale und Zeitungen der Aufklärung. Zur Entstehung, Entwicklung und Erschliessung deutschsprachiger Rezensionszeitungen des 18. Jahrhunderts* (Bremen: Édition Lumière, 2007)

Häberlein, Mark, *The Fuggers of Augsburg: Pursuing Wealth and Honor in Renaissance Germany* (Charlottesville, VA: University of Virginia Press, 2012)

Hadfield, Andrew, 'News of the Sussex Dragon', *Reformation*, 17 (2012), pp. 99–113

Haffemayer, Stéphane, *L'information dans la France du XVIIe siècle: La Gazette de Renaudot de 1647 à 1663* (Paris: Champion, 2002)

Haks, Donald, 'War, Government and the News: The Dutch Republic and the War of the Spanish Succession, 1702–1713' in Joop W. Koopmans, *News and Politics in Early Modern Europe (1500–1800)* (Louvain: Peeters, 2005)

Halasz, Alexandra, *The Marketplace of Print: Pamphlets and the Public Sphere in Early Modern England* (Cambridge: Cambridge University Press, 1997)

Hamy, E.-T. (ed.), 'Itinéraire de Bruges', in Gilles le Bouvier, *Le livre de la description des pays* (Paris: Leroux, 1908), pp. 157–216

Handover, P. M., *A History of the London Gazette, 1665–1965* (London: HMSO, 1965)

Hannis, Grant, 'Daniel Defoe's Pioneering Consumer Journalism in the *Review*', *British Journal for Eighteenth-Century Studies*, 30 (2007), pp. 13–26

Hanson, Laurence, *Government and the Press, 1695–1763* (Oxford: Oxford University Press, 1936; 1967)

Harline, Craig E., *Pamphlets, Printing, and Political Culture in the Early Dutch Republic* (Dordrecht: M. Nijhoff, 1987)

Harris, Bob, *Politics and the Rise of the Press: Britain and France, 1620–1800* (London: Routledge, 1996)

Harris, Michael, *London Newspapers in the Age of Walpole: A Study of the Origins of the Modern English Press* (London: Associated University Presses, 1987)

Harris, Michael, 'Timely Notices: The Uses of Advertising and its Relationship to News during the Late Seventeenth Century', *Prose Studies*, 21 (1998), pp. 141–56

Harris, Robert, *A Patriot Press: National Politics and the London Press in the 1740s* (Oxford: Oxford University Press, 1993)

Harris, Tim, *London Crowds in the Reign of Charles II: Propaganda and Politics from the Restoration until the Exclusion Crisis* (Cambridge: Cambridge University Press, 1987)

Haskins, C. H., 'The Lives of Medieval Students as Illustrated in their Letters', in his *Studies in Mediaeval Culture* (1929), pp. 1–35

Haynes, Alan, *Invisible Power: The Elizabethan Secret Services, c.1570–1603* (Stroud: Sutton, 1992)

Haywood, Eliza, *The Female Spectator*, ed. Gabrielle M. Firmager (Melksham: Bristol Classical Press, 1993)

Heise, Ulla, *Kaffee und Kaffeehaus. Eine Kulturgeschichte* (Hildesheim: Olms, 1987)

Helmers, Helmer, *The Royalist Republic: Literature, Politics and Religion in the Anglo-Dutch Public Sphere (1639–1660)* (Leiden: Leiden University Institute for Cultural Disciplines, 2011)

Hinds, Peter, 'Tales and Romantick Stories: Impostures, Trustworthiness and the Credibility of Information in the Late Seventeenth Century', in Anne Dunan-Page and Beth Lynch (eds), *Roger L'Estrange and the Making of Restoration Culture* (Aldershot: Ashgate, 2008), pp. 89–107

Hinds, Peter, *The Horrid Popish Plot: Roger L'Estrange and the Circulation of Political Discourse in Late Seventeenth-Century London* (Oxford: Oxford University Press, 2010)

Holmes, George, 'A Letter from Lucca to London in 1303', in Peter Denley and Caroline Elam (eds), *Florence and Italy: Renaissance Studies in Honour of Nicolai Rubinstein* (London: University of London Press, 1988), pp. 227–33

Hoppit, Julian, 'The Myths of the South Sea Bubble', *Transactions of the Royal Historical Society*, 6th ser., 12 (2002), pp. 141–65

Hunt, Edwin S., *The Medieval Super-Companies: A Study of the Peruzzi Company of Florence* (Cambridge: Cambridge University Press, 1994)

Hunt, Tamara L., *Defining John Bull: Political Caricature and National Identity in Late Georgian England* (Aldershot: Ashgate, 2003)

Hunter, J. Paul, *Before Novels: The Cultural Contexts of Eighteenth-Century English Fiction* (New York: Norton, 1990)

Hyde, J. Kenneth, 'The Role of Diplomatic Correspondence and Reporting: News and Chronicles', in his *Literacy and its Uses: Studies on Late Medieval Italy* (Manchester: Manchester University Press, 1993), pp. 217–59

Infelise, Mario, 'Le marché des informations à Venise au XVIIe siècle', in H. Duraton and P. Rétat (eds), *Gazettes et information politique sous l'Ancien Régime* (Saint-Etienne: Université de Saint-Etienne, 1999)

Infelise, Mario, 'The War, the News and the Curious: Military Gazettes in Italy', in B. Dooley and S. Baron (eds), *The Politics of Information in Early Modern Europe* (London: Routledge, 2001)

Infelise, Mario, *Prima dei giornali: alle origini della pubblica informazione (secoli XVI e XVII)* (Rome: Laterza, 2002)

Infelise, Mario, 'Roman Avvisi: Information and Politics in the Seventeenth Century', in Gianvittorio Signorotto and Maria Antonietta Visceglia (eds), *Court and Politics in Papal Rome, 1400–1800* (Cambridge: Cambridge University Press, 2002)

Infelise, Mario, 'From Merchants' Letters to Handwritten Political Avvisi: Notes on the Origins of Public Information', in Francisco Bethercourt and Florike Egmond (eds), *Correspondence and Cultural Exchange in Europe, 1400–1700* (Cambridge: Cambridge University Press, 2007), pp. 33–52

Infelise, Mario, 'Gazettes et information politique en Italie du XVIe au XVIIe siècle', in V. Millot, P. Minard and M. Porret (eds), *La grande chevauchée: faire de l'histoire avec Daniel Roche* (Geneva: Droz, 2011)

Jacob, Heinrich, *Coffee: The Epic of a Commodity* (London, 1935; reprinted Short Hills, NJ: Burford Books, 1998)

James, Carolyn (ed.), *The Letters of Giovanni Sabadino degli Arienti (1481–1510)* (Florence: Olschki, 2001)

Jensen, De Lamar, *Diplomacy and Dogmatism: Bernardino de Mendoza and the French Catholic League* (Cambridge, MA: Harvard University Press, 1964)

Jensen, Janus Møller, *Denmark and the Crusades, 1400–1650* (Leiden: Brill, 2007)

John, Richard R., *Spreading the News: The American Postal System from Franklin to Morse* (Cambridge, MA: Harvard University Press, 1975)

Jones, Colin, 'The Great Chain of Buying: Medical Advertisement, the Bourgeois Public Sphere, and the Origins of the French Revolution', *American Historical Review*, 101 (1996), pp. 13–40

Jones, Colin, *Contre Retz: sept pamphlets du temps de la Fronde* (Exeter: University of Exeter Press, 1982)

Jones, Norman, *The Birth of the Elizabethan Age: England in the 1560s* (Oxford: Blackwell, 1993)

Jouhaud, Christian, *Mazarinades: la Fronde des mots* (Paris: Aubier, 1985)

Jouhaud, Christian, 'Printing the Event: From La Rochelle to Paris', in Roger Chartier (ed.), *The Culture of Print: Power and Uses of Print in Early Modern Europe* (Princeton, NJ: Princeton University Press, 1989), pp. 290–333

Jouhaud, Christian, 'Readability and Persuasion: Political Handbills', in Roger Chartier (ed.), *The Culture of Print: Power and Uses of Print in Early Modern Europe* (Princeton, NJ: Princeton University Press, 1989), pp. 235–60

Jusserand, J. J., *English Wayfaring Life in the Middle Ages* (London: Unwin, 1901)

Kelly, Ian, *Mr Foote's Other Leg: Comedy, Tragedy and Murder in Georgian London* (Basingstoke: Picador, 2012)

Kemp, Peter, 'L'Estrange and the Publishing Sphere', in Jason McElligott (ed.), *Fear, Exclusion and Revolution* (Aldershot: Ashgate, 2006), pp. 67–90

Kingdon, Robert, *Myths about the St. Bartholomew's Day Massacres, 1572–1576* (Cambridge, MA: Harvard University Press, 1988)

Kirchner, Joachim, *Das Deutsche Zeitschriftenwesen. Seine Geschichte und seine Probleme. I: Von den Anfängen bis zum Zeitalter der Romantik* (Wiesbaden: Harrassowitz, 1958)

Kitch, Aaron W., 'Printing Bastards: Monstrous Birth Broadsides in Early Modern England', in Douglas A. Brooks (ed.), *Printing and Parenting in Early Modern England* (Aldershot: Ashgate, 2005), pp. 221–36

Klaits, Joseph, *Printed Propaganda under Louis XIV: Absolute Monarchy and Public Opinion* (Princeton, NJ: Princeton University Press, 1976)

Knight, Charles A., *A Political Biography of Richard Steele* (London: Pickering & Chatto, 2009)

Knights, Mark, *Politics and Opinion in the Exclusion Crisis, 1678–1681* (Cambridge: Cambridge University Press, 1994)

Knights, Mark, *Representation and Misrepresentation in Later Stuart Britain: Partisanship and Political Culture* (Oxford: Oxford University Press, 2005)

Knights, Mark, 'Judging Partisan News and the Language of Interest', in Jason McElligott (ed.), *Fear, Exclusion and Revolution* (Aldershot: Ashgate, 2006), pp. 204–20

Knights, Mark (ed.), *Faction Displayed: Reconsidering the Trial of Dr Henry Sacheverell* (London: Parliamentary Yearbook Trust, 2012)

Kobelt-Groch, M., 'Unter Zechern, Spielern und Häschern. Täufer im Wirtshaus', in N. Fischer and M. Kobelt-Groch (eds), *Aussenseiter zwischen Mittelalter und Neuzeit* (Leiden: Brill, 1997), pp. 111–26

Koopmans, Joop W., 'Supply and Speed of Foreign News in the Netherlands', in his *News and Politics in Early Modern Europe (1500–1800)* (Louvain: Peeters, 2005)

Koopmans, Joop W., *News and Politics in Early Modern Europe (1500–1800)* (Louvain: Peeters, 2005)

Kremer, Karl Heinz, 'Johann von den Birghden, 1582–1645', *Archiv für deutsche Postgeschichte* (1984), pp. 7–43

Kremer, Karl Heinz, *Johann von den Birghden, 1582–1645. Kaiserlicher und königlich-schwedischer Postmeister zu Frankfurt am Main* (Bremen: Lumière, 2005)

Kronick, David A., *'Devant le deluge' and Other Essays on Early Modern Scientific Communication* (Oxford: Scarecrow, 2004)

Kuhlmann, Erich, 'Aus Hamburgs älterer Postgeschichte', *Archiv für deutsche Postgeschichte, Sonderheft* (1984), pp. 36–68

Kümin, Beat, *Drinking Matters: Public Houses and Social Exchange in Early Modern Central Europe* (London: Palgrave Macmillan, 2007)

Kümin, Beat (ed.), *Political Space in Pre-Industrial Europe* (Aldershot: Ashgate, 2009).

Kümin, Beat and B. Ann Tlusty (eds), *The World of the Tavern: Public Houses in Early Modern Europe* (Aldershot: Ashgate, 2002)

Kutsch, Arnulf and Johannes Weber (eds), *350 Jahre Tageszeitung: Forschung und Dokumente* (Bremen: Lumière, 2010)

Labalme, Patricia H. and Laura Sanguieti White (eds), *Città Excelentissima: Selections from the Renaissance Diaries of Marin Sanudo* (Baltimore, MD: Johns Hopkins University Press, 2008)

Lake, Peter and Michael Questier, *The Antichrist's Lewd Hat: Protestants, Papists and Players in Post-Reformation England* (New Haven, CT, and London: Yale University Press, 2002)

Lambert, B. W., *The Croix de Gastines Affair (1568–1572): An Essay in Religious Controversy and Pamphlet Warfare* (Durham, NC: Duke University Press, 1971)

Lambert, B. W., *Pamphleteering in France during the Wars of Religion: Aspects of Ephemeral and Occasional Publications, 1562–1598* (Durham, NC: Duke University Press, 1975)

Lander, Jesse M., *Inventing Polemic: Religion, Print, and Literary Culture in Early Modern England* (Cambridge: Cambridge University Press, 2006)

Lane, Frederic C., *Andrea Barbarigo, Merchant of Venice, 1418–1449* (Baltimore, MD: Johns Hopkins University Press, 1944)

Lesger, Clé, 'Amsterdam as a Centre of Information Supply' in *The Rise of the Amsterdam Market and Information Exchange* (Aldershot: Ashgate, 2006)

Levin, Michael J., *Agents of Empire: Spanish Ambassadors in Sixteenth-Century Italy* (Ithaca, NY: Cornell University Press, 2005)

Levy, F. J., 'How Information Spread among the Gentry, 1550–1640', *Journal of British Studies*, 21 (1982), pp. 11–34

Levy, F. J., 'The Decorum of News', in Joad Raymond, *News, Newspapers, and Society in Early Modern Britain* (London: Frank Cass, 1999)

Levy, F. J., 'Staging the News', in Arthur F. Marotti and Michael D. Bristol (eds), *Print, Manuscript, & Performance: The Changing Relations of the Media in Early Modern England* (Columbus, OH: Ohio State University Press, 2001)

Levy, Leonard, *Emergence of a Free Press* (New York: Oxford University Press, 1985)

Lewis, Lawrence, *The Advertisements of the Spectator* (London: Houghton Mifflin, 1909)

Liemandt, Frank, *Die zeitgenössische literarische Reaktion auf den Tod des Königs Gustav II Adolf von Schweden* (Bern: Peter Lang, 1998)

Lopez, Robert S. and Irving W. Raymond, *Medieval Trade in the Mediterranean World: Illustrative Documents* (Oxford: Oxford University Press, 1955)

Lotz, Wolfgang, *Deutsche Postgeschichte. Essays und Bilder* (Berlin: Nicolai, 1989)

Love, Harold, *Scribal Publication in Seventeenth-Century England* (Oxford: Oxford University Press, 1993)

Lundell, Richard, 'Renaissance Diplomacy and the Limits of Empire: Eustace Chapuys, Habsburg Imperialisms, and Dissimulation as Method', in Tonio Andrade and William Reger (eds), *The Limits of Empire: European Imperial Formations in Early Modern World History: Essays in Honour of Geoffrey Parker* (Farnham: Ashgate, 2012), pp. 205–22

Lundin, Matthew, *Paper Memory: A Sixteenth-Century Townsman Writes his World* (Cambridge, MA: Harvard University Press, 2012)

Lunitz, Martin, *Diplomatie und Diplomaten im 16. Jahrhundert* (Constance: Hartung-Gorre Verlag, 1988)

Lüsebrink, Hans-Jürgen and Jeremy D. Popkin, *Enlightenment, Revolution, and the Periodical Press* (Oxford: Voltaire Foundation, 2004)

Lüsebrink, Hans-Jürgen and Rolf Reichardt, *The Bastille: A History of a Symbol of Despotism and Freedom* (Durham, NC: Duke University Press, 1997)

McAleer, John J., 'Ballads on the Spanish Armada', *Texas Studies in Literature and Language*, 4 (1963), pp. 602–12

McCusker, John J., 'The Business Press in England before 1775', *The Library*, 8 (1986), pp. 205–31

McCusker, John J., 'The Role of Antwerp in the Emergence of Commercial and Financial Newspapers in Early Modern Europe', in *La ville et la transmission des valeurs culturelles au bas moyen âge et aux temps modernes* (Brussels: Crédit communal, Collection histoire, 96, 1996), pp. 303–32

McCusker, John J., *Essays in the Economic History of the Atlantic World* (London: Routledge, 1997)

McCusker, John J. and Cora Gravesteijn, *The Beginnings of Commercial and Financial Journalism: The Commodity Price Currents, Exchange Rate Currents, and Money Currents of Early Modern Europe* (Amsterdam: NEHA, 1991)

McDowell, Paula, *The Women of Grub Street: Press, Politics and Gender in the London Literary Marketplace, 1678–1730* (Oxford: Oxford University Press, 1998)

McElligott, Jason, *Royalism, Print and Censorship in Revolutionary England* (Woodbridge: Boydell, 2007)

McEwen, Gilbert D., *The Oracle of the Coffee House: John Dunton's Athenian Mercury* (San Marino, CA: Huntington Library, 1972)

McHardy, A. K., 'Some Reflections on Edward III's Use of Propaganda', in James Bothwell (ed.), *The Age of Edward III* (Woodbridge: Boydell & Brewer, 2001), pp. 171–92

McKenzie, D. F., 'Speech – Manuscript – Print', in Peter D. McDonald and Michael F. Suarez (eds), *Making Meaning: Printers of the Mind* (Amherst, MA: University of Massachusetts Press, 2002), pp. 237–58

Mackie, Erin (ed.), *The Commerce of Everyday Life: Selections from the Tatler and the Spectator* (Boston, MA: Bedford, 1998)

McLeod, Jane, *Licensing Loyalty: Printers, Patrons and the State in Early Modern France* (University Park, PA: Pennsylvania State University Press, 2011)

McRae, Andrew, 'The Literary Culture of Early Stuart Libeling', *Modern Philology*, vol. 97 (2000), pp. 364–92

Madan, F., 'The Daily Ledger of John Dorne, 1520', in C. R. L. Fletcher (ed), *Collectanea* (Oxford: Oxford Historical Society, 1885), pp. 71–177

Madan, Francis F., *A New Bibliography of the Eikon Basilike* (Oxford: Oxford Bibliographical Society Publications, III, 1949)

Mareel, Samuel, 'Theatre and Politics in Brussels at the Time of Philip the Fair', in Hanno Wijsman (ed.), *Books in Transition at the Time of Philip the Fair*, in *Burgundia*, 15 (Turnhout: Brepols, 2010), pp. 213–30

Marotti, Arthur F. and Michael D. Bristol, *Print, Manuscript, & Performance: The Changing Relations of the Media in Early Modern England* (Columbus, OH: Ohio State University Press, 2001)

Marsh, Christopher, *Music and Society in Early Modern England* (Cambridge: Cambridge University Press, 2010)

Marshall, Alan, *Intelligence and Espionage in the Reign of Charles II* (Cambridge: Cambridge University Press, 1994)

Marshall, Alan, *The Strange Death of Edmund Godfrey: Plots and Politics in Restoration London* (Stroud: Sutton, 1999)

Marzi, C., 'Degli antecessori dei giornali', *Rivista delle biblioteche e degli archivi*, 24 (1913), pp. 181–5

Mason, Laura, 'Songs: Mixing Media', in Robert Darnton and Daniel Roche (eds), *Revolution in Print: The Press in France, 1775–1800* (Berkeley, CA: University of California Press, 1989), pp. 252–69

Mason, Laura, *Singing the French Revolution: Popular Culture and Politics, 1787–1799* (Ithaca, NY: Cornell University Press, 1996)

Matthews, George T. (ed.), *News and Rumor in Renaissance Europe: The Fugger Newsletters* (New York: Capricorn, 1959)

Mattingly, Garrett, *Renaissance Diplomacy* (London: Jonathan Cape, 1955)

Mauelshagen, Franz, *Wunderkammer auf Papier. Die 'Wickiana' zwischen Reformation und Volksglaube* (Zurich: Bibliotheca academica, 2011)

Melis, Federigo, 'Intensità e regolarità nella diffusione dell'informazione economica generale nel Mediterraneo e in Occidente alla fine del Medioevo', in *Mélanges en l'honneur de Fernand Braudel*, 2 vols (Toulouse: Privat, 1973), I, pp. 389–424

Melton, James van Horn, *The Rise of the Public in Enlightenment Europe* (Cambridge: Cambridge University Press, 2001)

Meserve, Margaret, 'News from Negroponte: Politics, Popular Opinion and Information Exchange in the First Decade of the Italian Press', *Renaissance Quarterly*, 59 (2006), pp. 440–80

Miller, John, *Religion in the Popular Prints, 1600–1832* (Cambridge: Chadwyck-Healey, 1986)

Mirowski, Philip, 'The Rise (and Retreat) of a Market: English Joint Stock Shares in the Eighteenth Century', *Journal of Economic History*, 41 (1981), pp. 559–77

Moran, Daniel, *Toward the Century of Words: Johann Cotta and the Politics of the Public Realm in Germany, 1795–1832* (Berkeley, CA: University of California Press, 1990)

Moureau, François, *Répertoire des nouvelles à la main. Dictionnaire de la presse manuscrite clandestine XVIe–XVIIIe siècle* (Oxford: Voltaire Foundation, 1999)

Moureau, François (ed.), *De bonne main. La communication manuscrite au XVIIIe siècle* (Paris: Universitas, and Oxford: Voltaire Foundation, 1993)

Muddiman, J. G., *The King's Journalist* (London: Bodley Head, 1923)

Murphy, Anne, *The Origins of English Financial Markets: Investment and Speculation before the South Sea Bubble* (Cambridge: Cambridge University Press, 2009)

Myers, Robin and Michael Harris (eds), *Censorship and the Control of Print in England and France, 1600–1900* (Winchester: St Paul's Bibliographies, 1992)

Neal, L., 'The Rise of a Financial Press: London and Amsterdam, 1681–1810', *Business History*, 30 (1988), pp. 163–78

Neal, L., *The Rise of Financial Capitalism: International Capital Markets in the Age of Reason* (Cambridge: Cambridge University Press, 1990)

Nelson, Caroline and Matthew Seccombe, *British Newspapers and Periodicals, 1641–1700: A Short-Title Catalogue* (New York: Modern Language Association of America, 1987)

Nicholls, David, 'The Theatre of Martyrdom in the French Reformation', *Past and Present*, 121 (188), pp. 49–73

Nord, David Paul, 'Teleology and News: The Religious Roots of American Journalism, 1630–1730', *Journal of American History*, 77 (1990), pp. 9–38

North, Michael, *Kommunikation, Handel, Geld und Banken in der Frühen Neuzeit* (Munich: Oldenbourg, 2000)

Novak, Maximillian E., *Daniel Defoe, Master of Fictions* (Oxford: Oxford University Press, 2001)

O'Connell, Sheila, *The Popular Print in England* (London: British Museum Press, 1999)

Oettinger, Rebecca Wagner, *Music as Propaganda in the German Reformation* (Aldershot: Ashgate, 2001)

Orden, Kate van, 'Cheap Print and Street Song Following the Saint Bartholomew's Massacres of 1572', in van Orden (ed.), *Music and the Cultures of Print* (New York: Garland, 2000), pp. 271–323

Origo, Iris, *The Merchant of Prato: Francesco di Marco Datini* (London: Jonathan Cape, 1957)

Ozouf, Mona, 'Public Opinion at the End of the Old Regime', *Journal of Modern History*, 60 (1988), pp. 9–13

Paas, Roger, *The German Political Broadsheet, 1600–1700*, 11 vols (Wiesbaden: O. Harrassowitz, 1985–2012)

Paas, Roger, 'The Use of the Popular Press to Influence Domestic and Foreign Opinion: Dutch Broadsheets from the Year of Disaster, 1672', in Heidrun Alzheimer et al. (eds), *Bilder – Sachen – Mentalitäten* (Regensburg: Schnell & Steiner, 2010), pp. 287–92

Palmer, J. J. N., *Froissart: Historian* (Woodbridge: Boydell & Brewer, 1981)

Parker, Geoffrey, *The Grand Strategy of Philip II* (New Haven, CT, and London: Yale University Press, 1998)

Parmelee, Lisa Ferraro, *Good Newes from Fraunce: French Anti-League Propaganda in Late Elizabethan England* (Rochester, NY: University of Rochester Press, 1996)

Paulus, Nikolaus, 'Raimund Peraudi als Ablasskommissar', *Historisches Jahrbuch*, 21 (1900), pp. 645–82

Payne, William L., *Mr Review: Daniel Defoe as Author of the Review* (New York: Crown Press, 1947)

Payne, William L., *The Best of Defoe's Review* (Freeport, NY: Books for Libraries Press, 1951)

Peacey, Jason, *Politicians and Pamphleteers: Propaganda during the English Civil Wars and Interregnum* (Aldershot: Ashgate, 2004)

Peacey, Jason, 'The Struggle for Mercurius Britanicus: Factional Politics and the Parliamentarian Press, 1643–6', *Huntington Library Quarterly*, 68 (2005), pp. 517–43

Peacey, Jason, 'Cromwellian England: A Propaganda State?', *History*, 91 (2006), pp. 176–99

Peacey, Jason and Chris R. Kyle, *Breaking News: Renaissance Journalism and the Birth of the Newspaper* (Baltimore, MD: Johns Hopkins University Press, 2009)

Pegolotti, F. Balducci (Francesco Balducci), *La pratica della mercatura*, ed. Allan Evans (Cambridge, MA: Mediaeval Academy of America, 1936)

Pettegree, Andrew, *Reformation and the Culture of Persuasion* (Cambridge: Cambridge University Press, 2005)

Pettegree, Andrew, *The Book in the Renaissance* (New Haven, CT, and London: Yale University Press, 2010)

Pettegree, Andrew, 'Catholic Pamphleteering', in Alexandra Bamji et al. (eds), *The Ashgate Research Companion to the Counter-Reformation* (Aldershot: Ashgate, 2013)

Picot, E. and H. Stein, *Recueil de pièces historiques imprimées sous le règne de Louis XI* (Paris: Société des bibliophiles français, F. Lefrançois, 1923)

Pieper, Renate, *Die Vermittlung einer neuen Welt: Amerika im Nachrichtennetz des Habsburgischen Imperium, 1493–1598* (Mainz: Von Zabern, 2000; 2009)

Pincus, Steve, 'Coffee Politicians Does Create: Coffeehouses and Restoration Political Culture', *Journal of Modern History*, 67 (1995), pp. 807–34

Plumb, J. H., *The Commercialisation of Leisure in Eighteenth-Century England* (Reading: University of Reading Press, 1973)

Popkin, Jeremy D., 'The Pre-Revolutionary Origins of Political Journalism', in Keith Michael Baker (ed.), *The French Revolution and the Creation of Modern Political Culture. Vol. I: The Political Culture of the Old Regime* (Oxford: Pergamon, 1987), pp. 203–23

Popkin, Jeremy D., *News and Politics in the Age of Revolution: Jean Luzac's Gazette de Leyde* (Ithaca, NY: Cornell University Press, 1989)

Popkin, Jeremy D., *Revolutionary News: The Press in France, 1789–1799* (Durham, NC: Duke University Press, 1990)

Popkin, Jeremy D., 'The Press and the French Revolution after Two Hundred Years', *French Historical Studies*, 16 (1990), pp. 664–83

Popkin, Jeremy D., 'Print Culture in the Netherlands on the Eve of the Revolution', in Margaret C. Jacob and Wijnand W. Mijnhardt (eds), *The Dutch Republic in the Eighteenth Century: Decline, Enlightenment, and Revolution* (Ithaca, NY: Cornell University Press, 1992), pp. 273–91

Popkin, Jeremy D., *Media and Revolution: Comparative Perspectives* (Lexington, KY: University Press of Kentucky, 1995)

Popkin, Jeremy D., 'Political Communication in the German Enlightenment: Gottlob Benedikt von Schirach's *Politische Journal*', *Eighteenth-Century Life*, 20, no. 1 (February 1996), pp. 24–41

Popkin, Jeremy D. and Jack Censer, *Press and Politics in Pre-Revolutionary France* (Berkeley, CA: University of California Press, 1987)

Porter, Roy, *Health for Sale: Quackery in England, 1660–1850* (Manchester: Manchester University Press, 1989)

Potter, David, *Renaissance France at War: Armies, Culture and Society, c. 1480–1560* (Woodbridge: Boydell, 2008)

Potter, David, 'War, Propaganda, Literature and National Identity in Renaissance France, c. 1490–1560', in Robert Stein and Judith Pollmann (eds), *Networks, Regions and Nations: Shaping Identity in the Low Countries, 1300–1650* (Leiden: Brill, 2010), pp. 173–93

Powell, William S., *John Pory, 1572–1636: The Life and Letters of a Man of Many Parts* (Chapel Hill, NC: University of North Carolina Press, 1976)

Price, Jacob M., 'Notes on Some London Price-Currents, 1667–1715', *Economic History Review*, 2nd ser., 7 (1954), pp. 240–50

Queller, Donald E., *Early Venetian Legislation on Ambassadors* (Geneva: Droz, 1967)

Queller, Donald E., *The Office of Ambassador in the Middle Ages* (Princeton, NJ: Princeton University Press, 1967)

Queller, Donald E., 'The Development of Ambassadorial Relazioni', in J. R. Hale (ed.), *Renaissance Venice* (London: Faber & Faber, 1973), pp. 174–96

Queller, Donald E., 'How to Succeed as an Ambassador', *Studia Gratiana*, 15 (1982), pp. 665–71

Racault, Luc, *Hatred in Print: Catholic Propaganda and Protestant Identity during the French Wars of Religion* (Aldershot: Ashgate, 2002)

Randall, David, *Credibility in Elizabethan and Early Stuart Military News* (London: Pickering & Chatto, 2008)

Randall, David, *English Military News Pamphlets, 1513–1637* (Tempe, AZ: ACMRS, 2011)

Ratia, Maura and Carla Suhr, 'Medical Pamphlets: Controversy and Advertising', in Irma Taavitsainen and Paivi Pahta (eds), *Medical Writings in Early Modern English* (Cambridge: Cambridge University Press, 2011), pp. 180–203

Raven, James, 'Serial Advertisement in 18th-Century Britain and Ireland', in Robin Myers and Michael Harris (eds), *Serials and their Readers, 1620–1914* (Winchester: St Paul's Bibliographies, 1993), pp. 103–22

Raymond, Joad, *Making the News: An Anthology of the Newsbooks of Revolutionary England 1641–1660* (Moreton-in-Marsh: Windrush Press, 1993)

Raymond, Joad, *The Invention of the Newspaper: English Newsbooks, 1641–1649* (Oxford: Oxford University Press, 1996)

Raymond, Joad, 'The Newspaper, Public Opinion and the Public Sphere in the Seventeenth Century', *Prose Studies*, 21 (1998), pp. 109–36

Raymond, Joad, *News, Newspapers, and Society in Early Modern Britain* (London: Frank Cass, 1999)

Raymond, Joad, *Pamphlets and Pamphleteering in Early Modern Britain* (Cambridge: Cambridge University Press, 2003)

Raymond, Joad (ed.), *News Networks in Seventeenth-Century Britain and Europe* (London: Routledge, 2006)

Rea, Robert R., *The English Press in Politics, 1760–1774* (Lincoln, NB: University of Nebraska Press, 1963)

Reichardt, Rolf, 'Prints: Images of the Bastille', in Robert Darnton and Daniel Roche (eds), *Revolution in Print: The Press in France, 1775–1800* (Berkeley, CA: University of California Press, 1989), pp. 235–51

Reichardt, R. and H. Schneider, 'Chanson et musique populaires devant l'histoire à la fin de l'Ancien Régime', *Dix-huitième siècle*, 18 (1986), pp. 117–36

Rein, Nathan, *The Chancery of God: Protestant Print, Polemic and Propaganda against the Emperor, Magdeburg 1546–1551* (Aldershot: Ashgate, 2008)

Reinders, Michel, *Printed Pandemonium: Popular Print and Politics in the Netherlands 1650–72* (Leiden: Brill, 2013)

Renouard, Yves, 'Comment les papes d'Avignon expédiaient leur courrier', *Revue historique*, 180 (1937), pp. 1–29

Renouard, Yves, 'Information et transmission des nouvelles', in Charles Samaran (ed.), *L'histoire et ses méthodes* (Paris: NRF, 1961)

Renouard, Yves, *The Avignon Papacy, 1305–1403* (London: Faber and Faber, 1970)

Rétat, Pierre, *Les Journaux de 1789. Bibliographie critique* (Paris: CNRS, 1988)

Rétat, Pierre, 'The Revolutionary World in the Newspaper in 1789', in Jeremy D. Popkin, *Media and Revolution: Comparative Perspectives* (Lexington, KY: University Press of Kentucky, 1995)

Richards, Gertrude R. B. (ed.), *Florentine Merchants in the Age of the Medici: Letters and Documents from the Selfridge Collection of Medici Manuscripts* (Cambridge, MA: Harvard University Press, 1932)

Richardson, Brian, *Manuscript Culture in Renaissance Italy* (Cambridge: Cambridge University Press, 2009)

Ries, Paul, 'The Anatomy of a Seventeenth-Century Newspaper', *Daphnis*, 6 (1977), pp. 171–232

Ries, Paul, 'Der Inhalt der Wochenzeitungen von 1609 im Computer', *Deutsche Presseforschung*, 26 (1987), pp. 113–25

Rivers, Isabel (ed.), *Books and their Readers in Eighteenth-Century England* (Leicester: Leicester University Press, 1982)

Rogers, C., 'Edward III and the Dialectics of Strategy, 1327–1360', *Transactions of the Royal Historical Society*, 6th ser., 4 (1994), pp. 83–102

Ross, Charles, 'Rumour, Propaganda and Popular Opinion during the Wars of the Roses', in R. A. Griffiths (ed.), *Patronage, the Crown and the Provinces in Late Medieval England* (Gloucester: Sutton, 1981)

Rosseaux, Ulrich, 'Die Entstehung der Messrelationen. Zur Entwicklung eines frühneuzeitlichen Nachrichtenmediums aus der Zeitgeschichtsschreibung des 16. Jahrhunderts', *Historisches Jahrbuch*, 124 (2004), pp. 97–123

Roth, Paul, *Die Neuen Zeitungen in Deutschland im 15. und 16. Jahrhundert* (Leipzig: B. G. Teubner, 1914)

Rublack, Ulinka, *The Crimes of Women in Early Modern Germany* (Oxford: Oxford University Press, 1999)

Rudé, George, *The Crowd in the French Revolution* (Oxford: Oxford University Press, 1959)

Salman, Jeroen, *Pedlars and the Popular Press: Itinerant Distribution Networks in England and the Netherlands, 1600–1850* (Leiden: Brill, 2014)

Salzberg, Rosa, 'The Lyre, the Pen and the Press: Performers and Cheap Print in Cinquecento Venice', in *The Books of Venice*, special issue of *Miscellanea Marciana*, ed. Craig Kallendorf and Lisa Pon (New Castle, DE: Oak Knoll Press, 2008)

Salzberg, Rosa, 'In the Mouths of Charlatans: Street Performers and the Dissemination of Pamphlets in Renaissance Italy', *Renaissance Studies*, (2010), pp. 1–16

Salzberg, Rosa and Massimo Rospocher, 'Street Singers in Italian Renaissance Urban Culture and Communication', *Cultural and Social History*, (2012), pp. 9–26

Salzberg, Rosa, 'An Evanescent Public Sphere: Voices, Spaces, and Publics in Venice during the Italian Wars', in Massimo Rospocher (ed.), *Beyond the Public Sphere: Opinions, Publics, Spaces in Early Modern Europe (XVI–XVIII)* (Bologna: Mulino, 2012)

Sapori, Armando, *Le marchand italien au Moyen Age: conférences et bibliographie* (Paris: Colin, 1952)

Sardella, Pierre, *Nouvelles et spéculations à Venise au début du XVIe siècle* (Paris: Colin, 1949)

Von Sautter, 'Auffindung einer grossen Anzahl verschlossener Briefe aus dem Jahre 1585', *Archiv für Post und Telegraphie*, 4 (1909), pp. 97–115

Sawyer, Jeffrey K., *Printed Poison: Pamphlet Propaganda, Faction Politics, and the Public Sphere in Early Seventeenth-Century France* (Berkeley, CA: University of California Press, 1990)

Schama, Simon, *Patriots and Liberators: Revolution in the Netherlands, 1780–1813* (London: Collins, 1977)

Scherbacher-Posé, Bridget, 'Die Entstehung einer weiblichen Öffentlichkeit im 18. Jahrhundert: Sophie von La Roche als Journalistin', *Jahrbuch für Kommunikationsgeschichte*, 2 (2000), pp. 24–51

Schilling, Michael, *Bildpublizistik der frühen Neuzeit. Aufgaben und Leistungen des illustrierten Flugblatts in Deutschland bis um 1700* (Tübingen: Niemeyer, 1990)

Schittenloher, Karl and J. Binkowshi, *Flugsblatt und Zeitung*, 2nd edn (Munich: Klinkhardt & Biermann, 1985)

Schlesinger, Arthur M., *Prelude to Independence: The Newspaper War on Britain, 1764–1776* (New York: Knopf, 1958)

Schneider, Maarten, *De Nederlandse Krant. Van Nieuwstydinghe tot dagblad* (Amsterdam: Van Kampen, 1949)

Schock, Flemming, 'Zur Kommunikation von Wunderzeichen in der ersten populärwissen-schaftlichen Zeitschriften Deutschlands, 1681–1691', *Jahrbuch für Kommunikationsgeschichte*, 9 (2007), pp. 76–100

Schöne, Walter, *Zeitungswesen und Statistik. Eine Untersuchung über den Einfluss der perio-dischen Presse auf die Entstehung und Entwicklung der staatswissenschaftlichen Literatur, speziell der Statistik* (Jena: Fischer, 1924)

Schöne, Walter, *Der Aviso des Jahres 1609. in Faksimiledruck* (Leipzig: O. Harrassowitz, 1939)

Schöne, Walter, *Die Relation des Jahres 1609. in Faksimiledruk* (Leipzig: O. Harrassowitz, 1940)

Schöne, Walter, *Die deutsche Zeitung des siebzehnten Jahrhunderts in Abbildungen, 400 Faksimiledrucke* (Leipzig: O. Harrassowitz, 1940)

Schroeder, E., *Das historisches Volkslied des dreissigjährige Krieges* (Marburg: Friedrich, 1916)

Schröder, Thomas, *Die ersten Zeitungen: Textgestaltung und Nachrichtenauswahl* (Tübingen: Gunter Narr Verlag, 1995)

Schwoebel, Robert, *The Shadow of the Crescent: The Renaissance Image of the Turk (1453–1517)* (Nieuwkoop: De Graaf, 1967)

Schwoerer, Lois G., *The Ingenious Mr Henry Care, Restoration Publicist* (Baltimore, MD: Johns Hopkins University Press, 2001)

Scott-Warren, Jason, 'Reconstructing Manuscript Networks: The Textual Transactions of Sir Stephen Powle', in Alexandra Shepard and Phil Withington (eds), *Communities in Early Modern Europe* (Manchester: Manchester University Press, 2000), pp. 18–37

Scribner, Robert, *For the Sake of Simple Folk: Popular Propaganda for the German Reformation* (Cambridge: Cambridge University Press, 1981)

Scurr, Ruth, *Fatal Purity: Robespierre and the French Revolution* (London: Chatto & Windus, 2006)

Seaver, Paul, *Wallington's World: A Puritan Artisan in Seventeenth-Century London* (Stanford, CA: Stanford University Press, 1985)

Seguin, Jean-Pierre, 'L'information à la fin du XVe siècle en France. Pièces d'actualité sous le règne de Charles VIII', *Arts et traditions populaires*, 4 (1956), pp. 309–30, 1–2; (1957), pp. 46–74

Seguin, Jean-Pierre, *L'information en France de Louis XII à Henri II* (Geneva: Droz, 1961)

Sgard, Jean, *Dictionnaire des Journaux 1600–1789* (Paris: Universitas, and Oxford: Voltaire Foundation, 1991)

Shaaber, Mathias A., *Some Forerunners of the Newspaper in England, 1476–1622* (Philadelphia, PA: Pennsylvania University Press, 1926)

Shagan, Ethan, 'Constructing Discord: Ideology, Propaganda and the English Responses to the Irish Rebellion of 1641', *Journal of British Studies*, 36 (1997), pp. 4–34

Shapin, Steven, *A Social History of Truth: Civility and Science in Seventeenth-Century England* (Chicago, IL: University of Chicago Press, 1994)

Sharpe, J. A., 'Last Dying Speeches: Religion, Ideology and Public Execution in Seventeenth-Century England', *Past and Present*, 107 (1985), pp. 144–67

Sharpe, Kevin, 'Thomas Witherings and the Reform of the Foreign Posts, 1632–1640', *Historical Research*, 57 (1984), pp. 149–63

Shepard, Alexandra and Phil Withington (eds), *Communities in Early Modern Europe* (Manchester: Manchester University Press, 2000), pp. 18–37

Sherman, Michael, 'Political Propaganda and Renaissance Culture: French Reactions to the League of Cambrai, 1509–1510', *Sixteenth Century Journal*, 8 (1977), pp. 97–128

Shevelow, Kathryn, *Women and Print Culture: The Construction of Femininity in the Early Periodical* (London; Routledge, 1989)

Shuger, Debora, *Censorship and Cultural Sensibility: The Regulation of Language in Tudor-Stuart England* (Philadelphia, PA: University of Pennsylvania Press, 2006)

Silver, Larry, *Marketing Maximilian: The Visual Ideology of a Holy Roman Emperor* (Princeton, NJ: Princeton University Press, 2008)

Simoni, Anna, 'Poems, Pictures and the Press: Observations on some Abraham Verhoeven Newsletters (1620–1621)', in Francine de Nave (ed.), *Liber amicorum Leon Voet* (Antwerp: Vereeniging der Antwerpsche Bibliophielen, 1985), pp. 353–73

Simpson, W. Sparrow, *Documents Illustrating the History of St. Paul's Cathedral* (London: Camden Society, 1880)

Smith, Helen, *'Grossly Material Things': Women and Book Production in Early Modern England* (Oxford: Oxford University Press, 2012)

Smith, Norman R., 'Portentous Births and the Monstrous Imagination in Renaissance Culture', in Timothy S. Jones and David A. Sprunger (eds), *Marvels, Monsters and Miracles* (Kalamazoo: Medieval Institute Publications, 2002), pp. 267–83

Smith, Woodruff D., 'The Function of Commercial Centers in the Modernization of European Capitalism: Amsterdam as an Information Exchange in the Seventeenth Century', *Journal of Economic History*, 44 (1984), pp. 985–1,005

Solomon, Howard M., *Public Welfare, Science, and Propaganda in Seventeenth-Century France: The Innovations of Théophraste Renaudot* (Princeton, NJ: Princeton University Press, 1972)

Solomon, Howard M., 'The *Gazette* and Antistatist Propaganda: The Medium of Print in the First Half of the Seventeenth Century', *Canadian Journal of History*, 9 (1974), pp. 1–17

Sommerville, C. John, *The News Revolution in England: Cultural Dynamics of Daily Information* (Oxford: Oxford University Press, 1996)

Spaans, Joke, *Graphic Satire and Religious Change: The Dutch Republic, 1676–1707* (Leiden: Brill, 2011)

Speakman Sutch, Susie, 'Politics and Print at the Time of Philip the Fair', in Hanno Wijsman (ed.), *Books in Transition at the Time of Philip the Fair*, in *Burgundia*, 15 (Turnhout: Brepols, 2010), pp. 231–55

Spiegel, Gabrielle M., *The Chronicle Tradition of Saint-Denis* (Brookline: Classical Folia, 1978)

Spiegel, Gabrielle M., *Romancing the Past: The Rise of Vernacular Prose Historiography in Thirteenth-Century France* (Berkeley, CA: University of California Press, 1993)

Spierenburg, Pieter, *The Spectacle of Suffering* (Cambridge: Cambridge University Press, 1984)

Spierenburg, Pieter, 'The Body and the State', in Norval Morris and David J. Rothman (eds), *The Oxford History of the Prison* (Oxford: Oxford University Press, 1998)

Spinks, Jennifer, *Monstrous Births and Visual Culture in Sixteenth-Century Germany* (London: Chatto & Pickering, 2009)

Spooner, Frank C., *The International Economy and Monetary Movements in France, 1493–1725* (Cambridge, MA: Harvard University Press, 1972)

Sporhan-Krempel, Lore, *Nürnberg als Nachrichtenzentrum zwischen 1400 und 1700* (Nuremberg: Vereins für Geschichte der Stadt Nürnberg, 1968)

Spufford, Peter, *Power and Profit: The Merchant in Medieval Europe* (London: Thames and Hudson, 2002)

Staff, Frank, *The Penny Post, 1680–1918* (London: Lutterworth, 1964)

Stearns, Bertha-Monica, 'The First English Periodical for Women', *Modern Philology*, 28 (1930–31), pp. 45–59

Stearns, Bertha-Monica, 'Early English Periodicals for Ladies (1700–1760)', *Proceedings of the Modern Languages Association*, 48 (1933), pp. 38–60

Steele, Ian K., *The English Atlantic, 1675–1740: An Exploration of Communication and Community* (New York: Oxford University Press, 1986)

Strauss, Walter L., *The German Single-Leaf Woodcut, 1550–1600*, 3 vols (New York: Abaris, 1975)

Stumpo, Enrico, *La gazzetta de l'anno 1588* (Florence: Giunti, 1988)

Styles, John, 'Print and Policing: Crime Advertising in Eighteenth-Century Provincial England', in Douglas Hay and Francis Snyder (eds), *Policing and Prosecution in Britain, 1750–1850* (Oxford: Oxford University Press, 1989), pp. 55–111

Sutherland, James, *The Restoration Newspaper and its Development* (Cambridge: Cambridge University Press, 1986)

Sutherland, James R., 'The Circulation of Newspapers and Literary Periodicals, 1700–1730', *The Library*, 4th series, XV (1934), pp. 110–24

Targett, S., 'Government and Ideology during the Age of Whig Supremacy: The Political Argument of Walpole's Newspaper Propagandists', *Historical Journal*, 37 (1994), pp. 289–318

Taylor, John, *English Historical Literature in the Fourteenth Century* (Oxford: Oxford University Press, 1987)

Thomas, Keith, 'The Meaning of Literacy', in G. Baumann (ed.), *The Written Word: Literacy in Transition* (Oxford: Oxford University Press, 1986)

Thomas, M. Halsey (ed.), *The Diary of Samuel Sewall*, 2 vols (New York: Farrar, Straus and Giroux, 1973)

Thomas, Peter D. G., 'The Beginnings of Parliamentary Reporting in Newspapers, 1768–1774', *English Historical Review*, 74 (1959), pp. 623–36

Thomas, Peter D. G., *John Wilkes: A Friend to Liberty* (Oxford: Oxford University Press, 1996)

Thomas, P. W., *Sir John Berkenhead, 1617–1679: A Royalist Career in Politics and Polemics* (Oxford: Oxford University Press, 1969)

Thompson, Peter, *Rum, Punch & Revolution: Tavern-Going & Public Life in Eighteenth-Century Philadelphia* (Philadelphia, PA: University of Pennsylvania Press, 1999)

Thomson, Elizabeth McClure, *The Chamberlain Letters* (London: John Murray, 1965)

Thornton, Tim, 'Propaganda, Political Communication and the Problem of English Responses to the Introduction of Printing', in Bertrand Taithe and Tim Thornton (eds), *Propaganda* (Stroud: Sutton, 1999), pp. 41–60

Tlusty, B. Ann, *Bacchus and Civic Order: The Culture of Drink in Early Modern Germany* (Charlottesville, VA: University of Virginia Press, 2001)

Todd, Christopher, *Political Bias, Censorship, and the Dissolution of the Official Press in Eighteenth-Century France* (Lampeter: Edwin Mellen Press, 1991)

Todd, Thomas, *William Dockwra and the Rest of the Undertakers: The Story of the London Penny Post, 1680–2* (Edinburgh: Cousland, 1952)

Tombeur, Jef, *Femmes & métiers du livre* (Soignies: Talus d'approche, 2004)

Tortarola, Eduardo, 'Censorship and the Conception of the Public in Late Eighteenth-Century Germany: or, Are Censorship and Public Opinion Mutually Exclusive?', in Dario Castiglione and Lesley Sharpe (eds), *Shifting the Boundaries: Transformation of the Languages of the Public and Private in the Eighteenth Century* (Exeter: University of Exeter Press, 1995), pp. 131–50

Trivellato, Francesca, 'Merchants' Letters across Geographical and Social Boundaries', in Francisco Bethercourt and Florike Egmond, *Correspondence and Cultural Exchange in Europe, 1400–1700* (Cambridge: Cambridge University Press, 2007), pp. 80–103

Tuchman, Gaye, 'Objectivity as a Strategic Ritual: An Examination of Newsmen's Notions of Objectivity', *American Journal of Sociology*, 77 (1972), pp. 660–79

Tucoo-Chala, Suzanne, *Charles-Joseph Panckoucke & la Librairie française, 1736–1798* (Paris: Éditions Marrimpouey jeune, 1977)

Varey, S. (ed.), *Lord Bolingbroke: Contributions to the Craftsman* (Oxford: Oxford University Press, 1982)

Venturi, Franco, *The End of the Old Regime in Europe, 1776–1789* (Princeton, NJ: Princeton University Press, 1991)

Vincent, Monique, *Mercure galant. Extraordinaire affaires du temps. Table analytique* (Paris: Champion, 1998).

Vivo, Filippo de, 'Paolo Sarpi and the Uses of Information in Seventeenth-Century Venice', *Media History*, 11 (2005), pp. 37–51

Vivo, Filippo de, *Information and Communication in Venice: Rethinking Early Modern Politics* (Oxford: Oxford University Press, 2007)

Voss, Paul J., *Elizabethan News Pamphlets: Shakespeare, Spenser, Marlowe and the Birth of Journalism* (Pittsburgh, NJ: Duquesne University Press, 2001)

Wahrman, Dror, *Mr. Collier's Letter Rack: A Tale of Art and Illusion at the Threshold of the Modern Information Age* (Oxford: Oxford University Press, 2012)

Walker, R. B., 'Advertising in London Newspapers, 1650–1750', *Business History*, 15 (1973), pp. 112–30

Walker, R. B., 'The Newspaper Press in the Reign of William III', *Historical Journal*, 17 (1974), pp. 691–709

Walker, Simon, 'Rumour, Sedition and Popular Protest in the Reign of Henry IV', *Past and Present*, 166 (2000), pp. 31–65

Walsham, Alexandra, *Providence in Early Modern England* (Oxford: Oxford University Press, 1999)

Walton, Charles, *Policing Public Opinion in the French Revolution: The Culture of Calumny and the Problem of Free Speech* (Oxford: Oxford University Press, 2011)

Ward, Stephen J. A., *The Invention of Journalism Ethics* (Montreal: McGill University Press, 2004)

Warner, Michael, *The Letters of the Republic: Publication and the Public Sphere in Eighteenth-Century America* (Cambridge, MA: Harvard University Press, 1990)

Watt, Tessa, 'Publisher, Pedlar, Pot-Poet: The Changing Character of the Broadside Trade, 1550–1640', in Robin Myers and Michael Harris (eds), *Spreading the Word: The Distribution Networks of Print, 1550–1850* (Winchester: St Paul's, 1990)

Watt, Tessa, *Cheap Print and Popular Piety, 1550–1640* (Cambridge: Cambridge University Press, 1991)

Watts, John, 'The Pressure of the Public on Later Medieval Politics', in Linda Clark and Christine Carpenter (eds), *The Fifteenth Century. Vol. IV. Political Culture in Late Medieval Britain* (Woodbridge: Boydell & Brewer, 2004), pp. 159–80

Weber, Harold, *Paper Bullets: Print and Kingship under Charles II* (Lexington, KY: University Press of Kentucky, 1996)

Weber, Johannes, '"Unterthenige Supplication Johann Caroli, Buchtruckers." Der Beginn gedruckter politischer Wochenzeitungen im Jahre 1605', *Archiv für Geschichte des Buchwesens*, 38 (1992), pp. 257–65

Weber, Johannes, 'Daniel Hartnack: ein gelehrter Streithahn und Avisen Schreiber am Ende des 17. Jahrhunders. Zum Beginn politisch kommentierenden Zeitungspresse', *Gutenberg Jahrbuch* (1993), pp. 140–58

Weber, Johannes, 'Neue Funde aus der Frühgeschichte des deutschen Zeitungswesen', *Archiv für Geschichte des Buchwesens*, 39 (1993), pp. 312–60

Weber, Johannes, *Götter-Both Mercurius: Die Urgeschichte der politischen Zeitschrift in Deutschland* (Bremen: Temen, 1994)

Weber, Johannes, 'Der grosse Krieg und die frühe Zeitung. Gestalt und Entwicklung der deutschen Nachrichtenpresse in der ersten Hälfte des 17. Jahrhunderts', *Jahrbuch für Kommunikationsgeschichte*, 1 (1999), pp. 23–61

Weber, Johannes, 'Kontrollmechanismen im deutschen Zeitungswesen des 17. Jahrhunderts: Ein kleiner Beitrag zur Geschichte der Zensur', *Jahrbuch für Kommunikationsgeschichte*, 6 (2005), pp. 56–73

Weber, Johannes, 'Strassburg 1605: The Origins of the Newspaper in Europe', *German History*, 24 (2006), pp. 387–412

Weller, Emil, *Die ersten deutschen Zeitungen* (Tübingen: Laupp, 1872)

Werkmeister, Lucyle, *A Newspaper History of England, 1792–1793* (Lincoln, NB: University of Nebraska Press, 1967)

Werner, Theodor Gustav, 'Regesten und Texte von Fuggerzeitungen der Öesterreichischen Nationalbibliothek in Wien', *Scripta Mercaturae* (1967), pp. 57–70

Werner, Theodor Gustav, 'Das kaufmännische Nachrichtenwesen im späten Mittelalter und in der frühen Neuzeit und sein Einfluss auf die Entstehung der handschriftlichen Zeitung', *Scripta Mercaturae* (1975), pp. 3–51

Wheale, Nigel, *Writing and Society: Literacy, Print and Politics in Britain, 1590–1660* (London: Routledge, 1999)

Whitehead, B. T., *Brags and Boasts: Propaganda in the Year of the Armada* (Stroud: Sutton, 1994)

Whyman, Susan E., *The Pen and the People: English Letter Writers 1660–1800* (Oxford: Oxford University Press, 2010)

Wiles, R. M., *Freshest Advices: Early Provincial Newspapers in England* (Columbus, OH: Ohio State University Press, 1965)

Williams, Gerhild Scholz and William Layher (eds), *Consuming News: Newspapers and Print Culture in Early Modern Europe (1500–1800)*, in *Daphnis*, 37 (2008)

Wilson, Dudley, *Signs and Portents: Monstrous Births from the Middle Ages to the Enlightenment* (London: Routledge, 1993)

Wiltenburg, Joy, *Disorderly Women and Female Power in the Street Literature of Early Modern England and Germany* (Charlottesville, VA: University Press of Virginia, 1992)

Wiltenburg, Joy, 'True Crime: The Origins of Modern Sensationalism', *American Historical Review*, 109 (2004), pp. 1,377–1,404

Wiltenburg, Joy, 'Crime and Christianity in Early Sensationalism', in Marjorie Plummer and Robin Barnes (eds), *Ideas and Cultural Margins in Early Modern Germany* (Aldershot: Ashgate, 2009), pp. 131–45

Woloch, Isser, 'The Contraction and Expansion of Democratic Space during the Period of the Terror', in K. M. Baker, *The French Revolution and the Creation of Modern Political Culture. Vol. IV: The Terror* (Oxford: Pergamon, 1994), pp. 309–25

Worden, Blair, *Literature and Politics in Cromwellian England: John Milton, Andrew Marvell, Marchamont Nedham* (Oxford: Oxford University Press, 2007)

Worden, Blair, 'Marchamont Nedham and the Beginnings of English Republicanism, 1649–1656', in David Wootton (ed.), *Republicanism, Liberty and Commercial Society, 1649–1776* (Stanford, CA: Stanford University Press, 1994), pp. 45–81

Wrightson, Keith, 'Alehouses, Order and Reformation in Rural England, 1590–1660', in Eileen Yeo and Stephen Yeo (eds), *Popular Culture and Class Conflict, 1590–1914* (Brighton: Harvester, 1981), pp. 1–27

Würzbach, Natasha, *The Rise of the English Street Ballad, 1550–1650* (Cambridge: Cambridge University Press, 1990)

Zilliacus, Laurin, *From Pillar to Post: The Troubled History of the Mail* (London: Heinemann, 1956)

Zuilen, Vincent van, 'The Politics of Dividing the Nation? News Pamphlets as a Vehicle of Ideology and National Consciousness in the Habsburg Netherlands (1585–1609)', in Joop W. Koopmans, *News and Politics in Early Modern Europe (1500–1800)* (Louvain: Peeters, 2005), pp. 61–78

Zulliger, Jürg, '"Ohne Kommunikation würde Chaos herrschen". Zur Bedeutung von Informationsaustauch, Briefverkehr und Boten bei Bernhard von Clairvaux', *Archiv für Kulturgeschichte*, 78 (1996), pp. 251–76

Index

Illustration Acknowledgements

Deutches Historisches Museum, Berlin, 0.1, 3.1; Folger Shakespeare Library, Washington, 3.2, 3.3, 4.2, 7.5, 7.6, 10.5, 11.4, 12.2, 13.3, 16.2, 17.1; Library Company of Philadelphia, Philadelphia, 16.3; Museum Plantin Moretus, Antwerp, 8.2, 9.3; National Gallery of Art, Washington, 2.1, 2.2; Princeton University Library, Folke Dahl collection, Princeton, 0.2, 6.3, 8.1, 9.1, 9.2, 9.4, 9.5, 9.6, 10.3, 11.2, 11.3, 12.4, 18.1; Staatsbibliothek, Berlin, 4.1; Trustees of the British Museum, London, 1.1, 1.2, 5.1, 5.2, 6.1, 6.2, 7.1, 7.2, 7.4, 8.3, 10.1, 10.2, 10.4, 11.1, 12.3, 13.2, 14.1, 14.2, 14.3, 15.1, 16.1, 18.2; Wikipedia Commons, 5.3, 13.1, 13.4, 15.2, 17.2; Zentralbibliothek, Zurich, 1.3, 4.3, 4.4, 7.3, 12.1.

Acknowledgements

T HE writing of this book has been enormous fun. I came to the project with a certain expertise in the history of the book, and a particular interest in cheap print. This alerted me to the importance of news, but I was aware that for a project of this nature I was going to have to expand my frame of reference to incorporate manuscripts and the spoken word, song and drama. The necessary research has given me the opportunity to range to the boundaries of the modern era and back into the medieval period. In the process I discovered the extraordinary world of the manuscript news writers, the wooden tablets of Vindolanda and Grub Street. This would not have been possible without access to an enormous amount of work already conducted by outstanding scholars in this field. It is one of the great glories of our university system that academic teachers are provided with time, indeed are under an obligation, to engage in research which in turn informs their teaching. In the course of this project I have come to know and admire enormously the work of many scholars who have written on aspects of the history of communications. Among current practitioners I thank Paul Arblaster, Wolfgang Behringer, Allyson Creasman, Gilles Feyel, Mario Infelise, Richard John, Mark Knights, Geoffrey Parker, Jason Peacey, Joad Raymond, Rosa Salzberg and many others for the penetrating studies that have helped form my own perceptions. But it is a characteristic – perhaps an idiosyncrasy – of history-writing that we can draw on work published many years, even decades, ago that remains wonderfully fresh and insightful; some of the material consulted for this book was published thirty, fifty or even one hundred years ago. Some of the most useful of this vintage scholarship was published by historians of the postal service in journals of philately. I thank in particular the Berlin Museum of Communications for making me welcome in their library, where I was able to consult a large amount of this material.

Other research was undertaken in a range of libraries in Britain, continental Europe and the United States. I thank particularly the Guildhall Library, London, the Royal Library in Copenhagen and the Library Company of Philadelphia for access to early newspapers; the Museum Plantin Moretus in Antwerp, the rare-book room of Amsterdam University Library and the Royal Library in Brussels for access to rare seventeenth-century serials and pamphlets. I was able to read *Mazarinades* in the Arsenal Library and the Bibliothèque Nationale in Paris, the John Rylands Library in Manchester and the Taylor Institute in Oxford. The Library of the Deutsches Historisches Museum in Berlin played host to a period of study of Reformation pamphlet literature, and I was able to explore a wonderful collection of official broadsheets in the Berlin Staatsbibliothek. The British Library played an essential part in this project, as it does for most British academic writers. At a late stage in my research I was able to work my way through the collection of the great scholar of early newspapers, Folke Dahl, now in Princeton University Library. I am especially grateful to the staff of the rare-book room for allowing me access to these papers, and to make free with my digital camera. I would also like to pay tribute to two parallel research projects: the Vienna project investigating the *Fuggerzeitungen*, and Joad Raymond's News Networks in Early Modern Europe, sponsored by the Leverhulme Trust. I thank Joad and his project manager Noah Moxham for making me welcome in the circle of scholars gathered by this initiative. Some of this work was tried out on audiences in Antwerp, Dublin, New York, Philadelphia and London, and I thank my hosts in all of those places. Flavia Bruni, Jacqueline Rose, Grant Tapsell and Peter Truesdale all very kindly read large chunks of the text, and suggested corrections, changes and further reading. I am extremely grateful to them all. Lucas Kriner kindly drew the maps. As ever, colleagues in the St Andrews Book History group have been a constant source of stimulating discoveries and sound advice, and I am grateful too to the project's technical managers, Graeme Kemp and before him Philip John, for helping me stay afloat in an age of testing media transformation. My co-director in the Book project group, Malcolm Walsby, has been for a decade my closest intellectual collaborator, and I am grateful for his help and advice as this project took shape. At Yale University Press Heather McCallum was a strong and imaginative supporter of this project from its incep-tion, and in its final stages it has benefited greatly from the professionalism and elegance of the copy-editor, Richard Mason. My wife Jane was the first person to read a complete text of this book; we wandered Vindolanda together; she has been a constant source of probing, insightful guidance in this and everything else. Jane, Megan and Sophie make it all worthwhile.

Andrew Pettegree
St Andrews, April 2013